THE BLUE BOOK OF
HOLLYWOOD MUSICALS

*Songs From The Sound Tracks and The
Stars Who Sang Them Since The Birth
Of The Talkies A Quarter-Century Ago*

BY

JACK BURTON

CENTURY HOUSE
WATKINS GLEN   NEW YORK

In memory of my son, Jack Burton Jr.,
who got a bigger kick out of a popular
song than anyone I ever knew.

Contents

Songs Awarded the Oscar

(By the Academy of Motion Picture Arts and Sciences)

1934—*The Continental* by Herbert Magidson and Con Conrad.
From the RKO picture *Gay Divorcee*

1935—*Lullaby Of Broadway* by Al Dubin and Harry Warren
From the First National picture *The Gold Diggers*

1936—*The Way You Look Tonight* by Dorothy Fields and Jerome Kern
From the RKO picture *Roberta*

1937—*Sweet Lelanie* by Harry Owens
From the Paramount picture *Waikiki Wedding*

1938—*Thanks For The Memory* by Leo Robin and Ralph Rainger
From the Paramount picture *The Big Broadcast*

1939—*Over The Rainbow* by E. Y. Harburg and Harold Arlen
From the M-G-M picture *The Wizard Of Oz*

1940—*When You Wish Upon A Star* by Ned Washington and Leigh Harline
From the RKO picture *Pinocchio*

1941—*The Last Time I Saw Paris* by Oscar Hammerstein II and Jerome Kern
From the M-G-M picture *Lady Be Good*

1942—*White Christmas* by Irving Berlin
From the Paramount picture *Holiday Inn*

1943—*You'll Never Know* by Mack Gordon and Harry Warren
From the 20th Century-Fox picture *Hello, Frisco, Hello*

1944—*Swinging On A Star* by Johnny Burke and Jimmy VanHeusen
From the Paramount picture *Going My Way*

1945—*It Might As Well Be Spring* by Oscar Hammerstein II and Richard Rodgers
From the 20th Century-Fox picture *State Fair*

1946—*On The Atchinson, Topeka and Santa Fe* by Johnny Mercer and Harry Warren
From the M-G-M picture *The Harvey Girls*

1947—*Zippa-Dee-Do-Da* by Ray Gilbert and Allie Wrubel
From the RKO picture *Song Of The South*

1948—*Buttons And Bows* by Ray Evans and Jay Livingston
From the Paramount picture *The Paleface*

1949—*Baby It's Cold Outside* by Frank Loesser
From the M-G-M picture *Neptune's Daughter*

1950—*Mona Lisa* by Ray Evans and Jay Livingston
From the Paramount picture *Capt. Carey of the U. S. A.*

1951—*In the Cool, Cool, Cool Of The Evening* by Johnny Mercer and Hoagy Carmichael
From the Paramount picture *Here Comes The Groom*

According to *Variety*, "the bible of show business," only thirty-four musicals and films with songs listed below are included in the eighty-eight films of all types that have grossed $4,000,000 or better at box offices in the U.S. and Canada.

Irving Berlin tops the songwriters with songs for four Golden Circle musicals: *This Is The Army, Blue Skies, Annie Get Your Gun* and *Easter Parade*. Bing Crosby, among the Hollywood singing stars, has paid off most handsomely with seven top-grossing pictures to his credit: *The Bells Of St. Mary's, Going My Way, Welcome Stranger, Blue Skies, Road To Rio, Road To Utopia* and *The Emperor Waltz*. Al Jolson is a three-time winner with *The Singing Fool, The Jolson Story* and *Jolson Sings Again*. And M-G-M, with twelve productions, has the most top-grossing musicals in the Golden Circle, Paramount taking place money with eight.

FOREWORD

Complementing The Blue Book Of Tin Pan Alley (1951) and *The Blue Book of Broadway Musicals* (1952), this present anthology completes a trilogy on popular music and covers a period of twenty-five years from October 6, 1927, when the first talkie was screened, to October 31, 1952.

The films, with their titles listed alphabetically, are divided into twenty-five chronological sections according to the year of their release, and then are subdivided into four classifications: Musicals, which include both bona fide song-and-dance productions and pictures in which songs play an important part; Feature Films With Songs; Western Films With Songs and Full Length Cartoon Films With Songs. No shorts like *Mickey Mouse* and *Donald Duck* have been included in this survey with the sole exception of *The Three Little Pigs,* the popularity of which led to the filming of full length cartoon pictures, while the title of the book is somewhat belied by the inclusion of several foreign films for one of three reasons: Their popularity in this country, the appearance of American players in the cast or because the songs are by American writers.

In addition to the annual volumes of the *Film Daily Year Book* and the *Motion Picture Almanac,* which provided much of the basic material for this anthology, the most valuable sources of reference were the music cue sheets that list the songs and instrumental numbers incorporated in each individual picture. In the early days of the talkies, however, these music cue sheets were far from complete, some producers failed to issue them, and several have been lost. This explains the incomplete listing of song titles in some instances.

In the research work that went into this book, Miss Carol Bridgman and two of her assistants in the Index Department of the American Society of Composers, Authors and Publishers, Miss Grace Morse and Mrs. Teresa Smith, were most helpful, and I am deeply indebted as well to Miss Cathy LéGall of the Motion Picture Association of America for clearing up many conflicting points and to Mrs. Joanne Godbout of the Museum of Modern Arts Film Library for supplying stills not available in the files of the producing companies.

Some of the illustrations, however, came from the following Hollywood studios: 20th Century-Fox (*State Fair* and *With A Song In My Heart*), Columbia Pictures (*The Jolson Story* and *Jolson Sings Again*) and RKO-Radio Pictures (*Snow White And The Seven Dwarfs*).

Jack Burton

Scarsdale Manor South
Scarsdale, New York

Al Jolson strikes a familiar pose in singing "My Mammy" in *The Jazz Singer*

1 9 2 7 — 1 9 2 8

Al Jolson Sounds Off For Sound

The time is October 6, 1927; the place, Warner Brothers' Theater in New York City; and the marquee boards scream:

"See and HEAR Al Jolson in 'The Jazz Singer'!"

That verb "hear", a comparatively new word in the vocabulary of the Hollywood drum-beater, proved to be loaded with both magic and TNT, for while there had been films with sound as early as 1923, they were experimental one-reelers and sparsely shown, whereas *The Jazz Singer* was the first full-length picture to bring both dialogue and music to the silver screen and sounded the death knell of the silent movie while intoning a requiem for Theda Bara, Bill Hart, and other inarticulate idols of the nation's movie-goers.

Viewed from any angle, *The Jazz Singer,* epochal though it proved to be, was truly a shot in the dark and anything but a great picture compared to the top-ranking films of 1927—the Oscar-winning *Seventh Heaven, Beau Geste, What Price Glory?* and *Ben Hur.* Its production was a desperate but winning gamble by the four Warner brothers, who having no nation-wide market for the films they made, decided they would have to come up with something sensationally new if they were to meet with any degree of success the competition of such theater-owning producers as Fox, First National and Paramount.

Al Jolson, too, was a second choice for the title role, being approached only after Georgie Jessel, who had starred in Samson Raphelson's stage play of the same name on which the film was to be based, refused to do the movie version, and Jolson, while a Broadway celebrity, was a screen unknown of tainted repute who had walked out of the studio in disgust during his first and only appearance before the movie cameras in 1923.

Even the dialogue in *The Jazz Singer* was an after-thought. Originally, the film was shot silent except for the singing sequences, but an ad lib by Jolson— "Wait a minute! Wait a minute! You ain't heard nothin' yet!"—voiced after he had finished singing *Dirty Hands, Dirty Face,* got such an enthusiastic reception from the studio extras in the cafe scene that the director decided to put it on the sound track and later dubbed in a dialogue sequence.

Although *The Jazz Singer* packed 'em in during its New York showing, the program for which listed shorts by Ohman and Arden, dual pianists; Eddie Peabody, the banjoist; William Demarest in a comedy sketch and an overture by a 107-piece orchestra under the direction of Louis Silvers, the top brass of Hollywood stamped this Father Adam of the talkies as nothing more than a short-lived novelty after its premiere, but when the Manhattan triumphs were repeated in Boston, Philadelphia, Chicago, St. Louis and other leading cities, their squints of cold disdain changed to wide-eyed looks of alarm.

"Talkies will wreck the industry!", they declared. "Millions of dollars worth of silent equipment will have to be junked. Many more millions will have to be spent for studio sound equipment and the wiring of more than 18,000 theaters for sound. And the first-run theaters with costly orchestras and stage shows will be empty if neighborhood theaters can buy the same deluxe show in a can!"

Consequently, sound, which travels at a speed of better than 1,000 feet a second, slowed down to a snail's pace after passing the boundaries of Hollywood, but eventually, the big movie tycoons, who had counseled against "rocking the boat" at first, were forced to take to the life rafts of sound—or sink. At the outset, there was chaos and confusion as traditions and precedents were shattered, but gradually order was restored. Wall Street came to the rescue with a loan of $300,000,000 for the conversion project, more than a thousand theaters were wired for sound in the twelve months following the premiere of *The Jazz Singer,* and during the closing months of 1928, such stars of the silent screen as John Gilbert, Greta Garbo, Joan Crawford, Ramon Novarro and Pola Negri appeared in pictures with both dialogue and musical sequences.

The advent of a new movie day that carried a threat to the prestige of those unable to speak lines or belt over a song was written on every studio wall, and it wouldn't be long before thousands of movie house pianists would be looking through the Help Wanted columns of their daily newspapers, when such titles as "Came the dawn" would be flashed on the screen for the last time, and the inarticulate stars of Hollywood would be seen in their final closeup. For *The Jazz Singer* not only had made history. It had remade the movies.

Feature Films With Songs

ALIAS JIMMY VALENTINE
An M-G-M picture starring William Haines, and directed by Jack Conway. Song by William Axt and David Mendoza:
LOVE DREAMS

ANNAPOLIS
A Pathe-RKO picture starring Hugh Allan and Jeanette Loff, and directed by Christy Cabanne. Song by Charles Weinberg and Irving Bibo:
MY ANNAPOLIS AND YOU

AWAKENING, THE
A United Artists' picture starring Vilma Banky and directed by Victor Fleming. Song by Irving Berlin:
MARIE

CAPTAIN SWAGGER
A Pathe-RKO picture starring Rod La-Roque and Sue Carol and directed by E. H.

Griffith. Song by Charles Weinberg and Irving Bibo:
CAPTAIN SWAGGER

CAVALIER, THE
A Tiffany-Stahl picture starring Barbara Bedford and directed by Irvin Willat. Song by Meredith Wilson and Hugh Riesenfeld:
MY CAVALIER

CLIMAX, THE
A Universal picture filmed with a cast headed by Jean Hersholt, Kathryn Crawford and Henry Armetta, and directed by Victor Schertzinger, who contributed the song:
YOU, MY MELODY OF LOVE

DIVINE LADY
A First National picture starring Corinne Griffith and directed by Frank Lloyd. Song by Joseph Pasternack and Richard Kountz:
LADY DIVINE

GANG WAR

A Film Booking Office release filmed with a cast headed by Olive Borden, Jack Pickford and Eddie Gribbon. Songs:

LOW DOWN by Jo Trent and Peter De-Rose; I LOVE ME by Will Mahoney; MY SUPPRESSED DESIRE by Ned Miller and Chester Cohn; and YA COMIN' UP TO-NIGHT—HUH? by Al Sherman, Al Lewis and Abe Lyman.

HIT OF THE SHOW

A Film Booking Office release filmed with a cast headed by Joe E. Brown and directed by Ralph Ince. Songs:

YOU'RE IN LOVE AND I'M IN LOVE by Walter Donaldson; WAITIN' FOR KATIE by Gus Kahn and Ted Shapiro.

JAZZ SINGER, THE

A Warner Brothers' picture, starring Al Jolson in a cast that included May Mc-Avoy, Warren Oland, Eugenie Besserer, Otto Lederer, Cantor Josef Rosenblatt, Bobbie Gordon, Richard Tucker, Nat Carr, William Demarest, Anders Randolf and Will Walling, and directed by Alan Crosland. In addition to the background music, which included *The Sidewalks of New York, My Gal Sal, In The Good Old Summer Time, Waiting For The Robert E. Lee* and *If A Girl Like You Loved A Boy Like Me,* Al Jolson sang the following songs:

BLUE SKIES by Irving Berlin; DIRTY HANDS DIRTY FACE by Edgar Leslie, Grant Clarke, Jolson and Jimmy Monaco; the Jewish chant KOL NIDRE; MOTHER I STILL HAVE YOU by Jolson and Louis Silvers; MY MAMMY by Sam Lewis, Joe Young and Walter Donaldson; and TOOT TOOT TOOTSIE GOODBYE by Gus Kahn, Ernie Erdman and Dan Russo.

LAUGHING LADY, THE

A Paramount picture starring Ruth Chatterton and Clive Brook and directed by Victor Schertzinger, who contributed the song:

ANOTHER KISS

LONESOME

A Universal picture starring Glenn Tryon and Barbara Kent and directed by Paul Fejos. Song by Dave Dreyer, Herman Ruby and Joseph Cherniovsky:

LONESOME

LOVE

A Paramount picture starring John Gilbert and Greta Garbo and directed by Edmund Goulding. Song by Howard Dietz and Walter Donaldson:

THAT MELODY OF LOVE

LOVES OF AN ACTRESS, THE

A Paramount picture starring Pola Negri and directed by Rowland W. Lee. Song by J. Keirn Brennan and Karl Hajos:

SUNBEAMS BRING DREAMS OF YOU

MAN WHO LAUGHS, THE

A Universal picture starring Mary Philbin and Conrad Veidt, and directed by Paul Leni. Song by Walter Hirsch, Lew Pollack and Erno Rapee:

WHEN LOVE COMES STEALING

MAN, WOMAN AND WIFE

A Universal picture filmed with a cast that included Norman Kerry, Pauline Stark and Marian Nixon, and directed by Edward Laemmle. Song by Herman Ruby and Joseph Cherniovsky:

LOVE CAN NEVER DIE

MANHATTAN COCKTAIL

A Fox picture starring Nancy Carroll and Richard Arlen, and directed by Victor Schertzinger, who also contributed the song:

GOTTA BE GOOD

MARRIAGE BY CONTRACT

A Tiffany-Stahl picture starring Patsy Ruth Miller and directed by James Flood. Songs:

COME BACK TO ME by Dave Goldberg and A. E. Joffe; WHEN THE RIGHT ONE COMES ALONG by L. Wolfe Gilbert and Mabel Wayne.

MASKS OF THE DEVIL, THE

An M-G-M picture starring John Gilbert in a cast that included Alma Rubens and Theodore Roberts, and directed by Victor Seastrom. Song by William Axt and David Mendoza:

LIVE AND LOVE

MATING CALL, THE

A Paramount picture starring Thomas Meighan and directed by James Cruze. Song by Francis Ring and Martin Broones:

THE MATING CALL

OUR DANCING DAUGHTERS

An M-G-M picture starring Joan Crawford in a cast that included Johnny Mack Brown, and directed by Harry Beaumont. Song by William Axt and David Mendoza:

I LOVED YOU THEN AS I LOVE YOU NOW

RED DANCE, THE

A Fox picture starring Dolores Del Rio in a cast that included Charles Farrell. Song by Lew Pollack and Erno Rapee:
SOMEDAY, SOMEWHERE WE'LL MEET AGAIN

ROMANCE OF THE UNDERWORLD

A Fox picture starring Mary Astor and John Boles, and directed by Irving Cummings. Song by Irving Kahal, Pierre Norman and Sammy Fain:
JUDY

SCARLET LADY, THE

A Columbia picture filmed with a cast that included Lya de Putti and Don Alvarado, and directed by Alan Crosland. Song by Lou Herscher:
MY HEART BELONGS TO YOU

SHOW FOLKS

A Pathe-RKO picture filmed with a cast headed by Eddie Quillan and Lina Basquette, and directed by Paul Stein. Song by Al Koppel, Billy Stone and Charles Weinberg:
NO ONE BUT ME

SHOW GIRL

A First National picture starring Alice White in a cast that included Lee Moran and Donald Reed, and directed by Alfred Santell. Songs by Bernie Grossman and Ed Ward:
BUY, BUY FOR BABY and SHOW GIRL (with Joseph Meyer)

SHOW PEOPLE

An M-G-M picture starring Marion Davies and William Haines, and directed by King Vidor. Song by William Axt and David Mendoza:
CROSS ROADS

SPEEDY

A Paramount picture starring Harold Lloyd and directed by Ted Wilde. Song by Ray Klages and Jesse Greer:
SPEEDY BOY

STEPPING HIGH

A Filming Booking Office release. Songs:
THERE'S A CRADLE IN CAROLIN' By Sam Lewis, Joe Young and Fred Ahlert; I'LL ALWAYS BE IN LOVE WITH YOU by Sammy Stept; THERE'S A PLACE IN THE SUN FOR YOU by B. Green & S. Fain; MY INSPIRATION IS YOU.

SUBMARINE

A Columbia picture filmed with a cast headed by Jack Holt and Dorothy Revier, and directed by Frank Capra. Song by Herman Ruby and Dave Dreyer:
PALS, JUST PALS

TIDE OF EMPIRE

An M-G-M picture filmed with a cast headed by Renee Adoree and George Duryea, and directed by Allan Dwan. Song by Ray Klages and Jesse Greer:
JOSEPHINE

TRAIL OF '98, THE

An M-G-M picture starring Dolores Del Rio in a cast that included Harry Carey and Tully Marshall, and directed by Clarence Brown. Song by Hazel Mooney, Evelyn Lyn and William Axt:
I FOUND GOLD WHEN I FOUND YOU

TWO LOVERS

A United Artists' picture starring Vilma Banky and Ronald Colman, and directed by Fred Niblo. Songs:
GRIEVING by Wayland Axtell; LEONORA by Abner Silver.

VARSITY

A Paramount picture filmed with a cast that included Charles "Buddy" Rogers and a group of Princeton University students, and directed by Frank Tuttle. Song by Al Bryan and W. Franke Harling:
MY VARSITY GIRL I'LL CLING TO YOU

WARMING UP

A Paramount picture filmed with a cast headed by Richard Dix, Jean Arthur and Roscoe Karns, and directed by Fred Newmeyer. Song by Walter Donaldson:
OUT OF THE DAWN

WEDDING MARCH, THE

A Paramount picture filmed with a cast that included George Fawcett, Maude George, Erich von Stroheim and Zasu Pitts, and directed by Erich von Stronheim. Song by Harry D. Kerr and J. S. Zamecnek:
PARADISE

WHITE SHADOWS IN THE SOUTH SEAS

An M-G-M picture filmed with a cast headed by Monte Blue, Raquel Torres and Robert Anderson, and directed by W. S. VanDyke. Song by William Axt and David Mendoza:
FLOWER OF LOVE

WOMAN DISPUTED

A United Artists' picture starring Norma Talmadge and directed by Henry King. Song by Bernie Grossman and Ed Ward:
WOMAN DISPUTED I LOVE YOU

1 9 2 9

Born: The Star-studded Revue and Technicolor Musical

In Tin Pan Alley and on Broadway, 1929 is fondly remembered to this day as the year of the California gold rush, a cross-country trek in which the fortune-hunters rode the Sante Fe Chief instead of traveling in covered wagons.

The die had been cast and the Rubicon crossed, just ahead stretched fresh and fertile fields for film exploitation, and Hollywood, now whole-heartedly committed to sound pictures although still producing silent films to fill the conversion gap, not only was in the market for songs and stage stars who could sing them but was ready to pay important money to get them.

Warner Brothers, stealing a march on their competitors, secured a backlog of music, valued at $10,000,000, by the outright purchase of three music publishing houses—Harms, Witmark and Remick, and rival studios soon followed suit by acquiring valuable music catalogues of their own. But that was only the beginning. The writers of popular songs, whose income from sheet music sales had been drastically cut when the radio set replaced the up-right piano in millions of homes, also struck pay dirt, finding in Hollywood both an eager market for their wares and fat long-term contracts that took them off the diet of lean royalties on which they had been subsisting, and such top-flight composers and lyricists as Walter Donaldson, Richard Whiting, Ray Henderson, Lew Brown, Abel Baer, Milton Ager, Con Conrad, Joe Burke, Buddy DeSylva, Sammy Fain, Grant Clarke and Leo Robin bought one-way tickets to California and switched their cheese-cake-and-coffee al-legiance from Lindy's on Broadway to Hollywood's Brown Derby.

But in this sunkist land of plenty, these members of the Manhattan chapter of the sharps-and-flats fraternity found competition worthy of envy upon their arrival in Hollywood in the person of Nacio Herb Brown, a Beverly Hills realtor who dabbled in songwriting—a hobby that enriched the sound tracks with five of the big song hits of 1929: *The Wedding of the Painted Doll, Singing In The Rain, You Were Meant For Me, Chant of The Jungle* and *Pagan Love Song*, all with lyrics by Arthur Freed, another Tin Pan Alley neophyte of 1929 and now credited with more successful film musicals than any other producer.

Like the Broadway songwriters, scores of Broadway stage stars also took Horace Greeley's sage advice and went west with Helen Morgan, Eddie Can-tor, Ann Pennington, Sophie Tucker, Jeanette MacDonald, Fanny Brice, Charlotte Greenwood, Rudy Vallee and the Four Marx Brothers breaking the trail that led to film fame and fortune, while Ted Lewis and his wailing

clarinet and Fred Waring's Pennsylvanians were the first bands to get headline billing on motion picture house marquees. Europe, too, contributed to
this galaxy of Hollywood-bound talent, Maurice Chevalier deserting the
French music halls to make his American film debut in *Innocents Of Paris,*
and Gertrude Lawrence, idol of London's West End, making her American
talkie premiere in *Battle Of Paris.*

Seven smash Broadway musicals—*The Desert Song, Rio Rita, Show Boat,
Sally, The Cocoanuts, So Long Letty* and *Little Johnny Jones*—were perpetu-
ated on film and played to more people in a single night than they had during
their entire record-breaking Broadway runs, and to insure a future crop of
song-and-dance shows, the motion picture studios started to finance the stag-
ing of Broadway productions.

Al Jolson, who had started the gold rush with *The Jazz Singer,* came
through with another history-maker, *The Singing Fool,* the first film musical
to gross $4,000,000 or better at the box office. Warner Brothers, who had
blazed the talkie trail, again played a pioneering role by filming two musicals
in Technicolor—*On With The Show* and *The Gold Diggers Of Broadway.*
Both Warner Brothers and Metro-Goldwyn-Mayer inaugurated the star-studded revue with *The Show of Shows* and *The Hollywood Revue,* respectively.
In the former picture, even Rin-Tin-Tin got feature billing for in those fabulous
days, even a dog's life in Hollywood merited envy. And with four musicals—
Broadway Melody, The Cockeyed World, Rio Rita and *Gold Diggers of
Broadway*—being voted among the ten best films of the year, the songwriters
had a field day and those who sang their songs had their eyes set on deluxe
swimming pools and Rolls-Royce motor cars.

Musicals

APPLAUSE
A Paramount picture filmed with a cast
headed by Helen Morgan, Joan Peters,
Fuller Melish, Jr., Jack Cameron, Henry
Wadsworth and Dorothy Cummings, and di-
rected by Rouben Mamoulian. Songs:
WHAT WOULDN'T I DO FOR THAT
MAN by E. Y. Harburg and Jay Gorney;
YAAKA HULA HICKEY DULA by E.
Ray Goetz, Joe Young and Pete Wendling;
GIVE YOUR LITTLE BABY LOTS OF
LOVIN' by Dolly Morse and Joe Burke and
I'VE GOT A FEELIN' I'M FALLIN' by
Billy Rose, Harry Link and "Fats" Waller.

BATTLE OF PARIS
A Paramount picture starring Gertrude
Lawrence in a cast that included Charles
Ruggles, Walter Petrie, Gladys DuBois and
Arthur Treacher, and directed by Robert
Flory. Songs:

THEY ALL FALL IN LOVE by Cole
Porter; WHAT MAKES MY BABY
BLUE? and HOUSEKEEPING FOR YOU
by Howard Dietz and Jay Gorney.

BLUE SKIES
A Fox picture starring Helen Twelve-
trees and Frank Albertson, and directed by
Alfred E. Werker. Songs by Walter Bullock
and Lew Pollack:
YOU NEVER CAN TELL; IT'S A
FINE HOW D'YA DO and HOW WERE
WE TO KNOW?

BROADWAY
A Universal picture filmed with a cast
headed by Glenn Tryon, Merna Kennedy,
Evelyn Brent and Otis Harlan, and directed
by Paul Fejos. Songs by Sidney Mitchell,
Archie Gottler and Con Conrad:
BROADWAY; THE CHICKEN OR

THE EGG; SING A LITTLE LOVE SONG; HITTIN' THE CEILING and HOT-FOOTN' IT.

BROADWAY BABIES
A First National picture filmed with a cast headed by Alice White, Sally Eilers and Fred Kohler, and directed by Mervyn LeRoy. Songs:
WISHING AND WAITING FOR LOVE by Grant Clarke and Harry Akst; BROADWAY BABY DOLL by Al Bryan and George W. Meyer.

BROADWAY MELODY
An M-G-M picture filmed with a cast headed by Bessie Love, Anita Paige and Charles King, and directed by Harry Beaumont. Songs:
GIVE MY REGARDS TO BROADWAY by George M. Cohan; THE WEDDING OF THE PAINTED DOLL; BROADWAY MELODY; LOVE BOAT; BOY FRIEND and YOU WERE MEANT FOR ME by Arthur Freed and Nacio Herb Brown; TRUTHFUL DEACON BROWN by Willard Robison.

BROADWAY SCANDALS
A Columbia picture filmed with a cast headed by Sally O'Neil, Jack Egan, Carmel Myers and John Hyams, and directed by George Archainbaud. Songs by James F. Hanley:
DOES AN ELEPHANT LOVE PEANUTS? KICKING THE BLUES AWAY and WHAT IS LIFE WTHOUT LOVE?

CLOSE HARMONY
A Paramount picture filmed with a cast headed by Nancy Carroll, Charles "Buddy" Rogers, Skeets Gallagher and Jack Oakie, and directed by John Cromwell and Edward Sutherland. Songs by Leo Robin and Richard J. Whiting:
I'M ALL A-TWITTER I'M ALL A-TWIRL and I WANT TO GO PLACES AND DO THINGS.

COCKEYED WORLD, THE
A Fox picture filmed with a cast that included Victor McLaglen, Edmund Lowe, Lily Damita, El Brendel, Bob Burns, Joe E. Brown and Stuart Erwin, and directed by Raoul Walsh. Musical numbers:
SEMPER FIDELIS by John Philip Sousa; OVER THERE by George M. Cohan; ROSE OF NO MAN'S LAND by James Caddigan and James Brennan; KA-KA-KATY by Geoffrey O'Hara; HINKY DINKY PARLEY VOO by Al Dubin, Irving Mills and Jimmy McHugh; SO LONG and SO DEAR TO ME by Sidney Mitchell, Archie Gottler and Con Conrad; YOUR'RE THE CREAM IN MY COFFEE by Lew Brown, B. G. DeSylva and Ray Henderson; GLORIANNA by Sidney Clare and Lew Pollack.

DANCE OF LIFE
A Paramount picture starring Hal Skelly and Nancy Carroll in a cast that included May Boley and Oscar Levant, and directed by John Cromwell and Edward Sutherland. Songs by Sam Coslow, Leo Robin and Richard Whiting:
TRUE BLUE LOU; THE FLIPPITY FLOP; LADIES OF THE DANCE; CUDDLESOME BABY, KING OF JAZZ-MANIA.

DESERT SONG, THE
A Warner Brothers' picture filmed with a cast headed by John Boles, Carlotta King, Louise Fazenda and Myrna Loy, and directed by Roy Del Ruth. Songs by Oscar Hammerstein II and Sigmund Romberg.
RIFF SONG; FRENCH MILITARY MARCHING SONG; THEN YOU WILL KNOW; LOVE'S DEAR YEARNING; DESERT SONG; SONG OF THE BRASS KEY; ONE FLOWER GROWS ALONE IN YOUR GARDEN; SABRE SONG and ROMANCE.

DEVIL MAY CARE
An M-G-M picture filmed with a cast headed by Ramon Novarro, and Marion Harris, and directed by Sidney Franklin. Songs by Clifford Grey & Herb Stothart:
SHEPHERD SERENADE; CHARMING; IF HE CARED and MARCH OF THE GUARD.

FOX MOVIETONE FOLLIES
A Fox picture filmed with a cast that included Sue Carol, Lola Lane, Sharon Lynn and Stepin Fetchit, and directed by David Butler. Songs by Sidney Mitchell, Archie Gottler and Con Conrad.
WALKING WITH SUSIE; WHY CAN'T I BE LIKE YOU?; LEGS; THE BREAKAWAY; THAT'S YOUR BABY; LOOK WHAT YOU'VE DONE TO ME; BIG CITY BLUES and PEARL OF OLD JAPAN.

GLORIFYING THE AMERICAN GIRL
A Paramount picture filmed with a cast headed by Mary Eaton, Dan Healy, Helen Morgan, Eddie Cantor and Rudy Vallee, and directed by Millard Webb. Songs:
BLUE SKIES by Irving Berlin; I'M

JUST A VAGABOND LOVER by Rudy Vallee and Leon Zimmerman; WHAT WOULDN'T I DO FOR THAT MAN by E. Y. Harburg and Jay Gorney; SAM THE OLD ACCORDIAN MAN; AT SUNDOWN and BEAUTIFUL CHANGES by Walter Donaldson.

GOLD DIGGERS OF BROADWAY

A Warner Borthers' picture filmed with a cast headed by Nancy Welford, Conway Tearle, Winnie Lightner, Ann Pennington, Lilyan Tashman and Nick Lucas, and directed by Roy Del Ruth. Songs by Al Dubin and Joe Burke:
TIP-TOE THROUGH THE THE TULIPS; IN A KITCHENETTE; GO TO BED; PAINTING THE CLOUDS WITH SUNSHINE; AND THEY STILL FALL IN LOVE and WHAT WILL I DO WITHOUT YOU?

HALLELUJAH

An M-G-M picture filmed with a cast that included Daniel L. Haymes, Mae McKinney, William Fountaine, Harry Gray and the Dixie Jubilee Singers, and directed by King Vidor. Songs by Irving Berlin:
WAITING AT THE END OF THE ROAD and SWANEE SHUFFLE.

HOLLYWOOD REVUE

An M-G-M- picture filmed with an all-star cast that included Marion Davies, Norma Shearer, Joan Crawford, Bessie Love, Conrad Nagel, Jack Benny, Lionel Barrymore, "Ukelele Ike" Edwards, Laurel and Hardy, John Gilbert, Anita Paige, William Haines, Buster Keaton, Marie Dressler, Charles King, Polly Moran, Natacha Nattova, the Brox Sisters and the Albertine Rasch Ballet, and directed by C. Reisner.
MINSTREL DAYS; YOUR MOTHER AND MINE; NOBODY BUT YOU; I NEVER KNEW I COULD DO A THING LIKE THAT; LON CHANEY WILL GET YOU IF YOU DON'T WATCH OUT; STROLLING THROUGH THE PARK ONE DAY and ORANGE BLOSSOM TIME, by Joe Goodwin and Gus Edwards: GOTTA FEELIN' FOR YOU by Jo Trent and Louis Alter; BONES AND TAMBOURINES; STRIKE UP THE BAND and TABLEAUX OF JEWELS by Fred Fisher: YOU WERE MEANT FOR ME; TOMMY ATKINS ON PARADE and SINGING IN THE RAIN by Arthur Freed and Nacio Herb Brown: LOW-DOWN RHYTHM by Raymond Klages and Jesse Greer; FOR I'M THE QUEEN by Andy Rice and Martin Broones.

HONKY TONK

A Warner Brothers' picture starring Sophie Tucker in a cast that included Lila Lee, Audrey Ferris, George Duryea and John T. Murray, and directed by Lloyd Bacon. Songs by Jack Yellen and Milton Ager:
I'M THE LAST OF THE RED-HOT MAMAS; I'M DOIN' WHAT I'M DOIN' FOR LOVE; HE'S A GOOD MAN TO HAVE AROUND; I'M FEATHERING A NEST (FOR A LTTLE BLUEBIRD) and I DON'T WANT TO GET THIN.

HOT FOR PARIS

A Fox picture filmed by a cast headed by Victor McLaglen, Fifi D'Orsay, El Brendel and Polly Moran, and directed by Raoul Walsh. Songs by Edgar Leslie and Walter Donaldson:
SWEET NOTHINGS OF LOVE; DUKE OF KAKIAK and SING YOUR LITTLE FOLK SONG.

INNOCENTS OF PARIS

A Paramount picture starring Maurice Chevalier in a cast that included Sylvia Beecher, Russell Simpson, George Fawcett and John Miljan, and directed by Richard Wallace. Songs by Leo Robin and Richard Whiting:
LOUISE; IT'S A HABIT OF MINE; ON TOP OF THE WORLD ALONE and WAIT TILL YOU SEE MY CHERIE.

IS EVERYBODY HAPPY?

A Warner Brothers' picture starring Ted Lewis in a cast that included Ann Pennington, and directed by Archie Mayo. Songs:
WOULDN'T IT BE WONDERFUL? I'M THE MEDICINE MAN FOR THE BLUES; SAMOA and NEW ORLEANS by Grant Clarke and Harry Akst: IN THE LAND OF JAZZ and START THE BAND by Ted Lewis: ST. LOUIS BLUES by W. C. Handy; TIGER RAG by the Original Dixieland Jazz Band.

I'TS A GREAT LIFE

An M-G-M picture starring Rosetta and Vivian Duncan in a cast that included Benny Rubin, Lawrence Gray and Jed Prouty, and directed by Sam Wood. Songs:
SMILE, SMILE, SMILE; I'M FOLLOWING YOU; IT MUST BE AN OLD SPANISH CUSTOM; HOOSIER HOP and I'M SAILING ON A SUNBEAM by Ballard MacDonald and Dave Dreyer: Let A SMILE BE YOUR UMBRELLA ON A RAINY DAY by Irving Kahal, Francis Wheeler and Sammy Fain.

LITTLE JOHNNY JONES

A First National picture filmed by a cast headed by Eddie Buzzell, Alice Day, Edna Murphy and Robert Edeson, and directed by Mervyn LeRoy. Songs:

YANKEE DOODLE BOY and GIVE MY REGARDS TO BROADWAY by George M. Cohan; STRAIGHT, PLACE AND SHOW by Herman Ruby and M. K. Jerome; GO FIND SOMEBODY TO LOVE by Herb Magidson and Michael Cleary; MY PARADISE by Herb Magidson and James Cavanaugh; PAINTING THE CLOUDS WITH SUNSHINE by Al Dubin and Joe Burke.

LOVE PARADE, THE

A Paramount picture starring Maurice Chevalier and Jeanette MacDonald in a cast that included Lupino Lane and Lillian Roth, and directed by Ernst Lubitsch. Songs by Clifford Grey and V. Schertzinger.

DREAM LOVER; MY LOVE PARADE; MARCH OF THE GRENADIERS; ANYTHING TO PLEASE THE QUEEN; LET'S BE COMMON; PARIS STAY THE SAME and NOBODY'S USING IT NOW.

LUCKY BOY

A Tiffany-Stahl picture starring Georgie Jessel in a cast that included Margaret Quimby and Gwen Lee, and directed by Norman Taurog and Charles C. Wilson.

LUCKY BOY and MY MOTHER'S EYES by L. Wolfe Gilbert and Abel Baer; CALIFORNIA HERE I COME by Al Jolson, B. G. DeSylva and Joseph Meyer; MY BLACKBIRDS ARE BLUEBIRDS NOW by Irving Caesar and Cliff Friend.

LUCKY IN LOVE

A Pathe-RKO picture filmed with a cast headed by Morton Downey, Betty Lawford, J. M. Kerrigan and Elizabeth Murray, and directed by Kenneth Webb. Songs by Bud Green and Sammy Stept:

LOVE IS A DREAMER; FOR THE LIKES OF YOU AND ME and WHEN THEY SING THE "WEARING OF THE GREEN" IN SYNCOPATED TIME.

MARIANNE

An M-G-M picture starring Marion Davies in a cast that included Lawrence Gray, Cliff Edwards, Benny Rubin and Oscar Shaw, and directed by Robert Z. Leonard.

WHEN I SEE MY SUGAR; MARIANNA and OO-LA-LA by Roy Turk and Fred Ahlert: HANG ON TO ME and JUST YOU, JUST ME by Ray Klages and Jesse Greer: BLONDY by Arthur Freed and Nacio Herb Brown.

MARRIED IN HOLLYWOOD

A Fox picture filmed with a cast headed by J. Harold Murray, Norma Terris and Walter Catlett, directed by Marcel Silver.

DANCE AWAY THE NIGHT and PEASANT LOVE SONG by Harlan Thompson and Dave Stamper: A MAN, A MAID and DEEP IN LOVE by Harlan Thompson Oscar Straus; BRIDAL CHORUS and NATIONAL ANTHEM by Harlan Thompson and Arthur Kay.

MELODY LANE

A Universal picture starring Eddie Leonard in a cast that included Josephine Dunn, and directed by Robert F. Hill. Songs :

ROLY BOLY EYES by Eddie Leonard: HERE I AM; THERE'S SUGAR CANE ROUND MY DOOR; BEAUTIFUL and THE BOOGY MAN IS HERE by Eddie Leonard and Grace and Jack Stern: THE SONG OF THE ISLANDS by Charles E. King.

MOTHER'S BOY

A Pathe-RKO picture starring Morton Downey in a cast that included Helen Chandler and Brian Donlevy, and directed by Bradley Barker. Songs by Bud Green and S. Stept:

THERE'LL BE YOU AND ME; COME TO ME; I'LL ALWAYS BE MOTHER'S BOY and THE WORLD IS YOURS AND MINE.

MY MAN

A Warner Brothers' picture starring Fanny Brice in a cast that included Guinn Williams, and directed by Archie Mayo. Songs:

SECOND-HAND ROSE by Grant Clarke and James Hanley; MY MAN by Channing Pollock and Maurice Yvain; IF YOU WANT A RAINBOW (YOU MUST HAVE THE RAIN) by Billy Rose, Mort Dixon and Oscar Levant; I'M AN INDIAN by Blanche Merrill and Leo Edwards; I WAS A FLORODORA BABY by Ballard MacDonald and Harry Carroll; I'D RATHER BE BLUE OVER YOU (THAN HAPPY WITH SOMEBODY ELSE) by B. Rose & F. Fisher.

ON WITH THE SHOW

A Warner Brothers' picture filmed with a cast headed by Betty Compson, Louise Fazenda, Sally O'Neil, Joe E. Brown, Ethel Waters and the Fairbanks Twins, and directed by Alan Crosland. Songs by Grant Clarke and Harry Akst:

BIRMINGHAM BERTHA; AM I BLUE? IN THE LAND OF LET'S PRETEND; LET ME HAVE MY DREAMS; WELCOME HOME; DON'T IT MEAN A

THING TO YOU?; and LIFT THE JUL-
EPS TO YOUR TWO LIPS.

RAINBOW MAN

A Paramount picture starring Eddie Dowl-
ing in a cast that included Frankie Darrow,
Marian Nixon and Sam Hardy, and directed
by Fred Newmeyer. Songs:
SLEEPY VALLEY by Andrew B. Sterling
and James Hanley; -LITTLE PAL and
RAINBOW MAN by Eddie Dowling and
James Hanley.

RIO RITA

An RKO picture starring Bebe Daniels in
a cast that included John Boles, Bert Wheel-
er, Robert Woolsey and Dorothy Lee, and
directed by Luther Reed. Songs:
YOU'RE ALWAYS IN MY ARMS
(BUT ONLY IN MY DREAMS);
SWEETHEART WE NEED EACH OTH-
ER; FOLLOWING THE SUN AROUND;
RIO RITA; IF YOU'RE IN LOVE
YOU'LL WALTZ; THE KINKAJOU and
THE RANGERS' SONG by Joseph McCar-
thy and Harry Tierney; LONG BEFORE
YOU CAME ALONG by E. Y. Harburg
and Harold Arlen.

SALLY

A First National picture starring Marilyn
Miller in a cast that included Alexander
Gray and Joe E. Brown, and directed by
John Francis Dillon. Songs:
LOOK FOR THE SILVER LINING by
B. G. DeSylva and Jerome Kern; WILD
ROSE by Clifford Grey and Jerome Kern;
SALLY by Al Dubin, Joe Burke and Jerome
Kern; WALKING OFF THOSE BALKAN
BLUES; AFTER BUSINESS HOURS
(THAT CERTAIN BUSINESS BEGINS);
ALL I WANT TO DO, DO, DO IS
DANCE; IF I'M DAY DREAMING
DON'T WAKE ME UP TOO SOON and
WHAT WILL I DO WITHOUT YOU?
by Al Dubin and Joe Burke.

SAY IT WITH SONGS

A Warner Brothers' picture starring Al
Jolson in a cast that included Davey Lee,
Marian Nixon and Fred Kohler, and directed
by Lloyd Bacon. Songs by Lew Brown, B. G.
DeSylva and Ray Henderson:
LITTLE PAL; I'M IN SEVENTH
HEAVEN; WHY CAN'T YOU? and USED
TO YOU.

SHOW BOAT

A Universal picture filmed with a cast
headed by Laura LaPlante, Otis Harlan,
Alma Rubens and Joseph Schildkraut, and
directed by Harry Pollard. Songs:
LOOK DOWN THAT LONESOME
ROAD by Gene Austin and Nathaniel Shil-
kret; HERE COMES THAT SHOW BOAT
by Billy Rose and Maceo Pinkard; LOVE
SINGS A SONG IN MY HEART by Joseph
Cherniovsky and Clarence J. Marks; OL'
MAN RIVER by Oscar Hammerstein II
and Jerome Kern.

SHOW OF SHOWS

A Warner Brothers' picture filmed with an
all-star cast that included Hobart Bosworth,
Johnny Arthur, H. B. Warner, Georges Car-
pentier, Monte Blue, Alice White, Frank
Fay, Beatrice Lillie, Ben Turpin, Louise Fa-
zenda, Richard Barthelmess, Dolores Cos-
tello, Alice Day, Loretta Young, Patsy Ruth
Miller, Winnie Lightner, Lila Lee, Irene
Bordoni, Myrna Loy, Sid Silvers, Marian
Nixon, Nick Lucas, Chester Morris, Douglas
Fairbanks Jr., Ted Lewis, Noah Beery, Bull
Montana, John Barrymore, Sally Eilers,
Betty Compson and Rin-Tin-Tin, and di-
rected by John Adolfi. Songs:
SINGING IN THE BATHTUB by Ned
Washington, Herb Magidson and Michael
Cleary; LADY LUCK by Ray Perkins; MO-
TION PICTURE PIRATES by M. K. Jer-
ome; IF I COULD LEARN TO LOVE by
Herman Ruby and M. K. Jerome; PINGO-
PONGO by Al Dubin and Joe Burke; THE
ONLY SONG I KNOW and MY SISTER
by J. Keirn Brennan and Ray Perkins;
YOUR MOTHER AND MINE by Joe
Goodwin and Gus Edwards; YOU WERE
MEANT FOR ME by Arthur Freed and
Nacio Herb Brown; JUST AN HOUR OF
LOVE and LI-PO-LI by Al Bryan and Ed
Ward; ROCK-A-BYE YOUR BABY WITH
A DIXIE MELODY by Joe Young, Sam
Lewis and Jean Schwartz; IF YOUR BEST
FRIENDS WON'T TELL YOU by Al Du-
bin and Joe Burke; JUMPING JACK by
Herman Ruby and Rube Bloom; YOUR
LOVE IS ALL I CRAVE by Al Dubin and
Arthur Johnston.

SINGING FOOL, THE

A Warner Brothers' picture starring Al
Jolson in a cast that included Betty Bronson,
Davey Lee and Josephine Dunn, and directed
by Lloyd Bacon. Songs:
SONNY BOY; IT ALL DEPENDS ON
YOU and I'M SITTIN' ON TOP OF THE
WORLD by Lew Brown, B. G. DeSylva and
Ray Henderson: THERE'S A RAINBOW
ROUND MY SHOULDER by Billy Rose,
Al Jolson and Dave Dreyer.

SMILING IRISH EYES

A First National picture starring Colleen Moore in a cast that included James Hall, and directed by William A. Seiter. Songs:

A WEE BIT OF LOVE; THEN I'LL RIDE HOME WITH YOU; OLD KILLARNEY FAIR by Herman Ruby and Norman Spencer: SMILING IRISH EYES by Ray Perkins.

SO LONG LETTY

A Warner Brothers' picture starring Charlotte Greenwood in a cast that included Grant Withers, Patsy Ruth Miller, Marion Brent, Helen Foster and Claude Gillingwater, and directed by Lloyd Bacon. Songs:

ONE SWEET LITTLE YES; CLOWNING; BEAUTY SHOP; AM I BLUE?; LET ME HAVE MY DREAMS and MY STRONGEST WEAKNESS IS YOU by Grant Clarke and Harry Akst: SO LONG LETTY by Earl Caroll; DOWN AMONG THE SUGAR CANE by Grant Clarke and Charles Tobias.

SO THIS IS COLLEGE

An M-G-M picture filmed with a cast headed by Elliott Nugent, Robert Montgomery, Cliff Edwards and Sally Starr, and directed by Sam Wood. Songs:

I DON'T WANT YOUR KISSES by Fred Fisher and Martin Broones; CAMPUS CAPERS by Charlotte Greenwood and Martin Broones; SOPHOMORE PROM by Ray Klages and Jesse Greer; UNTIL THE END by Al Boasberg and Martin Broones.

SONG OF LOVE

A Columbia picture filmed with a cast that included Belle Baker and Ralph Graves, and directed by Erle C. Kenton. Songs:

I'M SOMEBODY'S BABY NOW by Mack Gordon and Max Rich; I'M WALKING WITH THE MOONBEAMS (TALKING TO THE STARS) by Mack Gordon, Max Rich and Maurice Abrahams; I'LL STILL GO ON WANTING YOU by Bernie Grossman; WHITE WAY BLUES by Mack Gordon, Max Rich and George Weist.

STREET GIRL, THE

An RKO picture filmed with a cast headed by Betty Compson, Jack Oakie and Ned Sparks, and directed by Wesley Ruggles. Songs by Sidney Clare and Oscar Levant:

LOVEABLE AND SWEET; BROKEN UP TUNE and MY DREAMY MELODY.

SUNNY SIDE UP

A Fox picture starring Janet Gaynor and Charles Farrell in a cast that included Joe E. Brown and El Brendel, and directed by David Butler. Songs by Lew Brown, B. G. DeSylva and Ray Henderson:

TURN ON THE HEAT; KEEP YOUR SUNNY SIDE UP; IF I HAD A TALKING PICTURE OF YOU and (I'M A DREAMER) AREN'T WE ALL?

SWEETIE

A Paramount picture starring Nancy Carroll in a cast that included Helen Kane and Jack Oakie, and directed by Frank Tuttle.

MY SWEETER THAN SWEET; ALMA MAMMY; BEAR DOWN PELHAM; I THINK YOU'LL LIKE IT and PREP STEP by George Marion Jr. and Richard Whiting; HE'S SO UNUSUAL by Al Lewis, Abner Silver and Al Sherman.

SYNCOPATION

An RKO picture featuring Fred Waring's Pennsylvanians in a cast that included Morton Downey, Dorothy Lee, Osgood Perkins and Ian Hunter, and directed by Burt Glennon. Songs:

JERICHO by Leo Robin and Richard Myers; MINE ALONE by Herman Ruby and Richard Myers; DO SOMETHING and I'LL ALWAYS BE IN LOVE WITH YOU by Bud Green and Sammy Stept.

TANNED LEGS

An RKO picture starring Ann Pennington in a cast that included June Clyde, Arthur Lake, Dorothy Revier and Sally Blane, and directed by Marshall Neilan. Songs by Sidney Clare and Oscar Levant:

WITH YOU, WITH ME and YOU'RE RESPONSIBLE.

TIME, THE PLACE AND THE GIRL, THE

A Warner Brothers' picture starring Betty Compson in a cast that included Grant Withers, James Kirkwood and Vivian Oakland, and directed by Howard Bretherton. Songs:

I WONDER WHO'S KISSING HER NOW by Frank Adams, Will Hough and Joe Howard; COLLEGIATE by Moe Jaffe and Nat Bonx; COLLEGIANA by Dorothy Fields and Jimmy McHugh; DOIN' THE RACOON by Ray Klages, J. Fred Coots and Herb Magidson; FASHIONETTE by Robert King and Jack Glogau; JACK AND JILL by Larry Spier and Sam Coslow; HOW MANY TIMES by Irving Berlin; EVERYTHING I DO I DO FOR YOU by Al Sherman; IF YOU COULD CARE by E. Ray Goetz, Arthur Wimperus and Herman Darewski.

VAGABOND LOVER, THE
An RKO picture starring Rudy Vallee in a cast that included Sally Blane and Marie Dressler, and directed by Marshall Neilan.

A LITTLE KISS EACH MORNING and HEIGH-HO EVERYBODY by Harry M. Woods; PICCOLO PETE by Phil Baxter; I LOVE YOU BELIEVE ME I LOVE YOU by Ruby Cowen, Phil Bartholomae and Phil Boutelje; THEN I'LL BE REMINDED OF YOU.

WHY LEAVE HOME?
A Fox picture filmed with a cast that included Sue Carol, Nick Stuart, Dixie Lee, Jean Barry, Richard Keene, Jed Prouty, Walter Catlett and Ilka Chase, and directed by Raymond Cannon. Songs by Sidney Mitchel, Archie Gottler and Con Conrad:

DOING THE BOOM-BOOM and LOOK WHAT YOU'VE DONE TO ME.

WORDS AND MUSIC
A Fox picture filmed with a cast headed by Lois Moran, Helen Twelvetrees and Tom Patricola, and directed by James Tinling.

STEPPING ALONG by William Kernell; TOO WONDERFUL FOR WORDS by Dave Stamper, William Kernell, Edmund Joseph and Paul Gerard Smith; SHADOWS by Sidney Mitchell, Archie Gottler and Con Conrad.

Feature Films with Songs

BETRAYAL
A Paramount picture filmed with a cast headed by Emil Jannings, Gary Cooper and Esther Ralston, and directed by Lewis Milestone, Song by J. S. Zamecnck:

UNDER THE WEATHER

BIG TIME
A Fox picture filmed with a cast headed by Lee Tracy, Mae Clarke, Daphne Pollard, Josephine Dunn and Stepin Fetchit, and directed by Kenneth Hawks. Song by Sidney Lanfield:

NOBODY KNOWS YOU LIKE I DO

BLACK WATCH, THE
A Fox picture filmed with a cast headed by Victor McLaglen, Myrna Loy and David Torrence, and directed by John Ford. Song by William Kernell:

FLOWERS OF DELIGHT

BULLDOG DRUMMOND
A United Artists' picture starring Ronald Colman in a cast that included Joan Bennett, Lilyan Tashman and Montagu Love, and directed by F. Richard Jones. Song by Jack Yellen and Harry Akst:

(I SAYS TO MYSELF SAYS I) THERE'S THE ONE FOR ME

CAREERS
A First National picture starring Billie Dove in a cast headed by Antonio Moreno, Thelma Todd and Noah Beery, and directed by John Francis Dillon. Song by Al Bryan and George W. Meyer:

I LOVE YOU, I HATE YOU

CARELESS AGE, THE
A First National picture starring Douglas Fairbanks Jr. and Loretta Young in a cast that included Carmel Myers, and directed by John Griffith Wray. Song by Herman Ruby and Norman Spencer:

MELODY DIVINE

CHILDREN OF THE RITZ
A First National picture starring Dorothy Mackaill and Jack Mulhall, and directed by John Francis Dillon. Song by Lew Pollack and Nat Shilkret:

SOME SWEET DAY

CHRISTIANA
A Fox picture starring Janet Gaynor and Charles Morton, and directed by William K. Howard. Song by Sidney Mitchell, Archie Gottler and Con Conrad:

CHRISTIANA

COCOANUTS, THE
A Paramount picture starring the Four Marx Brothers in a cast that included Mary Eaton and Oscar Shaw, and directed by Joseph Santley and Robert Florey. Song by Irving Berlin:

WHEN MY DREAMS COME TRUE

COLLEGE LOVE
A Universal picture filmed with a cast headed by George Lewis, Eddie Phillips and Dorothy Gulliver, and directed by Nat Rose. Songs by Dave Silverstein and Lee Zahler:

IT'S YOU and OH HOW WE LOVE OUR COLLEGE

CONDEMNED
A United Artists' picture starring Ronald Colman and Ann Harding in a cast that included Louis Wolheim, and directed by Wesley Ruggles. Song by Jack Meskill and Pete Wendling:

SONG OF THE CONDEMNED

COQUETTE

A United Artists' picture starring Mary Pickford in a cast that included George Irving, Louise Beavers, Johnny Mack Brown, William Janning and Henry Kohler, and directed by Sam Taylor. Irving Berlin song:
COQUETTE

DARK SKIES

A Capital Film Exchange release starring Shirley Mason and Wallace MacDonald, and directed by Harry H. Webb. Song by Walter Sheridan and Lee Zahler:
JUANITA

DRAG

A First National picture starring Richard Barthelmess in a cast that included Lucian Littlefield, Katherine Parker, Alice Day and Lila Lee, and directed by Frank Lloyd. Songs by Al Bryan and George W. Meyer:
MY SONG OF THE NILE and I'M TOO YOUNG TO BE CAREFUL (AND TOO SWEET TO BE GOOD).

DUKE STEPS OUT, THE

An M-G-M picture starring William Haines and Joan Crawford, and directed by James Cruze. Song by William Axt and David Mendoza:
JUST YOU

DYNAMITE

An M-G-M picture filmed with a cast headed by Charles Bickford, Kay Johnson and Conrad Nagel, and directed by Cecil B. de Mille. Song by Dorothy Parker and Jack King:
HOW AM I TO KNOW?

EVIDENCE

A Warner Brothers' picture starring Pauline Frederick and Lowell Sherman, and directed by John Adolfi. Song by Al Dubin and M. K. Jerome:
LITTLE CAVALIER

FASHIONS IN LOVE

A Paramount picture starring Adolphe Menjou and Fay Compton, and directed by Victor Schertzinger. Songs by Leo Robin and Victor Schertzinger:
DELPHINE; I STILL BELIEVE IN YOU

FAST COMPANY

A Paramount picture filmed with a cast headed by Evelyn Brent, Jack Oakie, Skeets Gallagher and Sam Hardy, and directed by Edward Sutherland. Songs by S. Coslow:
YOU WANT LOVIN' I WANT LOVE

FAST LIFE

A First National picture starring Douglas Fairbanks Jr. and Loretta Young, and directed by John Francis Dillon. Song by Ray Perkins:
SINCE I FOUND YOU

FLYING FLEET, THE

An M-G-M picture co-starring Ramon Novarro and Anita Page, and directed by George Hill. Song by William Axt and David Mendoza:
YOU'RE THE ONLY ONE FOR ME

FLYING FOOL, THE

A Pathe-RKO picture filmed with a cast headed by William Boyd, Marie Prevost, Russell Gleason and Earl Burnett's orchestra, and directed by Tay Garnett. Song by George Waggner and George Green:
IF I HAD MY WAY

FOOTLIGHTS AND FOOLS

A First National picture starring Colleen Moore and Raymond Hackett, and directed by Wiliam A. Seiter. Songs by Al Bryan and George W. Meyer:
IF I CAN'T HAVE YOU and YOU CAN'T BELIEVE MY EYES.

FORWARD PASS, THE

A First National picture starring Douglas Fairbanks Jr. and Loretta Young, and directed by Eddie Cline. Song by Herb Magidson, Ned Washington and Michael Cleary:
HELLO, BABY

GIRL FROM HAVANA

A Fox picture filmed with a cast headed by Paul Page, Lola Lane and Natalie Moorhead, and directed by Benjamin Stoloff. Song by L. W. Gilbert and Abel Baer:
TIME WILL TELL

GIRL FROM WOOLWORTH'S, THE

A First National picture starring Alice White in a cast that included Charles Delancy, Wheeler Oakman and Ben Hall, and directed by William Beaudine. Song by Al Bryan and George W. Meyer:
CRYING FOR LOVE

GIRL ON THE BARGE, THE

A Universal picture filmed with a cast headed by Jean Hersholt, Sally O'Neil and Nancy Kelly, and directed by Edward Sloman. Song by Roy Turk, Fred Ahlert and Joseph Cherniovsky:
WHEN YOU WERE IN LOVE WITH NO ONE BUT ME

GLAD RAG DOLL

A Warner Brothers' picture starring Dolores Costello in a cast that included Claude Gillingwater and Ralph Graves, and direct-

ed by Mitchell Curtiz. Song by Jack Yellen, Dan Dougherty and Milton Ager:
GLAD RAG DOLL.

GRAND PARADE, THE
A Pathe-RKO picture filmed with a cast headed by Helen Twelvetrees, Fred Scott and Richard Carle, and directed by Fred Newmeyer. Songs by Dan Dougherty and Edmund Goulding:
MOANIN' FOR YOU and MOLLY.

GREAT GARBO, THE
A Sono Art-World Wide picture filmed with a cast headed by Erich von Stroheim, Betty Compson and Margie Kane, and directed by James Cruze. Song by Don Mc-Namee and King Zany:
I'M LAUGHING

HALF MARRIAGE
A Pathe-RKO picture filmed with a cast headed by Olive Borden, Morgan Farley and Ken Murray, and directed by William J. Cowan. Song by Sidney Clare and Oscar Levant:
AFTER THE CLOUDS ROLL BY

HARD TO GET
A First National picture filmed with a cast headed by Dorothy Mackaill, Jimmie Finlayson, Louise Fazenda and Jack Oakie, and directed by William Beaudine. Song by Al Bryan and George W. Meyer:
THINGS WE WANT MOST ARE HARD TO GET

HEARTS IN DIXIE
A Fox picture filmed with a cast headed by Stepin Fetchit and Clarence Muse, and directed by Paul Sloane. Song by Howard Jackson:
HEARTS OF DIXIE

HER PRIVATE LIFE
A First National picture filmed with a cast headed by Billie Dove, Walter Pidgeon, Holmes Herbert, Montagu Love, Thelma Todd and Zasu Pitts, and directed by Alexander Korda. Song by Al Bryan and George W. Meyer:
LOVE IS LIKE A ROSE

ILLUSION
A Paramount picture starring Charles "Buddy" Rogers and Nancy Carroll, and directed by L. Mendes. Song by L. Spier.
WHEN THE REAL THING COMES YOUR WAY

IN OLD ARIZONA
A Fox picture starring Warner Baxter, Edmund Lowe and Dorothy Burgess, and directed by Raoul Walsh and Irving Cummings. Song by Lew Brown, B. G. DeSylva and Ray Henderson:
MY TONIA

IRON MASK, THE
A United Artists' picture starring Douglas Fairbanks, and directed by Allan Dwan. Song by Ray Klages and Louis Alter:
ONE FOR ALL, ALL FOR ONE

JAZZ HEAVEN
A Pathe-RKO picture filmed with a cast headed by Johnny Mack Brown, Sally O'Neil and Joseph Cawthorn, and directed by Melville Brown. Song by Sidney Clare and Oscar Levant:
SOMEONE

KIBITZER, THE
A Paramount picture filmed with a cast headed by Harry Green, Mary Brian and Neil Hamilton, and directed by Edward Sloman. Song by Leo Robin & R. Whiting.
JUST WAIT AND SEE SWEETHEART

KING OF THE CONGO
A Mascot Pictures Corporation release filmed with a cast headed by Jacqueline Logan and Walter Miller. Song by Lois Leeson and Lee Zahler:
LOVE THOUGHTS OF YOU

LADY OF THE LAKE, THE
A Fitzpatrick picture starring Percy Marmont and Benita Hume, and directed by James A. Fitzpatrick. Song by Nat Shilkret:
EILEEN, SWEET EILEEN

LADY OF THE PAVEMENTS
A United Artists' picture filmed with a cast headed by Lupe Velez, William Boyd and Jetta Goudal, and directed by D. W. Griffith. Song by Irving Berlin:
WHERE IS THAT SONG OF SONGS FOR ME?

LEATHERNECK, THE
A Pathe-RKO picture filmed with a cast headed by William Boyd, Alan Hale and Robert Armstrong, and directed by Howard Higgin. Song by Josiah Zura, Francis Gromon and Charles Weinberg:
ONLY FOR YOU

LINDA
A First Division release filmed with a cast that included Warner Baxter, Helen Foster and Noah Beery, and directed by Mrs. Wallace Reid. Song by Al Sherman and Charles and Harry Tobias:
LINDA

LOOPING THE LOOP
A Paramount picture starring Werner Krause and Jenny Jugo, and directed by Arthur Robinson. Song by Joe Young, Sam Lewis and Lew Pollack:
POOR PUNCHINELLO

LOVE, LIVE AND LAUGH
A Fox picture filmed with a cast headed by George Jessel, Lila Lee, David Rollins and Henry Kohler, and directed by William K. Howard. Song by L. W. Gilbert & Abel Baer:
TWO LITTLE BABY ARMS

MADONNA OF AVENUE A
A Warner Brothers' picture starring Dolores Costello in a cast that included Grant Withers, Louise Dresser and Lee Moran, and directed by Michael Curtiz. Song by Fred Fisher and Louis Silvers:
MY MADONNA

MAN I LOVE, THE
A Paramount picture filmed with a cast headed by Richard Arlen, Mary Brian, Olga Baclanova, Harry Green, Jack Oakie and Pat O'Malley, and directed by William Wellman. Song by Leo Robin and Richard Whiting:
CELIA

MAN'S MAN, A
An M-G-M picture filmed with a cast headed by William Haines, Josephine Dunn, Sam Hardy and Mae Busch, and directed by James Cruze. Song by Al Bryan and Monte Wilhitt:
MY HEART IS BLUER THAN YOUR EYES, CHERIE

MISSISSIPPI GAMBLER
A Universal picture starring Joseph Schildkraut in a cast that included Joan Bennett and Otis Harlan, and directed by Reginald Barker and Harry Pollard. Song by L. Wolfe Gilbert and Harry Akst:
FATHER MISSISSIPPI

MOLLY AND ME
A Tiffany-Stahl picture filmed with a cast headed by Belle Bennett, Joe E. Brown and Alberta Vaughn, and directed by Albert Ray. Song by L. Wolfe Gilbert and Abel Baer:
IN THE LAND OF MAKE BELIEVE

NAVY BLUES
An M-G-M picture filmed with a cast headed by William Haines, Anita Paige and J. C. Nugent, and directed by Clarence Brown. Song by Roy Turk and Fred Ahlert:
NAVY BLUES

NEW ORLEANS
A Tiffany-Stahl picture filmed with a cast headed by William Collier Jr., Ricardo Cortez and Alma Bennett, and directed by Reginald Barker. Song by Ted Shapiro and Hugh Riesenfeld:
PALS FOREVER

NEW YORK NIGHTS
A United Artists' picture starring Norma Talmadge in a cast that included Gilbert Roland, John Wray and Lilyan Tashman, and directed by Lewis Milestone. Song by Al Jolson, Ballard MacDonald and Dave Dreyer:
A YEAR FROM TODAY

NOAH'S ARK
A Warner Brothers' picture starring Dolores Costello in a cast that included George O'Brien and Noah Beery, and directed by Michael Curtiz. Song by Billy Rose and Louis Silvers:
HEART O' MINE

NOTHING BUT THE TRUTH
A Paramount picture filmed with a cast headed by Richard Dix, Helen Kane, Berton Churchill, Louis Bartels and Ned Sparks, and directed by William Collier Sr. Song by Bud Green and Sammy Stept:
DO SOMETHING

OH! YEAH
A Pathe-RKO picture filmed with a cast headed by Robert Armstrong, James Gleason and Zasu Pitts, and directed by Tay Garnett. Song by Tay Garnett, George Waggner and George Green:
LOVE FOUND ME

PAGAN, THE
An M-G-M picture starring Ramon Novarro in a cast that included Renee Adoree, Dorothy Janis and Donald Crisp, and directed by W. S. VanDyke. Song by Arthur Freed and Nacio Herb Brown.
PAGAN LOVE SONG

PAINTED FACES
A Tiffany-Stahl picture filmed with a cast headed by Joe E. Brown, Helen Foster, Barton Hepburn and Richard Tucker, and directed by Al Rogell. Song by Abner Silver:
SOMEBODY JUST LIKE YOU

POINTED HEELS
A Paramount picture filmed with a cast headed by William Powell, Fay Wray, Helen Kane, Skeets Gallagher and Eugene Pallette, and directed by Edward Sutherland. Songs by Max Rich and Mack Gordon:
I HAVE TO HAVE YOU; AIN'T-CHA?

PORT OF DREAMS
A Universal picture filmed with a cast headed by Mary Philbin and Fred MacKaye. Song by Roy Turk, Fred Ahlert and Joseph Cherniovsky:
TODAY AND TOMORROW

RIVER OF ROMANCE, THE
A Paramount picture filmed with a cast headed by Charles "Buddy" Rogers, Mary Brian, June Collyer, Henry B. Walthall and Wallace Beery, and directed by Richard Wallace. Song by Leo Robin and Sam Coslow:
MY LADY LOVE

ROMANCE OF THE RIO GRANDE
A Fox picture filmed with a cast headed by Warner Baxter, Antonio Moreno, Mary Duncan and Robert Edeson, and directed by Alfred Santell. Song by L. Wolfe Gilbert and Abel Baer:
YOU'LL FIND YOUR ANSWER IN MY EYES

SACRED FLAME, THE
A Warner Brothers' picture starring Pauline Frederick in a cast that included Lila Lee and Conrad Nagel, and directed by Archie L. Mayo. Song by Grant Clarke and H. Akst.
THE SACRED FLAME

SAL OF SINGAPORE
A Pathe-RKO picture filmed with a cast headed by Phyllis Haver, Alan Hale and Fred Kohler, and directed by Howard Higgins. Song by Al Coppell, Billy Stone and Charles Weinberg:
SINGAPORE SAL

SATURDAY'S CHILDREN
A First National picture starring Corinne Griffith in a cast that included Grant Withers, Albert Conti and Alma Tell, and directed by Gregory La Cava. Song by Grant Clarke, Benny Davis and Harry Akst:
I STILL BELIEVE IN YOU

SHANGHAI LADY
A Universal picture starring Mary Nolan and James Murray, and directed by John S. Robertson. Song by Bernie Grossman and Arthur Sizemore:
I WONDER IF IT'S REALLY LOVE

SHANNONS OF BROADWAY, THE
A Universal picture starring James and Lucille Webster Gleason in a cast that included Mary Philbin and Slim Summerville, and directed by Emmett Flynn. Song by Ray Klages and Jesse Greer:
SOMEBODY TO LOVE ME

SHOPWORN ANGEL
A Paramount picture starring Nancy Carroll in a cast that included Gary Cooper and Paul Lukas, and directed by Richard Wallace. Song by Lou Davis and J. Fred Coots:
PRECIOUS LITTLE THING CALLED LOVE

SHOULD A GIRL MARRY?
A Rayart Pictures' release starring Helen Foster and Donald Keith, and directed by Scott Pembroke. Song by Irving Bibo:
HAUNTING MEMORIES

SKIN DEEP
A Warner Brothers' picture filmed with a cast headed by Monte Blue, Betty Compson, Tully Marshall and Davey Lee, and directed by Ray Enright. Song by Sidney Mitchell, Archie Gottler and Con Conrad:
I CAME TO YOU

SONG OF KENTUCKY, A
A Fox picture filmed with a cast headed by Lois Moran, Joseph Wagstaff, Dorothy Burgess and Hedda Hopper, and directed by Lewis Seiler. Song by Sidney Mitchell, Archie Gottler and Con Conrad:
A NIGHT OF HAPPINESS

SOPHOMORE, THE
A Pathe-RKO picture filmed with a cast that included Eddie Quillan, Sally O'Neil, Stanley Smith and Jeanette Loff, and directed by Leo McCarey. Song by Bobby Dolan and Walter O'Keefe:
LITTLE BY LITTLE

SOUTH SEA ROSE
A Fox picture starring Leonore Ulrich & Ilka Chase, and directed by Allan Dwan. Song by L. Wolfe Gilbert and Abel Baer:
SOUTH SEA ROSE

SQUALL, THE
A First National picture filmed with a cast headed by Myrna Loy, Alice Joyce, Richard Tucker, Carroll Nye and Loretta Young, and directed by Alexander Korda. Song by Grant Clarke and Harry Akst:
GYPSY CHARMER

SYNTHETIC SIN
A First National picture filmed with a cast headed by Colleen Moore, Antonio Moreno and Montagu Love, and directed by William A. Seiter. Song by H. Cristy & Nat Shilkret:
BETTY

THEY HAD TO SEE PARIS
A Fox picture starring Will Rogers and Irene Rich in a cast that included Marguerite Churchill, Fifi D'Orsay and Owen Davis, and directed by Frank Borzage. Song by Sidney Mitchell, Archie Gottler and Con Conrad:
I COULD DO IT FOR YOU

THIS IS HEAVEN
A United Artists' picture starring Vilma Banky in a cast that included James Hall and

Lucien Littlefield, and directed by Albert Santell. Song by Jack Yellen and H. Akst:
THIS IS HEAVEN

THROUGH DIFFERENT EYES
A Fox picture filmed with a cast headed by Warner Baxter, Mary Duncan and Edmund Lowe, and directed by John Blystone. Song by William Kernell and Dave Stamper:
I'M SAVING ALL MY LOVING

THUNDERBOLT
A Paramount picture starring George Bancroft in a cast that included Richard Arlen, Fay Wray and Tully Marshall, and directed by Joseph von Sternberg. Song by S. Coslow:
(SITTIN' AROUND) THINKIN' ABOUT MY BABY

TIGER ROSE
A Warner Brothers' picture starring Lupe Velez and Monte Blue, and directed by George Fitzmaurice. Song by Ned Washington, Herb Magidson and Michael Cleary:
THE DAY YOU FALL IN LOVE

TRESPASSER, THE
A United Artists' picture starring Gloria Swanson in a cast that included Robert Ames and Henry B. Walthall, and directed by Edmund Goulding. Song by Elsie Janis and Edmund Goulding:
LOVE YOUR MAGIC SPELL IS EVERYWHERE

TWO MEN AND A MAID
A Tiffany-Stahl picture starring William Collier Jr. and Alma Bennett, and directed by George Archainbaud. Song by L. Wolfe Gilbert and Abel Baer:
LOVE WILL FIND YOU

TWO WEEKS OFF
A First National picture starring Dorothy Mackaill and Jack Mulhall in a cast that included Gertrude Astor and Jed Prouty, and directed by William Beaudine. Song by Al Bryan and George W. Meyer:
LOVE THRILLS

UNTAMED
An M-G-M picture starring Joan Crawford in a cast that included Robert Montgomery and E. Torrence; J. Conway, director.
CHANT OF THE JUNGLE by Arthur Freed and Nacio Herb Brown; THAT WONDERFUL SOMETHING IS LOVE by Joe Goodwin and Louis Alter.

WEARY RIVER
A First National picture starring Richard Barthelmess in a cast that included Betty Compson and William Holden, and directed by Frank Lloyd. Song by Clark and Silvers:
WEARY RIVER

WELCOME DANGER
A Paramount picture starring Harold Lloyd in a cast that included Barbara Kent, and directed by Clyde Bruckman. Songs:
BILLIE by Lynn Cowan; WHEN YOU ARE MINE by Paul Titsworth.

WHEEL OF LIFE, THE
A Paramount picture starring Richard Dix and Esther Ralston in a cast that included O. P. Heggie, and directed by Victor Schertzinger, who contributed the following song:
I WONDER WHY YOU LOVE ME

WHY BE GOOD?
A First National picture starring Colleen Moore and Neil Hamilton, and directed by William A. Seiter. Song by Davis & Coots:
I'M THIRSTY FOR YOUR KISSES

WHY BRING THAT UP?
A Paramount picture starring Moran and and Mack in a cast that included Evelyn Brent and Harry Green; director, G. Abbott.
DO I KNOW WHAT I'M DOING WHILE I'M IN LOVE by Leo Robin and Richard Whiting; SHOO SHOO BOOGIE BOO by Sam Coslow and Richard Whiting.

WILD PARTY, THE
A Paramount picture filmed with a cast headed by Clara Bow, Frederic March, Marceline Day, Jack Oakie and Joyce Compton, and directed by Dorothy Arzner. Song by Leo Robin and Richard Whiting:
MY WILD PARTY GIRL

WOLF OF WALL STREET
A Paramount picture filmed with a cast headed by George Bancroft, Olga Baclanova, Paul Lukas and Nancy Carroll, and directed by Rowland V. Lee. Song by Harold Cristy and Joseph Meyer:
LOVE TAKE MY HEART

WOLF SONG, THE
A Paramount picture filmed with a cast headed by Gary Cooper, Lupe Velez and Louis Wolheim, and directed by Victor Fleming. Songs by Al Bryan and R. Whiting:
MI AMADO and YO TE AMO MEANS "I LOVE YOU".

WOMAN OF AFFAIRS
An M-G-M picture starring Greta Garbo and John Gilbert, and directed by Clarence Brown. Song by Wm. Axt and D. Mendoza:
LOVE'S FIRST KISS

WONDER OF WOMEN
An M-G-M picture filmed with a cast headed by Lewis Stone, Peggy Wood and Leila Haymes; directed by C. Brown. Songs:
ICH LIEBE DICH by Fred Fisher and Martin Broones; AT CLOSE OF DAY by Ray Klages, Jesse Greer and Martin Broones.

1930
A Groaner From Tacoma Makes His Film Debut

Of all the believe-it-or-not success stories that had their genesis in Holly-wood in the early days of the talkies, none is more incredible than that of a member of a troupe of musicians and singers that Paul Whiteman brought from New York City to the cinema capital in 1930 for filming *The King Of Jazz*.

An unknown singer in a male trio known as The Rhythm Boys, he alone of this entourage capitalized handsomely on this Universal picture, which repre-sented for the much-publicized Whiteman and all the others but a brief and fleeting hour of film glory that never struck again.

Although neither Luella Parsons nor Hedda Hopper gave him a tumble in their reviews, the talent scouts must have been impressed with this carefree guy who had both an ingratiating personality and a style all his own in wrapping up a song and giving it a sock delivery since two years later, he was back in Hollywood as a feature player in Paramount's *Big Broadcast;* inside the next twelve months, he had star billing in three musicals: *College Humor, Going Hollywood* and *Too Much Harmony,* and during the past decade he has be-come the most valuable bit of human property on the motion picture lots with seven top-grossing films to his credit, each of which has earned $4,000,000 or better at the box office.

But that's only one phase of this fabulous success story. As a side line, he has brought joy weekly to every American home that has a radio set, processed millions of cans of orange juice, manufactured toys for kiddies, promoted an-nual golf tournaments and provided Bob Hope with countless jokes. In addi-tion, you'll find his name on hundreds of Decca recordings. He is an Horatio Alger hero in the flesh with a penchant for blatant sports shirts—Bing Crosby.

In 1930, however, when Crosby was lurking in the shadows, the Hollywood spotlight played upon a coterie of Broadway stage stars who rushed eagerly into the open arms of the cinema magnates from legitimate theaters closed by the De-pression, and the names of Vivienne Segal, Ed Wynn, Grace Moore of the "Met", Ethelind Terry, Irene Bordoni, John McCormick, Everett Marshall, Lawrence Tibbett, Dennis King and Jimmy Durante appeared on the marquee boards of the country's movie theaters for the first time.

The Broadway stage also provided both scripts and music for at least ten musical films released during 1930: *Follow Through, Animal Crackers, Gold-en Dawn, Good News, Hit The Deck, The New Moon, Rain Or Shine, Sunny, Whoopie, The Vagabond King, Big Boy* and *Spring Is Here,* the latter with songs by Rodgers and Hart.

Jerome Kern, Sigmund Romberg and Harry Tierney, three composers par-tial to writing for Broadway productions, suddenly found in Hollywood a new field of opportunity and provided original music for *Three Sisters, Viennese Nights* and *Dixiana,* respectively, the first two with book and lyrics by Oscar Hammerstein II, while Irving Berlin, who previously had been cool to Hollywood proposals, warmed up to fresh overtures and contributed words-and-music to two of the year's top song-and-dance pictures: *Mammy,* starring Al Jolson, and *Puttin' on The Ritz,* which put a star on Harry Richman's dressing bungalow.

Maurice Chevalier continued to be a surefire box office lure, and in *The Big Pond* shared headline billing with Claudette Colbert, who in 1930 crossed the threshold leading to the talkie Hall of Fame to join Ginger Rogers, Irene Dunne, Myrna Loy, Charles King and Charles "Buddy" Rogers. The throaty voice of Marlene Dietrich, singing *Falling In Love Again,* was heard on the screen for the first time in *The Blue Angel.* And RKO, hoping to capitalize on the radio popularity of "Amos 'n' Andy", starred Freeman F. Cosden and Charles F. Correll in *Check and Double Check,* but this comedy film did not attract the crowds that had gathered around the nation's loud speakers when Madame Queen was suing Andy for a divorce and Amos was on trial for murder. This film, however, did produce one of the few talkie tunes that have sold a million or more sheet music copies, *Three Little Words* by Bert Kalmar and Harry Ruby, who had been brought to Hollywood to write special material as well as songs for the Four Marx Brothers and Wheeler and Woolsey and shared with Arthur Freed and Nacio Herb Brown the distinction of being the first of several Hollywood songwriting teams that made Tin Pan Alley history in the following decade.

Nineteen-thirty also marked the birth of the horse opera, songs being introduced in both *Near The Rainbow's End* and *Sons Of The Saddle* to relieve the monotony of the thundering hoofbeats of the posses, led by Bob Steele and Ken Maynard, as they rode hell-to-leather that wrong might be avenged and virtue triumph before the final fadeout. Enduring songs were hatched in two of the year's musicals, *Chasing Rainbows,* which introduced Jack Benny as a feature player, providing the followers of FDR with *Happy Days Are Here Again,* the rallying song of the 1932 Democratic National Convention, while the title tune for *Paramount On Parade,* a star-studded revue, has served as the play-on for the Paramount Weekly Newsreel for the past two decades.

But in the "E" for Excellence department, the musicals of 1930 failed to qualify, the judges who selected the ten best pictures of the year giving their votes to such highly dramatic productions as *All Quiet On The Western Front, Journey's End, Anna Christie, The Big House* and *Hell's Angels.* In fact, the movie makers had made a rather startling discovery: Movie goers went to the talkies to think as well as to feast their eyes on shapely legs and to listen to songs they'd already heard time and again on their loud speakers.

Musicals

ANIMAL CRACKERS
A Paramount picture starring the Four Marx Brothers in a cast that included Lillian Roth, and directed by Victor Heerman. Songs:
WHY AM I SO ROMANTIC? and HOORAY FOR CAPTAIN SPALDING by Bert Kalmar and Harry Ruby; COLLEGIATE by Moe Jaffe and Nat Bonx; SOME OF THESE DAYS by Shelton Brooks.

BE YOURSELF
A United Artists' picture starring Fanny Brice in a cast that included Harry Green and Robert Armstrong, and directed by Thornton Freeland. Songs:
WHEN A WOMAN LOVES A MAN by Billy Rose and Ralph Rainger; COOKING BREAKFAST FOR THE ONE I LOVE by Billy Rose and Henry Tobias; KICKING A HOLE IN THE SKY and SASHA THE PASSION OF THE PASCHA by Billy Rose, Ballard MacDonald and Jesse Greer.

BIG BOY
A Warner Brothers' picture starring Al Jolson in a cast that included Claudia Dell, Louise Closser Hale, Franklin Batie and Noah Berry, and directed by Alan Crosland. Musical numbers:
WHAT WILL I DO WITHOUT YOU? by Al Dubin and Joe Burke; TOMORROW IS ANOTHER DAY and LIZA LEE by Bud Green and Sammy Stept; DOWN SOUTH by Sigmund Spaeth and George Myddleton; THE HANDICAP MARCH by Dave Reed Jr. and George Rosey.

BIG POND, THE
A Paramount picture starring Maurice Chevalier and Claudette Colbert, and directed by Hobart Henley. Songs:
LIVIN' IN THE SUNLIGHT, LOVIN' IN THE MOONLIGHT by Al Lewis and Al Sherman; THIS IS MY LUCKY DAY by Lew Brown, B. G. DeSylva and Ray Henderson; MIA CARA and YOU BROUGHT A NEW KIND OF A LOVE TO ME by Irving Kahal, Pierre Norman and Sammy Fain.

BLAZE O' GLORY
A Sono Art—World Wide picture filmed with a cast headed by Eddie Dowling, Betty Compson, Henry Walthall and Frankie Darro, and directed by Renaud Hoffman and George Crone. Songs by Eddie Dowling, James Hanley and James Brockman:
DOUGHBOY'S LULLABY; PUT A LITTLE SALT ON THE BLUEBIRD'S TAIL and WRAPPED IN A RED, RED ROSE.

BRIDE OF THE REGIMENT
A First National picture starring Vivienne Segal in a cast that included Roger Pryor, Walter Pidgeon and Louise Fazenda, and directed by John Francis Dillon. Songs by Al Bryan and Ed Ward:
BROKEN-HEARTED LOVER; COOK'S SONG; DREAM AWAY; HEART OF HEAVEN; I'D LIKE TO BE A HAPPY BRIDE; ONE KISS, SWEETHEART, THEN GOODBYE; THROUGH THE MIRACLE OF LOVE; ONE LIFE ONE LOVE and YOU STILL RETAIN YOUR GIRLISH FIGURE.

CAPTAIN OF THE GUARD
A Universal picture starring Laura La-Plante and John Boles, and directed by John S. Robinson. Songs by William F. Dugan and Heinz Roemheld:
CAN IT BE; FOR YOU and MAIDS ON PARADE.

CHASING RAINBOWS
An M-G-M picture starring Bessie Love and Charles King in a cast that included Jack Benny, Polly Moran and Marie Dressler, and directed by Charles F. Reisner. Songs:
HAPPY DAYS ARE HERE AGAIN; LUCKY ME, LOVABLE YOU; DO I KNOW WHAT I'M DOING? and EVERYBODY TAP by Jack Yellen and Milton Ager; POOR BUT HONEST by Gus Edwards; DYNAMIC PERSONALITY by Fred Fisher, Edward Ward and Reggie Montgomery; LOVE AIN'T NOTHIN BUT THE BLUES by Joe Goodwin and Louis Alter; GOTTA FEELING FOR YOU by Jo Trent and Louis Alter.

CHECK AND DOUBLE CHECK
An RKO picture starring Freeman F. Cosden and Charles F. Correll (Amos 'n' Andy) in a cast that included Sue Carol, and directed by Melville Brown. Songs:
THREE LITTLE WORDS and RING DEM BELLS by Bert Kalmar and Harry Ruby; OLD MAN BLUES by Irving Mills and Duke Ellington.

CHEER UP AND SMILE
A Fox picture filmed with a cast headed by Arthur Lake, Dixie Lee, Olga Baclanova and Whispering Jack Smith, and directed by

Sidney Lanfield. Songs by Ray Klages and Jesse Greer:
THE SCAMP OF THE CAMPUS; WHERE CAN YOU BE? and YOU MAY NOT LIKE IT BUT IT'S A GREAT IDEA.

CHILDREN OF PLEASURE

An M-G-M picture filmed with a cast that included Lawrence Gray, Wynne Gibson, Helen Johnson, Kenneth Thompson, Lee Kohlmar and Benny Rubin, and directed by Harry Beaumont. Songs by Andy Rice and Fred Fisher:
LEAVE IT THAT WAY; DUST and A COUPLE OF BIRDS WITH THE SAME THOUGHT IN MIND.

COLLEGE LOVERS

A First National picture filmed with a cast headed by Jack Whiting, Marian Nixon and Frank McHugh, and directed by John Adolfi. Songs by Ned Washington, Herb Magidson and Michael Cleary:
UP AND AT 'EM and ONE MINUTE OF HEAVEN.

CUCKOOS, THE

An RKO picture, based on the Broadway musical *The Ramblers*, starring Bert Wheeler and Robert Woolsey in a cast that included June Clyde, and directed by Paul Sloane. Songs:
I LOVE YOU SO MUCH; KNOCK KNEES and LOOKING FOR THE LOVELIGHT IN YOUR EYES by Bert Kalmar and Harry Ruby; WHEREVER YOU ARE by Charles Tobias and Cliff Friend; IF I WERE A TRAVELING SALESMAN by Al Dubin and Joe Burke.

DANCING SWEETIES

A Warner Brothers' picture filmed with a cast that included Grant Withers, Sue Carol, Edna Murphy and Kate Price, and directed by Ray Enright. Songs:
WISHING AND WAITING FOR LOVE by Grant Clarke and Harry Akst; HULLABALOO by Bobby Dolan and Walter O'-Keefe; I LOVE YOU, I HATE YOU by Al Bryan and Joseph Meyer; THE KISS WALTZ by Al Dubin and Joe Burke.

DANGEROUS NAN McGREW

A Paramount picture starring Helen Kane in a cast that included Victor Moore, Stuart Erwin and Frank Morgan, and directed by Malcolm St. Clair. Songs:
I OWE YOU and DANGEROUS NAN McGREW by Don Hartman and Al Goodhart; ONCE A GYPSY TOLD ME (YOU WERE MINE) by Irving Kahal, Pierre

Norman and Sammy Fain; AW C'MON, WHATTA YA GOT TO LOSE? by Leo Robin and Richard Whiting.

DIXIANA

An RKO picture starring Bebe Daniels and Everett Marshall in a cast that included Bert Wheeler, Robert Woolsey and Joseph Cawthorn, and directed by Luther Reed. Songs by Anne Caldwell and Harry Tierney:
HERE'S TO THE OLD DAYS; A TEAR, A KISS, A SMILE; MY ONE AMBITION IS YOU; A LADY LOVED A SOLDIER; MR. AND MRS. SIPPI; GUIDING STAR and DIXIANA (lyrics by Benny Davis).

FOLLOW THE LEADER

A Paramount picture, based on the Broadway musical comedy *Manhattan Mary*, starring Ed Wynn in a cast that included Ginger Rogers, Lew Holtz and Ethel Merman, and directed by Norman Taurog. Songs:
BROADWAY (THE HEART OF THE WORLD) by Lew Brown, B. G. DeSylva and Ray Henderson; BROTHER JUST LAUGH IT OFF by E. Y. Harburg and Arthur Schwartz; SATAN'S HOLIDAY by Irving Kahal and Sammy Fain.

FOLLOW THROUGH

A Paramount picture, based on the Broadway musical of the same name, filmed by a cast that was headed by Charles "Buddy" Rogers, Nancy Carroll, Zelma O'Neal, Jack Haley and Thelma Todd, and directed by Laurance Schwab and Lloyd Corrigan. Songs:
BUTTON UP YOUR OVERCOAT and YOU WOULDN'T FOOL ME, WOULD YOU? by Lew Brown, B. G. DeSylva and Ray Henderson; I'M HARD TO PLEASE by Larry Hart and Richard Rodgers; A PEACH OF A PAIR by George Marion Jr. and Richard Whiting; IT MUST BE YOU by Ed Eliscu and Manning Sherwin.

FREE AND EASY

An M-G-M picture starring Buster Keaton in a cast that included Anita Paige, Robert Montgomery and Trixie Friganza, and directed by Edward Sedgwick. Songs:
THE FREE-AND-EASY by Roy Turk and Fred Ahlert; PENITENTIARY BLUES; CUBANITA and YOU'VE GOT ME THAT WAY by William Kernell.

GOLDEN DAWN

A Warner Brothers' picture starring Vivienne Segal in a cast that included Walter Woolf and Noah Beery, and directed by Ray Enright. Songs:

AFRICA SMILES NO MORE by Grant Clarke and Harry Akst; WHIP SONG; DAWN; MY BWANNA and WE TWO by Otto Harbach, Oscar Hammerstein II and Emmerich Kalman.

GOOD NEWS

An M-G-M picture, based on the Broadway musical of the same name, filmed with a cast headed by Bessie Love, Mary Lawlor, Stanley Smith and Cliff Edwards, and directed by Nick Grinde and Edgar J. McGregor. Songs:
HE'S A LADY'S MAN; THE BEST THINGS IN LIFE ARE FREE; VARSITY DRAG; GOOD NEWS; TAIT SONG and STUDENTS ARE WE by Lew Brown, B. G. DeSylva and Ray Henderson; IF YOU'RE NOT KISSING ME and FOOTBALL by Arthur Freed and Nacio Herb Brown; I FEEL PESSIMISTIC by J. Russell Robinson and George Waggner; I'D LIKE TO MAKE YOU HAPPY by Reggie Montgomery.

HAPPY DAYS

A Fox picture filmed with an all-star cast headed by Frank Albertson, Warner Baxter, El Brendel, Walter Catlett, Willie Collier, James J. Corbett, Charles Farrell, Janet Gaynor, George Jessel, Dixie Lee, Ann Pennington, Victor McLaglen, Will Rogers and George Olsen and his band, and directed by Benjamin Stoloff. Musical numbers:
CRAZY FEET and SNAKE HIPS by Sidney Mitchell, Con Conrad and Archie Gottler; I'M ON A DIET OF LOVE and MINSTREL MEMORIES by L. Wolfe Gilbert and Abel Baer; A TOAST TO THE GIRL I LOVE and WE'LL BUILD A LITTLE WORLD OF OUR OWN by James Brockman and James Hanley; HAPPY DAYS by B. G. DeSylva, Lew Brown and Ray Henderson; LAS GOLONDRINAS by Narciso Serradell; and *William Tell* and *Zampa Overtures*.

HEADS UP

A Paramount picture filmed with a cast headed by Charles "Buddy" Rogers, Helen Kane and Victor Moore, and directed by Victor Schertzinger. Songs:
MY MAN IS ON THE MAKE and A SHIP WITHOUT A SAIL by Lorenz Hart and Richard Rodgers; IF I KNEW YOU BETTER by Victor Schertzinger.

HIGH SOCIETY BLUES

A Fox picture starring Janet Gaynor and Charles Farrell in a cast that included William Collier Sr., and directed by David But-

ler. Songs by Joe McCarthy and James Hanley:
JUST LIKE IN A STORY BOOK; I'M IN THE MARKET FOR YOU; ELEANOR and THE SONG I SING IN MY DREAMS

HIT THE DECK

An RKO picture, based on the Broadway musical of the same name, starring Jack Oakie and Polly Walker, and directed by Luther Reed. Songs:
SOMETIMES I'M HAPPY and HALLELUJAH by Leo Robin, Clifford Grey and Vincent Youmans; KEEPING MYSELF FOR YOU by Sidney Clare and Vincent Youmans.

HOLD EVERYTHING

A Warner Brothers picture starring Winnie Lightner and Joe E. Brown in a cast that included Sally O'Neil and Georges Carpentier, the French heavyweight champion, and directed by Roy Del Ruth. Songs by Al Dubin and Joe Burke:
TAKE IT ON THE CHIN; WHEN LITTLE RED ROSES GET THE BLUES FOR YOU; SING A LITTLE THEME SONG; PHYSICALLY FIT; ISN'T THIS A COCK-EYED WORLD?; GIRLS WE REMEMBER and ALL ALONE TOGETHER.

HONEY

A Paramount picture starring Nancy Carroll in a cast that included Skeets Gallagher, Mitzi Green and Zasu Pitts, and directed by Wesley Ruggles. Songs by Sam Coslow and W. Franke Harling:
SING YOU SINNERS; IN MY LITTLE HOPE CHEST; LET'S BE DOMESTIC; I DON'T NEED ATMOSPHERE and WHAT IS THIS POWER I HAVE?

JUST IMAGINE

A Fox picture filmed with a cast headed by Maureen O'Sullivan and El Brendel, and directed by David Butler. Songs by Lew Brown, B. G. DeSylva and Ray Henderson:
THERE'S SOMETHING ABOUT AN OLD - FASHIONED GIRL; MOTHERS OUGHT TO TELL THEIR DAUGHTERS; I AM THE WORDS (YOU ARE THE MELODY); NEVER SWAT A FLY and DANCE OF VICTORY

KING OF JAZZ

A Universal picture starring Paul Whiteman and his orchestra in a cast that included John Boles, Laura LaPlante, the Rhythm Boys (Bing Crosby, Harry Barris and Al Ritter) and the Brox Sisters, and directed by John Murray Anderson. Songs:

HAPPY FEET; A BENCH IN THE PARK; MY BRIDAL VEIL; SONG OF THE DAWN; I LIKE TO DO THINGS FOR YOU, MUSIC HAS CHARMS and MY LOVER by Jack Yellen and Milton Ager: IN HAPPENED IN MONTEREY and RAGAMUFFIN ROMEO by Billy Rose and Mabel Wayne; SO THE BLUEBIRDS AND THE BLACKBIRDS GOT TOGETHER by Billy Moll and Harry Barris.

LADY'S MORALS, A
An M-G-M picture starring Grace Moore in a cast that included Reginald Denny and Wallace Beery, and directed by Sydney Franklin. Songs:
IS IT DESTINY?; STUDENT'S SONG and I HEAR YOUR VOICE by Clifford Grey and Oscar Straus: OH, WHY? by Arthur Freed, Herbert Stothart and Harry M. Woods; LOVELY HOUR by Carrie Jacobs Bond; SWEDISH PASTORALE by Howard Johnson and Herbert Stothart; CASTA DIVA from *Norma* by Vincenzo Bellini; RATAPLAN from *The Daughter Of The Regiment* by Gaetano Donizetti.

LET'S GO NATIVE
A Paramount picture starring Jeanette MacDonald in a cast that included Jack Oakie, Skeets Gallagher, Kay Francis and Eugene Pallette, and directed by Leo McCarey. Songs by George Marion Jr. and Richard Whiting:
I'VE GOT A YEN FOR YOU; IT SEEMS TO BE SPRING; LET'S GO NATIVE; MY MAD MOMENT; DON'T I DO? and PAMPA ROSE.

LET'S GO PLACES
A Fox picture filmed by a cast headed by Joseph Wagstaff, Lola Lane, Walter Catlett and Ilka Chase, and directed by Frank Strayer. Songs:
REACH OUT FOR A RAINBOW; UM, UM IN THE MOONLIGHT; OUT IN THE COLD; HOLLYWOOD NIGHTS and PARADE OF THE BLUES by Sidney Mitchell, Archie Gottler and Con Conrad; LET'S GO PLACES by Cliff Friend and Jimmy Monaco; FASCINATING DEVIL and SNOWBALL MAN by Joe McCarthy and Jimmy Monaco; BOOP - BOOP - A - DOOPA-DO TROT by Johnny Burke and George Little.

LIFE OF THE PARTY
A Warner Brothers' picture starring Winnie Lightner in a cast that included Irene Delroy, Jack Whiting and Charles Butterworth, and directed by Roy Del Ruth. Songs:

CAN IT BE POSSIBLE? by Sidney Mitchell, Archie Gottler and Joseph Meyer; ONE ROBIN DOESN'T MAKE A SPRING and SOMEHOW by Frederick Loewe and Earle Crooker.

LORD BYRON OF BROADWAY
An M-G-M picture starring Ethelind Terry in a cast that included Cliff Edwards and Benny Rubin, and directed by William Nigh and Harry Beaumont. Songs:
SHOULD I (REVEAL)?; THE WOMAN IN THE SHOE; BUNDLE OF OLD LOVE LETTERS and ONLY LOVE IS REAL by Arthur Freed and Nacio Herb Brown: LOVE AIN'T NOTHING BUT THE BLUES by Joe Goodwin and Louis Alter.

LOTTERY BRIDE
A United Artists' picture starring Jeanette MacDonald with a cast that included Zasu Pitts, Robert Chisholm, Joe E. Brown and John Garrick, and directed by Paul Stein. Songs:
YOU'RE AN ANGEL; I'LL FOLLOW THE TRAIL and MY NORTHERN LIGHT by J. Keirn Brennan and Rudolf Friml; HIGH AND LOW by Carter Desmond, Howard Dietz and Arthur Schwartz.

LOVE AMONG THE MILLIONAIRES
A Paramount picture starring Clara Bow in a cast that included Stanley Smith, Stuart Erwin, Mitzi Green and Skeets Gallagher, and directed by Frank Tuttle. Songs by L. Wolfe Gilbert and Abel Baer:
BELIEVE IT OR NOT I'VE FOUND MY MAN; DON'T BE A MEANIE; LOVE AMONG THE MILLIONAIRES; RARIN' TO GO and THAT IS WORTH WHILE WAITING FOR.

LOVE IN THE ROUGH
An M-G-M picture starring Dorothy Jardon and Robert Montgomery, and directed by Charles F. Reisner. Songs by Dorothy Fields and Jimmy McHugh:
GO HOME AND TELL YOUR MOTHER; LEARNING A LOT FROM YOU; I'M DOIN' THAT THING and ONE MORE WALTZ.

MAMMY
A Warner Brothers' picture starring Al Jolson in a cast that included Louise Dresser, Lois Moran and Lowell Sherman, and directed by Michael Curtiz. Songs by Irving Berlin:
TO MY MAMMY; ACROSS THE BREAKFAST TABLE LOOKING AT

YOU; LET ME SING AND I'M HAPPY and KNIGHTS OF THE ROAD.

MONTE CARLO

A Paramount picture starring Jeanette MacDonald in a cast that included Jack Buchanan and Zasu Pitts, and directed by Ernst Lubitsch. Songs by Leo Robin, W. Franke Harling and Richard Whiting:
GIVE ME A MOMENT PLEASE; BEYOND THE BLUE HORIZON; ALWAYS IN ALL WAYS; DAY OF DAYS; TRIMMIN' THE WOMEN; SHE'LL LOVE ME AND LIKE IT and WHATEVER IT IS, IT'S GRAND.

NEW MOON

An M-G-M picture starring Grace Moore and Lawrence Tibbett in a cast that included Adolphe Menjou, and directed by John Conway. Songs by Frederic Arnold Kummer and Sigmund Romberg:
MARIANNE; SOFTLY AS IN A MORNING SUNRISE; STOUT-HEARTED MEN; ONE KISS; WANTING YOU; FUNNY LITTLE SAILOR MEN and LOVER COME BACK TO ME.

NEW MOVIETONE FOLLIES OF 1930

A Fox picture filmed with a cast headed by El Brendel, Marjorie White and William Collier Jr., and directed by Benjamin Stoloff. Songs:
CHEER UP AND SMILE; DOIN' THE DERBY and HERE COMES EMILY BROWN by Jack Meskill and Con Conrad: I'D LOVE TO BE A TALKING PICTURE QUEEN by James Brockman and James Hanley.

NO, NO NANETTE

A First National picture filmed with a cast headed by Alexander Gray, Bernice Claire, Lucien Littlefield, Louise Fazenda and Lilyan Tashman, and directed by Clarence Badger. Songs:
AS LONG AS I'M WITH YOU by Grant Clarke and Harry Akst; KING OF THE AIR; NO. NO NANETTE and DANCING TO HEAVEN by Al Bryan and Ed Ward; DANCE OF THE WOODEN SHOES by Ned Washington, Herb Magidson and Michael Cleary.

OH! SAILOR BEHAVE!

A Warner Brothers' picture filmed with a cast headed by Irene Delroy, Charles King, Lotti Loder, Lowell Sherman, Vivian Oakland and Olsen and Johnson, and directed by Archie Mayo. Songs by Al Dubin and Joe Burke:

LOVE COMES IN THE MOONLIGHT; LEAVE A LITTLE SMILE; TELL US WHICH ONE DO YOU LOVE and HIGHWAY TO HEAVEN.

PARAMOUNT ON PARADE

A Paramount picture filmed with a cast of Paramount stars that included Maurice Chevalier, Nancy Carroll, Richard Arlen, Clara Bow, Evelyn Brent, Clive Brook, Gary Cooper, Kay Francis, Abe Lyman and his band, Helen Kane and Jack Oakie, and directed by the staff of Paramount directors. Songs:
SWEEPING THE CLOUDS AWAY by Sam Coslow; COME BACK TO SORRENTO by Leo Robin and Ernesto De Curtis; DANCING TO SAVE YOUR SOUL; DRINK TO THE GIRL OF MY DREAMS and I'M IN TRAINING FOR YOU by L. Wolfe Gilbert and Abel Baer; ALL I WANT IS JUST ONE by Leo Robin and Richard Whiting: MY MARINE by Ray Egan and Richard Whiting; ANYTIME IS THE TIME TO FALL IN LOVE; I'M TRUE TO THE NAVY NOW and PARAMOUNT ON PARADE by Elsie Janis and Jack King.

PARIS

A First National picture starring Irene Bordoni in a cast that included Jack Buchanan, Louise Closser Hale and Zasu Pitts, and directed by Clarence Badger. Songs:
CRYSTAL GIRL; MISS WONDERFUL; PARIS; I WONDER WHAT IS REALLY ON HIS MIND; I'M A LITTLE NEGATIVE; SOMEBODY MIGHTY LIKE YOU; and MY LOVER by Al Bryan and Ed Ward: AMONG MY SOUVENIRS by Edgar Leslie and Horatio Nicholls.

PLAYBOY OF PARIS

A Paramount picture starring Maurice Chevalier in a cast that included Frances Dee, O. P. Heggie and Stuart Erwin, and directed by Ludwig Berger. Songs by Leo Robin, Newell Chase and Richard Whiting:
MY IDEAL; IT'S A GREAT LIFE (IF YOU DON'T WEAKEN); IN THE HEART OF OLD PAREE and YVONNE'S SONG.

PUTTIN' ON THE RITZ

A United Artists' picture starring Harry Richman in a cast that included Joan Bennett, James Gleason and Lilyan Tashman, and directed by Edward H. Sloman. Songs:
WITH YOU; ALICE IN WONDERLAND and PUTTIN' ON THE RITZ by Irving Berlin; THERE'S DANGER IN YOUR EYES, CHERIE by Harry Richman, Jack Meskill and Pete Wendling.

QUEEN HIGH

A Paramount picture filmed with a cast headed by Ginger Rogers, Frank Morgan and Charles Ruggles, and directed by Fred Newmeyer. Songs:

BROTHER JUST LAUGH IT OFF by Arthur Schwartz and Ralph Rainger; SEEMS TO ME by Dick Howard and Ralph Rainger; I LOVE THE GIRLS IN MY OWN PECULIAR WAY by E. Y. Harburg and Henry Souvain; EVERYTHING WILL HAPPEN FOR THE BEST by B. G. DeSylva and Lewis Gensler.

RAIN OR SHINE

A Columbia picture starring Joe Cook in a cast that included Tom Howard, Joan Peers and Louise Fazenda, and directed by Frank Capra. Songs:

HAPPY DAYS ARE HERE AGAIN and RAIN OR SHINE by Jack Yellen and Milton Ager; SITTING ON A RAINBOW by Jack Yellen and Dan Dougherty.

ROGUE SONG, THE

An M-G-M picture starring Lawrence Tibbett in a cast that included Catherine Dale Owen and Laurel and Hardy, and directed by Lionel Barrymore. Songs:

WHEN I'M LOOKING AT YOU; SONG OF THE SHIRT and ROGUE SONG by Clifford Grey and Herbert Stothart: THE WHITE DOVE by Clifford Grey and Franz Lehar.

SAFETY IN NUMBERS

A Paramount picture starring Charles "Buddy" Rogers in a cast that included Josephine Dunn, Roscoe Karns, Virginia Bruce and Carol Lombard, and directed by Victor Schertzinger. Songs by George Marion Jr. and Richard Whiting:

MY FUTURE JUST PASSED; I'D LIKE TO BE A BEE IN YOUR BOUDOIR; BUSINESS GIRL; DO YOU PLAY, MADAME?; THE PICKUP and YOU APPEAL TO ME.

SHE COULDN'T SAY NO

A Warner Brothers' picture filmed with a cast headed by Winnie Lightner, Chester Morris, Sally Eilers and Tully Marshall, and directed by Lloyd Bacon. Songs by Al Dubin and Joe Burke:

DARN FOOL WOMAN LIKE ME; WATCHING MY DREAMS GO BY and BOUNCING THE BABY AROUND.

SHOW GIRL IN HOLLYWOOD

A First National picture starring Alice White in a cast that included Jack Mulhall, Ford Sterling and Blanche Sweet, and directed by Mervyn LeRoy. Songs by Bud Green and Sammy Stept:

HANG ON TO THE RAINBOW; I'VE GOT MY EYE ON YOU and THERE'S A TEAR FOR EVERY SMILE IN HOLLYWOOD.

SONG OF THE FLAME

A First National picture filmed with a cast that included Alexander Gray, Bernice Claire and Noah Beery, and directed by Alan Crosland. Songs:

LIBERTY SONG; PETROGRAD; THE GOOSE HANGS HIGH; PASSING FANCY and ONE LITTLE DRINK by Grant Clarke and Harry Akst: WHEN LOVE CALLS by Ed Ward.

SONG O' MY HEART

A Fox picture starring John McCormack in a cast that included Alice Joyce, Maureen O'Sullivan and J. M. Kerrigan, and directed by Frank Borzage. Songs:

I FEEL YOU NEAR ME; A PAIR OF BLUE EYES and SONG O' MY HEART by Charles W. Glover, William Kernell and James Hanley: PADDY ME LAD by Albert Malotte: ROSE OF TRALEE by Charles W. Glover and C. Mordaunt Spencer.

SONG OF THE WEST

A Warner Brothers' picture filmed with a cast headed by John Boles, Vivienne Segal and Joe E. Brown, and directed by Ray Enright. Songs:

COME BACK TO ME by Grant Clarke and Harry Akst; THE BRIDE WAS DRESSED IN WHITE and HAY-STRAW by Oscar Hammerstein II and Vincent Youmans.

SPRING IS HERE

A First National picture filmed with a cast headed by Alexander Gray and Bernice Claire, and directed by John Francis Dillon. Songs:

CRYING FOR THE CAROLINES and HAVE A LITTLE FAITH IN ME by Sam Lewis, Joe Young and Harry Warren: SPRING IS HERE IN PERSON; YOURS SINCERELY; RICH MAN, POOR MAN; BABY'S AWAKE NOW and WITH A SONG IN MY HEART by Lorenz Hart and Richard Rodgers.

SUNNY

A First National picture starring Marilyn Miller in a cast that included Lawrence Gray and O. P. Heggie, and directed by William A. Seiter. Songs by Otto Harbach, Oscar Hammerstein II and Jerome Kern:

SUNNY; WHO?; D'YA LOVE ME?; TWO LITTLE LOVE BIRDS and I WAS ALONE.

SWEETHEARTS ON PARADE
A Columbia picture filmed with a cast headed by Alice White, Lloyd Hughes and Marie Prevost, and directed by Marshall Neilan. Songs:
SWEETHEARTS ON PARADE by Charles Newman and Carmen Lombardo; DREAM OF ME by Henry Cohen and Irving Bibo; YEARNING JUST FOR YOU by Benny Davis and Joe Burke; MISSTEP by Irving Bibo.

SWING HIGH
An RKO picture filmed with a cast headed by Helen Twelvetrees, Fred Scott, Chester Conklin, Ben Turpin, Dorothy Burgess, Robert Edeson, Stepin Fetchit, Daphne Pollard and Sally Starr, and directed by Joseph Santley. Songs by Mack Gordon, Abner Silver and Ted Snyder:
DO YOU THINK I COULD GROW ON YOU?; IT MUST BE LOVE and WITH MY GUITAR AND YOU.

THEY LEARNED ABOUT WOMEN
An M-G-M picture filmed with a cast headed by Bessie Love, J. C. Nugent and Van and Schenck, and directed by John Conway and Sam Wood. Songs:
HARLEM MADNESS; HE'S THAT KIND OF A PAL; AIN'T YOU BABY?; A MAN OF MY OWN; DOES MY BABY LOVE?; THERE'LL NEVER BE ANOTHER MARY and TEN SWEET MAMMAS by Jack Yellen and Milton Ager: DOUGHERTY IS THE NAME by Van and Schenck.

THREE SISTERS
A Fox picture filmed with a cast headed by Louise Dresser, Tom Patricola, Joyce Compton and June Collyer, and directed by Paul Sloane. Songs by Oscar Hammerstein II and Jerome Kern:
LONELY FEET; HAND IN HAND; KEEP SMILING; WON'T DANCE; ROLL ON ROLLING ROAD; WHAT GOOD ARE WORDS? and YOU ARE DOING VERY WELL.

TOP SPEED
A First National picture filmed with a cast headed by Joe E. Brown, Bernice Claire, Jack Whiting and Frank McHugh, and directed by Mervyn LeRoy. Songs:

GOODNESS GRACIOUS; I'LL KNOW AND SHE'LL KNOW; KEEP YOUR UNDERSHIRT ON; WHAT WOULD I CARE?; and SWEETER THAN YOU by Bert Kalmar and Harry Ruby: AS LONG AS I HAVE YOU AND YOU HAVE ME by Al Dubin and Joe Burke.

TWO HEARTS IN WALTZ TIME
An Associated Cinemas of America release filmed in Germany with a cast headed by Walter Janseen, Oscar Karlweiss, Willy Forst and Gertl Theimer. Songs by Joe Young and Robert Stolz:
I SEE VIENNA IN YOUR EYES; THE SONG OF VIENNA; TWO HEARTS; YOU, TOO and TWO HEARTS IN ¾ TIME.

VAGABOND KING, THE
A Paramount picture starring Dennis King and Jeanette MacDonald in a cast that included O. P. Heggie, and directed by Ludwig Berger. Songs:
HUGUETTE WALTZ; LOVE FOR SALE; LOVE ME TONIGHT; ONLY A ROSE; SOME DAY and SONG OF THE VAGABONDS by Brian Hooker and Rudolf Friml: IF I WERE KING; KING LOUIE and MARY QUEEN OF HEAVEN by Leo Robin, Sam Coslow and Newell Chase.

VIENNESE NIGHTS
A Warner Brothers' picture starring Vivienne Segal in a cast that included Alexander Gray, Jean Hersholt and Bert Roach, and directed by Alan Crosland. Songs by Oscar Hammerstein II and Sigmund Romberg:
I BRING A LOVE SONG; I'M LONELY; WILL YOU REMEMBER VIENNA; HERE WE ARE; REGIMENTAL MARCH; YES, YES, YES and VIENNESE NIGHTS.

WHOOPIE
A United Artists' picture starring Eddie Cantor in a cast that included Eleanor Hunt, Paul Gregory, John Rutherford and Ethel Shutta, and directed by Thornton Freeland. Songs:
MAKING WHOOPIE; STETSON; MY BABY JUST CARES FOR ME and A GIRL FRIEND OF A BOY FRIEND OF MINE by Gus Kahn and Walter Donaldson: I'LL STILL BELONG TO YOU by Edward Eliscu and Nacio Herb Brown.

Feature Films With Songs

AFTER THE VERDICT
An International Photo Plays release filmed with a cast headed by Olga Tschechowa and Warwick Bond, and directed by Heinrich Gallen. Song by Magnus and Stuart:
TWO SMILING EYES

BLUE ANGEL, THE
A Paramount picture starring Emil Jannings and Marlene Dietrich, and directed by Josef von Sternberg. The story was by Dr. Karl Vollmoeller, author of *The Miracle* and a competitor in the first Paris-to-New-York round-the-world automobile race. Song by Sammy Lerner and Frederick Hollander:
FALLING IN LOVE AGAIN

BROTHERS
A Columbia picture filmed with a cast headed by Bert Lytell, Dorothy Sebastian and William Morris, and directed by Mervyn LeRoy. Song by Dan Dougherty:
I'M DREAMING

CALL OF THE FLESH
An M-G-M picture starring Ramon Novarro in a cast that included Dorothy Jordan and Renee Adoree, and directed by Charles Brabin. Song by Ramon Novarro and Herbert Stothart:
LONELY

CAMEO KIRBY
A Fox picture starring J. Harold Murray and Norma Terris in a cast that included Douglas Gilmore, Robert Edeson, Stepin Fetchit, Myrna Loy and John Hyams, and directed by Irving Cummings. Songs:
ROMANCE by Edgar Leslie and Walter Donaldson; AFTER A MILLION DREAMS by Walter Donaldson; DRINK TO THE GIRL OF MY DREAMS by L. Wolfe Gilbert and Abel Baer.

COCK O' THE WALK
A Sono Art-World Wide picture filmed with a cast headed by Joseph Schildkraut, Myrna Loy and Olive Tell, and directed by R. William Neil and Walter Lang. Song by Paul Titsworth:
PLAY ME A TANGO TUNE

DANGEROUS PARADISE
A Paramount picture starring Nancy Carroll and Richard Arlen, and directed by William A. Wellman. Song by Leo Robin and Richard Whiting:
SMILING SKIES

DANCERS, THE
A First National picture filmed with a cast headed by Lois Moran, Phillips Holmes, Mae Clarke and Mrs. Patrick Campbell, and directed by Chandler Sprague. Song by Cliff Friend and Jimmy Monaco:
LOVE HAS PASSED ME BY

DERELICT
A Paramount picture filmed with a cast headed by William Boyd, George Bancroft and Jessie Royce Landis, and directed by Rowland V. Lee. Song by Leo Robin and Jack King:
OVER THE SEA OF DREAMS

DEVIL'S HOLIDAY, THE
A Paramount picture starring Nancy Carroll and Phillip Holmes, and directed by Edmund Goulding. Song by Leo Robin and Edmund Goulding:
YOU ARE A SONG

GOLDEN CALF, THE
A Fox picture filmed with a cast that included Sue Carol, Jack Mulhall, Ilka Chase, El Brendel and Walter Catlett, and directed by Milton Webb. Song by Cliff Friend and Jimmy Monaco:
CAN I HELP IT IF I'M IN LOVE WITH YOU?

GREAT DIVIDE, THE
A First National picture starring Dorothy Mackaill with a cast that included Ian Keith, Lucien Littlefield and Myrna Loy, and directed by Reginald Barker. Song by Herman Ruby and Ray Perkins:
THE END OF THE LONESOME TRAIL

HALF-SHOT AT SUNRISE
An RKO picture starring Bert Wheeler and Robert Woolsey in a cast that included Dorothy Lee and Edna May Oliver, and directed by Paul Sloane. Song by Anne Caldwell and Harry Tierney:
NOTHING BUT LOVE

HARMONY AT HOME
A Fox picture filmed with a cast headed by Marguerite Churchill, Charles Eaton, Charlotte Henry, William Collier Sr., Rex Bell and Dixie Lee, and directed by Hamilton MacFadden. Song by James Brockman and James Hanley:
A LITTLE HOUSE TO DREAM BY A MOUNTAIN STREAM

HIDE OUT
A Universal picture starring James Murray and Kathryn Crawford, and directed by Reginald Barker. Song by Sam Perry and Clarence J. Marks:
JUST YOU AND I

IN GAY MADRID
An M-G-M picture starring Ramon Novarro in a cast that included Dorothy Jordan and Beryl Mercer, and directed by Robert Z. Leonard. Tango by Xavier Cugat:
DARK NIGHT

ISLE OF ESCAPE
A Warner Brothers' picture filmed with a cast headed by Monte Blue, Myrna Loy, Betty Compson and Noah Beery, and directed by Howard Bretherton. Song by Al Bryan and Ed Ward:
MY KALUA ROSE

LAST OF THE DUANES, THE
A Fox picture filmed with a cast that included George O'Brien, Lucille Browne, Lloyd Ingraham and Myrna Loy, and directed by Alfred L. Werker. Song by Cliff Friend:
COWBOY DAN

LAUGHTER
A Paramount picture filmed with a cast headed by Nancy Carroll, Fredric March and Frank Morgan, and directed by Harry D'Arrast. Song by Irving Kahal, Pierre Norman and Sammy Fain:
LITTLE DID I KNOW

LEATHERNECKING
An RKO picture filmed with a cast headed by Irene Dunne, Ken Murray, Louise Fazenda, Ned Sparks and Lilyan Tashman, and directed by Edward Cline. Song by Benny Davis and Harry Akst:
ALL MY LIFE

LILIES OF THE FIELD
A First National picture filmed with a cast headed by Corinne Griffith, John Loder, Freeman Wood, Patsy Paige and Eve Southern, and directed by Alexander Korda. Song by Ned Washington and Michael Cleary:
I'D LIKE TO BE A GYPSY

LOOSE ANKLES
A First National picture filmed with a cast headed by Loretta Young, Douglas Fairbanks Jr. and Louise Fazenda, and directed by Ed Wilde. Songs by Jack Meskill and Pete Wendling:
LOOSE ANKLES and WHOOPIN' IT UP.

LOVE COMES ALONG
An RKO picture filmed with a cast headed by Bebe Daniels, Lloyd Hughes, Montagu Love and Ned Sparks, and directed by Rupert Julian. Songs by Sidney Clare and Oscar Levant:
UNTIL LOVE COMES ALONG and NIGHT WINDS.

MADAM SATAN
An M-G-M picture starring Roland Young in a cast that included Reginald Denny, Kay Johnson, Lillian Roth and Elsa Peterson, and directed by Cecil B. de Mille. Songs by Elsie Janis and Jack King:
ALL I KNOW IS YOU ARE IN MY ARMS and LIVE AND LOVE TODAY.

MAN TROUBLE
A Fox picture filmed with a cast headed by Milton Sills, Dorothy Mackaill, Kenneth McKenna and Roscoe Karns, and directed by Berthold Viertel. Songs by Joseph McCarthy and James Hanley:
PICK YOURSELF UP, BRUSH YOURSELF OFF; and WHAT'S THE USE OF LIVING WITHOUT LOVE?

MATRIMONIAL BED, THE
A Warner Brothers' picture filmed with a cast headed by Frank Fay, Lilyan Tashman, James Gleason and Beryl Mercer, and directed by Michael Curtiz. Song by Sidney Mitchell and George W. Meyer:
FLEUR D'AMOUR

MAYBE IT'S LOVE
A Warner Brothers' picture starring Joan Bennett and Joe E. Brown and featuring the All-American football team of 1930; directed by William Wellman. Songs by Sidney Mitchell, Archie Gottler and George W. Meyer:
MAYBE IT'S LOVE and ALL-AMERICAN

MELODY MAN
A Columbia picture filmed with a cast headed by John St. Polis, William Collier Jr., Alice Day and Albert Conti, and directed by William Neill. Song by Ballard MacDonald, Arthur Johnston and Dave Dreyer:
BROKEN DREAMS

MONTANA MOON
An M-G-M picture starring Joan Crawford in a cast that included Johnny Mack Brown, Benny Rubin and Cliff Edwards, and directed by Malcolm St. Clair. Songs:
MONTANA CALL by Clifford Grey and Herbert Stothart; THE MOON IS LOW by Arthur Freed and Nacio Herb Brown.

MOROCCO

A Paramount picture starring Marlene Dietrich, Gary Cooper and Adolphe Menjou, and directed by Josef von Sternberg. Songs by Leo Robin and Karl Hajos:

GIVE ME THE MAN and WHAT AM I BID?

NIGHT WORK

An RKO picture filmed with a cast headed by Eddie Quillan, Sally Starr, Frances Upton and John T. Murray, and directed by Russell Mack. Songs by Mort Harris and Ted Snyder:

DEEP IN YOUR HEART and I'M TIRED OF MY TIRED MAN.

OH FOR A MAN

A Fox picture starring Jeanette MacDonald in a cast that included Reginald Denny, Marjorie White, Warren Hymer and Bella Lugosi, and directed by Hamilton MacFadden. Song by William Kernell:

I'M JUST NUTS ABOUT YOU

OFFICE WIFE, THE

A Warner Brothers' picture filmed with a cast headed by Joan Blondell, Lewis Stone and Dorothy Mackaill, and directed by Lloyd Bacon. Songs:

DAWN BROUGHT ME LOVE AND YOU by Richard Kountz; ALONG THE HIGHWAY OF LOVE by Tommy Christian and Blaine Stone; I FELL IN LOVE WITH YOU by Sammy Lerner and Max Previl.

ON THE LEVEL

A Fox picture starring Victor McLaglen in a cast that included William Harrigan, Lilyan Tashman and Leila McIntyre, and directed by Irving Cummings. Songs:

GOOD INTENTIONS by Cliff Friend and Jimmy Monaco; GOOD FOR NOTHING BUT LOVE by William Kernell.

ONE HEAVENLY NIGHT

A United Artists' picture starring Evelyn Laye and John Boles in a cast that included Leon Errol and Lilyan Tashman, and directed by George Fitzmaurice. Songs:

HEAVENLY NIGHT by Edward Eliscu and Nacio Herb Brown; ALONG THE ROAD OF DREAMS by Bruno Granichstaedten and Clifford Grey.

ONLY SAPS WORK

A Paramount picture filmed with a cast headed by Leon Errol, Mary Brian, Richard Arlen and Stuart Erwin, and directed by Cyril Gardner and Edwin H. Knopf. Song by Ballard MacDonald and Dave Dreyer:

FIND THE GIRL

PAINTED ANGEL, THE

A First National picture starring Billie Dove and Edmund Lowe in a cast that included George MacFarlane and J. Farrell MacDonald, and directed by Millard Webb. Songs by Herman Ruby and M. K. Jerome:

HELP YOURSELF TO LOVE and A BRIDE WITHOUT A GROOM

PARDON MY GUN

A Pathe-RKO picture filmed with a cast headed by Sally Starr, George Duryea, Mona Ray, Lee Moran, Robert Edeson and Abe Lyman's orchestra, and directed by Robert DeLacy. Song by George Green:

DEEP DOWN SOUTH

PARTY GIRL

A Tiffany-Stahl picture starring Douglas Fairbanks Jr. and Jeanette Loff, and directed by Victor Halperin. Songs by Marcy Klauber and Harry Stoddard:

FAREWELL and OH, HOW I ADORE YOU.

PLAYING AROUND

A First National picture starring Alice White and Chester Morris, and directed by Mervyn LeRoy. Songs by Bud Green and Sammy Stept:

THAT'S THE LOWDOWN ON THE LOWDOWN and WE LEARN ABOUT LOVE EVERY DAY.

ROADHOUSE NIGHTS

A Paramount picture filmed with a cast headed by Helen Morgan, Charles Ruggles, Fred Kohler and Jimmy Durante, and directed by Hobart Henley. Song by E. Y. Harburg and Jay Gorney:

IT CAN'T GO ON LIKE THIS

REMOTE CONTROL

An M-G-M picture filmed with a cast headed by William Haines, Mary Doran, Edward Nugent, John Miljan and Charles King, and directed by Malcolm St. Clair and Nick Grinde. Song by Howard Johnson and Joseph Meyer:

JUST A LITTLE CLOSER

RENO

A Sono Art—World Wide picture filmed with a cast that included Ruth Roland, Kenneth Thompson, Montagu Love and Sam Hardy, and directed by George Crone. Song by Leslie Barton (pseudonym for Sam Coslow) and Ben Bard:

AS LONG AS WE'RE TOGETHER

ROYAL ROMANCE

A Columbia picture filmed with a cast headed by William Collier Jr., Pauline Starke

and Clarence Muse, and directed by Erle C. Kenton. Song by Jack Meskill and Cyril Ray:
BLACK MINNIE'S GOT THE BLUES.

SAP FROM SYRACUSE, THE
A Warner Brothers' picture filmed with a cast headed by Ginger Rogers, Jack Oakie, George Barbier and Betty Starbuck, and directed by Edward Sutherland. Songs by E. Y. Harburg and Johnny Green:
AH, WHAT'S THE USE? and I WISH I COULD SING A LOVE SONG.

SEA BAT, THE
An M-G-M picture filmed with a cast headed by Charles Bickford, John Miljan, Raquel Torres and Nils Asther, and directed by Wesley Ruggles. Song by Reggie Montgomery and Ed Ward:
LO-LO

SEA LEGS
A Paramount picture starring Lillian Roth and Jack Oakie in a cast that included Harry Green and Eugene Pallette, and directed by Victor Heerman. Songs:
THIS MUST BE ILLEGAL by Ralph Rainger, W. Franke Harling and George Marion Jr.; TEN O'CLOCK TOWN by Arthur Swanstorm and Michael Cleary.

SILENT ENEMY, THE
A Paramount picture filmed with an all-native cast of Polynesian Islanders, and directed by H. P. Carver. Songs:
RAIN FLOWER by Sam Coslow and Newell Chase; SONG OF THE WATERS by Massard Kur Zhene.

SIT TIGHT
A Warner Brothers' picture filmed with a cast headed by Winnie Lightner, Joe E. Brown, Claudia Dell, Paul Gregory and Hobart Bosworth, and directed by Lloyd Bacon. Song by L. Wolfe Gilbert and Abel Baer:
FACE IT WITH A SMILE

SLIGHTLY SCARLET
A Paramount picture filmed with a cast headed by Evelyn Brent, Clive Brook, Paul Lukas, Helen Ware and Virginia Bruce, and directed by Louis Gasnier and Edwin H. Knopf. Song by Elsie Janis and Jack King:
YOU STILL BELONG TO ME

SON OF THE GODS
A First National picture starring Richard Barthelmess in a cast that included Constance Bennett and Dorothy Mathews, and directed by Frank Lloyd. Song by Ben Ryan and Sol Violinsky:
PRETTY LITTLE YOU

SUCH MEN ARE DANGEROUS
A Fox picture filmed with a cast headed by Warner Baxter, Catherine Dale Owen, Heddy Hopper and Bela Lugosi, and directed by Kenneth Hawks. Songs:
BRIDAL HYMN by Albert Malotte and George Gramlich; CINDERELLA BY THE FIRE by Dave Stamper.

TEXAN, THE
A Paramount picture starring Gary Cooper in a cast that included Fay Wray and Emma Dunn, and directed by John Cromwell. Songs by L. Wolfe Gilbert and Abel Baer:
CHICO and TO HOLD YOU

THEIR OWN DESIRE
An M-G-M picture starring Norma Shearer in a cast that included Belle Bennett, Lewis Stone and Robert Montgomery, and directed by E. Mason Hopper. Song by Fred Fisher:
BLUE IS THE NIGHT

THOSE THREE FRENCH GIRLS
An M-G-M picture starring Fifi D'Orsay in a cast that included Reginald Denny and Cliff Edwards, and directed by Harry Beaumont. Songs by Arthur Freed and Joseph Meyer:
YOU'RE SIMPLY DELISH and SIX POOR MORTALS.

TROOPERS THREE
A Tiffany-Stahl picture filmed with a cast headed by Rex Lease, Dorothy Gulliver, Slim Summerville and Roscoe Karns, and directed by William Taurog and Reaves Eason. Song by George Waggner and Abner Silver:
AS LONG AS YOU LOVE ME

TRUE TO THE NAVY
A Paramount picture starring Clara Bow in a cast that included Harry Green, Fredric March, Sam Hardy and Rex Bell, and directed by Frank Tuttle. Songs by L. Wolfe Gilbert and Abel Baer:
BELIEVE IT OR NOT, I LOST MY MAN and THERE'S ONLY ONE WHAT MATTERS TO ME.

UNDER A TEXAS MOON
A Warner Brothers' picture starring Frank Fay in a cast that included Raquel Torres, Myrna Loy, Armida and Noah Berry, and directed by Michael Curtiz. Song by Ray Perkins:
UNDER THE TEXAS MOON

WAY OUT WEST
An M-G-M picture filmed with a cast

headed by William Haines, Leila Hyams, Cliff Edwards and Polly Moran, and directed by Fred Niblo. Song by Howard Johnson and Joseph Meyer:
SINGING A SONG TO THE STARS

WEDDING RINGS

A First National picture filmed with a cast headed by H. B. Warner, Lois Wilson and Olive Borden, and directed by William Beaudine. Song by Al Bryan and Ed Ward:
LOVE WILL LAST FOREVER IF IT'S TRUE

WOMEN EVERYWHERE

A Fox picture filmed with a cast that included J. Harold Murray, Fifi D'Orsay and Clyde Cook, and directed by Alexander Korda. Songs by William Kernell:
BEWARE OF LOVE and ONE DAY.

YOUNG EAGLES

A Paramount picture starring Charles "Buddy" Rogers in a cast that included Jean Arthur, Paul Lukas, Virginia Bruce and Stuart Erwin, and directed by William A. Wellman. Songs:
LOVE HERE IS MY HEART by Ross Adrian and Leo Silesu; THE SUNRISE AND YOU by Arthur A. Penn.

YOUNG MAN OF MANHATTAN

A Paramount picture starring Claudette Colbert and Norman Foster in a cast that included Ginger Rogers and Charles Ruggles, and directed by Monte Bell. Songs by Irving Kahal, Pierre Norman and Sammy Fain:
I'VE GOT IT; I'D FALL IN LOVE ALL OVER AGAIN and I'LL BOB UP WITH THE BOB-O-LINK.

Western Films With Songs

NEAR THE RAINBOW'S END

A Tiffany-Stahl picture filmed with a cast headed by Bob Steele, "Lafe" McKee, Al Ferguson and Louise Lorraine, and directed by J. P. McGowan. Song by Murray Mencher, Billy Moll and Harry Richman:
RO-RO-ROLLIN' ALONG.

SONS OF THE SADDLE

A Universal picture starring Ken Maynard and Doris Hill, and directed by Harry J. Brown. Song by Bernie Grossman and Lou Handman:
DOWN THE HOME TRAIL WITH YOU.

Jeanette MacDonald and Maurice Chevalier in *The Love Parade*

1 9 3 1

Hollywood Sings The Blues As The Gold Rush Ends

There was no jubilant fanfare of trumpets to open the 1931 chapter of the Hollywood story. The happy ending also was missing from the script. But the final fadeout followed the tried and true Hollywood pattern—it was colossal.

Most of the writers of popular songs under contract to the studios were sent back to the music publishing houses in New York City to fashion tunes for deserted music counters in order to earn their fat pay checks. A legion of Broadway stage stars with unredeemed options to paste in their memory books joined them in the exodus from a land of milk and honey on which an economic blight had fallen. And the California gold rush of 1929, like the California gold rush of 1849, passed into history.

Retrenchment was the order of the day as the once prodigal spenders started nursing nickels and dimes, costly musicals were slashed from production schedules, and Hollywood concentrated on low-budget pictures, made with casts of players under long-term studio contracts, to keep the projection machines grinding in half-empty theaters. As the bread lines lengthened and the queues in front of the movie houses shortened, bank nights were inaugurated, Chevalier was offered with crockery and Garbo with glassware as box-office lure, and the double feature became an actuality even though the "two chickens in every pot" and the "two cars in every garage" President Herbert Hoover promised never did.

Even the few musicals produced in 1931 were lacking in lustre, and reflected the depressing environment in which they were made. George Gershwin made his debut on the sound track with four little-remembered songs that comprised the score for *Delicious,* starring Janet Gaynor and Charles Farrell. Cole Porter's introduction to movie-goers was equally inauspicious, the screen version of *Fifty Million Frenchmen* with Olsen and Johnson heading the cast failing to duplicate its Broadway triumph. The magic touch commonly associated with Rodgers and Hart was missing in the numbers they wrote for *Hot Heiress,* and their stage success, *A Connecticut Yankee,* fell far short of Jimmy Fidler's four bell rating when adapted to the screen. Even Sigmund Romberg missed the Hit Parade entirely with the music he composed for *Children of Dreams,* and the musicals again failed to place in the Ten Best Pictures of the Year derby, the honors going to such highly dramatic films as *Cimarron, Street Scene, Bad Girl, Five Star Final* and *A Free Soul.*

The top brass of Hollywood, in fact, lost all interest in music during 1931 except that already in the cans, and looked to stark drama to lift the talkies out of the Depression pit, and at one story conference, Samuel Goldwyn announced he was putting *The Well Of Loneliness* on the screen.

"You can't do that!", he was told. "Why, all the people in that book are Lesbians!"

"Can that stop us?", he asked, and then added with a shrug of his shoulders: "We'll make 'em Lithuanians."

Such was the desperation of Hollywood in a year when many swimming pools were dry because it cost too much money to fill them.

Musicals

ALONG CAME YOUTH

A Paramount picture starring Charles "Buddy" Rogers in a cast that included Frances Dee and Stuart Erwin, and directed by Lloyd Corrigan and Norman McLeod. Songs:
RARIN' TO GO by L. Wolfe Gilbert and Abel Baer; ANY TIME'S THE TIME TO FALL IN LOVE by Elsie Janis and Jack King; IT'S A GREAT LIFE and MY IDEAL by Leo Robin and Richard Whiting; I LOOK AT YOU AND A SONG IS BORN by George Marion Jr. and Ralph Rainger.

BLONDE CRAZY

A Warner Brothers' picture filmed with a cast headed by James Cagney, Joan Blondell, Louis Calhern, Guy Kibbe and Ray Milland, and directed by Roy Del Ruth. Songs:
WHEN YOUR LOVER HAS GONE by E. A. Swan; I CAN'T WRITE THE WORDS by Gerald Marks and Buddy Fields; I'M JUST A FOOL IN LOVE WITH YOU by Sidney Mitchell, Archie Gottler and George W. Meyer; AIN'T THAT THE WAY IT GOES? by Roy Turk and Fred Ahlert.

BRIGHT LIGHTS

A First National picture filmed with a cast headed by Dorothy Mackaill, Frank Fay, Noah Beery, Inez Courtney and Eddie Nugent, and directed by Michael Curtiz. Songs:
NOBODY CARES IF I'M BLUE by Grant Clarke and Harry Akst; I'M CRAZY FOR CANNIBAL LOVE by Al Bryan and Ed Ward; CHINATOWN by William Jerome and Jean Schwartz; SONG OF THE CONGO by Ned Washington, Benny Rubens and Herb Magidson; YOU'RE AN EYEFUL OF HEAVEN by Mort Dixon and Allie Wrubel.

CHILDREN OF DREAMS

A Warner Brothers' picture filmed with a cast headed by Margaret Schilling, Paul Gregory, Tom Patricola and Charles Winninger, and directed by Alan Crosland. Songs by Oscar Hammerstein II and Sigmund Romberg:
FRUIT PICKERS' SONG: OH, COULDN'T I LOVE THAT GIRL; HER PROFESSOR; CHILDREN OF DREAMS; SLEEPING BEAUTY; IF I HAD A GIRL LIKE YOU; SEEK LOVE and YES, SIR.

CONNECTICUT YANKEE, A

A Fox picture filmed with a cast that included Will Rogers, Maureen O'Sullivan, Myrna Loy and William Farnum, and directed by David Butler. Songs by Lorenz Hart and Richard Rodgers:
MY HEART STOOD STILL; THOU SWELL; ON A DESERT ISLAND WITH YOU; TO KEEP MY LOVE ALIVE; CAN'T YOU DO A FRIEND A FAVOR?; I FEEL AT HOME WITH YOU and ALWAYS LOVE THE SAME GIRL.

CUBAN LOVE SONG

An M-G-M picture starring Lawrence Tibbett in a cast that included Lupe Velez and Jimmy Durante, and directed by W. S. Van-Dyke. Songs by Dorothy Fields and Jimmy McHugh:
CUBAN LOVE SONG and TRAMPS AT SEA.

DANCE, FOOLS, DANCE

An M-G-M picture starring Joan Crawford in a cast that included Lester Vail and Cliff Edwards, and directed by Harry Beaumont. Songs:
A GAY CABALLERO by Frank Crumit and Lou Klein; ACCORDION JOE by Dale Winbrow and L. Cornell; FREE AND EASY by Roy Turk and Fred Ahlert; I'M LEARNING A LOT FROM YOU and GO HOME AND TELL YOUR MOTHER by Dorothy Fields and Jimmy McHugh.

DELICIOUS

A Fox picture starring Janet Gaynor and Charles Farrell, and directed by David Butler. Songs by Ira and George Gershwin:
DELISHIOUS; BLA-BLA-BLA; SOMEBODY FROM SOMEWHERE and KATINKITSCHKA.

FIFTY MILLION FRENCHMEN

A Warner Brothers' picture starring Olsen and Johnson in a cast that included William Gaxton, John Halliday, Helen Broderick and Claudia Dell, and directed by Lloyd Bacon: Songs:
YOU DO SOMETHING TO ME; WHY SHOULDN'T I HAVE YOU?; YOU'VE GOT THAT THING; PAREE, WHAT HAVE YOU DONE TO ME?; and AMERICAN EXPRESS NUMBER by Cole Porter: YOU REMIND ME OF MY MOTHER by George M. Cohan.

FLYING HIGH

An M-G-M picture starring Charlotte Greenwood and Bert Lahr in a cast that included Pat O'Brien, Kathryn Crawford, Charles Winninger and Hedda Hopper, and directed by Charles F. Reisner. Songs by Dorothy Fields and Jimmy McHugh:
HAPPY LANDING; DANCE TILL DAWN.

HOLY TERROR

A Fox picture filmed with a cast headed by George O'Brien, Sally Eilers, Rita LaRoy, Humphrey Bogart and James Kirkwood, and directed by Irving Cummings. Songs:
FOR YOU by Al Dubin and Joe Burke; DO YOU BELIEVE IN LOVE AT SIGHT? by Gus Kahn and Ted Fiorito; LONESOME LOVER by Al Bryan and Jimmy Monaco; I'M A DREAMER AREN'T WE ALL and I AM THE WORDS (YOU ARE THE MUSIC) by Lew Brown, B. G. DeSylva and Ray Henderson.

HONEYMOON LANE

A Paramount picture starring Eddie Dowling in a cast that included June Collyer, Ray Dooley, Raymond Hatton and Noah Beery, and directed by William J. Craft. Songs by Eddie Dowling and James Hanley:
LITTLE WHITE HOUSE AT THE END OF HONEYMOON LANE and HONEYMOON LANE.

HOT HEIRESS

A First National picture filmed with a cast headed by Ona Munson, Ben Lyon, Walter Pidgeon and Thelma Todd, and directed by Clarence Badger. Songs by Lorenz Hart and Richard Rodgers:
YOU'RE THE CATS; RIVETEER'S SONG and LIKE ORDINARY PEOPLE DO.

MONKEY BUSINESS

A Paramount picture starring the Four Marx Brothers in a cast that included Thelma Todd and Ruth Hall, and directed by Norman McLeod. Songs:
I'M DAFFY OVER YOU by Chico Marx and Sol Violinsky; YOU BROUGHT A NEW KIND OF A LOVE TO ME by Irving Kahal, Pierre Norman and Sammy Fain; BLUE BLAZES by Leo Robin and Richard Whiting; HO HUM by Edward Heyman and Dana Suesse; and WHEN I TAKE MY SUGAR TO TEA by Irving Kahal and Sammy Fain.

PALMY DAYS

A United Artists' picture starring Eddie Cantor in a cast that included Charlotte Greenwood and George Raft, and directed by Edward Sutherland. Songs:
BEND DOWN SISTER by Ballard MacDonald and Con Conrad; MY BABY SAID YES, YES by Cliff Friend; THERE'S NOTHING TOO GOOD FOR MY BABY by Eddie Cantor, Benny Davis and Harry Akst.

ROAD TO SINGAPORE, THE

A Warner Brothers' picture starring William Powell in a cast that included Mae Marsh and Doris Kenyon, and directed by Alfred E. Green. Songs:
AFRICAN LAMENT by Ernesto Lecuona and L. Wolfe Gilbert; HAND IN HAND by Jimmy Monaco, Edgar Leslie and Ned Washington; YES OR NO by Max Rich and Charles O'Flynn; SINGAPORE TANGO by Clyde Lucas; I'M JUST A FOOL IN LOVE WITH YOU by Sidney Mitchell and Archie Gottler.

SMILING LIEUTENANT, THE

A Paramount picture starring Maurice Chevalier and Claudette Colbert in a cast that included Charles Ruggles and Miriam Hopkins, and directed by Ernst Lubitsch. Songs by Clifford Grey and Oscar Straus:
WHILE HEARTS ARE SINGING; ONE MORE HOUR OF LOVE; JAZZ UP YOUR LINGERIE; TOUJOURS L'AMOUR IN THE ARMY and BREAKFAST TABLE LOVE.

Feature Films With Songs

AGE FOR LOVE, THE
A United Artists' picture filmed with a cast headed by Billie Dove, Charles Starrett, Lois Wilson and Edward Everett Horton, and directed by Frank Lloyd. Songs:
I'M CHUCK FULL OF KISSES by Alfred Newman and Dave Silverstein; JUST ANOTHER NIGHT by Alfred Newman, Silverstein and Con Conrad.

ALOHA
A Tiffany-Stahl picture filmed with a cast headed by Ben Lyon, Raquel Torres, Robert Edeson, Alan Hale and Thelma Todd, and directed by Albert Rogell. Songs:
POGO HULA by Joseph Perry; OAHU by Keoki and Sol Hoopii; A LA CUBANA by Murray Smith and ALOHA by Queen Liliuokalani.

ANNABELLE'S AFFAIRS
A Fox picture starring Victor McLaglen and Janet Gaynor in a cast that included Roland Young and Sam Hardy, and directed by Alfred Werker. Song by James Hanley:
IF SOMEONE SHOULD KISS YOU TONIGHT

BAD GIRL
A Fox picture starring James Dunn and Sally Eilers, and directed by Frank Borzage. Songs by James Hanley:
RED HEAD and COME ON BABY AND BEG FOR IT.

BUSINESS GIRL
A First National picture starring Loretta Young in a cast that included Frank Albertson, Ricardo Cortez, Virginia Sale and Joan Blondell, and directed by William Seiter. Song by Bud Green and Sammy Stept:
CONSTANTLY

CONSOLATION MARRIAGE
An RKO picture starring Irene Dunne and Pat O'Brien, and directed by Paul Sloane. Song by Marc Connelly and Max Steiner:
DEVOTION

DUDE RANCH
A Paramount picture filmed with a cast headed by Jack Oakie, Stuart Erwin, Eugene Pallette, Mitzi Green and June Collyer, and directed by Frank Tuttle. Songs:
(YOU CAME TO ME) OUT OF NO-WHERE by Ed Heyman and Johnny Green; CONSOLATION by Leo Robin and Richard Whiting.

HELL BOUND
A Tiffany-Stahl picture filmed with a cast headed by Leo Carrillo, Lola Lane and Lloyd Hughes, and directed by Walter Lang. Song by Russ Columbo:
IS IT LOVE?

HUSBAND'S HOLIDAY
A Paramount picture filmed with a cast headed by Clive Brook, Vivian Osborne and Charles Ruggles, and directed by Robert Milton. Song by Benny Davis and Harry Akst:
WHAT PRICE LOVE?

INDISCREET
A United Artists' picture starring Gloria Swanson in a cast that included Ben Lyon and Barbara Kent, and directed by Leo McCarey. Songs by Lew Brown, B. G. DeSylva and Ray Henderson:
COME TO ME and IF YOU HAVEN'T GOT LOVE

JUNE MOON
A Paramount picture filmed with a cast headed by Jack Oakie, Frances Dee, June MacCray, Ernest Wood, Wynne Gibson, Harry Akst and Sam Hardy, and directed by Edward Sutherland. Songs by Ring Lardner and George Kaufmann:
JUNE MOON; HELLO TOKIO; MONTANA MOON and GIVE OUR CHILD A NAME.

MAN WHO CAME BACK, THE
A Fox picture starring Janet Gaynor and Charles Farrell in a cast that included Kenneth McKenna, and directed by Raoul Walsh. Song by William Kernell:
SWEET HAWAIIAN MEM'RIES

POSSESSED
An M-G-M picture starring Clark Gable and Joan Crawford in a cast that included Wallace Ford, and directed by Clarence Brown. Song by Max Leif and Joseph Meyer:
HOW LONG WILL IT LAST?

REACHING FOR THE MOON
A United Artists' picture starring Douglas Fairbanks and Bebe Daniels in a cast that included Edward Everett Horton and Jack Mulhall, and directed by Edmund Goulding. Song by Irving Berlin:
REACHING FOR THE MOON

SALLY IN OUR ALLEY
An Associated Radio release starring

Gracie Fields. Song by William E. Haines, Harry Leon and Leo Towers:
SALLY

THEIR MAD MOMENT
A Fox picture starring Warner Baxter and Dorothy Mackaill, and directed by Hamilton MacFadden and Chandler Sprague. Songs by William Kernell:

HOLD MY HAND; LITTLE FLOWER OF LOVE and FIESTA SONG.

YOUNG SINNERS
A Fox picture starring Thomas Meighan and Dorothy Jordan, and directed by John Blystone. Song by James Hanley:
YOU CALLED IT LOVE

Western Films With Songs

FREIGHTERS OF DESTINY
An RKO picture starring Tom Keene and Barbara Kent, and directed by Fred Allen. Song by Johnny Lange and Bernie Grossman:
AT THE END OF THE TRAIL

TEXAS RANGER
A Columbia picture starring Buck Jones and Carmelita Geraghty, and directed by Ross Lederman. Song by Jack Scholl and Phil Boutelje:
I CAN'T PLAY MY BANJO

Bing Crosby (at left wearing hat) in his first movie *The King of Jazz*

1 9 3 2

"Happy Days Are Here Again" But Hollywood Is Skeptical

Although the dark clouds of the Depression still hovered over Hollywood in 1932, the sun broke through at times and there were rays of hope and future promise in several musicals that delivered a full measure of entertainment for the 25c admission price commonly charged at movie houses across the nation.

The *Big Broadcast* established an impressive milestone by introducing Bing Crosby as a featured player, and served as the tee-off for Leo Robin and Ralph Rainger as a songwriting team whose initial bid for fame as collaborators, *Please,* proved to be the first of many film songs destined for the Hit Parade.

Rodgers and Hart, the fair-haired boys of Broadway stage productions, finally found their place in the Hollywood spotlight with the songs they wrote for *Love Me Tonight,* starring Jeanette MacDonald and Maurice Chevalier: *Isn't It Romantic?, Mimi, Lover* and the title number. And millions of movie-goers who had never seen a stage production discovered that George Gershwin could write truly great and enduring music when *I Got Rhythm* and *Embraceable You* were recorded on the sound track in the 1932 adaptation of *Girl Crazy* to the screen.

As Pola Negri made her exit to the haunting strains of *Paradise,* George M. Cohan made his first talkie appearance in *The Phantom President.* A veteran showman who had produced shows on a shoestring and at incredible speed, the author-composer of *Over There* and *Give My Regards To Broadway* was both baffled and irritated by the waste of time and money on the picture lot and the last-minute changes and retakes the producers and directors demanded, and declared on his return to New York:

"If I had to choose between Hollywood and Atlanta, I'd take Leavenworth!"

But Hollywood no longer was dependent on the Broadway stage for talent and box office lure. It was discovering and developing fresh talent of its own, and refurbishing the dressing quarters of Mary Pickford and Douglas Fairbanks for such future screen celebrities as Ann Dvorak and Dick Powell. The songwriters, too, were mastering a new technique in which songs and story were more closely integrated than in the confusion that marked the talkies' infancy.

According to Tin Pan Alley, "every cloud has a silver lining", and so far as Hollywood was concerned, the Depression clouds were no exception. The song-and-dance film had reached a promising maturity on a starvation diet even though for the third straight year no musical made the Ten Best Films grade, the top honors for 1932 going to *Grand Hotel, The Champ, Arrowsmith, The Guardsman, Smiling Through, Dr. Jekyll and Mr. Hyde, Emma, Bill Of Divorcement, Back Street* and *Scarface.*

Musicals

BIG BROADCAST, THE

A Paramount picture filmed with a cast headed by Stuart Erwin, Bing Crosby, Leila Hyamns, Burns and Allen, Kate Smith, Mills Brothers, Boswell Sisters, Arthur Tracy and the orchestras of Vincent Lopez and Cab Calloway, and directed by Frank Tuttle. Musical numbers:

PLEASE and HERE LIES LOVE by Leo Robin and Ralph Rainger; HOT TODDY by Benny Carter; IN THE BLUE OF THE NIGHT by Roy Turk, Bing Crosby and Fred Ahlert; TIGER RAG by B. J. La-Rocca and the Original Dixieland Jazz Band; CRAZY PEOPLE by Edgar Leslie and Jimmy Monaco; IT WAS SO BEAU-TIFUL by Arthur Freed and Harry Barris; KICKING THE GONG AROUND by Ted Koehler and Richard Arlen.

BIG CITY BLUES

A Warner Brother's picture starring Joan Blondell in a cast that included Eric Linden, Inez Courtney, Evelyn Knapp, Guy Kibbe, Lyle Talbot, Gloria Shea and Jobyna Howland, and directed by Mervyn LeRoy. Songs:

BIG CITY BLUES and NEW YORK TOWN by Leo F. Forbstein; I'M IN LOVE WITH A TUNE by Ralph Rainger; MY BABY JUST CARES FOR ME by Gus Kahn and Walter Donaldson.

BLONDIE OF THE FOLLIES

An M-G-M picture filmed with a cast headed by Marion Davies, Robert Montgomery, Billie Dove, Jimmy Durante, James Gleason and Zasu Pitts, and directed by Edmund Goulding. Songs:

GOOD NIGHT MY LOVE by Harry Tobias, Gus Arnheim and Jules Lemare; TELL ME WHILE WE'RE DANCING by Harry Link and Nick Kenny; WHY DON'T YOU TAKE ME? by Edmund Goulding; THREE ON A MATCH by Ray Egan and Ted Fiorito; GOIN' FISHIN' by Walter Samuels and Leonard Whitcup; IT WAS SO BEAUTIFUL by Arthur Freed and Harry Barris; DON'T TAKE YOUR GIRL TO THE GRAND HOTEL by Dave Snell.

CARELESS LADY

A Fox picture filmed with a cast headed by Joan Bennett, John Boles and Minna Gombell, and directed by Kenneth McKenna. Songs:

WHEN YOU HEAR THAT SONG REMEMBER ME by Ralph Freed and James Hanley; SOUVENIR by James Hanley; and ALL OF ME by Gerald Marks and Seymour Simons.

CROONER, THE

A First National picture filmed with a cast headed by David Manners, Ann Dvorark, Guy Kibbe and Ken Murray, and directed by Lloyd Bacon. Songs:

I SEND MY LOVE WITH THE ROSES by Al Dubin and Joe Burke; THREE'S A CROWD by Al Dubin and Harry Warren; SWEETHEARTS FOREVER by Irving Caesar and Cliff Friend; NOW YOU'VE GOT ME WORRYING FOR YOU by Irving Kahal and Sammy Fain; BANKING ON THE WEATHER by Joe Young and Sammy Fain.

GIRL CRAZY

An RKO picture starring Bert Wheeler and Robert Woolsey in a cast that included Eddie Quillan and Dixie Lee, and directed by William A. Seiter. Songs by Ira and George Gershwin:

COULD YOU USE ME?; EMBRACE-ABLE YOU; SAM AND DELILAH; I GOT RHYTHM and BUT NOT FOR ME.

HYPNOTIZED

A Sono Art-World Wide picture starring Moran and Mack, and directed by Mack Sennett. Songs by Bernie Grossman and Desider Josef Vecsei:

ANYWHERE WITH YOU; IN A GYPSY'S HEART and LOVE BRING MY LOVE BACK TO ME.

KID FROM SPAIN, THE

A United Artists' picture starring Eddie Cantor in a cast that included Lyda Roberti, Robert Young and Noah Beery, and directed by Leo McCarey. Songs by Bert Kalmar and Harry Ruby:

IN THE MOONLIGHT; LOOK WHAT YOU'VE DONE and WHAT A PERFECT COMBINATION (with Harry Akst).

LOVE ME TONIGHT

A Paramount picture starring Maurice Chevalier and Jeanette MacDonald in a cast that included Charles Ruggles, Charles Butterworth and Myrna Loy, and directed by Rouben Mamoulian. Songs by Lorenz Hart and Richard Rodgers:

ISN'T IT ROMANTIC?; MIMI; LOVE ME TONIGHT; LOVER and THE POOR APACHE.

MANHATTAN PARADE
A Warner Brothers' picture starring Winnie Lightner in a cast that included Charles Butterworth, Walter Miller, Joe Smith, Charles Dale, Bobby Watson and Dickie Moore, and directed by Lloyd Bacon. Songs:
I LOVE A PARADE and TEMPORARILY BLUE by Ted Koehler and Richard Arlen; I'M HAPPY WHEN YOU'RE JEALOUS by Bert Kalmar and Harry Ruby.

ONE HOUR WITH YOU
A Paramount picture starring Maurice Chevalier and Jeanette MacDonald in a cast that included Genevieve Tobin, Charles Ruggles, Roland Young and Richard Carle, and directed by Ernst Lubitsch. Songs by Leo Robin, Oscar Straus and Richard Whiting:
(I'D LOVE TO SPEND) ONE HOUR WITH YOU; OH, THAT MITZI; WE WILL ALWAYS BE SWEETHEARTS; WHAT WOULD YOU DO? and THREE TIMES A DAY.

RED-HEADED WOMAN
An M-G-M picture starring Jean Harlow in a cast that included Chester Morris, Lewis Stone, Leila Hyams, Una Merkel and Henry Stephenson, and directed by Jack Conway. Songs:
RED-HEADED WOMAN by Ray Egan and Richard Whiting; NOBODY'S SWEETHEART by Gus Kahn, Ernie Erdman, Elmer Schoebel and Billy Meyers; WE'LL DANCE TILL DAWN by Dorothy Fields and Jimmy McHugh.

Feature Films With Songs

BIRD OF PARADISE
An RKO picture starring Dolores Del Rio and Joel McCrea, and directed by King Vidor. Song by Milia Rosa and Peter De Rose:
BIRD OF PARADISE

BLESSED EVENT
A Warner Brothers' picture filmed with a cast headed by Lee Tracy, Mary Brian, Emma Dunn and Dick Powell, and directed by Roy Del Ruth. Songs:
HOW CAN YOU SAY NO (WHEN ALL THE WORLD IS SAYING YES)? by Irving Kahal, Al Dubin and Joe Burke; and I'M MAKING HAY IN THE MOONLIGHT by Tot Seymour and Jesse Greer.

BLONDE VENUS
A Paramount picture starring Marlene Dietrich and Herbert Marshall in a cast that included Cary Grant and Dickie Moore, and directed by Josef Von Sternberg. Songs by Leo Robin and Sam Coslow:
HOT VOODOO and YOU LITLE SO-AND-SO.

CARNIVAL BOAT
An RKO picture filmed with a cast headed by Bill Boyd, Ginger Rogers, Fred Kohler and Hobart Bosworth, and directed by Albert Rogell. Songs:
HOW I COULD GO FOR YOU by Bernie Grossman and Harold Lewis; RUN AROUND by Max Steiner.

CENTRAL PARK
A First National picture starring Joan Blondell in a cast that included Wallace Ford, Guy Kibbe and Henry B. Walthall, and directed by John Adolfi. Songs by Cliff Hess:
YOUNG LOVE and CENTRAL PARK

COCK OF THE AIR
A United Artists' picture starring Billie Dove and Chester Morris, and directed by Tom Buckingham. Songs by Alfred Newman, Bernie Grossman and Dave Silverstein:
LOVE ME and PUPPETS ON PARADE

CONGRESS DANCES
A United Artists' picture filmed with a cast headed by Lilian Harvey, Conrad Veidt and Lil Dagover, and directed by Eric Charell. Songs by Robert Gilbert and Werner Heymann:
JUST ONCE FOR ALL TIME and LIVE, LAUGH AND LOVE.

DANCE TEAM
A Fox picture starring James Dunn and Sally Eilers in a cast that included Ralph Morgan, and directed by Sidney Lanfield. Song by James Hanley:
I SAW MY FUTURE IN YOUR EYES

HAT CHECK GIRL
A Fox picture starring Sally Eilers in a cast that included Ben Lyon, Ginger Rogers and Monroe Owsley, and directed by Sidney Lanfield. Song by L. Wolfe Gilbert and James Hanley:
YOU'RE WORTH WHILE WAITING FOR

HIGH PRESSURE

A Warner Brothers' picture starring William Powell in a cast that included Evelyn Brent, George Sidney, Frank McHugh, Guy Kibbe and Evelyn Knapp, and directed by Mervyn LeRoy. Song by Joe Young and Harry Akst:

I CAN'T GET MISSISSIPPI OFF MY MIND

HORSE FEATHERS

A Paramount picture starring the Four Marx Brothers in a cast that included Thelma Todd and Nat Pendleton, and directed by Norman McLeod. Songs by Bert Kalmar and Harry Ruby:

EVERYONE SAYS "I LOVE YOU" and I'M AGAINST IT

HOTEL VARIETY

A Screencraft release starring Hal Skelly and Olive Borden. Song by Paul Vincent and Lou Herscher:

I GAVE THE RIGHT KIND OF LOVE

LADY AND GENT

A Paramount picture starring George Bancroft and Wynne Gibson, directed by Stephen Roberts. Song by Sam Coslow and Arthur Johnston:

EVERYBODY KNOWS IT BUT YOU

MAGIC NIGHT

A United Artists' picture starring Jack Buchanan and Anna Neagle, and directed by Herbert Wilcox. Song by George Posford and Eric Maschwitz:

GOOD NIGHT, VIENNA

MAKE ME A STAR

A Paramount picture starring Stuart Erwin and Joan Blondell in a cast that included Zasu Pitts and Ben Turpin, and directed by William Beaudine. Song by Joe Young and Carmen Lombardo:

ROUND MY HEART

MILLION DOLLAR LEGS

A Paramount picture filmed with a cast headed by Jack Oakie, W. C. Fields, Andy Clyde, Lyda Roberti, Ben Turpin and Dickie Moore, and directed by Edward Cline. Song by Ralph Rainger:

IT'S TERRIFIC

OFFICE GIRL, THE

An RKO picture starring Renate Muller and Jack Hulbert, and directed by Victor Saville. Song by Paul Abraham, Desmond Carter and Frank Eyton:

I HAVE AN AUNT ELIZA

PAINTED WOMAN, THE

A Fox picture filmed with a cast headed by Peggy Shannon, William Boyd and Spencer Tracy, and directed by John Blystone. Songs by L. Wolfe Gilbert and James Hanley:

SAY YOU'LL BE GOOD TO ME and BESIDE THE CORAL SEA.

PHANTOM PRESIDENT, THE

A Paramount picture starring George M. Cohan in a cast that included Claudette Colbert, Jimmy Durante and George Barbier, and directed by Norman Taurog. Songs:

THE COUNTRY NEEDS A MAN; MAYBE SOMEONE OUGHT TO WAVE A FLAG and YOU'RE A GRAND OLD FLAG by George M. Cohan; GIVE HER A KISS by Lorenz Hart and Richard Rodgers.

STEPPING SISTERS

A Fox picture filmed with a cast headed by Louise Dresser, William Collier Sr. and Minna Gombell, and directed by Seymour Felix. Songs by James Hanley:

LOOK HERE COMES A RAINBOW and MY WORLD BEGINS AND ENDS WITH YOU

SUNSHINE SUSIE

A Gainsborough picture starring Renate Muller. Song by Paul Abraham, Desmond Carter and Frank Eyton:

TODAY I FEEL SO HAPPY.

THIS IS THE NIGHT

A Paramount picture filmed with a cast headed by Lili Damita, Charles Ruggles and Roland Young, and directed by Frank Tuttle. Song by Ralph Rainger and Sam Coslow:

THIS IS THE NIGHT

WAYWARD

A Paramount picture starring Nancy Carroll and Richard Arlen, and directed by Edward Sloman. Song by Ray Klages and Jesse Greer:

WHAT'S THE DIFFERENCE?

WOMAN COMMANDS, A

An M-G-M picture starring Pola Negri in a cast that included Basil Rathbone, Roland Young and H. B. Warner, and directed by Paul L. Stein. Song by Gordon Clifford and Nacio Herb Brown:

PARADISE

1 9 3 3

Round One In The Songwriters' Battle Royal

"We have nothing to fear but fear itself!" FDR declared in his first inaugural address, and apparently Hollywood believed him, for the talkies saluted the fourth year of the Depression with a musical razzberry, *Who's Afraid Of The Big Bad Wolf?*, from *The Three Little Pigs,* a Technicolor cartoon short that had such an enthusiastic box-office reception that Walt Disney, its progenitor, was prompted to produce similar films in full length three years later.

After taking it on the chin for two years, the top brass of the film capital got up off the floor groggy but fighting, determined to restore the movies to the eminent place they'd long occupied as the nation's most popular and dependable form of entertainment. Even a bank holiday couldn't stop them in such a high resolve. As far as they were concerned, the banks had been on a holiday since 1930 when any film tycoon seeking a loan found the welcome mat missing from a well-guarded door.

In the sharps-and-flats department, this renaissance marked the opening of a prolonged battle royal between four new teams of songwriters who punched their way to the top of the 1933 Hit Parade with such outstanding songs as *Just One More Chance, Down The Old Ox Road, Shuffle Off To Buffalo, Forty-second Street, The Gold Diggers' Song* and *Did You Ever See A Dream Walking?*, and at the end of Round 1 the score cards read:

Sam Coslow and Arthur Johnston: *College Coach, College Humor, Too Much Harmony, The Way To Love* and *Hello Everybody.*

Al Dubin and Harry Warren: *Forty-second Street, Gold Diggers of 1933* and *Roman Scandals.*

Leo Robin and Ralph Rainger: *International House, She Done Him Wrong* and *The Torch Singer.*

Mack Gordon and Harry Revel: *Broadway Through A Keyhole* and *Sitting Pretty.*

In addition, they were credited with scattered points—songs contributed to other than musical pictures.

Jimmy McHugh, who was about to become one of the most prolific composers for the talkies, first with Dorothy Fields and later with Harold Adamson as his lyricist, had a real smash hit in *Don't Blame Me,* introduced in *Dinner At Eight,* and Vincent Youmans, deserting Broadway for Hollywood, contributed enduring music to *Flying Down To Rio,* the picture marking the debut of Ginger Rogers and Fred Astaire as a dancing team that made an older generation of Americans forget the famous Castles.

Other debutantes of the 1933 film musical season were Kate Smith, who sang "the moon over the mountain" on the radio but failed to put *Hello Everybody* over at the movie box office; the curvaceous Mae West, whose innuendo-packed invitation, "Come up and see me sometime", was eagerly accepted by the crowds that flocked to the theaters where *I'm No Angel* and *She Done Him Wrong* were shown; and Ruby Keeler, whose dance on a taxicab roof in *Forty-second Street* put her in easy reach of Hollywood's firmament of stars.

Cauliflower ears challenged glamour on the studio lots and the pungent odor of arnica and rubbing alcohol mingled with the seductive scent of Chanel No. 5 when a stable of pugilists weighed in for their diction lessons before appearing in two 1933 releases: *Mr. Broadway,* a revue written and MC-ed by Ed Sullivan, in which Primo Carnera, Maxie Rosenbloom and Tony Canzoneri made a screen appearance, and *The Prize Fighter And The Lady,* a picture in which Max Baer, aided and abetted physically by Jack Dempsey, traded histrionic punches with Myrna Loy for a draw decision.

Reflecting the aggressive spirit that permeated the studios in 1933, two musicals belted their way into the championship division, *Forty-second Street* and *She Done Him Wrong* being voted among the Ten Best Films of the year in company with *Cavalcade, The Private Life Of Henry the VIII, Lady For A Day, State Fair, A Farewell To Arms, I Am A Fugitive From A Chain Gang, Maedchen In Uniform* and *Rasputin and The Empress.*

Musicals

ADORABLE
A Fox picture starring Janet Gaynor in a cast that included Henry Garat and C. Aubrey Smith, and directed by William Dieterle. Songs by George Marion Jr. and Richard Whiting:
MY FIRST LOVE TO LAST; ADORABLE and MY HEART'S DESIRE.

ALICE IN WONDERLAND
A Paramount picture filmed with a cast headed by Charlotte Henry, Richard Arlen, Roscoe Ates, Gary Cooper, Leon Errol and W. C. Fields, and directed by Norman McLeod. Songs:
ALICE IN WONDERLAND by Dmitri Tiomkin, Nathaniel Finston and Leo Robin; WALK A LITTLE FASTER by Lewis Carroll and Dave Franklin.

BEDTIME STORY, A
A Paramount picture starring Maurice Chevalier in a cast that included Helen Twelvetrees, Edward Everett Horton, Adri-enne Ames and Baby LeRoy, and directed by Norman Taurog. Songs by Leo Robin and Ralph Rainger:
MONSIEUR BABY; LOOK WHAT I'VE GOT; IN THE PARK IN PAREE and HOME MADE HEAVEN.

BEST OF ENEMIES
A Fox picture starring Charles "Buddy" Rogers in a cast that included Marian Nixon, Frank Morgan, and Joseph Cawthorn, and directed by Rian James. Songs by Val Burton and Will Jason:
WE BELONG TO ALMA MATER; ALL-AMERICAN GIRLS and HANS AND GRETCHEN.

BROADWAY BAD
A Fox picture filmed with a cast headed by Joan Blondell, Ricardo Cortez, Ginger Rogers, Victor Jory, Donald Crisp and Adrienne Ames, and directed by Sidney Lanfield. Songs by Sidney Mitchell and Harry Akst:

FORGET THE PAST; FORBIDDEN
MELODY; THE ISLANDS ARE CALL-
ING ME; TILL THE END OF TIME
and DERELICT SONG.

BROADWAY THROUGH A KEYHOLE
A United Artists' picture filmed with a
cast that included Constance Cummings,
Paul Kelly, Blossom Seeley, Texas Guinan,
Gregory Ratoff, Russ Columbo and Abe Ly-
man and his band, and directed by Lowell
Sherman. Songs by Mack Gordon and Harry
Revel:
DOING THE UPTOWN LOWDOWN;
I LOVE YOU PRINCE PIZZICATO:
YOU'RE MY PAST, PRESENT AND FU-
TURE and WHEN YOU WERE A GIRL
ON A SCOOTER AND I WAS A BOY
ON A BIKE.

COLLEGE COACH
A Warner Brothers' picture starring Dick
Powell and Ann Dvorak in a cast that
included Pat O'Brien, Lyle Talbot, Arthur
Byron, Hugh Herbert and Nat Pendleton,
and directed by William A. Wellman.
Songs:
LONELY LANE and MEN OF CAL-
VERT by Irving Kahal and Sammy Fain:
JUST ONE MORE CHANCE by Sam
Coslow and Arthur Johnston; MEET ME
IN THE GLOAMING by Arthur Freed,
Al Hoffman and Al Goodhart; WHAT
WILL I DO WITHOUT YOU? by Johnny
Mercer and Hilda Gottlieb.

COLLEGE HUMOR
A Paramount picture filmed with a cast
headed by Bing Crosby, Jack Oakie, Rich-
ard Arlen, Mary Carlisle, Burns and Allen
and Eddie Nugent, and directed by Wesley
Ruggles. Songs by Sam Coslow and Arthur
Johnston:
LEARN TO CROON; DOWN THE
OLD OX ROAD; MOON STRUCK; AL-
MA MATER; COLLEEN OF KILLAR-
NEY; CLASSROOM NUMBER; PLAY
BALL and I'M A BACHELOR OF THE
ART OF HA-CHA-CHA.

DANCE, GIRL, DANCE
An Invincible Films release filmed with a
cast headed by Alan Dinehart, Evelyn
Knapp and Eddie Nugent, and directed by
Frank Strayer. Songs:
IT TAKES A LOT OF JACK by J.
Keirn Brennan and George Grandee; SEE-
ING IS BELIEVING by James Morley
and Lee Zahler; PEANUT VENDOR'S
LITTLE MISSUS by Eugene Conrad and
Harry Carroll.

DANCING LADY
An M-G-M picture starring Joan Craw-
ford and Clark Gable and introducing Fred
Astaire to the screen. Directed by Robert
Z. Leonard. Songs:
MY DANCING LADY by Dorothy Fields
and Jimmy McHugh; RHYTHM OF THE
DAY by Lorenz Hart and Richard Rodgers;
EVERYTHING I HAVE IS YOURS;
LET'S GO BAVARIAN and HEIGH-HO
THE GANG'S ALL HERE by Harold Ad-
amson and Burton Lane.

DUCK SOUP
A Paramount picture starring the Four
Marx Brothers in a cast that included Ra-
quel Torres and Louis Calhern, and direct-
ed by Leo McCarey. Songs by Bert Kalmar
and Harry Ruby:
FREEDONIA HYMN; HIS EXCEL-
LENCY IS DUE and THE COUNTRY'S
GOING TO WAR.

FLYING DOWN TO RIO
An RKO picture starring Dolores Del Rio
in a cast that included Fred Astaire, Ginger
Rogers and Gene Raymond, and directed by
Thornton Freeland. Songs by Gus Kahn,
Edward Eliscu and Vincent Youmans:
THE CARIOCA; MUSIC MAKES ME;
ORCHIDS IN THE MOONLIGHT and
FLYING DOWN TO RIO.

FOOTLIGHT PARADE
A Warner Brothers' picture filmed with
a cast headed by James Cagney, Joan Blon-
dell, Ruby Keeler, Dick Powell, Guy Kibbe,
Frank McHugh and Hugh Herbert, and di-
rected by Lloyd Bacon. Songs:
BY A WATERFALL; AH, THE MOON
IS HERE and SITTING ON A BACK-
YARD FENCE by Irving Kahal and Sam-
my Fain: SHANGHAI LIL and HONEY-
MOON HOTEL by Al Dubin and Harry
Warren.

FORTY-SECOND STREET
A Warner Brothers' picture filmed with a
cast headed by Warner Baxter, Bebe Dan-
iels, George Brent, Ruby Keeler, Dick
Powell, Ginger Rogers and Guy Kibbe, and
directed by Lloyd Bacon. Songs by Al Dubin
and Harry Warren:
FORTY-SECOND STREET; SHUFFLE
OFF TO BUFFALO; YOUNG AND
HEALTHY and YOU'RE GETTING TO
BE A HABIT WITH ME.

GIRL WITHOUT A ROOM
A Paramount picture filmed with a cast
headed by Charles Farrell, Charles Ruggles,

Marguerite Churchill, Gregory Ratoff and Walter Woolf, and directed by Ralph Murphy. Songs by Val Burton and Will Jason:
YOU ALONE; ROOF-TOP SEREN-ADE and THE WHISTLE HAS TO BLOW.

GOING HOLLYWOOD
An M-G-M picture with Marion Davies, Bing Crosby, Fifi D'Orsay, Stuart Erwin, Ned Sparks, Patsy Kelly and Bobby Watson, and directed by Raoul Walsh. Songs by Arthur Freed and Nacio Herb Brown:
GOING HOLLYWOOD; OUR BIG LOVE SCENE; MAKE HAY WHILE THE SUN SHINES; CINDERELLA'S FELLA; AFTER SUNDOWN and TEMP-TATION.

GOLD DIGGERS OF 1933
A Warner Brothers' picture filmed with a cast headed by Warren William, Joan Blondell, Aline McMahon, Ruby Keeler, Dick Powell, Guy Kibbe, Ned Sparks and Ginger Rogers, and directed by Mervyn Le-Roy. Songs by Al Dubin and Harry Warren:
GOLD DIGGERS' SONG (WE'RE IN THE MONEY); I'VE GOT TO SING A TORCH SONG; REMEMBER MY FOR-GOTTEN MAN; PETTIN' IN THE PARK and SHADOW WALTZ.

HALLELUJAH, I'M A BUM
A United Artists' picture starring Al Jolson in a cast that included Madge Evans, Harry Langdon, Frank Morgan and Chester Conklin, and directed by Mervyn LeRoy. Songs by Lorenz Hart and Richard Rodgers:
HALLELUJAH, I'M A BUM; YOU ARE TOO BEAUTIFUL; I'LL DO IT AGAIN; WHAT DO YOU WANT WITH MONEY? and I'VE GOT TO GET BACK TO NEW YORK.

HELLO EVERYBODY
A Paramount picture starring Kate Smith in a cast that included Randolph Scott and Sally Blane, and directed by William Seiter. Songs by Sam Coslow and Arthur Johnston:
MOON SONG; GREAT OPEN SPACES; QUEEN OF LULLABY LAND; TWENTY MILLION PEOPLE and PICK-ANINNIES' HEAVEN.

I LOVED YOU WEDNESDAY
A Fox picture filmed with a cast headed by Warner Baxter, Elissa Landi, Victor Jory and Laura Hope Crews, and directed by Henry King. Songs:
I FOUND YOU, I LOST YOU, I

FOUND YOU AGAIN by L. Wolfe Gilbert and L. B. Kornblum; IT'S ALL FOR THE BEST by George Marian Jr. and Richard Whiting; HILLS OF OLD WYOMING by Will Vodery.

I'M NO ANGEL
A Paramount picture starring Mae West in a cast that included Cary Grant and Edward Arnold, and directed by Wesley Ruggles. Songs by Harvey Brooks, Gladys DuBois and Ben Ellison:
NO ONE LOVES ME LIKE THAT DALLAS MAN OF MINE; THEY CALL ME SISTER HONKY TONK; I WANT YOU, I NEED YOU; I'VE FOUND A NEW WAY TO GO TO TOWN and I'M NO ANGEL.

INTERNATIONAL HOUSE
A Paramount picture filmed with a cast headed by Peggy Hopkins Joyce, William C. Fields, Rudy Vallee, Stuart Erwin, Burns and Allen, Col. Stoopnagle and Budd, Baby Rose Marie and Cab Calloway, and directed by Edward Sutherland. Songs by Leo Robin and Ralph Rainger:
THANK HEAVEN FOR YOU; MY BLUEBIRD'S SINGING THE BLUES and TEA CUP.

IT'S GREAT TO BE ALIVE
A Fox picture filmed with a cast headed by Gloria Stuart, Raul Roulien, Edna May Oliver and Herbert Mundin, and directed by Alfred Werker. Songs by William Kernell:
GOODBYE LADIES; I'LL BUILD A NEST; WOMEN and IT'S GREAT TO BE THE ONLY MAN ALIVE.

JIMMY AND SALLIE
A Fox picture starring James Dunn and Claire Trevor, and directed by James Tinling. Songs by Sidney Clare and Jay Gorney:
YOU'RE MY THRILL; IT'S THE IR-ISH IN ME and EAT MARLOWE'S MEAT.

MELODY CRUISE
An RKO picture filmed with a cast headed by Charles Ruggles, Phil Harris, Greta Nissen and Helen Mack, and directed by Mark Sandrich. Songs by Val Burton and Will Jason:
I MET HER AT A PARTY; HE'S NOT THE MARRYING KIND; THIS IS THE HOUR and ISN'T THIS A NIGHT FOR LOVE!

MOONLIGHT AND PRETZELS
A Universal picture filmed with a cast headed by Leo Carrillo, Mary Brian, Roger Pryor, Lillian Miles and William Frawley, and directed by Karl Freund. Songs:
AH BUT IS IT LOVE?; MOONLIGHT AND PRETZELS; DUSTY SHOES and LET'S MAKE LOVE LIKE THE CROCODILES by E. Y. Harburg and Jay Gorney: THERE'S A LITTLE BIT OF YOU IN EVERY LOVE SONG by E. Y. Harburg and Sammy Fain: ARE YOU MAKING ANY MONEY? by Herman Hupfeld.

MR. BROADWAY
A Broadway-Hollywood production filmed with a cast of Broadway and Hollywood celebrities that included Ed Sullivan, Jack Dempsey, Ruth Etting, Bert Lahr, Hal Le-Roy, Josephine Dunn, Ted Husing, Blossom Seeley, Benny Fields, Jack Benny, Mary Livingston, Gus Edwards, Jack Haley, Lupe Velez, Joe Frisco, Primo Carnera, Maxie Rosenbloom, Tony Canzoneri and the orchestras of Eddie Duchin, Isham Jones and Abe Lyman.

MY LIPS BETRAY
A Fox picture starring Lilian Harvey and John Boles in a cast that included El Brendel, and directed by John Blystone. Songs by William Kernell:
HIS MAJESTY'S CAR; TO ROMANCE; WHY AM I HAPPY? and THE BAND IS GAILY PLAYING.

MY WEAKNESS
A Fox picture filmed with a cast that included Lew Ayres, Charles Butterworth, Sid Silvers, Harry Langdon and Lilian Harvey, and directed by David Butler. Songs by B. G. DeSylva, Leo Robin and Richard Whiting:
HOW DO I LOOK?; YOU CAN BE HAD, SO BE CAREFUL and GATHER LIP ROUGE WHILE YOU MAY.

ROMAN SCANDALS
A United Artists' picture starring Eddie Cantor in a cast that included Ruth Etting, Gloria Stuart, David Manners and Edward Arnold, and directed by Frank Tuttle. Songs by Al Dubin and Harry Warren:
KEEP YOUNG AND BEAUTIFUL; BUILD A LITTLE HOME; NO MORE LOVE; ROME WASN'T BUILT IN A DAY and PUT A TAX ON LOVE.

SHADY LADY, THE
An RKO picture filmed with a cast headed by Phyllis Haver, Robert Armstrong, Louis Wolheim and Russell Gleason, and directed by Edward H. Griffith. Songs by Bud Green and Sammy Stept:
ANY WAY THE WIND BLOWS; SWINGY LITTLE THINGY; TIME TO GO and GET HOT FOOT.

SHE DONE HIM WRONG
A Paramount picture starring Mae West in a cast that included Cary Grant, Owen Moore and Noah Beery, and directed by Lowell Sherman. Songs:
MAZIE; HAVEN'T GOT NO PEACE OF MIND; GOITY and a GUY WHO TAKES HIS TIME by Leo Robin and Ralph Rainger; EASY RIDER by Shelton Brooks.

SITTING PRETTY
A Paramount picture filmed with a cast headed by Jack Oakie, Jack Haley, Ginger Rogers, Thelma Todd, Gregory Ratoff, Lew Cody and Gordon and Revel, and directed by Harry Joe Brown. Songs by Mack Gordon and Harry Revel:
DID YOU EVER SEE A DREAM WALKING?; BALLAD OF THE SOUTH; I WANNA MEANDER WITH MIRANDA; YOU'RE SUCH A COMFORT TO ME; GOOD MORNING GLORY; MANY MOONS AGO; LUCKY LITTLE EXTRA; THERE'S A BLUEBIRD AT MY WINDOW; AND THEN WE WROTE— and LIGHTS, ACTION, CAMERA, LOVE.

TAKE A CHANCE
A Paramount picture filmed with a cast that included James Dunn, Cliff Edwards, June Knight, Lillian Roth and Charles "Buddy" Rogers, and directed by Laurence Schwab and Monte Brice. Songs:
EADIE WAS A LADY and TURN OUT THE LIGHT by B. G. DeSylva, Richard Whiting and Nacio Herb Brown; SHOULD I BE SWEET? and RISE 'N' SHINE by B. G. DeSylva and Vincent Youmans; IT'S ONLY A PAPER MOON by Billy Rose, E. Y. Harburg and Harold Arlen; COME UP AND SEE ME SOMETIME by Arthur Swanstrom and Louis Alter; NIGHT OWL by Herman Hupfeld.

TOO MUCH HARMONY
A Paramount picture starring Bing Crosby in a cast that included Jack Oakie, Skeets Gallagher, Judith Allen, Lilyan Tashman and Ned Sparks, and directed by Edward Sutherland. Songs by Sam Coslow and Arthur Johnston:
THANKS; THE DAY YOU CAME

ALONG; BLACK MOONLIGHT; BOO, BOO, BOO; BUCKIN' THE WIND; I GUESS IT HAD TO BE THAT WAY; TWO ARISTOCRATS and CRADLE ME WITH A HA-CHA LULLABY.

TORCH SINGER

A Paramount picture starring Claudette Colbert in a cast that included Ricardo Cortez, David Manners, Lyda Roberti, and Baby LeRoy, and directed by Alexander Hall and George Somnes. Songs by Leo Robin and Ralph Rainger:
DON'T BE A CRY BABY; GIVE ME LIBERTY OR GIVE ME LOVE; IT'S A LONG DARK NIGHT and THE TORCH SINGER.

WAY TO LOVE, THE

A Paramount picture starring Maurice Chevalier in a cast that included Ann Dvorak and Edward Everett Horton, and directed by Norman Taurog. Songs:
I'M A LOVER OF PAREE; IN A ONE-ROOM FLAT; IT'S OH, IT'S AH, IT'S WONDERFUL and THERE'S A LUCKY GUY by Leo Robin and Ralph Rainger; THE WAY TO LOVE by Sam Coslow and Arthur Johnston.

Feature Films With Songs

ABOVE THE CLOUDS

A Columbia picture filmed with a cast headed by Richard Cromwell, Robert Armstrong and Dorothy Wilson, and directed by R. William Neil. Song by Charles Rosoff:
ARE YOU MINE?

ANN CARVER'S PROFESSION

A Columbia picture starring Fay Wray and Gene Raymond, and directed by Edward Buzzell. Songs by Charles Rosoff:
THERE'S LIFE IN MUSIC and WHY CAN'T WE LOVE FOREVER?

BARBARIAN, THE

An M-G-M picture starring Ramon Novarro in a cast that included Myrna Loy, Reginald Denny, Louise Closser Hale, C. Aubrey Smith and Edward Arnold, and directed by Sam Wood. Song by Arthur Freed and Nacio Herb Brown:
LOVE SONGS OF THE NILE

BE MINE TONIGHT

A Universal picture filmed with a cast headed by Jan Kiepura, Sonnie Hale, Magda Schneider and Edmund Gwenn, and directed by Anatol Litwak. Song by Marcellus Schiffer, Frank Eyton and Mischa Spolianski:
TELL ME TONIGHT

BONDAGE

A Fox picture starring Dorothy Jordan and Alexander Kirkland, and directed by Alfred Santell. Songs by Hal Burton and Will Jason:
COMMAND TO LOVE and PENTHOUSE LAMENT.

BROADWAY TO HOLLYWOOD

An M-G-M picture filmed with a cast headed by Alice Brady, Frank Morgan, Madge Evans, Jackie Cooper, Mickey Rooney, Jimmy Durante, Fay Templeton, May Robson, Nelson Eddy and Una Merkel, and directed by Willard Mack. Songs:
WE ARE THE TWO HACKETS by Al Goodhart; WHEN OLD NEW YORK WAS YOUNG by Howard Johnson and Gus Edwards; BY BLUSHIN' ROSIE by Edgar Smith and John Stromberg; and COME DOWN MA EVENIN' STAR by Robert B. Smith and John Stromberg.

CAVALCADE

A Fox picture starring Clive Brook and Diana Wynyard. Song by Noel Coward:
TWENTIETH CENTURY BLUES

CHILD OF MANHATTAN

A Columbia picture starring Nancy Carroll and John Boles in a cast that included Buck Jones and Jane Darwell, and directed by Edward Buzzell. Song by Elmer Colby and Maurice Abrahams:
TAKE EVERYTHING BUT YOU

COCKTAIL HOUR

A Columbia picture starring Bebe Daniels in a cast that included Sidney Blackmer and Randolph Scott, and directed by Victor Schertzinger, who contributed the following song:
LISTEN HEART OF MINE

CRADLE SONG

A Paramount picture filmed with a cast headed by Dorothea Wieck, Evelyn Venable, Sir Guy Standing, Louise Dresser, Georgia Caine and Dickie Moore, and directed by Mitchell Leisen. Songs by Leo Robin and Ralph Rainger:
LONELY LITTLE SENORITA and CRADLE SONG

DESIGN FOR LIVING

A Paramount picture filmed with a cast headed by Miriam Hopkins, Gary Cooper and Fredric March, and directed by Ernst Lubitsch. Song by Mack Gordon and Harry Revel:
MY DESIGN FOR LIVING

DINNER AT EIGHT

An M-G-M picture filmed with a cast headed by Marie Dressler, John Barrymore, Wallace Beery, Jean Harlow, Lionel Barrymore, Lee Tracy, Edmund Lowe, Billie Burke, Madge Evans and Jean Hersholt, and directed by George Cukor. Songs by Dorothy Fields and Jimmy McHugh:
DON'T BLAME ME and DINNER AT EIGHT.

DIPLOMANIACS

An RKO picture starring Bert Wheeler and Robert Woolsey in a cast that included Marjorie White, and directed by William A. Seiter. Song by Edward Eliscu and Harry Akst:
SING TO ME

DISGRACED

A Paramount picture filmed with a cast headed by Helen Twelvetrees, Bruce Cabot, Adrienne Ames and Ken Murray, and directed by Erle C. Kenton. Song by Sam Coslow and Stephen Pasternack:
ANY PLACE IS PARADISE (AS LONG AS YOU ARE THERE).

FACE IN THE SKY

A Fox picture starring Marian Nixon in a cast that included Spencer Tracy and Stuart Erwin, and directed by Harry Lachman. Song by Val Burton and Will Jason:
JUST ANOTHER DREAM

FROM HELL TO HEAVEN

A Paramount picture starring Carole Lombard in a cast that included Jack Oakie, Adrienne Ames, David Manners and Sidney Blackmer, and directed by Erle C. Kenton. Songs:
NOVA SCOTIA MOONLIGHT by Sam Coslow and Arthur Johnston; PLEASE by Leo Robin and Ralph Rainger.

HER BODYGUARD

A Paramount picture filmed with a cast headed by Edmund Lowe, Wynne Gibson, Edward Arnold and Alan Dinehart, and directed by William Beaudine. Song by Sam Coslow and Arthur Johnston:
WHERE HAVE I HEARD THAT MELODY?

HIS DOUBLE LIFE

A Fox picture filmed with a cast headed by Roland Young, Lillian Gish and Montagu Love, and directed by Arthur Hopkins. Songs by James Hanley and Karl Stark:
SOMEDAY, SOMETIME, SOMEWHERE and SPRINGTIME IN OLD GRANADA.

HOLD YOUR MAN

An M-G-M picture starring Jean Harlow and Clark Gable in a cast that included Stuart Erwin and Dorothy Burgess, and directed by Sam Wood. Song by Arthur Freed and Nacio Herb Brown:
HOLD YOUR MAN

HOT PEPPER

A Fox picture starring Lupe Velez and Edmund Lowe in a cast that included Victor McLaglen, and directed by John Blystone. Songs by Val Burton and Will Jason:
MON PAPA and AIN'T IT GONNA RING NO MORE?

I COVER THE WATERFRONT

A United Artists' picture starring Claudette Colbert and Ben Lyon in a cast that included Ernest Torrence, and directed by James Cruze. Song by Edward Heyman and Johnny Green:
I COVER THE WATERFRONT

MAN WHO DARED, THE

A Fox picture filmed with a cast headed by Norman Foster, Zita Johann and Joan Marsh, and directed by Hamilton MacFadden. Song by Val Burton and Will Jason:
BOHEMIAN DRINKING SONG

MEET THE BARON

An M-G-M picture starring Jack Pearl in a cast that included Jimmy Durante and Zasu Pitts, and directed by Walter Lang. Song by Dorothy Fields and Jimmy McHugh:
CLEAN AS A WHISTLE

MIDNIGHT CLUB

A Paramount picture filmed with a cast headed by Clive Brook, George Raft, Helen Vinson, Sir Guy Standing and Alison Skipworth, and directed by Alexander Hall and George Somnes. Song by Leo Robin and Ralph Rainger:
IN A MIDNIGHT CLUB

PADDY THE NEXT BEST THING

A Fox picture starring Janet Gaynor and Warner Baxter in a cast that included Walter Connolly, Harvey Stephens and Fiske O'-

Hara, and directed by Harry Lachman. Song
by Lester O'Keefe and L. E. Francesco:
PADDY

PEG O' MY HEART
An M-G-M picture starring Marion Davies
in a cast that included Onslow Stevens and
Alan Mowbray, and directed by Robert Z.
Leonard. Songs:
I'LL REMEMBER ONLY YOU by Ar-
thur Freed and Nacio Herb Brown: SWEET-
HEART DARLIN' by Gus Kahn and Herb-
ert Stothart.

PLEASURE CRUISE
A Fox picture starring Genevieve Tobin
in a cast that included Roland Young and
Ralph Forbes, and directed by Frank Tuttle.
Song by Val Burton and Will Jason:
IS THIS A SOUVENIR?

PRIZE FIGHTER AND THE LADY, THE
An M-G-M picture starring Myrna Loy in
a cast that included Max Baer, Primo Can-
era, Jack Dempsey, Walter Huston and Otto
Kruger, and directed by W. S. Van Dyke.
Songs:
YOU'VE GOT EVERYTHING by Gus
Kahn and Walter Donaldson; LUCKY
FELLA by Dorothy Fields and Jimmy Mc-
Hugh; DOWNSTREAM DRIFTER by Gus
Kahn, Ray Egan and Dave Snell.

PROFESSIONAL SWEETHEART
An RKO picture starring Ginger Rogers
and Norman Foster in a cast that included
Zasu Pitts, Frank McHugh, Allen Jenkins
and Gregory Ratoff, and directed by William
A. Seiter. Song by Edward Eliscu and Harry
Akst:
MY IMAGINERY SWEETHEART

SAILOR'S LUCK
A Fox picture starring James Dunn and
Sally Eilers in a cast that included Frank
Morgan and Victor Jory, and directed by
Raoul Walsh. Song by Ben Ryan, Hal Burton
and Will Jason:
A SAILOR'S LUCK

SECRET OF MADAME BLANCHE
An M-G-M picture starring Irene Dunne
in a cast that included Phillips Holmes,
Lionel Atwill and Una Merkel, and directed
by Charles Brabin. Song by M. L. Wells and
William Axt:
IF LOVE WERE ALL

SENSATION HUNTERS
A Monogram picture filmed with a cast
headed by Arline Judge, Preston Foster and
Marion Burns, and directed by Charles

Vidor. Song by Bernie Grossman and J. Harold Lewis:
SOMETHING IN THE AIR

SONG OF THE EAGLE
A Paramount picture filmed with a cast
headed by Charles Bickford, Richard Arlen,
Jean Hersholt, Mary Brian, Louise Dresser
and Andy Devine, and directed by Ralph
Murphy. Song by Bernie Grossman and J.
Harold Lewis:
HEY, HEY WE'RE GONNA BE FREE

SONG OF SONGS
A Paramount picture starring Marlene
Dietrich in a cast that included Brian
Aherne and Lionel Atwill, and directed by
Rouben Mamoulian. Songs by Edward Hey-
man and Frederick Hollander:
JOHNNY and YOU ARE MY SONG OF
SONGS.

STAGE MOTHER
An M-G-M picture starring Alice Brady
in a cast that included Maureen O'Sullivan,
Franchot Tone and Phillips Holmes, and di-
rected by Charles R. Brabin. Songs by Arthur
Freed and Nacio Herb Brown:
BEAUTIFUL GIRL and I'M DANCING
ON A RAINBOW.

STATE FAIR
A Fox picture starring Janet Gaynor in a
cast that included Sally Eilers, Victor Jory,
Louise Dresser, Will Rogers and Lew Ayers,
and directed by Henry King. Song by Val
Burton and Will Jason:
ROMANTIC

STORM AT DAYBREAK
An M-G-M picture starring Nils Asther
and Kay Francis, and directed by Richard
Boleslavsky. Songs by Gus Kahn and William
Axt:
I WILL BE A SOLDIER'S BRIDE and
OH, HOW WEARY.

SWEETHEART OF SIGMA CHI
A Monogram picture filmed with a cast
headed by Mary Carlisle, Buster Crabbe and
Charles Starrett, and directed by Edward L.
Marin. Songs by George Waggner and Ed
Ward:
FRATERNITY WALK and IT'S
SPRING AGAIN.

THREE-CORNERED MOON
A Paramount picture starring Claudette
Colbert in a cast that included Richard Arlen, Mary Boland and Wallace Ford, and directed by Elliott Nugent. Song by Leo Robin
and Ralph Rainger:
THREE-CORNERED MOON

WARRIOR'S HUSBAND, THE

A Fox film filmed with a cast headed by Elissa Landi, Ernest Truex, Majorie Rambeau and David Manners, and directed by Walter Lang. Song by Arthur Lange, Val Burton and Will Jason:

AMAZON BLUES

WHITE SISTER, THE

An M-G-M picture starring Helen Hayes and Clark Gable, and directed by Victor Fleming. Song by Gus Kahn and Herbert Stothart:

DRIFTING ON A BLUE LAGOON

WHITE WOMAN

A Paramount picture starring Charles Laughton and Carole Lombard in a cast that included Charles Bickford, and directed by Stuart Walker. Songs by Mack Gordon and Harry Revel:

YES, MY DEAR and HE'S A CUTE BRUTE (A GENTLEMAN AND A SCHOLAR).

WINE, WOMEN AND SONG

A Chadwick Pictures' release filmed with a cast headed by Lilyan Tashman, Lew Cody, Marjorie Moore, Paul Gregory and Bobbe Arnst, and directed by Herbert Brenon. Songs by Sidney Mitchell, Archie Gottler and Con Conrad:

WHEN YOU ARE MINE and WINE, WOMEN AND SONG.

WORST WOMAN IN PARIS, THE

A Fox picture filmed with a cast headed by Benita Hume, Adolphe Menjou, Harvey Stephens and Helen Chandler, and directed by Monte Blue. Song by Arthur Lange, Allan Stuart and Robert Burnhardt:

LOVE PASSES ME BY

Western Films With Songs

FIGHTING TEXANS

A Monogram picture starring Rex Bell and directed by Armand Shaefer. Song by Ruth and Louis Herscher:

HE'S MINE ALL MINE

ROBBERS' ROOST

A Fox picture starring George O'Brien in

a cast that included Maureen O'Sullivan, Reginald Owen and William Frawley, and directed by Louis King. Songs by Val Burton and Will Jason:

COWBOY'S HEAVEN; THE GAL FROM AMARILLO and YOU TO ADORE.

Cartoon Film With Songs

THREE LITTLE PIGS, THE

A Walt Disney production with a song by Ann Ronell and Frank Churchill:

WHO'S AFRAID OF THE BIG BAD WOLF?

Eddie Cantor in an early starring film, *Roman Scandals*.

1934

"Twinkle, Twinkle Little Star" and Her Name Is Shirley Temple

She was only five years old — a small bundle of energy and irresistable glamour. Jay Gorney, the songwriter, discovered her during the Christmas holidays in the lobby of a Los Angeles movie house, and persuaded Lew Brown, who was writing songs and producing pictures for Fox, to give her a screen test in which she proved herself a born actress who could both sing and dance. So Shirley Temple was put under contract.

In April, she made her film bow in *Stand Up And Cheer,* and that's just what theater audiences did. A month later, when *Little Miss Marker* was released, she stole that picture away from such seasoned performers as Adolphe Menjou and Charles Bickford. She was a star in her own right in *Baby Take A Bow* in June, then shared top billing with Gary Cooper and Carole Lombard in *Now And Forever,* and as the year closed, had millions of housewives itching to get their infuriated hands on Jane Withers, a seven-year-old brat who had pulled Shirley's golden curls in a scene of *Bright Eyes.*

But Shirley Temple wasn't the only Hollywood discovery of 1934. Metro-Goldwyn-Mayer dug down in the old music catalogues and finding music there worthy of revival on the sound track, introduced Stan Laurel and Oliver Hardy in a film version of Victor Herbert's *Babes In Toyland* and starred Jeanette MacDonald and Maurice Chevalier in Franz Lehar's *The Merry Widow.*

A singing cowboy from Tioga, Texas, Gene Autry, wandered onto the Mascot Pictures' lot, corraled some film experience in several shorts, and branded *In Old Sante Fe* with a style of singing on which his future fame was founded. Jerome Kern also was welcomed as a new and permanent resident of Hollywood where for the next eleven years he repeated his Broadway triumphs in a new medium for him—sound pictures—that both challenged and proved his amazing talent and versatility, and as his break-in assignment, he edited for the films the scores of two of his greatest stage musicals: *The Cat And The Fiddle,* starring Jeanette MacDonald and Ramon Novarro, and *Music In The Air* with Gloria Swanson and John Boles heading the cast.

The first film edition of *George White's Scandals* went before the cameras in 1934. Jimmy Durante nosed his way into the sharps-and-flats fraternity by writing *Inka Dinka Doo* for his starring picture, *Palooka.* Mort Dixon and Allie Wrubel became contenders in the songwriters' battle royal with the tunes they wrote for *Flirtation Walk,* starring Dick Powell and Ruby Keeler, and *Happiness Ahead.* And the Academy of Motion Picture Arts and Sciences decided that music as well as histrionic ability merited recognition, and awarded the first song Oscar to *The Continental,* written by Herb Magidson and Con Conrad and introduced by Ginger Rogers and Fred Astaire in *The Gay Divorcee.*

The 1934 sound tracks were loaded with new song hits, Mack Gordon and Harry Revel leading the field with *Love Thy Neighbor, Stay As Sweet As You Are, Take A Number From One To Ten* and *With My Eyes Wide Open I'm Dreaming.* But they had strenuous competition in the record shops and on the air from such songs, now classified as standards, as *June In January* by Leo Robin and Ralph Rainger, *Love Is Just Around The Corner* by Leo Robin and Lewis Gensler, *Lost In A Fog* by Dorothy Fields and Jimmy McHugh, *Cocktails For Two* by Sam Coslow and Arthur Johnston and the musical stepping stone to fame for Carl Brisson, *Waiting At The Gate For Katie* by Gus Kahn and Richard Whiting, *Boulevard Of Broken Dreams, I Only Have Eyes For You* and *I'll String Along With You* by Al Dubin and Harry Warren, and *One Night Of Love* by Gus Kahn and Victor Schertzinger, sung by Grace Moore in the film of the same name—the only musical to be included in the Ten Best Films of 1934, a year when top honors also went to *The Barretts of Wimpole Street, The House of Rothschild, The Thin Man, Viva Villa, Count Of Monte Cristo, Berkeley Square* and *It Happened One Night,* the last picture almost wrecking the underwear business when millions of high school and college students followed Clark Gable's example and ceased to wear undershirts.

And if the Golden Age of screen musicals hadn't arrived, it was like the love Bing Crosby sang about in *Here Is My Heart*—it was "just around the corner."

Musicals

BABES IN TOYLAND
An M-G-M picture filmed with a cast headed by Laurel and Hardy, Charlotte Henry, Harry Kleinbach and Johnny Downs, and directed by Gus Meins and Charles Rogers. Songs:
TOYLAND; MARCH OF THE TOYS; I CAN'T DO THAT SUM; NEVER MIND BO-PEEP; GO TO SLEEP, SLUMBER DEEP and JANE by Glen MacDonough and Victor Herbert; WHO'S AFRAID OF THE BIG BAD WOLF? by Ann Ronell and Frank Churchill.

BACHELOR OF ARTS
A Fox picture filmed with a cast headed by Tom Brown, Anita Louise, Henry Walthall, Arline Judge and Mae Marsh, and directed by Louis King. Songs:
PHI! PHI! PHI! and WHEN THE LAST YEAR ROLLS AROUND by Sidney Clare and Richard Whiting; I'M COUNTING ON YOU by Milton Drake and Ben Oakland; WHAT A NIGHT! by Cliff Friend and Carmen Lombardo; EASY COME, EASY GO by Edward Heyman and Johnny Green.

BELLE OF THE NINETIES
A Paramount picture starring Mae West in a cast that included Roger Pryor, Johnny Mack Brown and Duke Ellington, and directed by Leo McCarey. Songs by Sam Coslow and Arthur Johnston:
MY OLD FLAME; TROUBLED WATERS; MY AMERICAN BEAUTY and WHEN A ST. LOUIS WOMAN GOES DOWN TO NEW ORLEANS.

BOTTOMS UP
A Fox picture filmed with a cast headed by Spencer Tracy, John Boles, Pat Patterson, Herbert Mundin, Sid Silvers and Thelma Todd, and directed by David Butler. Songs:
TURN ON THE MOON; THROWIN' MY LOVE AWAY and LITTLE DID I DREAM by Harold Adamson and Burton Lane; WAITING AT THE GATE FOR KATIE by Gus Kahn and Richard Whiting.

CAT AND THE FIDDLE, THE

An M-G-M picture starring Ramon Novarro and Jeanette MacDonald in a cast that included Frank Morgan, Charles Butterworth, Jean Hersholt and Vivienne Segal, and directed by William K. Howard. Songs by Otto Harbach and Jerome Kern:

SHE DIDN'T SAY YES; THE NIGHT WAS MADE FOR LOVE; TRY TO FORGET; A NEW LOVE IS OLD; DON'T ASK ME NOT TO SING; I WATCHED THE LOVE PARADE; ONE MOMENT ALONE; POOR PIERROT and HA! CHA! CHA!

COCKEYED CAVALIERS

An RKO picture starring Bert Wheeler and Robert Woolsey in a cast that included Dorothy Lee, Noah Beery and Thelma Todd, and directed by Mark Sandrich. Songs:

AND THE BIG BAD WOLF WAS DEAD and DILLY-DALLY by Val Burton and Will Jason; COQUETTE by Gus Kahn, Carmen Lombardo and Johnny Green.

COLLEGE RHYTHM

A Paramount picture filmed with a cast headed by Jack Oakie, Joe Penner, Lyda Roberti, Lanny Ross, Helen Mack and George Barbier, and directed by Norman Taurog. Songs by Mack Gordon and Harry Revel:

STAY AS SWEET AS YOU ARE; COLLEGE RHYTHM; GOO GOO (I'M GA-GA OVER YOU); LET'S GIVE THREE CHEERS FOR LOVE and TAKE A NUMBER FROM ONE TO TEN.

DAMES

A Warner Brothers' picture starring Joan Blondell and Dick Powell in a cast that included Ruby Keeler, Zasu Pitts, Guy Kibbe, Phil Regan and Sammy Fain, and directed by Ray Enright. Songs:

WHEN YOU WERE A SMILE ON YOUR MOTHER'S LIPS (AND A TWINKLE IN YOUR DADDY'S EYE) by Irving Kahal and Sammy Fain; I ONLY HAVE EYES FOR YOU; DAMES and THE GIRL AT THE IRONING BOARD by Al Dubin and Harry Warren; TRY TO SEE IT MY WAY by Mort Dixon and Allie Wrubel.

DOWN TO THEIR LAST YACHT

An RKO picture filmed with a cast headed by Mary Boland, Polly Moran and Ned Sparks, and directed by Paul Sloane. Songs:

TINY LITTLE FINGER ON YOUR HAND by Val Burton and Will Jason; THERE'S NOTHING ELSE TO DO IN MA-LA-KA-MO-KA-LU BUT LOVE by Sidney Mitchell and Cliff Friend; BEACH BOY; FUNNY LITTLE WORLD; QUEEN MARCH and BEACH BOY BOLERO by Ann Ronell and Max Steiner.

EMBARRASSING MOMENTS

A Universal picture starring Chester Morris and Marian Nixon, and directed by Edward Laemmle. Songs:

I WON'T THINK ABOUT TOMORROW by Sammy Lerner and Jay Gorney; BROTHER CAN YOU SPARE A DIME by E. Y. Harburg and Jay Gorney; WHAT A FOOL AM I by George Waggner and Edward Ward.

FLIRTATION WALK

A First National picture starring Dick Powell and Ruby Keeler in a cast that included Pat O'Brien and Ross Alexander, and directed by Frank Borzage. Songs by Mort Dixon and Allie Wrubel:

FLIRTATION WALK; MR. AND MRS. IS THE NAME; NO HORSE, NO WIFE, NO MOUSTACHE; WHEN DO WE EAT?; I SEE TWO LOVERS and SMOKING IN THE DARK.

GAY DIVORCEE, THE

An RKO picture starring Fred Astaire and Ginger Rogers in a cast that included Alice Brady, Edward Everett Horton and Eric Blore, and directed by Mark Sandrich. Songs:

LOOKING FOR A NEEDLE IN A HAYSTACK and THE CONTINENTAL by Herb Magidson and Con Conrad; DON'T LET IT BOTHER YOU and LET'S K-NOCK K-NEES by Mack Gordon and Harry Revel; NIGHT AND DAY by Cole Porter.

GEORGE WHITE'S SCANDALS

A 20th Century-Fox picture filmed with a cast headed by Rudy Vallee, Jimmy Durante, Alice Faye, Gregory Ratoff, Adrienne Ames, Cliff Edwards, George White, Dixie Dunbar and Richard Carle, and directed by George White, Thornton Freeland and Harry Lachman. Songs by Jack Yellen, Irving Caesar and Ray Henderson:

OH YOU NASTY MAN!; SO NICE; SWEET AND SIMPLE; FOLLOWING IN MOTHER'S FOOTSTEPS; EVERY DAY IS FATHER'S DAY WITH BABY; SIX WOMEN; MY DOG LOVES YOUR DOG and HOLD MY HAND.

GIFT OF GAB, THE

A Universal picture filmed with a cast headed by Edmund Lowe, Gloria Stuart, Paul Lukas, Boris Karloff, Roger Pryor, June

Knight, Ruth Etting, Phil Baker, Chester Morris, Bela Lugosi, Alice White, Alexander Woollcott, Victor Moore, Hugh O'Connell and Graham McNamee, and directed by Karl Freund. Songs:

TALKING TO MYSELF, I AIN'T GONNA SIN NO MORE and GIFT OF GAB by Herb Magidson and Con Conrad; SOMEBODY LOOKS GOOD by George Whiting and Albert VonTilzer; DON'T LET THIS WALTZ MEAN GOODBYE and WALKIN' ON AIR by Jack Meskill and Albert VonTilzer; WHAT A WONDERFUL DAY by Harry Tobias and Al Sherman; TOMORROW—WHO CARES by Murray Mencher and Charles Tobias.

GIRL FROM MISSOURI
An M-G-M picture starring Jean Harlow and Franchot Tone, and directed by Jack Conway. Songs:

HOT DOGS AND SASPARELLA by Walter Samuels and Leonard Whitcup; FEELIN' HIGH by Howard Dietz and Walter Donaldson; I'VE HAD MY MOMENTS by Gus Kahn and Walter Donaldson; THANK YOU FOR A LOVELY EVENING by Dorothy Fields and Jimmy McHugh; BORN TO BE KISSED by Howard Dietz and Arthur Schwartz; A HUNDRED YEARS FROM TODAY by Ned Washington and Victor Young; MOONLIGHT WALTZ by Ned Washington and Joe Burke; EV'RYBODY LOVES A SAILOR by Mitchell Parish, James Cavanaugh and Nat Simon.

HAPPINESS AHEAD
A First National picture starring Dick Powell in a cast that included Josephine Hutchinson, John Halliday, Dorothy Dare, Frank McHugh, Allen Jenkins, Ruth Donnelly and J. M. Kerrigan, and directed by Mervyn LeRoy. Songs:

BEAUTY MUST BE LOVED by Irving Kahal and Sammy Fain; THERE MUST BE HAPPINESS AHEAD; POP GOES YOUR HEART and ALL ON ACCOUNT OF A STRAWBERRY SUNDAE by Mort Dixon and Allie Wrubel; THE WINDOW-CLEANERS by Bert Kalmar and Harry Ruby.

HAROLD TEEN
A Warner Brothers' picture starring Hal LeRoy in a cast that included Rochelle Hudson, Patricia Ellis, Hugh Herbert, Guy Kibbe and Richard Carle, and directed by Murray Roth. Songs by Irving Kahal and Sammy Fain:

HOW DO YOU KNOW IT'S SUN-DAY?; SIMPLE AND SWEET; TWO LITTLE FLIES ON A LUMP OF SUGAR and COLLEGIATE WEDDING.

HEAT WAVE
A Gainsborough film starring Anna Lee and Les Allen. Songs by Maurice Sigler, Al Goodhart and Al Hoffman:

IF YOUR FATHER ONLY KNEW and SAN FELIPE.

HEI TIKI
A Principal Films' release filmed with a cast of South Sea Islanders. Songs by Alexander Markey:

CAN THIS BE HEAVEN? THE HEY-HA and SWEETHEARTS IN PARADISE.

HERE IS MY HEART
A Paramount picture starring Bing Crosby in a cast that included Kitty Carlisle, Roland Young, Alison Skipworth and Reginald Owen, and directed by Frank Tuttle. Songs:

LOVE IS JUST AROUND THE CORNER by Leo Robin and Lewis Gensler; WITH EVERY BREATH I TAKE; JUNE IN JANUARY; HERE IS MY HEART and YOU CAN'T MAKE A MONKEY OF THE MOON by Leo Robin and Ralph Rainger.

HIPS, HIPS HOORAY
An RKO picture starring Bert Wheeler and Robert Woolsey in a cast that included Ruth Etting and Thelma Todd, and directed by Mark Sandrich. Songs by Bert Kalmar and Harry Ruby:

KEEP ON DOIN' WHAT YOU'RE DOIN'; TIRED OF IT ALL and KEEP ROMANCE ALIVE.

HOLLYWOOD PARTY
An M-G-M picture filmed with a cast headed by Stan Laurel, Oliver Hardy, Jimmy Durante, Charles Butterworth, Polly Moran, Lupe Velez, Frances Williams and Jack Pearl, and directed by Ray Rowland. Songs:

I'VE HAD MY MOMENTS by Gus Kahn and Walter Donaldson; FEELIN' HIGH by Howard Dietz and Walter Donaldson; HOT CHOCOLATE SOLDIERS by Arthur Freed and Nacio Herb Brown.

I AM SUZANNE
A Fox picture filmed with a cast headed by Lilian Harvey, Gene Raymond and Leslie Banks, and directed by Rowland V. Lee. Songs by Frederick Hollander:

JUST A LITTLE GARRET; OH HOW I'VE SINNED!; ONE WORD; SAN MORITZ; WOODEN WOMAN and OSKI-O-LAY LI-O-MO.

I LIKE IT THAT WAY

A Universal picture filmed with a cast headed by Gloria Stuart, Roger Pryor, Marian Marsh, Lucile Gleason and Mickey Rooney, and directed by Harry Lachman. Songs:

BLUE SKY AVENUE by Herb Magidson and Con Conrad; LET'S PUT TWO AND TWO TOGETHER; I LIKE IT THAT WAY and GOIN' TO TOWN by Sidney Mitchell and Archie Gottler.

KID MILLIONS

A United Artists' picture starring Eddie Cantor in a cast that included Ann Sothern, Ethel Merman and George Murphy, and directed by Roy Del Ruth. Songs:

OKAY TOOTS; AN EARFUL OF MUSIC; WHEN MY SHIP COMES IN and ICE CREAM FANTASY by Gus Kahn and Walter Donaldson; YOUR HEAD ON MY SHOULDER and I WANT TO BE A MINSTREL MAN by Harold Adamson and Burton Lane; MANDY by Irving Berlin.

KING KELLY OF THE U.S.A.

A Monogram picture filmed with a cast headed by Guy Robertson, Irene Ware, Franklin Pangborn, Joyce Compton and Otis Harlan, and directed by Leonard Fields. Songs by Bernie Grossman and Joe Sanders:

RIGHT NEXT DOOR TO LOVE; BELIEVE ME and THERE'S A LOVE SONG IN THE AIR.

LET'S FALL IN LOVE

A Columbia picture starring Ann Sothern in a cast that included Edmund Lowe and Gregory Ratoff, and directed by David Burton. Songs by Ted Koehler and Richard Arlen:

LET'S FALL IN LOVE; BREAKFAST BALL; THIS IS ONLY THE BEGINNING and LOVE IS LOVE ANYWHERE.

LET'S TALK IT OVER

A Universal picture filmed with a cast headed by Chester Morris, Mae Clark, Frank Craven and Andy Devine, and directed by Kurt Neumann. Songs:

HEAVEN ON EARTH by Roy Turk and Harry Akst; LONG LIVE LOVE by Walter Donaldson; WHERE WILL I FIND THE ONE? by Gordon Clifford and Sid Cutler; SOMEONE TO LOVE by Lynn Cowan and David Klatzkin.

LITTLE MISS MARKER

A Paramount picture filmed with a cast headed by Shirley Temple, Adolphe Menjou, Charles Bickford and Dorothy Dell, and directed by Alexander Hall. Songs by Leo Robin and Ralph Rainger:

LOW-DOWN LULLABY; I'M A BLACK SHEEP WHO'S BLUE and LAUGH YOU SON-OF-A-GUN.

LOUD SPEAKER

A Monogram picture filmed with a cast headed by Ray Walker, Jacqueline Wells, Noel Francis and Charles Grapevine, and directed by Joseph Santley. Songs:

WHO BUT YOU and DOO AH, DOO AH, DOO AH KNOW WHAT I'M DOING? by Lew Brown and Harry Akst; THROUGH THE COURTESY OF LOVE and YOU ON MY MIND by Jack Scholl and M. K. Jerome.

MANY HAPPY RETURNS

A Paramount picture filmed with a cast headed by Guy Lombardo and his Royal Canadians, Burns and Allen, Jean Marsh, George Barbier, Ray Milland and Veloz and Yolando, and directed by Norman McLeod. Songs:

FARE-THEE-WELL; I DON'T WANNA PLAY and BOOGY MAN by Sam Coslow and Arthur Johnston; THE SWEETEST MUSIC THIS SIDE OF HEAVEN by Carmen Lombardo and Cliff Friend.

MELODY IN SPRING

A Paramount picture starring Ann Sothern and Lanny Ross in a cast that included Mary Boland and Charles Ruggles, and directed by Norman McLeod. Songs by Harlan Thompson and Lewis Gensler:

MELODY IN SPRING; THE OPEN ROAD; IT'S PSYCHOLOGICAL and ENDING WITH A KISS.

MERRY WIDOW, THE

An M-G-M picture starring Jeanette MacDonald and Maurice Chevalier, and directed by Ernst Lubitsch. Music by Franz Lehar with new lyrics by Gus Kahn and Lorenz Hart:

VILIA; MAXIM'S; GIRLS, GIRLS, GIRLS and THE MERRY WIDOW WALTZ.

MOULIN ROUGE

A United Artists' picture filmed with a cast headed by Constance Bennett, Franchot Tone, Tullio Carminati and Helen Wesley, and directed by Sidney Lanfield. Songs by Al Dubin and Harry Warren:

BOULEVARD OF BROKEN DREAMS; SONG OF SURRENDER and COFFEE IN THE MORNING AND KISSES AT NIGHT.

MURDER AT THE VANITIES

A Paramount picture starring Carl Brisson in a cast that included Victor McLaglen, Jack Oakie, Kitty Carlisle, Dorothy Stickney, Gail Patrick, Donald Meek and Duke Ellington and his orchestra, and directed by Mitchell Leisen. Songs by Johnny Burke, Sam Coslow and Arthur Johnston:

LOVELY ONE; WHERE DO THEY COME FROM? MARAHUANA; LIVE AND LOVE TONIGHT; COCKTAILS FOR TWO and EBONY RHAPSODY.

MUSIC IN THE AIR

A Fox picture starring Gloria Swanson and John Boles in a cast that included June Lang, Al Shean, Reginald Owen, Joseph Cawthorn and Hobart Bosworth, and directed by Joe May. Songs by Oscar Hammerstein II and Jerome Kern:

MUSIC IN THE AIR; I AM SO EAGER; I'VE TOLD EV'RY LITTLE STAR; ONE MORE DANCE; THE SONG IS YOU and WE BELONG TOGETHER.

MYRT AND MARGE

A Universal picture filmed with a cast headed by Myrtle Vail, Donna Damerell and Eddie Foy Jr., and directed by Al Boasberg. Songs by Joan Jasmin and M. K. Jerome:

DRAGGIN' MY HEELS AROUND; ISLE OF BLUES and WHAT IS SWEETER?

ONE NIGHT OF LOVE

A Columbia picture starring Grace Moore and Tullio Carminati, and directed by Victor Schertzinger. In addition to several arias from leading grand operas, there was one song by Gus Kahn and Victor Schertzinger:
ONE NIGHT OF LOVE

PALOOKA

A United Artists' picture starring Jimmy Durante in the title role of Joe Palooka with a supporting cast that included Lupe Velez, Stuart Erwin, Marjorie Rambeau, Mary Carlisle and Thelma Todd, and directed by Benjamin Stoloff. Songs:

LIKE ME A LITTLE BIT LESS (LOVE ME A LITTLE BIT MORE); by Harold Adamson and Burton Lane; PALOOKA IT'S A GRAND OLD NAME by Ann Ronell and Joe Burke; COUNT YOUR BLESSINGS by Irving Caesar and Ferde Grofe; INKA DINKA DOO by Ben Ryan and Jimmy Durante.

RAINBOW OVER BROADWAY

A Chesterfield Film release starring Joan Marsh and Frank Albertson, and directed by Richard Thorpe. Songs by Neville Fleeson, Elizabeth Morgan and Harry Von Tilzer:

DANCE MY BLUES AWAY; I MUST BE IN LOVE WITH LOVE; THERE AIN'T NO SUBSTITUTE FOR LOVE and WHILE I'M IN THE MOOD (with Richard Whiting).

SHE LEARNED ABOUT SAILORS

A Fox picture in which Alice Faye made her film debut in a cast that included Lew Ayers. Songs:

HERE'S THE KEY TO MY HEART and SHE LEARNED ABOUT SAILORS by Sidney Clare and Richard Whiting; IF I WERE ADAM AND YOU WERE EVE by James F. Hanley.

SHE LOVES ME NOT

A Paramount picture starring Bing Crosby and Miriam Hopkins in a cast that included Kitty Carlisle, Henry Stephenson, Lynne Overmann, Eddie Nugent and George Barbier, and directed by Elliott Nugent. Songs:

LOVE IN BLOOM by Leo Robin and Ralph Rainger; AFTER ALL YOU'RE ALL I'M AFTER by Edward Heyman and Arthur Schwartz; STRAIGHT FROM THE SHOULDER (RIGHT FROM THE HEART); I'M HUMMIN', I'M WHISTLIN', I'M SINGIN' and PUT A LITTLE RHYTHM IN EVERYTHING YOU DO by Mack Gordon and Harry Revel.

SHOOT THE WORKS

A Paramount picture filmed with a cast headed by Jack Oakie, Dorothy Dell, Arline Judge, Alison Skipworth, Roscoe Karns, William Frawley, Lew Cody and Ben Bernie and his orchestra, and directed by Wesley Ruggles. Songs:

DO I LOVE YOU? and TAKE A LESSON FROM THE LARK by Leo Robin and Ralph Rainger; WERE YOUR EARS BURNING? and WITH MY EYES WIDE OPEN I'M DREAMING by Mack Gordon and Harry Revel; A BOWL OF CHOP SUEY AND YOU-EY by Al Goering and Ben Bernie.

STAND UP AND CHEER

A Fox picture filmed with a cast headed by Shirley Temple, Warner Baxter, Madge Evans, James Dunn, John Boles, Ralph Morgan, Aunt Jemima, Nigel Bruce and Stepin Fetchit, and directed by Hamilton MacFadden. Songs:

STAND UP AND CHEER; NOW I'LL TELL; FOOLING WITH OTHER WOMEN; BABY TAKE A BOW; THIS IS OUR LAST NIGHT TOGETHER; BROAD-

WAY'S GONE HILLBILLY; I'M LAUGH-ING and SHE'S WAY UP THAR by Lew Brown and Harry Akst; WE'RE OUT OF THE RED by Lew Brown and Jay Gorney.

STRICTLY DYNAMITE
An RKO picture starring Jimmy Durante and Lupe Velez in a cast that included Irene Franklin and the Mills Brothers, and directed by Elliott Nugent. Songs:
MONEY IN MY CLOTHES by Irving Kahal and Sammy Fain; SWING IT SIS-TER and OH ME, OH MY, OH YOU by Harold Adamson and Burton Lane.

STUDENT TOUR
An M-G-M picture starring Jimmy Dur-ante in a cast that included Charles Butter-worth, Maxine Doyle, Phil Regan, Monte Blue and Betty Grable, and directed by Charles Reisner. Songs:
A NEW MOON IS OVER MY SHOUL-DER; THE CARLO; SNAKE DANCE; BY THE TAJ MAHAL; FROM NOW ON and FIGHT 'EM by Arthur Freed and Nacio Herb Brown; I SAY IT WITH MUSIC by Jimmy Durante.

THAT'S A GOOD GIRL
A United Artists' release filmed with a cast headed by Jack Buchanan, Elsie Randolph and Vera Pearce. Songs:
FANCY OUR MEETING and LET YOURSELF GO by Phil Charig and Joseph Meyer; SO GREEN by Douglas Furber and Walter Jurmann; THE ONE I'M LOOK-ING FOR by Douglas Furber, Ira Gershwin, Joseph Meyer and Phil Charig.

TRANSATLANTIC MERRY-GO-ROUND
A United Artists' picture filmed with a cast headed by Jack Benny, Gene Raymond, Nancy Carroll, Sidney Howard, Mitzi Green and Ralph Morgan, and directed by Ben-jamin Stoloff. Songs:
IT WAS SWEET OF YOU; ROCK AND ROLL; OH, LEO, IT'S LOVE and MOON OVER MONTE CARLO by Sidney Clare and Richard Whiting; IF I HAD A MIL-LION DOLLARS by Johnny Mercer and Matt Malneck.

TWENTY MILLION SWEETHEARTS
A First National picture starring Dick Powell and Ginger Rogers in a cast that in-cluded Pat O'Brien, Allen Jenkins and Jos-eph Cawthorn, and directed by Ray Enright. Songs by Al Dubin and Harry Warren:
FAIR AND WARMER; OUT FOR NO GOOD; WHAT ARE YOUR INTEN-TIONS and (YOU MAY NOT BE AN ANGEL BUT) I'LL STRING ALONG WITH YOU.

WAKE UP AND DREAM
A Universal picture filmed with a cast headed by Russ Columbo, June Knight, Roger Pryor, Winnie Shaw and Andy Devine, and directed by Kurt Neumann. Songs by Russ Columbo, Grace Hamilton and Jack Stern:
TOO BEAUTIFUL FOR WORDS; WHEN YOU'RE IN LOVE and LET'S PRETEND THERE'S A MOON.

WE'RE NOT DRESSING
A Paramount picture starring Bing Crosby and Carole Lombard in a cast that included George Burns, Gracie Allen, Ethel Merman and Leon Errol, and directed by Norman Taurog. Songs:
ONCE IN A BLUE MOON; MAY I?; LOVE THY NEIGHGOR; IT'S THE ANI-MAL IN ME; GOODNIGHT LOVELY LITTLE LADY and SHE WALKS LIKE YOU SHE TALKS LIKE YOU by Mack Gordon and Harry Revel; LIVE AND LOVE TONIGHT by Sam Coslow and Ar-thur Johnston; WHEN THE GOLDEN GATE WAS SILVER by Leo Robin and Ralph Rainger.

WHARF ANGEL
A Paramount picture starring Victor Mc-Laglen, Dorothy Dell and Preston Foster, and directed by William C. Menzies and George Somnes. Songs:
DOWN HOME by Leo Robin and Ralph Rainger; HELLO FRISCO HELLO by Gene Buck and Louis Hirsch; I WISH THAT I HAD A GIRL by Gus Kahn and Grace LeBoye; OH YOU BEAUTIFUL DOLL by A. Seymour Brown and Nat D. Ayer; UNDER THE YUM-YUM TREE by Andrew B. Sterling and Harry VonTilzer; DOIN' THE GRIZZLY BEAR by Irving Berlin and George Botsford; YOU MADE ME LOVE YOU by Joe McCarthy and Jimmy Monaco.

WONDER BAR
A Warner Brothers' picture starring Al Jolson in a cast that included Kay Francis, Dick Powell, Dolores Del Rio and Ricardo Cortez, and directed by Lloyd Bacon. Songs by Al Dubin and Harry Warren:
GOING TO HEAVEN ON A MULE; WHY DO I DREAM THOSE DREAMS?; DON'T SAY GOOD NIGHT; WONDER BAR; VIVE LA FRANCE and TANGO DEL RIO.

Feature Films With Songs

ALL MEN ARE ENEMIES
A Fox picture filmed with a cast headed by Helen Twelvetrees, Hugh Williams, Mona Barrie, Herbert Mundin and Henry Stephenson, and directed by George Fitzmaurice. Song by William Kernell and L. E. DeFrancesco:
HEART OF MY HEART

AS HUSBANDS GO
A Fox picture filmed with a cast headed by Warner Baxter, Helen Vinson and Warner Oland, and directed by Hamilton MacFadden. Song by Robert Browning and L. E. DeFrancesco:
AH LOVE BUT A DAY

BABY TAKE A BOW
A Fox picture filmed with a cast headed by Shirley Temple, James Dunn, Claire Trevor and Alan Dinehart, and directed by Harry Lachman. Song by Bud Green and Sammy Stept:
ON ACCOUNTA I LOVE YOU

BAND PLAYS ON, THE
An M-G-M picture with Robert Young, Stuart Erwin, Leo Carrillo and Betty Furness, and directed by Russell Mack. Song by Harold Adamson and Burton Lane:
ROLL UP THE SCORE

BELOVED
A Universal picture starring John Boles in a cast that included Gloria Stuart, Albert Conti, Dorothy Peterson and Mickey Rooney, and directed by Victor Schertzinger, who contributed the following song:
BELOVED

BRIGHT EYES
A Fox picture filmed with a cast that included Shirley Temple, James Dunn, Judith Allen and Jane Withers, and directed by David Butler. Song by Sidney Clare and Richard Whiting:
ON THE GOOD SHIP LOLLIPOP

CALL IT LUCK
A Fox picture with Georgia Caine, Pat Patterson and Herbert Mundin, and directed by James Tinling. Songs:
I'LL BET ON YOU by George Marion Jr. and Richard Whiting; A MERRY CHEERIO and DRINKING SONG by Sidney Clare and Richard Whiting.

CARAVAN
A Fox picture filmed with a cast headed by Charles Boyer, Loretta Young, Jean Parker, Phillip Holmes, Louise Fazenda and Eugene Pallete, and directed by Eric Charrell. Songs by Gus Kahn and Werner H. Heymann:
HA-CHA-CHA; HAPPY I AM and WINE SONG.

CAROLINA
A Fox picture starring Janet Gaynor and Lionel Barrymore in a cast that included Robert Young and Richard Cromwell, and directed by Henry King. Songs:
CAROLINA by Lew Brown and Jay Gorney; MOANIN' and PUT ON YO' WORKIN' SHOES by L. E. DeFrancesco; BRIGHT NEW MORNIN' by Frederick Hollander; THE SUN SHINES BRIGHTER WHEN YOU GO SINGING ALONG by William Kernell.

CAT'S PAW
A Fox picture starring Harold Lloyd and Una Merkel, and directed by Sam Taylor. Song by Roy Turk and Harry Akst:
I'M JUST THAT WAY

CHANGE OF HEART
A Fox picture starring Janet Gaynor and Charles Farrell in a cast that included James Dunn and Ginger Rogers, and directed by John G. Blystone. Song by Harry Akst:
SO WHAT?

COME ON MARINES
A Paramount picture starring Richard Arlen and Ida Lupino, and directed by Henry Hathaway. Songs by Leo Robin and Ralph Rainger:
TEQUILA; HULA HOLIDAY and OH BABY OBEY

COMING OUT PARTY
A Fox picture filmed with a cast headed by Frances Dee, Gene Raymond, Alison Skipworth and Nigel Bruce, and directed by John G. Blystone. Song by Harold Adamson and Burton Lane:
I THINK YOU'RE WONDERFUL

COUNT OF MONTE CRISTO
A United Artists' picture starring Robert Donat and Elissa Landi in a cast that included Louis Calhern, O. P. Heggie and Sidney Blackmer, and directed by Rowland V. Lee. Song by E. Y. Harburg and Johnny Green:
THE WORLD IS MINE

COUNTESS OF MONTE CRISTO, THE
A Universal picture filmed with a cast headed by Fay Wray, Paul Lukas, Reginald

Owen and Patsy Kelly, and directed by Karl Freund. Song by Allen Grey and Harry Tobias:
NO ONE WORRIES NO ONE CARES.

CRIME OF HELEN STANLEY
A Columbia picture filmed with a cast headed by Ralph Bellamy, Shirley Grey and Gail Patrick, and directed by D. Ross Lederman. Song by Charles Rosoff:
THERE'S LIFE IN MUSIC

DESIRABLE
A Warner Brothers' picture filmed with a cast headed by Jean Muir, George Brent, Verree Teasdale and John Halliday, and directed by Archie Mayo. Song by Irving Kahal and Sammy Fain:
DESIRABLE

EASY TO LOVE
A Warner Brothers' picture starring Genevieve Tobin and Adolphe Menjou in a cast that included Mary Astor, Guy Kibbe and Edward Everett Horton, and directed by William Keighley. Song by Irving Kahal and Sammy Fain:
EASY TO LOVE

EVENSONG
A Gaumont-British picture starring Evelyn Laye in a cast that included Fritz Kortner, Alice Delysia and Carl Esmond, and directed by Victor Saville. Song by Edward Knoblock and Maurice Spoliansky:
I WAIT FOR YOU

EVER SINCE EVE
A Fox picture starring George O'Brien and Mary Brian in a cast that included Herbert Mundin and Betty Blythe, and directed by George Marshall. Song by George Marshall and Cally Holden:
HORSEY

FASHIONS OF 1934
A First National picture starring Bette Davis and William Powell in a cast that included Frank McHugh, Verree Teasdale and Reginald Owen, and directed by William Dieterle. Song by Irving Kahal and Sammy Fain:
SPIN A LITTLE WEB OF DREAMS.

FORSAKING ALL OTHERS
An M-G-M picture filmed with a cast headed by Joan Crawford, Robert Montgomery, Clark Gable and Billie Burke, and directed by W. S. VanDyke. Song by Gus Kahn and Walter Donaldson.
FORSAKING ALL OTHERS

FUGITIVE LOVERS
An M-G-M picture starring Madge Evans and Robert Montgomery, and directed by Richard Boleslavsky. Song by Dorothy Fields and Jimmy McHugh:
I'M FULL OF THE DEVIL

GAY BRIDE, THE
An M-G-M picture starring Carole Lombard and Chester Morris, and directed by John Conway. Song by Gus Kahn and Walter Donaldson:
MISSISSIPPI HONEYMOON

GLAMOUR
A Universal picture starring Constance Cummings and Paul Lukas, and directed by William Weyler. Song by Roy Turk and Harry Askt:
HEAVEN ON EARTH

GOOD DAME
A Paramount picture starring Sylvia Sidney and Fredric March, and directed by Marion Gering. Song by Leo Robin and Ralph Rainger:
SHE'S A GOOD DAME

GOODBYE LOVE
An RKO picture filmed with a cast headed by Charles Ruggles, Verree Teasdale and Sidney Blackmer, and directed by H. Bruce Humberstone. Songs by Sidney Mitchell, Archie Gottler and Con Conrad:
ALIMONY BLUES and GOODBYE LOVE

HANDY ANDY
A Fox picture starring Will Rogers in a cast that included Peggy Wood and Mary Carlisle, and directed by David Butler. Song by George Marion Jr. and Richard Whiting:
ROSES IN THE RAIN

HAVE A HEART
An M-G-M picture starring Jean Parker and James Dunn in a cast that included Una Merkel and Stuart Erwin, and directed by David Butler. Songs by Dorothy Fields and Jimmy McHugh:
LOST IN A FOG and THANK YOU FOR A LOVELY EVENING

HE WAS HER MAN
A Fox picture starring Joan Blondell and James Cagney in a cast that included Victor Jory, and directed by Lloyd Bacon. Song by Sidney Mitchell and Lew Pollack:
MY ONLY ROMANCE

HERE COMES THE GROOM

A Paramount picture filmed with a cast headed by Jack Haley, Mary Boland, Patricia Ellis, Neil Hamilton, Sidney Toler and Arthur Treacher, and directed by Edward Sedgwick. Song by Mack Gordon and Harry Revel:
I'LL BLAME THE WALTZ NOT YOU

HERE COMES THE NAVY

A Warner Brothers' picture starring James Cagney and Pat O'Brien in a cast that included Frank McHugh and Gloria Stuart, and directed by Lloyd Bacon. Song by Irving Kahal and Sammy Fain:
HEY, SAILOR!

HIDEOUT

An M-G-M picture filmed with a cast headed by Robert Montgomery, Maureen O'Sullivan, Edward Arnold and Mickey Rooney, and directed by W. S. VanDyke. Song by Arthur Freed and Nacio Herb Brown:
THE DREAM WAS SO BEAUTIFUL

HOLD THAT GIRL

A Fox picture filmed with a cast headed by James Dunn, Claire Trevor and Alan Edwards, and directed by Hamilton Mac-Fadden. Songs:
IT'S ALL FOR THE BEST by George Marion Jr. and Richard Whiting; FAN DANCE by Furman Brown and Frederick Hollander.

HOUSEWIFE

A Warner Brothers' picture starring Bette Davis and George Brent in a cast that included Ann Dvorak and John Halliday, and directed by Alfred E. Green. Song by Mort Dixon and Allie Wrubel:
COSMETICS BY DUPREE

I BELIEVED IN YOU

A Fox picture filmed with a cast headed by Rosemary Ames, Victor Jory and John Boles, and directed by Irving Cummings. Song by William Kernell:
OUT OF A BLUE SKY

I'VE BEEN AROUND

A Universal picture filmed with a cast headed by Chester Morris, Rochelle Hudson, G. P. Huntley, Phyllis Brooks, Gene Lockhart and Ralph Morgan, and directed by Phil Cahn. Song by Jack Meskill and Jack Stern:
I'VE BEEN AROUND

JUDGE PRIEST

A Fox picture starring Will Rogers in a cast that included Tom Brown, Anita Louise, Henry Walthall, Rochelle Hudson, Hattie McDaniels and Stepin Fetchit, and directed by John Ford. Songs by Cyril F. Mockridge:
MASSA JESUS WROTE ME A NOTE and AUNT DILSEY'S SONG

KENTUCKY KERNELS

An RKO picture starring Bert Wheeler and Robert Woolsey in a cast that included Mary Carlisle and Noah Beery, and directed by George Stevens. Song by Bert Kalmar and Harry Ruby:
ONE LITTLE KISS

KEY, THE

A Warner Brothers' picture starring William Powell and Edna Best, and directed by Michael Curtiz. Song by Mort Dixon and Allie Wrubel:
THERE'S A COTTAGE IN KILLAR-NEY

KISMET

An M-G-M picture starring Marlene Dietrich and Ronald Colman in a cast that included Edward Arnold and James Craig, and directed by William Dieterle. Songs by E. Y. Harburg and Richard Arlen:
WILLOW IN THE WIND and TELL ME, TELL ME EVENING STAR

KISS AND MAKE UP

A Paramount picture filmed with a cast headed by Cary Grant, Helen Mack, Genevieve Tobin and Edward Everett Horton, and directed by Harlan Thompson. Songs by Leo Robin and Ralph Rainger:
LOVE DIVIDED BY TWO; CORN BEEF AND CABBAGE I LOVE YOU and MIRROR SONG

LAUGHING BOY

An M-G-M picture starring Ramon Novarro and Lupe Velez in a cast that included William Davidson and Chief Thunderbird, and directed by W. S. VanDyke. Song by Gus Kahn and Herbert Stothart:
THE CALL OF LOVE

LIMEHOUSE BLUES

A Paramount picture starring Anna May Wong and George Raft in a cast that included Jean Parker, and directed by Alexander Hall. Song by Sam Coslow:
LIMEHOUSE NIGHTS

LONG LOST FATHER

An RKO picture starring John Barrymore in a cast that included Helen Chandler and Donald Cook, and directed by Ernest B. Schoedsack. Song by Harold Adamson and Burton Lane:

IT ISN'T SO MUCH THAT I WOULDN'T

MANDALAY

A First National picture starring Kay Francis and Ricardo Cortez in a cast that included Lyle Talbot, Warner Oland, Ruth Donnelly and Reginald Owen, and directed by Michael Curtiz. Song by Irving Kahal and Sammy Fain:
WHEN TOMORROW COMES

MARIE GALANTE

A Fox picture starring Spencer Tracy and Ketti Gallian in a cast that included Helen Morgan, Ned Sparks, Arthur Byron and Stepin Fetchit, and directed by Henry King. Songs:
ON A LITTLE SIDE STREET and JE T'ADORE by Bernie Grossman and Harry Akst; SONG OF A DREAMER by Don Hartman and Jay Gorney; SERVES ME RIGHT FOR TREATING HIM WRONG by Maurice Sigler, Al Hoffman and Al Goodhart.

MILLION DOLLAR RANSOM

A Universal picture filmed wtih a cast headed by Phillips Holmes, Edward Arnold, Winnie Shaw, Mary Carlisle and Andy Devine, and directed by Murray Roth. Songs:
YOU'LL NEVER KNOW by Walter Donaldson; HAVE A GOOD TIME by Ben Ryan and Sol Violinsky.

NANA

A United Artists' picture starring Anna Sten in a cast that included Lionel Atwill and Phillips Holmes, and directed by Dorothy Arzner. Song by Lorenz Hart and Richard Rodgers:
THAT'S LOVE

NOW AND FOREVER

A Paramount picture filmed with a cast that included Shirley Temple, Gary Cooper and Carole Lombard, and directed by Henry Hathaway. Song by Larry Morey and Leigh Harline:
THE WORLD OWES ME A LIVING

NOW I'LL TELL

A Fox picture starring Spencer Tracy and Helen Twelvetrees in a cast that included Alice Faye, and directed by Edwin Burke. Songs by Lew Brown and Harry Akst:
FOOLIN' WITH THE OTHER WOMAN'S MAN and HARLEM VERSUS THE JUNGLE

OLD FASHIONED WAY, THE

A Paramount picture starring W. C. Fields in a cast that included Joe Morrison, Judith Allen, Jan Duggan, Baby LeRoy, Richard Carle, Otis Harlan and Tammany Young, and directed by William Beaudine. Songs by Mack Gordon and Harry Revel:
ROLLING IN LOVE and A LITTLE BIT OF HEAVEN KNOWN AS MOTHER

OPERATOR 13

An M-G-M picture starring Marion Davies in a cast that included Gary Cooper, Ned Sparks, Henry B. Walthall, Larry Adler, Hattie McDaniels and the Four Mills Brothers, and directed by Richard Boleslavsky. Songs by Gus Kahn and Walter Donaldson:
SLEEPY HEAD and ONCE IN A LIFETIME

PURSUED

A Fox picture starring Rosemary Ames and Victor Jory, and directed by Louis King. Song by Sidney Clare and Harry Akst:
WANTED: SOMEONE

RIPTIDE

An M-G-M picture starring Norma Shearer in a cast that included Herbert Marshall, Robert Montgomery and Mrs. Patrick Campbell, and directed by Edmund Goulding. Songs:
WE'RE TOGETHER AGAIN by Arthur Freed and Nacio Herb Brown; RIPTIDE by Gus Kahn and Walter Donaldson.

ROMANCE IN THE RAIN

A Universal picture filmed with a cast headed by Roger Pryor, Heather Angel, Esther Ralston and Victor Moore, and directed by Stuart Walker. Songs by Don Hartman and Jay Gorney:
LOVE AT LAST and F'R INSTANCE TAKE ME

SADIE McKEE

An M-G-M picture starring Joan Crawford in a cast that included Gene Raymond, Franchot Tone and Edward Arnold, and directed by Clarence Brown. Songs by Arthur Freed and Nacio Herb Brown:
PLEASE MAKE ME CARE and ALL I DO IS DREAM OF YOU

SEARCH FOR BEAUTY, THE

A Paramount picture starring Ida Lupino and Buster Crabbe, and directed by Erle C. Kenton. Song by Sam Coslow and Arthur Johnston:
I'M A SEEKER OF BEAUTY

SOCIAL REGISTER, THE

A Columbia picture filmed with a cast headed by Colleen Moore, Alexander Kirk-

land, Charles Winninger, Pauline Frederick and Robert Benchley, and directed by Marshall Neilan. Songs by Sidney Mitchell and Con Conrad:
WHY NOT? and I DON'T WANT TO LOVE YOU

SPRINGTIME FOR HENRY
A Fox picture filmed with a cast headed by Otto Kruger, Nancy Carroll and Heather Angel, and directed by Frank Tuttle. Song by Don Hartman and Jay Gorney:
FORBIDDEN LIPS

STINGAREE
An RKO picture starring Irene Dunne and Richard Dix in a cast that included Mary Boland, Conway Tearle, Andy Devine and Henry Stephenson, and directed by William Wellman. Songs:
TONIGHT IS MINE by Gus Kahn and W. Franke Harling; ONCE YOU'RE MINE by Edward Eliscu and Max Steiner.

STRAIGHT IS THE WAY
An M-G-M picture filmed with a cast headed by Franchot Tone, Karen Morley, May Robson and Gladys George, and directed by Paul Sloane. Song by Ned Washington, Joe Young and Victor Young:
A HUNDRED YEARS FROM TODAY

THREE HUNDRED AND SIXTY-FIVE NIGHTS IN HOLLYWOOD
A Fox picture starring Alice Faye and James Dunn, and directed by George Marshall. Songs by Sidney Clare and Richard Whiting:
MY FUTURE STAR and YES TO YOU

THREE ON A HONEYMOON
A Fox picture filmed with a cast headed by Sally Eilers, Zasu Pitts, Charles Starrett, Johnny Mack Brown and Henrietta Crosman, and directed by James Tinling. Song by William Kernell:
DESERT NIGHTS

TRUMPET BLOWS, THE
A Paramount picture filmed with a cast headed by George Raft, Adolphe Menjou, Frances Drake and Sidney Toler, and directed by Stephen Roberts. Songs by Leo Robin and Ralph Rainger:
THE RED CAPE; PANCHO and THIS NIGHT MY HEART DOES THE RHUMBA

WE'RE RICH AGAIN
An RKO picture filmed with a cast headed by Edna May Oliver, Billie Burke, Marian Nixon and Reginald Denny, and directed by William A. Seiter. Songs:
SENORITA by Albert Hay Malotte; ARABELLA by Roy Webb.

WILD GOLD
A Fox picture starring John Boles and Claire Trevor, and directed by George Marshall. Songs by Sidney Clare and Jay Gorney:
I'VE GOT YOU ON THE TOP OF MY LIST and CUTE LITTLE RHUMBA (RUM-TI-DI-UM-BA-BAY)

YOU BELONG TO ME
A Paramount picture filmed with a cast headed by Lee Tracy, Helen Mack, Helen Morgan and Lynne Overman, and directed by Alfred Werker. Songs:
WHEN HE COMES HOME TO ME by Leo Robin and Sam Coslow; THE BAD NEWS by Milan Roder and Sam Coslow.

YOU'RE TELLING ME
A Paramount picture starring W. C. Fields in a cast that included Joan Marsh and Buster Crabbe, and directed by Erle C. Kenton. Song by Sam Coslow and Arthur Johnston:
SYMPATHIZIN' WITH ME

Western Films With Songs

BEYOND THE LAW
A Columbia picture starring Tim McCoy and Shirley Grey, and directed by Ross Lederman. Song by Charles Rosoff:
YOU ARE MINE

FRONTIER MARSHALL
A Fox picture starring George O'Brien in a cast that included Irene Bentley, George E. Stone and Alan Edwards, and directed by Lewis Seiler. Song by William Kernell and Hugh Friendhofer:
SOME DAY

IN OLD SANTE FE
A Mascot picture filmed with a cast headed by Ken Maynard, Evelyn Knapp, H. B. Warner, Gene Autry and Smiley Burnette, and directed by David Howard. Songs:
MAMA DON'T ALLOW NO MUSIC by M. M. Hathaway and Floyd Ray; SOME DAY IN WYOMING by Gene Autry and Smiley Burnette; DOWN IN OLD SANTA FE and AS LONG AS I'VE GOT MY DOG by Bernie Grossman and J. Harold Lewis.

1935

A Former Bass Drummer Starts Collecting Oscars

Harry Warren and his lyricist, Al Dubin, certainly caught on fire in 1935, and during the inspirational conflagration that followed, collaborated on seven songs that millions hummed and whistled as they filed out of the country's movie theaters:

The Rose In Her Hair and *Lulu's Back In Town* from *Broadway Gondolier, About A Quarter Of Nine* and *She's A Latin From Manhattan* from Al Jolson's starring picture *Go Into Your Dance, Don't Give Up The Ship,* introduced in *Shipmates Forever* and now one of the official songs of the U. S. Naval Academy; *September In The Rain* from *Stars Over Broadway,* and *Lullaby Of Broadway* from *Gold Diggers Of Broadway,* a song which won for its composer the first of three Oscars—a distinction of which no other Hollywood songwriter can boast.

What makes this record even more notable is the fact that Harry Warren is a self-taught musician who started his career in show business as a bass drummer with a traveling carnival company and worked as a stage hand and studio pianist in the early days of the silent pictures before striking pay dirt in Tin Pan Alley in 1922 with *Rose Of The Rio Grande.*

Dubin and Warren, however, weren't the only Hollywood songwriters that could afford caviar and vintage champagne in 1935 since other top members of the words-and-music colony added to their laurels with such outstanding hits as *A Little White Gardenia* by Sam Coslow, *You Are My Lucky Star, I Gotta Feelin' You're Foolin'* and *Alone* by Arthur Freed and Nacio Herb Brown, *I'm In The Mood Love* and *I Feel A Song Coming On* by Dorothy Fields and Jimmy McHugh, *The Lady In Red* by Mort Dixon and Allie Wrubel, *When I Grow Too Old To Dream* by Oscar Hammerstein II and Sigmund Romberg, and *Here Comes Cookie* and *From The Top Of Your Head To The Tip Of Your Toes* by Mack Gordon and Harry Revel.

Rodgers and Hart provided Bing Crosby with three hits—*Soon, It's Easy To Remember* and *Down By The River*—for his starring picture *Mississippi.* Irving Berlin did even better by Ginger Rogers and Fred Astaire by dealing them five aces for *Top Hat: Cheek To Cheek, The Piccolino, No Strings (I'm Fancy Free), What A Lovely Day To Be Caught In The Rain* and *Top Hat White Tie And Tails.* And Jerome Kern was represented on the 1935 sound tracks with an original score for *I Dream Too Much* in which Lily Pons of the "Met" made her talkie debut and by the music he had written for *Roberta* and *Sweet Adeline,* Broadway musicals adapted to the screen as starring vehicles for Irene Dunne.

Victor Herbert again received posthumous recognition when Nelson Eddy and Jeanette MacDonald revived on the screen the immortal music composed for *Naughty Marietta* soon after the century's turn, and while the songs in *Old Man Rhythm* and *To Beat The Band* were far from distinguished, they served to introduce Johnny Mercer, who had been strumming a ukelele in one of Baron Long's roadhouses, as a lyricist destined to write words for long-remembered hits.

A long-stemmed American Beauty from Mount Vernon, N.Y., Eleanor Powell, tapped her way to fame in *George White's Scandals Of 1935* and *Broadway Melody Of 1936,* and even the low-budget westerns made history in 1935, Bill Boyd, a veteran of the silent days, donning ten-gallon hat, chaps and high-heeled boots to take the lead in three rootin'-tootin'-shootin' pictures in one of which he created his perennial role of Hopalong Cassidy, while Gene Autry rode to horse opera stardom in five films and introduced in one of them the first of the present day sagebrush classics, *Tumbling Tumbleweeds,* written by Bob Nolan.

Four musicals were included in the Ten Best Films of 1935: *Naughty Marietta, Top Hat, Broadway Melody Of 1936* and *Roberta* in a year that yielded such other top-ranking films as *David Copperfield, Lives Of A Bengal Lancer, Les Miserables, Ruggles Of Red Gap* and *Anna Karenina.* But in this year of notable achievement and mounting prosperity, a cinema empire, founded in 1904 on a $1400 shoestring and valued at $300,000,000 at the time of the 1929 stock market crash, crumbled and collapsed, and William Fox, its founder, joined in the valley of oblivion the many stars that had reached the heights under his banner.

Musicals

ABDUL THE DAMNED
A Gaumont-British picture starring Nils Asther, released in this country through M-G-M, and directed by Karl Grune. Songs by Clifford Grey and Hans Eisler:
SULTAN'S HYMN; SONG OF FREEDOM; TERESA'S SONG; I BRING A SONG and KAN-KAN

AFTER THE DANCE
A Columbia picture filmed with a cast headed by Nancy Carroll, George Murphy, Thelma Todd and Jack LaRue, and directed by Lee Bulgakov. Songs:
WITHOUT YOU I'M JUST DRIFTING and TOMORROW NIGHT by Harry Akst; I HEARD A BLIND MAN SINGING IN THE STREET by Clarence Muse.

ALL THE KING'S HORSES
A Paramount picture starring Carl Brisson

in a cast that included Mary Ellis, Edward Everett Horton and Eugene Pallette, and directed by Frank Tuttle. Songs by Sam Coslow:
A LITTLE WHITE GARDENIA; BE CAREFUL YOUNG LADY; DANCING THE VIENNESE; A KING CAN DO NO WRONG and WHEN MY PRINCE CHARMING COMES ALONG

BIG BROADCAST OF 1936
A Paramount picture filmed with a cast headed by Jack Oakie, Burns and Allen, Lyda Roberti, Wendy Berrie, "Amos 'n' Andy", Bing Crosby, Ethel Merman, Charles Ruggles, Bill Robinson and Ray Noble and his orchestra, and directed by Norman Taurog. Songs:
MISS BROWN TO YOU and THROUGH THE DOORWAY OF DREAMS I SAW YOU by Leo Robin and

Richard Whiting; DOUBLE TROUBLE and WHY DREAM? by Leo Robin, Richard Whiting and Ralph Rainger; AMARGURA by Leo Robin and Ralph Rainger; I WISHED ON THE MOON by Dorothy Parker and Ralph Rainger; CROONER'S LULLABY by Sam Coslow and Arthur Johnston; WHY STARS COME OUT AT NIGHT by Ray Noble.

BREWSTER'S MILLIONS

A United Artists' picture filmed with a cast headed by Jack Buchanan, Lili Damiti and Nancy O'Neil, and directed by Thornton Freeland. Songs by Douglas Furber and Ray Noble:
THE CARRANGA; I THINK I CAN; ONE GOOD TURN DESERVES ANOTHER and PULL DOWN THE BLINDS.

BRIGHT LIGHTS

A First National picture filmed with a cast headed by Joe E. Brown, Ann Dvorak, Patricia Ellis, William Gargan and Joseph Cawthorn, and directed by Busby Berkeley. Songs:
SHE WAS AN ACROBAT'S DAUGHTER by Bert Kalmar and Harry Ruby; TODDLING ALONG WITH YOU and YOU'RE AN EYEFUL OF HEAVEN by Mort Dixon and Allie Wrubel; NOBODY CARES IF I'M BLUE by Grant Clarke and Harry Akst.

BROADWAY GONDOLIER

A Warner Brothers' picture starring Joan Blondell and Dick Powell in a cast that included Louise Fazenda, Adolphe Menjou and William Gargan, and directed by Lloyd Bacon. Songs by Al Dubin and Harry Warren:
THE ROSE IN HER HAIR; LONELY GONDOLIER; OUTSIDE OF YOU; LULU'S BACK IN TOWN; YOU CAN BE KISSED; SWEET AND LOW and THE PIG AND THE COW

BROADWAY HOSTESS

A First National picture filmed with a cast headed by Winnie Shaw, Genevieve Tobin, Lyle Talbot, Phil Regan, Marie Wilson and Spring Byington, and directed by Frank McDonald. Songs:
HE WAS HER MAN; LET IT BE ME; WEARY; WHO BUT YOU and PLAYBOY OF PAREE by Mort Dixon and Allie Wruble; ONLY THE GIRL by Herman Ruby and M. K. Jerome.

BROADWAY MELODY OF 1936

An M-G-M picture filmed with a cast headed by Jack Benny, Eleanor Powell, Robert Taylor, Una Merkel, Sid Silvers, Frances Langford and June Knight, and directed by Roy Del Ruth. Songs by Arthur Freed and Nacio Herb Brown:
YOU ARE MY LUCKY STAR; SING BEFORE BREAKFAST; I'VE GOTTA FEELIN' YOU'RE FOOLIN'; BROADWAY RHYTHM and ON A SUNDAY AFTERNOON.

COME OUT OF THE PANTRY

A Cinephonic release filmed in England with a cast headed by Jack Buchanan. Songs by Maurice Sigler, Al Hoffman and Al Goodhart:
EVERYTHING STOPS FOR TEA and FROM ONE MINUTE TO ANOTHER.

CORONADO

A Paramount picture filmed with a cast headed by Johnny Downs, Betty Burgess, Jack Haley, Leon Errol and Eddy Duchin and his orchestra, and directed by Norman McLeod. Songs:
ALL'S WELL IN CORONADO BY THE SEA; YOU TOOK MY BREATH AWAY; HOW DO I RATE WITH YOU; KEEP YOUR FINGERS CROSSED; MIDSUMMER MADNESS; DOWN ON THE BEACH AT OOMPH and MASHED POTATOES by Sam Coslow and Richard Whiting; I'VE GOT SOME NEW SHOES by Sam Coslow, Walter Bullock and Richard Whiting; WHICH IS WHICH? by Sidney Clare and Troy Sanders.

CURLY TOP

A 20th Century-Fox picture starring Shirley Temple in a cast that included John Boles, Rochelle Hudson and Jane Darwell, and directed by Irving Cummings. Songs by Ted Koehler, Irving Caesar and Ray Henderson:
ANIMAL CRACKERS IN MY SOUP; CURLY TOP; IT'S ALL SO NEW TO ME; WHEN I GROW UP and THE SIMPLE THINGS IN LIFE.

DANCE BAND

An Alliance Films' release starring Charles "Buddy" Rogers in a cast that included June Clyde and Steve Geray, and directed by Marcell Barnell. Songs:
LOVEY DOVEY by Arthur Young; VALPARAISO by Desmond Carter and Mabel Wayne.

EVERGREEN

A Gaumont-British picture starring Jessie Mathews and Sonnie Hale, and directed by Victor Saville. Songs:

DANCING ON THE CEILING; DEAR, DEAR and HARLEMANIA by Lorenz Hart and Richard Rodgers; OVER MY SHOULDER; WHEN YOU'VE GOT A LITTLE SPRINGTIME IN YOUR HEART and TINKLE, TINKLE, TINKLE by Harry M. Woods.

EVERY NIGHT AT EIGHT
A Paramount picture filmed with a cast headed by George Raft, Alice Faye, Frances Langford and Patsy Kelly, and directed by Raoul Walsh. Songs:
TAKE IT EASY; SPEAKING CONFIDENTIALLY; I'M IN THE MOOD FOR LOVE; IT'S GREAT TO BE IN LOVE AGAIN and I FEEL A SONG COMING ON by Dorothy Fields and Jimmy McHugh; THEN YOU'VE NEVER BEEN BLUE by Joe Young, Sam Lewis, Frances Langford and Ted Fiorito.

FIRST A GIRL
A Gaumont-British picture starring Jessie Mathews. Songs by Maurice Sigler, Al Goodhart and Al Hoffman:
EVERYTHING'S IN RHYTHM WITH MY HEART; I CAN WIGGLE MY EARS; SAY THE WORD AND IT'S YOURS; THE SILKWORM and HALF AND HALF.

FOLIES BERGERE
A United Artists' picture starring Maurice Chevalier in a cast that included Merle Oberon, Ann Dvorak and Eric Blore, and directed by Roy Del Ruth. Songs:
I WAS LUCKY; RHYTHM OF THE RAIN; SINGING A HAPPY SONG and AU REVOIR L'AMOUR by Jack Meskill and Jack Stern; YOU TOOK THE WORDS RIGHT OUT OF MY MOUTH by Harold Adamson and Burton Lane; I DON'T STAND A GHOST OF A CHANCE WITH YOU by Bing Crosby, Ned Washington and Victor Young.

FRANKIE AND JOHNNY
An RKO picture starring Helen Morgan and Chester Morris in a cast that included Florence Reed and Lilyan Tashman, and directed by John H. Auer. Songs:
GIVE ME A HEART TO SING TO by Ned Washington and Victor Young; GET RHYTHM IN YOUR FEET by Bill Livingston; IF YOU WANT MY HEART by J. Russel Robinson.

GEORGE WHITE'S SCANDALS
A 20th Century-Fox picture filmed with a cast heeded by Alice Faye, James Dunn, Eleanor Powell, Lyda Roberti, Cliff Edwards

and George White, and directed by George White. Songs:
ACCORDING TO THE MOONLIGHT; OH, I DIDN'T KNOW YOU'D GET THAT WAY and IT'S TIME TO SAY GOOD NIGHT by Jack Yellen, Herb Magidson and Joseph Meyer; IT'S AN OLD SOUTHERN CUSTOM by Jack Yellen and Joseph Meyer; I GOT SHOES YOU GOT SHOESIES and HUNKADOLA by Jack Yellen, Cliff Friend and Joseph Meyer; I WAS BORN TOO LATE by Jack Yellen and Joseph Meyer; I LIKE IT WITH MUSIC by Herb Magidson and Cliff Friend; THE PIED PIPER OF HARLEM and SCANDALERO by Jack Yellen and Ray Henderson.

GIRL FRIEND, THE
A Columbia picture starring Ann Sothern in a cast that included Jack Haley and Roger Pryor, and directed by Eddie Buzzell. Songs by Gus Kahn and Arthur Johnston:
WHAT IS THIS POWER? TWO TOGETHER AND WELCOME TO NAPOLEON.

GO INTO YOUR DANCE
A First National picture starring Al Jolson in a cast that included Ruby Keeler, Glenda Farrell, Benny Rubin, Phil Regan, Helen Morgan, Patsy Kelly and the songwriters, Al Dubin and Harry Warren, and directed by Archie Mayo. Songs by Al Dubin and Harry Warren:
ABOUT A QUARTER TO NINE; GO INTO YOUR DANCE; MAMMY I'LL SING ABOUT YOU; A GOOD OLD-FASHIONED COCKTAIL WITH A GOOD OLD-FASHIONED GIRL; LITTLE THINGS YOU USED TO DO; CASINO DE PAREE and SHE'S A LATIN FROM MANHATTAN.

GOIN' TO TOWN
A Paramount picture starring Mae West and Paul Cavanaugh in a cast that included Marjorie Gateson and Fred Kohler, and directed by Alexander Hall. Songs by Irving Kahal, Sam Coslow and Sammy Fain:
LOVE IS LOVE IN ANY WOMAN'S HEART; NOW I'M A LADY and HE'S A BAD MAN.

GOLD DIGGERS OF BROADWAY
A First National picture starring Dick Powell in a cast that included Gloria Stuart, Adolphe Menjou, Alice Brady, Glenda Farrell, Frank McHugh, Hugh Herbert and Joseph Cawthorn, and directed by Busby

Berkeley. Songs by Al Dubin and Harry Warren:

LULLABY OF BROADWAY; THE WORDS ARE IN MY HEART and I'M GOIN' SHOPPING WITH YOU.

HERE COMES THE BAND

An M-G-M picture starring Ted Lewis in a cast that included Virginia Bruce, Ted Healy and Nat Pendleton, and directed by Paul Sloane. Songs:

HEADIN' HOME by Ned Washington and Herbert Stothart; ROLL ALONG PRAIRIE MOON by Ted Fiorito, Cecil Mack and Albert VonTilzer; TENDER IS THE NIGHT by Harold Adamson and Walter Donaldson; YOU'RE MY THRILL by Ned Washington and Burton Lane; I'M BOUND FOR HEAVEN and THE ARMY BAND by Harold Adamson and Burton Lane.

HERE COMES COOKIE

A Paramount picture starring George Burns and Gracie Allen in a cast that included George Barbier, Betty Furness, Andrew Tombes, Lee Kohlmar, Edward Gargan and Richard Carle, and directed by William LeBaron. Songs:

VAMP OF THE PAMPAS by Leo Robin and Richard Whiting; LAZY MOON by Bob Cole and A. Rosamond Johnson.

HOORAY FOR LOVE

An RKO picture filmed with a cast headed by Ann Sothern, Gene Raymond, Bill Robinson, Fats Waller, Sam Hardy and Georgia Caine, and directed by Walter Lang. Songs by Dorothy Fields and Jimmy McHugh:

HOORAY FOR LOVE; I'M IN LOVE ALL OVER AGAIN; I'M LIVING IN A GREAT BIG WAY; YOU'RE AN ANGEL; PALSIE WALSIE and GOTTA SNAP IN MY FINGERS.

HYDE PARK CORNER

A Grosvenor Sound Film picture filmed with a cast headed by Binnie Hale. Songs by Maurice Sigler, Al Hoffman and Al Goodhart:

DID YOU GET THAT OUT OF A BOOK? and YOU DON'T THE HALF OF IT.

I DREAM TOO MUCH

An RKO picture starring Lily Pons in a cast that included Henry Fonda, Eric Blore, Osgood Perkins, Lucille Ball and Mischa Auer, and directed by John Cromwell. Songs by Dorothy Fields and Jerome Kern:

I DREAM TOO MUCH; JOCKEY ON THE CAROUSEL (With Jimmy McHugh); I'M THE ECHO—YOU'RE THE SONG and I GOT LOVE.

I LIVE FOR LOVE

A Warner Brothers' picture starring Dolores Del Rio in a cast that included Everett Marshall, Guy Kibbe and Allen Jenkins, and directed by Busby Berkeley. Songs by Mort Dixon and Allie Wrubel:

MINE ALONE; SILVER WINGS; I LIVE FOR LOVE and I WANNA PLAY HOUSE WITH YOU.

IN CALIENTE

A First National picture starring Dolores Del Rio in a cast that included Pat O'Brien, Leo Carrillo, Edward Everett Horton, Glenda Farrell, Phil Regan and the DeMarco Sisters, and directed by Lloyd Bacon. Songs:

THE LADY IN RED; IN CALIENTE and TO CALL YOU MY OWN by Mort Dixon and Allie Wrubel; MUCHACHA by Al Dubin and Harry Warren.

IN PERSON

An RKO picture starring Ginger Rogers and George Brent, and directed by William A. Seiter. Songs by Dorothy Fields and Oscar Levant:

DON'T MENTION LOVE TO ME; GOT A NEW LEASE ON LIFE and OUT OF SIGHT OUT OF MIND.

JACK OF ALL TRADES

A Gainsborough picture starring Jack Hulbert. Songs by Maurice Sigler, Al Goodhart and Al Hoffman:

WHERE THERE'S YOU THERE'S ME; YOU'RE SWEETER THAN I THOUGHT and TAP YOUR TOOTSIES.

KING OF BURLESQUE

A 20th Century-Fox picture filmed with a cast headed by Warner Baxter, Jack Oakie, Alice Faye, Mona Barrie, Dixie Dunbar, Arline Judge, Kenny Baker, Gregory Ratoff and Fats Waller, and directed by Sidney Lanfield. Songs:

I'VE GOT MY FINGERS CROSSED; LOVELY LADY; SPREADIN' RHYTHM AROUND; WHO'S BIG BABY ARE YOU? and I'M SHOOTING HIGH by Ted Koehler and Jimmy McHugh; I LOVE TO RIDE THE HORSES by Jack Yellen and Lew Pollack.

KING SOLOMON OF BROADWAY

A Universal picture filmed with a cast headed by Edmund Lowe, Dorothy Page, Pinky Tomlin and Louise Henry, and directed by Alan Crosland. Songs:

MOANING IN THE MOONLIGHT and A FLOWER IN MY LAPEL by Herb Magidson and Con Conrad; THAT'S WHAT

YOU THINK by Pinky Tomlin, Coy Poe and Raymond Jasper.

LOTTERY LOVER

A 20th Century-Fox picture filmed with a cast headed by Lew Ayers, Pat Patterson, Peggy Fears, Reginald Denny, Alan Dinehart and Eddie Nugent, and directed by William Thiele. Songs by Don Hartman and Jay Gorney:

THERE'S A BIT OF PAREE IN YOU; TING-A-LING-A-LING; CLOSE YOUR EYES AND SEE and ALL FOR THE LOVE OF A GIRL.

LOVE IN BLOOM

A Paramount picture starring George Burns and Gracie Allen in a cast that included Dixie Lee, J. C. Nugent, Lee Kohlmar and Richard Carle, and directed by Elliott Nugent. Songs by Mack Gordon and Harry Revel:

MY HEART IS AN OPEN BOOK; HERE COMES COOKIE; GOT ME DOING THINGS and LET ME SING YOU TO SLEEP WITH A LOVE SONG.

MILLIONS IN THE AIR

A Paramount picture starring Willie and Eugene Howard in a cast that included Robert Cummings and Inez Courtney, and directed by Ray McCarey. Songs:

LAUGHING AT THE WEATHER MAN and A PENNY IN MY POCKET by Leo Robin and Ralph Rainger; YOU TELL HER, I STUTTER by Billy Rose and Cliff Friend.

MISSISSIPPI

A Paramount picture starring Bing Crosby in a cast that included W. C. Fields, Joan Bennett, Queenie Smith and Gail Patrick, and directed by Edward A. Sutherland. Songs by Lorenz Hart and Richard Rodgers:

IT'S EASY TO REMEMBER (AND SO HARD TO FORGET); SOON; DOWN BY THE RIVER; PABLO YOU ARE MY HEART and ROLL MISSISSIPPI.

MUSIC IS MAGIC

A 20th Century-Fox picture filmed with a cast headed by Alice Faye, Bebe Daniels and Ray Walker, and directed by George Marshall. Songs:

HONEY CHILE; LOVE IS SMILING AT ME and MUSIC IS MAGIC by Sidney Clare and Oscar Levant; LA LOCUMBA by Raul Roulien and Sidney Clare.

NAUGHTY MARIETTA

An M-G-M picture starring Jeanette Mac-Donald and Nelson Eddy in a cast that included Frank Morgan, Elsa Lanchester and Joseph Cawthorn, and directed by W. S. VanDyke. Songs by Rita Johnson Young, Gus Kahn and Victor Herbert:

LIVE FOR TODAY; TRAMP, TRAMP, TRAMP ALONG THE HIGHWAY; DANCE OF THE MARIONETTES; I'M FALLING IN LOVE WITH SOMEONE; ITALIAN STREET SONG; 'NEATH THE SOUTHERN MOON; AH SWEET MYSTERY OF LIFE and STUDENT'S SONG (music by Herbert Stothart).

NIGHT AT THE OPERA, A

An M-G-M picture starring Groucho, Chico and Harpo Marx in a cast that included Allan Jones and Kitty Carlisle, and directed by Sam Wood. Songs:

ALONE by Arthur Freed and Nacio Herb Brown; COSI COSA by Ned Washington, Bronislaw Kaper and Walter Jurmann.

NIGHT IS YOUNG, THE

An M-G-M picture starring Ramon Novarro and Evelyn Laye in a cast that included Charles Butterworth, Una Merkel, Edward Everett Horton, Rosalind Russell and Henry Stephenson, and directed by Dudley Murphy. Songs by Oscar Hammerstein II and Sigmund Romberg:

MY OLD MARE; WHEN I GROW TOO OLD TO DREAM; THE NOBLE DUCHESS; LIFT YOUR GLASS; THERE'S A RIOT IN HAVANA and THE NIGHT IS YOUNG.

OH! DADDY

A Gainsborough picture starring Leslie Henson. Songs by Sam Coslow:

NOW I UNDERSTAND and YOU BRING OUT THE SAVAGE IN ME.

OLD HOMESTEAD, THE

A Liberty picture starring Mary Carlisle and Lawrence Gray, and directed by William Nigh. Songs:

MOONLIGHT IN HEAVEN by Jack Scholl and Louis Alter; SOMEHOW I KNOW by Harry Tobias, Neil Moret and Charles Rosoff; THE PLOWBOY by J. Keirn Brennan and Ted Snyder; WHEN THE OLD AGE PENSION CHECK COMES TO OUR DOOR by Manny Stone.

OLD MAN RHYTHM

An RKO picture starring Charles "Buddy" Rogers in a cast that included George Barbier, Barbara Kent, Eric Blore, Johnny Mercer and Betty Grable, and directed by

Eddie Ludwig. Songs by Johnny Mercer and Lewis Gensler:

OLD MAN RHYTHM; I NEVER SAW A BETTER NIGHT; THERE'S NOTHING LIKE A COLLEGE EDUCATION; BOYS WILL BE BOYS; WHEN YOU ARE IN MY ARMS and COMES THE REVOLUTION BABY.

PARIS IN THE SPRING

A Paramount picture filmed with a cast headed by Mary Ellis, Tullio Carminati, Ida Lupino, Lynne Overman and Jessie Ralph, and directed by Lewis Milestone. Songs by Mack Gordon and Harry Revel:

PARIS IN THE SPRING; BON JOUR MAM'SELLE; WHY DO THEY CALL IT GAY PAREE? and JEALOUSY.

PRINCESS CHARMING

A Gaumont-British picture starring Evelyn Laye in a cast that included Henry Wilcoxson and Yvonne Arnaud, and directed by Maurice Elvey. Songs by Max Kester and Ray Noble:

LOVE IS A SONG; NEAR AND YET SO FAR; WHEN GAY ADVENTURE CALLS and ON THE WINGS OF THE DAWN.

RECKLESS

An M-G-M picture starring Jean Harlow and William Powell in a cast that included Rosalind Russell, Franchot Tone and May Robson, and directed by Victor Fleming. Songs:

CYCLONE by Gus Kahn and Walter Donaldson; RECKLESS by Oscar Hammerstein II and Jerome Kern; HI DIDDLE DEE DUM by Herbert Magidson and Con Conrad; HEAR WHAT MY HEART IS SAYING and TROCADERO by Harold Adamson and Burton Lane; EVERYTHING'S BEEN DONE BEFORE by Harold Adamson, Ed H. Knopf and Jack King.

RED HEADS ON PARADE

A 20th Century-Fox picture filmed with a cast headed by John Boles, Dixie Lee, Jack Haley and Alan Dinehart, and directed by Norman McLeod. Songs by Dan Hartman and Jay Gorney:

I FOUND A DREAM; GOOD NIGHT KISS; I LIKE MYSELF FOR LIKING YOU; RED HEADS ON PARADE; I'VE GOT YOUR FUTURE ALL PLANNED; TINSEL TOWN and YOU BEAUTIFUL THING.

ROBERTA

An RKO picture starring Irene Dunne, Fred Astaire and Ginger Rogers in a cast that included Randolph Scott and Helen Westley. Songs by Otto Harbach, Oscar Hammerstein II and Jerome Kern:

I WON'T DANCE; I'LL BE HARD TO HANDLE; SMOKE GETS IN YOUR EYES; THE TOUCH OF YOUR HAND; YESTERDAYS and LOVELY TO LOOK AT (with Jimmy McHugh).

RUMBA

A Paramount picture starring Carole Lombard and George Raft in a cast that included Margo and Lynne Overman, and directed by Marion Gering. Songs by Leo Robin and Ralph Rainger:

I'M YOURS FOR TONIGHT; THE MAGIC OF YOU; THE RHYTHM OF THE RUMBA; YOUR EYES HAVE SAID and IF I KNEW.

ST. LOUIS WOMAN

A Showmen Pictures' release filmed with a cast headed by Jeanette Loff, Johnny Mack Brown, Earl Foxe and Roberta Gale, and directed by Al Ray. Songs by Betty Laidlow and Bob Lively:

ST. LOUIS WOMAN; CO-ED DRAG; LEAVE ME ALONE and YOU'RE INDISPENSABLE TO ME.

SCANDALS OF PARIS

A Regal picture filmed with a cast headed by Wendy Barrie, Zelma O'Neal, Gene Gerrard and Gus McNaughton, and directed by John Stafford and W. Victor Handbury. Songs by Sonny Miller, Nikolas Schwalb and Otto Strosky.

SHE SHALL HAVE MUSIC

A Twickenham Film production starring Jack Hylton and his band and June Clyde, and directed by Lester H. Hiscott. Songs by Maurice Sigler, Al Hoffman and Al Goodhart:

THE BAND THAT JACK BUILT; MOANIN' MINNIE; SAILING ALONG ON A CARPET OF DREAMS; NOTHIN' ON EARTH; DON'T ASK ME ANY QUESTIONS; THE RUN-AROUND; MAY ALL YOUR TROUBLES BE LITTLE ONES and MY FIRST THRILL.

SHIP CAFE

A Paramount picture starring Carl Brisson in a cast that included Arline Judge, Mady Christians and William Frawley, and directed by Robert Florey. Songs:

A FATAL FASCINATION; I WON'T TAKE NO FOR AN ANSWER; IT'S A GREAT LIFE; I LOST MY HEART and

LAZYBONES GOTTA JOB NOW by Harlan Thompson and Lewis Gensler; CHANGE YOUR MIND by Ray Noble.

SHIPMATES FOREVER
A First National picture starring Dick Powell, Ruby Keeler and Lewis Stone, and directed by Frank Borzage. Songs by Al Dubin and Harry Warren:
DON'T GIVE UP THE SHIP; I'D RATHER LISTEN TO YOUR EYES; ALL ABOARD THE NAVY; I'D LOVE TO TAKE ORDERS FROM YOU and DO I LOVE MY TEACHER?

STARS OVER BROADWAY
A Warner Brothers' picture starring James Melton in a cast that included Jane Froman and Pat O'Brien, and directed by William Keighley. Songs:
BROADWAY CINDERELLA; DON'T LET ME DOWN; AT YOUR SERVICE MADAME; WHERE AM I (AM I IN HEAVEN?); SEPTEMBER IN THE RAIN and OVER YONDER MOON by Al Dubin and Harry Warren; CARRY ME BACK TO THE LONE PRAIRIE by Carson J. Robison.

STOLEN HARMONY
A Paramount picture filmed with a cast headed by George Raft, Grace Bradley, Iris Adrian and Ben Bernie and his orchestra, and directed by Alfred Werker. Songs by Mack Gordon and Harry Revel:
WOULD THERE BE LOVE; LET'S SPILL THE BEANS; I NEVER HAD A MAN TO CRY OVER and FAGIN YOUSE A VIPER.

SWEET ADELINE
A Warner Brothers' picture starring Irene Dunne in a cast that included Donald Woods, Hugh Herbert, Ned Sparks and Joseph Cawthorn, and directed by Mervyn LeRoy. Songs by Arthur Hammerstein II and Jerome Kern:
DON'T EVER LEAVE ME; HERE AM I; OUT OF THE BLUE; 'TWAS NOT SO LONG AGO; WHY WAS I BORN? and WE WERE SO YOUNG.

SWEET MUSIC
A Warner Brothers' picture starring Rudy Vallee and Ann Sothern in a cast that included Helen Morgan, Al Shean, Alice White, Joseph Cawthorn and Allen Jenkins, and directed by Alfred E. Green. Songs:
GOOD GREEN ACRES OF HOME; EV'RY DAY; DON'T GO ON A DIET; WINTER OVERNIGHT; THERE'S A DIFF'RENT YOU IN YOUR HEART; SELZER THEME SONG and SWEET MUSIC by Irving Kahal and Sammy Fain; FARE-THEE-WELL ANNABELLE and SNAKE CHARMER'S SONG by Mort Dixon and Allie Wrubel.

SWEET SURRENDER
A Universal picture filmed with a cast headed by Tamara, Frank Parker, Helen Lynd, Russ Brown, Jack Dempsey and Abe Lyman and his orchestra, and directed by Monte Brice. Songs:
LOVE MAKES THE WORLD GO 'ROUND; TAKE THIS RING; I'M SO HAPPY I COULD CRY and THE DAY YOU WERE BORN by Edward Heyman and Dana Suesse; TWENTY-FOUR HOURS A DAY by Arthur Swanstrom and James Hanley.

THANKS A MILLION
A 20th Century-Fox picture starring Dick Powell and Ann Dvorak in a cast that included Fred Allen, Patsy Kelly, Ramona, Rubinoff, the Yacht Club Boys and Paul Whiteman and his orchestra, and directed by Roy Del Ruth. Songs:
THANKS A MILLION; SITTING HIGH ON A HILLTOP; SUGAR PLUM; NEW O'LEANS; SING BROTHER and I'VE GOT A POCKETFUL OF SUNSHINE by Gus Kahn and Arthur Johnston; WHAT A BEAUTIFUL NIGHT by Bert Kalmar and Harry Ruby.

THIS IS THE LIFE
A 20th Century-Fox picture filmed with a cast headed by Sally Blaine, Sidney Toler and Jane Withers, and directed by Marshall Neilan. Songs by Sidney Clare and Sammy Stept:
GOTTA NEW KIND OF RHYTHM; SANDY AND ME and FRESH FROM THE COUNTRY.

TO BEAT THE BAND
An RKO picture filmed with a cast headed by Hugh Herbert, Helen Broderick, Roger Pryor, Fred Keating, Eric Blore, Phyllis Brooks, Johnny Mercer and the California Collegians, and directed by Benjamin Stoloff. Songs by Johnny Mercer and Matt Malneck:
EENEY-MEENEY-MINEY-MO; I SAW HER AT EIGHT O'CLOCK; IF YOU WERE MINE; MEET MISS AMERICA and SANTA CLAUS CAME IN THE SPRING.

TOP HAT

An RKO picture starring Ginger Rogers and Fred Astaire in a cast that included Edward Everett Horton, Helen Broderick and Eric Blore, and directed by Mark Sandrich. Songs by Irving Berlin:

THE PICCOLINO; TOP HAT, WHITE TIE AND TAILS; ISN'T THIS A LOVELY DAY TO BE CAUGHT IN THE RAIN?; CHEEK TO CHEEK and NO STRINGS (I'M FANCY FREE).

TWO FOR TONIGHT

A Paramount picture starring Bing Crosby in a cast that included Joan Bennett, Mary Boland, Lynne Overman and Thelma Todd, and directed by Frank Tuttle. Songs by Mack Gordon and Harry Revel:

WITHOUT A WORD OF WARNING; TWO FOR TONIGHT; IT TAKES TWO TO MAKE A BARGAIN; FROM THE TOP OF YOUR HEAD TO THE TIP OF YOUR TOES and I WISH I WERE ALADDIN.

UNDER THE PAMPAS MOON

A 20th Century-Fox picture starring Warner Baxter and Ketti Gallian in a cast that included J. Carroll Nash, Jack LaRue and Veloz and Yolanda, and directed by James Tinling. Musical numbers:

THE GAUCHO by B. G. DeSylva and Walter Samuels; QUERIDA MIA by Paul Francis Webster and Lew Pollack; ZAMBA by Arthur Wynter-Smith; LOVE SONG OF THE PAMPAS by Cyril J. Mockridge and Miguel De Zarraga.

UNDER PRESSURE

A 20th Century-Fox picture starring Edmund Lowe and Victor McLaglen in a cast that included Florence Rice, Marjorie Rambeau and Charles Bickford, and directed by Raoul Walsh. Songs by Jack Yellen and Dan Dougherty:

EAST RIVER; FICKLE FLO; IT'S THE IRISH IN YOU; I'LL GO TO FLANNIGAN and A MAN OF YOUR OWN.

Feature Films With Songs

ACCENT ON YOUTH

A Paramount picture starring Sylvia Sidney and Herbert Marshall, and directed by Wesley Ruggles. Song by Tot Seymour and Vee Lawnhurst:

ACCENT ON YOUTH

ALICE ADAMS

An RKO picture starring Katherine Hepburn and Fred MacMurray, and directed by George Stevens. Song by Dorothy Fields and Max Steiner:

I CAN'T WALTZ ALONE

BLACK SHEEP

A 20th Century-Fox picture starring Edmund Lowe and Claire Trevor in a cast that included Adrienne Ames, Tom Brown and Herbert Mundin, and directed by Allan Dwan. Song by Sidney Clare and Oscar Levant:

IN OTHER WORDS I'M IN LOVE

CAR OF DREAMS

A Gaumont-British picture starring Greta Mosheim and John Mills. Song by Maurice Sigler, Al Hoffman and Al Goodhart:

CAR OF DREAMS

CHINA SEAS

An M-G-M picture starring Jean Harlow and Clark Gable in a cast that included Wallace Beery, Lewis Stone, Rosalind Russell, Dudley Diggs, C. Aubrey Smith and Robert Benchley, and directed by Tay Garnett. Song by Arthur Freed and Nacio Herb Brown:

CHINA SEAS

COLLEGE SCANDAL

A Paramount picture filmed with a cast headed by Arline Judge, Kent Taylor, Wendy Barrie, Mary Nash and William Frawley, and directed by Elliott Nugent. Song by Sam Coslow:

IN THE MIDDLE OF A KISS

CONVENTION GIRL

A Universal picture filmed with a cast headed by Rose Hobart, Sally O'Neil and Herbert Rawlinson, and directed by Luther Reed. Songs by Arthur Swanstrom and Louis Alter:

I'VE GOT SAND IN MY SHOES and YOU OUGHTA BE ARRESTED (FOR BREAKING MY HEART).

CRUSADES, THE

A Paramount picture starring Loretta Young and Henry Wilcoxson in a cast that included Ian Keith, and directed by Cecil B. de Mille. Song by Leo Robin, Richard Whiting and Rudolph Kopp:

SONG OF THE CRUSADES

DEVIL IS A WOMAN, THE

A Paramount picture starring Marlene Dietrich and Lionel Atwill in a cast that included Cesar Romero, Edward Everett Horton and Alison Skipworth, and directed by

Josef von Sternberg. Song by Leo Robin and Ralph Rainger:
(IF IT ISN'T PAIN) THEN IT ISN'T LOVE

DRESSED TO THRILL
A 20th Century-Fox picture starring Tutta Rolf and Clive Brook, and directed by Henry Lachman. Songs by Paul Francis Webster and Lew Pollack:
MY ONE BIG MOMENT and MY HEART IS A VIOLIN.

EAST OF JAVA
A Universal picture filmed with a cast headed by Charles Bickford, Frank Albertson and Elizabeth Young, and directed by George Melford. Songs:
ONE MAN WOMAN by Jack Brooks and Milton Schwartzwald; BLUE LAGOON by Arnold Hughes and Frederick Herbert.

ESCAPADE
An M-G-M picture starring Luise Rainer and William Powell in a cast that included Frank Morgan, Virginia Bruce, Mady Christians, Reginald Owen, Laura Hope Crews and Henry Travers, and directed by Robert Z. Leonard. Song by Gus Kahn, Bronislaw Kaper and Walter Jurmann:
YOU'RE ALL I NEED

FIRE HAS BEEN ARRANGED, A
A Twickenham Film production starring the English comedians, Flanagan and Allen. Song by Maurice Sigler, Al Goodhart and Al Hoffman:
IT DOES'T COST A THING TO SMILE

FOUR HOURS TO KILL
A Paramount picture starring Richard Barthelmess in a cast that included Joe Morrison, Helen Mack, Ray Milland, Henry Travers and Lee Kohlmar, and directed by Mitchell Leisen. Songs by Leo Robin and Ralph Rainger:
HATE TO TALK ABOUT MYSELF; WALKING THE FLOOR and LET'S MAKE A NIGHT OF IT.

GILDED LILY, THE
A Paramount picture starring Claudette Colbert and Fred MacMurray in a cast that included Roger Pryor, Ray Milland, C. Aubrey Smith and Edward Gargan, and directed by Wesley Ruggles. Song by Sam Coslow and Arthur Johnston:
SOMETHING ABOUT ROMANCE

GOING HIGHBROW
A Warner Brothers' picture filmed with a cast headed by Guy Kibbe, Zasu Pitts, Ed-ward Everett Horton, Ross Alexander and Judy Canova, and directed by Robert Florey. Songs by Jack Scholl and Louis Alter:
ONE IN A MILLION and MOON CRAZY.

GREAT GOD GOLD
A Monogram picture filmed with a cast headed by Sidney Blackmer, Gloria Shea and Martha Sleeper, and directed by Arthur Lubin. Song by Charles Rosoff:
WHY CAN'T WE LOVE FOREVER?

HERE'S TO ROMANCE
A 20th Century-Fox picture filmed with a cast headed by Nino Martini, Genevieve Tobin, Anita Louise, Maria Gambarelli. Madame Schumann-Heink and Reginald Denny, and directed by Alfred E. Green. Songs by Herb Magidson and Con Conrad:
MIDNIGHT IN PARIS and HERE'S TO ROMANCE

HITCH HIKE LADY
A Republic picture filmed with a cast headed by Alison Skipworth, Mae Clarke and Arthur Treacher, and directed by Aubrey Scott. Song by Wallace McDonald and Smiley Burnette:
MARCHING FEET

JACK AHOY
A Gaumont-British picture starring Jack Hurlbert and Nancy O'Neil, and directed by Walter Forde. Song by Harry M. Woods:
MY HAT'S ON THE SIDE OF MY HEAD

KIND LADY
An M-G-M picture filmed with a cast headed by Aline McMahon, Basil Rathbone, Mary Carlisle, Frank Albertson and Dudley Diggs, and directed by George B. Seitz. Song by Ned Washington, Bronislaw Kaper and Walter Jurmann:
THE DUCHESS HAS A TWINKLE IN HER EYE

LAST OF THE PAGANS
An M-G-M picture filmed with a cast of Polynesian natives headed by Mala and Lotus, and directed by Richard Thorpe. Song by Gus Kahn, Bronislaw Kaper and Walter Jurmann:
SHADOWS ON THE STARLIT WA-TERS

LET'S LIVE TONIGHT
A Columbia picture starring Lilian Harvey and Tullio Carminati in a cast that included Janet Beecher, and directed by Victor Schertzinger. Songs by Jack Scholl and Victor Schertzinger:

LOVE PASSES BY and I'LL LIVE IN MY DREAMS

LIMELIGHT
A Herbert Wilcox production starring Anna Neagle and the Street Singer. Songs by Maurice Sigler, Al Goodhart and Al Hoffman:
STRANDED and STAY AWHILE

LITTLE BIG SHOT
A Warner Brothers' picture filmed with a cast headed by Sybil Jason, Glenda Farrell, Robert Armstrong, Edward Everett Horton, Jack LaRue, Emma Dunn and Arthur Treacher, and directed by Michael Curtiz. Song by Mort Dixon and Allie Wrubel:
I'M A LITTLE BIG SHOT NOW

LITTLE COLONEL, THE
A 20th Century-Fox picture starring Shirley Temple and Lionel Barrymore in a cast that included Evelyn Venable, John Lodge and Bill Robinson, and directed by David Butler. Song by Thomas Moore:
LOVE'S YOUNG DREAM

LIVING ON VELVET
A First National picture starring Kay Francis and George Brent, and directed by Frank Borzage. Song by Al Dubin and Harry Warren:
LIVING ON VELVET

LOVE ME FOREVER
A Columbia picture starring Grace Moore in a cast that included Leo Carrillo, Robert Allen and Spring Byington, and directed by Victor Schertzinger. Songs by Gus Kahn and Victor Schertzinger:
WHOA! and LOVE ME FOREVER.

MAN ON THE FLYING TRAPEZE, THE
A Paramount picture starring W. C. Fields in a cast that included Mary Brian, and directed by Clyde Bruckman. Song by Tot Seymour and Vee Lawnhurst:
THE MAN ON THE FLYING TRAPEZE

MILLION DOLLAR BABY
A Monogram picture filmed with a cast headed by Jimmy Fay, Arline Judge, Ray Walker and George Stone, and directed by Joseph Santley. Songs:
WHO IS IN YOUR DREAMS TO-NIGHT? by Frederick Hollander; I FOUND A MILLION DOLLAR BABY AT A 5-AND-10 CENT STORE by Billy Rose, Mort Dixon and Harry Warren.

MILKY WAY, THE
A Paramount picture starring Harold Lloyd in a cast that included Adolphe Menjou, and directed by Leo McCarey. Song by Tot Seymour and Vee Lawnhurst:
THE MILKY WAY

MUTINY ON THE BOUNTY
An M-G-M picture starring Clark Gable, Franchot Tone and Charles Laughton, and directed by Frank Lloyd. Song by Gus Kahn, Bronislaw Kaper and Walter Jurmann:
LOVE SONG OF TAHITI

MY SONG FOR YOU
A Gaumont-British picture filmed with a cast headed by Jan Kiepura, Sonnie Hale and Aileen Marson, and directed by Maurice Elvey. Song by Frank Eyton and Mischa Spoliansky:
MY SONG FOR YOU

NITWITS
An RKO picture starring Bert Wheeler and Robert Woolsey in a cast that included Betty Grable, and directed by George Stevens. Songs:
YOU OPENED MY EYES by L. Wolfe Gilbert and Felix Bernard; MUSIC IN MY HEART by Dorothy Fields and Jimmy McHugh.

ONE HOUR LATE
A Paramount picture filmed with a cast headed by Helen Twelvetrees, Joe Morrison, Conrad Nagel, Arline Judge, Gail Patrick, Ray Milland and Jed Prouty, and directed by Ralph Murphy. Songs:
A LITTLE ANGEL TOLD ME SO by Sam Coslow; (I CAN'T IMAGINE) ME WITHOUT YOU by Leo Robin and Lewis Gensler.

OUR LITTLE GIRL
A 20th Century-Fox picture starring Shirley Temple in a cast that included Rosemary Ames, Joel McCrea, Lyle Talbot, Erin-O'-Brien Moore and Poodles Hanniford and his family of circus bareback riders, and directed by John Robertson. Song by Paul Francis Webster and Lew Pollack:
OUR LITTLE GIRL

PADDY O'DAY
A 20th Century-Fox picture filmed with a cast headed by Jane Withers, Pinky Tomlin, Rita Casino, Jane Darwell and George Givot, and directed by Lewis Seiler. Songs:
KEEP THAT TWINKLE IN YOUR EYE and I LIKE A BALALAIKA by Sidney Clare, Edward Eliscu and Harry Akst.

PAGE MISS GLORY
A Warner Brothers' picture starring Mar-

ion Davies in a cast that included Pat O'-
Brien, Dick Powell, Mary Astor and Frank
McHugh, and directed by Mervyn LeRoy.
Song by Al Dubin and Harry Warren:
PAGE MISS GLORY

PEG OF OLD DRURY
A Gaumont-British production starring
Anna Neagle. Song by Maurice Sigler, Al
Goodhart and Al Hoffman:
A LITTLE DASH OF DUBLIN

PERFECT GENTLEMAN, A
An M-G-M picture starring Frank Morgan
in a cast that included Cicely Courtneidge
and Heather Angel, and directed by Tim
Whelan. Songs:
IT'S ONLY HUMAN by Harold Adamson
and Burton Lane; THERE'S SOMETHING
IN A BIG PARADE and TILLIE THE
TIGHT ROPE WALKER by Ned Washing-
ton, Bronislaw Kaper and Walter Jurmann.

RAINMAKERS, THE
An RKO picture starring Bert Wheeler
and Robert Woolsey in a cast that included
Dorothy Lee, and directed by Fred Guiol.
Song by Jack Scholl and Louis Alter:
ISN'T LOVE THE GRANDEST
THING?

REMEMBER LAST NIGHT
A Universal picture filmed with a cast
headed by Edward Arnold, Constance Cummings, Sally Eilers and Robert Young, and
directed by J. Whale. Song by S. Coslow.
REMEMBER LAST NIGHT

SHADOW OF A DOUBT
An M-G-M picture filmed with a cast
headed by Ricardo Cortez, Virginia Bruce,
Constance Collier, Betty Furness and Arthur
Byron, and directed by William B. Seiter.
Song by Harold Adamson and Burton Lane:
BEYOND THE SHADOW OF A
DOUBT

SPRING TONIC
A 20th Century-Fox picture filmed with
a cast headed by Lew Ayers, Claire Trevor,
Zasu Pitts and Jack Haley, and directed by
Clyde Brockman. Song by Jay Gorney:

TONIGHT THERE'S A SPELL ON
THE MOON

STORMY WEATHER
A Gainsborough picture filmed with a cast
headed by Tom Wallis, Ralph Lynn and
Yvonne Arnaud. Song by Maurice Sigler,
Al Goodhart and Al Hoffman:
TELL ME WITH YOUR EYES

TIMES SQUARE LADY
An M-G-M picture filmed with a cast
headed by Robert Taylor, Virginia Bruce,
Helen Twelvetrees, Nat Pendleton, Henry
Kolker, Jack LaRue and Fred Kohler, and
directed by George B. Seitz. Songs by Coy
Poe, Jimmy Grier and Pinky Tomlin:
THE OBJECT OF MY AFFECTION
and WHAT'S THE REASON I'M NOT
PLEASIN' YOU?

WATERFRONT LADY
A Republic picture filmed with a cast
headed by Ann Rutherford, Frank Albert-
son, Farrell McDonald, Barbara Pepper and
Jack LaRue, and directed by Joseph Santley.
Songs by Smiley Burnette:
DEEP DARK RIVER and WHAT
WOULDN'T I DO?

WE'RE IN THE MONEY
A Warner Brothers' picture filmed with a
cast headed by Joan Blondell, Glenda Farrell, Ross Alexander, Phil Regan and Ed
Gargan, and directed by Ray Enright. Song
by Mort Dixon and Allie Wrubel:
SO NICE SEEING YOU AGAIN

WHEN KNIGHTS WERE BOLD
A Capitol Film production starring Jack
Buchanan. Songs by Maurice Sigler, Al Hoff-
man and Al Goodhart:
I'M STILL DREAMING and LET'S
PUT SOME PEOPLE TO WORK.

WOMAN IN RED, THE
A First National picture starring Barbara
Stanwyck in a cast that included Gene Ray-
mond, Genevieve Tobin, John Eldredge,
Phillip Reed, Claude Gillingwater and Ar-
thur Treacher, and directed by Robert
Florey. Song by J. Young and L. Reginald.
SO CLOSE TO THE FOREST

Western Films With Songs

BAR 20 RIDES AGAIN
A Paramount picture starring William
Boyd in a cast that included Jimmy Ellison
and Jean Rouverol, and directed by Howard
Bretherton. Song by Dave Franklin and
Sammy Stept:
THE MOON HANGS HIGH

EAGLE'S BROOD, THE
A Paramount picture starring William
Boyd in a cast that included James Ellison
and William Farnum, and directed by Harry
Lachman. Song by Sidney Mitchell and Sam-
my Stept:
DRUNK WITH LOVE

80

HOPALONG CASSIDY

A Paramount picture starring William Boyd in a cast that included Jimmy Ellison and Paula Stone, and directed by Howard Bretherton. Song by Dave Franklin and Sammy Stept:

FOLLOWING THE STARS

MELODY TRAIL

A Republic picture starring Gene Autry in a cast that included Smiley Burnette and Ann Rutherford, and directed by Joseph Kane. Songs by Gene Autry and Smiley Burnette:

ON THE MELODY TRAIL; WESTERN LULLABY; WHERE WILL THE WEDDING SUPPER BE?; HOLD ON, LITTLE DOGIES, HOLD ON and MY NEIGHBOR HATES MUSIC.

MOONLIGHT ON THE PRAIRIE

A Warner Brothers' picture starring Dick Foran in a cast that included Herbert Heywood and Sheila Manners, and directed by D. Ross Lederman. Songs:

COVERED WAGON DAYS by Joan Jasmin and M. K. Jerome; MOONLIGHT ON THE PRAIRIE by Tim Spencer and Bob Nolan.

SAGEBRUSH TROUBADOR

A Republic picture starring Gene Autry in a cast that included Barbara Pepper, Smiley Burnette and Fred Kelsey, and directed by Joseph Kane. Songs by Gene Autry and Smiley Burnette:

END OF THE TRAIL and LOST CHORD.

SINGING VAGABOND, THE

A Republic picture starring Gene Autry in a cast that included Ann Rutherford, Smiley Burnette, Barbara Pepper, Frank La-Rue and Bob Burns, and directed by Carl Pierson. Songs by Gene Autry and Smiley Burnette:

WAGON TRAIN and FAREWELL FRIENDS OF THE PRAIRIE.

TUMBLING TUMBLEWEEDS

A Republic picture starring Gene Autry in a cast that included Smiley Burnette, Lucille Brown and Norma Taylor, and directed by Joseph Kane. Songs:

CORNFED AND RUSTY; THE OLD COVERED WAGON and RIDIN' DOWN THE CANYON by Gene Autry and Smiley Burnette: TUMBLING TUMBLEWEEDS by Bob Nolan.

The "I Won't Dance" number from Jerome Kern's *Roberta*

1 9 3 6
An Oscar For "Ziegfeld"; A Sarong For Lamour

Nine years after *The Jazz Singer* ushered in the talkie era, the Hollywood muscial in 1936 finally reached the charmed circle reserved exclusively for Oscar winners with the selection of *The Great Ziegfeld* as the outstanding picture of the year and Luise Rainer, for added measure, being voted the best actress for her portrayal of Anna Held, Ziggy's first wife, in the same film. But a far more enduring triumph was scored by a package of pulchritude from New Orleans, who spent days under a sun lamp before making her film debut in *Jungle Princess* with a sarong draped about her bronzed body to become the perennial favorite of sailors, who voted Dorothy Lamour the gal they'd like best to be shipwrecked with on a lonely island in the Pacific.

The year of 1936, in fact, was loaded with newcomers to the screen who were destined for future greatness—and soon. Sonja Henie, winner of gold medals at three Olympics, introduced ice skating on the screen in *One In A Million;* Betty Grable, a blonde bombshell from St. Louis, uncorked her tremendous vitality in *Collegiate;* Judy Garland revealed a charm and a talent in *The Pigskin Parade* that not only carried her to Hollywood heights but sparked the rebirth of big-time vaudeville at the Palace fifteen years later; Martha Raye made the shift from night clubs to the screen with a resounding bang in *Rhythm On The Range;* and Gladys Swarthout, in the higher realms of music, challenged the popularity of three other songbirds from the "Met", Jeanette MacDonald, Grace Moore and Lily Pons, in her screen debut in two 1936 releases: *Give Us This Night* and *Rose Of The Rancho.*

Shirley Temple, now nine year old, continued to be a sensational box-office draw in four pictures: *Captain January, Dimples, The Poor Little Rich Girl* and *Stowaway,* and her success prompted 20th Century-Fox to star another moppet, Jane Withers, in *Little Miss Nobody* and *Can This Be Dixie?* while RKO introduced Bobby Breen, a nine-year-old singing discovery of Eddie Cantor, in *Rainbow On The River* and *Let's Sing Again* as a counter attraction. Catch-'em-young-and-sprinkle-'em-with-stardust-instead-of-talcum-powder was the order-of-the-day in Hollywood that was carried out to the last letter two years later when the Dionne Quintuplets made their film debut at the age of four in *Five Of A Kind.*

In addition to winning an Oscar for the best song of the year—*The Way You Look Tonight,* Jerome Kern had two four-bell pictures to his credit in the retake of his immortal *Show Boat* and the melodious *Swing Time,* starring Ginger Rogers and Fred Astaire, who had a second 1936 success in *Follow The Fleet* with such distinguished Irving Berlin songs as *I'm Putting All My Eggs In One Basket* and *Let's Face The Music And Dance.*

Cole Porter also hit his high Broadway level in Hollywood with the songs he wrote for *Born To Dance,* starring Eleanor Powell, and Bing Crosby and Ethel Merman made his *Anything Goes* equally as captivating on the screen as it had been on the stage two seasons before.

Jack Benny, Burns and Allen, Frances Langford and Bob Burns, the bazooka virtuoso from Van Buren, Ark., capitalized on their radio popularity as film celebrities in a year that yielded such Ten Best Pictures as *Mr. Deeds Goes To Town, San Francisco, Dodsworth, The Story Of Louis Pasteur, A Tale Of Two Cities, Anthony Adverse* and *The Green Pastures,* but the sun was about to set for the dynamic personality who had been instrumental in making all this multifold success possible—Al Jolson.

Musicals

ANYTHING GOES
A Paramount picture starring Bing Crosby and Ethel Merman in a cast that included Charles Ruggles and Ida Lupino, and directed by Lewis Milestone. Songs:
YOU'RE THE TOP; ANYTHING GOES; ALL THROUGH THE NIGHT; BLOW GABRIEL BLOW; I GET A KICK OUT OF YOU and THERE'LL ALWAYS BE A LADY FAIR by Cole Porter: MOONBURN by Edward Heyman and Hoagy Carmichael; SAILOR BEWARE by Leo Robin and Richard Whiting; SHANGHI-DE-HO; MY HEART AND I; AM I AWAKE? and HOPELESSLY IN LOVE by Leo Robin and Frederick Hollander.

BIG BROADCAST OF 1937
A Paramount picture filmed with a cast headed by Burns and Allen, Jack Benny, Bob Burns and Martha Raye, and directed by Mitchell Leisen. Songs by Leo Robin and Ralph Rainger:
I'M TALKING THROUGH MY HEART; YOU CAME TO MY RESCUE; HERE'S LOVE IN YOUR EYE; VOTE FOR MR. RHYTHM; LA BOMBA and NIGHT IN MANHATTAN.

BORN TO DANCE
An M-G-M picture starring Eleanor Powell in a cast that included James Stewart, Virginia Bruce, Una Merkel, Sid Silvers and Frances Langford, and directed by Roy Del Ruth. Songs by Cole Porter:
I'VE GOT YOU UNDER MY SKIN; EASY TO LOVE; I'M NUTS ABOUT YOU; RAP-TAP ON WOOD; SWINGING THE JINX AWAY; ROLLING HOME; HEY, BABE, HEY and LOVE ME LOVE MY PEKINESE.

CAIN AND MABEL
A Warner Brothers' picture starring Marion Davies and Clark Gable in a cast that included Allen Jenkins, Roscoe Karns and Walter Catlett, and directed by Lloyd Bacon. Songs by Al Dubin and Harry Warren:
I'LL SING YOU A THOUSAND LOVE SONGS; CONEY ISLAND and HERE COMES CHIQUITA.

CAN THIS BE DIXIE?
A 20th Century-Fox picture filmed with a cast headed by Jane Withers, Slim Summerville, Helen Wood and Thomas Beck, and directed by George Marshall. Songs by Sidney Clare and Harry Akst:
PICK - PICK - PICKANINNY; UNCLE TOM'S CABIN IS A CABARET NOW; DOES YOU WANNA GO TO HEAVEN? and IT'S JULEP TIME IN DIXIELAND.

CAPTAIN JANUARY
A 20th Century-Fox picture starring Shirley Temple in a cast that included Guy Kibbe and Slim Summerville, and directed by David Butler. Songs by Jack Yellen and Lew Pollack:
EARLY BIRD; AT THE CODFISH BALL and THE RIGHT SOMEBODY TO LOVE.

CHARLEY CHAN AT THE OPERA
A 20th Century-Fox picture starring Warner Oland in a cast that included Boris Karloff, Keye Luke and Charlotte Henry, and directed by H. Bruce Humberson. Songs by William Kernell and Oscar Levant:
CARNIVAL; KING AND COUNTRY CALL; AH, ROMANTIC LOVE DREAM, CARNIVAL and CARNIVAL, THEN FAREWELL.

COLLEEN

A Warner Brothers' picture starring Ruby Keeler and Dick Powell in a cast that included Joan Blondell, Hugh Herbert and Jack Oakie, and directed by Alfred E. Green. Songs by Al Dubin and Harry Warren:

I DON'T HAVE TO DREAM AGAIN; YOU'VE GOTTA KNOW HOW TO DANCE; AN EVENING WITH YOU and A BOULEVARDIER FROM THE BRONX.

COLLEGE HOLIDAY

A Paramount picture filmed with a cast headed by Jack Benny, Burns and Allen, Mary Boland, Martha Raye and Marsha Hunt, and directed by Frank Tuttle. Songs:

WHO'S THAT KNOCKING AT MY HEART and THE SWEETHEART WALTZ by Ralph Freed and Burton Lane: A RHYME FOR LOVE; I ADORE YOU and SO WHAT! by Leo Robin and Ralph Rainger.

COLLEGIATE

A Paramount picture filmed with a cast headed by Joe Penner, Jack Oakie, Ned Sparks, Frances Langford and Betty Grable, and directed by Ralph Murphy. Songs by Mack Gordon and Harry Revel:

I FEEL LIKE A FEATHER IN THE BREEZE; YOU HIT THE SPOT; RYTHMATIC; MY GRANDFATHER'S CLOCK IN THE HALLWAY; WHO AM I?; WILL I EVER KNOW?; GUESS AGAIN and LEARN TO BE LOVELY.

DANCING FEET

A Republic picture filmed with a cast headed by Ben Lyon, Joan Marsh and Eddie Nugent, and directed by Joseph Santley. Songs by Sidney Mitchell and Sammy Stept:

EVERY TIME I LOOK AT YOU; DANCING FEET; IN AND OUT; LAND OF DREAMS; AND THEN—; GET IN STEP; HERE I AM AGAIN; HERE COMES LOVE; WATER WHEEL; I'M GLAD IT'S ME; DREAMING OF YOU; NEVER GIVE UP and RECOLLECTIONS OF LOVE.

DEVIL ON HORSEBACK

A Grand National picture starring Lili Damiti and Fred Keating, and directed by Crane Wilbur. Songs by Harry Tobias and Jack Stern:

SO DIVINE; OH BELLA MIA; OUT OF THE HILLS and THE LOVE FIESTA.

DIMPLES

A 20th Century-Fox picture starring Shirley Temple in a cast that included Frank Morgan, Helen Westley, Robert Kent and Stepin Fetchit, and directed by William A. Seiter. Songs by Ted Koehler and Jimmy McHugh:

WHAT DID THE BLUEBIRD SAY?; HE WAS A DANDY; PICTURE ME WITHOUT YOU and OH MISTER MAN UP IN THE MOON.

DIZZY DAMES

A Liberty picture filmed with a cast headed by Marjorie Rambeau, Florine McKinney and Lawrence Gray, and directed by William Nigh. Songs:

LOVE IS THE THING by Harry Tobias and Neil Moret; THE MARTINIQUE by Arthur Swanstrom, George Waggner and Louis Alter; I WAS TAKEN BY STORM by Edward Heyman and Louis Alter; and LET'S BE FRIVOLOUS by Howard Jackson and George Waggner.

FIRST BABY, THE

A 20th Century-Fox picture filmed with a cast headed by Johnny Downs, Shirley Dean, Jane Darwell, Dixie Dunbar and Hattie McDaniels, and directed by Lewis Seiler. Musical numbers:

JOAN OF ARKANSAS by Edward Heyman and Johnny Green; PHI-PHI-PHI by Sidney Clare and Richard Whiting; SPREADIN' RHYTHM AROUND by Ted Koehler and Jimmy McHugh; SHE AND I by Bill Robinson and Cyril J. Mockridge.

FOLLOW THE FLEET

An RKO picture starring Ginger Rogers and Fred Astaire, and directed by Mark Sandrich. Songs by Irving Berlin:

I'M PUTTING ALL MY EGGS IN ONE BASKET; WE SAW THE SEA; LET'S FACE THE MUSIC AND DANCE; LET YOURSELF GO; BUT WHERE ARE YOU?; I'D RATHER LEAD A BAND and GET THEE BEHIND ME SATAN.

FOLLOW YOUR HEART

A Republic picture filmed with a cast headed by Marion Talley, Michael Bartlett and Nigel Bruce, and directed by Aubrey Scotto. Songs by Sidney Mitchell, Walter Bullock and Victor Schertzinger:

MAGNOLIAS IN THE MOONLIGHT; WHO MINDS 'BOUT ME and FOLLOW YOUR HEART.

GIVE US THIS NIGHT

A Paramount picture starring Gladys Swarthout and Jan Kiepura, and directed by Alexander Hall. Songs by Oscar Hammerstein II and Erich Korngold:

SWEET MELODY OF NIGHT; I MEAN TO SAY I LOVE YOU; MY LOVE AND I; MUSIC IN THE NIGHT; GIVE US THIS NIGHT and WAS THERE EVER A VOICE.

GOLD DIGGERS OF 1937
A First National picture starring Dick Powell and Joan Blondell in a cast that included Glenda Farrell and Victor Moore, and directed by Lloyd Bacon. Songs:
WITH PLENTY OF MONEY AND YOU and ALL'S FAIR IN LOVE AND WAR by Al Dubin and Harry Warren; SPEAKING OF THE WEATHER; LET'S PUT OUR HEADS TOGETHER and LIFE INSURANCE SONG by E. Y. Harburg and Harold Arlen.

GREAT ZIEGFELD, THE
An M-G-M picture filmed with a cast headed by William Powell, Myrna Loy, Luise Rainer, Frank Morgan, Virginia Bruce, Fanny Brice and Harriet Hoctor, and directed by Robert Z. Leonard. Songs:
IT'S BEEN SO LONG; YOU NEVER LOOKED SO BEAUTIFUL; YOU; SHE'S A FOLLIES' GIRL; YOU GOTTA PULL STRINGS and QUEEN OF THE JUNGLE by Harold Adamson and Walter Donaldson: A PRETTY GIRL IS LIKE A MELODY by Irving Berlin.

HATS OFF
A Grand National picture filmed with a cast headed by Mae Clarke, John Payne, Helen Lynd, Luis Alberni and Skeets Gallagher, and directed by Boris Petroff. Songs by Herb Magidson and Ben Oakland:
WHERE HAVE YOU BEEN ALL MY LIFE? LITTLE OLD RHYTHM; TWINKLE, TWINKLE LITTLE STAR; LET'S HAVE ANOTHER and HATS OFF.

HEAD OVER HEELS
A Gaumont-British picture filmed with a cast headed by Jessie Mathews and Louis Borrell. Songs by Mack Gordon and Harry Revel:
THROUGH THE COURTESY OF LOVE; HEAD OVER HEELS IN LOVE; MAY I HAVE THE NEXT ROMANCE WITH YOU; LOOKING AROUND CORNERS FOR YOU; THERE'S THAT LOOK IN YOUR EYE and DON'T GIVE A GOOD GOSH DARN.

HI GAUCHO
An RKO picture filmed with a cast headed by Steffi Duna, John Carroll and Montagu Love, and directed by Tommy Atkins. Songs by Albert Hay Malotte:
SONG OF THE OPEN ROAD; BANDIT SONG; MY LITTLE WHITE ROSE and PANCHITA.

IT'S LOVE AGAIN
A Gaumont-British picture starring Jessie Mathews and Robert Young, and directed by Victor Saville. Songs:
I NEARLY LET LOVE GO SLIPPING THROUGH MY FINGERS by Harry M. Woods; IT'S LOVE AGAIN and I'VE GOT TO DANCE MY WAY TO HEAVEN by Sam Coslow.

KING STEPS OUT, THE
A Columbia picture starring Grace Moore in a cast that included Franchot Tone, and directed by William Perlberg. Songs by Dorothy Fields and Fritz Kreisler:
STARS IN MY EYES; MADLY IN LOVE; LEARN HOW TO LOSE and WHAT SHALL REMAIN?

KLONDIKE ANNIE
A Paramount picture starring Mae West and Victor McLaglen, and directed by Raoul Walsh. Songs:
MY MEDICINE MAN by Sam Coslow: MISTER DEEP BLUE SEA; OCCIDENTAL WOMAN; CHEER UP LITTLE SISTER; I HEAR YOU KNOCKIN' BUT YOU CAN'T COME IN; IT'S NEVER TOO LATE TO SAY NO; THIS MAY NOT BE LOVE BUT IT'S WONDERFUL; IT'S BETTER TO GIVE THAN TO RECEIVE and OPEN UP YOUR HEART AND LET THE SUNSHINE IN by Gene Austin.

LAUGHING IRISH EYES
A Republic picture filmed with a cast headed by Phil Regan, Walter Kelly and Evelyn Knapp, and directed by Joseph Santley. Songs by Sidney Mitchell and Sammy Stept:
ALL MY LIFE; BLESS YOU DARLING MOTHER and LAUGHING IRISH EYES.

MUSIC GOES ROUND, THE
A Columbia picture starring Harry Richman in a cast that included Rochelle Hudson and Walter Connolly, and directed by Victor Schertzinger. Songs by Lew Brown, Harry Richman and Harry Akst:
ROLLING ALONG; THIS IS LOVE; SUSANNAH I'M BETTING ON YOU; TAKING CARE OF YOU; THERE'LL BE NO SOUTH and LIFE BEGINS WHEN YOU'RE IN LOVE (music by Victor Schertzinger).

ONE IN A MILLION

A 20th Century-Fox picture starring Sonja Heine in a cast that included Adolphe Menjou, Don Ameche, Ned Sparks, Jean Hersholt, Arline Judge and the Ritz Brothers, and directed by Sidney Lanfield. Songs by Sidney Mitchell and Lew Pollack:
LOVELY LADY IN WHITE; WE'RE BACK IN CIRCULATION AGAIN; THE MOONLIGHT WALTZ; ONE IN A MILLION and WHO'S AFRAID OF LOVE?

PALM SPRINGS

A Paramount picture filmed with a cast headed by Frances Langford, Smith Ballew, Sir Guy Standing and Ernest Cossart, and directed by Aubrey Scotto. Songs:
THE HILLS OF OLD WYOMING; I DON'T TO MAKE HISTORY (I JUST WANT TO MAKE LOVE); PALM SPRINGS and DREAMING OUT LOUD by Leo Robin and Ralph Rainger: WILL I EVER KNOW? by Mack Gordon and Harry Revel.

PENNIES FROM HEAVEN

A Columbia picture starring Bing Crosby in a cast that included Madge Evans, Edith Fellows and Louis Armstrong, and directed by Norman Z. McLeod. Songs by Johnny Burke and Arthur Johnston:
ONE, TWO BUTTON MY SHOE; PENNIES FROM HEAVEN; SO DO I; SKELETON IN THE CLOSET; LET'S CALL A HEART A HEART; NOW I'VE GOT SOME DREAMING TO DO and WHAT THIS COUNTRY NEEDS.

PIGSKIN PARADE

A 20th Century-Fox picture filmed with a cast headed by Stuart Erwin, Patsy Kelly, Jack Haley, Judy Garland, Dixie Dunbar, Betty Grable and the Yacht Club Boys, and directed by David Butler. Songs by Sidney Mitchell and Lew Pollack:
IT'S LOVE I'M AFTER; BALBOA; YOU'RE SLIGHTLY TERRIFIC; YOU DO THE DARNDEST THINGS BABY; T. S. U. ALMA MATER; HOLD THAT BULLDOG and THE TEXAS TORNADO.

POOR LITTLE RICH GIRL

A 20th Century-Fox picture starring Shirley Temple in a cast that included Alice Faye, Gloria Stuart, Jack Haley and Michael Whalen, and directed by Irving Cummings. Songs by Mack Gordon and Harry Revel:
OH, MY GOODNESS!; BUY A BAR OF BARRY'S; WHEN I'M WITH YOU; BUT DEFINITELY; YOU GOTTA EAT YOUR SPINACH BABY and MILITARY MAN.

POPPY

A Paramount picture starring W. C. Fields in a cast that included Rochelle Hudson and Richard Cromwell. Songs:
POPPY by Sam Coslow and Frederick Hollander; A RENDEZVOUS WITH A DREAM by Leo Robin and Ralph Rainger; HANG YOUR SORROWS IN THE SUN and A PICNIC PARTY WITH YOU by John Egan and Dorothy Donnelly.

PRINCESS COMES ACROSS, THE

A Paramount picture starring Carole Lombard and Fred MacMurray, and directed by William K. Howard. Songs:
MY CONCERTINA by Jack Scholl and Phil Boutelje; PAMPA ROSE by George Marion Jr. and Richard Whiting; PARIS IN THE SPRING and IT'S YOU I'M TALKING ABOUT by Mack Gordon and Harry Revel; AWAKE IN A DREAM by Leo Robin and Frederick Hollander.

RAINBOW ON THE RIVER

An RKO picture filmed with a cast headed by Bobby Breen, May Robson, Charles Butterworth and Benita Hume, and directed by Kurt Neumann. Songs:
RAINBOW ON THE RIVER; YOU ONLY LIVE ONCE and A THOUSAND DREAMS OF YOU by Paul Francis Webster and Louis Alter; WAITING FOR THE SUN TO RISE by Arthur Swanstrom and Karl Hajos.

RAMONA

A 20th Century-Fox picture starring Loretta Young and Don Ameche in a cast that included Kent Taylor, Pauline Frederick, Jane Darwell, Katherine de Mille and John Carradine, and directed by Henry King. Songs:
LA FIESTA; BLESSED BE THE DAWNING; UNDER THE REDWOOD TREE and HOW THE RABBIT LOST HIS TAIL by William Kernell; PIERRE by Alfred Newman.

RHYTHM ON THE RANGE

A Paramount picture starring Bing Crosby in a cast that included Frances Farmer, Bob Burns and Martha Raye, and directed by Norman Taurog. Songs:
I CAN'T ESCAPE FROM YOU by Leo Robin and Richard Whiting; EMPTY SADDLES by Billy Hill; I'M AN OLD COWHAND by Johnny Mercer; IF YOU CAN'T SING IT YOU'LL HAVE TO SWING IT MR. PAGANINI by Sam Coslow; THE HOUSE JACK BUILT FOR JILL by Leo Robin and Frederick Hollander; DRINK IT

DOWN by Leo Robin and Ralph Rainger;
HANG UP MY SADDLE and RHYTHM
ON THE RANGE by Walter Bullock and
Richard Whiting; MEMORIES by Richard
Whiting and Frederick Hollander.

ROSE MARIE
An M-G-M picture starring Nelson Eddy
and Jeanette MacDonald in a cast that in-
cluded Reginald Owen, Allan Jones and
James Stewart, and directed by W. S. Van-
Dyke. Songs:
ROSE MARIE; SONG OF THE MOUN-
TIES; LAK JEEM; INDIAN LOVE CALL
and TOTEM TOM TOM by Otto Harbach,
Oscar Hammerstein II and Rudolf Friml;
PARDON ME MADAME by Gus Kahn and
Herbert Stothart: JUST FOR YOU by Gus
Kahn, Herbert Stothart and Rudolf Friml:
DINAH by Sam Lewis, Joe Young and Harry
Akst: SOME OF THESE DAYS by Shelton
Brooks.

ROSE OF THE RANCHO
A Paramount picture starring Gladys
Swarthout and John Boles in a cast that
included Charles Bickford and Willie How-
ard, and directed by Marion Gering. Songs
by Leo Robin and Ralph Rainger:
IF I SHOULD LOSE YOU; THUN-
DER OVER PARADISE; LITTLE ROSE
OF THE RANCHO; GOT A GIRL IN
CALIFORN-I-A; THERE'S GOLD IN
MONTEREY; WHERE IS MY LOVE?
and THE PADRE AND THE BRIDE.

SHOW BOAT
A Universal picture filmed with a cast
headed by Irene Dunne, Allan Jones,
Charles Winninger, Paul Robeson, Helen
Morgan, Helen Westley and Hattie Mc-
Daniels, and directed by James Whale.
Songs by Oscar Hammerstein II and Jer-
ome Kern:
MAKE BELIEVE; OL' MAN RIVER;
CAN'T HELP LOVIN' DAT MAN; GAL-
LIVANTIN' AROUND; YOU ARE
LOVE; BILL; AH STILL SUITS ME and
I HAVE THE ROOM ABOVE.

SING BABY SING
A 20th Century-Fox picture filmed with a
cast headed by Alice Faye, Adolphe Men-
jou, Ted Healy, Dixie Dunbar and Gregory
Ratoff, and directed by Sidney Lanfield.
WHEN DID YOU LEAVE HEAVEN?
by Walter Bullock and Richard Whiting;
LOVE WILL TELL and SING BABY
SING by Jack Yellen and Lew Pollack;
YOU TURNED THE TABLES ON ME
by Sidney Mitchell and Louis Alter.

SING ME A LOVE SONG
A First National picture filmed with a
cast headed by James Melton, Patricia Ellis,
Hugh Herbert, Zasu Pitts and Allen Jen-
kins, and directed by Ray Enright. Songs:
SUMMER NIGHT; THE LITTLE
HOUSE THAT LOVE BUILT and
THAT'S THE LEAST YOU CAN DO
FOR A LADY by Al Dubin and Harry
Warren: YOUR EYES HAVE TOLD ME
SO by Gus Kahn, Walter Blaufuss and Al-
bert Von Tilzer.

SINGING KID, THE
A First National picture starring Al Jol-
son in a cast that included Sybil Jason,
Edward Everett Horton, Lyle Talbot and
Allen Jenkins, and directed by William
Keighley. Songs:
MY HOW THIS COUNTRY HAS
CHANGED; I LOVE TO SING A; SAVE
ME SISTER; YOU'RE THE CURE FOR
ALL THAT AILS ME and HERE'S
LOOKING AT YOU by E. Y. Harburg and
Harold Arlen; KEEP THAT HI-DI-HO
IN YOUR SOUL by Irving Mills and Cab
Calloway.

SITTING ON THE MOON
A Republic picture starring Roger Pryor
and Grace Bradley, and directed by Ralph
Staub. Songs by Sidney Mitchell and Sam-
my Stept:
LOST IN MY DREAMS; SITTING ON
THE MOON and HOW AM I DOIN'
WITH YOU?

SKY'S THE LIMIT, THE
A British-Gaumont picture starring Jack
Buchanan in a cast that included the Mills
Brothers. Songs by Al Sherman and Abner
Silver:
DOIN' THE MONTREAL; SWING
MADAM; MY BELOVED and JUST
WHISPER I LOVE YOU.

SMARTEST GIRL IN TOWN
An RKO picture starring Ann Sothern
and Gene Raymond, and directed by Joseph
Santley. Songs:
GOT A NEW LEASE ON LIFE and
DON'T MENTION LOVE TO ME by
Dorothy Fields and Oscar Levant: SWING
IT SISTER by Harold Adamson and Burton
Lane; WILL YOU? by Gene Raymond.

SONG AND DANCE MAN
A 20th Century-Fox picture filmed with
a cast headed by Claire Trevor, Paul Kelly,
Michael Whalen and Ruth Donnelly, and
directed by Allan Dwan. Songs by Sidney
Clare and Lew Pollack:

YOU'RE MY FAVORITE ONE; ON A HOLIDAY IN MY PLAYROOM; JOIN THE PARTY; LET'S GET GOING; AIN'T HE GOOD LOOKING? and DANCING IN THE OPEN.

SQUIBS
A Twickenham Film production starring Betty Balfour with songs by Maurice Sigler, Al Goodhart and Al Hoffman:
ONE WAY STREET; SQUIBS and DID YOU EVER HAVE A FEELING YOU'RE FLYING?

STAR FOR A NIGHT
A 20th Century-Fox picture filmed with a cast headed by Clair Trevor, Jane Darwell, Evelyn Venable, Arline Judge and J. Edward Bromberg, and directed by Lewis Seiler. Songs by Sidney Clare and Harry Akst:
DOWN AROUND MALIBU WAY; OVER A CUP OF COFFEE and AT THE BEACH AT MALIBU.

STOWAWAY
A 20th Century-Fox picture starring Shirley Temple in a cast that included Robert Young, Alice Faye and Helen Westley, and directed by William A. Seiter. Songs:
YOU GOTTA SMILE TO BE H-A-DOUBLE P-Y; GOOD NIGHT MY LOVE; ONE NEVER KNOWS, DOES ONE? I WANNA GO TO THE ZOO and A DREAMLAND CHOO-CHOO TO LULLABY TOWN by Mack Gordon and Harry Revel; THAT'S WHAT I WANT FOR CHRISTMAS by Irving Caesar and Gerald Marks.

STRIKE ME PINK
A United Artists' picture starring Eddie Cantor in a cast that included Ethel Merman and Sally Eilers, and directed by Norman Taurog. Songs by Lew Brown and Harold Arlen:
THE LADY DANCES; CALABASH PIPE; IF I FEEL THIS WAY TOMORROW THEN IT'S LOVE and FIRST YOU HAVE ME HIGH (THEN YOU HAVE ME LOW).

SWING TIME
An RKO picture starring Ginger Rogers and Fred Astaire in a cast that included Helen Broderick and Victor Moore, and directed by George Stevens. Songs by Dorothy Fields and Jerome Kern:
THE WAY YOU LOOK TONIGHT; BOJANGLES OF HARLEM; WALTZ IN SWING TIME; PICK YOURSELF UP; NEVER GONNA DANCE and A FINE ROMANCE (THIS IS).

THAT GIRL FROM PARIS
An RKO picture starring Lili Pons in a cast that included Jack Oakie, Gene Raymond, Lucille Ball and Mischa Auer, and directed by Leigh Jason. Songs by Edward Heyman and Arthur Schwartz:
LOVE AND LEARN; SEAL IT WITH A KISS; THE CALL TO ARMS; MY NEPHEW FROM NICE and MOONFACE.

THIS'LL MAKE YOU WHISTLE
A Herbert Wilcox production, starring Jack Buchanan. Songs by Maurice Sigler, Al Goodhart and Al Hoffman:
I'M IN A DANCING MOOD; THERE ISN'T ANY LIMIT TO MY LOVE; WITHOUT RHYTHM; YOU'VE GOT THE WRONG RHUMBA; I'M NEVER TOO BUSY FOR YOU; COCKTAIL TIME; KEEP YOUR EYE ON THE SKY; I DON'T GIVE A CONTINENTAL; I MAKE A MOTION; MY RED LETTER DAY and CRAZY WITH LOVE.

THREE CHEERS FOR LOVE
A Paramount picture filmed with a cast headed by Eleanor Whitney, Robert Cummings, William Frawley, Elizabeth Patterson and Roscoe Karns, and directed by Ray McCarey. Songs by Leo Robin and Ralph Rainger:
WHERE IS MY HEART?; THE SWING TAP; LONG AGO AND FAR AWAY and TAP YOUR FEET.

UNDER YOUR SPELL
A 20th Century-Fox picture starring Lawrence Tibbett in a cast that included Wendy Barrie. Gregory Ratoff and Arthur Treacher, and directed by Otto Perminger. Songs by Howard Dietz and Arthur Schwartz:
AMIGO; MY LITTLE MULE WAGON and UNDER YOUR SPELL.

WALKING ON AIR
An RKO picture starring Gene Raymond and Ann Sothern in a cast that included Jessie Ralph and Henry Stephenson, and directed by Joseph Santley. Songs by Bert Kalmar and Harry Ruby:
CABIN ON A HILLTOP; LET'S MAKE A WISH and MY HEART WANTS TO DANCE.

WITH LOVE AND KISSES
A Melody Pictures' production filmed with a cast headed by Pinky Tomlin, Toby

Wing and Kane Richmond, and directed by
Leslie Goodwins. Songs:
DON'T EVER LOSE IT and I'M
RIGHT BACK WHERE I STARTED by
Coy Poe and Pinky Tomlin; THE
TROUBLE WITH ME IS YOU by Harry
Tobias and Pinky Tomlin; SWEET by
Buddy LeRoux, Pinky Tomlin and Al
Health; WITH LOVE AND KISSES by
Connie Lee; SITTING ON THE EDGE
OF MY CHAIR by Paul Parks, Coy Poe
and Pinky Tomlin.

Feature Films With Songs

ACCUSED, THE
A United Artists' picture starring Dolores
Del Rio and Douglas Fairbanks Jr., and di-
rected by Thornton Freeland. Song by Vic-
tor Young:
LATIN RHYTHM

AFTER THE THIN MAN
An M-G-M picture starring William
Powell and Myrna Loy, and directed by
W. S. Van Dyke. Songs:
SMOKE DREAMS by Arthur Freed and
Nacio Herb Brown; BLOW THAT HORN
by Bob Wright, Chet Forrest and Walter
Donaldson.

BANJO ON MY KNEE
A 20th Century-Fox picture starring Barbara Stanwyck in a cast that included Joel
McCrea and Walter Brennan, and directed
by John Cromwell. Songs by Harold Adamson and Jimmy McHugh:
WHERE THE LAZY RIVER GOES BY;
THERE'S SOMETHING IN THE AIR
and WITH MY BANJO ON MY KNEE.

CAPTAIN'S KID, THE
A First National picture filmed with a
cast headed by May Robson, Sybil James,
Guy Kibbe, Jane Bryan, Fred Lawrence and
Dick Purcell, and directed by Nick Grinde.
Songs by Jack Scholl and M. K. Jerome:
DRIFTING ALONG and I'M THE
CAPTAIN'S KID.

CRACK-UP
A 20th Century-Fox picture starring Peter
Lorre in a cast that included Brian Donlevy,
Helen Wood and Ralph Morgan, and di-
rected by Malcolm St. Clair. Song by Sidney
Clare and Harry Akst:
TOP GALLANTE

DANCING PIRATE
An RKO picture filmed with a cast head-
ed by Charles Collins, Frank Morgan, Steffi
Duna and Luis Alberni, and directed by
Lloyd Corrigan. Songs by Lorenz Hart and
Richard Rodgers:
ARE YOU MY LOVE? and WHEN
YOU'RE DANCING THE WALTZ.

DESIRE
A Paramount picture starring Marlene
Dietrich and Gary Cooper, and directed by
Frank Borzage. Songs by Leo Robin and
Frederick Hollander:
WHISPERS IN THE DARK and
AWAKE IN A DREAM.

DEVIL IS A SISSY, THE
An M-G-M picture filmed with a cast
headed by Freddie Bartholomew, Jackie
Cooper, Mickey Rooney, Ian Hunter and
Peggy Conklin, and directed by W. S. Van
Dyke. Song by Arthur Freed and Nacio
Herb Brown:
SAY "AH!"

EVERY SATURDAY NIGHT
A 20th Century-Fox picture filmed with
a cast headed by June Lang, Thomas Beck,
Jed Prouty and Spring Byington, and di-
rected by James Tinling. Song by Herb
Magidson and Burton Lane:
BREATHES THERE A MAN

FATAL LADY
A Paramount picture filmed with a cast
headed by Mary Ellis, Walter Pidgeon, Ruth
Donnelly, Norman Foster and Guy Bates
Post, and directed by Edward Ludwig.
Songs by Sam Coslow and Victor Young:
BAL MASQUE and JE VOUS ADORE.

FLORIDA SPECIAL
A 20th Century-Fox picture filmed with
a cast headed by Jack Oakie, Sally Eilers,
Kent Taylor and Frances Drake, and directed by Ralph Murphy. Song by Mack Gordon and Harry Revel:
IT'S YOU I'M TALKING ABOUT

FRESHMAN LOVE
A Warner Brothers' picture filmed with a
cast headed by Frank McHugh, Patricia
Ellis, Warren Hull and Joseph Cawthorn,
and directed by William McGann. Song by
Jack Scholl and M. K. Jerome:
COLLEGIANA

GAY DESPERADO, THE
A United Artists' picture filmed with a
cast headed by Nino Martini, Ida Lupino,
Leo Carrillo and Mischa Auer, and direct-

ed by Rouben Mamoulian. Song by Holt Marvell and George Posford:
THE WORLD IS MINE TONIGHT.

GO WEST YOUNG MAN
A Paramount picture starring Mae West in a cast that included Warren William, Randolph Scott and Alice Brady, and directed by Henry Hathaway. Songs by Johnny Burke and Arthur Johnston:
I WAS SAYING TO THE MOON; ON A TYPICAL TROPICAL NIGHT and GO WEST YOUNG MAN.

HAPPY GO LUCKY
A Republic picture starring Phil Regan and Evelyn Venable, and directed by Aubrey Scotto. Songs:
RIGHT OR WRONG by Ted Koehler and Sammy Stept; A TREAT FOR THE EYES by Cliff Friend and Sammy Stept.

HEARTS DIVIDED
A First National picture starring Marion Davies and Dick Powell in a cast that included Edward Everett Horton, Charles Ruggles and Claude Rains, and directed by Frank Borzage. Songs by Al Dubin and Harry Warren:
TWO HEARTS DIVIDED and MY KINGDOM FOR A KISS.

HER MASTER'S VOICE
A Paramount picture filmed with a cast headed by Edward Everett Horton, Peggy Conklin and Laura Hope Crews, and directed by Joseph Santley. Song by Gus Kahn and Jimmy McHugh:
WITH ALL MY HEART

HERE COMES CARTER
A First National picture filmed with a cast headed by Ross Alexander, Glenda Farrell, Anne Nagel and Craig Reynolds, and directed by William Clemons. Songs by Jack Scholl and M. K. Jerome:
YOU ON MY MIND and THROUGH THE COURTESY OF LOVE.

HIGH TENSION
A 20th Century-Fox picture filmed with a cast headed by Brian Donlevy, Glenda Farrell and Norman Foster, and directed by Allan Dwan. Song by Sidney Clare:
AND THAT WOMAN MADE A MONKEY OUT OF ME

HIS BROTHER'S WIFE
An M-G-M picture starring Barbara Stanwyck and Robert Taylor in a cast that included Jean Hersholt and Joseph Calleia, and directed by W. S. Van Dyke. Song

by Harold Adamson and Walter Donaldson:
CAN'T WE FALL IN LOVE?

HOT MONEY
A Warner Brothers' picture starring Ross Alexander and Beverly Roberts, and directed by William McGann. Song by Ruth and Louis Herscher:
WHAT CAN I DO? I LOVE HIM

I'D GIVE MY LIFE
A Paramount picture filmed with a cast headed by Sir Guy Standing, Frances Drake, Tom Brown and Janet Beecher, and directed by Edward L. Marin. Song by Herb Magidson and Con Conrad:
SOME DAY WE'LL MEET AGAIN

IT'S A GREAT LIFE
A Paramount picture filmed with a cast headed by Joe Morrison, Paul Kelly, Chic Sale, Rosalind Keith and Baby LeRoy, and directed by Edward F. Cline. Songs by Leo Robin and Lewis Gensler:
I LOST MY HEART AND LAZYBONES GOTTA JOB NOW.

JUNGLE PRINCESS
A Paramount picture filmed with a cast headed by Dorothy Lamour, Ray Milland, Akim Tamiroff and Lynne Overman, and directed by William Thiele. Song by Leo Robin and Frederick Hollander:
MOONLIGHT AND SHADOWS

LET'S SING AGAIN
An RKO picture filmed with a cast headed by Bobby Breen, Henry Armetta, George Houston and Vivienne Osborne, and directed by Kurt Neumann. Song by Gus Kahn and Jimmy McHugh:
LET'S SING AGAIN

LITTLE MISS NOBODY
A Fox picture starring Jane Withers in a cast that included Jane Darwell, Ralph Morgan, Sarah Padden and Harry Carey, and directed by John Blystone. Song by Harry Tobias and Jack Stern:
THEN CAME THE INDIANS

LONGEST NIGHT, THE
An M-G-M picture filmed with a cast headed by Robert Young, Florence Rice and Ted Healy, and directed by Errol Taggart. Song by Bob Wright and Chet Forrest:
THE LONGEST NIGHT

LOVE ON THE RUN
An M-G-M picture starring Joan Crawford and Clark Gable in a cast that in-

cluded Franchot Tone, and directed by W. S. Van Dyke. Song by Gus Kahn and Franz Waxman:
GONE

MOON'S OUR HOME, THE
A Paramount picture filmed with a cast headed by Margaret Sullavan, Henry Fonda and Charles Butterworth, and directed by William A. Seiter. Song by Leo Robin and Frederick Hollander:
THE MOON'S OUR HOME

ONCE IN A BLUE MOON
A Paramount picture starring Jimmy Savo and Nikita Balieff, and directed by Ben Hecht and Charles McArthur. Song by Billy Rose and Mabel Wayne:
SUGAR COOKIE MOUNTAIN

ONE RAINY AFTERNOON
A United Artists' picture filmed with a cast headed by Frances Lederer, Ida Lupino, Hugh Herbert and Roland Young, and directed by Rowland V. Lee. Song by Harry Tobias, Ralph Irwin and Jack Stern:
ONE RAINY AFTERNOON

PICCADILLY JIM
An M-G-M picture filmed with a cast headed by Robert Montgomery, Frank Morgan, Madge Evans, Billie Burke, Robert Benchley and Ralph Forbes, and directed by Robert Z. Leonard. Songs:
NIGHT OF NIGHTS by Walter Donaldson; IN THE SHADOW OF AN OLD OAK TREE by Bob Wright and Chet Forrest.

PREVIEW MURDER MYSTERY
A Paramount picture filmed with a cast headed by Reginald Denney, Frances Drake, Gail Patrick and Rod LaRocque, and directed by Robert Florey. Song by Leo Robin and Charles Kisco:
PROMISE WITH A KISS

SAN FRANCISCO
An M-G-M picture filmed with a cast headed by Jeanette MacDonald, Clark Gable, Spencer Tracy and Jack Holt, and directed by W. S. Van Dyke. Songs:
SAN FRANCISCO by Gus Kahn and Bronislaw Kaper; WOULD YOU? by Arthur Freed and Nacio Herb Brown; THE ONE LOVE by Gus Kahn, Bronislaw Kaper and Walter Jurmann.

SINNER TAKE ALL
An M-G-M picture filmed with a cast headed by Bruce Cabot, Margaret Lindsay and Joseph Calleia, and directed by Errol Taggart. Song by Walter Donaldson:
I'D BE LOST WITHOUT YOU

SMALL TOWN GIRL
An M-G-M picture starring Janet Gaynor in a cast that included Robert Taylor, Binnie Barnes, Lewis Stone and Andy Devine, and directed by William A. Wellman. Song by Gus Kahn, Ed Ward and Herbert Stothart:
SMALL TOWN GIRL

SMART BLONDE
A Warner Brothers' picture filmed with a cast headed by Glenda Farrell, Barton MacLane, Winnie Shaw and Jane Wyman, and directed by Frank McDonald. Song by Jack Scholl and M. K. Jerome:
WHY DO I HAVE TO SING A TORCH SONG?

SONS O' GUNS
A Warner Brothers' picture starring Joe E. Brown and Joan Blondell in a cast that included Eric Blore and Winnie Shaw, and directed by Lloyd Bacon. Song by Al Dubin and Harry Warren:
FOR A BUCK AND A QUARTER A DAY.

STAGE STRUCK
A First National picture starring Joan Blondell and Dick Powell in a cast that included Warren William and Frank McHugh, and directed by Busby Berkeley. Songs by E. Y. Harburg and Richard Arlen:
IN YOUR OWN QUIET WAY and FANCY MEETING YOU.

STOLEN HOLIDAY
A Warner Brothers' picture starring Kay Francis in a cast that included Claude Rains and Ian Hunter, and directed by Michael Curtiz. Song by Al Dubin and Harry Warren:
STOLEN HOLIDAY

SUZI
An M-G-M picture starring Jean Harlow in a cast that included Franchot Tone, Cary Grant and Lewis Stone, and directed by George Fitzmaurice. Song by Harold Adamson and Walter Donaldson:
DID I REMEMBER?

TRAIL OF THE LONESOME PINE
A Paramount picture filmed with a cast headed by Sylvia Sidney, Fred MacMurray, Henry Fonda and Fred Stone, and directed by Henry Hathaway. Songs by Paul Francis Webster and Louis Alter:

MELODY FROM THE SKY and TWI-
LIGHT ON THE TRAIL.

TWO AGAINST THE WORLD
A First National picture starring Hum-
phrey Bogart and Beverly Roberts, and di-
rected by William McGann. Song by Jack
Scholl and M. K. Jerome:
THE MOON DOES THINGS TO ME

VOICE OF BUGLE ANN, THE
An M-G-M picture starring Lionel Barry-
more in a cast that included Maureen
O'Sullivan, Eric Linden and Dudley Digges,
and directed by Richard Thorpe. Songs by
Harold Adamson and Jimmy McHugh:
THERE'S A HOME IN THE MOUN-
TAINS and THERE'S NO TWO WAYS
ABOUT IT.

Western Films With Songs

CALIFORNIA MAIL
A Warner Brothers' picture starring Dick
Foran, Linda Perry and Ed Cobb, and di-
rected by Noel Smith. Songs by Jack Scholl
and M. K. Jerome:
LOVE BEGINS AT EVENING and
RIDIN' THE MAIL

CALL OF THE PRAIRIE
A Paramount picture starring Bill Boyd
in a cast that included Jimmy Ellison and
Muriel Evans, and directed by Howard
Bretherton. Song by Tot Seymour and Vee
Lawnhurst:
CALL OF THE PRAIRIE

HEART OF THE WEST
A Paramount picture starring Bill Boyd
in a cast that included Jimmy Ellison, Gabby Hayes and Sidney Blackmer, and directed
by Howard Bretherton. Song by Sam Coslow and Victor Young:
MY HEART'S IN THE HEART OF
THE WEST

MOONLIGHT ON THE RANGE
A DeLuxe Picture Corporation picture
filmed with a cast headed by Fred Scott
and Lois January. Songs by June Hershey
and Don Swander:
AS TIME GOES ON; RIDIN' DOWN
THE SUNDOWN TRAIL and THERE'S
GONNA BE A SHINDIG.

RED RIVER VALLEY
A Republic picture starring Gene Autry,
and directed by B. Reeves Eason. Songs by
Smiley Burnette and Gene Autry:
RED RIVER SWEETHEART; KEEN
GOIN' LITTLE PONY and HAND ME
DOWN MY TRUSTY 45.

RIO GRANDE RANGER
A Columbia picture starring Charles
Starrett and Ann Doran, and directed by
Spencer Gordon Bennett. Song by Dave
Ormont and Lee Zahler:
IN THE GLOAMIN' IN WYOMIN'

SONG OF THE SADDLE
A First National picture starring Dick
Foran and Alma Lloyd, and directed by
Louis King. Song by Jack Scholl, Ted Fior-
ito and M. K. Jerome:
UNDERNEATH A WESTERN SKY.

SONG OF THE TRAIL
An Ambassador picture starring Kermit
Maynard in a cast that included Evelyn
Brent and Fuzzy Knight, and directed by
Russell Hopton. Songs by Didheart Conn:
SONG OF THE TRAIL; MY HEART'S
ON THE PLAIN; LET ME WHISPER
MY LOVE and NELL WAS THE BELLE
OF THE PRAIRIE.

TRAIL DUST
A Paramount picture starring Bill Boyd,
and directed by Nute Watt. Songs:
TAKE ME BACK TO THOSE WIDE
OPEN SPACES and BENEATH A WEST-
ERN SKY by Harry Tobias and Jack Stern;
TRAIL DUST by Claudia Humphrey.

TRAILIN' WEST
A First National picture starring Dick
Foran and Paula Stone, and directed by
Noel Smith. Songs by Jack Scholl and M.
K. Jerome:
MOONLIGHT VALLEY and DRUMS
OF GLORY.

TREACHERY RIDES THE RANGE
A Warner Brothers' picture starring Dick
Foran and Paula Stone in a cast that in-
cluded Craig Reynolds and Monte Blue, and
directed by Frank McDonald. Songs by
Jack Scholl and M. K. Jerome:
RIDIN' HOME and LEATHER AND
STEEL.

UNKNOWN RANGER, THE
A Columbia picture starring Robert Al-
len and Martha Tibbett, and directed by
Spencer G. Bennett. Songs by Dave Ormont
and Lee Zahler:
I LOST MY HEART ON THE LONE
PRAIRIE; FRANKIE'S FLAMING FAN-
DANGO and COWBOY, COWBOY
WHERE HAVE YOU BEEN?

1 9 3 7

The "Seven Little Dwarfs" Are Box-Office Giants

It just couldn't happen, but it did! Glamour, Hollywood's chief stock in trade, suddenly ceased to be the principal magnet that drew thousands to the motion picture theater, and the flesh-and-blood stars with their gorgeous gams, come-hither eyes and seductive voices finished as runners-up in the 1937 Popularity Sweepstakes to a group of whimsical characters created with pen and brush by the artists in the Walt Disney studios—the seven little dwarfs who "whistled while they worked", broke the spell cast by the wicked old witch on Snow White, and made her wish—*Some Day My Prince Will Come*—come true.

And their fame was international. The band of the Royal British Grenadiers switched from *Pomp and Circumstance* to *Heigh Ho, Heigh Ho As Off To Work We Go* for the changing of the guard at Buckingham Palace, and even Adolf Hitler was powerless to purge them out of Germany. They were just what the doctor ordered—the shot in the arm America and the world needed as the lifting Depression clouds were joined by gathering war clouds that threatened the peace of five continents.

But the "seven little dwarfs", which drew $6,000,000 at American and Canadian box-offices alone, weren't the only out-of-place characters that came to Hollywood in 1937. "Jolting Joe" DiMaggio of the New York Yankees went down swinging as a screen personality in *Manhattan Merry-Go-Round,* and Walter Winchell, the columnist, demonstrated that the pen is mightier than the movie script in two pictures—*Love and Hisses* and *Wake Up And Live,* both with songs by Mack Gordon and Harry Revel, who owed their start in Tin Pan Alley to the rave notices Winchell gave them.

Out of the storied past of the theater came Joe Weber and Lew Fields to make their Hollywood bow in *Blossoms On Broadway* and revive on the screen the stage characters of "Mike Dillpickle" and "Meyer Bockheister" that made their music hall famous in the Gay Nineties' days of Lillian Russell's glory, and Metro-Goldwyn-Mayer in a nostalgic moment dusted off the scores of Sigmund Romberg's *Maytime* and Rudolf Friml's *The Firefly* to provide Jeanette MacDonald with songs to sing in her two starring films of 1937.

Dick Powell rode high as a singing lead in *Hollywood Hotel, Varsity Show, The Singing Marine* and *On The Avenue,* the latter with *I've Got My Love To Keep Me Warm, This Year's Kisses, The Girl On The Police Gazette* and other Irving Berlin songs. George Murphy, an amateur boxing champion in his college days and the son of Mike Murphy, the University of Pennsyl-

vania track coach, with Alice Faye faced the cameras for the first time as
a song-and-dance team. Deanna Durbin's golden voice gave her star billing in *Three Smart Girls* and *One Hundred Men And A Girl*. And Kenny
Baker springboarded from the Jack Benny radio program onto the screen to
be featured in *The King And The Chorus Girl* and *Turn Off The Moon* and
to be starred in *Mr. Dodd Takes The Air*.

George Gershwin, breaking away from Broadway, found inspiration in
the sunkist California climate for two musicals: *Damsel in Distress,* starring
Joan Fontaine and Fred Astaire, and *Shall We Dance?* with Ginger Rogers
sharing headline honors with Astaire, while Cole Porter's *Rosalie,* starring
Eleanor Powell and Nelson Eddy, was made memorable by both the title
song and *In The Still Of The Night*.

But an author-composer from Hawaii, Harry Owens, took the top honors
in the sharps-and-flats department with *Sweet Leilani,* the Oscar-winning
song of 1937 that was inspired by his infant daughter and introduced by
Bing Crosby in *Waikiki Wedding*. That, however, was the only Oscar to be
garnered by a Hollywood musical in a year when the Ten Best Picture
awards went to *The Life Of Emil Zola, The Good Earth, Captains Cour-
ageous, Lost Horizon, A Star Is Born, Romeo And Juliet, Stage Door, Dead
End, Winterset* and *The Awful Truth*.

Musicals

ALI BABA GOES TO TOWN
A 20th Century-Fox picture starring Ed-
die Cantor in a cast that included Tony
Martin, Roland Young and June Lang, and
directed by David Butler. Songs:
LAUGH YOUR WAY THROUGH
LIFE; SWING IS HERE TO SWAY; I'VE
GOT MY HEART SET ON YOU; VOTE
FOR HONEST ABE and ARABANIA by
Mack Gordon and Harry Revel; TWI-
LIGHT IN TURKEY by Raymond Scott.

ARTISTS AND MODELS
A Paramount picture filmed with a cast
headed by Jack Benny, Ida Lupino, Gail
Patrick, Richard Arlen, Martha Raye and
Connee Boswell, and directed by Raoul
Walsh. Songs:
POP GOES THE BUBBLE, PUBLIC
ENEMY NO. 1 and STOP YOU'RE
BREAKING MY HEART by Ted Koehler
and Burton Lane; WHISPERS IN THE
DARK by Leo Robin and Frederick Hol-
lander; I HAVE EYES by Leo Robin and
Ralph Rainger; MR. ESQUIRE by Ted
Koehler and Victor Young.

BLOSSOMS ON BROADWAY
A Paramount picture filmed with a cast
headed by Edward Arnold, Shirley Ross,
Lew Fields and Joe Weber, and directed by
Richard Wallace. Songs:
BLOSSOMS ON BROADWAY by Leo
Robin and Ralph Rainger; NO RING ON
HER FINGER and YOU CAN'T TELL
A MAN BY HIS HAT by Frank Loesser
and Manning Sherwin.

BROADWAY MELODY OF 1937
An M-G-M picture filmed with a cast
headed by Eleanor Powell, Robert Taylor,
George Murphy, Judy Garland, Sophie
Tucker, Willie Howard and Robert Bench-
ley, and directed by Roy Del Ruth. Songs
by Arthur Freed and Nacio Herb Brown:
I'M FEELING LIKE A MILLION;
YOUR BROADWAY AND MY BROAD-
WAY; A PAIR OF NEW SHOES; YOURS
AND MINE; SUN SHOWERS and
BROADWAY RHYTHM.

CHAMPAGNE WALTZ, THE
A Paramount picture starring Gladys
Swarthout in a cast that included Fred

94   [1937]

MacMurray, Jack Oakie and Volez and
Yolanda, and directed by Edward Suther-
land. Songs:
BLUE DANUBE WALTZ by Leo Robin
and Johann Strauss; COULD I BE IN
LOVE? by Leo Robin and William Daly;
THE MERRY-GO ROUND by Ann Ron-
ell; PARADISE IN WALTZ TIME by Sam
Coslow and Frederick Hollander; WHEN
IS A KISS NOT A KISS? by Leo Robin
and Burton Lane; THE CHAMPAGNE
WALTZ by Milton Drake, Ben Oakland
and Con Conrad.

DAMSEL IN DISTRESS

An RKO picture starring Fred Astaire
and Joan Fontaine in a cast that included
Burns and Allen and Ray Noble and his
orchestra, and directed by George Stevens.
Songs by Ira and George Gershwin:
FOGGY DAY; THINGS ARE LOOK-
ING UP; I CAN'T BE BOTHERED
NOW; NICE WORK IF YOU CAN GET
IT; THE JOLLY TAR AND THE MILK-
MAID and STIFF UPPER LIP.

DAY AT THE RACES, A

An M-G-M picture starring the Marx
Brothers in a cast that included Allan Jones
and Maureen O'Sullivan, and directed by
Sam Wood. Songs by Gus Kahn, Walter
Jurmann and Bronislaw Kaper:
BLUE VENETIAN WATERS; ALL
GOD'S CHILLUN GOT RHYTHM; TO-
MORROW IS ANOTHER DAY and A
MESSAGE FROM THE MAN IN THE
MOON.

DOUBLE OR NOTHING

A Paramount picture starring Bing Crosby
in a cast that included Martha Raye, Mary
Carlisle and Andy Devine, and directed by
Theodore Reed. Songs:
IT'S ON, IT'S OFF and AFTER YOU
by Al Siegal and Sam Coslow; DOUBLE
OR NOTHING by Johnny Burke and Vic-
tor Young; DON'T LOOK NOW by Irving
Kahal and Johnny Green; LISTEN MY
CHILDREN AND SMARTY (YOU
KNOW IT ALL SMARTY) by Arthur
Freed and Burton Lane; ALL YOU WANT
TO DO IS DANCE; THE MOON GOT
IN MY EYES and IT'S THE NATURAL
THING TO DO by Johnny Burke and Ar-
thur Johnston.

EVERY DAY'S A HOLIDAY

A Paramount picture starring Mae West
in a cast that included Edmund Lowe,
Charles Butterworth, Charles Winninger

and Louis Armstrong, and directed by A.
Edward Sutherland. Songs:
JUBILEE by Stanley Adams and Hoagy
Carmichael; FIFI and FLUTTER BY LIT-
TLE BUTTERFLY by Sam Coslow; EV-
ERY DAY'S A HOLIDAY and ALONG
THE BROADWAY TRAIL by Barry Triv-
ers and Sam Coslow.

EVERYBODY DANCE

A Gaumont-British picture filmed with a
cast headed by Ernest Truex and Cicely
Courtneidge. Songs by Mack Gordon and
Harry Revel:
MY WHAT A DIFFERENT NIGHT!;
EVERYBODY DANCE; WHAT DOES IT
GET ME? and WHY DID I MARRY A
WRESTLER?

FIFTY-SECOND STREET

A United Artists' picture filmed with a
cast headed by Ian Hunter, Leo Carrillo,
Pat Patterson, Ella Logan, Sid Silvers, Zasu
Pitts and Kenny Baker, and directed by
Harold Young. Songs by Walter Bullock and
Harold Spina:
I STILL LOVE TO KISS YOU GOOD
NIGHT; NOTHING CAN STOP ME
NOW; I'D LIKE TO SEE SOME MO' OF
SAMOA; DON'T SAVE YOUR LOVE
FOR A RAINY DAY; FIFTY-SECOND
STREET; 23-SKIDOO; LET DOWN
YOUR HAIR AND SING and WE LOVE
THE SOUTH.

FIREFLY, THE

An M-G-M picture starring Jeanette Mac-
Donald and Allan Jones, and directed by
Robert Z. Leonard. Songs:
A WOMAN'S KISS; GIANNINA MIA;
HE WHO LOVES AND RUNS AWAY;
LOVE IS LIKE A FIREFLY; SYMPA-
THY and WHEN A MAID COMES
KNOCKING AT YOUR HEART by Otto
Harbach and Rudolf Friml; DONKEY
SERENADE by Bob Wright, Chet Forrest
and Rudolf Friml.

GANGWAY

A Gaumont-British picture starring Jessie
Mathews and Barry Mackay, and directed
by Sonny Hale. Songs by Sol Lerner, Al
Hoffman and Al Goodhart:
WHEN YOU GOTTA SING YOU
GOTTA SING; LORD AND LADY
WHOOZIS; MOON OR NO MOON and
GANGWAY.

HIDEAWAY GIRL

A Paramount picture filmed with a cast
headed by Shirley Ross, Robert Cummings

and Martha Raye, and directed by George Archinbaud. Songs:

DANCING INTO MY HEART and TWO BIRDIES UP A TREE by Ralph Freed and Burton Lane; WHAT IS LOVE? by Leo Rubin, Ralph Rainger and Victor Young; BEETHOVEN, MENDELSSOHN AND LISZT by Sam Coslow.

HIGH, WIDE AND HANDSOME

A Paramount picture starring Irene Dunne in a cast that included Randolph Scott, Dorothy Lamour and Alan Hale, and directed by Rouben Mamoulian. Songs by Oscar Hammerstein II and Jerome Kern:

CAN I FORGET YOU?; ALLEGHANY AL; FOLKS WHO LOVE ON THE HILL; HIGH, WIDE AND HANDSOME; THE THINGS I WANT and CAN YOU MARRY ME TOMORROW MARIA?

HIT PARADE

A Republic picture filmed with a cast headed by Frances Langford and Phil Regan in a cast that included the orchestras of Duke Ellington and Eddie Duchin, and directed by Gus Meins. Songs:

SWEET HEARTACHE by Ned Washington and Sammy Stept; HAIL ALMA MATER by Sammy Stept; LAST NIGHT I DREAMED OF YOU; YOU'D LIKE IT; I'LL REACH FOR A STAR; THE LADY WANTS TO DANCE; WAS IT RAIN? and LOVE IS GOOD FOR ANYTHING THAT AILS YOU by Lou Handman and Walter Hirsch.

HITTING A NEW HIGH

An RKO picture starring Lili Pons in a cast that included Edward Everett Horton, Eric Blore and Jack Oakie, and directed by Raoul Walsh. Songs by Harold Adamson and Jimmy McHugh:

YOU'RE LIKE A SONG; I HIT A NEW HIGH; LET'S GIVE LOVE ANOTHER CHANCE and THIS NEVER HAPPENED BEFORE.

HOLLYWOOD HOTEL

A Warner Brothers' picture filmed with a cast headed by Dick Powell, Rosemary and Lola Lane, Hugh Herbert, Ted Healy, Glenda Farrell, Luella Parsons, Alan Mowbray and Frances Langford, and directed by Busby Berkeley. Songs by Johnny Mercer and Richard Whiting:

I'M LIKE A FISH OUT OF WATER; I'VE HITCHED MY WAGON TO A STAR; LET THAT BE A LESSON TO YOU; SILHOUETTED IN THE MOONLIGHT; HOORAY FOR HOLLYWOOD

and CAN'T TEACH MY HEART NEW TRICKS.

HOLY TERROR, THE

A 20th Century-Fox picture starring Jane Withers in a cast that included Tony Martin, Leah Ray, El Brendel and Joe Lewis, and directed by James Tinling. Songs by Sidney Clare and Harry Akst:

THERE I GO AGAIN; DON'T KNOW MYSELF SINCE I KNOW YOU; DON'T SING, EVERYBODY SWING and THE CALL OF THE SIREN.

I'LL TAKE ROMANCE

A Columbia picture starring Grace Moore in a cast that included Melvyn Douglas, Stuart Erwin and Helen Westley, and directed by Edward H. Griffith. Songs:

I'LL TAKE ROMANCE by Oscar Hammerstein II and Ben Oakland; A FRANGESA by Milton Drake and Marie Costa.

LIFE BEGINS IN COLLEGE

A 20th Century-Fox picture starring the Ritz Brothers in a cast that included Joan Davis, Tony Martin, Gloria Stuart and Fred Stone, and directed by William A. Seiter. Songs:

BIG CHIEF SWING IT; OUR TEAM IS ON THE WARPATH; FAIR LOMBARDY and WHY TALK ABOUT LOVE? by Sidney Mitchell and Lew Pollack; SWEET VARSITY SUE by Al Lewis, Charles Tobias and Murray Mencher.

LIFE OF THE PARTY

An RKO picture filmed with a cast headed by Joe Penner, Gene Raymond, Harriet Hilliard, Victor Moore and Parkyakarkas, and directed by William A. Seiter. Songs:

LET'S HAVE ANOTHER CIGARETTE; LIFE OF THE PARTY; SO YOU WON'T SING; YANKEE DOODLE BAND AND CHIRP A LITTLE DITTY by Herb Magidson and Allie Wrubel; ROSES IN DECEMBER by Herb Magidson, George Jessel and Ben Oakland.

LONDON MELODY

A Herbert Wilcox production starring Anna Neagle and Tullio Carminati. Songs by Sol Lerner, Al Goodhart and Al Hoffman:

JINGLE OF THE JUNGLE and THE EYES OF THE WORLD ARE UPON YOU.

LOVE AND HISSES

A 20th Century-Fox picture filmed with a cast headed by Walter Winchell, Ben Bernie, Simone Simon, Bert Lahr and Joan Davis, and directed by Sidney Lanfield. Songs by Mack Gordon and Harry Revel: SWEET SOMEONE; BROADWAY'S GONE HAWAIIAN; I WANT TO BE IN WINCHELL'S COLUMN; BE A GOOD SPORT and LOST IN YOUR EYES.

MAKE A WISH
An RKO picture starring Bobby Breen in a cast that included Basil Rathbone, Marion Claire, Henry Armetta, Ralph Forbes and Leon Errol, and directed by Kurt Neumann. Songs:
MAKE A WISH; MUSIC IN MY HEART and BIRCH LAKE FOREVER by Paul Francis Webster, Louis Alter and Oscar Straus; MY CAMPFIRE DREAMS and OLD MAN RIP by Paul Francis Webster and Louis Alter.

MANHATTAN MERRY-GO-ROUND
A Republic picture filmed with a cast that included Phil Regan, Leo Carrillo, Ann Dvorak, Tamara Geva, Jimmy Gleason, Ted Lewis, Cab Calloway, Kay Thompson, Joe DiMaggio, Louis Prima and Gene Autry, and directed by Charles F. Reiser. Songs:
MAMMA I WANNA MAKE RHYTHM by Jerome Jerome, Richard Byron and Walter Kent; MANHATTAN MERRY-GO-ROUND by Herman Pinkus; HAVE YOU EVER BEEN IN HEAVEN?; I OWE YOU and IT'S ROUNDUP TIME IN RENO by Jack Lawrence and Peter Tinturin.

MAYTIME
An M-G-M picture starring Jeanette MacDonald and Nelson Eddy in a cast that included John Barrymore, and directed by Robert Z. Leonard. Songs:
WILL YOU REMEMBER (SWEETHEART)?; JUMP JIM CROW; ROAD TO PARADISE and DANCING WILL KEEP YOU YOUNG by Rida Johnson Young, Cyrus Wood and Sigmund Romberg; MAYPOLE by Ed Ward; STUDENTS' DRINKING SONG; VIVE L'OPERA and STREET SINGER by Bob Wright, Chet Forrest and Herbert Stothart.

MEET THE BOY FRIEND
A Republic picture filmed with a cast headed by David Carlisle, Carol Hughes and Warren Hymer, and directed by Ralph Staub. Songs by Harry Tobias and Roy Ingraham:
SWEET LIPS (KISS MY BLUES AWAY); THIS BUSINESS OF LOVE and TO KNOW YOU CARE.

MELODY FOR TWO
A Warner Brothers' picture starring James Melton in a cast that included Patricia Ellis, Marie Wilson and Fred Keating, and directed by Louis King. Songs:
A FLAT IN MANHATTAN; AN EXCUSE FOR DANCING and JOSE O'NEILL THE CUBAN HEEL by Jack Scholl and M. K. Jerome: MELODY FOR TWO and SEPTEMBER IN THE RAIN by Al Dubin and Harry Warren.

MERRY-GO-ROUND OF 1938
A Universal picture filmed with a cast headed by Bert Lahr, Jimmy Savo and Alice Brady, and directed by Irving Cummings. Songs by Harold Adamson and Jimmy McHugh:
YOU'RE MY DISH; I'M IN MY GLORY; MORE POWER TO YOU; SIX OF ONE, HALF DOZEN OF THE OTHER and THE GRAND STREET COMEDY FOUR.

MR. DODD TAKES THE AIR
A Warner Brothers' picture starring Kenny Baker and Jane Wyman in a cast that included Frank McHugh and Alice Brady, and directed by Alfred E. Green. Songs by Al Dubin and Harry Warren:
AM I IN LOVE?; IF I WERE A LITTLE POND LILY; THE GIRL YOU USED TO BE; HERE COMES THE SANDMAN and REMEMBER ME?

MOUNTAIN MUSIC
A Paramount picture starring Martha Raye and Bob Burns, and directed by Robert Florey. Songs by Sam Coslow:
GOOD MORNIN'; IF I PUT MY HEART IN A SONG; CAN'T YOU HEAR THAT MOUNTAIN MUSIC?; THAR SHE COMES and HILLBILLY WEDDING SONG.

MUSIC FOR MADAME
An RKO picture starring Nino Martini in a cast that included Joan Fontaine, Alan Mowbrey and Billy Gilbert, and directed by John Blystone. Songs:
I WANT THE WORLD TO KNOW and MY SWEET BAMBINO by Gus Kahn and Rudolf Friml; KING OF THE ROAD by Eddie Cherkose and Nat Skilkret; MUSIC FOR MADAME by Herb Magidson and Allie Wrubel.

NEW FACES OF 1937
An RKO picture filmed with a cast headed by Joe Penner, Milton Berle and Harriet Hilliard, and directed by Leigh Jason. Songs:

LOVE IS NEVER OUT OF SEASON; IT GOES TO YOUR FEET; OUR PENTHOUSE ON THIRD AVENUE; TAKE THE WORLD OFF YOUR SHOULDERS; IF I DIDN'T HAVE YOU and IT'S THE DOCTOR'S ORDERS by Lew Brown and Sammy Fain: WIDOW IN LACE by Walter Bullock and Harold Spina: NEW FACES by Charles Henderson: PECKIN' by Ben Pollack and Harry James.

NOBODY'S BABY
An M-G-M picture with Patsy Kelly, Lyda Roberti and Lynne Overman, and directed by Gus Meins. Songs by Walter Bullock and Marvin Hatley:
QUIEN SABE; I DREAMED ABOUT THIS; ALL DRESSED UP IN RHYTHM and NOBODY'S BABY.

ON THE AVENUE
A 20th Century-Fox picture filmed with a cast headed by Dick Powell, Alice Faye, Madeleine Carroll and the Ritz Brothers, and directed by Roy Del Ruth. Songs by Irving Berlin:
HE AIN'T GOT RHYTHM; I'VE GOT MY LOVE TO KEEP ME WARM; THIS YEAR'S KISSES; THE GIRL ON THE POLICE GAZETTE; SLUMMING ON PARK AVENUE and YOU'RE LAUGHING AT ME.

READY, WILLING AND ABLE
A Warner Brothers' picture filmed with a cast headed by Ruby Keeler, Lee Dixon, Allen Jenkins, Louise Fazenda, Carol Hughes and Teddy Hart, and directed by Ray Enright. Songs by Johnny Mercer and Richard Whiting:
TOO MARVELOUS FOR WORDS; JUST A QUIET EVENING and SENTIMENTAL AND MELANCHOLY.

RENFREW OF THE MOUNTED
A Grand National picture filmed with a cast headed by James Newell, Carol Hughes, William Royle, Herbert Corthell and Chief Thundercloud, and directed by Al Herman. Songs by Betty Laidlow and Robert Lively:
TALE OF LOVE; BARBECUE BILL WAS A MOUNTIE; LITTLE SON and WE'RE MOUNTED MEN.

ROSALIE
An M-G-M picture filmed with a cast headed by Eleanor Powell, Nelson Eddy, Frank Morgan and Ray Bolger, and directed by W. S. Van Dyke. Songs by Cole Porter:
IN THE STILL OF THE NIGHT; ROSALIE; CLOSE; WHO KNOWS?; WHY

SHOULD I CARE?; I'VE A STRANGE NEW RHYTHM IN MY HEART; IT'S ALL OVER BUT THE SHOUTING; IT WASN'T MEANT FOR ME and SPRING LOVE IS IN THE AIR.

SHALL WE DANCE?
An RKO picture starring Ginger Rogers and Fred Astaire in a cast that included Harriet Hoctor, Eric Blore and Edward Everett Horton, and directed by Mark Sandrich. Songs by Ira and George Gershwin:
SLAP THAT BASS; LET'S CALL THE WHOLE THING OFF; THEY CAN'T TAKE THAT AWAY FROM ME; SHALL WE DANCE?; THEY ALL LAUGHED; I'VE GOT BEGINNER'S LUCK and WAKE UP BROTHER AND DANCE.

SING AND BE HAPPY
A 20th Century-Fox picture filmed with a cast headed by Tony Martin, Leah Ray, Joan Davis, Helen Westley and Dixie Dunbar, and directed by James Tinling. Songs by Sidney Clare and Harry Akst:
PICKLES; TRAVELIN' LIGHT; WHAT A BEAUTIFUL BEGINNING and SING AND BE HAPPY.

SINGING MARINE, THE
A Warner Brothers' picture filmed with a cast headed by Dick Powell, Doris Weston, Lee Dixon and Doc Rockwell, and directed by Ray Enright. Songs by Al Dubin, Johnny Mercer and Harry Warren:
'CAUSE MY BABY SAYS IT'S SO; I KNOW NOW; SONG OF THE MARINES; NIGHT OVER SHANGHAI; YOU CAN'T RUN AWAY FROM LOVE TONIGHT and THE LADY WHO COULDN'T BE KISSED.

SOMETHING TO SING ABOUT
A First National picture filmed with a cast headed by James Cagney, Evelyn Daw, William Frawley, Mona Barry and Gene Lockhart, and directed by Victor Swertzinger, who also contributed the following songs:
LOVING YOU; OUT OF THE BLUE; RIGHT OR WRONG; ANY OLD LOVE and SOMETHING TO SING ABOUT.

SWING HIGH SWING LOW
A Paramount picture starring Carole Lombard and Fred MacMurray in a cast that included Dorothy Lamour and Charles Butterworth, and directed by Mitchell Leisen. Songs:
IF IT ISN'T PAIN THEN IT ISN'T LOVE by Leo Robin and Ralph Rainger; SWING HIGH SWING LOW by Ralph

Freed and Burton Lane; I HEAR A CALL TO ARMS and PANAMANIA by Al Siegal and Sam Coslow; SPRING IS IN THE AIR by Ralph Freed and Charles Kisco.

SWING IT PROFESSOR

A Conn-Ambassador picture filmed with a cast headed by Pinky Tomlin and Paula Stone, and directed by Marshall Neilan. Songs by Al Heath, Connie Lee and Buddy LeRoux:
I'M SORTA KINDA GLAD I MET YOU; AN OLD-FASHIONED MELODY and I'M RICHER THAN A MILLIONAIRE.

SWING WHILE YOU'RE ABLE

A Melody Pictures' production filmed with a cast headed by Pinky Tomlin, Toby Wing, Suzanne Kaaren and Michael Romanoff. Songs:
SWING BROTHER SWING by Al Heath and Buddy LeRoux; YOU'RE MY STRONGEST WEAKNESS by Coy Poe, Buddy LeRoux and Al Heath; I'M JUST A COUNTRY BOY AT HEART by Pinky Tomlin, Connie Lee and Paul Parks; ONE GIRL IN MY ARMS by Harry Tobias and Roy Ingraham; LEAVE IT UP TO UNCLE JAKE by Paul Parks, Connie Lee, Al Heath and Buddy LeRoux; I'M GONNA SWING WHILE I'M ABLE by Paul Parks and Connie Lee.

THIN ICE

A 20th Century-Fox picture starring Sonja Henie in a cast that included Tyrone Power, Arthur Treacher and Joan Davis, and directed by Sidney Lanfield. Songs by Sidney Mitchell and Lew Pollack:
MY SECRET LOVE AFFAIR; OVER NIGHT and MY SWISS HILLBILLY.

THIS IS MY AFFAIR

A 20th Century-Fox picture starring Robert Taylor and Barbara Stanwyck in a cast that included Victor McLaglen and Brian Donlevy, and directed by William A. Seiter. Songs by Mack Gordon and Harry Revel:
I HUM A WALTZ; FILL IT UP; PUT DOWN YOUR GLASSES and PICK UP YOUR GIRL AND DANCE.

THIS WAY PLEASE

A Paramount picture starring Charles "Buddy" Rogers in a cast that included Mary Livingston, Betty Grable and Ned Sparks, and directed by Robert Florey. Songs:
IS IT LOVE OR IS IT INFATUATION? by Sam Coslow and Frederick Hollander; THIS WAY PLEASE; DELIGHTED TO MEET YOU and WHAT THIS COUNTRY NEEDS IS VOOM VOOM by Al Siegal and Sam Coslow; I'M THE SOUND EFFECTS MAN by "Jock" and George Gray.

THRILL OF A LIFETIME, THE

A Paramount picture filmed with a cast headed by Dorothy Lamour, Ben Blue, Johnny Downs and the Yacht Club Boys, and directed by George Archainbaud. Songs:
KEENO, SCREENO AND YOU; I'LL FOLLOW MY BABY; THRILL OF A LIFETIME; PARIS IN SWING and SWEETHEART TIME by Sam Coslow and Frederick Hollander; IT'S BEEN A WHOLE YEAR and IF WE COULD RUN THE COUNTRY FOR A DAY by the Yacht Club Boys.

TOP OF THE TOWN

A Universal picture filmed with a cast headed by George Murphy, Hugh Herbert, Ella Logan and Gertrude Niesen, and directed by Ralph Murphy. Songs by Harold Adamson and Jimmy McHugh:
JAMBOREE; BLAME IT ON THE RHUMBA; TOP OF THE TOWN; THAT FOOLISH FEELING; FIREMAN, FIREMAN SAVE MY CHILD; WHERE ARE YOU? and POST OFFICE (I'VE GOT TO BE KISSED).

TURN OFF THE MOON

A Paramount picture filmed with a cast headed by Johnny Downs, Charles Ruggles, Eleanor Whitney, Kenny Baker and Phil Harris and his orchestra, and directed by Lewis Seiler. Songs by Sam Coslow:
EASY ON THE EYES; LITTLE WOODEN SOLDIER; JAMMIN'; TURN OFF THE MOON and THAT'S SOUTHERN HOSPITALITY.

TWENTY-THREE AND A HALF HOURS' LEAVE

A Grand National picture starring James Ellison and Terry Walker, and directed by John G. Blystone. Songs by Ted Koehler and Sammy Stept:
GOOD NIGHT MY LUCKY DAY; NOW YOU'RE TALKING MY LANGUAGE; IT MUST BE LOVE and WE HAPPEN TO BE IN THE ARMY.

VARSITY SHOW

A Warner Brothers' picture filmed with a cast headed by Dick Powell, Ted Healy, Rosemary and Priscilla Lane, Walter Catlett, Emma Dunn, Johnny Davis, Buck and

Bubbles and Fred Waring and His Pennsylvanians, and directed by William Keighley. Songs by Johnny Mercer and Richard Whiting:

HAVE YOU GOT ANY CASTLES BABY?; WE'RE WORKING OUR WAY THROUGH COLLEGE; OLD KING COLE; ON WITH THE DANCE; YOU'VE GOT SOMETHING THERE; MOONLIGHT ON THE CAMPUS; LOVE IS ON THE AIR TONIGHT; LET THAT BE A LESSON TO YOU and WHEN YOUR COLLEGE DAYS ARE GONE.

WAIKIKI WEDDING

A Paramount picture starring Bing Crosby in a cast that included Bob Burns, Martha Raye and Shirley Ross, and directed by Frank Tuttle. Songs:

SWEET IS THE WORD FOR YOU; IN A LITTLE HULA HEAVEN; BLUE HAWAII; OKOLEHAO and NANI ONA PUA by Leo Robin and Ralph Rainger: SWEET LEILANI by Harry Owens.

WAKE UP AND LIVE

A 20th Century-Fox picture filmed with a cast headed by Walter Winchell, Alice Faye, Ben Bernie and Patsy Kelly, and directed by Sidney Lanfield. Songs by Mack Gordon and Harry Revel:

NEVER IN A MILLION YEARS; THERE'S A LULL IN MY LIFE; WAKE UP AND LIVE; IT'S SWELL OF YOU; OH, BUT I'M HAPPY; I LOVE YOU TOO MUCH MUCHACHA and I'M BUBBLING OVER.

WALLABY JIM OF THE ISLANDS

A First National picture filmed with a cast headed by George Houston, Ruth Coleman and Douglas Walton, and directed by Charles Lamont. Songs:

HI-HO-HUM; LA ORANA; MOON OVER THE ISLANDS and THE LADY WITH TWO LEFT FEET by Felix Bernard

and Irving Bibo: FAIR HAWAII and WHEN A BLUEJACKET RIDES THE WAVES by Betty Laidlow and Robert Lively.

WALTER WANGER'S VOGUES OF 1938

A United Artists' picture starring Joan Bennett and Warren Baxter, and directed by Irving Cummings. Songs:

LOVELY ONE by Frank Loesser and Manning Sherwin; TURN ON THE RED HOT HEAT (BURN THE BLUES AWAY) by Paul Francis Webster and Louis Alter; THAT OLD FEELING by Lew Brown and Sammy Fain; KING OF JAM by Louis Alter.

YOU CAN'T HAVE EVERYTHING

A 20th Century-Fox picture starring Alice Faye and Don Ameche in a cast that included the Ritz Brothers, Tony Martin, Louis Prima and Rubinoff, and directed by Norman Taurog. Songs:

YOU CAN'T HAVE EVERYTHING; AFRAID TO DREAM; THE LOVELINESS OF YOU; PLEASE PARDON US WE'RE IN LOVE and DANGER — LOVE AT WORK by Mack Gordon and Harry Revel; RHYTHM ON THE RADIO by Louis Prima; IT'S A SOUTHERN HOLIDAY by Louis Prima, Jack Loman and Dave Franklin.

YOU'RE A SWEETHEART

A Universal picture starring Alice Faye and George Murphy in a cast that included Ken Murray and Charles Winninger, and directed by David Butler. Songs:

YOU'RE A SWEETHEART; BROADWAY JAMBOREE; MY FINE FEATHERED FRIEND; WHO KILLED MAGGIE? and OH, OH OKLAHOMA by Harold Adamson and Jimmy McHugh; HONKY DORY by Charles Henderson; SCRAPING THE TOAST by Murray Mencher and Charles Tobias; SO IT'S LOVE by Mickey Bloom and Arthur Quenzer.

Feature Films With Songs

ANGEL

A Paramount picture starring Marlene Dietrich in a cast that included Herbert Marshall, Melvyn Douglas, Edward Everett Horton and Laura Hope Crews, and directed by Ernest Lubitsch. Song by Leo Robin and Frederick Hollander:

ANGEL

AWFUL TRUTH, THE

A Columbia picture starring Irene Dunne in a cast that included Cary Grant and

Ralph Bellamy, and directed by Leo McCarey. Songs by M. Drake and Ben Oakland:

MY DREAMS ARE GONE WITH THE WIND and I DON'T LIKE MUSIC.

BARRIER, THE

A Paramount picture filmed with a cast headed by Jean Parker and Leo Carrillo, and directed by Leslie Selander. Songs by Harry Tobias and Jack Stern:

MOONLIT PARADISE and SONG OF THE WILD.

BIG TOWN GIRL

A 20th Century-Fox picture filmed with a cast headed by Claire Trevor, Donald Woods and Alan Dinehart, and directed by Alfred Werker. Songs by Sidney Clare and Harry Akst:

ARGENTINE SWING; I'LL SETTLE FOR LOVE and DON'T THROW KISSES.

BREEZING HOME

A Universal picture filmed with a cast headed by William Gargan, Binnie Barnes and Wendy Barrie, and directed by Milton Carruth. Songs:

YOU'RE IN MY HEART AGAIN and I'M HITTING THE HIGH SPOTS by Harold Adamson and Jimmy McHugh; UNWANTED by Charles Previn.

BRIDE WORE RED, THE

An M-G-M picture starring Joan Crawford in a cast that included Franchot Tone, Robert Young, Billie Burke and Reginald Owen, and directed by Dorothy Arzner. Song by Gus Kahn and Franz Waxman:

WHO WANTS LOVE?

CAPTAINS COURAGEOUS

An M-G-M picture starring Freddie Bartholomew and Lionel Barrymore in a cast that included Spencer Tracy and Melvyn Douglas, and directed by Victor Fleming. Songs by Gus Kahn and Franz Waxman:

DON'T CRY LITTLE FISH and OOH, WHAT A TERRIBLE MAN!

CONFESSION

A Warner Brothers' picture starring Kay Francis in a cast that included Ian Hunter and Basil Rathbone, and directed by Joseph May. Song by Jack Scholl and Peter Kreuder:

ONE HOUR OF ROMANCE

CRIMINAL LAWYER

An RKO picture filmed with a cast headed by Lee Tracy, Eduardo Ciannelli, Erik Rhodes and Betty Lawford, and directed by Christy Cabanne. Song by Harry Tobias and Jack Stern:

TONIGHT LOVER TONIGHT

DANGER: LOVE AT WORK

An M-G-M picture starring Ann Sothern in a cast that included Jack Haley, Mary Boland, Edward Everett Horton and John Carradine, and directed by Otto L. Preminger. Song by Mack Gordon and Harry Revel:

DANGER: LOVE AT WORK

DANGER PATROL

An RKO picture filmed with a cast headed by Sally Eilers, John Beal and Harry Carey, and directed by Lew Landers. Songs:

SWEETER ALL THE TIME by Lyle Tomerlin and Andy Iona Long; I CAN'T WALTZ ALONE by Dorothy Fields and Max Steiner; MORNING GLORY by Joe Young and Max Steiner.

DAUGHTER OF SHANGHAI

A Paramount picture starring Anna May Wong in a cast that included Buster Crabbe and Charles Bickford, and directed by Robert Florey. Song by Ralph Freed and Frederick Hollander:

IT'S RAINING IN SHANGHAI

EASY LIVING

A Paramount picture starring Jean Arthur and Edward Arnold, and directed by Mitchell Leisen. Song by Leo Robin and Ralph Rainger:

EASY LIVING

EBBTIDE

A Paramount picture filmed with a cast headed by Oscar Homolka, Frances Farmer, Ray Milland, Lloyd Nolan and Barry Fitzgerald, and directed by James Hogan. Songs by Leo Robin and Ralph Rainger:

I KNOW WHAT ALOHA MEANS and EBBTIDE.

ECSTACY

A Jewell production, filmed in Europe, that introduced Hedy Lamarr to American audiences in the few theaters where this picture was permitted to be shown over the protests of the League Of Deceny. Musical numbers:

DOWN THE GYPSY TRAIL; LOST IN ECSTACY; LOVE AWAKENS IN THE SPRING; OH PLAY TZIGANI; WHAT DO GYPSIES DREAM? and THIS MUST BE LOVE by a number of Viennese composers.

EVER SINCE EVE

A Warner Brothers' picture starring Marion Davies and Robert Montgomery in a cast that included Frank McHugh and Patsy Kelly, and directed by Lloyd Bacon. Songs:

WREATHS OF FLOWERS by S. Hoopii Haaia; EVER SINCE EVE by Jack Scholl and M. K. Jerome; SHINE ON HARVEST MOON by Jack Northworth and Nora Bayes.

FIGHT FOR YOUR LADY

An RKO picture starring John Boles and Ida Lupino, and directed by Ben Stoloff. Song by Frank Loesser and Harry Akst:

BLAME IT ON THE DANUBE

GO-GETTER, THE
A Warner Brothers' picture filmed with a cast headed by George Brent, Anita Louise and Charles Winninger, and directed by Busby Berkeley. Song by Jack Scholl and M. K. Jerome:
IT SHALL BE DONE

GOLD RACKET, THE
A Grand National picture filmed with a cast headed by Conrad Nagel, Eleanor Hunt and Fuzzy Knight, and directed by Louis J. Gasnier. Songs:
HITCH HIKE LADY by Arthur Kay; BROKEN DOWN MAMA by Fuzzy Knight; I'D LIKE TO BE THE BUTTONS ON YOUR VEST by Julie Cruze; IF YOU'RE NICE TO ME by Sammy Stept.

GOOD MORNING, BOYS
A British-Gaumont picture starring Lilli Palmer. Song by Sol Lerner, Al Goodhart and Al Hoffman:
BABY WHATCHA GONNA DO TO-NIGHT?

HEIDI
A 20th Century-Fox picture starring Shirley Temple in a cast that included Jean Hersholt, Helen Westley, Arthur Treacher, Mary Nash and Mady Christians, and directed by Allan Dwan. Songs by Sidney Mitchell and Lew Pollack:
MY LITTLE WOODEN SHOES and HAPPY ENDING.

HER HUSBAND LIES
A Paramount picture filmed with a cast headed by Gail Patrick, Ricardo Cortez, Akim Tamiroff and Tom Brown, and directed by Edward Ludwig. Songs by Ralph Freed and Burton Lane:
NO MORE TEARS and YOU GAMBLED WITH LOVE.

HIGH FLYERS
An RKO picture starring Bert Wheeler and Robert Woolsey in a cast that included Lupe Velez, and directed by Edward Cline. Song by Herman Ruby and Dave Dreyer:
KEEP YOUR HEAD ABOVE WATER

HURRICANE, THE
A United Artists's picture starring Dorothy Lamour and Jon Hall in a cast that included Mary Astor, C. Aubrey Smith, Thomas Mitchell and Raymond Massey, and directed by John Ford. Song by Frank Loesser and Alfred Newman:
MOON OF MANAKOORA

I MET HIM IN PARIS
A Paramount picture starring Claudette Colbert in a cast that included Melvyn Douglas and Robert Young, and directed by Wesley Ruggles. Song by Helen Meinardi and Hoagy Carmichael:
I MET HIM IN PARIS

IT'S ALL YOURS
A Columbia picture starring Madeleine Carroll in a cast that included Francis Lederer and Mischa Auer, and directed by Elliott Nugent. Song by Milton Drake and Ben Oakland:
IF THEY GAVE ME A MILLION

KID GALAHAD
A Warner Brothers' picture starring Bette Davis and Edward G. Robinson in a cast that included Humphrey Bogart and Wayne Morris, and directed by Michael Curtiz. Song by Jack Scholl and M. K. Jerome:
THE MOON IS IN TEARS TONIGHT

KING AND THE CHORUS GIRL, THE
A Warner Brothers' picture starring Joan Blondell and Fernand Gravet in a cast that included Edward Everett Horton, Alan Mowbrey, Mary Nash, Jane Wyman, Kenny Baker and Shaw and Lee, and directed by Mervyn LeRoy. Songs by Ted Koehler and Werner Heymann:
FOR YOU and RUE DE LA PAIX

KING OF GAMBLERS
A Paramount picture starring Claire Trevor and Lloyd Nolan, and directed by Robert Florey. Song by Ralph Freed and Burton Lane:
I'M FEELING HIGH

KING SOLOMON'S MINES
A Gaumont-British picture filmed with a cast headed by Sir Cedric Hardwicke, Paul Robeson, Roland Young, John Loder and Anna Lee, and directed by Robert Stevenson. Songs by Eric Maschwitz and Mischa Spoliansky:
CLIMBING UP, CLIMBING UP and HO! HO!

LIFE BEGINS WITH LOVE
A Columbia picture starring Jean Parker and Douglas Montgomery, and directed by Raymond B. McCarey. Song by Bennee Russell and Ben Oakland:
WHAT MAKES YOU SO SWEET?

LIVING ON LOVE
An RKO picture filmed with a cast headed by James Dunn, Whitney Bourne and Joan

Woodbury, and directed by Lew Landers. Song by Dorothy Fields and Oscar Levant:
DON'T MENTION LOVE TO ME

LOVE IS NEWS
A 20th Century-Fox picture filmed with a cast headed by Loretta Young, Don Ameche and Tyrone Power, and directed by Tay Garnett. Song by Sidney Mitchell and Lew Pollack:
LOVE IS NEWS

MADAME X
An M-G-M picture starring Gladys George in a cast that included John Beal, Warren William and Reginald Owen, and directed by Sam Wood. Song by Bob Wright, Chet Forrest and Walter Donaldson:
YOU'RE SETTING ME ON FIRE

MAKE WAY FOR TOMORROW
A Paramount picture filmed with a cast headed by Victor Moore, Beulah Bondi, Fay Bainter and Thomas Mitchell, and directed by Leo McCarey. Song by Leo Robin, Sam Coslow and Jean Schwartz:
MAKE WAY FOR TOMORROW

MAMA STEPS OUT
An M-G-M picture filmed with a cast headed by Guy Kibbe, Alice Brady and Betty Furness, and directed by George B. Seitz. Songs by Bob Wright and Chet Forrest:
BURNT FINGERS and BE CAREFUL OF MY HEART.

MAN OF THE PEOPLE
An M-G-M picture filmed with a cast headed by Joseph Calleia, Florence Rice and Thomas Mitchell, and directed by Edwin L. Marin. Song by Chet Forrest, Bob Wright and Walter Donaldson:
LET ME DAY-DREAM

MANNEQUIN
An M-G-M picture starring Joan Crawford in a cast that included Spencer Tracy and Ralph Morgan, and directed by Frank Borzage. Song by Chet Forrest, Bob Wright and Edward Ward:
ALWAYS AND ALWAYS

MARKED WOMAN
A Warner Brothers' picture starring Bette Davis and Humphrey Bogart in a cast that included Lola Lane. Song by Al Dubin and Harry Warren:
MY SILVER DOLLAR MAN

MIDNIGHT MADONNA
A Paramount picture filmed with a cast headed by Warren William, Mady Correll,

Kitty Clancy and Edward Ellis, and directed by James Flood. Song by Johnny Burke and Arthur Johnston:
LOVE DIDN'T KNOW ANY BETTER

O. H. M. S.
A Gaumont-British picture filmed with a cast headed by Wallace Ford, John Mills and Anna Lee. Song by Sol Lerner, Al Goodhart and Al Hoffman:
TURNING THE TOWN UPSIDE DOWN

OFF TO THE RACES
A 20th Century-Fox picture filmed with a cast headed by Slim Summerville, Jed Prouty, Shirley Deane and Spring Byington, and directed by Frank Strayer. Song by L. Wolfe Gilbert and Felix Bernard:
MEET THE FAMILY

OLD SOAK, THE
An M-G-M picture starring Wallace Beery in a cast that included Janet Beecher and Una Merkel, and directed by J. Walter Ruben. Song by Chet Forrest, Bob Wright and Walter Donaldson:
YOU'VE GOT A CERTAIN SOMETHING

ON AGAIN, OFF AGAIN
An RKO picture starring Bert Wheeler and Robert Woolsey in a cast that included Majorie Lord, and directed by Edward Cline. Songs by Herman Ruby and Dave Dreyer:
THANKS TO YOU and ONE HAPPY FAMILY.

ONE HUNDRED MEN AND A GIRL
A Universal picture starring Deanna Durbin in a cast that included Adolphe Menjou, Alice Brady and Leopold Stokowski and his symphony orchestra, and directed by Henry Koster. Songs:
IT'S RAINING SUNBEAMS by Sam Coslow and Frederick Hollander; A HEART THAT'S FREE by R. J. Robyn and T. Railey.

OVER THE WALL
A Warner Brothers' picture filmed with a cast headed by Dick Foran and June Travis, and directed by Frank McDonald. Songs by Jack Scholl and M. K. Jerome:
HAVE YOU MET MY LULU? and THE LITTLE WHITE HOUSE ON THE HILL.

PICK A STAR
An M-G-M picture filmed with a cast headed by Patsy Kelly, Jack Haley, Rosina Lawrence, Mischa Auer and Lyda Roberti,

and directed by Edward Sedgwick. Song by
Johnny Lange and Fred Stryker:
WITHOUT YOUR LOVE

RACKETEERS IN EXILE
A Columbia picture starring George Ban-
croft and Evelyn Venable, and directed by
Erle C. Kenton. Song by Milton Royce and
Joseph Myrow:
SOMETHING HAS HAPPENED

RHYTHM IN THE CLOUDS
A Republic picture starring Patricia Ellis
and Warren Hull, and directed by John H.
Auer. Songs by Walter Hirsch and Lou
Handman:
DON'T EVER CHANGE; HAWAIIAN
HOSPITALITY and TWO HEARTS ARE
DANCING.

RIDING ON AIR
An RKO picture starring Joe E. Brown
in a cast that included Guy Kibbe and Flor-
ence Rice, and directed by Edward Sedg-
wick. Song by Henry Cohen and Edward
Sedgwick:
I'M TIRED OF TRYING TO MAKE
YOU CARE

SAN QUENTIN
A First National picture starring Humph-
rey Bogart in a cast that included Ann Sheri-
dan and Pat O'Brien, and directed by Lloyd
Bacon. Song by Al Dubin and Harry Warren:
HOW COULD YOU?

SARATOGA
An M-G-M picture starring Jean Harlow
and Clark Gable in a cast that included
Lionel Barrymore, Frank Morgan, Walter
Pidgeon, Una Merkel and Cliff Edwards,
and directed by John Conway. Songs by Chet
Forrest, Bob Wright and Walter Donaldson:
THE HORSE WITH THE DREAMY
EYES and SARATOGA.

SEVENTH HEAVEN
A 20th Century-Fox picture starring Simone Simon and James Stewart, and directed by Henry King. Song by Sidney Mitchell and Lew Pollack:
SEVENTH HEAVEN

SHEIK STEPS OUT, THE
A Republic picture filmed with a cast
headed by Ramon Novarro, Lola Lane and
Gene Lockhart, and directed by Irving Pich-
el. Songs:
RIDE WITH THE WIND by Felix Bern-
ard and Dick Tharp; SONG OF THE
SANDS by Elsie Janis and Alberto Columbo.

SOULS AT SEA
A Paramount picture filmed with a cast
headed by Gary Cooper, George Raft and
Frances Dee, and directed by Henry Hatha-
way. Song by Leo Robin and Ralph Rainger:
SUSIE SAPPLE

SUNSET IN VIENNA
A Gaumont-British picture starring Lilli
Palmer and Tullio Carminati. Songs by Sol
Lerner, Al Goodhart and Al Hoffman:
WE'LL NEVER RUN SHORT OF
LOVE and SUNSET IN VIENNA.

SWEETHEART OF THE NAVY
A Grand National picture filmed with a
cast headed by Eric Linden, Cecilia Parker,
Roger Imhof and Bernadene Hayes, and di-
rected by Duncan Mansfield. Songs by Harry
Tobias and Jack Stern:
I WANT YOU TO WANT ME and
SWEETHEART OF THE NAVY.

TAKE MY TIP
A Herbert Wilcox production starring Jack
Hulbert and Cicely Courtneidge. Songs by
Sol Lerner, Al Goodhart and Al Hoffman:
I WAS ANYTHING BUT SENTIMEN-
TAL and BIRDIE OUT OF A CAGE.

TALENT SCOUT
A Warner Brothers' picture starring Donald Woods and Jeanne Madden, and directed
by William Clemons. Song by Jack Scholl
and M. K. Jerome:
BORN TO LOVE

THEY GAVE HIM A GUN
An M-G-M picture filmed with a cast
headed by Gladys George, Spencer Tracy
and Franchot Tone, and directed by W. S.
Van Dyke. Song by Gus Kahn and Sigmund
Romberg:
A LOVE SONG OF LONG AGO

THINK FAST MR. MOTO
A 20th Century-Fox picture starring Peter
Lorre in a cast that included Virginia Field
and Thomas Beck, and directed by Norman
Foster. Song by Sidney Clare and Harry
Akst:
THE SHY VIOLET

THOROUGHBREDS DON'T CRY
An M-G-M picture starring Judy Garland
and Mickey Rooney in a cast that included
Sophie Tucker, and directed by Alfred E.
Green. Songs by Arthur Freed and Nacio
Herb Brown:
SUN SHOWERS and GOT A PAIR OF
NEW SHOES.

THREE SMART GIRLS
A Universal picture filmed with a cast headed by Deanna Durbin, Binnie Barnes, Alice Brady, Ray Milland and Charles Winninger, and directed by Henry Koster. Songs by Gus Kahn, Bronislaw Kaper and Walter Jurmann:
SOMEONE TO CARE FOR ME and MY HEART IS SINGING.

TOAST OF NEW YORK
An RKO picture filmed with a cast headed by Edward Arnold, Cary Grant, Jack Oakie and Frances Farmer, and directed by Rowland V. Lee. Songs by Allie Wrubel and Nat Shilkret:
THE FIRST TIME I SAW YOU and OOH LA LA.

TOPPER, THE
An M-G-M picture filmed with a cast headed by Constance Bennett, Cary Grant, Roland Young and Billie Burke, and directed by Norman Z. McLeod. Song by Hoagy Carmichael:
OLD MAN MOON

TRUE CONFESSION
A Paramount picture starring Carole Lombard and Fred MacMurray in a cast that included John Barrymore and Una Merkel, and directed by Wesley Ruggles. Song by Sam Coslow and Frederick Hollander:
TRUE CONFESSION

WELLS FARGO
A Paramount picture filmed with a cast headed by Joel McCrea, Bob Burns, Frances Dee, Lloyd Nolan and Johnny Mack Brown, and directed by Frank Lloyd. Song by Ralph Freed and Burton Lane:
WHERE I AIN'T BEEN BEFORE

WHEN LOVE IS YOUNG
A Universal picture filmed with a cast headed by Virginia Bruce, Kent Taylor and Walter Brennan, and directed by Hal Mohr. Songs by Harold Adamson and Jimmy McHugh:
DID ANYONE EVER TELL YOU? and WHEN LOVE IS YOUNG.

WHEN YOU'RE IN LOVE
A Columbia picture starring Grace Moore in a cast that included Cary Grant, Aline MacMahon and Thomas Mitchell, and directed by Robert Raskin. Songs by Dorothy Fields and Jerome Kern:
OUR SONG and THE WHISTLING SONG.

WHEN'S YOUR BIRTHDAY?
An RKO picture filmed with a cast headed by Joe E. Brown, Marian Nash and Fred Keating, and directed by Harry Beaumont. Song by Basil Adlam, Alex Hager and Al Stillman:
I LOVE YOU FROM COAST TO COAST

WILD AND WOOLLY
A 20th Century-Fox picture starring Jane Withers in a cast that included Walter Brennan, Pauline Moore and Jackie Searl, and directed by Alfred Werker. Song by Sidney Clare and Harry Akst:
WHOA WHOOPIE, WHOA WHIPPY

WINGS OVER HONOLULU
A Universal picture starring Wendy Barrie and Ray Milland, and directed by H. C. Potter. Song by Frank Skinner and Charles Henderson:
WASN'T IT YOU?

YOU ONLY LIVE ONCE
A United Artists' picture starring Sylvia Sidney and Henry Fonda in a cast that included Barton MacLane. Song by Paul Francis Webster and Louis Alter:
A THOUSAND DREAMS OF YOU

Western Films With Songs

BIG SHOW, THE
A Republic picture starring Gene Autry in a cast that included Smiley Burnette, Kay Hughes and Sally Payne, and directed by Mack V. Wright. Songs:
THE LADY KNOWN AS LULU by Ned Washington and Sammy Stept; MAD ABOUT YOU by Ted Koehler and Sammy Stept.

DEVIL'S SADDLE LEGION
A Warner Brothers' picture starring Dick Foran and Anne Nagel, and directed by Bobby Connolly. Song by Jack Scholl and M. K. Jerome:
MY TEXAS HOME

DODGE CITY TRAIL
A Columbia picture starring Charles Starrett in a cast that included Donald Grayson and Marian Weldon, and directed by C. C. Coleman. Songs by Ned Washington and Sammy Stept:
STRIKE WHILE THE IRON IS HOT; PANCHO'S WIDOW; LONESOME RIVER and OUT IN THE COW COUNTRY.

GUNS OF THE PECOS

A First National picture starring Dick Foran and Anne Nagel, and directed by Noel Smith. Songs by Jack Scholl and M. K. Jerome:

WHEN A COWBOY TAKES A WIFE and THE PRAIRIE IS MY HOME.

PARTNERS OF THE PLAINS

A Paramount picture starring Bill Boyd in a cast that included Harvey Clark, Russell Hayden and Gwen Gaze, and directed by Leslie Selander. Song by Ralph Freed and Burton Lane:

MOONLIGHT ON THE SUNSET TRAIL

ROLL ALONG COWBOY

A 20th Century-Fox picture starring Smith Ballew, and directed by Gus Meins. Songs by Harry Tobias and Roy Ingraham:

ON THE SUNNY SIDE OF THE ROCKIES and STARS OVER THE DESERT.

ROLLIN' PLAINS

A Grand National picture starring Tex Ritter and Harriet Spencer, and directed by Al Herman. Song by Walter Samuels, Leonard Whitcup and Teddy Powell:

ROLLIN' PLAINS

ROUGH RIDING RHYTHM

An Ambassador-Conn picture starring Kermit Maynard and Mary Hayes. Song by Gene Autry and Odie Thompson:

I HATE TO SAY GOODBYE TO THE PRAIRIE

SANDFLOW

A Universal picture starring Buck Jones and Lita Chevret, and directed by Leslie Selander. Song by Betty Laidlow and Robert Lively:

WE ARE THE RANGERS

SPRINGTIME IN THE ROCKIES

A Republic picture starring Gene Autry in a cast that included Smiley Burnette and Polly Rowles, and directed by Joseph Kane. Songs:

GIVE ME A PONY AND AN OPEN PRAIRIE by Gene Autry and Frank Harford; DOWN IN THE LAND OF ZULU and HAYRIDE WEDDIN' IN JUNE by Gene Autry and Johnny Marvin.

Feature Cartoon With Songs

SNOW WHITE AND THE SEVEN DWARFS

An RKO-Walt Disney production with songs by Larry Morey and Frank Churchill:

HEIGH HO; JUST WHISTLE WHILE YOU WORK; SOME DAY MY PRINCE WILL COME; I'M WISHING; ONE SONG; WITH A SMILE AND A SONG; THE WASHING SONG; ISN'T THIS A SILLY SONG?; BUDDLE-UDDLE-UM-DUM; MUSIC IN YOUR SOUP and YOU'RE NEVER TOO OLD TO BE YOUNG.

The *Seven Dwarfs* sing "Heigh Ho, Heigh Ho, It's Off To Work We Go."

1 9 3 8

Bob Hope Acquires A Theme Song And The Midas Touch

The gold rush that marked the early days of the talkies was ancient history in 1938, but a sharp-nosed comedian, English-born, Cleveland-bred and Broadway-trained, had a hunch "thar was gold in them thar hills" man-made on the Paramount lot and started to do a bit of prospecting. He was no stranger to the moving picture camera, having worked for two years in Universal and Vitaphone shorts, and in his first feature length film, *The Big Broadcast of 1938,* he not only discovered a theme song, *Thanks For The Memory,* which incidentally won the Oscar as the best song of the year, but struck gold—tons of it, not only for himself but for the studio that hired him as proven by the fact that Bob Hope has been one of the biggest box-office draws for the past fifteen years.

Although Bing Crosby, Bob Hope's vis-a-vis on the screen and the golf course, continued to be a top attraction in *Dr. Rhythm* and *Sing You Sinners,* Hollywood's singing kids—the moppets and the teen-agers—stole the 1938 spotlight. Shirley Temple was starred in *Little Miss Broadway, Just Around The Corner* and *Rebecca Of Sunnybrook Farm,* and Bobby Breen had headline billing in *Breaking The Ice* and *Hawaii Calls,* the latter introducing Irvin S. Cobb as a film actor. Judy Garland at the age of fifteen gained fresh laurels in *Listen Darling, Everybody Sing* and *Love Finds Andrew Hardy,* the first of the series in which she co-starred with Mickey Rooney, a year her senior, and Deanna Durbin at sixteen was a full-fledged songbird in *Mad About Music* and *That Certain Age.* In fact, the pint-size stars brought such king-size receipts to the box-office that Columbia featured a troupe of midgets as synthetic competition in *The Terror Of Tiny Town.*

In this year of "youth must be served", however, the adult performers managed to garner their share of rave notices. Don Ameche, who later specialized on inventor's roles, raised his baritone voice in song in two pictures that were voted among the Ten Best Films of the year: *Alexander's Ragtime Band* and *In Old Chicago,* in each of which he shared headline billing with Tyrone Power and Alice Faye.

Ginger Rogers and Fred Astaire continued to dance to starlit heights in *Carefree,* which with *Alexander's Ragtime Band,* gave Irving Berlin credit for contributing songs to two top-rated musicals of 1938. Nelson Eddy and Jeanette MacDonald revived some of Victor Herbert's immortal music in a screen version of *Sweethearts,* and in addition, appeared in *The Girl Of The Golden West* with an original score by Sigmund Romberg. And Irene Dunne found the music written by Jerome Kern for *The Joy Of Living* ideally suited to her voice.

The Republic studios, which had Gene Autry under contract, added another singing cowboy to its roster of hard-ridin', gun-totin' heroes by putting its brand on Leonard Slye, a radio singer from the wide open spaces of Cincinnati, who changed his name to Roy Rogers and rode to stardom in four 1938 films, while 20th Century-Fox put spurs, chaps and a ten-gallon hat on Lou Gerhig and featured the indestructible first baseman of the New York Yankees in the western thriller *Rawhide*.

Nineteen-thirty-eight also found two comparatively new Hollywood lyricists on the threshold of Tin Pan Alley fame: Johnny Burke, who later became with Jimmy Van Heusen, Bing Crosby's favorite songwriters and Frank Loesser, who had three 1938 smash song hits to his credit in *I Fall In Love With You Every Day, Small Fry* and *Two Sleepy People,* the last two with music by Hoagy Carmichael.

But this year of triumph had its note of sorrow, since it brought to the screen the last music to be written by George Gershwin, who had suffered a fatal brain tumor during the summer of 1937 while he was working on the score for the *Goldwyn Follies*. Gershwin, who had first caught the popular fancy with his *Swanee,* exited from the stage of life as he had made his entrance into Tin Pan Alley—with a hit, the haunting *Love Walked In*. And that's exactly how this musical perfectionist would have wanted to walk out.

Musicals

ALEXANDER'S RAGTIME BAND
A 20th Century-Fox picture filmed with a cast headed by Tyrone Power, Alice Faye, Don Ameche, Jack Haley and Ethel Merman, and directed by Henry King. Songs by Irving Berlin:
NOW IT CAN BE TOLD; MY WALKING STICK; ALEXANDER'S RAGTIME BAND and I'M MARCHING ALONG WITH TIME.

ALL-AMERICAN SWEETHEART
A Columbia picture filmed with a cast headed by Patricia Farr, Scott Colton and Gene Morgan, and directed by Lambert Hillyer. Songs by Milton Drake and Ben Oakland:
POP GOES THE BOTTLE; TURN ON THE TAP; MY KID SISTER and THE FIGHT SONG (with Paul Mertz).

ARTISTS AND MODELS ABROAD
A Paramount picture filmed with a cast headed by Jack Benny, Joan Bennett, Mary Boland and the Yacht Club Boys, and directed by Mitchell Leisen. Songs:
WHAT HAVE YOU GOT THAT GETS ME?; YOU'RE LOVELY MADAME and

DO THE BUCKAROO by Leo Robin and Ralph Rainger; YOU'RE BROKE YOU DOPE by Jack Rock and the Yacht Club Boys.

BIG BROADCAST OF 1938
A Paramount picture filmed with a cast headed by W. C. Fields, Martha Raye, Dorothy Lamour, Shirley Ross and Bob Hope, and directed by Mitchell Leisen. Songs:
THANKS FOR THE MEMORY; DON'T TELL A SECRET TO A ROSE; YOU TOOK THE WORDS RIGHT OUT OF MY HEART; MAMA THAT MOON IS HERE AGAIN; THIS LITTLE RIPPLE HAS RHYTHM and THE WALTZ LIVES ON by Leo Robin and Ralph Rainger; ZUNI ZUNI by Tito Guizar; SAWING A WOMAN IN HALF by Jack Rock.

BREAKING THE ICE
An RKO picture starring Bobby Breen in a cast that included Dolores Costello and Charles Ruggles, and directed by Edward F. Cline. Songs:
HAPPY AS A LARK; PUT YOUR HEART IN A SONG and THE SUNNY SIDE OF THINGS by Paul Francis Webster

and Frank Churchill; TELLING MY
TROUBLES TO A MULE and GOOD-
BYE MY DREAMS GOODBYE by Paul
Francis Webster and Victor Young.

CAREFREE

An RKO picture starring Ginger Rogers
and Fred Astaire in a cast that included
Jack Carson and Ralph Bellamy, and di-
rected by Mark Sandrich. Songs by Irving
Berlin:
CHANGE PARTNERS; I USED TO BE
COLOR BLIND; THE YAM and THE
NIGHT IS FILLED WITH MUSIC.

COCOANUT GROVE

A Paramount picture starring Fred Mac-
Murray and Harriet Hilliard in a cast that
included Ben Blue, Eve Arden and the
Yacht Club Boys, and directed by Alfred
Santell. Songs:
YOU LEAVE ME BREATHLESS by
Ralph Freed and Frederick Hollander;
SAYS MY HEART by Frank Loesser and
Burton Lane; DREAMY HAWAIIAN
MOON and COCOANUT GROVE by
Harry Owens; TEN EASY LESSONS by
"Jock", Frank Loesser and Burton Lane;
TWO BITS A PAIR by "Jock"; SWAMI
SONG by Alfred Santell and Burton Lane;
THE MUSKETEERS' SONG by Bert Kal-
mar, Harry Ruby and the Yacht Club Boys;
THE FOUR OF US WENT TO SEA by
the Yacht Club Boys.

COLLEGE SWING

A Paramount picture filmed with a cast
headed by Burns and Allen, Bob Hope, Mar-
tha Raye, Betty Grable and Jackie Cooper,
and directed by Raoul Walsh. Songs:
I FALL IN LOVE WITH YOU EVERY
DAY; WHAT A RHUMBA DOES TO
ROMANCE and THE OLD SCHOOL
BELL by Frank Loesser and Manning Sher-
win; MOMENTS LIKE THIS; HOW'DJA
LIKE TO LOVE ME and WHAT DID
ROMEO SAY TO JULIET? by Frank Loes-
ser and Burton Lane; COLLEGE SWING by
Frank Loesser and Hoagy Carmichael.

COWBOY FROM BROOKLYN

A Warner Brothers' picture filmed with a
cast headed by Dick Powell, Pat O'Brien,
Priscilla Lane, Dick Foran and Ann Sheri-
dan, and directed by Lloyd Bacon. Songs:
I'VE GOT A HEARTFUL OF MUSIC;
I'LL DREAM TONIGHT and RIDE TEN-
DERFOOT RIDE by Johnny Mercer and
Richard Whiting; COWBOY FROM
BROOKLYN by Johnny Mercer and Harry
Warren.

DOCTOR RHYTHM

A Paramount picture starring Bing Crosby
in a cast that included Mary Carlisle, Bea-
trice Lillie, Andy Devine and Sterling Hollo-
way, and directed by Frank Tuttle. Songs by
Johnny Burke and Jimmy Monaco:
MY HEART IS TAKING LESSONS;
THIS IS MY NIGHT TO DREAM; ON
THE SENTIMENTAL SIDE; DOCTOR
RHYTHM; ONLY A GYPSY KNOWS;
P. S. 43 and TRUMPET PLAYER'S LA-
MENT.

EVERYBODY SING

An M-G-M picture filmed with a cast
headed by Allan Jones, Fanny Brice, Judy
Garland, Reginald Owen and Billie Burke,
and directed by Edwin L. Marin. Songs:
SWING MR. MENDELSSOHN SWING;
THE ONE I LOVE; DOWN ON MELODY
FARM; THE SHOW MUST GO ON; THE
SUN NEVER SETS ON SWING and
NEVER WAS THERE SUCH A PERFECT
DAY by Gus Kahn, Bronislaw Kaper and
Walter Jurmann; BETWIXT AND BE-
TWEEN by Neville Fleeson and Mabel
Wayne; QUAINTY DAINTY ME and
WHY? BECAUSE by Bert Kalmar and
Harry Ruby.

FRESHMAN YEAR, THE

A Universal picture filmed with a cast
headed by Constance Moore, William Lundi-
gan, Dixie Dunbar and Ernest Truex, and
directed by Frank McDonald. Songs:
CHASIN' YOU AROUND by Frank
Loesser and Irving Actman; AIN'T THAT
MARVELOUS and SWING THAT
CHEER by Joe McCarthy and Harry Barris.

GAIETY GIRLS

A United Artists' picture starring Jack
Hulbert and Patricia Ellis, and directed by
Thornton Freeland. Songs by William Ker-
nell and Mischa Spoliansky:
WHEN YOU HEAR MUSIC; IT'S A
PARADISE FOR TWO and KISS ME
GOOD NIGHT.

GARDEN OF THE MOON

A Warner Brothers' picture filmed with
a cast headed by Pat O'Brien, Margaret
Lindsay and John Payne, and directed by
Busby Berkeley. Songs:
THE GIRL FRIEND OF THE WHIRL-
ING DERVISH; THE GARDEN OF THE
MOON; LOVE IS WHERE YOU FIND
IT; THE LADY ON THE 2c STAMP and
CONFIDENTIALLY by Johnny Mercer and
Harry Warren; THE UMBRELLA MAN
by V. Rose, Larry Stock and J. Cavanaugh.

GIRL OF THE GOLDEN WEST
An M-G-M picture starring Nelson Eddy and Jeanette MacDonald in a cast that included Walter Pidgeon, Leo Carrillo and Cliff Edwards, and directed by Robert Z. Leonard. Songs by Gus Kahn and Sigmund Romberg:
SENORITA; SOLDIERS OF FORTUNE; FROM SUN-UP TO SUNDOWN; WHO ARE WE TO SAY?; THERE'S A BRAND NEW SONG IN TOWN; MARIACHIE; THE GOLDEN WEST and THE WEST AIN'T WILD ANYMORE.

GIVE ME A SAILOR
A Paramount picture filmed with a cast headed by Bob Hope, Martha Raye and Betty Grable, and directed by Elliott Nugent. Songs by Leo Robin and Ralph Rainger:
WHAT GOES ON HERE IN MY HEART?; THE U. S. A. AND YOU; A LITTLE KISS AT TWILIGHT and IT DON'T MAKE SENSE.

GOING PLACES
A Warner Brothers' picture filmed with a cast headed by Dick Powell, Anita Louise and Allen Jenkins, and directed by Ray Enright. Songs by Johnny Mercer and Harry Warren:
JEEPERS - CREEPERS; MUTINY IN THE NURSERY; OH WHAT A HORSE WAS CHARLEY and SAY IT WITH A KISS.

GOLD DIGGERS IN PARIS
A Warner Brothers' picture filmed with a cast headed by Rudy Vallee, Rosemary Lane and Hugh Herbert, and directed by Ray Enright. Songs by Al Dubin and Harry Warren:
THE LATIN QUARTER; I WANNA GO BACK TO BALI; DAY DREAMING ALL NIGHT LONG (Lyrics by Johnny Mercer); A STRANGER IN PAREE; PUT THAT DOWN IN WRITING; WALTZ OF THE FLOWERS and MY ADVENTURE (Lyrics by Johnny Mercer).

GOLDWYN FOLLIES
A United Artists' picture filmed with a cast that included Adolphe Menjou, the Ritz Brothers, Zorina, Kenny Baker, Andrea Leeds, Helen Jepson, Phil Baker, Ella Logan and Bobby Clark, and directed by George Marshall. Songs:
LOVE WALKED IN; LOVE IS HERE TO STAY; I LOVE TO RHYME and I WAS DOING ALL RIGHT by Ira and George Gershwin; SPRING AGAIN and I'M NOT COMPLAINING by Ira Gershwin and Kurt Weill; HERE PUSSY PUSSY by Ray Golden and Sid Kuller.

GREAT WALTZ, THE
An M-G-M picture starring Luise Rainer and Fernand Gravet, and directed by Julien Duvivier. Songs by Oscar Hammerstein II, based on the melodies of Johann Strauss:
TALES OF THE VIENNA WOODS; VOICES OF SPRING; DU UNT DU; THE BAT; I'M IN LOVE WITH VIENNA; ONE DAY WHEN WE WERE YOUNG; REVOLUTIONARY MARCH and THERE'LL COME A TIME.

HAPPY LANDING
A 20th Century-Fox picture starring Sonja Henie in a cast that included Don Ameche, Cesar Romero and Ethel Merman, and directed by Roy Del Ruth. Songs:
HOT AND HAPPY; YONNY AND HIS OOMPAH; YOU ARE THE MUSIC TO THE WORDS IN MY HEART and A GYPSY TOLD ME by Jack Yellen and Samuel Pokrass; YOU APPEAL TO ME by Walter Bullock and Harold Spina.

HAVING A WONDERFUL TIME
An RKO picture starring Ginger Rogers and Douglas Fairbanks Jr. in a cast that included Lucille Ball and Peggy Conklin, and directed by Alfred Santell. Songs:
NIGHTY NIGHT and THE BAND PLAYED OUT OF TUNE by Charles Tobias and Sammy Stept; MY FIRST IMPRESSION OF YOU and HAVING A WONDERFUL TIME by Bill Livingston.

HOLD THAT CO-ED
A 20th Century-Fox picture filmed with a cast headed by John Barrymore, George Murphy, Marjorie Weaver and Joan Davis, and directed by George Marshall. Songs:
HERE AM I DOING IT and HOLD THAT CO-ED by Mack Gordon and Harry Revel; LIMPY DIMP by Sidney Clare, Nick Castle and Jule Styne; HEADS HIGH by Lew Brown and Lew Pollack.

JOSETTE
A 20th Century-Fox picture starring Simone Simon and Don Ameche in a cast that included Robert Young, Bert Lahr and Joan Davis, and directed by Allan Dwan. Songs by Mack Gordon and Harry Revel:
WHERE IN THE WORLD; IN ANY LANGUAGE and MAY I DROP A PETAL IN YOUR GLASS OF WINE?

JOY OF LIVING
An RKO picture starring Irene Dunne in a cast that included Douglas Fairbanks Jr.,

Alice Brady, Guy Kibbe and Lucille Ball, and directed by Tay Garnett. Songs by Dorothy Fields and Jerome Kern:
YOU COULDN'T BE CUTER; JUST LET ME LOOK AT YOU; WHAT'S GOOD ABOUT GOOD NIGHT? and A HEAVENLY PARTY.

JUST AROUND THE CORNER
A 20th Century-Fox picture starring Shirley Temple in a cast that included Joan Davis, Charles Farrell, Bill Robinson and Bert Lahr, and directed by Irving Cummings. Songs by Walter Bullock and Harold Spina:
THIS IS A HAPPY LITTLE DITTY; BRASS BUTTONS AND EPAULETS; I LOVE TO WALK IN THE RAIN; I'M NOT MYSELF TODAY and I'LL ALWAYS BE LUCKY WITH YOU.

KENTUCKY MOONSHINE
A 20th Century-Fox picture starring the Ritz Brothers in a cast that included Tony Martin, Marjorie Weaver, Slim Summerville and John Carradine, and directed by David Butler. Songs:
MOONSHINE OVER KENTUCKY; ISN'T IT WONDERFUL, ISN'T IT SWELL?; SING A SONG OF HARVEST and REUBEN, REUBEN I'VE BEEN SWINGING by Sidney Mitchell and Lew Pollack; KENTUCKY OPERA by Sidney Clare and Jule Styne.

LADY OBJECTS, THE
A Columbia picture starring Lanny Ross and Gloria Stuart in a cast that included Joan Marsh, and directed by Clifford Boughton. Songs by Oscar Hammerstein II and Ben Oakland:
A MIST OVER THE MOON; THAT WEEK IN PARIS; HOME IN YOUR ARMS; WHEN YOU'RE IN THE ROOM; SKY HIGH; NAUGHTY NAUGHTY (I'M SURPRISED AT YOU) and VICTORY SONG (Lyrics by Milton Drake).

LISTEN DARLING
An M-G-M picture starring Judy Garland in a cast that included Freddie Bartholomew, Mary Astor and Walter Pidgeon, and directed by Edward L. Marin. Songs:
TEN PINS IN THE SKY by Joseph McCarthy and Milton Ager; ON THE BUMPY ROAD TO LOVE by Al Lewis, Al Hoffman and Murray Mencher; ZING WENT THE STRINGS OF MY HEART by James Hanley.

LITTLE MISS BROADWAY
A 20th Century-Fox picture starring Shirley Temple in a cast that included George Murphy, Jimmy Durante, Phyllis Brooks and Edna May Oliver, and directed by Irving Cummings. Songs by Walter Bullock and Harold Spina:
WE SHOULD BE TOGETHER; BE OPTIMISTIC; HOW CAN I THANK YOU?; IF ALL THE WORLD WERE PAPER; SWING ME AN OLD-FASHIONED SONG; LITTLE MISS BROADWAY; I'LL BUILD A BROADWAY FOR YOU and HOP, SKIP AND JUMP (with Jimmy Durante).

LITTLE MISS ROUGHNECK
A Columbia picture filmed with a cast headed by Edith Fellows, Leo Carrillo, Jacqueline Wells and Scott Colton, and directed by Aubrey Scotto. Songs by Milton Drake, George Jessel and Ben Oakland:
AS LONG AS I LOVE; PICKANINNY PARADISE and WHEN I TRUCK ON DOWN.

LOVE FINDS ANDY HARDY
An M-G-M picture starring Judy Garland and Mickey Rooney in a cast that included Lewis Stone and Lana Turner, and directed by George B. Seitz. Songs:
WHAT DO YOU KNOW ABOUT LOVE?; MEET THE BEAT OF MY HEART and IT NEVER RAINS BUT IT POURS by Mack Gordon and Harry Revel; IN BETWEEN by Roger Edens.

LOVE ON TOAST
A Paramount picture filmed with a cast headed by John Payne, Stella Ardler, Luis Alberni and Kenny Baker, and directed by E. A. Dupont. Songs:
I'D LOVE TO PLAY A LOVE SCENE OPPOSITE YOU and MY MISTAKE by Sam Coslow; I WANT A NEW ROMANCE by Sam Coslow and Burton Lane; I'D RATHER CALL YOU BABY by Tot Seymour and Vee Lawnhurst.

MAD ABOUT MUSIC
A Universal picture starring Deanna Durbin in a cast that included Herbert Marshall and Gail Patrick, and directed by Norman Taurog. Songs by Harold Adamson and Jimmy McHugh.
CHAPEL BELLS; I LOVE TO WHISTLE; SERENADE TO THE STARS and THERE ISN'T A DAY GOES BY.

MY LUCKY STAR
A 20th Century-Fox picture starring Sonja Henie in a cast that included Richard Green, Cesar Romero and Joan Davis, and

directed by Roy Del Ruth. Songs by Mack Gordon and Harry Revel:
I'VE GOT A DATE WITH A DREAM; COULD YOU PASS IN LOVE? THIS MAY BE THE NIGHT and THE ALL-AMERICAN SWING.

OUTSIDE OF PARADISE
A Republic picture starring Phil Regan and Penny Singleton, and directed by John H. Auer. Songs by Jack Lawrence and Peter Tinturin:
A SWEET IRISH SWEETHEART OF MINE; OUTSIDE OF PARADISE; SHENANIGANS; ALL FOR ONE AND ONE FOR ALL and A LITTLE BIT OF EVERYTHING.

RADIO CITY REVELS
An RKO picture filmed with a cast headed by Bob Burns, Jack Oakie, Kenny Baker, Ann Miller and Victor Moore, and directed by Benjamin Stoloff. Songs by Herb Magidson and Allie Wrubel:
GOOD NIGHT ANGEL; SPEAK YOUR HEART; TAKE A TIP FROM THE TULIP; I'M TAKING A SHINE TO YOU; SWINGING IN THE CORN; THERE'S A NEW MOON OVER THE OLD MILL; YOU'RE THE APPLE OF MY EYE YOU LITTLE PEACH; MORNING GLORIES IN THE MOONLIGHT; WHY MUST I LOVE YOU? and (I PROMISE TO) LOVE HONOR AND OH, BABY.

RASCALS
A 20th Century-Fox picture starring Jane Withers in a cast that included Rochelle Hudson, Robert Wilcox and Borah Minnevitch and His Harmonica Rascals, and directed by H. Bruce Humberstone. Songs by Sidney Clare and Harry Akst:
BLUE IS THE EVENING; TAKE A TIP FROM A GYPSY, WHAT A GAY OCCASION and SONG OF THE GYPSY BAND.

REBECCA OF SUNNYBROOK FARM
A 20th Century-Fox picture starring Shirley Temple in a cast that included Randolph Scott, Jack Haley, Gloria Stuart, Helen Westley, Slim Summerville and Bill Robinson, and directed by Allan Dwan. Songs:
CRACKLY CORN FLAKES; ALONE WITH YOU; HAPPY ENDING and AU REVOIR by Sidney Mitchell and Lew Pollack; AN OLD STRAW HAT by Mack Gordon and Harry Revel; COME AND GET YOUR HAPPINESS by Jack Yellen and Samuel Pokrass; TOY TRUMPET by Sidney Mitchell, Lew Pollack and Raymond Scott.

ROMANCE IN THE DARK
A Paramount picture starring Gladys Swarthout and John Boles in a cast that included John Barrymore, and directed by H. C. Potter. Songs:
TONIGHT WE LOVE by Leo Robin and Ralph Rainger; BLUE DAWN by Ned Washington and Phil Boutelje; BEWITCHED BY THE NIGHT by Jay Gorney; ROMANCE IN THE DARK by Gertrude Niesen and Sam Coslow.

SALLY, IRENE AND MARY
A 20th Century-Fox picture starring Alice Faye in a cast that included Tony Martin, Fred Allen and Joan Davis, and directed by William A. Seiter. Songs:
HALF MOON ON THE HUDSON; I COULD USE A DREAM; THIS IS WHERE I CAME IN; WHO STOLE THE JAM? and HELP WANTED: MALE by Walter Bullock and Harold Spina; SWEET AS A SONG and GOT MY MIND ON MUSIC by Mack Gordon and Harry Revel.

SING YOU SINNERS
A Paramount picture starring Bing Crosby in a cast that included Fred MacMurray, Donald O'Connor, Ellen Drew and Elizabeth Patterson, and directed by Wesley Ruggles. Songs:
I'VE GOT A POCKETFUL OF DREAMS; LAUGH AND CALL IT LOVE; DON'T LET THE MOON GET AWAY and WHERE IS CENTRAL PARK? by Johnny Burke and Jimmy Monaco; SMALL FRY by Frank Loesser and Hoagy Carmichael.

START CHEERING
A Columbia picture starring Jimmy Durante in a cast that included Joan Perry, and directed by Albert S. Rogell. Songs:
MY HEAVEN ON EARTH by Charles Tobias, Phil Baker and Samuel Pokrass; YOU WALKED INTO MY LIFE and START CHEERING by Milton Drake and Ben Oakland; ROCKIN' THE TOWN and HAIL SIGMA PSI by Ted Koehler and Johnny Green; WHEN I STRUT AWAY IN MY CUTAWAY by Jimmy Durante.

STRAIGHT, PLACE AND SHOW
A 20th Century-Fox picture starring the Ritz Brothers in a cast that included Ethel Merman, Richard Arlen and Phyllis Brooks, and directed by David Butler. Songs:

WITH YOU ON MY MIND and WHY NOT STRING ALONG WITH ME? by Lew Brown and Lew Pollack: INTERNATIONAL COWBOYS by Ray Golden, Sid Kuller and Jule Styne.

SWEETHEARTS
An M-G-M picture starring Nelson Eddy and Jeanette MacDonald in a cast that included Frank Morgan, Ray Bolger, Florence Rice and Mischa Auer, and directed by W. S. Van Dyke. Songs by Chet Forrest, Bob Wright and Victor Herbert: ANGELUS; EVERY LOVER MUST MEET HIS FATE; THE GAME OF LOVE; GRANDMOTHER; IRON, IRON, IRON; MADEMOISELLE ON PARADE; PRETTY AS A PICTURE; SUMMER SERENADE; SWEETHEARTS; WAITING FOR THE BRIDE and WOODEN SHOES.

SWING SISTER SWING
A Universal picture filmed with a cast headed by Ken Murray, Johnny Downs, Kathryn Kane, Eddie Quillan and Ernest Truex, and directed by Joseph Santley. Songs by Frank Skinner and Charles Henderson: GINGHAM GOWN; JUST A BORE; WASN'T IT YOU?; KANESKI WALTZ and THE BALTIMORE BUBBLE.

SWING YOUR LADY
A Warner Brothers' picture filmed with a cast headed by Humphrey Bogart, Frank McHugh, Louise Fazenda, Nat Pendleton and Penny Singleton, and directed by Ray Enright. Songs by Jack Scholl and M. K. Jerome: THEY CUT DOWN THE OLD APPLE TREE; HILLBILLY FROM TENTH AVENUE; MOUNT SWINGAROO; SWING YOUR LADY and DIG ME A GRAVE IN MISSOURI.

SWISS MISS
An M-G-M picture starring Laurel and Hardy in a cast that included Della Lind, Walter Woolf King and Eric Blore, and directed by John Blystone. Songs by Arthur Quenzer and Phil Charig: THE CRICKET SONG; COULD YOU SAY NO TO ME? and MINE TO LOVE.

TERROR OF TINY TOWN
A Columbia picture filmed with a cast headed by Billy Curtis, Yvonne Moray and Little Billy, and directed by Sam Newfield. Songs by L. Wolfe Gilbert and Lew Porter: MR. JACK AND MRS. JILL; DOWN ON THE SUNSET TRAIL; THE DAUGHTER OF SWEET CAROLINE; LAUGH YOUR TROUBLES AWAY and HEY, LOOK OUT (I'M GONNA MAKE LOVE TO YOU).

THANKS FOR EVERYTHING
A 20th Century-Fox picture filmed with a cast headed by Adolphe Menjou, Jack Oakie, Jack Haley, Arleen Whalen, Tony Martin and Binny Barnes, and directed by William S. Seiter. Songs by Mack Gordon and Harry Revel: YOU'RE THE WORLD'S FAIREST; THREE CHEERS FOR HENRY SMITH; PUFF-A-PUFF and THANKS FOR EVERYTHING.

THAT CERTAIN AGE
A Universal picture starring Deanna Durbin in a cast that included Melvyn Douglas, Jackie Cooper and Irene Rich, and directed by Edward Ludwig. Songs by Harold Adamson and Jimmy McHugh: MY OWN; THAT CERTAIN AGE; YOU'RE AS PRETTY AS A PICTURE; BE A GOOD SCOUT and HAS ANYONE EVER TOLD YOU BEFORE?

TROPIC HOLIDAY
A Paramount picture starring Dorothy Lamour and Ray Milland, and directed by Theodore Reed. Songs: LAMP ON THE CORNER; TONIGHT WE LIVE; MY FIRST LOVE and TROPIC NIGHT by Ned Washington and Augustin Lara; HAVING MYSELF A TIME by Leo Robin and Ralph Rainger.

Feature Films With Songs

ALGIERS
A United Artists' picture starring Charles Boyer in a cast that included Sigrid Gurie, Hedy Lamarr and Joseph Calleia, and directed by John Cromwell. Songs by Ann Ronell and Vincent Scotto: C'EST LA VIE and ALGIERS

ANGELS WITH DIRTY FACES
A Warner Brothers' picture filmed with a cast headed by Jimmy Cagney, Pat O'Brien, Humphrey Bogart and Ann Sheridan, and directed by Michael Curtiz. Song by Fred Fisher and Maurice Spitalny: ANGELS WITH DIRTY FACES.

BAD MAN FROM BRIMSTONE

An M-G-M picture starring Wallace Beery in a cast that included Virginia Bruce, Dennis O'Keefe, Joseph Calleia and Lewis Stone, and directed by J. Wallace Ruben. Song by Arthur Freed, Chet Forrest and Bob Wright:
SAVE THAT LAST GRAVE FOR ME

BARRICADE

A 20th Century-Fox picture starring Alice Faye and Warner Baxter, and directed by Gregory Ratoff. Song by Lew Brown and Lew Pollack.
THERE'LL BE OTHER NIGHTS

BATTLE OF BROADWAY

A 20th Century--Fox picture filmed with a cast headed by Victor McLaglen, Brian Donlevy, Louise Hovick, Raymond Walburn and Lynn Bari, and directed by George Marshall. Song by Sidney Clare and Harry Akst:
DAUGHTER OF MADEMOISELLE

BLOCKADE

A United Artists' picture starring Madeleine Carroll and Henry Fonda in a cast that included Leo Carrillo and John Halliday, and directed by William Dieterle. Song by Ann Ronell and Werner Janssen:
BELOVED YOU'RE LOVELY

BOOLOO

A Paramount picture filmed with a cast headed by Colin Tapley, Jayne Regan and Mamo Clark, and directed by Clyde Elliott. Songs by Sam Coslow and Frederick Hollander:
BESIDE A MOONLIT STREAM and BOOLOO.

BOY MEETS GIRL

A Warner Brothers' picture filmed with a cast headed by Jimmy Cagney, Pat O'Brien, Marie Wilson, Ralph Bellamy, Frank McHugh and Dick Foran, and directed by Lloyd Bacon. Song by Jack Scholl and M. K. Jerome:
WITH A PAIN IN MY HEART.

BROADWAY MUSKETEERS

A Warner Brothers' picture starring Margaret Lindsay, Ann Sheridan and Marie Wilson in a cast that included John Litel. Songs by Jack Scholl and M. K. Jerome:
WHO SAID THAT THIS ISN'T LOVE? and HAS IT EVER OCCURRED TO YOU?

BROTHER RAT

A Warner Brothers' picture filmed with a cast headed by Priscilla Lane, Wayne Morris, Johnny Davis, Jane Bryan and Eddie Albert, and directed by William Keighly. Songs by Jack Scholl and M. K. Jerome:
THE DAY IS DONE and MY KATE.

COWBOY AND THE LADY, THE

A United Artists' picture starring Merle Oberon and Gary Cooper in a cast that included Patsy Kelly and Walter Brennan, and directed by Henry C. Potter. Songs by L. Wolfe Gilbert, Arthur Quenzer and Lionel Newman:
ER-RU-TI-TU-TI and THE COWBOY AND THE LADY.

DEVIL'S PARTY, THE

A Universal picture starring Victor McLaglen in a cast that included William Gargan, Paul Kelly and Beatrice Roberts, and directed by Ray McCarey. Song by Harold Adamson and Jimmy McHugh:
THINGS ARE COMING MY WAY

DOWN IN ARKANSAS

A Republic picture filmed with a cast headed by Ralph Byrd, Leon Weaver and Elvira, and directed by Nick Grinde. Song by Eddie Cherkose and Walter Kent:
THE FARMER'S NOT IN THE DELL

FIRST ONE HUNDRED YEARS, THE

An M-G-M picture starring Robert Montgomery and Virginia Bruce in a cast that included Warren William and Binnie Barnes, and directed by Richard Thorpe. Song by Chet Forrest and Bob Wright:
MISUNDERSTOOD

FIVE OF A KIND

A 20th Century-Fox picture filmed with a cast headed by Jean Hersholt, Claire Trevor and Cesar Romero and featuring the Dionne Quintuplets. Directed by Herbert I. Leeds. Song by Sidney Clare and Samuel Pokrass:
ALL MIXED UP

FLIRTING WITH FATE

An M-G-M picture filmed with a cast headed by Joe E. Brown, Leo Carrillo, Beverly Roberts and Wynne Gibson, and directed by Frank McDonald. Songs by Walter Samuels and Charles Newman:
RIDE BANDALEROS; MATE; THE GAUCHO GONZALES.

FOOLS FOR SCANDAL

A Warner Brothers' picture starring Carole Lombard in a cast that included Fernand Gravet, Ralph Bellamy and Allen Jenkins, and directed by Mervyn LeRoy.

Songs by Lorenz Hart and Richard Rodgers:
HOW CAN YOU FORGET? and THERE'S A BOY IN HARLEM.

GLADIATOR, THE
A Columbia picture starring Joe E. Brown in a cast that included Man Mountain Dean, June Travis and Dickie Moore, and directed by Edward Sedgwick. Song by Charles Newman and Walter Samuels:
ON TO VICTORY!

HARD TO GET
A Warner Brothers' picture starring Dick Powell and Olivia DeHaviland, and directed by Ray Enright. Songs by Johnny Mercer and Harry Warren:
YOU MUST HAVE BEEN A BEAUTIFUL BABY and THERE'S A SUNNY SIDE TO EVERY SITUATION.

HAWAII CALLS
An RKO picture starring Bobby Breen in a cast that included Ned Sparks and Irvin S. Cobb, and directed by Edward F. Cline. Songs by Harry Owens:
DOWN WHERE THE TRADE WINDS BLOW and HAWAII CALLS.

HER JUNGLE LOVE
A Paramount picture starring Dorothy Lamour and Ray Milland, and directed by George Archainbaud. Songs:
COFFEE AND KISSES and JUNGLE LOVE by Leo Robin and Ralph Rainger; LOVELIGHT IN THE STARLIGHT by Ralph Freed and Frederick Hollander.

IF I WERE KING
A Paramount picture starring Ronald Colman in a cast that included Frances Dee and Basil Rathbone, and directed by Frank Lloyd. Song by Leo Robin, Sam Coslow and Newell Chase:
IF I WERE KING

I'LL GIVE A MILLION
A 20th Century-Fox picture starring Warner Baxter in a cast that included Marjorie Weaver, Jean Hersholt and John Carradine, and directed by Walter Lang. Song by Mack Gordon and Harry Revel:
FOND OF YOU

IN OLD CHICAGO
A 20th Century-Fox picture filmed with a cast headed by Tyrone Power, Don Ameche, Alice Faye and Alice Brady, and directed by Henry King. Songs:
IN OLD CHICAGO by Mack Gordon and Harry Revel; I'LL NEVER LET YOU CRY; I'VE TAKEN A FANCY TO YOU and TAKE A DIP IN THE SEA by Sidney Clare and Lew Pollack.

INTERNATIONAL SETTLEMENT
A 20th Century-Fox picture filmed with a cast headed by Dolores Del Rio, George Sanders and June Lang, and directed by Eugene Ford. Songs:
YOU MAKE ME THAT WAY by Sidney Clare and Harry Akst; THINK TWICE by Harold Spina.

JEZEBEL
A Warner Brothers' picture starring Bette Davis in a cast that included Henry Fonda and George Brent, and directed by William Wyler. Song by Johnny Mercer and Harry Warren:
JEZEBEL

LET'S MAKE A NIGHT OF IT
A Universal picture starring Charles "Buddy" Rogers in a cast that included June Clyde and Claire Luce, and directed by Graham Cutts. Song by Michael Carr and Ord Hamilton:
ANGEL WHY DON'T YOU COME DOWN TO EARTH?

LOVE, HONOR AND BEHAVE
A Warner Brothers' picture filmed with a cast headed by Wayne Morris, Priscilla Lane, John Litel, Thomas Mitchell and Dick Foran, and directed by Stanley Logan. Song by Jacob Jacobs, Sammy Cahn and Saul Chaplin:
BEI MIR BIST DU SCHON (MEANS THAT YOU'RE GRAND)

MARIE ANTOINETTE
An M-G-M picture starring Norma Shearer in a cast that included Tyrone Power, John Barrymore, Robert Morley and Anita Louise, and directed by W. S. Van Dyke. Song by Bob Wright, Chet Forrest and Herbert Stothart:
AMOUR ETERNAL AMOUR

MEN WITH WINGS
A Paramount picture starring Fred MacMurray and Ray Milland, and directed by William A. Wellman. Song by Frank Loesser and Hoagy Carmichael:
MEN WITH WINGS

MR. CHUMP
A Warner Brothers' picture filmed with a cast headed by Johnny Davis, Lola Lane and Penny Singleton, and directed by William Clemons. Song by Johnny Mercer and Bernard Hanighen:
AS LONG AS YOU LIVE

NIGHT HAWK, THE

A Republic picture filmed with a cast headed by Robert Livingston, June Travis and Robert Armstrong, and directed by Sidney Salkow. Song by Mann Curtiss, Al Sherman and Walter Kent:
NEVER A DREAM GOES BY

PORT OF MISSING GIRLS

A Monogram picture filmed with a cast headed by Judith Allen, Milburn Stone, Harry Carey and Betty Compson, and directed by Karl Brown. Songs by Charles Rosoff:
ONE NIGHT ONE KISS AND YOU; DREAM CARGO and I'VE CHANGED MY ROUTINE.

RECKLESS LIVING

A Universal picture filmed with a cast headed by Robert Wilcox, Nan Grey and Jimmy Savo, and directed by Frank McDonald. Song by Harold Adamson and Jimmy McHugh:
WHEN THE STARS GO TO SLEEP

ROAD TO RENO, THE

A Universal picture filmed with a cast headed by Randolph Scott, Hope Hampton and Helen Broderick, and directed by S. Sylvan Simon. Songs by Harold Adamson and Jimmy McHugh:
RIDING HOME; I GAVE MY HEART AWAY and TONIGHT IS THE NIGHT.

ROMANCE ON THE RUN

A Republic picture filmed with a cast headed by Donald Wood, Craig Reynolds and Patricia Ellis, and directed by Gus Meins. Song by Jack Lawrence and Peter Tinturin:
ARE YOU A DREAMER?

ROSE OF THE RIO GRANDE

A Monogram picture starring Movita and John Carroll, and directed by William Nigh. Songs by Eddie Cherkose and Charles Rosoff:
RIDE AMIGOS RIDE; SONG OF THE ROSE and WHAT CARE I?

SAY IT IN FRENCH

A Paramount picture filmed with a cast headed by Ray Milland, Olympe Bradna, Irene Hervey, Janet Beecher and Mary Carlisle, and directed by Andrew L. Stone. Song by Helen Meinardi and Hoagy Carmichael:
APRIL IN MY HEART

SHE'S GOT EVERYTHING

An RKO picture starring Ann Sothern and Gene Raymond in a cast that included Victor Moore and Helen Broderick, and directed by Joseph Santley. Song by Leon and Otis Rene:
IT'S SLEEPY TIME IN HAWAII

SLIGHT CASE OF MURDER, A

A Warner Brothers' picture starring Edward G. Robinson in a cast that included Jane Bryant, Allen Jenkins and Ruth Donnelly, and directed by Lloyd Bacon. Song by Jack Scholl and M. K. Jerome:
HOW DO YOU DO MR. MARCO.

SONS OF THE LEGION

A Paramount picture filmed with a cast headed by Lynne Overman, Evelyn Keyes, Donald O'Connor and Elizabeth Patterson, and directed by James Hogan. Song by Ralph Freed and Frederick Hollander:
SONS OF THE LEGION

SPAWN OF THE NORTH

A Paramount picture filmed with a cast headed by George Raft, Henry Fonda and Dorothy Lamour, and directed by Henry Hathaway. Songs by Frank Loesser and Burton Lane:
I WISH I WAS THE WILLOW and I LIKE HUMP-BACKED SALMON.

STATE POLICE

A Universal picture starring John King and Constance Moore, and directed by John Rawlins. Songs by Jack Scholl and M. K. Jerome:
THE SONG IS THE THING; YOU, YOU DARLING and I'M AN OFFICER OF THE LAW.

STOLEN HEAVEN

A Paramount picture filmed with a cast headed by Gene Raymond, Olympe Bradna and Lewis Stone, and directed by Andrew L. Stone. Songs:
THE BOYS IN THE BAND by Frank Loesser and Manning Sherwin; STOLEN HEAVEN by Ralph Freed and Frederick Hollander.

SWING THAT CHEER

A Universal picture filmed with a cast headed by Tom Brown, Robert Wilcox, Andy Devine and Constance Moore, and directed by Harold Schuster. Song by Frank Loesser and Irving Actman:
CHASIN' YOU AROUND

TARNISHED ANGEL

An RKO picture filmed with a cast headed by Sally Eilers, Lee Bowman and Ann

Miller, and directed by Leslie Goodwins.
Song by Lew Brown and Sammy Fain:
IT'S THE DOCTOR'S ORDERS

TEXANS, THE
A Paramount picture starring Randolph
Scott and Joan Bennett in a cast that in-
cluded May Robson and Walter Brennan,
and directed by James Hogan. Song by Leo
Robin and Ralph Rainger:
SILVER ON THE SAGE

THANKS FOR THE MEMORY
A Paramount picture starring Bob Hope
and Shirley Ross, and directed by George
Archainbaud. Song by Frank Loesser and
Hoagy Carmichael:
TWO SLEEPY PEOPLE

THREE BLIND MICE
A 20th Century-Fox picture starring Loretta Young and Joel McCrea, and directed
by William A. Seiter. Song by Sidney Mitchell and Lew Pollack:
ISN'T IT WONDERFUL, ISN'T IT
SWELL?

THREE COMRADES
An M-G-M picture filmed with a cast
headed by Robert Taylor, Margaret Sulla-
van, Franchot Tone and Robert Young, and
directed by Frank Borzage. Songs by Chet
Forrest, Bob Wright and Franz Waxman:
YANKEE RAGTIME COLLEGE JAZZ;
COMRADE SONG; HOW CAN I LEAVE
THEE and MIGHTY FOREST.

UP THE RIVER
A 20th Century-Fox picture filmed with
a cast headed by Preston Foster, Tony Martin and Phyllis Brooks, and directed by Alfred Werker. Song by Sidney Clare and
Harry Akst:
IT'S THE STRANGEST THING

VACATION FROM LOVE
An M-G-M picture filmed with a cast
that included Dennis O'Keefe, Florence
Rice, Reginald Owen and June Knight,
and directed by George Fitzmaurice. Song
by Chet Forrest, Bob Wright and Edward
Ward:
LET'S PRETEND IT'S TRUE

VIVACIOUS LADY
An RKO picture starring Ginger Rogers
and James Stewart in a cast that included
James Ellison, Beulah Bondi and Charles

Coburn, and directed by George Stevens.
Song by George Jessel, Jack Meskill and
Ted Shapiro:
YOU'LL BE REMINDED OF ME

WALKING DOWN BROADWAY
A 20th Century-Fox picture filmed with
a cast headed by Claire Trevor, Leah Ray,
Phyllis Brooks, Dixie Dunbar, Lynn Bari,
Jayne Regan and Michael Whalen, and di-
rected by Norman Foster. Songs:
GOODBYE MY HEART (GOOD
LUCK TO YOU) by Sidney Clare and
Harry Akst; THINK TWICE by Harold
Spina.

WHO KILLED GAIL PRESTON?
A Columbia picture filmed with a cast
headed by Rita Hayworth, Don Terry and
Robert Payne, and directed by Leon Barsha.
Songs by Milton Drake and Ben Oakland:
TWELVE O'CLOCK AND ALL'S NOT
WELL and THE GREATEST ATTRAC-
TION IN THE WORLD

YOU AND ME
A Paramount picture starring Sylvia Sid-
ney and George Raft in a cast that included
Robert Cummings and Burton Lane, and
directed by Fritz Lang. Songs:
THE RIGHT GUY FOR ME by Sam
Coslow and Kurt Weill; YOU AND ME by
Ralph Freed and Frederick Hollander.

YOUNG IN HEART
A United Artists' picture starring Janet
Gaynor and Douglas Fairbanks Jr., and di-
rected by Richard Wallace. Song by Harry
Tobias and Franz Waxman:
YOUNG IN HEART

YOU'RE ONLY YOUNG ONCE
An M-G-M picture filmed with a cast
headed by Lewis Stone, Cecilia Parker,
Mickey Rooney, Fay Holden and Frank
Craven, and directed by George B. Seitz.
Song by Chet Forrest, Bob Wright and Al-
exander Hyde:
YOU'RE ONLY YOUNG ONCE

YOUTH TAKES A FLING
A Universal picture starring Andrea
Leeds and Joel McCrea, and directed by
Archie Mayo. Songs by Harold Adamson
and Jimmy McHugh:
FOR THE FIRST TIME and HEIGH-
HO THE MERRY-O.

Western Films With Songs

BILLY THE KID RETURNS
A Republic picture starring Gene Autry in a cast that included Smiley Burnette and Lynne Roberts, and directed by Joseph Kane. Songs:
BORN TO THE SADDLE and TRAIL BLAZIN' by Eddie Cherkose; SING A LITTLE SONG ABOUT ANYTHING by Eddie Cherkose and Smiley Burnette; WHEN THE SUN IS SETTING ON THE PRAIRIE by Eddie Cherkose and Alberto Columbo; WHEN I CAMPED UNDER THE STARS by Vern and Tim Spencer.

BLACK BANDIT
A Universal picture starring Bob Baker and Marjorie Reynolds, and directed by George Waggner. Songs by Fleming Allan:
MY OLD PAINT PONY AND ME; STARLIGHT ON THE PRAIRIE and COWBOY SONG FOR SALE.

BORN TO BE WILD
A Republic picture starring Ralph Byrd and Doris Weston, and directed by Joseph Kane. Songs by Jack Lawrence and Peter Tinturin:
DANGER AHEAD and A STORY AS OLD AS THE HILLS.

COME ON RANGERS
A Republic picture starring Roy Rogers and Mary Hart, and directed by Joseph Kane. Songs:
SONG OF THE WEST and LET ME HUM A WESTERN SONG by Eddie Cherkose and Walter Kent; I'VE LEARNED A LOT ABOUT WOMEN by Gene Autry and Johnny Marvin.

GHOST TOWN RIDERS
A Universal picture starring Bob Baker and Fay Shannon, and directed by George Waggner. Songs by Fleming Allan:
DOWN THE OLD HOME TRAIL; HEADIN' HOME and IT AIN'T SO ROSY ON THE RANGE.

GOLD MINE IN THE SKY
A Republic picture starring Gene Autry in a cast that included Smiley Burnette and Carol Hughes, and directed by Joseph Kane. Songs:
HUMMIN' WHEN WE'RE COMIN' ROUND THE BEND by Eddie Cherkose and Alberto Columbo; THERE'S A GOLD MINE IN THE SKY by Nick and Charles Kenny; THAT'S HOW DONKEYS WERE BORN by Eddie Cherkose and Smiley Bur-

nette; I'D LOVE TO CALL YOU SWEETHEART by Paul Ash, Joe Goodwin and Larry Shay; HIKE YA by Smiley Burnette; TUMBLEWEED TENOR by Eddie Cherkose and Smiley Burnette; AS LONG AS I HAVE MY HORSE by Gene Autry, Johnny Marvin and Fred Rose.

GUILTY TRAILS
A Universal picture starring Bob Baker and Marjorie Reynolds, and directed by George Waggner. Song by Fleming Allan:
GIVE ME A HOME ON THE PLAINS

HEADIN' EAST
A Columbia picture starring Buck Jones and Ruth Coleman, and directed by Ewing Scott. Song by Harry Tobias and Roy Ingraham:
IRRESISTIBLE YOU

LAST BARRIER, THE
A Grand National picture with songs by Milton Drake, Al Sherman and Walter Kent:
I FEEL AT HOME IN THE SADDLE; WHEN A COWBOY SINGS A DOGIE LULLABY and LET'S GO ON LIKE THIS FOREVER.

MAN FROM MUSIC MOUNTAIN
A Republic picture starring Gene Autry in a cast that included Smiley Burnette and Carol Hughes, and directed by Joseph Kane. Songs:
LOVE BURNING LOVE; THERE'S A LITTLE DESERTED TOWN; I'M BEGINNING TO CARE and GOODBYE PINTO by Gene Autry, Johnny Marvin and Fred Rose; ALL NICE PEOPLE and SHE WORKS THIRD TUB AT THE LAUNDRY by Smiley Burnette.

OLD BARN DANCE, THE
A Republic picture starring Gene Autry in a cast that included Smiley Burnette and Helen Valkis, and directed by Joseph Kane. Songs:
YOU'RE THE ONLY STAR IN MY BLUE HEAVEN by Gene Autry; THE OLD MILL by Johnny Marvin; TEN LITTLE MILES and AT THE OLD BARN DANCE by Jack Lawrence and Peter Tinturin.

PRAIRIE MOON
A Republic picture starring Gene Autry in a cast that included Smiley Burnette and Shirley Deane, and directed by Ralph Staub. Songs:

THE GIRL IN THE MIDDLE OF MY
HEART; WELCOME STRANGERS and
THE STORY OF TRIGGER JOE by Ed-
die Cherkose and Walter Kent; IN THE
JAILHOUSE NOW by Jimmy Rodgers;
THE WEST, A NEST AND YOU by
Larry Yoell and Billy Hill; RHYTHM OF
THE HOOFBEATS by Johnny Marvin.

RANGERS ROUNDUP
A Spectrum picture starring Fred Scott
in a cast that included Al St. John and
Christine McIntyre, and directed by Sam
Newfield. Song by Johnny Lange and Lew
Porter:
WILDER THAN THE WOOLLY WEST

RAWHIDE
A 20th Century-Fox picture starring Lou
Gerhig and Smith Ballew in a cast that in-
cluded Evelyn Knapp, and directed by Ray
Taylor. Songs:
WHEN A COWBOY GOES TO TOWN
by Cecil Mack and Albert Von Tilzer; A
COWBOY'S LIFE by Eddie Cherkose and
Charles Rosoff; A ROLLIN' STONE by
Bob Russell and Lionel Newman.

RHYTHM OF THE SADDLE
A Republic picture starring Gene Autry
in a cast that included Smiley Burnette and
Peggy Moran, and directed by George Sher-
man. Songs by Gene Autry, Johnny Marvin
and Fred Rose:
THE OLD TRAIL; OH, LADIES! and
MERRY-GO-ROUNDUP.

SHINE ON HARVEST MOON
A Republic picture starring Roy Rogers
in a cast that included Mary Hart and Lulu
Bell and Scotty, and directed by Joseph
Kane. Songs:
LET ME BUILD A CABIN by Eddie
Cherkose and R. Kraushner; HEADIN'
FOR THE OPEN PLAIN by Eddie Cher-
kose and Walter Kent; THE MAN IN THE
MOON IS A COWHAND by Roy Rogers.

SINGING COWGIRL, THE
A Grand National picture filmed with a
cast headed by Dorothy Page, David O'-
Brien and Vince Barnett. Songs by Milton
Drake, Al Sherman and Walter Kent:
PRAIRIE BOY; LET'S ROUNDUP
OUR DREAMS and YA GOTTA SING
LAH-DEE-DAH.

SIX GUN TRAIL
A Victory Pictures film starring Tim Mc-
Coy and Nora Lane, and directed by Sam
Newfield. Song by Johnny Lange and Lew
Porter:

MOON OVER THE PLAINS

SONGS AND BULLETS
A Spectrum picture filmed with a cast
headed by Fred Scott, Al St. John and Alice
Ardell, and directed by Sam Newfield. Song
by Johnny Lange and Lew Porter:
PRAIRIE MOON

STARLIGHT OVER TEXAS
A Monogram picture starring Tex Ritter
and Carmel LeRoux, and directed by Al
Herman. Song by Harry Tobias and Roy
Ingraham:
STARLIGHT OVER TEXAS

SUNSET TRAIL, THE
A Paramount picture starring Bill Boyd
in a cast that included Gabby Hayes and
Charlotte Wynters. Song by Stanley Cowan
and Bobby Worth:
A COWGIRL DREAMS

UNDER WESTERN SKIES
A Republic picture starring Roy Rogers
and directed by Joseph Kane. Songs:
BACK TO THE BACKWOODS; SEND
MY MAIL TO THE COUNTY JAIL;
DUST OVER THE WEST and WHEN A
COWBOY SINGS A SONG by Jack Law-
rence and Peter Tinturin; LISTEN TO THE
RHYTHM OF THE RANGE by Gene
Autry and Johnny Marvin.

UTAH TRAIL, THE
A Grand National picture starring Tex
Ritter and Adele Pearce. Songs by Frank
Harford:
GIVE ME BACK MY SADDLE (GIVE
ME BACK MY GUN); A ROAMIN' I
WILL BE and MIGHTY GOOD HOSS.

WESTERN JAMBOREE
A Republic picture starring Gene Autry
in a cast that included Smiley Burnette,
Jean Rouverol, Esther Muir and Joe Frisco,
and directed by Ralph Staub. Songs:
BALLOON SONG and I LOVE THE
MORNING by Gene Autry, Johnny Mar-
vin and Fred Rose; OLD NOVEMBER
MOON by Johnny Marvin and Gene Autry.

WHERE THE BUFFALO ROAM
A Monogram picture starring Tex Ritter.
Songs:

IN THE HEART OF THE WEST by
J. W. Smith; WHERE THE BUFFALO
ROAM and TROUBADOUR OF THE
PRAIRIE by Tex Ritter and Frank Har-
ford; IN THE HEART OF THE PRAI-
RIE and BUNKHOUSE JAMBOREE by
Larry Wollington and Louise Massey.

1 9 3 9

Judy Gets An Oscar and Jolson Gets The Gate

As a girl of sixteen, Judy Garland in 1939 scored a series of triumphs that a seasoned trouper twice her age might well have envied. She starred in the film version of Rodger and Hart's Broadway musical, *Babes In Arms,* and made it one of the most successful box-office attractions of the year. In *The Wizard Of Oz,* which was selected as one of the Ten Best Films of 1939, she not only hit the jackpot again but introduced in it the Oscar-winning song, *Over The Rainbow.* And she was voted a special Oscar by the Motion Picture Academy of Arts and Sciences for her distinguished services to the screen.

While Judy Garland was garnering these fresh garlands, the sun of another great singing star of the screen went into full eclipse as Hollywood gave Al Jolson the polite brush-off and relegated him to secondary billing, the Mammy Singer making his exit from the Hollywood scene singing the songs of another forgotten man of song—Stephen Foster—in *Swanee River* and reviving *Toot Toot Tootsie Goodbye* in *Rose Of Washington Square* as an appropriate bow-off number.

And although Hollywood forgot to remember the debt it owed the man who was largely responsible for the initial success of the talkies, the movie tycoons were in a nostalgic mood when the shooting schedules for 1939 were under discussion, and turned back the pages of Tin Pan Alley and Broadway history to the early years of the century to gain song-and-story material on which to base three film biographies.

The first was released in March when Ginger Rogers and Fred Astaire played the roles of Irene and Vernon Castle on the screen and revived the dance steps this famous pair of ballroom dancers created in the golden age of the cabaret. Five months later, movie-goers first flocked to the theaters where Bing Crosby was headlined in the *Star Maker,* a musical inspired by the achievements of Gus Edwards, a songwriter who not only wrote such enduring hits as *School Days* and *In My Merry Oldsmobile* but discovered talent in short pants and pigtails and developed scores of future stage and screen stars in his kid revues. And in December, Paramount released *The Great Victor Herbert,* a picture that paid posthumous tribute to the dean of American light opera composers and brought to the screen a Texas girl who became the toast of Broadway ten years later—Mary Martin, who "washed that man"—Ezio Pinza—"right out of her hair" in *South Pacific.*

The achievements of Judy Garland, the exit of Al Jolson, the screen debut of Mary Martin all emphasized a Hollywood trend. Like Gus Edwards, Hollywood was constantly on the prowl for new talent, discovering it in the most unusual places, and grooming it for stardom. Neither was this quest confined solely to acting talent. It led to the discovery of new songwriters, new directors, new producers. In the latter category was a former lyricist who with Nacio Herb Brown wrote some of the early hits of the talkies, Arthur Freed, who made his debut as a producer with *Babes In Arms* and now tops the field in fashioning screen musicals that make top money at the box-office.

Musicals

BABES IN ARMS
An M-G-M picture starring Judy Garland and Mickey Rooney in a cast that included Charles Winninger and Guy Kibbe, and directed by Busby Berkeley. Songs: WHERE OR WHEN; THE LADY IS A TRAMP and BABES IN ARMS by Lorenz Hart and Richard Rodgers; I CRIED FOR YOU by Arthur Freed, Gus Arnheim and Abe Lyman; GOD'S COUNTRY by E. Y. Harburg and Harold Arlen; GOOD MORNING and YOU ARE MY LUCKY STAR by Arthur Freed and Nacio Herb Brown.

BALALAIKA
An M-G-M picture starring Nelson Eddy and Ilona Massey in a cast that included Charles Ruggles, Frank Morgan, Joyce Compton, Walter Woolf King and C. Aubrey Smith, and directed by Reinhold Schunzel. Songs: AT THE BALALAIKA; TANYA; RIDE COSSACK RIDE; SHADOWS ON THE SAND and TALE OF THE TAILORS by Bob Wright, Chet Forrest and Herbert Stothart; BENEATH THE WINTER'S SNOWS; IN A HEART AS BRAVE AS YOUR OWN and SOLDIERS OF THE CZAR by Gus Kahn and Sigmund Romberg; HOW MANY MILES TO GO by M. Glinka and Herbert Stothart; THE MAGIC OF YOUR LOVE by Gus Kahn and Franz Lehar; MY HEART IS A GYPSY by Gus Kahn and Bronislaw Kaper.

BROADWAY SERENADE
An M-G-M picture starring Jeanette MacDonald in a cast that included Ian Hunter, Lew Ayers and Frank Morgan, and directed by Robert Z. Leonard. Songs: NO TIME TO ARGUE by Gus Kahn and Sigmund Romberg; TIME CHANGES EVERYTHING BUT LOVE by Gus Kahn and Walter Donaldson; FOR EVERY LONELY HEART and BROADWAY SERENADE by Gus Kahn and Herbert Stothart; HIGH FLYIN' and ONE LOOK AT YOU by Bob Wright, Chet Forrest and Ed Ward.

CAFE SOCIETY
A Paramount picture starring Madeleine Carroll and Fred MacMurray in a cast that included Shirley Ross, and directed by Edward H. Gifford. Songs: KISS ME WITH YOUR EYES by Frank Loesser and Burton Lane; PARK AVENUE GIMP by Frank Loesser and Leo Shuken; WITHOUT YOUR LOVE by Harry Tobias and Dave Oppenheim.

DAY AT THE CIRCUS, A
An M-G-M picture starring Groucho, Chico and Harpo Marx in a cast that included Kenny Baker and Eve Arden, and directed by Mervyn Le Roy. Songs by E. Y. Harburg and Harold Arlen: LYDIA THE TATTOOED LADY; TWO BLIND LOVES; STEP UP AND TAKE A BOW and SWINGALI.

EAST SIDE OF HEAVEN
A Universal picture starring Bing Crosby in a cast that included Joan Blondell, Mischa Auer, C. Aubrey Smith and Irene Hervey, and directed by David Butler. Songs by Johnny Burke and Jimmy Monaco: HANG YOUR CLOTHES ON A HICKORY LIMB; THAT SLY OLD GENTLEMAN FROM FEATHERBED LANE; SING A SONG OF MOONBEAMS and EAST SIDE OF HEAVEN.

FIRST LOVE
A Universal picture starring Deanna Durbin in a cast that included Robert Stack, Helen Parrish and Eugene Pallette, and directed by Henry Koster. Songs: SYMPATHY; A CHANGE OF HEART and DESERTED by Ralph Freed and Frank Skinner; SPRING IN MY HEART (based on a melody by Johann Strauss); AMAPOLA by Reginald Connelly and Joseph M. Lacalle.

GREAT VICTOR HERBERT, THE

A Paramount picture starring Walter Connolly in the title role in a cast that included Allan Jones, Mary Martin, Lee Bowman, Judith Barrett and Susanna Foster, and directed by Andrew L. Stone. Music by Victor Herbert with names of lyricists in parentheses:

SOMEDAY (William LeBaron); AL FRESCO; THINE ALONE (Henry Blossom); PUNCHINELLO; ALL FOR YOU (Henry Blossom); KISS ME AGAIN (Henry Blossom); ABSINTHE FRAPPE (Glen MacDonough); ROSE OF THE WORLD (Glen MacDonough); A KISS IN THE DARK (B. G. DeSylva); MARCH OF THE TOYS (Glen MacDonough); NEAPOLITAN LOVE SONG (Henry Blossom); THERE ONCE WAS AN OWL (Harry B. Smith); AH SWEET MYSTERY OF LIFE (Rida Johnson Young); TO THE LAND OF MY OWN ROMANCE (Harry B. Smith); I'M FALLING IN LOVE WITH SOMEONE (Rida Johnson Young) and I MIGHT BE YOUR ONCE IN A WHILE (Robert B. Smith).

GULLIVER'S TRAVELS

A Paramount picture starring Jessica Dragonette and Lanny Ross, and directed by Dave Fleisher. Songs:

BLUEBIRDS IN THE MOONLIGHT; ALL'S WELL; WE'RE ALL TOGETHER AGAIN; FAITHFUL; FOREVER; FAITHFUL FOREVER and I HEAR A DREAM by Leo Robin and Ralph Rainger; IT'S A HAP-HAP-HAPPY DAY by Sammy Timberg, Winston Sharples and Al J. Neiburg.

HAWAIIAN NIGHTS

A Universal picture filmed with a cast headed by Mary Carlisle, Constance Moore and Johnny Downs, and directed by Albert Rogell. Songs by Frank Loesser and Matt Malneck:

HAWAII SANG ME TO SLEEP; HEY, GOOD LOOKIN'; I FOUND MY LOVE and THEN I WROTE THE MINUET IN G (based on a Ludwig Beethoven melody).

HONOLULU

An M-G-M picture starring Eleanor Powell in a cast that included Robert Young and Burns and Allen, and directed by Eddie Buzzell. Songs by Gus Kahn and Harry Warren:

THE LEADER DOES'NT LIKE MUSIC; THIS NIGHT WILL BE MY SOUVENIR and HONOLULU.

ICE FOLLIES OF 1939

An M-G-M picture starring Joan Crawford in a cast that included James Stewart and Lew Ayers, and directed by Reinhold Schunzel. Songs:

LOVELAND IN THE WINTERTIME by Cliff Friend and Dave Franklin; SOMETHING'S GOTTA HAPPEN SOON by Arthur Freed and Nacio Herb Brown; IT'S ALL SO NEW TO ME by Bernice Petkere and Marty Symes; CINDERELLA REEL and BLACKBIRDS by Roger Edens and Franz Waxman.

LAUGH IT OFF

A Universal picture filmed with a cast headed by Johnny Downs, Constance Moore, Majorie Rambeau and Hedda Hopper, and directed by Albert S. Rogell. Songs by Sam Lerner and Ben Oakland:

MY DREAM AND I; DOIN' THE 1940; LAUGH IT OFF and WHO'S GONNA KEEP YOUR WIGWAM WARM?

LET FREEDOM RING

An M-G-M picture starring Nelson Eddy in a cast that included Virginia Bruce, Victor McLaglen, Lionel Barrymore, Edward Arnold and Guy Kibbe, and directed by John Conway. Songs:

WHERE ELSE BUT HERE by Edward Heyman and Sigmund Romberg; LOVE SERENADE by Chet Forrest, Bob Wright and R. Drigo; DUSTY ROAD by Leon and Otis Rene; PAT SEZ HE by Foster Carling and Phil Ohman.

MAN ABOUT TOWN

A Paramount picture filmed with a cast headed by Jack Benny, Betty Grable, Edward Arnold, Dorothy Lamour and Phil Harris and his orchestra, and directed by Mark Sandrich. Songs:

STRANGE ENCHANTMENT, THAT SENTIMENTAL SANDWICH and MAN ABOUT TOWN by Frank Loesser and Frederick Hollander; FIDGETY JOE by Frank Loesser and Matt Malneck; BLUEBIRDS IN THE MOONLIGHT by Leo Robin and Ralph Rainger.

NAUGHTY BUT NICE

A Warner Brothers' picture starring Ann Sheridan and Dick Powell in a cast that included Gale Page, and directed by Ray Enright. Songs by Johnny Mercer and Harry Warren:

CORN PICKIN'; HOORAY FOR SPINACH; I'M HAPPY ABOUT THE WHOLE THING; IN A MOMENT OF WEAKNESS and I DON'T BELIEVE IN SIGNS.

ON YOUR TOES

A Warner Brothers' picture starring Zorina in a cast that included Eddie Albert, James Gleason, Alan Hale and Frank McHugh, and directed by Ray Enright. Musical numbers by Lorenz Hart and Richard Rodgers:

THERE'S A SMALL HOTEL; QUIET NIGHT; ON YOUR TOES and SLAUGHTER ON TENTH AVENUE.

ONE DARK NIGHT

A Gold Seal picture filmed with an all-Negro cast headed by Manton Moreland. Songs by Johnny Lange and Lew Porter:

SHARPEST MAN IN TOWN; WEST OF HARLEM; ALONE AGAIN; SHAKE IT AND BREAK IT and GIT ALONG MULE.

PARIS HONEYMOON

A Paramount picture starring Bing Crosby in a cast that included Franciska Gaal, Akim Tamiroff and Shirley Ross, and directed by Frank Tuttle. Songs by Leo Robin and Ralph Rainger:

I HAVE EYES; YOU'RE A SWEET LITTLE HEADACHE; FUNNY OLD HILLS; JOOBALAI; THE MAIDEN BY THE BROOK and WORK WHILE YOU MAY.

ROSE OF WASHINGTON SQUARE

A 20th Century-Fox picture filmed with a cast headed by Tyrone Power, Alice Faye, Al Jolson, William Frawley and Joyce Compton, and directed by Gregory Ratoff. Songs:

I NEVER KNEW HEAVEN COULD SPEAK by Mack Gordon and Harry Revel; MY MAN by Channing Pollock and Maurice Yvain; TOOT TOOT TOOTSIE GOODBYE by Gus Kahn, Ernie Erdman and Dan Russo.

ST. LOUIS BLUES

A Paramount picture starring Dorothy Lamour in a cast that included Lloyd Nolan, Tito Guizar and Maxine Sullivan, and directed by Raoul Walsh. Songs:

JUNIOR; BLUE NIGHTFALL and THE SONG IN MY HEART IS THE RHUMBA by Frank Loesser and Burton Lane; I GO FOR THAT by Frank Loesser and Matt Malneck; LET'S DREAM IN THE MOONLIGHT by Raoul Walsh and Matt Malneck; KINDA LONESOME by Leo Robin, Sam Coslow and Hoagy Carmichael.

SECOND FIDDLE

A 20th Century-Fox picture starring Sonja Henie and Tyrone Power in a cast that included Rudy Vallee, Edna May Oliver and Mary Healy, and directed by Sidney Lanfield. Songs by Irving Berlin:

I POURED MY HEART INTO A SONG; WHEN WINTER COMES; AN OLD-FASHIONED TUNE ALWAYS IS NEW; I'M SORRY FOR MYSELF; BACK TO BACK and SONG OF THE METRONOME.

SHE MARRIED A COP

A Republic picture starring Phil Regan and Jean Parker, and directed by Sidney Salkow. Songs by Ralph Freed and Burton Lane:

I CAN'T IMAGINE; I'LL REMEMBER and HERE'S TO LOVE.

STAR MAKER, THE

A Paramount picture starring Bing Crosby in a cast that included Louise Campbell, Linda Ware, Ned Sparks and Laura Hope Crews, and directed by Roy Del Ruth. Songs by Johnny Burke and Jimmy Monaco:

GO FLY A KITE; AN APPLE FOR THE TEACHER; STILL THE BLUEBIRD SINGS and A MAN AND HIS DREAM.

STORY OF THE CASTLES, THE

An RKO picture starring Ginger Rogers and Fred Astaire, and directed by Henry C. Potter. Songs:

ONLY WHEN YOU'RE IN MY ARMS by Bert Kalmar and Harry Ruby; BY THE BEAUTIFUL SEA by Harold Atteridge and Harry Carroll; YAMA YAMA MAN by Colin Davis and Karl Hoschna; COME JOSEPHINE IN MY FLYING MACHINE by Albert Bryan and Fred Fisher; OH YOU BEAUTIFUL DOLL by A. Seymour Brown and Nat D. Ayer; CUDDLE UP A LITTLE CLOSER by Otto Harbach and Karl Hoschna; WHILE THEY WERE DANCING AROUND by Joseph McCarthy and Jimmy Monaco; WAITING FOR THE ROBERT E. LEE by L. Wolfe Gilbert and Lewis E. Muir; DARKTOWN STRUTTERS' BALL by Shelton Brooks; TOO MUCH MUSTARD by Cecil Macklin; CHICAGO by Fred Fisher; HELLO, HELLO WHO'S YOUR LADY FRIEND? by Worton David and Bert Lee.

SWANEE RIVER

A 20th Century-Fox picture filmed with a cast headed by Don Ameche, Al Jolson and Andrea Leeds, and directed by Sidney Lanfield. Songs:

CURRY A MULE by Sidney Lanfield and Louis Silvers; GWINE DOWN THE RIVER by William O. Davis; MULE SONG by Hall Johnson; OH, SUSANNA; DE CAMPTOWN RACES; MY OLD KENTUCKY HOME; RING, RING DE BANJO; JEANIE WITH THE LIGHT BROWN HAIR; OLD BLACK JOE; SWANEE RIVER and BEAUTIFUL DREAMER by Stephen Foster.

THAT'S RIGHT, YOU'RE WRONG

An RKO picture starring Kay Kyser in a cast that included Adolphe Menjou, May Robson, Lucille Ball and Dennis O'Keefe, and directed by David Butler. Songs:

I'M FIT TO BE TIED by Walter Donaldson; SCATTERBRAIN by Johnny Burke and Frankie Masters; LITTLE RED FOX by James Kern, Hy Heath, Johnny Lange and Lew Porter; THE ANSWER IS LOVE by Charles Newman and Sammy Stept; CHATTERBOX by Jerome Brainin and Allan Roberts and HAPPY BIRTHDAY TO LOVE by Dave Franklin.

THREE MUSKETEERS

A 20th Century-Fox picture starring the Ritz Brothers in a cast that included Don Ameche, Lionel Atwill, Gloria Stuart, Pauline Moore, Binnie Barnes and John Carradine, and directed by Allan Dwan. Songs by Walter Bullock and Samuel Pokrass:

VIOLA; MY LADY and SONG OF THE MUSKETEERS.

WIZARD OF OZ, THE

An M-G-M picture starring Judy Garland in a cast that included Bert Lahr, Ray Bolger and Jack Haley, and directed by Victor Fleming. Songs by E. Y. Harburg and Harold Arlen:

MERRY OLD LAND OF OZ; IF I ONLY HAD A HEART; IF I ONLY HAD A BRAIN; IF I ONLY HAD THE NERVE; OVER THE RAINBOW; MUNCHKINLAND; WE'RE OFF TO SEE THE WIZARD; DING, DONG THE WITCH IS DEAD and THE JITTERBUG.

Feature Films With Songs

ALL WOMEN HAVE SECRETS

A Paramount picture starring Jeanne Cagney and Joseph Allen, and directed by Kurt Neumann. Song by Ned Washington and Victor Young:

I LIVE AGAIN BECAUSE I'M IN LOVE AGAIN

BIG TOWN CZAR

A Universal picture starring Barton MacLane in a cast that included Tom Brown and Eve Arden, and directed by Arthur Lubin. Songs by Frank Skinner:

GETTING DRESSED UP and YOU'RE THE ONLY ONE I ADORE.

BLONDIE MEETS THE BOSS

A Columbia picture starring Penny Singleton and Arthur Lake, and directed by Frank Strayer. Song by Sam Lerner and Ben Oakland:

YOU HAD IT COMIN' TO YOU

BOY FRIEND

A 20th Century-Fox picture starring Jane Withers in a cast that included Arleen Whalen and Richard Bond, and directed by James Tinling. Song by Sidney Clare and Harry Akst:

DOIN' THE SOCIALITE

BRIDAL SUITE

An M-G-M picture starring Annabella and Robert Young in a cast that included Walter Connolly and Reginald Owen, and directed by William Thiele. Songs:

WHEN I GAVE MY SMILE TO YOU by Gus Kahn and Bill Buddie; ONE LITTLE DRINK TO YOU by Gus Kahn and Arthur Gutmann; WHEN I CALLED YOU MY SWEETHEART by Jeff Orban and Bill Buddie.

BURN 'EM UP O'CONNOR

An M-G-M picture filmed with a cast headed by Dennis O'Keefe, Cecilia Parker and Nat Pendleton, and directed by Edgar Sedgwick. Song by William Axt:

AT THE FAIR

CHARLEY McCARTHY DETECTIVE

A Universal picture starring Edgar Bergen in a cast that included Robert Cummings and Constance Moore, and directed by Frank Tuttle. Songs:

ALMOST by Sam Lerner and Ben Oakland; HOW WAS I TO KNOW? by Eddie Cherkose and Jacques Press; CHARLEY McCARTHY DETECTIVE by Eddie Cherkose, Jacques Press and Hal Block.

DANCING CO-ED

An M-G-M picture filmed with a cast that included Lana Turner, Richard Carlson and Artie Shaw and his orchestra, and directed by S. Sylvan Simon. Musical number:

JUNGLE DRUMS by Ernesto Lecuona, Carmen Lombardo and Charles O'Flynn.

DARK VICTORY
A Warner Brothers' picture starring Bette Davis in a cast that included George Brent and Humphrey Bogart, and directed by Edmund Goulding. Song by Elsie Janis and Edmund Goulding:
OH GIVE ME TIME FOR TENDERNESS

DESTRY RIDES AGAIN
A Universal picture starring Marlene Dietrich in a cast that included James Stewart, Charles Winninger, Brian Donlevy, Una Merkel and Jack Carson, and directed by George Marshall. Songs by Frank Loesser and Frederick Hollander:
LI'L JOE THE WRANGLER; YOU'VE GOT THAT LOOK THAT LEAVES ME WEAK and (SEE WHAT) THE BOYS IN THE BACK ROOM (WILL HAVE).

DUST BE MY DESTINY
A Warner Brothers' picture starring John Garfield and Priscilla Lane, and directed by Lewis Seiler. Song by Jack Scholl and Max Steiner:
DUST BE MY DESTINY

ETERNALLY YOURS
A United Artists' picture starring Loretta Young in a cast that included David Niven, Hugh Herbert, C. Aubrey Smith, Billie Burke and Broderick Crawford, and directed by Tay Garnett. Song by L. Wolfe Gilbert and Werner Janssen:
ETERNALLY YOURS

EVERYTHING'S ON ICE
An RKO picture starring Irene Dunne in a cast that included Roscoe Karns, Edgar Kennedy and Lynne Roberts, and directed by Erle C. Kenton. Songs by Milton Drake and Frank Stryker:
GEORGIE PORGIE and EVERYTHING'S ON ICE.

FAMILY NEXT DOOR, THE
A Universal picture starring Joy Hodges and Hugh Herbert, and directed by Joseph Santley. Song by Harold Adamson and Jimmy McHugh:
IT'S A DOG'S LIFE

FISHERMAN'S WHARF
An RKO picture starring Bobby Breen in a cast that included Leo Carrillo, Henry Armetta and Lee Patrick, and directed by Bernard Vorhaus. Songs:
FISHERMAN'S CHANTEY by William

Howe and Harlan Myers; SELL YOUR CARES FOR A SONG by Charles Newman and Victor Young; BLUE ITALIAN WATERS by Paul Francis Webster and Frank Churchill.

FLIGHT AT MIDNIGHT
A Paramount picture filmed with a cast headed by Col. Roscoe Turner, Phil Regan, Jean Parker and Robert Armstrong, and directed by Sidney Salkow. Song by Ralph Freed and Burton Lane:
I NEVER THOUGHT I'D FALL IN LOVE AGAIN

GIRL DOWNSTAIRS
An M-G-M picture starring Franchot Tone and Franciska Gaal, and directed by Norman Taurog. Song by Bob Wright and Chet Forrest:
WHEN YOU'RE IN LOVE

GIRL FROM MEXICO
An RKO picture starring Lupe Velez in a cast that included Donald Woods and Leon Errol, and directed by Leslie Goodwins. Musical numbers:
NEGRA CONSENTIDA by Joaquin Pardave; CHIAPANECAS by Romero, Garuse and De Torre.

GIRL FROM RIO, THE
A Monogram picture starring Movita in a cast that included Warren Hull and Alan Baldwin, and directed by Lambert Hillyer. Songs:
ROMANCE IN RIO by Johnny Lange and Lew Porter; THE SINGING BURRO by Emil De Recat.

GRACIE ALLEN MURDER CASE
A Paramount picture starring Gracie Allen in a cast that included Warren William, and directed by Alfred E. Green. Song by Frank Loesser and Matt Malneck:
SNUG AS A BUG IN A RUG

HERITAGE OF THE DESERT
A Paramount picture starring Evelyn Venable and Donald Woods, and directed by Leslie Selander. Song by Frank Loesser and Victor Young:
HERE'S A HEART

HOTEL IMPERIAL
A Paramount picture starring Isa Miranda and Ray Milland in a cast that included Reginald Owen and Gene Lockhart, and directed by Robert Florey. Song by Ralph Freed and Frederick Hollander:
THERE'S SOMETHING MAGIC SAYING "NITCHEVO".

IDIOT'S DELIGHT
An M-G-M picture starring Norma Shearer and Clark Gable in a cast that included Edward Arnold, Charles Coburn, Joseph Schildkraut and Burgess Meredith, and directed by Clarence Brown. Song by Gus Kahn and Herbert Stothart:
HOW STRANGE

INTERMEZZO
A United Artists' picture starring Leslie Howard and Ingrid Bergman in a cast that included Edna Best and John Halliday, and directed by Gregory Ratoff. Song by Robert Henning and Heinz Provost:
INTERMEZZO

INVITATION TO HAPPINESS
A Paramount picture starring Irene Dunne and Fred MacMurray, and directed by Wesley Ruggles. Song by Frank Loesser and Frederick Hollander:
INVITATION TO HAPPINESS

ISLAND OF LOST MEN
A Paramount picture starring Anna May Wong in a cast that included J. Carroll Naish and Anthony Quinn, and directed by Kurt Neumann. Song by Frank Loesser and Frederick Hollander:
MUSIC ON THE SHORE

KID FROM TEXAS, THE
An M-G-M picture filmed with a cast headed by Dennis O'Keefe, Florence Rice, Anthony Allan, Jessie Ralph and Buddy Ebsen, and directed by S. Sylvan Simon. Song by Albert Mannheimer, Milton Merlin and Ormand Ruthven:
RIGHT IN THE MIDDLE OF TEXAS

KID NIGHTINGALE
A Warner Brothers' picture filmed with a cast headed by John Payne, Jane Wyman, Harry Burns and Walter Catlett, and directed by George Amy. Songs:
WHO TOLD YOU I CARED by George Whiting and Bert Reisfield; HARK, HARK THE MEADOW LARK by Jack Scholl and M. K. Jerome.

LADY OF THE TROPICS
An M-G-M picture starring Hedy Lamarr and Robert Taylor, and directed by John Conway. Song by Foster G. Carling and Phil Ohman:
EVERY TIME YOU SAY GOODBYE I DIE A LITTLE

LOVE AFFAIR
An RKO picture starring Irene Dunne and Charles Boyer, and directed by Leo McCarey. Songs:
WISHING by B. G. DeSylva; SING MY HEART by Ted Koehler and Harold Arlen.

MADE FOR EACH OTHER
A United Artists' picture starring Carole Lombard and James Stewart, and directed by John Cromwell. Song by Harry Tobias and Oscar Levant:
MADE FOR EACH OTHER

MAISIE
An M-G-M picture starring Ann Sothern and Robert Young. Songs:
LITTLE JOE THE WRANGLER by Frank Loesser and Victor Hollander; WHOO-PEE-TI-YI-YO.

MIDNIGHT
A Paramount picture starring Claudette Colbert and Don Ameche in a cast that included John Barrymore and Francis Lederer, and directed by Mitchell Leisen. Song by Ralph Freed and Frederick Hollander:
MIDNIGHT

NEVER SAY DIE
A Paramount picture starring Martha Raye and Bob Hope, and directed by Elliott Nugent. Song by Leo Robin and Ralph Rainger:
THE TRA-LA-LA AND OOM-PAH-PAH

ONE THOUSAND DOLLARS A TOUCHDOWN
A Paramount picture starring Joe E. Brown and Martha Raye in a cast that included Eric Blore and Susan Hayward, and directed by James Hogan. Song by Leo Robin and Ralph Rainger:
LOVE WITH A CAPITAL "U"

PACK UP YOUR TROUBLES
A 20th Century-Fox picture starring Jane Withers and the Ritz Brothers, and directed by H. Bruce Humberstone. Song by Sidney Clare and Jule Styne:
WHO'LL BUY MY FLOWERS?

RAINS CAME, THE
A 20th Century-Fox picture starring Tyrone Power, Myrna Loy and George Brent, and directed by Clarence Brown. Songs:
THE RAINS CAME by Mack Gordon and Harry Revel; HINDOO SONG OF LOVE by Lal Chand Mehra.

RIO
A Universal picture filmed with a cast headed by Basil Rathbone, Victor MacLaglen, Sigrid Gurie, Robert Cummings and

Leo Carrillo, and directed by John Brahm.
Songs:
LOVE OPENED MY EYES by Ralph Freed and Jimmy McHugh; HEART OF MINE and AFTER THE RAIN by Ralph Freed and Frank Skinner.

SHIPYARD SALLY
A 20th Century-Fox picture starring Gracie Fields and Sydney Howard. Song by Harry Parr-Davies and Phil Park:
WISH ME LUCK AS YOU WAVE GOODBYE

SOCIETY LAWYER
An M-G-M picture starring Virginia Bruce and Walter Pidgeon in a cast that included Leo Carrillo, Eduardo Cianelli and Lee Bowman, and directed by Edward L. Marin. Song by Sam Coslow:
I'M IN LOVE WITH THE HONORABLE MR. SO AND SO

SOME LIKE IT HOT
A Paramount picture starring Bob Hope and Shirley Ross, and featuring Gene Krupa and his band. Directed by George Archainbaud. Songs:
THE LADY'S IN LOVE WITH YOU by Frank Loesser and Burton Lane; SOME LIKE IT HOT by Frank Loesser, Gene Krupa and Remo Biondi.

SPIRIT OF CULVER
A Universal picture starring Jackie Cooper and Freddie Bartholomae in a cast that included Tim Holt and Henry Hull, and directed by Joseph Santley. Songs:
GIVE THE MILITARY BAND A HAND by Harry Brown and Clarence Marks; YOU ARE THE WORDS TO A SONG by Charles Henderson and Frank Skinner.

STOP, LOOK AND LOVE
A 20th Century-Fox picture starring Jean Rogers and Robert Kelland, and directed by Otto Brower. Song by Sidney Clare and Jule Styne:
LET'S START WHERE WE LEFT OFF

TAIL SPIN
A 20th Century-Fox picture filmed with a cast headed by Alice Faye, Constance Bennett, Nancy Kelly, Joan Davis, Charles Farrell and Jane Wyman, and directed by Roy Del Ruth. Song by Mack Gordon and Harry Revel:
ARE YOU IN THE MOOD FOR MISCHIEF?

THESE GLAMOUR GIRLS
An M-G-M picture filmed with a cast headed by Lew Ayers, Lana Turner, Tom Brown, Richard Carlson, Jane Bryan, Anita Louise, Marsha Hunt and Ann Rutherford, and directed by S. Sylvan Simon. Song by Chet Forrest, Bob Wright and Ed Ward:
LOVELINESS

THEY SHALL HAVE MUSIC
A United Artists' picture filmed with a cast headed by Jascha Heifetz, Andrea Leeds, Joel McCrea, Gene Reynolds and Walter Brennan, and directed by Archie Mayo. The score consisted of classical numbers.

WAY DOWN SOUTH
An RKO picture starring Bobby Breen in a cast that included Alan Mowbrey, Ralph Morgan, Clarence Muse, Steffi Duna and Sally Blane, and directed by Bernard Vorhaus. Songs by Langston Hughes and Clarence Muse:
GOOD GROUND and LOUISIANA.

WHILE NEW YORK SLEEPS
A 20th Century-Fox picture starring Michael Whalen and Joan Woodbury, and directed by Allan Dwan. Songs by Sidney Clare:
AIN'T HE GOOD LOOKIN' and I'LL NEVER CHANGE.

WIFE, HUSBAND AND FRIEND
A 20th Century-Fox picture starring Loretta Young and Warner Baxter in a cast that included Binnie Barnes, George Barbier, Helen Westley and Cesar Romero, and directed by Gregory Ratoff. Song by Walter Bullock and Samuel Pokrass:
DRINK FROM THE CUP OF TOMORROW

WINTER CARNIVAL
A United Artists' picture starring Ann Sheridan and Richard Carlson in a cast that included Helen Parrish, Robert Armstrong and Marsha Hunt, and directed by Charles F. Reisner. Song by L. Wolfe Gilbert and Werner Janssen:
WINTER BLOSSOMS

WOMEN, THE
An M-G-M picture filmed with a cast headed by Norma Shearer, Joan Crawford, Rosalind Russell, Mary Boland, Paulette Goddard and Joan Fontaine, and directed by George Cukor. Song by Bob Wright, Chet Forrest and Ed Ward:
FOREVERMORE

ZAZA

A Paramount picture starring Claudette Colbert and Herbert Marshall, and directed by George Cukor. Songs by Frank Loesser

and Frederick Hollander:
HELLO MY DARLING; FORGET ME and ZAZA.

Western Films With Songs

ARIZONA KID, THE

A Republic picture starring Roy Rogers in a cast that included Gabby Hayes and Dorothy Sebastian, and directed by Joseph Kane. Songs by Walter G. Samuels:
IT'S HOME SWEET HOME TO ME and LAZY OLD MOON.

BLUE MONTANA SKIES

A Republic picture starring Gene Autry in a cast that included Smiley Burnette and June Storey, and directed by B. Reeves Eason. Songs by Gene Autry, Johnny Marvin and Fred Rose:
ROCKING IN THE SADDLE; OLD GEEZER; NEATH THE BLUE MONTANA SKY; I JUST WANT YOU and AWAY OUT YONDER.

BRONZE BUCKAROO, THE

A Sack Amusement Company picture filmed with an all-Negro cast headed by Herbert Jeffries and Artie Young, and directed by Richard Kahn. Songs by Johnny Lange and Lew Porter:
PAY DAY BLUES and WHEN A COWBOY'S DAY IS ENDED.

COLORADO SUNSET

A Republic picture starring Gene Autry in a cast that included Smiley Burnette, June Storey and Barbara Pepper, and directed by George Sherman. Songs:
POOR LITTLE DOGIES by Fred Rose; THE MERRY WAY BACK HOME by Walter G. Samuels.

DAYS OF JESSE JAMES

A Republic picture starring Roy Rogers in a cast that included Gabby Hayes and Pauline Moore, and directed by Joseph Kane. Songs by Peter Tinturin:
I'M THE SON OF A COWBOY; ECHO MOUNTAIN and SADDLE YOUR DREAMS.

DOWN THE WYOMING TRAIL

A Monogram picture starring Tex Ritter and Mary Brodel, and directed by Al Herman. Songs:
AND HE LOOKS SO PEACEFUL NOW and IN ELK VALLEY by Johnny Lange and Lew Porter; GOING BACK TO TEXAS by Carson Robison; IT MAKES

NO DIFFERENCE NOW by Jimmy Davis and Floyd Tillman.

EL DIABLO RIDERS

A Metropolitan picture starring Bob Steele and Claire Rochelle, and directed by Ira Webb. Songs by Johnny Lange and Lew Porter:
DOWN BY THE OLD CORRAL and HI, COWBOY.

FRONTIER PONY EXPRESS

A Republic picture starring Roy Rogers in a cast that included Mary Hart and Raymond Hatton, and directed by Joseph Kane. Song by Walter G. Samuels:
THE MAIL MUST GO THROUGH

HARLEM RIDES THE RANGE

A Hollywood Pictures' production filmed with an all-Negro cast headed by Herbert Jeffries and Lucius Brooks, and directed by Richard C. Kahn. Songs by Johnny Lange and Lew Porter:
PRAIRIE FLOWER and ALMOST TIME FOR ROUNDUP.

HOME ON THE PRAIRIE

A Republic picture starring Gene Autry in a cast that included Smiley Burnette and June Storey, and directed by Jack Townley. Songs:
I'M GONNA ROUND UP MY BLUES by Johnny Marvin; MOONLIGHT ON THE RANCH HOUSE and BIG BULLFROG by Walter G. Samuels.

HONOR OF THE WEST

A Universal picture starring Bob Baker, and directed by George Waggner. Songs by Fleming Allan:
PRIDE OF THE PRAIRIE; AS THE OLD CHUCK WAGON ROLLS ALONG and HEADIN' FOR THE OLD CORRAL.

IN OLD CALIENTE

A Republic picture starring Roy Rogers in a cast that included Mary Hart, Gabby Hayes and Jack LaRue, and directed by Joseph Kane. Songs:
WE'RE NOT COMIN' OUT TONIGHT and THE MOON SHE WILL BE SHINING TONIGHT by Walter G. Samuels; SUNDOWN ON THE RANGE LAND by Fred Rose.

IN OLD MONTANA

A Spectrum picture starring Fred Scott and Jean Carmen, and directed by Raymond Johnson. Songs by Johnny Lange and Lew Porter:
I'M A MOTHER'S HELPER and RATTLE-SNAKE JOE.

IN OLD MONTEREY

A Republic picture starring Gene Autry in a cast that included Smiley Burnette and June Storey, and directed by Joseph Kane. Songs:
LITTLE PARDNER by Gene Autry and Fred Rose; BORN IN THE SADDLE by Gene Autry and Johnny Marvin.

MEXACALI ROSE

A Republic picture starring Gene Autry in a cast that included Smiley Burnette, Noah Beery and Luana Walters, and directed by George Sherman. Songs:
MEXACALI ROSE by Jack Tenney and Helen Stone; YOU'RE THE ONLY STAR IN MY BLUE HEAVEN by Gene Autry; MY ORCHESTRA'S DRIVING ME CRAZY by Smiley Burnette; ALLA EN EL RANCHO GRANDE by Bartley Costello, Del Morales and Emilio Uranga.

MOUNTAIN RHYTHM

A Republic picture starring Gene Autry in a cast that included Smiley Burnette and June Storey, and directed by B. Reeves Eason. Songs by Fred Rose:
KNIGHTS OF THE OPEN ROAD; ONLY A HOBO'S DREAM and A GOLD MINE IN YOUR HEART.

RACKETEERS OF THE RANGE

An RKO picture starring George O'Brien and Majorie Reynolds, and directed by D. Ross Lederman. Songs by Fred Rose:
RED BALL TRAIN and SLEEPY WRANGLER.

RENEGADE TRAIL

A Paramount picture starring Bill Boyd in a cast that included Russell Hayden, Gabby Hayes and Charlotte Wynters, and directed by Leslie Selander. Songs by Foster Carling and Phil Ohman:
LAZY ROLLS THE RIO GRANDE; HI THAR STRANGER! and LULLABY OF THE HERD.

RIDE 'EM COWGIRL

A Grand National picture starring Dorothy Page, and directed by Samuel Diege. Songs by Milton Drake and Walter Kent:
I LOVE THE WIDE OPEN SPACES and A CAMPFIRE, A PRAIRIE MOON AND YOU.

ROLL WAGONS ROLL

A Monogram picture starring Tex Ritter, Nelson McDowell and Muriel Evans, and directed by Al Herman. Song by Dorcas Cochran and Charles Rosoff:
ROLL WAGONS ROLL

ROLLIN' WESTWARD

A Monogram picture starring Tex Ritter, and directed by Al Herman. Songs:
BACK IN '67 by Johnny Lange and Lew Porter; ROLLIN' WESTWARD by Bert Pellish and Ted Choate.

ROUGH RIDER ROUNDUP

A Republic picture starring Roy Rogers in a cast that included Mary Hart and Raymond Hatton, and directed by Joseph Kane. Songs:
RIDIN' DOWN THE TRAIL by Eddie Cherkose and C. Feuer; HERE ON THE RANGE by Tim Spencer.

ROVIN' TUMBLEWEEDS

A Republic picture starring Gene Autry in a cast that included Mary Carlisle and Smiley Burnette, and directed by George Sherman. Songs:
HURRAY by Eddie Cherkose and Smiley Burnette; A GIRL LIKE YOU AND A NIGHT LIKE THIS by Johnny Marvin and Gene Autry; SUNNY SIDE OF A CELL by Gene Autry, Johnny Marvin and Fred Rose.

SAGA OF DEATH VALLEY

A Republic picture starring Roy Rogers in a cast that included Gabby Hayes and Doris Day, and directed by Joseph Kane. Songs:
SONG OF THE BANDIT by Bob Nolan; SHADOWS ON THE PRAIRIE and RIDE by Walter G. Samuels; I'VE SOLD MY SADDLE FOR AN OLD GUITAR by Fleming Allan.

SIX GUN RHYTHM

A Grand National picture starring Tex Fletcher, and directed by Sam Newfield. Songs:
A SERENADE TO A LOVELY SENORITA; THEY WON'T STRETCH MY NECK; BACK ON THE RANGE; CABIN IN THE VALLEY and I'M A LONESOME COWBOY by Johnny Lange and Lew Porter; ROCK ME IN THE CRADLE OF THE ROCKIES by Al Jacobs and Dave Oppenheim.

SONG OF THE BUCKAROO

A Monogram picture starring Tex Ritter in a cast that included Jinx Falkenburg, and

Bing Crosby puts "Please" on hit parade in *The Big Broadcast*

The first technicolor musical, *"Gold Diggers of Broadway"*

The title song number from *"Forty-second Street"*

Jimmy Cagney as George M. Cohan in *The Yankee Doodle Boy*

Fred Astaire in a scene from *Top Hat*

Lionel Barrymore, Shirley Temple and Bill Robinson in *The Little Colonel*

Louise Rainer and William Powell in *The Great Ziegfeld*

Judy Garland in *Wizard of Oz* with woodman, scarecrow and lion.

Sonja Henie skates to stardom in *One In A Million*

Judy Garland sings "Sunny" in *Till the Clouds Roll By*

Fred Astaire dance routine in *Blue Skies*

Finale of the all-star revue *Thank Your Lucky Stars*

"I hate to get up in the morning" scene from *This Is The Army*

"Swinging on a Star" number from *Going My Way*

Gene Kelly, Rita Hayworth and Phil Silvers in *Cover Girl*

Title number from *The Easter Parade*

directed by Al Herman. Songs:
LITTLE TENDERFOOT by Johnny Lange; I PROMISED YOU by Tex Ritter and Frank Harford; TEXAS DAN by Carson Robison.

SOUTH OF THE BORDER

A Republic picture starring Gene Autry in a cast that included Lupita Tovar, Smiley Burnette and June Storey, and directed by George Sherman. Songs:
COME TO THE FIESTA by Art Wenzel; HORSE OP'RY by Fred Rose; MOON OF MANANA and WHEN THE CACTUS BLOOMS AGAIN by Gene Autry and Johnny Marvin.

SOUTHWARD HO!

A Republic picture starring Roy Rogers in a cast that included Mary Hart and Gabby Hayes, and directed by Joseph Kane. Songs:
WALK THE OTHER WAY and HEADIN' FOR TEXAS by Walter G. Samuels; I HOPE I'M NOT DREAMING AGAIN by Fred Rose.

SUNDOWN ON THE PRAIRIE

A Monogram picture starring Tex Ritter, and directed by Al Herman. Songs:
CACTUS PETE FROM TEXAS by Johnny Lange and Lew Porter; SUNDOWN ON THE PRAIRIE by Cecil Mack and Albert Von Tilzer.

TRIGGER PALS

A Grand National picture filmed with a cast headed by Art Jarrett, Lee Powell and Dorothy Faye, and directed by Sam Newfield. Song by Johnny Lange and Lew Porter:
WHEN A COWBOY SINGS A LULLABY

WALL STREET COWBOY

A Republic picture starring Roy Rogers in a cast that included Gabby Hayes, Raymond Hatton and Ann Baldwin, and directed by Joseph Kane. Songs by Walter G. Samuels:
RIDE 'EM COWBOY! RIDIN' DOWN THE RAINBOW TRAIL; THAT'S MY LOUISIANA and ME AND THE ROLLING HILLS.

Bob Hope, Dorothy Lamour and Bing Crosby in *The Road to Singapore*

1940

Bing, Bob And Dottie Start Hitting "The Road"

They traveled light with some songs for Bing, some snappy sayings for Bob and a sarong for Dottie, but they certainly were bonanza-bound in *The Road To Singapore,* the first of six "road" pictures that now have taken Crosby, Hope and Lamour to such distant and exotic places as Zanzibar in 1941, Morocco in 1942, Utopia in 1945, Rio in 1947 and Bali in 1952, and these treks will probably continue until they have to depend on wheelchairs for locomotion since all six pictures kept the ticket spools spinning with two yielding a gross return of $4,500,000 each.

The Groaner continued to be a triple threat at the box-office with two other musicals released in 1940—*If I Had My Way* and *Rhythm On The River,* which like *The Road To Singapore* had songs by Johnny Burke, a comparatively newcomer to Tin Pan Alley, and the veteran "Ragtime Jimmy" Monaco; and Brother Bob, the orchestra leader, also got into the Hollywood act by making his screen debut in *Let's Make Music.*

Judy Garland matched Bing Crosby's 1940 output by appearing in three films with music: *Little Nellie Kelly, Strike Up The Band* and *Andy Hardy Meets Debutante,* while Jack Benny continued to make screen capital of his radio popularity in *Love Thy Neighbor* in which he shared headline billing with Mary Martin, and *Buck Benny Rides Again,* a travesty on the horse op'ries with which Hollywood was infested.

In fact, the westerns were riding high, wide and handsome on the 1940 shooting schedules with Roy Rogers appearing in seven pictures and Gene Autry in six, and Universal unloosed a new cowboy star in Johnny Mack Brown, the former Alabama end whose phenomenal pass-catching won the 1925 Rose Bowl classic, who became the villain-catching hero of eight 1940 sagebrush epics.

Carmen Miranda made her screen debut in *Down Argentine Way,* which with *Argentine Nights* and *La Conga Nights* tied in musically with FDR's Good Neighbor Policy, and Anna Neagle, the Gaumont-British singing star, left bomb-shattered London to find temporary peace and security in Hollywood where she faced the cameras in the film versions of two Broadway musicals: Harry Tierney's *Irene* and Vincent Youman's *No, No, Nanette.*

The London and the Broadway stage provided Jeanette MacDonald and Nelson Eddy with scenarios and songs for their 1940 screen appearances in Noel Coward's *Bitter Sweet* and Sigmund Romberg's *The New Moon.* Alice Faye sported ostrich plumes and an hour-glass figure in the film biography of Lillian Russell in which Edward Arnold played Diamond Jim Brady and

Weber and Fields played their English-murdering selves. And Fred Astaire was forced to find a new song-and-dance partner when Ginger Rogers hung up her dancing shoes to play a straight dramatic role in *Kitty Foyle,* and was co-starred with Eleanor Powell in Cole Porter's *Broadway Melody* and with Paulette Goddard in *Second Chorus.*

The Oscar for the best song of 1930 was awarded the writers of *When You Wish Upon A Star,* introduced in Walt Disney's full-length cartoon picture *Pinocchio,* but musical pictures failed to place among the Ten Best Films of a year surcharged with actual and impending drama that was reflected in the choice of such highly dramatic films as *Rebecca, The Grapes Of Wrath, Abe Lincoln in Illinois* and *All This And Heaven Too* for top honors.

Musicals

ARGENTINE NIGHTS

A Universal picture starring the Ritz Brothers in a cast that included Constance Moore and the Andrews Sisters, and directed by Albert S. Rogell. Musical numbers:

OH, OFFICER by Frank Skinner; HIT THE ROAD by Don Raye, Vic Shoen and Hughie Prince; RUM BOOGIE by Don Raye and Hughie Prince; THE SPIRIT OF 77B and BROOKLYNONGA by Hal Borne, Sid Kuller and Ray Golden; AMIGO WE GO RIDING TONIGHT and THE DOWRY SONG by Sammy Cahn and Saul Chaplin.

BARNYARD FOLLIES

A Republic picture filmed with a cast headed by Mary Lee, Rufe Davis, June Storey and Ted Prouty, and directed by Frank McDonald. Songs:

BIG BOY BLUES; BARNYARD HOLIDAY and LOLLIPOP LANE by Johnny Marvin and Fred Rose; MAMA DON'T ALLOW IT by Charles Davenport.

BITTER SWEET

An M-G-M picture starring Jeanette MacDonald and Nelson Eddie in a cast that included George Sanders, and directed by W. S. Van Dyke. Songs by Noel Coward:

I'LL SEE YOU AGAIN; LOVE IN ANY LANGUAGE (lyrics by Gus Kahn); TOKAY; WHAT IS LOVE?; KISS ME; DEAR LITTLE CAFE (lyrics by Gus Kahn); LADIES OF THE TOWN (lyrics by Gus Kahn); ZIGEUNER and IF YOU COULD ONLY COME TO ME.

BLUEBIRD, THE

A 20th Century-Fox picture starring Shirley Temple in a cast that included Spring Byington, Nigel Bruce, Gale Sondergaard, Jessie Ralph and Laura Hope Crews, and directed by Walter Lang. Songs by Walter Bullock and Alfred Newman:

LAY-DE-O; KINGDOM OF THE FUTURE; I CAN'T BELIEVE MY EYES and SOMEDAY YOU'LL FIND YOUR BLUEBIRD.

BOYS FROM SYRACUSE

A Universal picture filmed with a cast headed by Joe Penner, Allan Jones, Martha Raye and Rosemary Lane, and directed by A. Edward Sutherland. Songs by Lorenz Hart and Richard Rodgers:

WHO ARE YOU?; THIS CAN'T BE LOVE; FALLING IN LOVE WITH LOVE; THE GREEKS HAVE NO WORD FOR IT; SING FOR YOUR SUPPER and HE AND SHE.

BROADWAY MELODY

An M-G-M picture starring Fred Astaire and Eleanor Powell in a cast that included Frank Morgan and George Murphy, and directed by Norman Taurog. Songs by Cole Porter:

I CONCENTRATE ON YOU; BETWEEN YOU AND ME; I'VE GOT MY EYES ON YOU; BEGIN THE BEGUINE; PLEASE DON'T MONKEY WITH BROADWAY and I HAPPEN TO BE IN LOVE.

BUCK BENNY RIDES AGAIN

A Paramount picture starring Jack Benny in a cast that included Eddie "Rochester"

Anderson; Lillian Cornell, Dennis Day and Andy Devine, and directed by Mark Sandrich. Songs by Frank Loesser and Jimmy McHugh:
DRUMS IN THE NIGHT; MY, MY; MY KIND OF COUNTRY and SAY IT (OVER AND OVER AGAIN).

CAPTAIN CAUTION
A United Artists' picture filmed with a cast headed by Victor Mature, Louise Platt, Leo Carrillo and Bruce Cabot, and directed by Richard Wallace. Songs by Foster G. Carling and Phil Ohman:
ON A LITTLE ISLAND BY A SUNLIT SEA; HILDA; APPLE SONG; ONLY ONE and WHAT CAN I DO?

DANCE GIRL DANCE
An RKO picture filmed with a cast headed by Maureen O'Hara, Louis Hayward, Lucille Ball, Virginia Field, Ralph Bellamy, Maria Ouspenskaya, Walter Abel and Ernest Truex, and directed by Dorothy Arzner. Songs by Chet Forrest and Bob Wright:
MORNING STAR; OH MOTHER, WHAT DO I DO NOW? and THE JITTERBUG BIT (with Ed Ward).

DOWN ARGENTINE WAY
A 20th Century-Fox picture starring Don Ameche, Betty Grable and Carmen Miranda in a cast that included Charlotte Greenwood, and directed by Robert Cummings. Songs:
TWO DREAMS MET; DOWN ARGENTINE WAY; NENITA and SING TO YOUR SENORITA by Mack Gordon and Harry Warren; I WANT MY MAMA by Al Stillman and Jaraca and Vincente Paiva; DOIN' THE CONGA by Gene Rose; SOUTH AMERICAN WAY by Al Dubin and Jimmy McHugh.

GO WEST
An M-G-M picture starring Groucho, Chico and Harpo Marx in a cast that included John Carroll, Diana Lewis, Walter Woolf King and Tully Marshall, and directed by Eddie Buzzell. Songs:
RIDIN' THE RANGE by Gus Kahn and Roger Edens; YOU CAN'T ARGUE WITH LOVE and AS IF I DON'T KNOW by Gus Kahn and Bronislaw Kaper; GO WEST; THERE'S A NEW MOON OVER THE OLD CORRAL; I'M THE GUY WHO LOVES YOU and I CAN'T GET ALONG WITH HORSES by Gus Kahn and Earl Brent; HOT TAMALES and DO YOU REMEMBER? by Bert Kalmar and Harry Ruby.

HIT PARADE OF 1941
A Republic picture starring Kenny Baker and Frances Langford in a cast that included Hugh Herbert, Mary Boland, Ann Miller, Patsy Kelly and Phil Silvers, and directed by John H. Auer. Songs by Walter Bullock and Jule Styne:
IN THE COOL OF THE EVENING; MAKE YOURSELF AT HOME; WHO AM I? and SWING LOW SWEET RHYTHM.

I CAN'T GIVE YOU ANYTHING BUT LOVE BABY
A Universal picture filmed with a cast headed by Broderick Crawford, Peggy Moran and Johnny Downs, and directed by Albert S. Rogell. Songs:
SWEETHEART OF SCHOOL 59 and DAY BY DAY by Paul Gerard Smith and Frank Skinner; I CAN'T GIVE YOU ANYTHING BUT LOVE by Dorothy Fields and Jimmy McHugh.

IF I HAD MY WAY
A Universal picture starring Bing Crosby in a cast that included Gloria Jean, Charles Winninger, El Brendel, Allyn Joslyn, Blanche Ring, Trixie Friganza and Julian Eltinge, and directed by David Butler.
APRIL PLAYED THE FIDDLE; MEET THE SUN HALF WAY; THE PESSIMISTIC CHARACTER and I HAVEN'T TIME TO BE A MILLIONAIRE by Johnny Burke and Jimmy Monaco; IF I HAD MY WAY by Lew Klein and James Kendis.

I'M NOBODY'S SWEETHEART NOW
A Universal picture filmed with a cast headed by Dennis O'Keefe, Constance Moore, Laura Hope Crews and Berton Churchill, and directed by Arthur Lubin. Songs:
GOT LOVE and THERE GOES MY ROMANCE by Everett Carter and Milton Rosen; NOBODY'S SWEETHEART by Gus Kahn, Ernie Erdman, Billy Meyers and Elmer Schoebel.

IRENE
An RKO picture starring Anna Neagle in a cast that included Ray Milland, Roland Young, Alan Marshall, May Robson, Billie Burke and Arthur Treacher, and directed by Herbert Wilcox. Songs by Joseph McCarthy and Harry Tierney:
IRENE; CASTLE OF DREAMS; YOU'VE GOT ME OUT ON A LIMB; THERE'S SOMETHING IN THE AIR; WORTHY OF YOU; SWEET VERMOSA BROWN and SWEET LITTLE ALICE BLUE GOWN.

IT'S A DATE

A Universal picture starring Deanna Durbin in a cast that included Kay Francis, and directed by William A. Seiter. Songs:

LOVE IS ALL by Pinky Tomlin and Harry Tobias; IT HAPPENED IN KALOHA by Ralph Freed and Frank Skinner; RHYTHM OF THE ISLANDS by Eddie Cherkose, L. Belasco and Jacques Press; HAWAIIAN WAR CHANT by Johnny Noble and Leleiohaku.

JOHNNY APOLLO

A 20th Century-Fox picture starring Dorothy Lamour and Tyrone Power in a cast that included Lloyd Nolan and Edward Arnold, and directed by Henry Hathaway. Songs:

DANCING FOR NICKELS AND DIMES by Frank Loesser and Lionel Newman; THIS IS THE BEGINNING OF THE END by Frank Loesser and Alfred Newman; YOUR KISS by Mack Gordon.

LA CONGA NIGHTS

A Universal picture filmed with a cast headed by Hugh Herbert, Dennis O'Keefe, Constance Moore and Joe E. Brown Jr., and directed by Lew Landers. Songs by Sammy Lerner and Frank Skinner:

CARMENITA McCOY; HAVANA and CHANCE OF A LIFETIME.

LET'S MAKE MUSIC

An RKO picture filmed with a cast headed by Bob Crosby, Jean Rogers, Elizabeth Risden and Joseph Buloff, and directed by Leslie Goodwins. Musical numbers:

FIGHT ON NEWTON HIGH by Dave Dreyer; YOU FORGOT ABOUT ME by Dick Robertson, Sammy Mysels and James Hanley; THE BIG NOISE FROM WINNETKA by Gil Rodin, Bob Haggart, Ray Baudau and Bob Crosby; CENTRAL PARK by Johnny Mercer and Matt Malneck.

LILLIAN RUSSELL

A 20th Century-Fox picture starring Alice Faye and Don Ameche in a cast that included Henry Fonda, Edward Arnold, William Warren, Leo Carrillo, Helen Westley, Joe Weber and Lew Fields, and directed by Irving Cummings. Songs:

BLUE LOVE BIRD by Gus Kahn and Bronislaw Kaper; ADORED ONE by Mack Gordon and Alfred Newman; WALTZ IS KING by Mack Gordon and Charles Henderson; BACK IN THE DAYS OF OLD BROADWAY by Charles Henderson and Alfred Newman.

LITTLE BIT OF HEAVEN, A

A Universal picture filmed with a cast headed by Gloria Jean, Robert Stack, Hugh Herbert, J. Aubrey Smith and Stuart Erwin, and directed by Andrew Marton. Songs:

A LITTLE BIT OF HEAVEN by J. Keirn Brennan and Ernest Ball; WHAT DID WE LEARN AT SCHOOL by Vivian Ellis; DAWN OF LOVE by Ralph Freed and Charles Previn; AFTER EVERY RAIN STORM by Sam Lerner and Frank Skinner.

LITTLE NELLIE KELLY

An M-G-M picture starring Judy Garland in a cast that included George Murphy and Charles Winninger, and directed by Norman Taurog. Songs:

IT'S A GREAT DAY FOR THE IRISH; NELLIE IS A DARLIN' and PRETTY GIRL MILKING HER COW by Roger Edens; SINGIN' IN THE RAIN by Arthur Freed and Nacio Herb Brown.

LOVE THY NEIGHBOR

A Paramount picture starring Jack Benny in a cast that included Mary Martin and Fred Allen, and directed by Mark Sandrich. Songs by Johnny Burke and Jimmy Van Heusen:

DO YOU KNOW WHY? ISN'T THAT JUST LIKE LOVE and DEAREST DAREST I?

MELODY AND MOONLIGHT

A Republic picture filmed with a cast headed by Johnny Downs, Barbara Allen, Jerry Colonna and Jane Frazee, and directed by Joseph Santley. Songs by George H. Brown, Sol Meyer and Jule Styne:

ROOFTOP SERENADE; TAHITI HONEY; TOP O' THE MORNIN'; I CLOSE MY EYES and MELODY AND MOONLIGHT.

MUSIC IN MY HEART

A Columbia picture starring Tony Martin and Rita Hayworth in a cast that included Edith Fellows, Alan Mowbray and Eric Blore, and directed by Joseph Santley. Songs by Chet Forrest and Bob Wright:

I'VE GOT MUSIC IN MY HEART; IT'S A BLUE WORLD; PUNCHINELLO; OH, WHAT A LOVELY DREAM; NO OTHER LOVE; HEARTS IN THE SKY and PRELUDE TO LOVE.

NEW MOON, THE

An M-G-M picture starring Jeanette MacDonald and Nelson Eddy in a cast that included H. B. Warner and Mary Boland, and directed by Robert Z. Leonard. Songs by Oscar Hammerstein II and Sigmund Romberg:

MARIANNA; TAKE A FLOWER; ONE KISS; GORGEOUS ALEXANDER; SOFT AS IN A MORNING SUNRISE; WANTING YOU; LOVER COME BACK TO ME; STOUT-HEARTED MEN and FUNNY LITTLE SAILOR MAN.

NIGHT AT EARL CARROLL'S, A
A Paramount picture filmed with a cast headed by Ken Murray and Rose Hobart, and directed by Kurt Neumann. Musical numbers:

LI'L BOY LOVE by Frank Loesser and Frederick Hollander; I WANNA MAKE WITH THE HAPPY TIMES by Frank Loesser and Gertrude Niesen; CALI-CON-GA by Earl Carroll, Dorcas Cochran and Milo Menendez; ONE LOOK AT YOU by Earl Carroll, Ned Washington and Victor Young.

NO, NO, NANETTE
An RKO picture starring Anna Neagle in a cast that included Richard Carlson, Victor Mature, Roland Young, Helen Broderick, Zasu Pitts and Tamara, and directed by Herbert Wilcox. Songs by Irving Caesar, Otto Harbach and Vincent Youmans:

TEA FOR TWO; I WANT TO BE HAPPY; WHERE HAS MY HUBBY GONE? TAKE A LITTLE ONE-STEP and NO, NO, NANETTE.

OH, JOHNNY HOW YOU CAN LOVE
A Universal picture filmed with a cast headed by Tom Brown, Peggy Moran, Allen Jenkins and Donald Meek, and directed by Charles Lamont. Songs by Paul Gerard Smith and Frank Skinner:

MAYBE I LIKE WHAT YOU LIKE; SWING CHARIOT SWING and MAKE UP YOUR MIND.

ONE NIGHT IN THE TROPICS
A Universal picture starring Abbott and Costello in a cast that included Allan Jones, Nancy Kelly and Leo Carrillo, and directed by A. Edward Sutherland. Songs by Dorothy Fields and Jerome Kern:

BACK IN MY SHELL; REMIND ME; YOU AND YOUR KISS and YOUR DREAM IS THE SAME AS MY DREAM (Lyrics by Oscar Hammerstein II and Otto Harbach).

POT OF GOLD
A United Artists' picture starring James Stewart and Paulette Goddard in a cast that included Charles Winninger, Mary Gordon, Jed Prouty and Horace Heidt and his orchestra, and directed by George Marshall. Songs:

DO YOU BELIEVE IN FAIRY TALES? by Mack David and Vee Lawnhurst; WHEN JOHNNY TOOTS HIS HORN by Hy Heath and Fred Rose; A KNIFE, A FORK AND A SPOON by Dave Franklin; BROADWAY CABALLERO; PETE THE PIPER; HI, CY, WHAT'S COOKIN'? and SLAP HAPPY BAND by Lou Forbes and Henry Sullivan.

RHYTHM ON THE RIVER
A Paramount picture starring Bing Crosby in a cast that included Mary Martin, Basil Rathbone and Oscar Levant, and directed by Victor Schertzinger. Songs:

ONLY FOREVER; AIN'T IT A SHAME ABOUT MAME?; WHEN THE MOON COMES OVER MADISON SQUARE GARDEN; THAT'S FOR ME; RHYTHM ON THE RIVER and WHAT WOULD SHAKESPEARE HAVE SAID by Johnny Burke and Jimmy Monaco; I DON'T WANT TO CRY ANYMORE by Johnny Burke and Victor Schertzinger.

ROAD TO SINGAPORE
A Paramount picture starring Bing Crosby, Bob Hope and Dorothy Lamour in a cast that included Charles Coburn and Jerry Colonna, and directed by Victor Schertzinger. Songs:

SWEET POTATO PIPER; TOO ROMANTIC and KAIGOON by Johnny Burke and Jimmy Monaco; CAPTAIN CUSTARD and THE MOON AND THE WILLOW TREE by Johnny Burke and Victor Schertzinger.

SECOND CHORUS
A Paramount picture starring Fred Astaire and Paulette Goddard in a cast that included Burgess Meredith and Artie Shaw's orchestra, and directed by Henry C. Potter. Musical numbers:

I AIN'T HEP TO THAT STEP and DIG IT by Johnny Mercer and Hal Borne; POOR MR. CHISHOLM and ME AND THE GHOST UPSTAIRS by Johnny Mercer and Bernie Hanighen; SWING CONCERTO by Artie Shaw; (HOW WOULD YOU LIKE TO BE) THE LOVE OF MY LIFE? by Johnny Mercer and Artie Shaw.

SING, DANCE AND PLENTY HOT
A Republic picture filmed with a cast headed by Ruth Terry, Johnny Downs, Barbara Allen and Billy Gilbert, and di-

rected by Lew Landers. Songs by Lew Brown and Jule Styne:
I'M JUST A WEAKIE; TOO TOY; WHEN A FELLA'S GOT A GIRL; WHAT YOU GONNA DO WHEN THERE AIN'T NO SWING?; TEQUILA and WHAT FOOLS THESE MORTALS BE.

SPRING PARADE
A Universal picture starring Deanna Durbin in a cast that included Robert Cummings, Mischa Auer and Henry Stephenson, and directed by Henry Koster. Songs:
THE DAWN OF LOVE (based on the Eili Eili melody) by Ralph Freed and Charles Previn; BLUE DANUBE DREAM (based on a Johann Strauss melody with lyrics by Gus Kahn); IN A SPRING PARADE by Gus Kahn and Charles Previn.

STRIKE UP THE BAND
An M-G-M picture starring Judy Garland and Mickey Rooney in a cast that included June Presser, William Tracey and Paul Whiteman's orchestra. Songs:
OUR LOVE AFFAIR by Arthur Freed and Roger Edens; STRIKE UP THE BAND by Ira and George Gershwin; DRUMMER BOY; NOBODY; DO THE CONGA and NELL OF NEW ROCHELLE by Roger Edens.

TOO MANY GIRLS
An RKO picture filmed with a cast headed by Lucille Ball, Richard Carlson, Ann Miller, Eddie Bracken, Hal LeRoy, Desi Arnaz and Frances Langford, and directed by George Abbott. Songs by Lorenz Hart and Richard Rodgers:
YOU'RE NEARER; I DIDN'T KNOW WHAT TIME IT WAS; SPIC AND SPANISH; LOVE NEVER WENT TO COLLEGE; 'CAUSE WE ALL GOT CAKE; HEROES IN THE FALL and POTTAWATOMIE.

TWO GIRLS ON BROADWAY
An M-G-M picture filmed with a cast headed by Lana Turner, Joan Blondell and George Murphy, and directed by S. Sylvan Simon. Songs:
RANCHO SANTA FE and TRUE LOVE by Gus Kahn and Walter Donaldson; MY WONDERFUL ONE LET'S DANCE by Arthur Freed, Nacio Herb Brown and Roger Edens; MAYBE IT'S THE MOON by Bob Wright, Chet Forrest and Walter Donaldson; BROADWAY'S STILL BROADWAY by Ted Fetter and Jimmy McHugh.

YOU'LL FIND OUT
An RKO picture filmed with a cast headed by Kay Kyser, Peter Lorre, Boris Karloff, Bela Lugosi and Helen Parrish, and directed by David Butler. Songs by Johnny Mercer and Jimmy McHugh:
YOU'VE GOT ME THIS WAY; I'D KNOW YOU ANYWHERE; THE BAD HUMOR MAN; I'VE GOT A ONE-TRACK MIND; LIKE THE FELLER ONCE SAID and DON'T THINK IT AIN'T BEEN CHARMING.

YOUNG PEOPLE
A 20th Century-Fox picture starring Shirley Temple in a cast that included Jack Oakie and Charlotte Greenwood, and directed by Allan Dwan. Songs by Mack Gordon and Harry Revel:
MASON-DIXON LINE; FIFTH AVENUE; I WOULDN'T TAKE A MILLION; YOUNG PEOPLE and TRA-LA-LA-LA.

Feature Films With Songs

ALL THIS AND HEAVEN TOO
A Warner Brothers' picture starring Bette Davis and Charles Boyer, and directed by Anatole Litvak. Songs by Jack Scholl and M. K. Jerome:
LOTUS SONG and THE WAR OF ROSES.

AND ONE WAS BEAUTIFUL
An M-G-M picture filmed with a cast headed by Laraine Day, Robert Cummings, Jean Muir and Billie Burke, and directed by Robert B. Sinclair. Song by Chet Forrest and Bob Wright:
I WANT TO WRITE A SONG

ANDY HARDY MEETS A DEBUTANTE
An M-G-M picture starring Judy Garland and Mickey Rooney in a cast that included Lewis Stone and Cecilia Parker, and directed by George B. Seitz. Songs:
I'M NOBODY'S BABY by Lester Santley, Benny Davis and Milton Ager; ALONE by Arthur Freed and Nacio Herb Brown.

ARISE MY LOVE
A Paramount picture starring Claudette Colbert and Ray Milland in a cast that included Walter Abel and Dennis O'Keefe, and directed by Mitchell Leisen. Song by Ned Washington and Frederick Hollander:
ARISE MY LOVE

BEYOND TOMORROW

An RKO picture filmed with a cast headed by Harry Carey, C. Aubrey Smith, Charles Winninger, Maria Ouspenskaya, Helen Vinson and Rod LaRocque, and directed by A. Edward Sutherland. Song by Charles Newman and Harold Spina:
IT'S RAINING DREAMS

BRIGHAM YOUNG, FRONTIERSMAN

A 20th Century-Fox picture starring Tyrone Power in a cast that included Linda Darnell, Dean Jagger, Brian Donlevy and John Carradine, and directed by Henry Hathaway. Song by Sam Coslow:
THERE'S A HAPPY HUNTING GROUND

BROTHER ORCHID

A Warner Brothers' picture starring Edward G. Robinson, Ann Sothern and Humphrey Bogart, and directed by Lloyd Bacon. Songs by M. K. Jerome:
THREE CHEERS FOR US; STARRY NIGHT and IT ALL BELONGS TO YOU.

BROTHER RAT AND THE BABY

A Warner Brothers' picture starring Wayne Morris and Priscilla Lane, and directed by Ray Enright. Musical numbers by M. K. Jerome:
BUDGET MARCH; VICTORY MARCH and BROTHER RAT MARCH.

CHEROKEE STRIP, THE

A Paramount picture starring Richard Dix and Florence Rice, and directed by Leslie Selander. Song by Jack Scholl and M. K. Jerome:
MY LITTLE BUCKAROO

CURTAIN CALL

An RKO picture filmed with a cast headed by Barbara Reed, Alan Mowbray and Helen Vinson, and directed by Frank Woodruff. Songs by M. K. Jerome:
A KISS FOR MADAME; ORIENTAL MOON and TONIGHT IS MINE.

DANGER AHEAD

A Monogram picture starring James Newill and Dorothea Kent, and directed by Ralph Staub. Song by Johnny Lange and Lew Porter:
SPARE THE ROD AND SPOIL THE CHILD

DEVIL'S ISLAND

A Warner Brothers' picture starring Boris Karloff in a cast that included Nedda Harrigan and James Stephenson, and directed by William Clemons. Song by Jack Scholl and M. K. Jerome:
SONG OF THE DOOMED

DREAMING OUT LOUD

An RKO picture starring Lum and Abner in a cast that included Frances Langford and Phil Harris and his orchestra, and directed by Harold Young. Song by Sam Coslow:
DREAMING OUT LOUD

FARMER'S DAUGHTER, THE

A Paramount picture starring Martha Raye in a cast that included Charles Ruggles and Richard Denning, and directed by James Hogan. Song by Frank Loesser and Frederick Hollander:
JUNGLE JINGLE

FORTY LITTLE MOTHERS

An M-G-M picture starring Eddie Cantor in a cast that included Judith Anderson, Ralph Morgan, Rita Johnson and Bonita Granville, and directed by Busby Berkeley. Songs by Harry Tobias and Nat Simon:
LITTLE CURLY HAIR IN A HIGH CHAIR and YOUR DAY WLL COME.

GIRL FROM HAVANA

A Republic picture filmed with a cast headed by Dennis O'Keefe, Victor Jory, Claire Carleton and Steffi Duna, and directed by Lew Landers. Songs by George R. Brown and Jule Styne:
QUERIDA (TAKE ME TONIGHT) and THE GIRL FROM HAVANA.

GLAMOUR FOR SALE

A Columbia picture starring Anita Louise in a cast that included Roger Pryor and June MacClay, and directed by D. Ross Lederman. Song by Milton Drake and Ben Oakland:
IF THEY GAVE ME A MILLION

GOLDEN FLEECING, THE

An M-G-M picture filmed with a cast headed by Lew Ayres, Rita Johnson, Lloyd Nolan, Virginia Grey, Nat Pendleton and Leon Errol, and directed by Leslie Fenton. Song by Gus Kahn and David Snell:
MARCH, MARCH THE BOYS ARE TRAMPING

HE STAYED FOR BREAKFAST

A Columbia picture starring Loretta Young and Melvyn Douglas in a cast that included Una O'Connor, Eugene Pallette and Alan Marshall, and directed by Alexander Hall. Song by Milton Drake:
WORKERS' SONG

HOUSE ACROSS THE BAY

A United Artists' picture starring George Raft and Joan Bennett in a cast that in-

cluded Lloyd Nolan, Gladys George, Walter
Pidgeon and June Knight, and directed by
Archie Mayo. Songs:
CHULA CHIHUAHUA by Sidney Clare,
Nick Castle and Jule Styne; I'LL BE A
FOOL AGAIN by Al Siegel; A HUNDRED
KISSES FROM NOW by George R. Brown
and Irving Actman.

HOUSE OF SEVEN GABLES
A Universal picture starring George San-
ders, Margaret Lindsay and Vincent Price,
and directed by Joe May. Song by Ralph
Freed and Frank Skinner:
THE COLOR OF YOUR EYES

HULLABALOO
An M-G-M picture filmed with a cast
headed by Frank Morgan, Virginia Grey,
Dan Dailey Jr. and Billie Burke, and di-
rected by Edwin L. Marin. Songs:
CARRY ME BACK TO OLD VIR-
GINNY by James Bland; WE'VE COME
A LONG WAY TOGETHER by Ted
Koehler and Sammy Stept; A HANDFUL
OF STARS by Jack Lawrence and Ted
Shapiro.

IT ALL CAME TRUE
A Warner Brothers' picture starring Ann
Sheridan and Humphrey Bogart in a cast
that included Jeffery Lynn and Zasu Pitts,
and directed by Lewis Seiler. Song by Kim
Gannon, Stephen Weiss and Paul Mann:
ANGEL IN DISGUISE

KIT CARSON
A United Artists' picture filmed with a
cast headed by Jon Hall, Lynn Bari and
Dana Andrews, and directed by George B.
Seitz. Songs by Chet Forrest, Bob Wright
and Ed Ward:
WITH MY CONCERTINA and PRAI-
RIE SCHOONER (SAIL ALONG).

LADIES MUST LIVE
A Warner Brothers' picture starring
Wayne Morris and Priscilla Lane, and di-
rected by Noel Smith. Song by Sammy
Cahn and Saul Chaplin:
I COULD MAKE YOU CARE

LADY WITH RED HAIR
A Warner Brothers' picture starring Mir-
iam Hopkins and Claude Rains, and direct-
ed by Kurt Bernhard. Song by Bickley
Reichner and Guy Wood:
LADY WITH RED HAIR

LI'L ABNER
An RKO picture filmed with a cast head-
ed by Granville Owen, Martha O'Driscoll
and Mona Ray. Song by Milton Drake,
Milton Berle and Ben Oakland:
LI'L ABNER

LITTLE OLD NEW YORK
A 20th Century-Fox picture starring Alice
Faye and Fred MacMurray in a cast that
included Branda Joyce, Richard Greene and
Henry Stephenson, and directed by Henry
King. Song by Mack Gordon:
WHO IS THE BEAU OF THE BELLE
OF NEW YORK?

MA, HE'S MAKING EYES AT ME
A Universal picture starring Tom Brown
and Constance Moore in a cast that in-
cluded Richard Carle and Anne Nagel, and
directed by Harold Schuster. Songs:
UNFAIR TO LOVE by Sam Lerner and
Frank Skinner; A LEMON IN THE GAR-
DEN OF LOVE by M. E. Rourke and
Richard Carle; MA, HE'S MAKING EYES
AT ME by Sidney Clare and Con Conrad.

MARGIE
A Universal picture filmed with a cast
headed by Tom Brown, Nan Grey, Mischa
Auer, Edgar Kennedy and Allen Jenkins,
and directed by Otis Garrett and Paul Gerard Smith. Songs:
WHEN BANANA BLOSSOMS BLOOM
by Sam Lerner and Charles Previn; OH,
FLY WITH ME by Paul Gerard Smith
and Charles Previn; MARGIE by Benny
Davis, J. Russell Robinson and Con Conrad.

MOON OVER BURMA
A Paramount picture starring Dorothy
Lamour in a cast that included Robert
Preston and Preston Foster, and directed
by Louis King. Songs:
MEXICAN MAGIC by Frank Loesser
and Harry Revel; MOON OVER BURMA
by Frank Loesser and Frederick Hollander.

MY LITTLE CHICKADEE
A Universal picture starring Mae West
and W. C. Fields in a cast that included
Joseph Calleia and Dick Foran, and directed
by Edward F. Cline. Song by Milton Drake
and Ben Oakland:
WILLIE OF THE VALLEY

MY SON, MY SON
A United Artists' picture starring Made-
leine Carroll in a cast that included Brian
Aherne, Louis Heyward, Laraine Day and
Henry Hull, and directed by Charles Vidor.
Song by L. Wolfe Gilbert and Lew Pollack:
MY SON, MY SON

NOBODY'S CHILDREN
A Columbia picture filmed with a cast

headed by Edith Fellows, Billy Lee, Georgia Caine and Lois Wilson, and directed by Charles Barton. Song by Sidney Mitchell, Con Conrad and Archie Gottler:
SO DEAR TO ME

NORTHWEST MOUNTED POLICE
A Paramount picture starring Gary Cooper and Madeleine Carroll in a cast that included Paulette Goddard, Preston Foster, Robert Preston and George Bancroft, and directed by Cecil B. De Mille. Song by Frank Loesser and Victor Young:
DOES THE MOON SHINE THROUGH THE TALL PINE?

PARDON MY RHYTHM
A Universal picture starring Gloria Jean and Patric Knowles in a cast that included Marjorie Weaver, Walter Catlett, Mel Torme and Bob Crosby's orchestra, and directed by Felix E. Feist. Song by Irving Bibo, Don George and Al Piantadosi:
DO YOU BELIEVE IN DREAMS?

QUARTERBACK, THE
A Paramount picture filmed with a cast headed by Wayne Morris, Virginia Dale and Edgar Kennedy, and directed by H. Bruce Humberstone. Songs:
OUT WITH YOUR CHEST (AND UP WITH YOUR CHIN) by Frank Loesser and Matt Malneck; SENTIMENTAL ME by Jack Lawrence, Stephen Weiss and Paul Mann.

RAMPARTS WE WATCH, THE
An RKO picture filmed with a cast headed by John Adair, John Sammers and Julia Kent, and directed by Louis de Rochemont. Song by W. Gordon Beecher:
THE RAMPARTS WE WATCH

SANTA FE TRAIL
A First National picture starring Errol Flynn and Olivia De Haviland in a cast that included Raymond Massey and Ronald Reagan, and directed by Michael Curtiz. Songs:
HOLIDAY WAGON SONG by Jack Scholl and M. K. Jerome; ALONG THE SANTA FE TRAIL by Al Dubin and Will Grosz.

SCATTERBRAIN
A Republic picture starring Judy Canova in a cast that included Alan Mowbray, Ruth Donnelly and Eddie Foy Jr., and directed by Gus Meins. Song by Hy Heath, Johnny Lange and Lew Porter:
BENNY THE BEAVER (YOU BETTER BE LIKE THAT, YEAH, YEAH).

SEVEN SINNERS
A Universal picture starring Marlene Dietrich and John Wayne, and directed by Tay Garnett. Songs by Frank Loesser and Frederick Hollander:
I'VE FALLEN OVERBOARD; I'VE BEEN IN LOVE BEFORE and THE MAN'S IN THE NAVY.

SEVENTEEN
A Paramount picture starring Jackie Cooper and Betty Field, and directed by Louis King. Song by Frank Loesser:
SEVENTEEN

SIDEWALKS OF LONDON, THE
A Paramount picture starring Charles Laughton and Vivian Leigh in a cast that included Rex Harrison and Larry Adler, and directed by Tim Whelan. Songs by Ed Pola and Arthur Johnston:
WEAR A STRAW HAT IN THE RAIN and LONDON LOVE SONG.

SLIGHTLY HONORABLE
A United Artists' picture filmed with a cast headed by Pat O'Brien, Edward Arnold, Broderick Crawford and Ruth Terry, and directed by Tay Garnett. Song by George R. Brown and Jule Styne:
CUPID'S AFTER ME

SOUTH OF PAGO PAGO
A United Artists' picture filmed with a cast headed by Victor McLaglen, Jon Hall, Frances Farmer, Gene Lockhart and Olympe Bradna, and directed by Alfred E. Green. Song by Bob Wright, Chet Forrest and Lew Pollack:
SOUTH OF PAGO PAGO

STAR DUST
A 20th Century-Fox picture starring Linda Darnell and John Payne in a cast that included Roland Young, William Gargan, Charlotte Greenwood, Mary Beth Hughes, Donald Meek and Mary Healy, and directed by Walter Lang. Songs by Mack Gordon:
SECRETS IN THE MOONLIGHT and DON'T LET IT GET YOU DOWN.

STRANGE CARGO
An M-G-M picture starring Joan Crawford and Clark Gable in a cast that included Ian Hunter, Peter Lorre, Albert Dekker and Paul Lukas, and directed by Frank Borzage. Song by Bob Wright and Chet Forrest:
STAR OF THE SEA

THIEF OF BAGDAD, THE
An Alexander Korda-United Artists' pic-

ture filmed with a cast headed by Conrad Veidt, Sabu, June Duprez and Rex Ingram, and directed by Ludwig Berger, Michael Powell and Tim Whelan. Songs:
SINCE TIME BEGAN by Nic Roger and William Kernell; I WANT TO BE A SAILOR by Milton Rozsa and R. Denham.

THIRD FINGER LEFT HAND
An M-G-M picture starring Myrna Loy and Melvyn Douglas, and directed by Robert Z. Leonard. Song by Earl Brent and David Snell:
ROUND AT THE ENDS AND HIGH IN THE MIDDLE

'TIL WE MEET AGAIN
A First National picture starring Merle Oberon and George Brent, and directed by

Edmund Goulding. Song by Al Dubin and W. Franke Harling:
WHERE WAS I?

TIN PAN ALLEY
A 20th Century-Fox picture filmed with a cast headed by Alice Faye, Betty Grable, Jack Oakie and John Payne, and directed by Walter Lang. Song by Mack Gordon and Harry Revel:
YOU SAY THE SWEETEST THINGS BABY

TYPHOON
A Paramount picture starring Dorothy Lamour and Robert Preston, and directed by Louis King. Song by Frank Loesser and Frederick Hollander:
PALMS OF PARADISE

Western Films With Songs

ARIZONA GANG BUSTERS
A Producers Releasing Corporation picture starring Tim McCoy. Song by Johnny Lange and Lew Porter:
PEPITO MIO

BAD MAN FROM RED BUTTE
A Universal picture starring Johnny Mack Brown in a cast that included Fuzzy Knight, Bob Baker and Anne Gwynne, and directed by Ray Taylor. Songs by Everett Carter and Milton Rosen:
GABBY THE LAWYER and WHERE THE PRAIRIE MEETS THE SKY.

BORDER LEGION, THE
A Republic picture starring Roy Rogers in a cast that included Gabby Hayes and Carol Hughes, and directed by Joseph Kane. Song by Mort Harris, Edward Heyman and Ted Snyder:
WITH MY GUITAR AND YOU

CAROLINA MOON
A Republic picture starring Gene Autry in a cast that included Smiley Burnette and June Storey, and directed by Frank McDonald. Songs by Gene Autry and Johnny Marvin:
AT THE RODEO and DREAMS THAT WON'T COME TRUE (with Harry Tobias).

CARSON CITY KID
A Republic picture starring Roy Rogers in a cast that included Gabby Hayes and Pauline Moore, and directed by Joseph Kane. Songs by Peter Tinturin:
GOLD DIGGERS' SONG; ARE YOU THE ONE? and SONORA MOON.

CHIP OF THE FLYING U
A Universal picture starring Johnny Mack Brown in a cast that included Doris Weston and Fuzzy Knight, and directed by Ralph Staub. Songs by Everett Carter and Milton Rosen:
MR. MOON; RIDE ON and GIT ALONG.

COLORADO
A Republic picture starring Roy Rogers in a cast that included Pauline Moore and Gabby Hayes, and directed by Joseph Kane. Songs:
NIGHT ON THE PRAIRIE by A. Hamilton and Nate Gluck; RING DE BANJO; DE CAMPTOWN RACES and OH, SUSANNA by Stephen Foster.

GAUCHO SERENADE
A Republic picture starring Gene Autry in a cast that included Smiley Burnette and June Storey, and directed by Frank McDonald. Songs:
KEEP ROLLIN' LAZY LONGHORNS by Gene Autry and Johnny Marvin; A SONG AT SUNSET and HEADIN' FOR THE WIDE OPEN SPACES by Gene Autry, Johnny Marvin and Harry Tobias.

GOLDEN TRAIL
A Monogram picture starring Tex Ritter in a cast that included Slim Andrews and Ina Guest, and directed by Al Herman. Song by Johnny Lange and Lew Porter:
THEY'RE HANGIN' PAPPY IN THE MORNIN'.

KID FROM SANTA FE
A Monogram picture starring Jack Ran-

dall and Clarence Curtis, and directed by Raymond K. Johnson. Song by Johnny Lange and Lew Porter:
UNDER WESTERN SKIES

KNIGHTS OF THE RANGE

A Paramount picture filmed with a cast headed by Russell Hayden, Victor Jory, Jean Parker, Bret Wood and the King's Men, and directed by Leslie Selander. Songs by Foster Carling and Phil Ohman:
PRAYER ON THE PRAIRIE; MORNIN' ON THE TRAIL; WHERE THE CIMARRON FLOWS and ROLL ALONG COVERED WAGON.

LAND OF SIX GUNS

A Monogram picture starring Jack Randall and Louise Stanley, and directed by Raymond K. Johnson. Song by Johnny Lange and Lew Porter:
THE PRIDE OF THE VALLEY

LAW AND ORDER

A Universal picture starring Johnny Mack Brown in a cast that included Fuzzy Knight and Nell O'Day, and directed by Ray Taylor. Songs by Everett Carter and Milton Rosen:
RIDE 'EM COWBOY and THOSE HAPPY OLD DAYS.

MELODY RANCH

A Republic picture starring Gene Autry and Jimmy Durante in a cast that included Ann Miller, Barton McLane, Barbara Allen and Gabby Hayes, and directed by Joseph Santley. Songs:
TORPEDO JOE; WHAT ARE COWBOYS MADE OF? RODEO ROSE and STAKE YOUR DREAMS ON MELODY RANCH by Eddy Cherkose and Jule Styne; WE NEVER DREAM THE SAME DREAM TWICE by Gene Autry and Fred Rose.

PALS OF THE SILVER SAGE

A Republic picture starring Tex Ritter and Sugar Dawn, and directed by Al Herman. Song by Johnny Lange and Lew Porter:
PRAIRIE FAIRYLAND

PONY POST

A Universal picture starring Johnny Mack Brown, Fuzzy Knight and Nell O'Day, and directed by Ray Taylor. Song by Everett Carter and Milton Rosen:
I DON'T LIKE NO COWS

PRAIRIE STRANGER

A Columbia picture filmed with a cast headed by Cliff Edwards, Charles Starrett,

Patti McCarty and Frank LaRue, and directed by Lambert Hillyer. Songs:
I'M JUST A SMALL TOWN SCALLYWAG; RIDE COWBOY RIDE and DOING IT RIGHT by Lew Preston; I'LL BE A COWBOY TILL I DIE by Lopez Willingham.

RAGTIME COWBOY JOE

A Universal picture starring Johnny Mack Brown in a cast that included Fuzzy Knight and Nell O'Day, and directed by Ray Taylor. Songs by Everett Carter and Milton Rosen:
CROSS-EYED KATE and DO THE OO-LA-LA.

RAINBOW OVER THE RANGE

A Monogram picture filmed with a cast headed by Tex Ritter, Slim Andrews and Dorothy Ray, and directed by Al Herman. Songs:
POOR SLIM by Johnny Lange and Lew Porter; RAINBOW OVER THE RANGE by Allan Fleming.

RANCHO GRANDE

A Republic picture starring Gene Autry, and directed by Frank McDonald. Songs:
THERE'LL NEVER BE ANOTHER PAL LIKE YOU by Johnny Marvin, Gene Autry and Harry Tobias; I DON'T BELONG IN YOUR WORLD by Gene Autry, Johnny Marvin and Fred Rose; WHISTLE by Johnny Marvin and Fred Rose; SWING OF THE RANGE by Johnny Marvin and Harry Tobias.

RANGE BUSTERS

A Monogram picture filmed with a cast headed by John King, Ray Corrigan and Max Terhune, and directed by S. Roy Luby. Song by Johnny Lange and Lew Porter:
GIT ALONG COWBOY

RANGER AND THE LADY, THE

A Republic picture starring Roy Rogers in a cast that included Gabby Hayes and Jacqueline Wells, and directed by Joseph Kane. Songs by Peter Tinturin:
CHIQUITA and AS LONG AS WE'RE DANCING.

RIDE TENDERFOOT RIDE

A Republic picture starring Gene Autry in a cast that included Smiley Burnette and June Storey, and directed by Frank McDonald. Songs:
ELEVEN MORE MONTHS AND TEN MORE DAYS (I'll BE OUT OF THE CALABOOSE) by Fred Hall and Arthur Fields; RIDE TENDERFOOT RIDE by

Johnny Mercer and Richard Whiting; WOODPECKER'S SONG by Harold Adamson and Eldo Di Lazzaro; THAT WAS ME BY THE SEA by Smiley Burnette; LEANIN' ON THE OLD TOP RAIL by Nick and Charles Kenny; OH, OH, OH! and ON THE RANGE by Johnny Marvin and Gene Autry.

RIDERS OF PASCO BASIN

A Universal picture starring Johnny Mack Brown in a cast that included Bob Baker and Fuzzy Knight, and directed by Ray Taylor. Songs by Everett Carter and Milton Rosen:
SONG OF THE PRAIRIE and I'M TYING UP MY BRIDLE TO THE DOOR OF YOUR HEART.

SHOOTING HIGH

A 20th Century-Fox picture starring Gene Autry and Jane Withers, and directed by Alfred E. Green. Songs:
ONLY ONE LOVE IN A LIFETIME by Gene Autry and Harry Tobias; IN OUR LITTLE SHANTY OF DREAMS by Gene Autry and Johnny Marvin; ON THE RANCHO WITH MY PANCHO by Sidney Clare and Harry Akst.

SHOWDOWN, THE

A Paramount picture starring Bill Boyd in a cast that included Russell Hayden, Britt Wood, Jane Clayton and the King's Men, and directed by Howard Bretherton. Song by Foster Carling and Phil Ohman:
MY SOLO AMOUR

SKY BANDITS

A Monogram picture starring James Newill and Louise Stanley. Songs by Johnny Lange and Lew Porter:
YOU'RE THE KIND OF A GIRL FOR ME; ALLEZ OOP and LADY IN THE CLOUDS.

SON OF ROARING DAN

A Universal picture starring Johnny Mack Brown in a cast that included Fuzzy Knight and Nell O'Day, and directed by Ford Beebe. Songs by Everett Carter and Milton Rosen:
SING YIPPI KI YI and THEN I GOT MARRIED.

STAGECOACH WAR

A Paramount picture starring Bill Boyd in a cast that included Russell Hayden and Julie Carter, and directed by Leslie Selander. Songs by Foster Carling and Phil Ohman:
THE HOP-ALONG ROAD; WESTWARD HO and HOLD YOUR HORSES.

TAKE ME BACK TO OKLAHOMA

A Monogram picture starring Tex Ritter and Terry Walker. Songs:
VILLAGE BLACKSMITH by Slim Andrews and Tex Ritter; YOU ARE MY SUNSHINE by Jimmy Davis and Charles Mitchell; CALAMITY KATE by Johnny Lange and Lew Porter; GOOD OLD OKLAHOMA; TAKE ME BACK TO TULSA; LONE STAR RAG and GOIN' INDIAN by Bob Wills and Tommy Duncan.

TRAILING DOUBLE TROUBLE

A Monogram picture filmed with a cast headed by Ray Corrigan, John Dusty King and Max Terhune, and directed by S. Ray Luby. Song by Johnny Lange and Lew Porter:
UNDER THE WESTERN SKIES

TULSA KID

A Republic picture filmed with a cast headed by Don "Red" Barry, Noah Beery and Luana Walters, and directed by George Sherman. Song by James Bland:
OH DEM GOLDEN SLIPPERS

UNDER WESTERN STARS

A Republic picture starring Roy Rogers in a cast that included Smiley Burnette and Carole Hughes. Song by Johnny Marvin:
OL' PEACEFUL RIVER

WEST OF CARSON CITY

A Universal picture starring Johnny Mack Brown in a cast that included Bob Baker, Fuzzy Knight and Peggy Moran, and directed by Ray Taylor. Songs by Everett Carter and Milton Rosen:
ON THE TRAIL OF TOMORROW and LET'S GO.

WEST OF PINTO BASIN

A Monogram picture filmed with a cast headed by Ray "Crash" Corrigan, and directed by S. Roy Luby. Songs by Johnny Lange and Lew Porter:
THAT LITTLE PRAIRIE GAL OF MINE and A RAINBOW IS RIDIN' THE RANGE

WESTBOUND STAGE

A Monogram picture starring Tex Ritter in a cast that included Muriel Evans, and directed by Spencer Bennett. Song by Johnny Lange and Lew Porter:
IT'S ALL OVER NOW (I WON'T WORRY)

WINNERS OF THE WEST

A Universal picture filmed with a cast

headed by Dick Foran, Harry Woods and Anne Nagel. Song by Everett Carter and Milton Rosen:

THE DRINKS ARE ON THE HOUSE

YOUNG BILL HICKOK

A Republic picture starring Roy Rogers in a cast that included Gabby Hayes and Jacqueline Wells, and directed by Joseph Kane. Songs:

I'LL KEEP ON SINGIN' A SONG by Roy Rogers; WHEN THE SHADOWS FALL ACROSS THE ROCKIES by Peter Tinturin; CHOLLIE'S TAMALES by Eddie Cherkose and Raoul Kraushaar; I'M GONNA HAVE A COWBOY WEDDIN' by Mila Sweet and Nat Vincent.

YOUNG BUFFALO BILL

A Republic picture starring Roy Rogers in a cast that included Pauline Moore and Gabby Hayes, and directed by Joseph Kane. Songs:

ROLLIN' DOWN TO SANTA FE by Walter G. Samuels; BLOW BREEZE BLOW by Peter Tinturin.

Feature Cartoon With Songs

PINOCCHIO

An RKO-Walt Disney production with songs by Ned Washington and Leigh Harline:

AS I WAS SAY'N' TO THE DUCHESS; GIVE A LITTLE WHISTLE; GOT NO STRINGS; LITTLE WOODEN HEAD; PINOCCHIO; THREE CHEERS FOR ANYTHING; HI-DIDDLE-DEE-DEE; WHEN YOU WISH UPON A STAR; TURN ON THE OLD MUSIC BOX and JIMINY CRICKET.

Gene Kelly and Judy Garland in *For Me and My Gal*

1 9 4 1

The Fall Of Paris Inspires An Oscar-winning Song

There was little spectacular or colossal about the musicals that Hollywood released in 1941 when an aroused America started to marshal her military and economic might for an inevitable war of survival, but in this year of national anxiety and watchful waiting, the cinema capital came through with an Oscar-winning song that was destined to endure because it struck deep into the hearts of the people.

Oscar Hammerstein II, the lyricist, just had to write it to relieve the emotional tension that gripped him when he read of the fall of the French capital. He could think of nothing else, concentrate on nothing else but the plight of a city he knew and loved and the shame of its proud people. So finally brushing aside all his other work, he sat down and dashed off the words and sent them to Jerome Kern, who was equally as inspired when he started to compose a melody. Thus *The Last Time I Saw Paris* was conceived—a poignant tribute to a city of beauty, charm and gaiety now betrayed and enslaved.

And while *I Like New York In June How About You?*, *Blues In The Night*, *Dolores* and *Chattanooga Choo-Choo*, all Hollywood-born, also rode high on the 1941 Hit Parade, it was a lack-lustre year in which the two biggest box-office attractions appeared in only two musicals each: Bing Crosby in *Birth Of The Blues* and *The Road To Zanzibar* and Judy Garland in *Babes On Broadway* and *Ziegfeld Girl*.

Hollywood again turned to Broadway for ready-made song-and-dance material, and adapted to the screen George Gershwin's *Lady Be Good* in which *The Last Time I Saw Paris* was interpolated, Irving Berlin's *Louisiana Purchase*, Jerome Kern's *Sunny* in which Anna Neagle, the English singing star, appeared, *The Chocolate Soldier* in which the "Met" soprano, Risé Stevens, made her film debut, and *Hellzapoppin'*, which was far from the success on the screen that it had been in New York where it ran for 1404 performances.

As the training camps were being constructed or opened to house thousands of selective service men, the Hollywood studios besieged the costume houses for Army and Navy uniforms, and Abbott and Costello were starred in three pictures with a military background: *Buck Privates*, *In The Navy* and *Keep 'Em Flying*, Bob Crosby had headline billing in *Rookies On Parade*, Bob Hope donned khaki in *Caught In The Draft*, and Mary Martin became the sweetheart of the services in *Kiss The Boys Goodbye*.

A limited shooting schedule for musicals gave the song-and-dance stars a chance to relax in their swimming pools and on the beach at Malibu, but the cartoonists in the Walt Disney studios worked around-the-clock to get *Dumbo*, *Mr. Bug Goes To Town* and *The Reluctant Dragon* before the cameras.

Musicals

ALL-AMERICAN CO-ED
A United Artists' picture starring Frances Langford in a cast that included Johnny Downs, Marjorie Woodworth, Noah Beery Jr., Esther Dale, Harry Langdon, Alan Hale Jr. and Joe E. Brown Jr., and directed by Le Roy Prinz. Songs:
I'M A CHAP WITH A CHIP ON MY SHOULDER; UP AT THE CRACK OF DAWN and THE FARMER'S DAUGHTER by Charles Newman and Walter G. Samuels; OUT OF THE SILENCE by Lloyd Norlin.

ANGELS WITH BROKEN WINGS
A Republic picture filmed with a cast headed by Binnie Barnes, Gilbert Roland, Mary Lee, Billy Gilbert and Jane Frazee, and directed by Donald Vorhaus. Songs by Eddie Cherkose and Jule Styne:
BYE-LO BABY; HAS TO BE; IN BUENOS AIRES; THREE LITTLE WISHES and WHERE DO WE DREAM FROM HERE?

ARKANSAS JUDGE
A Republic picture filmed with a cast headed by Leon, Frank and Joan Weaver and Roy Rogers, and directed by Frank McDonald. Songs:
NAOMI WISE by Carson J. Robison; PEACEFUL VALLEY by Willard Robison; KEEP ON THE SUNNY SIDE by A. P. Carter; HAPPY LITTLE HOME IN ARKANSAS (Traditional)

BABES ON BROADWAY
An M-G-M picture starring Judy Garland and Mickey Rooney in a cast that included Fay Bainter, and directed by Busby Berkeley. Songs:
(I LIKE NEW YORK IN JUNE) HOW ABOUT YOU? and BABES ON BROADWAY by Ralph Freed and Burton Lane; ANYTHING CAN HAPPEN IN NEW YORK and CHIN UP, CHEERIO, CARRY ON by E. Y. Harburg and Burton Lane; HOE DOWN by Ralph Freed and Roger Edens; BOMBSHELL FROM BRAZIL by Roger Edens; F. D. R. Jones by Harold Rome; MAMA YO QUIERO (I WANT MY MAMA) by Al Stillman and Jararaca and Vincente Paiva.

BIG STORE, THE
An M-G-M picture starring Chico, Harpo and Groucho Marx in a cast that included Tony Martin, Virginia Grey, Margaret Dumont and Six Hits and A Miss, and directed by Charles Reisner. Songs:
TENEMENT SYMPHONY and SING WHILE YOU SELL by Sid Kuller, Ray Golden and Hal Borne; IF IT'S YOU by Milton Drake, Artie Shaw and Ben Oakland.

BIRTH OF THE BLUES
A Paramount picture starring Bing Crosby in a cast that included Mary Martin, Brian Donlevy, Carolyn Lee, Eddie "Rochester" Anderson and Jack Teagarden, and directed by Victor Schertzinger. Musical numbers:
THE WAITER AND THE PORTER AND THE UPSTAIRS MAID by Johnny Mercer; GOTTA GO TO THE JAIL HOUSE by Robert E. Dolan and Harry Tugend; MEMPHIS BLUES and ST. LOUIS BLUES by W. C. Handy; BY THE LIGHT OF THE SILVERY MOON by Edward Madden and Gus Edwards; TIGER RAG by the Original Dixieland Jazz Band; WAITING AT THE CHURCH by Henry Pether and F. W. Leigh; CUDDLE UP A LITTLE CLOSER by Otto Harbach and Karl Hoschna; WAIT TILL THE SUN SHINES NELLIE by Andrew Sterling and Harry Von Tilzer; THAT'S WHY THEY CALL ME SHINE by Lew Brown, Cecil Mack and Ford Dabney; MELANCHOLY BABY by George Norton and Ernie Burnett; ST. JAMES INFIRMARY by Joe Primrose; BIRTH OF THE BLUES by B. G. DeSylva, Lew Brown and Ray Henderson.

BLONDIE GOES LATIN
A Columbia picture starring Penny Singleton and Arthur Lake in a cast that included Larry Simms, Tito Guizar and Ruth Terry, and directed by Frank R. Strayer. Songs by Chet Forrest and Bob Wright:
YOU DON'T PLAY A DRUM (YOU BEAT IT); I HATE MUSIC LESSONS; QUERIDA; YOU CAN'T CRY ON MY SHOULDER and CASTILLIAN COTILLION.

BLUES IN THE NIGHT
A Warner Brothers' picture starring Priscilla Lane in a cast that included Richard Whorf, Eddie Field, Lloyd Nolan and Jack Carson, and directed by Anatole Litvak. Songs by Johnny Mercer and Harold Arlen:
HANG ON TO YOUR LIDS KIDS; BLUES IN THE NIGHT; THIS TIME THE DREAM'S ON ME and SAYS WHO? SAYS YOU SAYS I.

BUCK PRIVATES

A Universal picture filmed with a cast headed by Lee Bowman, Al Curtis, Bud Abbott, Lou Costello, the Andrews Sisters, Jane Frazee and Nat Pendleton, and directed by Arthur Lubin. Songs by Don Raye and Hughie Prince:

BOUNCE ME WITH A SOLID FOUR; WISH YOU WERE HERE; WHEN PRIVATE BROWN MEETS A SERGEANT and YOU'RE A LUCKY FELLOW, MR. SMITH (With Sonny Burke).

CADET GIRL

A 20th Century-Fox picture starring Carole Landis and George Montgomery, and directed by Ray McCarey. Songs by Leo Robin and Ralph Rainger:

MY OLD MAN WAS AN ARMY MAN; SHE'S A GOOD NEIGHBOR; I'LL SETTLE FOR YOU; IT HAPPENED, IT'S OVER, LET'S FORGET IT; IT WON'T BE FUN (BUT IT'S GOT TO BE DONE); MAKING A PLAY FOR YOU and UNCLE SAM GETS AROUND.

CHOCOLATE SOLDIER, THE

An M-G-M picture starring Risé Stevens and Nelson Eddy in a cast that included Nigel Bruce, Florence Bates and Dorothy Gilmore, and directed by Roy Del Ruth. Songs:

MY HERO: LETTER SONG; ALEXIUS THE HEROIC; SYMPATHY; SEEK THE SPY and THE CHOCOLATE SOLDIER by Stanislaus Stange and Oscar Straus; WHILE MY LADY SLEEPS by Gus Kahn and Bronislaw Kaper.

DANCING ON A DIME

A Paramount picture filmed with a cast headed by Grace McDonald, Robert Paige and Peter Lind Hayes, and directed by Joseph Santley. Songs:

I HEAR MUSIC; MANANA and DANCING ON A DIME by Frank Loesser and Burton Lane; LOVEABLE SORT OF PERSON by Frank Loesser and Victor Young.

FIESTA

A United Artists' picture filmed with a cast headed by Anne Ayars, George Negrete and Armida, and directed by Le Roy Prinz. Songs:

EL RALAJO by Lamberto Layva, Jesus Castillion and Oscar Felix; I'LL NEVER FORGET FIESTA by Bob Wright, Chet Forrest and Nilo Menendez; NEVER TRUST A JUMPING BEAN and QUIEN SABE by Bob Wright, Chet Forrest and Ed Ward; LA GOLONDRINA by Narciso Serradell.

FOUR JACKS AND A JILL

An RKO picture filmed with a cast headed by Ray Bolger, Anne Shirley, Desi Arnaz and June Havoc, and directed by Jack Hively. Songs by Mort Greene and Harry Revel:

I'M IN GOOD SHAPE (FOR THE SHAPE I'M IN); KARANINA; WHEREVER YOU ARE; I HAVEN'T A THING TO WEAR; BOOGIE WOOGIE CONGA and YOU GO YOUR WAY (AND I'LL GO CRAZY).

GO WEST YOUNG LADY

A Columbia picture filmed with a cast headed by Penny Singleton, Glenn Ford, Ann Miller, Charles Ruggles, Allen Jenkins and Bob Wills and His Texas Playboys, and directed by Frank B. Strayer. Songs by Sammy Cahn and Saul Chaplin:

SOMEWHERE ALONG THE TRAIL; GO WEST YOUNG LADY; MOST GENTLEMEN PREFER A LADY; I WISH I COULD BE A SINGING COWBOY; DOGIE TAKE YOUR TIME and RISE TO ARMS (THE POTS AND PANS PARADE).

GREAT AMERICAN BROADCAST

A 20th Century-Fox picture filmed with a cast headed by Alice Faye, John Payne, Jack Oakie, Cesar Romero, Mary Beth Hughes and the Ink Spots, and directed by Archie Mayo. Songs by Mack Gordon and Harry Warren:

I'VE GOT A BONE TO PICK WITH YOU; I TAKE TO YOU; IT'S ALL IN A LIFETIME; LONG AGO LAST NIGHT; WHERE ARE YOU and THE GREAT AMERICAN BROADCAST.

HELLZAPOPPIN'

A Universal picture starring Olsen and Johnson in a cast that included Martha Raye, Mischa Auer, Jane Frazee, Hugh Herbert and Robert Paige, and directed by Henry C. Potter. Songs by Gene DePaul and Don Raye:

WHAT KIND OF LOVE IS THIS?; WATCH THE BIRDIE; YOU WERE THERE; HEAVEN FOR TWO; HELLZAPOPPIN'; PUTTING ON THE DOG; CONGEROO and CONGA BESO.

IN THE NAVY

A Universal picture starring Abbott and Costello in a cast that included Dick Powell, the Andrew Sisters, Claire Dodd and Dick

Foran, and directed by Arthur Lubin. Songs by Gene De Paul and Don Raye:

WE'RE IN THE NAVY; HULA-BA-LUA; OFF TO SEE THE WORLD; GIM-ME SOME SKIN MY FRIEND; A SAIL-OR'S LIFE FOR ME and STARLIGHT, STAR BRIGHT.

KEEP 'EM FLYING

A Universal picture starring Abbott and Costello in a cast that included Carol Bruce, Martha Raye, William Gargan and Dick Foran, and directed by Arthur Lubin. Songs by Don Raye and Gene DePaul:

TOGETHER; YOU DON'T KNOW WHAT LOVE IS; THE BOY WITH THE WISTFUL EYES; PIGFOOT PETE and LET'S KEEP 'EM FLYING.

KISS THE BOYS GOODBYE

A Paramount picture starring Mary Martin and Don Ameche in a cast that included Oscar Levant, directed by Victor Schertzinger, who wrote with Frank Loesser the following songs for this film:

FIND YOURSELF A MELODY; I'LL NEVER LET A DAY PASS BY; KISS THE BOYS GOODBYE; SAND IN MY SHOES and THAT'S HOW I GOT MY START.

LADY BE GOOD

An M-G-M picture filmed with a cast headed by Eleanor Powell, Ann Sothern, Robert Young, Lionel Barrymore, Red Skelton and Virginia O'Brien, and directed by Norman Z. McLeod. Songs:

HANG ON TO ME; FASCINATING RHYTHM and OH, LADY BE GOOD by Ira and George Gershwin; THE LAST TIME I SAW PARIS by Oscar Hammerstein II and Jerome Kern; YOU'LL NE-VER KNOW and YOUR WORDS AND MY MUSIC by Arthur Freed and Roger Edens.

LAS VEGAS NIGHTS

A Paramount picture filmed with a cast headed by Phil Regan, Bert Wheeler, Constance Moore and Tommy Dorsey's orchestra, and directed by Frank Murphy. Songs:

I'VE GOTTA RIDE and MARY, MARY QUITE CONTRARY by Frank Loesser and Burton Lane; DOLORES by Frank Loesser and Louis Alter.

LOUISIANA PURCHASE

A Paramount picture filmed with a cast headed by Bob Hope, Vera Zorina, Victor Moore, Irene Bordoni, Dona Drake, Raymond Walburn and Maxie Rosenbloom, and directed by Irving Cummings. Songs by Irving Berlin:

YOU'RE LONELY AND I'M LONELY; LOUISIANA PURCHASE; IT'S A LOVE-LY DAY TOMORROW and DANCE WITH ME AT THE MARDI GRAS.

MELODY LANE

A Universal picture filmed with a cast headed by the Merry Macs (Judd, Ted, Joe Mitchell and Mary Lou Cook), Sandy, Leon Errol, Butch and Buddy and Robert Paige, and directed by Charles Lamont. Songs by Jack Brooks and Norman Berens:

CHANGEABLE HEART; PEACEFUL ENDS THE DAY; CHEROKEE CHAR-LIE; LET'S GO TO CALIACABU; SWING-A-BYE MY BABY; IF IT'S A DREAM (DON'T WAKE ME) and SINCE THE FARMER IN THE DELL LEARNED TO SWING.

MOON OVER MIAMI

A 20th Century-Fox picture filmed with a cast headed by Don Ameche, Betty Grable, Charlotte Greenwood, Jack Haley, Carole Landis, Cobina Wright Jr. and Robert Cummings, and directed by Walter Lang. Songs by Leo Robin and Ralph Rainger:

SOLITARY SEMINOLE; LOVELI-NESS AND LOVE; YOU STARTED SOMETHING; HURRAY FOR TODAY; MIAMI; I'VE GOT YOU ALL TO MY-SELF; IS THAT GOOD? and KINDER-GARTEN CONGA (RING AROUND THE ROSIE).

MOONLIGHT IN HAWAII

A Universal picture filmed with a cast headed by Jane Frazee, Johnny Downs, Leon Errol, Mischa Auer, Richard Carle, Maria Montez and the Merry Macs, and directed by Charles Lamont. Songs by Don Raye and Gene DePaul:

POI; WE'LL HAVE A LOT OF FUN; IT'S PEOPLE LIKE YOU; MOON-LIGHT IN HAWAII and ALOHA LOW DOWN.

NAVY BLUES

A Warner Brothers' picture filmed with a cast headed by Ann Sheridan, Jack Oakie, Martha Raye, Jack Haley, Jack Carson and Jackie Gleason, and directed by Lloyd Bacon. Songs by Johnny Mercer and Arthur Schwartz:

IN WAIKIKI; YOU'RE A NATURAL; NAVY BLUES and WHEN ARE WE GO-ING TO LAND ABROAD?

NICE GIRL?

A Universal picture starring Deanna

Durbin and Franchot Tone in a cast that included Walter Brennan, Robert Stack, Robert Benchley and Helen Broderick, and directed by William A. Seiter. Songs:

LOVE AT LAST by Eddie Cherkose and Jacques Press; PERHAPS by Aldo Franchetti and Androsde Sequrola; BENEATH THE LIGHTS OF HOME and THANK YOU AMERICA by Bernie Grossman and Walter Jurmann.

PLAYMATES

An RKO picture filmed with a cast headed by Kay Kyser, Lupe Velez, John Barrymore, May Robson, Peter Lind Hayes, Ginny Simms and Patsy Kelly, and directed by David Butler. Songs by Johnny Burke and Jimmy Van Heusen:

HUMPTY DUMPTY HEART; ROMEO SMITH AND JULIET JONES; HOW LONG DID I DREAM?; QUE CHICA and THANK YOUR LUCKY STARS AND STRIPES.

PUDDIN' HEAD

A Republic picture starring Judy Canova in a cast that included Francis Lederer and Raymond Walburn, and directed by Joseph Santley. Songs by Eddie Cherkose, Sol Meyer and Jule Styne:

HEY JUNIOR; YOU'RE TELLING I; MANHATTAN HOLIDAY and PUDDIN' HEAD.

RISE AND SHINE

A 20th Century-Fox picture filmed with a cast headed by Jack Oakie, Linda Darnell, George Murphy, Walter Brennan, Donald Meek and Ruth Donnelly, and directed by Allan Dwan. Songs by Leo Robin and Ralph Rainger:

I'M MAKING A PLAY FOR YOU; CENTRAL TWO TWO OH OH; I WANT TO BE THE GUY; HEIL TO BOLENCIEWEZ and GET THEE BEHIND ME CLAYTON.

ROAD TO ZANZIBAR, THE

A Paramount picture starring Bing Crosby, Bob Hope and Dorothy Lamour in a cast that included Una Merkel, Eric Blore and Luis Alberni, and directed by Victor Schertzinger. Songs by Johnny Burke and Jimmy Van Heusen:

BIRDS OF A FEATHER; IT'S ALWAYS YOU; YOU'RE DANGEROUS and YOU LUCKY PEOPLE YOU.

ROAD SHOW

A United Artists' picture filmed with a cast headed by Adolphe Menjou, Carole

Landis, John Hubbard, Charles Butterworth and Patsy Kelly, and directed by Hal Roach Jr. and Gordon Douglas. Songs by Hoagy Carmichael:

CALLIOPE JANE; I SHOULD HAVE KNOWN YOU YEARS AGO; SLAV ANNIE and YUM! YUM!

ROOKIES ON PARADE

A Republic picture filmed with a cast headed by Bob Crosby, Ruth Terry, Gertrude Niesen, Eddie Foy Jr., Marie Wilson, Cliff Nazarro, William Demarest and Horace MacMahon, and directed by Joseph Santley. Songs:

THE ARMY BUILDS MEN; I LOVE YOU MORE; MOTHER NEVER TOLD ME WHY; MY KINDA LOVE; YOU'LL NEVER GET RICH; WHAT MORE DO YOU WANT and MY KINDA MUSIC by Sammy Cahn and Saul Chaplin; ROOKIES ON PARADE by Eddie Cherkose and Jule Styne.

SAN ANTONIO ROSE

A Universal picture filmed with a cast headed by Jane Frazee, Robert Paige, Eve Arden and Lon Chaney Jr., and directed by Charles Lamont. Songs:

ONCE UPON A SUMMERTIME by Jack Brooks and Norman Berens; MEXICAN JUMPING BEAT and YOU'VE GOT WHAT IT TAKES by Don Raye and Gene DePaul; HUT SUT SONG by Leo Killion, Ted McMichael and Jack Owens; HI NEIGHBOR by Jack Owens; SAN ANTONIO ROSE by Bob Wills; YOU'RE EVERYTHING WONDERFUL and BUGLE WOOGIE BOY by Henry Russell; BOUNCE ME BROTHER WITH A SOLID FOUR by Don Raye and Hughie Prince; SWEEP IT by Frank Skinner.

SING ANOTHER CHORUS

A Universal picture starring Jane Frazee and Johnny Downs, and directed by Charles Lamont. Songs by Everett Carter and Milton Rosen:

BOOGIE WOOGIE BOOGIE MAN; DANCING ON AIR; WALK WITH ME; TWO WEEKS' VACATION WITH PAY; MR. YANKEE DOODLE and WE TOO CAN SING.

SIS HOPKINS

A Republic picture starring Judy Canova and Bob Crosby in a cast that included Charles Butterworth, Jerry Colonna and Susan Hayward, and directed by Joseph Santley. Songs by Frank Loesser and Jule Styne:

CRACKER BARREL COUNTY; IF YOU'RE IN LOVE; LOOK AT YOU LOOK AT ME; WELL! WELL! and IT AIN'T HAY (IT'S THE U. S. A.).

SUN VALLEY SERENADE
A 20th Century-Fox picture starring Sonja Henie in a cast that included John Payne, Milton Berle, Joan Davis, the Nicholas Brothers and Glenn Miller's orchestra, and directed by H. Bruce Humberstone. Songs by Mack Gordon and Harry Warren:
CHATTANOOGA CHOO-CHOO; IT HAPPENED IN SUN VALLEY; I KNOW WHY (AND SO DO YOU); THE KISS POLKA and AT LAST.

SUNNY
An RKO picture starring Anna Neagle in a cast that included Ray Bolger, John Carroll, Martha Tilton, Benny Rubin and Grace and Paul Hartman, and directed by Herbert Wilcox. Songs by Otto Harbach, Oscar Hammerstein II and Jerome Kern:
WHO?; SUNNY; TWO LITTLE LOVE BIRDS and D'YE LOVE ME?

SWEETHEART OF THE CAMPUS
A Columbia picture filmed with a cast headed by Ruby Keeler, Ozzie Nelson, Harriet Hilliard and the Four Spirits of Rhythm, and directed by Edward Dmytryk. Songs:
WHEN THE GLEE CLUB SWINGS THE ALMA MATER by Charles Newman and Walter G. Samuels; WHERE by Jacques Krakeur; TOM, TOM THE ELEVATOR BOY by Walter G. Samuels; TAP HAPPY; ZIG ME BABY WITH A GENTLE ZAG and HERE WE GO AGAIN by Eddie Cherkose and Jacques Press.

TALL, DARK AND HANDSOME
A 20th Century-Fox picture filmed with a cast headed by Cesar Romero, Virginia Gilmore and Milton Berle, and directed by H. Bruce Humberstone. Songs by Leo Robin and Ralph Rainger:
HELLO MA I DONE IT AGAIN; WISHFUL THINKING and I'M ALIVE AND KICKIN'.

THAT NIGHT IN RIO
A 20th Century-Fox picture filmed with a cast headed by Alice Faye, Don Ameche and Carmen Miranda, and directed by Irving Cummings. Songs by Mack Gordon and Harry Warren:
CHICA CHICA BUM CHIC; I YI YI YI YI YI LIKE YOU VERY MUCH; THEY MET IN RIO; BOA NOITE and THE BARON IS IN CONFERENCE.

THEY MET IN ARGENTINA
An RKO picture filmed with a cast headed by Maureen O'Hara, James Ellison and Buddy Ebsen, and directed by Leslie Goodwins and Jack Hively. Songs by Lorenz Hart and Richard Rodgers:
SIMPATICA; NORTH AMERICA MEETS SOUTH AMERICA; YOU'VE GOT THE BEST OF ME; AMARILLO; LOLITA; NEVER GO TO ARGENTINE and CUTTING THE CANE.

TIME OUT FOR RHYTHM
A Columbia picture filmed with a cast headed by Ann Miller, Rudy Vallee, Rosemary Lane, Allen Jenkins, Joan Merrill and Richard Lane, and directed by Sidney Salkow. Songs by Sammy Cahn and Saul Chaplin:
DID ANYONE EVER TELL YOU? BOOGIE WOOGIE MAN; TIME OUT FOR RHYTHM; TWIDDLIN' MY THUMBS; OBVIOUSLY THE GENTLEMAN PREFERS TO DANCE; AS IF YOU DIDN'T KNOW; THE RIO DE JANEIRO and SHOWS HOW WRONG A GAL CAN BE.

TOO MANY BLONDES
Universal picture filmed with a cast headed by Rudy Vallee, Helen Parrish, Lon Chaney Jr., Eddie Quillan and Jeanne Kelly, and directed by Thornton Freeland. Songs:
WHISTLE YOUR BLUES TO A BLUEBIRD; DON'T MIND IF I DO and LET'S LOVE AGAIN by Everett Carter and Milton Rosen; THE MAN ON THE FLYING TRAPEZE.

TWO LATINS FROM MANHATTAN
A Columbia picture filmed with a cast headed by Joan Davis, Jinx Falkenburg, Joan Woodbury, Fortunio Bonanova and Don Beddoe, and directed by Charles Barton. Songs:
HOW DO YOU SAY IT? and THE KID WITH THE DRUM by Sammy Cahn and Saul Chaplin; DADDY by Bob Troup.

VIRGINIA
A Paramount picture starring Madeleine Carroll and Fred MacMurray, and directed by Edward H. Griffith. Songs by Howard Dietz and Arthur Schwartz:
GOODBYE JONAH; IF YOU WERE SOMEONE ELSE; AN OLD FLAME NEVER DIES and YOU AND I KNOW.

WEEK-END IN HAVANA
A 20th Century-Fox picture filmed with a cast headed by Alice Faye, Carmen Mir-

anda, John Payne and Cesar Romero, and directed by Walter Lang. Songs by Mack Gordon and Harry Warren:
MAN WITH THE LOLLIPOP SONG; THE NANGO; TROPICAL MAGIC; WHEN I LOVE I LOVE; WEEK-END IN HAVANA and ROMANCE AND THE RHUMBA (music by Jimmy Monaco).

YOU'LL NEVER GET RICH
A Columbia picture starring Fred Astaire and Rita Hayworth, and directed by Sidney Lanfield. Songs by Cole Porter:
DREAM DANCING; SINCE I KISSED MY BABY GOODBYE; SO NEAR AND YET SO FAR; BOOGIE WOOGIE BARCAROLE; SHOOTING THE WORKS FOR UNCLE SAM and WEDDING CAKE WALK.

YOU'RE THE ONE
A Paramount picture filmed with a cast headed by Bonnie Baker, Orrin Tucker, Albert Dekker, Jerry Colonna and Edward Everett Horton, and directed by Ralph Murphy. Songs by Johnny Mercer and Jimmy McHugh:
STRAWBERRY LANE; YOU'RE THE ONE FOR ME; GEE, I WISH I'D LISTENED TO MY MOTHER; I COULD KISS YOU FOR THAT and THE YOGI WHO LOST HIS WILL POWER.

ZIEGFELD GIRL
An M-G-M picture filmed with an all-star cast headed by James Stewart, Judy Garland, Hedy Lamarr, Lana Turner, Tony Martin, Jackie Cooper, Paul Kelly, Eve Arden, Dan Dailey Jr., Al Shean, Ian Hunter, Charles Winninger and Edward Everett Horton, and directed by Robert Z. Leonard. Songs:
MINNIE FROM TRINIDAD; ZIEGFELD GIRLS and LAUGH? I THOUGHT I'D SPLIT MY SIDES by Roger Edens; CARIBBEAN LOVE SONG by Ralph Freed and Roger Edens; YOU STEPPED OUT OF A DREAM by Gus Kahn and Nacio Herb Brown; I'M ALWAYS CHASING RAINBOWS by Joseph McCarthy and Harry Carroll; WHISPERING by John Schonberger, Richard Coburn and Vincent Rose; MR. GALLAGHER AND MR. SHEAN by Gallagher and Shean; YOU NEVER LOOKED SO BEAUTIFUL BEFORE by Walter Donaldson.

ZIS BOOM BAH
A Monogram picture filmed with a cast headed by Grace Hayes, Peter Lind Hayes, Mary Healy, Skeets Gallagher and Benny Rubin, and directed by William Nigh. Songs:
ANNABELLA and IT MAKES NO DIFFERENCE WHEN YOU'RE IN THE ARMY by Johnny Lange and Lew Porter; PUT YOUR TRUST IN THE MOON by June Baldwin and Charles Callender; ZIS BOOM BAH by Elaine Cannon; GOOD NEWS TOMORROW and I'VE LEARNED TO SMILE AGAIN by Neville Fleeson.

Feature Films With Songs

ALOMA OF THE SOUTH SEAS
A Paramount picture starring Dorothy Lamour and Jon Hall, and directed by Alfred Santell. Song by Frank Loesser and Frederick Hollander:
THE WHITE BLOSSOMS OF TAH-NI

ANDY HARDY'S PRIVATE SECRETARY
An M-G-M picture starring Mickey Rooney and Ann Rutherford in a cast that included Lewis Stone and Kathryn Grayson, and directed by George B. Seitz. Song by Cole Porter:
I'VE GOT MY EYES ON YOU

BAD LANDS OF DAKOTA
A Universal picture filmed with a cast headed by Robert Stack, Ann Rutherford, Richard Dix, Frances Farmer, Broderick Crawford, Hugh Herbert, Andy Devine and Lon Chaney Jr., and directed by Al Green.
NO ONE TO LOVE and GOIN' TO HAVE A BIG TIME TONIGHT by Carson Robison; MacNAMARA'S BAND by Shamus O'Connor and J. J. Stamford.

BARNACLE BILL
An M-G-M picture starring Wallace Beery in a cast that included Majorie Main, Leo Carrillo, Virginia Weidler, Donald Meek and Barton MacLane, and directed by Richard Thorpe. Songs by Harry Leon, Leo Towers and Victor Robins:
I'LL MEET YOU BY THE BLUE LAGOON and THE MISSUS AND ME

BILLY THE KID
An M-G-M picture starring Robert Taylor in a cast that included Brian Donlevy, Ian Hunter, Mary Howard, Gene Lockhart and Lon Chaney Jr., and directed by David Miller. Song by Ormand Ruthven and Albert Mannheimer:
VIVA LA VIDA

BREAK THE NEWS

A Monogram picture, filmed in England, starring Maurice Chevalier, Jack Buchanan and June Knight, and directed by Rene Clair. Song by Cole Porter:

IT ALL BELONGS TO YOU (THE LAUGH OF THE TOWN)

CAUGHT IN THE DRAFT

A Paramount picture starring Bob Hope and Dorothy Lamour in a cast that included Lynne Overman and Eddie Bracken, and directed by David Butler. Song by Frank Loesser and Louis Alter:

LOVE ME AS I AM

DANCE HALL

A 20th Century-Fox picture starring Carole Landis and Cesar Romero in a cast that included William Henry, June Storey and J. Edward Bromberg, and directed by Irving Pichel. Song by Joyce Cochrane and Christopher Hassall:

YOU'RE ONLY DREAMING

DOCTOR'S DON'T TELL

A Republic picture filmed with a cast headed by John Beal, Florence Rice, Edward Norris and Ward Bond, and directed by Jacques Tourneur. Songs:

LILLY AND BILLY by Sol Meyer and Jule Styne; TAKE MY HEART (FOR INSTANCE) and QUERIDA by Eddie Cherkose and Jule Styne.

FLAME OF NEW ORLEANS, THE

A Universal picture starring Marlene Dietrich in a cast that included Bruce Cabot and Roland Young, and directed by Rene Clair. Song by Sol Lerner and Charles Previn:

SALT O' THE SEA

FOOTSTEPS IN THE DARK

A Warner Brothers' picture filmed with a cast headed by Errol Flynn, Brenda Marshall, Ralph Bellamy, Alan Hale and Lee Patrick, and directed by Lloyd Bacon. Song by Jack Scholl and M. K. Jerome:

LOVE ME

FOUR MOTHERS

A Warner Brothers' picture filmed with a cast headed by Priscilla, Rosemary and Lola Lane, Gale Page, Claude Rains, Jeffry Lynn and Eddie Albert, and directed by William Keighley. Song by Jack Scholl and Heinz Roemheld:

MOONLIGHT AND TEARS

GIRL MUST LIVE, A

A Universal picture filmed with a cast headed by Margaret Lockwood, Lilli Palmer and Renee Houston, and directed by Carol Reed. Songs by George Scott and Wood Vedey:

I'M A SAVAGE and WHO'S YOUR LOVE?

GLAMOUR BOY

A Paramount picture starring Jackie Cooper and Susanna Foster, and directed by Ralph Murphy. Songs by Frank Loesser and Victor Schertzinger:

LOVE IS SUCH AN OLD-FASHIONED THING and THE MAGIC OF MAGNOLIAS

GOLDEN HOOFS

A 20th Century-Fox picture starring Jane Withers and Charles "Buddy" Rogers, and directed by Lynn Shores. Song by Walter Bullock and Harold Spina:

CONSIDER YOURSELF IN LOVE

HOLD BACK THE DAWN

A Paramount picture starring Charles Boyer, Olivia De Haviland and Paulette Goddard, and directed by Mitchell Leisen. Song by Frank Loesser, Jimmy Berg, Fred Spielman and Fred Jacobson:

MY BOY, MY BOY

HOLD THAT GHOST

A Universal picture starring Abbott and Costello, and directed by Arthur Lubin. Songs:

SLEEPY SERENADE by Mort Greene and Lou Singer; AURORA by Harold Adamson, Maria Logo and Roberto Roberti.

HOW GREEN WAS MY VALLEY

A 20th Century-Fox picture filmed with a cast headed by Walter Pidgeon, Maureen O'Hara, Donald Crisp, Anna Lee, Rody McDowell, John Loder, Sara Allgood and Barry Fitzgerald, and directed by John Ford. Song by Alfred Newman:

HOW GREEN WAS MY VALLEY

I WAKE UP SCREAMING

A 20th Century-Fox picture starring Betty Grable and Victor Mature in a cast that included Carole Landis, Laird Cregar, William Gargan, Alan Mowbray and Allyn Joslyn, and directed by H. Bruce Humberstone. Song by Harold Barlow and Lewis Harris:

THE THINGS I LOVE

I WANTED WINGS

A Paramount picture filmed with a cast headed by Ray Milland, William Holden, Wayne Morris, Brian Donlevy, Constance

Moore and Veronica Lake, and directed by
Mitchell Leisen. Song by Ned Washington
and Victor Young:
  BORN TO LOVE

ICE-CAPADES
A Republic picture filmed with a cast
headed by James Ellison, Jerry Colonna,
Dorothy Lew and Barbara Jo Allen, and
directed by Joseph Santley. Song by Sol
Meyer, George R. Brown and Jule Styne:
  FOREVER AND EVER

IT STARTED WITH EVE
A Universal picture starring Deanna Durbin, Charles Laughton and Robert Cummings, and directed by Henry Koster. Song
by Sam Lerner based on a melody by Peter
Tschaikowsky:
  WHEN I SING

LOVE CRAZY
An M-G-M picture starring William Powell and Myrna Loy in a cast that included
Gail Patrick and Jack Carson, and directed
by Jack Conway. Song by Dave Oppenheim
and Art Kahn:
  THAT NIGHT IN BRAZIL

MOON OVER HER SHOULDER
A 20th Century-Fox picture filmed with a
cast headed by Lynn Bari, John Sutton,
Dan Dailey Jr. and Alan Morbray, and di-
rected by Alfred Werker. Song by Walter
Bullock and Alfred Newman:
  THE GIRL WITH THE SUGAR-
BROWN HAIR

NEW YORK TOWN
A Paramount picture starring Mary Mar-
tin and Fred MacMurray, and directed by
Charles Vidor. Songs:
  TROPICAL SERENADE by Phil Bou-
telje; LOVE IN BLOOM by Leo Robin
and Ralph Rainger; YIP I ADDY I AY by
Will Cobb and John H. Flynn.

PAPER BULLETS
A Producers Releasing Corporation pic-
ture filmed with a cast that included Joan
Woodbury, Jack LaRue, Linda Ware, John
Archer and Alan Ladd, and directed by
Franklin Kozinsky. Songs by Johnny Lange
and Lew Porter:
  I KNOW, I KNOW and BLUE IS THE
DAY

PARACHUTE BATTALION
An RKO picture filmed with a cast head-
ed by Robert Preston, Nancy Kelly, Edmond
O'Brien, Harry Carey, Buddy Ebsen, Paul
Kelly and Richard Cromwell, and directed

by Leslie Goodwins. Song by Herman Ruby
and Roy Webb:
  SONG OF THE PARACHUTE BAT-
TALION

RAGS TO RICHES
A Republic picture starring Alan Baxter
and Mary Carlisle, and directed by Joseph
Kane. Songs by Sol Meyer and Jule Styne:
  THE CALL OF LOVE and NEVER,
NEVER, NEVER

RED HEAD
A Monogram picture starring June Lange
and Johnny Downs, and directed by Edward Cahn. Songs:
  DON'T KID YOURSELF by B. Watters
and Howard Steiner; SANTO DOMINGO
by B. Watters and Harvey Brooks.

REG'LAR FELLERS
A Producers Releasing Corporation pic-
ture filmed with a cast headed by Billy Lee,
Carl Alfalfa Switzer, Janet Dempsey, Buddy
Boles, Sarah Padden and Pat O'Malley, and
directed by Arthur Dreifuss. Songs by Ethel
Meglin and Dean Marmon:
  HOORAY FOR FUN and REG'LAR
FELLERS

RINGSIDE MAIZIE
An M-G-M picture filmed with a cast
headed by Ann Sheridan, George Murphy,
Robert Sterling, Virginia O'Brien, Maxie
Rosenbloom, Jack LaRue and Rags Rag-
land, and directed by Edward L. Marin.
Song by Arthur J. Lamb and Harry Von
Tilzer:
  A BIRD IN A GILDED CAGE

ROMANCE OF THE RIO GRANDE
A 20th Century-Fox picture starring Ces-
ar Romero and Lynne Roberts in a cast
that included Patricia Morison, Ricardo
Cortez and Pedro de Cordova, and directed
by Herbert I. Leeds. Songs:
  YOU'LL FIND YOUR ANSWER IN
MY EYES and RIDE ON VAQUERO by
Abel Baer; LA CUCARACHA (Mexican
folk song with English lyrics by Mitchell
Parish).

SAILORS ON LEAVE
A Republic picture starring William Lun-
digan and Shirley Ross, and directed by
Herbert Dalmas. Song by Frank Loesser and
Jule Styne:
  SINCE YOU

SHEPHERD OF THE HILLS
A Paramount picture starring John
Wayne and Betty Field in a cast that in-

cluded Harry Carey, Beulah Bondi and James Barton, and directed by Henry Hathaway. Song by Sam Coslow:
THERE'S A HAPPY HUNTING GROUND

SING FOR YOUR SUPPER
A Columbia picture starring Jinx Falkenburg and Charles "Buddy" Rogers, and directed by Charles Barton. Song by Sammy Cahn and Saul Chaplin:
WHY IS IT SO?

SIX LESSONS FROM MADAME LaZONGA
A Universal picture starring Lupe Velez in a cast that included Leon Errol, Helen Parrish, William Frawley, Eddie Quillan and Big Boy Williams, and directed by John Rawling. Songs:
THE MATADOR'S WIFE and JITTERUMBA by Everett Carter and Milton Rosen; SIX LESSONS FROM MADAME LaZONGA by Charles Newman and Jimmy Monaco.

SOUTH OF TAHITI
A Universal picture filmed with a cast headed by Brian Donlevy, Broderick Crawford, Andy Devine and Maria Montez, and directed by George Waggner. Song by Frank Skinner and George Waggner:
MELAHI

SUNDOWN
A United Artists' picture starring Gene Tierney in a cast that included Bruce Cabot, George Sanders, Harry Carey and Joseph Calleia, and directed by Henry Hathaway. Song by Jack Betzner and Irving Mills:
I'LL MEET YOU AT SUNDOWN

SWING IT SOLDIER
A Universal picture starring Frances Langford and Ken Murray, and directed by Harold Young. Song by Eddie Cherkose and Jacques Press:
I'M GONNA SWING MY WAY TO HEAVEN

THERE'S MAGIC IN MUSIC
A Paramount picture filmed with a cast headed by Allan Jones, Susanna Foster, Margaret Lindsay, Lynne Overman, Grace Bradley, William Collier and Deems Taylor, and directed by Andrew W. Stone. Song by Ann Ronell:
FIREFLIES ON PARADE

TOM, DICK AND HARRY
An RKO picture starring Ginger Rogers and George Murphy in a cast that included

Alan Marshall, Burgess Meredith, Jane Seymour and Phil Silvers, and directed by Carson Kanin. Song by Gene Rose and Roy Webb:
TOM COLLINS

TOP SERGEANT MULLIGAN
A Monogram picture filmed with a cast headed by Nat Pendleton, Carol Hughes, Sterling Holloway, Marjorie Reynolds, Tom Neal and Betty Blythe, and directed by Jean Yarbrough. Songs:
THAT'S WHAT I THINK ABOUT YOU by Harry Tobias and Edward Kay; TWENTY-ONE DOLLARS A DAY ONCE A MONTH by Ray Klages and Felix Bernard.

UNHOLY PARTNERS
An M-G-M picture starring Edward G. Robinson in a cast that included Edward Arnold, Laraine Day and Marsha Hunt, and directed by Mervyn Le Roy. Song by Turner Layton and Henry Creamer:
AFTER YOU'RE GONE

UP IN THE AIR
A Monogram picture filmed with a cast headed by Frankie Daro, Martin Moreland and Marjorie Reynolds, and directed by Howard Bretherton. Song by Johnny Lange and Lew Porter:
DOIN' THE CONGA

VANISHING VIRGINIAN
An M-G-M picture starring Frank Morgan, Kathryn Grayson and Spring Byington, and directed by Frank Borzage. Song by Minnaletha White and Earl K. Brent:
THE WORLD WAS MADE FOR YOU

WHERE DID YOU GET THAT GIRL?
A Universal picture filmed with a cast that included Helen Parrish, Charles Lang, Leon Errol, Stanley Fields, Tom Dugan, Franklin Pangborn, Eddie Quillan and Joe E. Brown Jr., and directed by Arthur Lubin. Songs by Everett Carter and Milton Rosen:
RUG-CUTTIN' ROMEO and SERGEANT SWING

WORLD PREMIERE
A Paramount picture starring John Barrymore and Frances Farmer, and directed by Ted Tetzlaff. Song by Frank Loesser and Burton Lane:
DON'T CRY LITTLE CLOUD

YANK IN THE R.A.F., A
A 20th Cenutry-Fox picture starring Tyrone Power and Betty Grable in a cast that

included Reginald Gardiner and John Sutton, and directed by Henry King. Songs by Leo Robin and Ralph Rainger:
ANOTHER LITTLE DREAM WON'T DO US ANY HARM and HI-YA LOVE

YUKON FLIGHT
A Monogram picture starring James Newill and Louise Stanley, and directed by Ralph Staub. Songs by Johnny Lange and Lew Porter:

MY WEAKNESS IS EYES OF BLUE and MOUNTED MEN ON PARADE

YOUTH WILL BE SERVED
A 20th Century-Fox picture starring Jane Withers in a cast that included Jane Darwell and Robert Conway, and directed by Otto Brower. Song by Frank Loesser and Louis Alter:
HOT CATFISH AND CORN DODGERS

Western Films With Songs

ACROSS THE SIERRAS
A Columbia picture starring Bill Elliott and Luana Walters, and directed by D. Ross Lederman. Songs by Milton Drake:
HONEYMOON RANCH; STAR-SPANGLED PRAIRIE and I GOTTA MAKE MUSIC.

BACK IN THE SADDLE
A Republic picture starring Gene Autry in a cast that included Smiley Burnette and Mary Lee, and directed by Lew Landers. Songs:
SWINGING SAM THE COWBOY MAN and WHERE THE RIVER MEETS THE RANGE by Sol Meyer and Jule Styne; NINETY-NINE BULLFROGS by Smiley Burnette.

BAD MAN OF DEADWOOD
A Republic picture starring Roy Rogers in a cast that included Gabby Hayes and Carol Adams, and directed by Joseph Kane. Song by Sol Meyer and Jule Styne:
JOE O'GRADY

BANDIT TRAIL, THE
An RKO picture filmed with a cast headed by Tim Holt, Ray Whitley, Janet Waldo and Lee 'Lasses White, and directed by Edward Killy. Song by Ray Whitley and Fred Rose:
ON THE OUTLAW TRAIL

BEYOND THE SACRAMENTO
A Columbia picture starring Bill Elliott and Evelyn Keyes, and directed by Lambert Hillyer. Songs by Milton Drake:
RIDIN' FOR THE LAW and THE WEST GETS UNDER MY SKIN

BURY ME NOT ON THE LONE PRAIRIE
A Universal picture starring Johnny Mack Brown in a cast that included Fuzzy Knight and Nell O'Day. Song by Everett Carter and Milton Rosen:
THE BEARS GIVE ME THE BIRD

COME ON DANGER
An RKO picture starring Tim Holt in a cast that included Frances Neal, Lee 'Lasses White and Ray Whitley, and directed by Edward Killy. Songs by Ray Whitley and Fred Rose:
ON THE TRAIL AGAIN and OLD BOWLEGGED JONES

CYCLONE ON HORSEBACK
An RKO picture starring Tim Holt in a cast that included Marjorie Reynolds, Ray Whitley and Lee 'Lasses White, and directed by Edward Killy. Songs by Ray Whitley and Fred Rose:
BANGTAIL; TUMBLEWEED COWBOY and BLUE NIGHTFALL

DOUBLE TROUBLE
A Monogram picture filmed with a cast headed by Harry Langdon, Charles Rogers, Catherine Lewis, Louis Curry and Benny Rubin, and directed by William West. Song by Johnny Lange and Lew Porter:
UNDER WESTERN SKIES

DOWN MEXICO WAY
A Republic picture starring Gene Autry in a cast that included Smiley Burnette, Fay McKenzie and Sidney Blackmer, and directed by Joseph Santley. Song by Eddie Cherkose and Jule Styne:
DOWN MEXICO WAY

IN OLD CHEYENNE
A Republic picture starring Roy Rogers in a cast that included Gabby Hayes, Joan Woodbury and J. Farrell MacDonald, and directed by Joseph Kane. Song by Sol Meyer and Jule Styne:
BONITA

JESSE JAMES AT BAY
A Republic picture starring Roy Rogers in a cast that included Gabby Hayes and Sally Payne, and directed by Joseph Kane. Song by Sol Meyer and Jule Styne:
JUST FOR YOU

LAND OF THE OPEN RANGE

An RKO picture starring Tim Holt in a cast that included Ray Whitley, Janet Waldo and Lee 'Lasses White, and directed by Edward Killy. Songs by Ray Whitley and Fred Rose:

KI-O and LAND OF THE OPEN RANGE

LAW OF THE RANGE

A Universal picture starring Johnny Mack Brown in a cast that included Fuzzy Knight and Nell O'Day, and directed by Ray Taylor. Songs by Everett Carter and Milton Rosen:

I PLUMB FORGOT and FORGET YOUR BOOTS AND SADDLE

LONE RIDER AMBUSHED, THE

A Producers Releasing Corporation picture filmed with a cast headed by George Houston, Al St. John and Maxine Leslie, and directed by Sam Newfield. Song by Johnny Lange and Lew Porter:

RIDIN', ROAMIN' ON THE PRAIRIE

LONE RIDER FIGHTS BACK, THE

A Producers Releasing Corporation picture filmed with a cast headed by George Houston, Al St. John and Dorothy Moore, and directed by Sam Newfield. Songs by Johnny Lange and Lew Porter:

WHERE THE WEST BEGINS and THE SHOOTIN' SONG

MAN FROM MONTANA

A Universal picture starring Johnny Mack Brown in a cast that included Fuzzy Knight and Nell O'Day, and directed by Ray Taylor. Songs by Everett Carter and Milton Rosen:

THE CALL OF THE RANGE; THE WESTERN TRAIL and BANANAS MAKE ME TOUGH

MASKED RIDER, THE

A Universal picture starring Johnny Mack Brown in a cast that included Fuzzy Knight and Nell O'Day, and directed by Ford Beebe. Song by Everett Carter and Milton Rosen:

CARMENCITA

NEVADA CITY

A Republic picture starring Roy Rogers in a cast that included Gabby Hayes and Sally Payne, and directed by Joseph Kane. Songs:

LONELY HILLS and PRAIRIE SERENADE by Eddie Cherkose, Sol Meyer and Jule Styne; STARS OVER THE PRAIRIE by Peter Tinturin.

NORTH FROM THE LONE STAR

A Columbia picture filmed with a cast headed by Bill Elliott, Richard Fiske, Dorothy Fay and Dub Taylor, and directed by Lambert Hillyer. Songs by Milton Drake:

SATURDAY NIGHT IN SAN ANTONE and OF COURSE IT'S YOUR HORSE

PALS OF THE PECOS

An RKO picture filmed with a cast headed by Bob Livingston, Bob Steele, Rufe Davis and June Johnson, and directed by Lester Orlebeck. Song by Eddie Cherkose and Jule Styne:

DON PEDRO PISTACHIO

RAWHIDE RANGERS

A Universal picture starring Johnny Mack Brown. Songs by Everett Carter and Milton Rosen:

A COWBOY IS HAPPY and HUCKLEBERRY PIE

RED RIVER VALLEY

A Republic picture starring Roy Rogers in a cast that included Gabby Hayes, Sally Payne and the Sons of the Pioneers, and directed by Joseph Kane. Songs:

SUNSET ON THE TRAIL and SPRINGTIME ON THE RANGE TODAY by Tim Spencer; CHANT OF THE WANDERER and WHEN PAY DAY ROLLS AROUND by Bob Nolan.

RIDERS OF DEATH VALLEY

A Universal picture filmed with a cast headed by Dick Foran, Leo Carrillo, Buck Jones and Charles Bickford. Song by Everett Carter and Milton Rosen:

RIDE ALONG

RIDIN' ON A RAINBOW

A Republic picture starring Gene Autry in a cast that included Smiley Burnette, Mary Lee, Carol Adams and Georgia Caine, and directed by Lew Landers. Songs:

HUNKY DORY; SING A SONG OF LAUGHTER; WHAT'S YOUR FAVORITE HOLIDAY and I'M THE ONE WHO'S LONELY by Sol Meyer and Jule Styne; STEAMBOAT BILL by the Leighton Brothers and Ren Shields; RIDIN' ON A RAINBOW by Don George, Jean Herbert and Teddy Hall.

RIDIN' THE WIND

An RKO picture starring Tim Holt in a cast that included Ray Whitley, Mary Douglas and Lew 'Lasses White, and directed by Edward Killy. Songs by Ray Whitley and Fred Rose:

I'LL LIVE UNTIL I DIE; GOIN' ON A HAYRIDE and RIDIN' THE WIND.

ROBIN HOOD OF THE PECOS
A Republic picture starring Roy Rogers in a cast that included Gabby Hayes, Marjorie Reynolds and Sally Payne, and directed by Joseph Kane. Songs:
A SAD, SAD STORY by Peter Tinturin; A CERTAIN PLACE I KNOW by Eddie Cherkose.

ROLLING HOME TO TEXAS
A Monogram picture filmed with a cast headed by Tex Ritter, Slim Andrews, Virginia Carpenter and Eddie Dean, and directed by Al Herman. Songs:
WHY DID I GET MARRIED? by Carson J. Robison; UNDER TEXAS STARS; ROLLING HOME and DESERT MOONLIGHT by Hal Blair and Bob Hoag; WABASH CANNON BALL by A. P. Carter; COWBOY SWING by Jules L. Fox and S. Friedman; GIVE ME A HORSE AND A SADDLE AND YOU by Buck Nation.

SADDLEMATES
A Republic picture filmed with a cast headed by Robert Livingston, Bob Steele, Rufe Davis and Gale Storm, and directed by Lester Orlebeck. Song by Smiley Burnette:
JUST IMAGINE THAT

SECRETS OF THE WASTELANDS
A Paramount picture starring Bill Boyd in a cast that included Andy Clyde and Barbara Britton, and directed by Derwin Abrahams. Song by Ralph Freed and Sammy Stept:
BLUE MOON ON THE SILVER SAGE

SHERIFF OF TOMBSTONE
A Republic picture starring Roy Rogers in a cast that included Gabby Hayes, Elyse Knox and Sally Payne, and directed by Joseph Kane. Songs:
RIDIN' ON A ROCKY ROAD and YA SHOULD'A SEEN PETE by Sol Meyer and Jule Styne; DON'T GAMBLE WITH ROMANCE by Peter Tinturin.

SIERRA SUE
A Republic picture starring Gene Autry in a cast that included Gabby Hayes and Fay MacKenzie, and directed by William Morgan. Songs:
BE HONEST WITH ME and I'LL BE TRUE WHILE YOU'RE GONE by Gene Autry and Fred Rose; HEEBIE JEEBIE BLUES by Oliver Drake and Harry Grey;

SIERRA SUE by Joseph Carey; RIDIN' THE RANGE by Gene Autry and Nelson Shawn.

SINGING HILL, THE
A Republic picture starring Gene Autry in a cast that included Smiley Burnette, Virginia Dale, Mary Lee and Spencer Charters, and directed by Lew Landers. Songs:
RIDIN' DOWN THE OLD TEXAS TRAIL by M. Mabre and D. Massey; TUMBLE DOWN SHACK IN HAVANA by Sol Meyer, Eddie Cherkose and Jule Styne; BLUEBERRY HILL by Al Lewis, Larry Stock and Vincent Rose; SAIL THE SEVEN SEAS by Smiley Burnette; GOOD OLD-FASHIONED HOE DOWN by Gene Autry; LAST ROUNDUP by Billy Hill.

STICK TO YOUR GUNS
A Paramount picture starring Bill Boyd in a cast that included Brad King, Andy Clyde and Jacqueline Holt, and directed by Leslie Selander. Song by Smiley Burnette:
ON THE STRINGS OF MY GUITAR

SUNSET IN WYOMING
A Republic picture starring Gene Autry in a cast that included Smiley Burnette, George Cleveland, Sarah Edwards and Monte Blue, and directed by William Morgan. Songs:
I WAS BORN IN OLD WYOMING by Carson J. Robison; THERE'S A HOME IN WYOMING by Billy Hill and Peter DeRose; TWENTY-ONE YEARS by Bob Nolan; CASEY JONES by Eddie Newton and T. Lawrence Siebert; SING ME A SONG OF THE SADDLE by Gene Autry and Frank Harford.

TEXAS MARSHALL
A Producers Releasing Corporation picture filmed with a cast headed by Tim McCoy, Art Davis and Kay Leslie, and directed by Peter Stewart. Song by Johnny Lange and Lew Porter:
DOWN ON THE MOONLIT TRAIL

THUNDERING HOOFS
An RKO picture starring Tim Holt in a cast that included Ray Whitley, Lee 'Lasses White and Luana Walters, and directed by Leslie Selander. Songs by Ray Whitley and Fred Rose:
RAMBLE ON; THUNDERING HOOFS and AS LONG AS I RIDE THE TRAIL

TRAIL OF THE SILVER SPURS
A Monogram picture filmed with a cast

headed by Ray Corrigan, John King, Max Terhune, Dorothy Short and Eddie Dean, and directed by S. Roy Luby. Song by Johnny Lange and Lew Porter:
A RAINBOW IS RIDIN' THE RANGE

TWILIGHT ON THE TRAIL
A Paramount picture filmed with a cast headed by Bill Boyd, Brad King, Andy Clyde, Jack Rockwell, Wanda McKay and Norma Wills, and directed by Howard Bretherton. Songs:
THE FUNNY OLD HLLS by Leo Robin and Ralph Rainger; CIMARRON ROLL ON by Johnny Bond; TWILIGHT ON THE TRAIL by Sidney Mitchell and Louis Alter.

UNDER ARIZONA SKIES
A Monogram picture starring Johnny Mack Brown in a cast that included Raymond Hatton and Reno Blair, and directed by Lambert Hillyer. Songs:
YOU CAN BET YOUR BOOTS AND SADDLES by Louis Herscher and Roy Newell; DUSTY TRAIL by Louis Herscher; DRIFTIN' by Louis Herscher and Ed Kay.

UNDER FIESTA STARS
A Republic picture starring Gene Autry in a cast that included Gabby Hayes and Carol Hughes, and directed by Frank McDonald. Song by Smiley Burnette:
KEEP IT IN THE FAMILY

WEST OF THE CIMARRON
A Republic picture filmed with a cast headed by Bob Steele, Tom Tyler, Rufe Davis and Lois Collier, and directed by Lester Orlebeck. Song by Sol Meyer and Jule Styne:
WA-WA-WATERMELON

WILDCAT OF TUCSON, THE
A Columbia picture filmed with a cast headed by Bill Elliott, Stanley Brown, Evelyn Young and Dub Taylor, and directed by Lambert Hillyer. Songs by Milton Drake:
INSIDE LOOKING OUT and WILD BILL

Feature Cartoons With Songs

DUMBO
An RKO-Walt Disney production with songs by Ned Washington, Oliver Wallace and Frank Churchill:
BABY MINE; CASEY JUNIOR; LOOK OUT FOR MR. STORK and SONG OF THE ROUSTABOUTS

MR. BUG GOES TO TOWN
A Paramount-Walt Disney production with the following songs:
BOY, OH BOY! by Frank Loesser and Sammy Timberg; I'LL DANCE AT YOUR WEDDING; KATY DID KATY DIDN'T and WE'RE THE COUPLE IN THE CASTLE by Frank Loesser and Hoagy Carmichael.

RELUCTANT DRAGON, THE
An RKO-Walt Disney production with Robert Benchley, Frances Gifford and Nana Bryant as the speaking voices. Songs:
OH FLEECY CLOUD; TO AN UPSIDE DOWN CAKE; RADISH SO RED and 'TIS EVENING by Frank Churchill; I'M A RELUCTANT DRAGON by Charles Wolcott.

Bing Crosby in *Star Spangled Rhythm.*

1 9 4 2

Hollywood Takes Its Wartime Cue From "Yankee Doodle Boy"

The sneak attack on Pearl Harbor on "the day that will live in infamy" didn't catch Hollywood napping. It must have had a better crystal ball than Washington did, since in 1942, it was fully prepared for the boom business that America's entry into World War II created, and had in the cans a bumper crop of musicals, packed with easy-to-remember songs and gorgeous pin-up gals, to strengthen the morale of the war workers at home and the millions of soldiers, sailors and airmen in training or fighting overseas.

The top brass of Warner Brothers must have been blessed with occult powers when they decided in 1941 to make the life story of George M. Cohan the basis for a biographical film, for the author-composer of *Over There* and *You're A Grand Old Flag* was a 100 proof, bottled-in-bond patriot who glorified America and the American way of life in both the songs and the plays he wrote, and *Yankee Doodle Boy*, starring Jimmy Cagney in the Oscar-winning title role, sounded a high patriotic keynote and became the standard-bearer of the other wartime musicals that Hollywood produced.

But *Yankee Doodle Boy* was hard pressed for top honors by such other distinguished musicals as *The Fleet's In* in which Betty Hutton qualified for a star's bungalow; *For Me And My Gal* with Gene Kelly making his first screen appearance with Judy Garland as his co-star; *My Gal Sal*, which paid tribute to another songwriter, Paul Dresser; the star-studded *Star-Spangled Rhythm; The Road To Morocco; Panama Hattie* in which Ann Sheridan sang Cole Porter's *Let's Be Buddies; You Were Never Lovelier* with music by Jerome Kern and like *My Gal Sal*, introducing Rita Hayworth as a singing star; and *Holiday Inn* for which Irving Berlin wrote a song that will be sung as long as children believe in Santa Claus—*White Christmas*.

Both from these and other less notable musicals as well as from several screen dramas of 1942 came songs that captured the hearts of soldiers, sailors and airmen who were capturing island bases on the long hop across the Pacific: *I Remember You, Arthur Murray Taught Me Dancing In A Hurry, I've Got A Gal In Kalamazoo, Be Careful It's My Heart, That Old Black Magic, Moonlight Becomes You, Three Little Sisters, Don't Sit Under The Apple Tree (With Anyone Else But Me), Jim, Deep In The Heart of Texas, I've Got Spurs That Jingle, Jangle, Jingle, As Time Goes By* and *I Don't Want To Walk Without You*, the latter the first of many Hollywood-born song hits to be written by Sammy Cahn and Jule Styne in the years when GI Joe was avenging Pearl Harbor and making Hitler and Mussolini cry

"Uncle!" And *Saludos Amigos,* which with *Bambi* comprised the 1942 feature-length cartoon output of the Walt Disney studios, was highlighted by two lend-lease tango numbers by Latin-American composers: *Brazil* and *Tico Tico.*

With such a galaxy of outstanding musicals, the golden age of the screen's song-and-dance shows enjoyed a revival, and Hollywood's "finest hour" had begun.

Musicals

ALMOST MARRIED
A Universal picture filmed with a cast headed by Jane Frazee, Robert Paige, Eugene Pallette and Elizabeth Patterson, and directed by Charles Lamont. Songs:
AFTER ALL THESE YEARS; TAKE YOUR PLACE IN THE SUN and THE RHUMBA by Eddie Cherkose and Jacques Press; JUST TO BE NEAR YOU by Don Raye and Gene DePaul.

BEHIND THE EIGHT BALL
A Universal picture starring the Ritz Brothers in a cast that included Carol Bruce, Dick Foran, Grace McDonald, Johnny Downs and William Demarest, and directed by William Morgan. Songs by Don Raye and Gene DePaul:
KEEP 'EM LAUGHING; RIVERBOAT JAMBOREE; GOLDEN WEDDING DAY; WASN'T IT WONDERFUL, BRAVEST OF THE BRAVE; ATLAS and MR. FIVE BY FIVE.

BORN TO SING
An M-G-M picture filmed with a cast headed by Virginia Weidler, Ray McDonald, Leo Gorcey and Rags Ragland, and directed by Edward Ludwig. Songs:
I HATE THE CONGA by Earl Brent; ALONE and YOU ARE MY LUCKY STAR by Arthur Freed and Nacio Herb Brown; I LOVE YA by Lennie Hayton and Earl Brent; BALLAD FOR AMERICANS by John LaTouche and Earl Robinson.

BROADWAY
A Universal picture starring George Raft and Pat O'Brien in a cast that included Janet Blair, Broderick Crawford and Marjorie Rambeau, and directed by William A. Seiter. Songs:
DINAH by Joe Young, Sam Lewis and Harry Akst; SWEET GEORGIA BROWN by Ben Bernie, Kenneth Casey and Maceo Pinkard; I'M JUST WILD ABOUT HARRY by Noble Sissle and Eubie Blake; DARKTOWN STRUTTERS' BALL and SOME OF THESE DAYS by Shelton Brooks; YES SIR THAT'S MY BABY by Gus Kahn and Walter Donaldson; ALABAMY BOUND by B. D. DeSylva, Lew Brown and Ray Henderson.

CAIRO
An M-G-M picture starring Jeanette MacDonald and Robert Young in a cast that included Ethel Waters and Reginald Owen, and directed by W. S. VanDyke II. Songs by E. Y. Harburg and Arthur Schwartz:
THE WALTZ IS OVER; BUD'S WON'T BUD; CAIRO and KEEP THE LIGHT BURNING BRIGHT IN THE HARBOR

CALL OUT THE MARINES
An RKO picture filmed with a cast headed by Victor MacLaglen, Edmund Lowe and Binnie Barnes, and directed by Frank Ryan and William Hamilton. Songs by Mort Greene and Harry Revel:
BEWARE; THE LIGHT IN MY LIFE; CALL OUT THE MARINES; ZANA ZORANDA and HANDS ACROSS THE BORDER

DON'T GET PERSONAL
A Universal picture filmed with a cast headed by Hugh Herbert, Mischa Auer, Jane Frazee and Robert Paige, and directed by Charles Lamont. Songs by Jack Brooks and Norman Behens:
IT DON'T MAKE SENSE; NOW WHAT DO WE DO? and EVERY TIME A MOMENT GOES BY

FLEET'S IN, THE
A Paramount picture starring Dorothy Lamour and William Holden in a cast that included Eddie Bracken, Cass Daley, Betty Hutton and Jimmy Dorsey's orchestra, and directed by Victor Schertzinger. Songs:
I REMEMBER YOU; WHEN YOU

HEAR THE TIME SIGNAL; THE FLEET'S IN; TOMORROW YOU BELONG TO UNCLE SAM; ARTHUR MURRAY TAUGHT ME DANCING IN A HURRY; IF SOMEBODY BUILDS A BETTER MOUSETRAP and SOMEBODY ELSE'S MOON (NOT MINE) by Johnny Mercer and Victor Schertzinger; TANGERINE by Frank Loesser and Victor Schertzinger; CONGA FROM HONGA by Joseph J. Lilley.

FOOTLIGHT SERENADE

A 20th Century-Fox picture filmed with a cast headed by John Payne, Betty Grable, Victor Mature, Jane Wyman, James Gleason, Phil Silvers and Cobina Wright Jr., and directed by Gregory Ratoff. Songs by Leo Robin and Ralph Rainger:
LIVING HIGH (ON A WESTERN HILL); I'LL BE MARCHING TO A LOVE SONG; I'M STILL CRAZY FOR YOU; I HEARD THE BIRDIES SING; ARE YOU KIDDIN'? and LAND ON YOUR FEET.

FOR ME AND MY GAL

An M-G-M picture starring Judy Garland and Gene Kelly in a cast that included George Murphy, Marta Eggerth and Ben Blue, and directed by Busby Berkeley. Songs:
OH YOU BEAUTIFUL DOLL by A. Seymour Brown and Milton Ager; AFTER YOU'VE GONE by Henry Creamer and Turner Layton; WHAT ARE YOU GOING TO DO TO HELP THE BOYS? by Gus Kahn and Egbert VanAlstyne; BALLING THE JACK by Chris Smith; HOW YOU GONNA KEEP 'EM DOWN ON THE FARM? by Joe Young, Sam Lewis and Walter Donaldson; WHERE DO WE GO FROM HERE? by Howard Johnson and Percy Wenrich.

GET HEP TO LOVE

A Universal picture starring Gloria Jean and Donald O'Connor in a cast that included Jane Frazee and Robert Paige, and directed by Charles Lamont. Songs:
SIBONEY by Dolly Morse and Ernesto Lecuona; LET'S HITCH A HORSIE TO THE AUTOMOBILE by Al Hoffman, Mann Curtis and Jerry Livingston; HEAVEN FOR TWO by Don Raye and Gene DePaul.

GIVE OUT SISTERS

A Universal picture starring the Andrews Sisters in a cast that included Grace MacDonald, Dan Dailey Jr., Charles Butter-

worth and Walter Catlett, and directed by Edward F. Cline. Songs:
YOU'RE JUST A FLOWER FROM AN OLD BOUQUET by Gwynne and Lucien Denni; THE NEW GENERATION by Walter Donaldson; WHO DO YOU THINK YOU'RE FOOLING? by Ray Stillwell and Ray Gold; PENNSYLVANIA POLKA by Lester Lee and Zeke Manners; JIGGERS (THE BEAT) by Al Lerner and Sid Robin.

HARD WAY, THE

A Warner Brothers' picture filmed with a cast headed by Ida Lupino, Dennis Morgan, Joan Leslie, Jack Carson, Gladys George and Faye Emerson, and directed by Vincent Sherman. Songs:
AM I BLUE by Grant Clarke and Harry Akst; YOUTH MUST HAVE ITS FLING and GOOD NIGHT OH MY DARLING by Jack Scholl and M. K. Jerome.

HI NEIGHBOR

A Republic picture filmed with a cast headed by Jean Parker, John Archer and Janet Beecher, and directed by Charles Lamont. Songs:
HAIL TO GREENFIELD by S. and B. Magowan and Raoul Kraushaar; HI NEIGHBOR by Jack Owens; WHEN A FELLA'S GOT A GIRL by Sol Meyer, George R. Brown and Jule Styne; MOO WOO WOO and PASS THE BISCUITS MIRANDY by Carl Hoefle and Del Porter; STUCK UP BLUES and I KNOW WE ARE SAYING GOODBYE by Roy Acuff; DEEP IN THE HEART OF TEXAS by Don Swander and June Hershey.

HOLIDAY INN

A Paramount picture starring Bing Crosby and Fred Astaire in a cast that included Marjorie Reynolds, and directed by Mark Sandrich. Songs by Irving Berlin:
BE CAREFUL IT'S MY HEART; WHITE CHRISTMAS; ABRAHAM; YOU'RE EASY TO DANCE WITH; LET'S START THE NEW YEAR RIGHT; PLENTY TO BE THANKFUL FOR; I'LL CAPTURE YOUR HEART SINGING and HAPPY HOLIDAY.

I MARRIED AN ANGEL

An M-G-M picture starring Jeanette MacDonald and Nelson Eddy in a cast that included Edward Everett Horton and Binnie Barnes, and directed by W. S. Van Dyke II. Songs:
LITTLE WORK-A-DAY WORLD; I MARRIED AN ANGEL; I'LL TELL THE

MAN IN THE STREET; SPRING IS HERE; A TWINKLE IN YOUR EYE and AT THE ROXY MUSIC HALL by Lorenz Hart and Richard Rodgers; MAY I PRESENT THE GIRL? YOU'VE MET THE ANGEL and BUT WHAT OF THE TRUTH by Chet Forrest, Bob Wright and Herbert Stothart.

ICE-CAPADES REVUE

A Republic picture filmed with a cast headed by Ellen Drew, Richard Denning, Jerry Colonna and Barbara Jo Allen, and directed by Bernard Vorhaus. Songs:
TEQUILA by Sol Meyer, George R. Brown and Jule Styne; THE GUY WITH THE POLKA-DOTTED TIE by Sol Meyer and Jule Styne; SONG OF THE ISLANDS by Charles E. King; AFTER ALL by Sol Meyer and Walter Scharf; THE CAISSONS GO ROLLING ALONG by Edmund L. Gruber; ARMY AIR CORPS SONG by Robert Crawford.

ICELAND

A 20th Century-Fox picture starring Sonja Henie in a cast that included John Payne, Jack Oakie and Sammy Kaye and his orchestra, and directed by H. Bruce Humberstone. Songs by Mack Gordon and Harry Warren:
THERE WILL NEVER BE ANOTHER YOU; YOU CAN'T SAY NO TO A SOLDIER; LET'S BRING NEW GLORY TO OLD GLORY; I LIKE A MILITARY TUNE and IT'S THE LOVER'S KNOT.

JOHNNY DOUGHBOY

A Republic picture starring Jane Withers in a cast that included Henry Wilcoxson, Patrick Brook and William Demarest, and directed by John F. Auer. Songs:
BABY'S A BIG GIRL NOW; ALL DONE ALL THROUGH; IT TAKES A GUY LIKE I and VICTORY CARAVAN by Sammy Cahn and Jule Styne; ALL MY LIFE by Sidney Mitchell and Sammy Stept; JOHNNY DOUGHBOY FOUND A ROSE IN IRELAND and BETTER NOT ROLL THOSE BIG BLUE EYES (AT SOMEBODY ELSE) by Kay Twomey and Al Goodhart.

JUKE BOX JENNIE

A Universal picture starring Harriet Hilliard and Ken Murray, and directed by Harold Young. Songs:
SWING IT MOTHER GOOSE; GIVE OUT and MACUMBA by Everett Carter and Milton Rosen; FIFTY MILLION NICKELS by Charles Barnet.

JUKE GIRL

A Warner Brothers' picture starring Ann Sheridan and Ronald Reagan in a cast that included Richard Whorf, Gene Lockhart, Betty Brewer and Faye Emerson, and directed by Curtis Bernhardt. Songs:
I GOT ME A BLUE BELL and I HATES LOVE by Jack Scholl and M. K. Jerome; SOMEONE'S ROCKING MY DREAM BOAT by Leon and Otis Rene and Emerson Scott.

MAYOR OF 44th STREET

An RKO picture starring George Murphy and Anne Shirley in a cast that included William Gargan, Richard Bartholomess and Joan Merrill, and directed by John Paddy Carstairs. Songs by Mort Greene and Harry Revel:
YOUR FACE LOOKS FAMILIAR; HEAVENLY, ISN'T IT? LET'S FORGET IT; YOU'RE BAD FOR ME; A MILLION MILES FROM MANHATTAN and WHEN THERE'S A BREEZE ON LAKE LOUISE.

MOONLIGHT IN HAVANA

A Universal picture starring Allan Jones and Jane Frazee in a cast that included William Frawley and Marjorie Lord, and directed by Anthony Mann. Songs by Dave Franklin:
I DON'T NEED MONEY; ONLY YOU; GOT MUSIC; ISN'T IT LOVELY?; RHYTHM OF THE TROPICS and MOONLIGHT IN HAVANA.

MY GAL SAL

A 20th Century-Fox picture starring Rita Hayworth and Victor Mature in a cast that included Carole Landis and James Gleason, and directed by Irving Cummings. Songs:
MY GAL SAL; MR. VOLUNTEER and COME TELL ME YOUR ANSWER— YES OR NO by Paul Dresser; OH THE PITY OF IT ALL; HERE YOU ARE; ON THE GAY WHITE WAY; MIDNIGHT AT THE MASQUERADE and ME AND MY FELLA AND A BIG UMBRELLA by Leo Robin and Ralph Rainger.

OLD HOMESTEAD, THE

A Republic picture starring the Weaver Brothers. Songs:
FERRIS WHEEL by Fred Stryker; DIG, DIG, DIG FOR VICTORY by Sol Meyer and Jule Styne; IN THE TOWN WHERE I WAS BORN by Al Harriman, Dick Howard and Bill Tracey.

ORCHESTRA WIVES

A 20th Century-Fox picture starring

George Montgomery and Ann Rutherford in a cast that included Lynn Bari, Carole Landis and Glenn Miller's orchestra, and directed by Archie Mayo. Songs by Mack Gordon and Harry Warren:
I'VE GOT A GAL IN KALAMAZOO; SERENADE IN BLUE; PEOPLE LIKE YOU AND ME; AT LAST and THAT'S SABOTAGE.

PANAMA HATTIE
An M-G-M picture starring Ann Sheridan in a cast that included Red Skelton, Rags Ragland, Ben Blue, Marsha Hunt and Virginia O'Brien, and directed by Norman Z. McLeod. Songs:
FRESH AS A DAISY and LET'S BE BUDDIES by Cole Porter; GOOD NEIGHBORS by Roger Edens; THE SON OF A GUN THAT PICKS ON UNCLE SAM by E. Y. Harburg and Burton Lane; DID I GET STINKING AT THE CLUB SAVOY! by E. Y. Harburg and Walter Donaldson.

PARDON MY SARONG
A Universal picture starring Abbott and Costello in a cast that included Virginia Bruce, Robert Paige, the Ink Spots and the Katherine Dunham Dancers, and directed by Erle C. Kenton. Songs:
ISLAND OF THE MOON; LOVELY LUANA and VINGO JINGO by Don Raye and Gene DePaul; DO I WORRY? by Bobby North and Stanley Cowan.

POWERS GIRL
A United Artists' picture starring Anne Shirley and George Murphy, and directed by Norman Z. McLeod. Songs by Kim Gannon and Jule Styne:
THREE DREAMS; OUT OF THIS WORLD; THE LADY WHO DIDN'T BELIEVE IN LOVE; PARTNERS and WE'RE LOOKING FOR THE BIG BAD WOLF.

PRIORITIES ON PARADE
A Paramount picture filmed with a cast headed by Ann Miller, Johnny Johnston, Jerry Colonna and Betty Rhodes, and directed by Albert S. Rogell. Songs by Herb Magidson and Jule Styne:
I'D LOVE TO KNOW YOU BETTER; HERE COMES KATRINKA; CO-OPERATE WITH YOUR AIR RAID WARDEN; CONCHITA, MARQUITA, LOLITA, PEPITA, ROSETTA, JUANITA LOPEZ and YOU'RE IN LOVE WITH SOMEONE ELSE BUT I'M IN LOVE WITH YOU (Lyrics by Frank Loesser).

PRIVATE BUCKAROO
A Universal picture starring the Andrews Sisters in a cast that included Dick Foran and Joe E. Lewis, and directed by Edward F. Cline. Songs:
THREE LITTLE SISTERS by Irving Taylor and Vic Mizzy; PRIVATE BUCKAROO by Charles Newman and Allie Wrubel; DON'T SIT UNDER THE APPLE TREE WITH ANYBODY ELSE BUT ME by Sammy Stept and Charles Tobias; JOHNNY GET YOUR GUN AGAIN by Don Raye and Gene DePaul; WE'VE GOT A JOB TO DO by Vickie Knight; YOU MADE ME LOVE YOU by Joseph McCarthy and Jimmy Monaco; SIX JERKS IN A JEEP by Sid Robin; THAT'S THE MOON MY SON by Art Kassel and Sammy Gallop.

RHYTHM PARADE
A Monogram picture filmed with a cast headed by Nils T. Grunland, Gale Storm, Robert Lowery, the Mills Brothers and Ted Fiorito and his orchestra, and directed by Dave Gould and Howard Bretherton. Songs:
'NEATH THE YELLOW MOON IN OLD TAHITI and TOOTIN' MY OWN HORN by Eddie Cherkose and Edward Kay; MIMI FROM TAHITI and YOU'RE DRAFTED by Dave Oppenheim and Roy Ingraham; WAIT TILL THE SUN SHINES NELLIE by Andrew B. Sterling and Harry VonTilzer; SWEET SUE by Will J. Harris and Victor Young.

RIDE 'EM COWBOY
A Universal picture starring Abbott and Costello in a cast that included Dick Foran, Anne Gwynne, Ella Fitzgerald and the Merry Macs, and directed by Arthur Lubin. Songs by Don Raye and Gene DePaul:
GIVE ME MY SADDLE; WAKE UP JACOB; BESIDE THE RIO TONTO; RIDE 'EM COWBOY; ROCKIN' AND REELIN' and I'LL REMEMBER APRIL AND BE GLAD (With Patricia Johnston).

RIO RITA
An M-G-M picture starring Abbott and Costello in a cast that included John Carroll and Kathryn Grayson, and directed by S. Sylvan Simon. Musical numbers:
RANGER'S SONG and RIO RITA by Joseph McCarthy and Harry Tierney; LONG BEFORE YOU CAME ALONG by E. Y. Harburg and Harold Arlen; BRAZILIAN DANCE by Nilo Barnet; ORA O CONGA by Lacerdo.

ROAD TO MOROCCO, THE

A Paramount picture starring Bing Crosby, Bob Hope and Dorothy Lamour, and directed by David Butler. Songs by Johnny Burke and Jimmy Van Heusen: ALADDIN'S DAUGHTER; CONSTANTLY; MOONLIGHT BECOMES YOU and AIN'T GOT A DIME TO MY NAME.

SEVEN DAYS LEAVE

An RKO picture starring Lucille Ball and Victor Mature, and directed by Tom Whelan. Songs by Frank Loesser and Jimmy McHugh: CAN'T GET OUT OF THE MOOD; A TOUCH OF TEXAS; I GET THE NECK OF THE CHICKEN; PLEASE WON'T YOU LEAVE MY GIRL ALONE; BABY; YOU SPEAK MY LANGUAGE; PUERTO RICO and SOFT-HEARTED.

SHIP AHOY

An M-G-M picture starring Eleanor Powell and Red Skelton in a cast that included Bert Lahr, Virginia O'Brien and Tommy Dorsey's orchestra, and directed by Eddie Buzzell. Songs: TAMPICO by Walter Ruick; I'LL TAKE TALLULAH; POOR YOU and THE LAST CALL FOR LOVE (With Margery Cummings) by E. Y. Harburg and Burton Lane.

SING YOUR WORRIES AWAY

An RKO picture filmed with a cast headed by Bert Lahr, June Havoc, Buddy Ebsen and Patsy Kelly, and directed by Edward Sutherland. Songs by Mort Greene and Harry Revel: CINDY LOU McWILLIAMS; IT JUST HAPPENED TO HAPPEN; SING YOUR WORRIES AWAY and SALLY MY DEAR SALLY.

SLEEPY TIME GAL

A Republic picture starring Judy Canova and Tom Brown in a cast that included Ruth Terry and Billy Gilbert, and directed by Albert S. Rogell. Songs: I DON'T WANT ANYBODY AT ALL; WHEN THE CAT'S AWAY and BARRELHOUSE BESSIE by Herb Magidson and Jule Styne; SLEEPY TIME GAL by Ray Egan and Richard Whiting.

SONG OF THE ISLANDS

A 20th Century-Fox picture starring Betty Grable and Victor Mature, and directed by Walter Lang. Songs: BLUE SHADOWS AND WHITE GARDENIAS; O'BRIEN HAS GONE HAWAIIAN; MALUNA MALALO MAWAENA; WHAT'S BUZZIN' COUSIN? and DOWN ON AMI-ONI-ONI ISLE by Mack Gordon and Harry Owens; SING ME A SONG OF THE ISLANDS by Mack Gordon and Harry Warren.

SPRINGTIME IN THE ROCKIES

A 20th Century-Fox picture starring Betty Grable and John Payne in a cast that included Carmen Miranda, Cesar Romero and Harry James and his orchestra, and directed by Irving Cummings. Songs by Mack Gordon and Harry Warren: I HAD THE CRAZIEST DREAM; A POEM SET TO MUSIC; PAN-AMERICAN JUBILEE; RUN LITTLE RAINDROP RUN and I LIKE TO BE LOVED BY YOU.

STAR-SPANGLED RHYTHM

A Paramount picture filmed with a cast headed by Bing Crosby, Ray Milland, Vera Zorina, Bob Hope, Mary Martin, Veronica Lake, Fred MacMurray, Dick Powell, Dorothy Lamour and Betty Hutton, and directed by George Marshall. Songs by Johnny Mercer and Harold Arlen: THAT OLD BLACK MAGIC; HIT THE ROAD TO DREAMLAND; OLD GLORY; A SWEATER, A SARONG AND A PEEKABOO BANG; I'M DOING IT FOR DEFENSE; SHARP AS A TACK; ON THE SWING SHIFT and HE LOVED ME TILL THE ALL-CLEAR CAME.

STRICTLY IN THE GROOVE

A Universal picture filmed with a cast headed by Martha Tilton, the Dinning Sisters, Mary Healy, Leon Errol, Donald O'Connor and Ozzie Nelson's orchestra, and directed by Vernon Keays. Musical numbers: RIDIN' HOME by Harold Adamson and Jimmy McHugh; ELMER'S TUNE by Elmer Albrecht and Dick Jurgens; BE HONEST WITH ME by Gene Autry and Fred Rose; DANCING ON AIR by Everett Carter and Milton Rosen; YOU ARE MY SUNSHINE by Jimmy Davis and Charles Mitchell; MISS YOU by Harry, Charles and Henry Tobias; I NEVER COULD LOVE ANYBODY (LIKE I'M LOVING YOU) by Tom Pitts and Roy Marsh; SOMEBODY ELSE IS TAKING MY PLACE by Dick Howard and Bob Ellsworth; HAPPY COWBOY by Bob Nolan; JERSEY JIVE by Ozzie Nelson.

SWEATER GIRL

A Paramount picture starring Eddie Bracken, June Priesser and Betty Jane

Rhodes, and directed by William Clemons.
Songs by Frank Loesser and Jule Styne:
 I DON'T WANT TO WALK WITH-
OUT YOU; I SAID "NO"; WHAT
GIVES OUT NOW? and SWEATER
GIRL.

SYNCOPATION

An RKO picture filmed with a cast
headed by Adolphe Menjou, Jackie Cooper,
Bonita Granville, George Bancroft, Connee
Boswell and the Hall Johnson Choir, and
directed by William Dieterle. Songs:
 GOIN' UP THE RIVER by Dave Tor-
bett and Leith Stevens; ONLY WORRY
FOR A PILLOW and CHICAGO RAG-
TIME by Leith Stevens; UNDER A FALL-
ING STAR by Rich Hall and Leith Stevens;
YOU MADE ME LOVE YOU by Joseph
McCarthy and Jimmy Monaco; SLAVE
MARKET by Hall Johnson.

TRUE TO THE ARMY

A Paramount picture starring Judy Can-
ova and Allan Jones in a cast that included
Jerry Colonna and Ann Miller, and directed
by Albert S. Rogell. Songs:
 NEED I SPEAK? JITTERBUG'S LUL-
LABY; SPANGLES ON MY TIGHTS;
IN THE ARMY and WACKY FOR
KHAKI by Frank Loesser and Harold
Spina; SWING IN LINE by Frank Loesser
and Joseph J. Lilley; LOVE in BLOOM
by Leo Robin and Ralph Rainger; I
CAN'T GIVE YOU ANYTHING BUT
LOVE by Dorothy Fields and Jimmy Mc-
Hugh.

WHAT'S COOKING?

A Universal picture starring the Andrews
Sisters in a cast that included Gloria Jean,
Jane Frazee, Leo Carrillo, Robert Paige,
Billie Burke, Charles Butterworth and
Woody Herman and his orchestra, and di-
rected by Edward F. Cline. Musical num-
bers:
 YOU CAN'T HOLD A MEMORY IN
YOUR ARMS by Hy Zaret and Arthur
Altman; I'LL PRAY FOR YOU by Kim
Gannon and Arthur Altman; WOOD-
CHOPPER'S BALL by Joe Bishop and
Woody Herman; PACK UP YOUR
TROUBLES IN YOUR OLD KIT BAG
by Felix Powell and George Asaf; IF and
LOVE LAUGHS AT ANYTHING by Don
Raye and Gene DePaul; BLUE FLAME
by James Noble; WHAT TO DO by Sid
Robin.

WHEN JOHNNY COMES
MARCHING HOME

A Universal picture filmed with a cast
headed by Allan Jones, Gloria Jean, Donald O'Connor, Jane Frazee, Peggy Ryan
and Phil Spitalny and his All-Girl Orchestra, and directed by Charles Lamont. Songs:
 WE MUST BE VIGILANT by Edgar
Leslie and Joe Burke; THIS IS WORTH
FIGHTING FOR by Edgar DeLange and
Sammy Stept; SAY IT WITH DANCING
and THIS IS IT by Don Raye and Gene
DePaul; ONE OF US HAS GOTTA GO
by Inez James and Buddy Pepper; WHEN
JOHNNY COMES MARCHING HOME
by Buddy Kaye.

WHO DONE IT?

A Universal picture starring Abbott and
Costello in a cast that included Louise All-
britton and Patric Knowles, and directed by
Erle C. Kenton. Songs by Don Raye and
Gene DePaul:
 PLEASE LOUISE; HE'S MY GUY and
MR. FIVE BY FIVE.

YANKEE DOODLE DANDY

A Warner Brothers' picture starring
Jimmy Cagney in a cast that included Wal-
ter Huston, Joan Leslie, Richard Whorf,
Irene Manning, Rosemary DeCamp, Jeanne
Cagney and Eddie Foy Jr., and directed by
Michael Curtiz. Songs:
 I WAS BORN IN VIRGINIA; THE
WARMEST BABY IN THE BUNCH;
GIVE MY REGARDS TO BROADWAY;
MARY'S A GRAND OLD NAME; SO
LONG MARY; YANKEE DOODLE BOY;
OVER THERE; HARRIGAN; FORTY-
FIVE MINUTES FROM BROADWAY
and YOU'RE A GRAND OLD FLAG by
George M. Cohan; ALL ABOARD FOR
OLD BROADWAY by Jack Scholl and M.
K. Jerome.

YOKEL BOY

A Republic picture filmed with a cast
headed by Albert Dekker, Joan Davis, Eddie
Foy Jr., Alan Mowbray and Roscoe Karns,
and directed by Joseph Santley. Songs:
 COMES LOVE; IT'S ME AGAIN;
LET'S MAKE MEMORIES TONIGHT
and I CAN'T AFFORD TO DREAM by
Lew Brown, Charles Tobias and Sammy
Stept; JIM by Caesar Petrillo, Nelson
Shawn and Edward Ross.

YOU WERE NEVER LOVELIER

A Columbia picture starring Rita Hayworth and Fred Astaire in a cast that included Adolphe Menjou and Xavier Cugat
and his orchestra, and directed by William
A. Seiter. Musical numbers:

YOU WERE NEVER LOVELIER; DEARLY BELOVED; I'M OLD FASHIONED; WEDDING IN THE SPRING; ON THE BEAM and THE SHORTY GEORGE by Johnny Mercer and Jerome Kern.

Feature Films With Songs

ALL THROUGH THE NIGHT
A Warner Brothers' picture starring Humphrey Bogart in a cast that included Conrad Veidt and Kaaren Verne, and directed by Vincent Sherman. Song by Johnny Mercer and Arthur Schwartz:
ALL THROUGH THE NIGHT

BEYOND THE BLUE HORIZON
A Paramount picture starring Dorothy Lamour in a cast that included Richard Denning, Jack Haley and Walter Abel, and directed by Alfred Santell. Songs:
PAGAN LULLABY by Frank Loesser and Jule Styne; A FULL MOON AND AN EMPTY HEART by Mort Greene and Harry Revel.

BIG STREET, THE
An RKO picture starring Henry Fonda and Lucille Ball in a cast that included Barton MacLane, Sam Levene and Ozzie Nelson's orchestra, and directed by Irving Reis. Song by Mort Greene and Harry Revel:
WHO KNOWS?

BLONDIE GOES TO COLLEGE
A Columbia picture starring Penny Singleton and Arthur Lake, and directed by Frank B. Strayer. Songs by Sammy Cahn and Saul Chaplin:
DO I NEED YOU? and LOYAL SONS OF LEIGHTON

BLONDIE'S BLESSED EVENT
A Columbia picture starring Penny Singleton and Arthur Lake, and directed by Frank B. Strayer. Song by Sammy Cahn and Saul Chaplin:
AH LOO LOO

CASABLANCA
A Warner Brothers' picture starring Humphrey Bogart and Ingrid Bergman in a cast that included Dewey Wilson, Claude Rains, Sydney Greenstreet and Peter Lorre, and directed by Michael Curtiz. Songs:
AS TIME GOES BY by Herman Hupfeld; KNOCK ON WOOD by Jack Scholl and M. K. Jerome.

COMMANDOS STRIKE AT DAWN, THE
A Columbia picture starring Paul Muni and Lillian Gish, and directed by John Farrow. Musical numbers:
COMMANDOS MARCH by Ann Ronell and Louis Gruenberg; OUT TO PICK THE BERRIES by Ann Ronell.

CROSSROADS
An M-G-M picture starring William Powell and Hedy Lamarr in a cast that included Claire Trevor and Basil Rathbone, and directed by Jack Conway. Song by Howard Dietz and Arthur Schwartz:
TILL YOU RETURN

DRUMS OF THE CONGO
A Universal picture filmed with a cast headed by Ona Munson, Stuart Erwin, Peggy Moran, Don Terry, Richard Lane, Jules Bledsoe and Turhan Bey, and directed by Christy Cabanne. Songs by Everett Carter and Milton Rosen:
ROUND THE BEND; HEAR THE DRUMS BEAT OUT and RIVER MAN.

DUDES ARE PRETTY PEOPLE
A United Artists' picture filmed with a cast headed by Jimmy Rogers, Noah Beery Jr., and Marjorie Woodworth, and directed by Hal Roach Jr. Song by Chet Forrest, Bob Wright and Edward Ward:
WEST WIND WHISTLIN'

FOREST RANGERS
A Paramount picture starring Fred MacMurray, Paulette Goddard and Susan Hayward, and directed by George Marshall. Songs:
I'VE GOT SPURS THAT JINGLE, JANGLE JINGLE by Joseph J. Lilley; TALL GROWS THE TIMBER by Frank Loesser and Frederick Hollander.

HELLO ANNAPOLIS
A Columbia picture filmed with a cast headed by Tom Brown, Jean Parker and Larry Parks, and directed by Charles Barton. Song by Morris Stoloff and Nico Grigor:
CAPTAIN MY CAPTAIN

HER CARDBOARD LOVER
An M-G-M picture starring Norma Shearer and Robert Taylor in a cast that included George Sanders and Frank McHugh, and directed by George Cukor. Song by Ralph Freed and Burton Lane:
I DARE YOU

HERE WE GO AGAIN

An RKO picture filmed with a cast headed by Edgar Bergen, Jim Jordan, Marian Jordan, Harold Perry, Ginny Simms and Ray Noble, and directed by Allan Dwan. Songs by Mort Greene and Harry Revel:
DELICIOUS DELIRIUM and UNTIL I LIVE AGAIN.

HONOLULU LU

A Columbia picture starring Lupe Velez and Bruce Bennett, and directed by Charles Barton. Songs by Sammy Cahn and Saul Chaplin:
THAT'S THE KIND OF WORK I DO and HONOLULU LU

JOAN OF THE OZARKS

A Republic picture starring Judy Canova and Joe E. Brown in a cast that included Eddie Foy Jr. and Anne Jeffreys, and directed by Joseph Santley. Songs:
BACKWOODS BARBECUE and THE LADY AT LOCKHEED by Mort Greene and Harry Revel; WABASH BLUES by Dave Ringle and Fred Meinken.

LADY IS WILLING, THE

A Columbia picture starring Marlene Dietrich and Fred MacMurray in a cast that included Arline MacMahon and Arline Judge, and directed by Mitchell Leisen. Song by Gordon Clifford and Jack King:
STRANGE THING (AND I FIND LOVE).

LAUGH YOUR BLUES AWAY

A Columbia picture starring Bert Gordon and Jinx Falkenburg, and directed by Charles Barton. Song by Larry Markes and Dick Charles:
PRAIRIE PARADE

MAISIE GETS HER MAN

An M-G-M picture starring Ann Sothern and Red Skelton in a cast that included Leo Gorcey and Allen Jenkins, and directed by Roy Del Ruth. Song by Lennie Hayton and Roger Edens:
COOKIN' WITH GAS

MISSISSIPPI GAMBLER

A Universal picture starring Frances Langford, Kent Taylor and John Litel, and directed by John Rawlins. Songs by Everett Carter and Milton Rosen:
GOT LOVE and THERE GOES MY ROMANCE.

MOONLIGHT MASQUERADE

A Republic picture filmed with a cast headed by Dennis O'Keefe, Jane Frazee and Eddie Foy Jr., and directed by John H. Auer. Song by Mort Greene and Harry Revel:
WHAT AM I DOING HERE IN YOUR ARMS?

MOONTIDE

A 20th Century-Fox picture starring Ida Lupino and Jean Gabin, and directed by Archie Mayo. Song by Alfred Newman and Charles Henderson:
MOONTIDE

MRS. MINIVER

An M-G-M picture starring Greer Garson and Walter Pidgeon in a cast that included Teresa Wright, and directed by William Wyler. Song by Gene Lockhart:
MIDSUMMER'S DAY

MY FAVORITE SPY

An RKO picture filmed with a cast headed by Kay Kyser, Ellen Drew, Jane Wyman and Robert Armstrong, and directed by Tay Garnett. Songs by Johnny Burke and Jimmy Van Heusen:
JUST PLAIN LONESOME and GOT THE MOON IN MY POCKET

MYSTERY OF MARY ROGET

A Universal picture filmed with a cast headed by Patric Knowles, Maria Montez and John Litel, and directed by Phil Rosen. Songs by Everett Carter and Milton Rosen:
MAMA DIT MOI and DO THE OO-LA-LA

NORTHWEST RANGERS

An M-G-M picture filmed with a cast headed by James Craig, William Lundigan, Patricia Dane, John Carradine, Jack Holt and Keenan Wynn, and directed by Joseph Newman. Song by Ralph Freed and Earl Brent:
THAT GOOD FOR NOTHIN' MAN OF MINE

NOW VOYAGER

A Warner Brothers' picture starring Bette Davis in a cast that included Paul Henreid, Claude Rains, Bonita Granville and Ilka Chase, and directed by Irving Rapper. Song by Kim Gannon and Max Steiner:
IT CAN'T BE WRONG

PIERRE OF THE PLAINS

An M-G-M picture filmed with a cast headed by John Carroll, Ruth Hussey, Bruce Cabot, Phil Brown, Reginald Owen and Henry Travers, and directed by George B. Seitz. Song by Ralph Freed and Herbert Stothart:
SASKATCHEWAN

REAP THE WILD WIND

A Paramount picture starring Ray Milland, Paulette Goddard and Raymond Massey, and directed by Melvyn Le Roy. Songs: SEA CHANTEY by Frank Loesser and Victor Young; 'TIS BUT A LITTLE FADED FLOWER by J. R. Thomas and Troy Sanders.

REMEMBER PEARL HARBOR

A Republic picture starring Fay McKenzie and Don Barry, and directed by Joseph Santley. Song by Emily Robinson Head: BECAUSE WE ARE AMERICANS

RINGS ON HER FINGERS

A 20th Century-Fox picture starring Henry Fonda and Gene Tierney, and directed by Rouben Mamoulian. Song by Alfred Newman: THE MOON LOOKED THE OTHER WAY

SEVEN SWEETHEARTS

An M-G-M picture starring Kathryn Grayson, Van Heflin and Marsha Hunt, and directed by Frank Borzage. Song by Paul Francis Webster and Walter Jurmann: YOU AND THE WALTZ AND I

SHEPHERD OF THE OZARKS

A Republic picture starring the Weaver Brothers and June Weaver, and directed by Frank McDonald. Songs: LONELY HILLBILLY by Jesse O. Rodgers; WELL, WELL by Frank Loesser and Jule Styne.

SONG OF FURY

A 20th Century-Fox picture starring Tyrone Power and Gene Tierney in a cast that included George Sanders, Frances Farmer and John Carradine, and directed by John Cromwell. Song by Mack Gordon: BLUE TAHITIAN MOON

SWAMP WOMAN

A Producers Releasing Corporation picture starring Ann Corio and Jack LaRue, and directed by Elmer Clifton. Song by Ken Darby: STARRY HILL

SWEETHEART OF THE FLEET

A Columbia picture filmed with a cast headed by Joan Davis, Jinx Falkenburg, Joan Woodbury, Brenda and Cobina Wright and Robert Stevens, and directed by Charles Barton. Song by Cliff Friend and Charles Tobias: WE DID IT BEFORE (AND WE'LL DO IT AGAIN).

TALES OF MANHATTAN

A 20th Century-Fox picture filmed with an all-star cast that included Charles Boyer, Rita Hayworth, Ginger Rogers, Henry Fonda, Charles Laughton, Edward G. Robinson, Eddie "Rochester" Anderson, Paul Robeson and Ethel Waters, and directed by Julien Duvivier. Songs: GLORY DAY by Leo Robin and Ralph Rainger; FARE THEE WELL TO EL DORADO; A JOURNEY TO YOUR LIPS and A TALE OF MANHATTAN by Paul Francis Webster and Saul Chaplin.

THIS GUN FOR HIRE

A 20th Century-Fox picture starring Veronica Lake and Robert Preston in a cast that included Laird Cregar, Alan Ladd and Tully Marshall, and directed by Frank Tuttle. Songs by Frank Loesser and Jacques Press: NOW YOU SEE IT and I'VE GOT YOU

THIS TIME FOR KEEPS

An M-G-M picture starring Ann Rutherford and Robert Sterling and directed by Charles Riesner. Song by Benny Davis and Harry Akst: WHY DON'T THEY LET ME SING A LOVE SONG?

TORPEDO BOAT

A Paramount picture starring Richard Arlen and Jean Parker, and directed by John Rawlins. Song by Marion Boyle and Nat Winecoff: HEAVEN IS A MOMENT IN YOUR ARMS

TORTILLA FLAT

An M-G-M picture starring Spencer Tracy and Hedy Lamarr in a cast that included John Garfield, Frank Morgan and Akim Tamiroff, and directed by Victor Fleming. Songs by Frank Loesser and Franz Waxman: OH HOW I LOVE A WEDDING and AI-PAISANO (Based on the melody of a Mexican folk song).

TWO YANKS IN TRINIDAD

A Columbia picture starring Pat O'Brien and Brian Donlevy in a cast that included Janet Blaire, and directed by Gregory Ratoff. Song by Sammy Cahn and Saul Chaplin: TWO YANKS IN TRINIDAD

YOUTH ON PARADE

A Republic picture filmed with a cast

headed by John Hubbard, Ruth Terry, Martha O'Driscoll and Tom Brown, and directed by Albert S. Rogell. Songs by

Sammy Cahn and Jule Styne:
I'VE HEARD THAT SONG BEFORE and YOU'RE SO GOOD TO ME

Western Films With Songs

ALONG THE SUNSET TRAIL
A Producers Releasing Corporation film starring Bill Boyd in a cast that included Art Davis and Lee Powell. Song by Johnny Lange and Lew Porter:
YOU WAITED JUST A LITTLE TOO LONG

BANDIT RANGER
An RKO picture starring Tim Holt in a cast that included Cliff Edwards and Joan Barclay, and directed by Leslie Selander. Song by Ray Whitley and Fred Rose:
MOVE ALONG

BELLS OF CAPISTRANO
A Republic picture starring Gene Autry in a cast that included Smiley Burnette and Virginia Grey, and directed by William Morgan. Songs:
FORGIVE ME by Jack Yellen and Milton Ager; AT SUNDOWN by Walter Donaldson; FORT WORTH JAIL by Richard Rinehart; IN OLD CAPISTRANO by Jerry Charleston and Fred Stryker; DON'T BITE THE HAND THAT'S FEEDING YOU by Thomas Hoier and James Morgan; AMERICA THE BEAUTIFUL by Katherine Lee Bates and Samuel E. Ward.

BOSS OF HANGTOWN MESA
A Universal picture starring Johnny Mack Brown in a cast that included Fuzzy Knight, William Farnum and Helen Deverell, and directed by Joseph H. Lewis. Song by Oliver Drake, Jimmy Wakely and Milton Rosen:
TRAIL DREAMIN'

CALL OF THE CANYON
A Republic picture starring Gene Autry in a cast that included Smiley Burnette and Ruth Terry, and directed by Joseph Santley. Songs:
SOMEBODY ELSE IS TAKING MY PLACE by Dick Howard and Bob Ellsworth; TAKE ME BACK TO MY BOOTS AND SADDLE by Teddy Powell, Walter Samuels and Leonard Whitcup; MONTANA PLAINS by Patsy Montana; WHEN IT'S CHILLY DOWN IN CHILE by Sol Meyer and Jule Styne; CALL OF THE CANYON by Billy Hill.

CALLING WILD BILL ELLIOTT
A Republic picture starring Bill Elliott in a cast that included Gabby Hayes and Anne Jeffreys, and directed by Spencer Bennett. Song by Thomas H. Bayly:
LONG, LONG AGO

CODE OF THE OUTLAW
A Republic picture filmed with a cast headed by Tom Tyler, Bob Steele and Melinda Leighton, and directed by John English. Song by Hy Heath:
ROOTIN' TOOTIN' TERROR OF THE WEST

COWBOY SERENADE
A Republic picture starring Gene Autry in a cast that included Smiley Burnette and Fay McKenzie, and directed by William Morgan. Songs:
SWEETHEARTS OR STRANGERS by Jimmy Davis; TAHITI HONEY by George R. Brown, Sol Meyer and Jule Styne; NOBODY KNOWS by George R. Brown and Jule Styne; COWBOY SERENADE by Rich Hall.

FIGHTING BILL FARGO
A Universal picture starring Johnny Mack Brown in a cast that included Fuzzy Knight and Jeanne Kelly, and directed by Ray Taylor. Songs by Everett Carter and Milton Rosen:
HAPPINESS CORRAL and GERALDINE

HEART OF THE GOLDEN WEST
A Republic picture starring Roy Rogers in a cast that included Smiley Burnette, Gabby Hayes and Ruth Terry, and directed by Joseph Kane. Songs:
RIVER ROBIN; NIGHT FALLS ON THE PRAIRIE and WHO'S GONNA HELP ME SING? by Bob Nolan; COWBOYS AND INDIANS by Tim Spencer; RIVER CHANT by Hall Johnson.

HEART OF THE RIO GRANDE
A Republic picture starring Gene Autry in a cast that included Smiley Burnette and Fay McKenzie, and directed by William Morgan. Songs:
LET ME RIDE DOWN ROCKY CANYON by Ray Whitley, Gene Autry and Fred Rose; DEEP IN THE HEART OF TEXAS

by June Hershey and Don Swander; DUSK ON THE PAINTED DESERT by Al Frisch, Don George and Helen Bernard; A RUMBLE SEAT FOR TWO by Johnny and Frank Marvin; RANCHO PILLOW by Charles Newman and Allie Wrubel; RAINBOW IN THE NIGHT by Sol Meyer and Jule Styne; CIMARRON by Johnny Bond; I'LL WAIT FOR YOU by Gene Autry and Fred Rose.

HOME IN WYOMING

A Republic picture starring Gene Autry in a cast that included Smiley Burnette and Olin Howard, and directed by Frank Morgan. Song by Gene Autry and Fred Rose: TWEEDLE O' TWILL

IN OLD CALIFORNIA

A Republic picture filmed with a cast headed by John Wayne, Binnie Barnes and Albert Dekker, and directed by William McGann. Songs:
THERE'S GOLD IN THE HILLS by Sol Meyer and David Buttolph; CALIFORNIA JOE by Johnny Marvin and Fred Rose.

LONE RIDER IN CHEYENNE

A Producers Releasing Corporation picture filmed with a cast headed by George Houston and Al St. John. Songs by Johnny Lange and Lew Porter:
THE WEST WILL ALWAYS REMEMBER; WHEN A COWBOY PLAYS HIS TRUSTY GUITAR and PRAIRIE TRAIL

MAN FROM CHEYENNE

A Republic picture starring Roy Rogers in a cast that included Gabby Hayes and Sally Payne, and directed by Joseph Kane. Songs:
HOME AGAIN IN OL' WYOMING and WHEN A COWBOY STARTS COURTIN' by Tim Spencer; HAPPY COWBOY; YOU AIN'T HEARD NOTHIN' TILL YOU HEAR HIM ROAR and MY OLD PAL, PAL OF MINE by Bob Nolan; LONG AFTER SUNDOWN by Tim and Glen Spencer.

RAIDERS OF THE RANGE

A Republic picture filmed with a cast headed by Tom Tyler, Bob Steele, Lois Collier and Rufe Davis. Song by Sol Meyer and Raoul Kraushaar:
THE WHISTLE OF THE 5:27

RAIDERS OF THE WEST

A Producers Releasing Corporation picture starring Bill Boyd and Lee Powell.

Song by Johnny Lange and Lew Porter: WHISPERIN' WINDS

RIDERS OF THE NORTHLAND

A Columbia picture filmed with a cast headed by Charles Starrett, Russell Hayden, Shirley Patterson and Cliff Edwards. Song by Johnny Marvin, Jimmy Wakely and Jack Briggs:
WE'LL CARRY THE TORCH FOR MISS LIBERTY

RIDIN' DOWN THE CANYON

A Republic picture starring Roy Rogers in a cast that included Gabby Hayes and Linda Hayes, and directed by Joseph Kane. Songs:
SAGEBRUSH SYMPHONY and CURLY JOE by Tim Spencer; RIDIN' DOWN THE CANYON by Gene Autry and Smiley Burnette; BLUE PRAIRIE by Tim Spencer and Bob Nolan; MY LITTLE BUCKAROO by Jack Scholl and M. K. Jerome; IN A LITTLE SPANISH TOWN by Joe Young and Mabel Wayne.

ROMANCE OF THE RANGE

A Republic picture starring Roy Rogers in a cast that included Gabby Hayes, Sally Payne and Linda Hayes, and directed by Joseph Kane. Songs:
COYOTE SERENADE and SING AS YOU WORK by Bob Nolan; OH WONDERFUL WORLD by Tim Spencer and Sam Allen; ROCKY MOUNTAIN LULLABY by Tim Spencer; WHEN ROMANCE RIDES THE RANGE by Glen Spencer.

SHADOWS ON THE SAGE

A Republic picture filmed with a cast headed by Bob Steele, Tom Tyler, Jimmy Dodd and Cherle Walker, and directed by Leslie Orlebeck. Song by Jimmy Dodd:
HAPPY COWBOY

SILVER BULLET, THE

A Universal picture starring Johnny Mack Brown in a cast that included Fuzzy Knight, William Farnum and Jennifer Holt, and directed by Joseph Lewis. Songs by Oliver Drake, Jimmy Wakely and Milton Rosen:
MY GAL SHE WORKS IN THE LAUNDRY; SWEETHEART OF THE RIO GRANDE and VOTE FOR EMILY MORGAN

SONS OF THE PIONEERS

A Republic picture starring Roy Rogers in a cast that included Gabby Hayes and

Maria Wrixon, and directed by Joseph Kane. Songs:

COME AND GET IT and LILY OF HILLBILLY VALLEY by Tim Spencer; THE WEST IS IN MY SOUL; THINGS ARE NEVER WHAT THEY SEEM and TRAIL HERDIN' COWBOY by Bob Nolan; HE'S GONE UP THE TRAIL by Vern Spencer.

SOUTH OF SANTA FE

A Republic picture starring Roy Rogers in a cast that included Gabby Hayes and Linda Hayes, and directed by Joseph Kane. Songs:

HEADIN' FOR THE HOME CORRAL and YODEL YOUR TROUBLES AWAY by Tim Spencer; SONG OF THE VAQUERO; DOWN THE TRAIL and OPEN RANGE AHEAD by Bob Nolan.

STAGECOACH BUCKAROO

A Universal picture starring Johnny Mack Brown in a cast that included Anne Nagel and Nell O'Day, and directed by Ray Taylor. Songs by Everett Carter and Milton Rosen:

PUT IT THERE and DON'T YOU EVER BE A COWBOY

STARDUST ON THE SAGE

A Republic picture starring Gene Autry in a cast that included Gabby Hayes and

Edith Fellows, and directed by William Morgan. Songs:

PERFIDA by Milton Leeds and A. Dominguez; GOOD NIGHT SWEETHEART by Jimmy Campbell, Reg Connelly and Ray Noble; YOU'LL BE SORRY by Gene Autry and Fred Rose; WOULDN'T YOU LIKE TO KNOW? by Smiley Burnette; I'LL NEVER LET YOU GO by Jimmy Wakely; WHEN THE ROSES BLOOM AGAIN by Nat Burton and Walter Kent.

SUNSET ON THE DESERT

A Republic picture starring Roy Rogers in a cast that included Gabby Hayes and Lynne Carver, and directed by Joseph Kane. Songs:

YIP PEE YI AY YOUR TROUBLES AWAY; DON JUAN and FAITHFUL PAL O' MINE by Tim Spencer; REMEMBER ME? by Bob Nolan; RIDIN' ON A ROCKY ROAD by Sol Meyer and Jule Styne.

SUNSET SERENADE

A Republic picture starring Roy Rogers in a cast that included Gabby Hayes and Helen Parrish, and directed by Joseph Kane. Songs:

COWBOY ROCKEFELLER; MAVOURNEEN O'SHEA and SONG OF THE SAN JOAQUIN by Tim Spencer; SANDMAN LULLABY and HE'S A NO GOOD SON OF A GUN by Bob Nolan.

Feature Cartoons With Songs

BAMBI

An RKO-Walt Disney production with songs by Edward H. Plumb and Frank Churchill:

LET'S SING A LITTLE SPRING SONG; LITTLE APRIL SHOWER and LOVE IS A SONG.

SALUDOS AMIGOS

An RKO-Walt Disney production with the following songs:

BRAZIL by Bob Russell and Ary Barroso; TICO TICO by Ervin Drake and Zequinta Abreu; SALUDOS AMIGOS by Ned Washington and Charles Wolcott.

Tom Drake, Margaret O'Brien and Judy Garland in *Meet Me In St. Louis.*

1 9 4 3

"To Irving Berlin: Paid In Full, Uncle Sam"

"I owe America a debt I can never repay!"

Irving Berlin has said this time and again, and this adopted son of Uncle Sam who started his musical career as a singing waiter in a Bowery dive to zoom to towering heights as a songwriter, means it, too.

But the books were more than balanced when Berlin wrote, produced and trouped the world with *This Is The Army*, the all-soldier stage revue that when adapted to the screen, grossed $8,500,000 at the box-office, a record yet to be smashed by any other Hollywood musical. And he did it all for free—for love of country.

His, however, was the common pattern followed by the Hollywood stars during those years of blood, sweat and tears when as soldiers in grease paint, they traveled to the far-flung theaters of war to bring the solace of laughter and song to millions of battle-weary and homesick GIs, and although they gave unsparingly of their time and talent, their work before the cameras didn't suffer, and the musicals of 1943 were the equal if not the superior of the song-and-dance films that had made 1942 a banner year in Hollywood screen history.

At least twenty of the musicals released in 1943 merited four-bell rating, and included screen adaptations of five of Broadway's top productions: *Best Foot Forward* with songs by Hugh Martin and Ralph Blane, newcomers to Hollywood; *Cabin In The Sky* with music by Vernon Duke and memorable performances by Ethel Waters and Lena Horne; Sigmund Romberg's *The Desert Song,* Cole Porter's *DuBarry Was A Lady,* and *Girl Crazy* in which Judy Garland and Mickey Rooney revived such all-time hits by Ira and George Gershwin as *Bidin' My Time, I Got Rhythm, Embraceable You* and *Fascinating Rhythm.*

Harry Warren was credited with the music of three films: *Sweet Rosie O'Grady,* starring Betty Grable; *The Gang's All Here* with Alice Faye and Carmen Miranda heading the cast; and *Hello, Frisco, Hello,* distinguished by the song, *You'll Never Know,* which won a second Oscar for this former bass drummer with a traveling carnival show, while Cole Porter's *You'd Be So Nice To Come Home To* from *Something To Shout About* couldn't help but be a hit with the lonesome GI, sweating out the war and the time when he could return to the girl back in the states.

Bing Crosby introduced one of his biggest hits, *Sunday, Monday And Always,* in *Dixie;* Ted Lewis and his wailing clarinet revived the oldtime songs of more peaceful days in *Is Everybody Happy?;* and Frank Sinatra escaped from his frenzied army of shrieking bobby-soxers long enough to make his screen debut in *Higher And Higher,* aided and abetted by the studio makeup men who covered his scars and bruises with grease paint, and two ballads by Harold Adamson and Jimmy McHugh: *I Couldn't Sleep A Wink Last Night* and *A Lovely Way To Spend An Evening.*

Three all-star revues packed the movie houses: Metro-Goldwyn-Mayer's *Thousands Cheer;* Warner Brothers' *Thank Your Lucky Stars* in which Bette Davis stepped out of character to sing *They're Either Too Young Or Too Old;* and United Artists' *Stage Door Canteen,* which was voted one of the Ten Best Films of the year and grossed $4,300,000 at the box-office—a take that admitted it to the Golden Circle of top money-producers.

Again, as in 1942, songs bearing the Made-in-Hollywood trademark poured out of the nation's loud speakers and produced a bumper crop of nickels in the juke boxes, and included *I Left My Heart At The Stage Door Canteen, This Is The Army, Mr. Jones, Mandy* and *Oh, How I Hate To Get Up In The Morning!,* all from Irving Berlin's all-soldier revue; *Taking A Chance On Love, Take It From There, Do I Love You?, No Love No Nothing, Let's Get Lost, My Heart Tells Me, My Shining Hour, One For My Baby (And One More For The Road), Cool Water, Say A Prayer For The Boys Over There,* and *I'll Get By (As Long As I Have You),* the latter introduced in *A Guy Named Joe.*

All in all, it was a good year musically even though the master, Jerome Kern, came up with only one song and that in the light of what is happening today, had best be forgotten. It was a tribute to the Soviet Union, and bore the title: *And Russia Is Her Name.*

Musicals

ALWAYS A BRIDESMAID
A Universal picture starring the Andrews Sisters in a cast that included Patric Knowles, Grace McDonald, Billy Gilbert and Charles Butterworth, and directed by Erle C. Kenton. Songs:
THAT'S MY AFFAIR by Hy Zaret and Irving Weiser; YOO-HOO by Vic Shoen, Ray Jacobs and John Wilforth; AS LONG AS I HAVE YOU by Earl Hanbrich, Al Lewis and Howard Simon; THANKS FOR THE BUGGY RIDE by Jules Buffano.

AROUND THE WORLD
An RKO picture filmed with a cast headed by Kay Kyser, Mischa Auer and Joan Davis, and directed by Allan Dwan. Songs by Harold Adamson and Jimmy Mc-Hugh:
CANDLELIGHT AND WINE; THEY CHOPPED DOWN THE OLD APPLE TREE; DON'T BELIEVE EVERYTHING YOU DREAM; HE'S GOT A SECRET WEAPON; GREAT NEWS IN THE MAKING; A MOKE FROM SHAMOKIN and ROODLE-DE-DOO.

BEST FOOT FORWARD
An M-G-M picture starring Lucille Ball and William Gaxton in a cast that included Virginia Weidler, Tommy Dix, Nancy Walker, Gloria DeHaven, June Allyson and Harry James and his orchestra, and directed by Eddie Buzzell. Songs by Hugh Martin and Ralph Blane:
BUCKLE DOWN WINSOCKIE; WISH I MAY; THREE MEN ON A DATE; EV'RYTIME; THE THREE B'S; ALIVE AND KICKING and YOU'RE LUCKY.

CABIN IN THE SKY

An M-G-M picture starring Ethel Waters in a cast that included Lena Horne, Eddie "Rochester" Anderson; Louis Armstrong, Rex Ingram, Duke Ellington and his orchestra and the Hall Johnson choir, and directed by Vincent Minnelli. Songs:

LI'L BLACK SHEEP; HAPPINESS IS JUS' A THING CALLED JOE; AIN'T IT DE TRUTH and DAT OLD DEBBIL CONSEQUENCE by E. Y. Harburg and Harold Arlen; HONEY IN THE HONEYCOMB; TAKING A CHANCE ON LOVE and IN MY OLD VIRGINIA HOME by John LaTouche, Ted Fetter and Vernon Duke; GOING UP by Duke Ellington; THINGS AIN'T WHAT THEY USED TO BE by Mercer Ellington, SHINE by Lew Brown, Ford Dabney and Cecil Mack.

CAMPUS RHYTHM

A Monogram picture filmed with a cast headed by Johnny Downs, Gale Storm, Robert Lowery, Candy Candido and Gee-Gee Pearson, and directed by Arthur Dreifuss. Songs:

SWING YOUR WAY THROUGH COLLEGE by Andy Iona Long and Louis Herscher; WALKING THE CHALK LINE by Jules Loman and Louis Herscher; IT'S GREAT TO BE A COLLEGE GIRL and COLLEGE SWEETHEART by Louis Herscher.

CAREER GIRL

A Producers Releasing Corporation picture starring Frances Langford in a cast that included Edward Norris, Iris Adrian and Craig Wood, and directed by Wallace W. Fox. Songs:

THAT'S HOW THE RHUMBA BEGAN and SOME DAY by Morey Amsterdam and Tony Ramano; BLUE IN LOVE AGAIN and A DREAM COME TRUE by Michael Breen and Sam Neuman.

CHATTERBOX

A Republic picture starring Joe E. Brown and Judy Canova in a cast that included Rosemary Lane, John Hubbard, Anne Jeffreys, Spade Cooley and the Mills Brothers, and directed by Joseph Santley. Songs:

MAD ABOUT HIM, SAD WITHOUT HIM, HOW CAN I BE GLAD WITHOUT HIM BLUES by Larry Markes and Dick Charles; SWEET LUCY BROWN by Leon and Otis Rene; WHY CAN'T I SING A LOVE SONG? by Sol Meyer and Harry Akst.

CONEY ISLAND

A 20th Century-Fox picture starring Betty Grable in a cast that included George Montgomery, Cesar Romero and Charles Winninger, and directed by Walter Lang. Songs by Leo Robin and Ralph Rainger:

TAKE IT FROM THERE; BEAUTIFUL CONEY ISLAND; MISS LULU FROM LOUISVILLE; GET THE MONEY; THERE'S DANGER IN A DANCE and OLD DEMON RUM.

COWBOY IN MANHATTAN

A Universal picture starring Frances Langford and Robert Paige in a cast that included Leon Errol, Walter Catlett and Dorothy Grainger, and directed by Frank Woodruff. Songs by Everett Carter and Milton Rosen:

PRIVATE COWBOY JONES; WHISTLE YOUR BLUES TO A BLUEBIRD; DANCIN' ON AIR; GOT LOVE; NEED I SAY MORE; MR. MOON and A COWBOY IS HAPPY.

CRAZY HOUSE

A Universal picture starring Olsen and Johnson in a cast that included Martha O'Driscoll, Allan Jones, Patric Knowles, Cass Daley, Leo Carrillo, Robert Paige, Lon Chaney, Andy Devine, the DeMarco Sisters, Glenn Miller Chorus, Delta Rhythm Boys and Count Basie and his orchestra, and directed by Edward Cline. Musical numbers:

POCKETFUL O' PENNIES by Eddie Cherkose and Franz Steininger; CRAZY HOUSE by Eddie Cherkose and Milton Rosen; LAMENT OF A LAUNDRY GIRL by Jerry Seelan, Lester Lee and Ted Shapiro; MY RAINBOW SONG by Mitchell Parish, Matt Malneck and Frank Signorelli; TROPICANA and GET ON BOARD LITTLE CHILDREN by Don Raye and Gene DePaul; MY SONG WITHOUT WORDS by John LaTouche and Vernon Duke; I OUGHT TO DANCE by Sammy Cahn and Saul Chaplin.

DESERT SONG, THE

A Warner Brothers' picture filmed with a cast headed by Dennis Morgan, Irene Manning, Bruce Cabot, Lynne Overman, Faye Emerson and Gene Lockhart, and directed by Robert Florey. Songs:

SONG OF THE RIFFS; DESERT SONG; ONE ALONE; ROMANCE and FRENCH MILITARY MARCHING SONG by Otto Harbach, Oscar Hammerstein II and Sigmund Romberg; FIFI'S SONG by Jack Scholl and Sigmund Romberg; LONG LIVE THE NIGHT by Jack

Scholl, Mario Silva and Sigmund Romberg; GAY PARISIENNE by Jack Scholl and Serge Walters.

DIXIE
A Paramount picture starring Bing Crosby in a cast that included Dorothy Lamour, Billy DeWolf and Marjorie Reynolds, and directed by A. Edward Sutherland. Songs by Johnny Burke and Jimmy Van Heusen:
SUNDAY, MONDAY AND ALWAYS; SHE'S FROM MISSOURI; MISS JEMIMA WALKS BY; IF YOU PLEASE; KINDA PECULIAR BROWN and A HORSE THAT KNOWS HIS WAY BACK HOME.

DuBARRY WAS A LADY
An M-G-M picture starring Red Skelton, Lucille Ball and Gene Kelly in a cast that included Virginia O'Brien, Rags Ragland and Tommy Dorsey's orchestra, and directed by Roy Del Ruth. Songs:
DO I LOVE YOU? KATIE WENT TO HAYTI and FRIENDSHIP by Cole Porter; I LOVE AN ESQUIRE GIRL by Lew Brown, Ralph Freed and Roger Edens; MADAME I LOVE YOUR CREPE SUZETTES by Ralph Freed, Lew Brown and Burton Lane; DuBARRY WAS A LADY by Ralph Freed and Burton Lane; SALOME by E. Y. Harburg, Ralph Freed and Burton Lane; LADIES OF THE BATH by Roger Edens.

FOLLIES' GIRL
A Producers Releasing Corporation picture filmed with a cast headed by Wendy Barrie, Doris Nolan, Gordon Oliver, Anne Barrett, J. C. Nugent, Lew Hearn, Cliff Hall and Patsy Flick, and directed by William Rowland. Songs:
KEEP THE FLAG A-FLYING AMERICA by Mary Schaefer; I TOLD A LIE by Nick Kenny, Kim Gannon and Ken Lane; THOITY POIPLE BOIDS; I KNEW YOUR FATHER SON and FASCINATION by Fred Wise, Buddy Kaye and Sidney Lippman; SHALL WE GATHER AT THE RHYTHM? by Nick and Charles Kenny, Sonny Burke and John Murphy; NO MAN IN THE HOUSE by Nick and Charles Kenny and Sonny Burke; SOMEONE TO LOVE by Robert Warren.

FOLLOW THE BAND
A Universal picture filmed with a cast headed by Leon Errol, Eddie Quillan, Mary Beth Hughes, Skinny Ennis, Robert Mitchum, Leo Carrillo, Frances Langford, Ray Eberle and Alvino Rey and his orchestra, and directed by Jean Yarbrough. Songs:

SWINGING THE BLUES and SPELLBOUND by Everett Carter and Milton Rosen; MY DEVOTION by Roc Hillman and Johnny Napton; HILO HATTIE by Harold Adamson and Johnny Noble; WHAT KIND OF LOVE IS THIS? and HE'S MY GUY by Don Raye and Gene DePaul; ARMY AIR CORPS SONG by Robert Crawford.

FOOTLIGHT GLAMOUR
A Columbia picture starring Penny Singleton and Arthur Lake, and directed by Frank Strayer. Songs by Ray Evans and Jay Livingston:
BAMBOOLA; MISSISSIPPI SIREN and WHAT'S UNDER YOUR MASK, MADAME?

GALS, INC.
A Universal picture filmed with a cast headed by Leon Errol, Harriet Hilliard, David Bacon, Maureen Cannon, Betty Keane, the Pied Pipers and Glen Gray and his orchestra, and directed by Leslie Goodwins. Songs by Everett Carter and Milton Rosen:
ALL THE TIME IT'S YOU; HEP HEP HOORAY and HERE'S YOUR KISS.

GANG'S ALL HERE, THE
A 20th Century-Fox picture starring Alice Faye and Carmen Miranda in a cast that included Phil Baker and Benny Goodman and his orchestra, and directed by Busby Berkeley. Songs by Leo Robin and Harry Warren:
NO LOVE NO NOTHING; JOURNEY TO A STAR; THE LADY IN THE TUTTI-FRUITI HAT; THE POLKA-DOT POLKA; YOU DISCOVER YOU'RE IN NEW YORK; PADUCAH; MINNIE'S IN THE MONEY; PICKIN' ON YOUR MAMA; SLEEPY MOON and DRUMS AND DREAMS.

GIRL CRAZY
An M-G-M picture starring Judy Garland and Mickey Rooney in a cast that included Gil Stratton, Robert E. Strickland, Rags Ragland, June Allyson, Nancy Walker, Guy Kibbe and Tommy Dorsey and his orchestra, and directed by Norman Taurog. Songs by Ira and George Gershwin:
TREAT ME ROUGH; SAM AND DELILAH; BIDIN' MY TIME; EMBRACEABLE YOU; FASCINATING RHYTHM; I GOT RHYTHM; BUT NOT FOR ME; BARBARY COAST and CACTUS TIME IN ARIZONA.

GIRL FROM MONTEREY

A Producers Releasing Corporation picture starring Armida, and directed by Sam Wood. Songs by Louis Herscher:

JIVE BROTHER JIVE; LAST NIGHT'S ALL OVER and THE GIRL FROM MONTEREY (with Harold Raymond).

HAPPY GO LUCKY

A Paramount picture starring Mary Martin and Dick Powell in a cast that included Betty Hutton, Eddie Bracken and Rudy Vallee, and directed by Curtis Bernhardt. Songs by Frank Loesser and Jimmy McHugh:

LET'S GET LOST; MURDER HE SAYS; HAPPY GO LUCKY; FUDDY DUDDY WATCHMAKER and SING A TROPICAL SONG.

HARVEST MELODY

A Producers Releasing Corporation picture filmed with a cast headed by Rosemary Lane, Johnny Downs, Luis Alberni and Eddie LaBaron and his orchestra, and directed by Sam Newfield. Songs:

PUT IT IN REVERSE; YOU COULD HAVE KNOCKED ME OVER WITH A FEATHER and LET'S DRIVE OUT TO A DRIVE-IN by Benny Davis and Harry Akst; TENDERLY by Leo Shuken and Walter Colmes.

HEAT'S ON, THE

A Columbia picture starring Mae West, Victor Moore and William Gaxton in a cast that included Lester Allen, Hazel Scott and Xavier Cugat and his orchestra, and directed by Gregory Ratoff. Musical numbers:

I'M JUST A STRANGER IN TOWN; THEY LOOKED SO PRETTY ON THE ENVELOPE; THERE GOES THAT GUITAR; THE WHITE KEYS AND THE BLACK KEYS and HELLO MI AMIGO by Henry Meyers, Edward Eliscu and Jay Gorney; ANTONIO by Leo Huntley, John Blackburn and Fabian Andre; THE CAISSONS GO ROLLING ALONG by Edmund L. Gruber.

HELLO FRISCO HELLO

A 20th Century-Fox picture starring Alice Faye and John Payne in a cast that included Jack Oakie, Lynn Bari and June Havoc, and directed by H. Bruce Humberstone. Songs:

YOU'LL NEVER KNOW and I GOTTA HAVE YOU by Mack Gordon and Harry Warren; RAGTIME COWBOY JOE by Grant Clarke, Maurice Abrahams and Lewis E. Muir.

HERE COMES ELMER

A Republic picture starring Al Pearce and Dale Evans, and directed by Joseph Santley. Songs:

STRAIGHTEN UP AND FLY RIGHT by Nat "King" Cole and Irving Mills; DON'T BE AFRAID TO TELL MOTHER by Pinky Tomlin, Coy Poe and Jimmy Grier; YOU'RE SO GOOD TO ME by Sammy Cahn and Jule Styne; HITCH OLD DOBBIN TO THE SHAY AGAIN by J. C. Lewis Jr. and Jud Conlon.

HI, BUDDY

A Universal picture starring Harriet Hilliard, Dick Foran and Robert Paige in a cast that included Marjorie Lord, and directed by Harold Young. Songs:

HI, BUDDY, HI; WE'RE THE MARINES and MR. YANKEE DOODLE by Everett Carter and Milton Rosen; WE'RE IN THE NAVY by Don Raye and Gene DePaul; HERE'S TO TOMORROW by Charles Newman and Lew Pollack; TAKE ME IN YOUR ARMS by Mitchell Parish, Fritz Rotter and Fred Markush.

HIGHER AND HIGHER

An RKO picture filmed with a cast headed by Michele Morgan, Jack Haley, Frank Sinatra, Leon Errol, Marcy McGuire and Victor Borge, and directed by Tim Whelan. Songs by Harold Adamson and Jimmy McHugh:

I COULDN'T SLEEP A WINK LAST NIGHT; A LOVELY WAY TO SPEND AN EVENING; THE MUSIC STOPPED; HIGHER AND HIGHER; IT'S A MOST IMPORTANT AFFAIR; YOU'RE ON YOUR OWN; MINUET IN BOOGIE; I SAW YOU FIRST; TODAY I'M A DEBUTANTE and MRS. WHIFFEN.

HI'YA CHUM

A Universal picture starring the Ritz Brothers in a cast that included Jane Frazee, Robert Paige and June Clyde, and directed by Harold Young. Songs by Don Raye and Gene DePaul:

TWO ON A BIKE; HE'S MY GUY; THE DOO DAT; I'M HITTING A HIGH SPOT and YOU GOTTA HAVE PERSONALITY.

HI'YA SAILOR

A Universal picture filmed with a cast headed by Donald Woods, Elyse Knox, Eddie Quillan, Phyllis Brooks, the Delta

Rhythm Boys and the orchestras of Ray Eberle and Wingy Manone, and directed by Jean Yarbrough. Songs:

A DREAM AGO; HI'YA SAILOR; SO GOOD NIGHT and JUST A STEP AWAY FROM HEAVEN by Everett Carter and Milton Rosen; THE MORE I GO OUT WITH SOMEBODY ELSE by Billy Post, Don Pierce and Pierre Norman; OH, BROTHER! by Maxine Manners and Jean Miller.

HIT PARADE OF 1943

A Republic picture filmed with a cast headed by John Carroll, Susan Hayward, Gail Patrick, Melville Cooper, Walter Catlett, the Music Maids, Golden Gate Quartet and the orchestras of Freddy Martin, Count Basie and Ray McKinley, and directed by Albert S. Rogell. Songs by Harold Adamson and Jule Styne:

A CHANGE OF HEART; DO THESE OLD EYES DECEIVE ME? HARLEM SANDMAN; THAT'S HOW TO WRITE A SONG; WHO TOOK ME HOME LAST NIGHT? and TAHM-BOOM-BAH.

HIT THE ICE

A Universal picture starring Abbott and Costello in a cast that included Ginny Simms, Patric Knowles, Elyse Knox and Johnny Long's orchestra, and directed by Charles Lamont. Songs by Paul Francis Webster and Harry Revel:

I'D LIKE TO SET YOU TO MUSIC; I'M LIKE A FISH OUT OF WATER; HAPPINESS BOUND and THE SLAP POLKA.

HONEYMOON LODGE

A Universal picture filmed with a cast headed by David Bruce, June Vincent, Rod Cameron, Harriet Hilliard, Franklin Pangborn and Ozzie Nelson and his orchestra, and directed by Edward Lilley. Musical numbers:

I NEVER KNEW I COULD LOVE ANYBODY LIKE I'M LOVING YOU by Tom Pitts, Ray Egan and Roy K. Marsh; I'M THROUGH WITH LOVE by Gus Kahn, Matt Malneck and Fud Livingston; JERSEY JIVE by Minor Hassel and Ozzie Nelson; (AS LONG AS YOU'RE NOT IN LOVE WITH ANYONE ELSE) WHY DON'T YOU FALL IN LOVE WITH ME? by Al Lewis and Mabel Wayne; DO I WORRY? by Bobby Worth and Stanley Cowan.

HOW'S ABOUT IT?

A Universal picture starring the Andrews Sisters and Robert Paige, and directed by

Erle C. Fenton. Songs:

DON'T MIND THE RAIN by Ned Miller and Chester Cohn; TAKE IT AND GIT by William and Melvin Chapman, James T. Marshall and Johnny Green; EAST OF THE ROCKIES by Sid Robin; GOING UP by Irving Gordon and Allen Roth; I'M ON MY WAY and I DO by Buddy Pepper and Inez James; HERE COME'S THE NAVY by Lew Brown, W. A. Timm, J. Vejvoda and Clarence P. Oakes.

I DOOD IT

An M-G-M picture starring Red Skelton in a cast that included Lena Horne, Eleanor Powell, Sam Levene and Hazel Scott, and directed by Vincent Minnelli. Songs:

SWINGING THE JINX AWAY by Cole Porter; SO LONG SARAH JANE by Lew Brown, Ralph Freed and Sammy Fain; STAR EYES by Don Raye and Gene De-Paul; TAKING A CHANCE ON LOVE by Ted Fetter, John LaTouche and Vernon Duke; JERICHO by Leo Robin and Richard Myers; HOLA E PAE by Johnny Noble.

IS EVERYBODY HAPPY?

A Columbia picture starring Ted Lewis in a cast that included Nan Wynn, Bob Haymes and Larry Parks, and directed by Charles Barton. Songs:

JUST AROUND THE CORNER by Dolph Singer and Harry Von Tilzer; ON THE SUNNY SIDE OF THE STREET by Dorothy Fields and Jimmy McHugh; BE YOURSELF by Harry Harris; CUDDLE UP A LITTLE CLOSER by Otto Harbach and Karl Hoscha; WAY DOWN YONDER IN NEW ORLEANS by Henry Creamer and Turner Layton; CHINATOWN by William Jerome and Jean Schwartz; I'M JUST WILD ABOUT HARRY by Noble Sissle and Eubie Blake; PRETTY BABY by Gus Kahn, Tony Jackson and Egbert VanAlstyne; AM I BLUE by Grant Clarke and Harry Akst; MORE THAN ANYTHING ELSE IN THE WORLD by Charles Kenny and Ruth Lowe; ST. LOUIS BLUES by W. C. Handy; TELL ME WHY NIGHTS ARE LONELY by Will Callahan and Max Kortlander.

JITTERBUGS

A 20th Century-Fox picture starring Laurel and Hardy in a cast that included Vivian Blaine, Bob Bailey and Lee Patrick, and directed by Mal St. Clair. Songs by Charles Newman and Lew Pollack:

THE MOON KISSED THE MISSIS-

SIPPI; I'VE GOTTA SEE FOR MYSELF
and IF THE SHOE FITS YOU WEAR
IT.

LARCENY WITH MUSIC
A Universal picture starring Allan Jones
and Kitty Carlisle, and directed by Edward
Lilley. Songs:
DO YOU HEAR MUSIC? and PLEASE
LOUISE by Don Raye and Gene DePaul;
ONLY IN DREAMS by Sam Lerner and
Charles Previn; FOR THE WANT OF
YOU by Eddie Cherkose and Jule Styne.

LET'S FACE IT
A Paramount picture starring Bob Hope
and Betty Hutton in a cast that included
Zasu Pitts and Eve Arden, and directed by
Sidney Lanfield. Songs:
LET'S NOT TALK ABOUT LOVE by
Cole Porter; PLAIN JANE DOE and
WHO DID? I DID, YES I DID by Sammy
Cahn and Jule Styne.

MELODY PARADE
A Monogram picture filmed with a cast
headed by Mary Beth Hughes, Eddie Quil-
lan, Tim and Irene Ryan and the orchestras
of Anson Weeks and Ted Fiorito, and di-
rected by Arthur Dreifuss. Songs by Eddie
Cherkose and Edward Kay:
THE WOMAN BEHIND THE MAN
BEHIND THE GUN; WHATEVER POS-
SESSED ME? DON'T FALL IN LOVE;
SPEECHLESS; AMIGO and MR. AND
MRS. COMMANDO.

MR. BIG
A Universal picture starring Gloria Jean
and Donald O'Connor in a cast that in-
cluded Peggy Ryan, Robert Paige, Elyse
Knox, Ray Eberle and his orchestra, Eddie
Miller's Bob Cats and the Ben Carter Choir,
and directed by Charles Lamont. Songs by
Inez James and Buddy Pepper:
KITTENS WITH THEIR MITTENS
LACED; THE SPIRIT IS IN ME; THEE
AND ME; WE'RE NOT OBVIOUS; ALL
THE THINGS I WANTA SAY; RUDE,
CRUDE AND UNATTRACTIVE and
THIS MUST BE A DREAM.

MOONLIGHT IN VERMONT
A Universal picture starring Gloria Jean
in a cast that included Ray Malone and
George Dolenz, and directed by Edward
Lilley. Songs:
SOMETHING TELLS ME; BE A
GOOD, GOOD GIRL; THEY GOT ME
IN THE MIDDLE OF THINGS; PICKIN'
THE BEETS; DOBBIN AND A WAGON
OF HAY and AFTER THE BEAT by

Inez James and Sidney Miller; LOVER
by Lorenz Hart and Richard Rodgers.

PRESENTING LILY MARS
An M-G-M picture starring Judy Gar-
land and Van Heflin in a cast that in-
cluded Fay Bainter, Richard Carlson, Spring
Byington, Martha Eggerth and the orches-
tras of Tommy Dorsey and Bob Crosby,
and directed by Norman Taurog. Songs:
KULEBIAKA; WHEN I LOOK AT
YOU and IS IT LOVE (OR THE GYP-
SY IN ME)? by Paul Francis Webster and
Walter Jurmann; SWEETHEARTS OF
AMERICA by Ralph Freed and Burton
Lane; PAGING MR. GREENBACK by
Lew Brown, E. Y. Harburg, Sammy Fain
and Roger Edens.

RED HEAD FROM MANHATTAN
A Columbia picture starring Lupe Velez
in a cast that included Michael Duane, Tim
Ryan and Gerald Mohr, and directed by
Lew Landers. Songs:
WHY BE DOWN-HEARTED?; AN
OUNCE OF BOUNCE; THE FIESTIGO;
LET'S FALL IN LINE and I'M UNDE-
CIDED (CAN'T MAKE UP MY MIND)
by Walter G. Samuels and Saul Chaplin;
TWIDDLIN' MY THUMBS by Sammy
Cahn and Saul Chaplin.

RHYTHM OF THE ISLANDS
A Universal picture starring Allan Jones
and Jane Frazee in a cast that included
Andy Devine, Ernest Truex, Marjorie Gate-
son and the Step Brothers, and directed by
Roy William Neill. Songs:
NANI LOA; BLUE MIST; TWILIGHT
MEMORIES; HURA HURA and DRIFT-
ING IN THE MOONLIGHT by Andy
Iona Long and Louis Herscher; TROPIC
LULLABY and SAVAGE SERENADE by
Dave Franklin; CHANT OF THE TOM-
TOM by Inez James and Buddy Pepper.

RIDING HIGH
A Paramount picture starring Dorothy
Lamour and Dick Powell in a cast that in-
cluded Victor Moore, Gil Lamb, Cass Daley
and Milton Britton's orchestra, and directed
by George Marshall. Songs:
GET YOUR MAN; WHISTLING IN
THE DARK and YOU'RE THE RAIN-
BOW by Leo Robin and Ralph Rainger;
I'M THE SECRETARY TO THE SUL-
TAN by Leo Robin; INJUN GAL HEAP
HEP by Leo Robin, Ralph Rainger and
Joseph J. Lilley; WILLIE THE WOLF
OF THE WEST by Johnny Mercer and
Joseph J. Lilley.

SALUTE FOR THREE

A Paramount picture filmed with a cast headed by Betty Rhodes, MacDonald Carey, Marty May and Cliff Edwards, and directed by Ralph Murphy. Songs:
DON'T WORRY; I'D DO IT FOR YOU; WHA' D'YA DO WHEN IT RAINS?; MY WIFE'S A WAC and LEFT-RIGHT (with Sol Meyer) by Kim Gannon and Jule Styne; VALSE CONTINENTAL by Victor Young.

SILVER SKATES

A Monogram picture filmed with a cast headed by Kenny Baker, Patricia Morison and Ted Fiorito's orchestra, and directed by Leslie Goodwins. Songs:
DANCING ON TOP OF THE WORLD; LOVE IS A BEAUTIFUL SONG; CAN'T YOU HEAR ME CALLING FROM THE MOUNTAIN?; A BOY LIKE YOU AND A GIRL LIKE ME and COWBOY JOE by Dave Oppenheim and Roy Ingraham; SING A SONG OF THE SEA by Dave Oppenheim and Archie Gottler.

SKY'S THE LIMIT, THE

An RKO picture starring Fred Astaire in a cast that included Joan Leslie and Robert Benchley, and directed by Edward H. Griffith. Musical numbers:
I'VE GOT A LOT IN COMMON WITH YOU; MY SHINING HOUR; ONE FOR MY BABY (AND ONE MORE FOR THE ROAD) and HARVEY THE VICTORY GARDEN MAN by Johnny Mercer and Harold Arlen; CUBAN SUGAR MILL by Freddie Slack.

SLEEPY LAGOON

A Republic picture starring Judy Canova and Dennis Day in a cast that included Ruth Donnelly, Ernest Truex, Herbert Corthell and Mike Riley's orchestra, and directed by Joseph Santley. Songs:
IF YOU ARE THERE; YOU'RE THE FONDEST THING I AM OF and I'M NOT MYSELF ANYMORE by Ned Washington and Phil Ohman; SLEEPY LAGOON by Jack Lawrence and Eric Coates.

SOMETHING TO SHOUT ABOUT

A Columbia picture filmed with a cast headed by Don Ameche, Janet Blair, Jack Oakie, William Gaxton, Cobina Wright and Hazel Scott, and directed by Gregory Ratoff. Songs by Cole Porter:
YOU'D BE SO NICE TO COME HOME TO; SOMETHING TO SHOUT ABOUT; I ALWAYS KNEW; HASTA LA VISTA; LOTUS BLOOM; THROUGH THICK AND THIN; I CAN DO WITHOUT TEA IN MY TEAPOT and IT MIGHT HAVE BEEN.

STAGE DOOR CANTEEN

A United Artists' picture filmed with an all-star cast headed by Kenny Baker, Tallulah Bankhead, Ralph Bellamy, Edgar Bergen, Ray Bolger, Ina Claire, Katherine Cornell, Jane Cowl, Gracie Fields, Lynn Fontaine, Helen Hayes, Katherine Hepburn, George Jessel, Gertrude Lawrence, Gypsy Rose Lee, Ethel Merman, Harpo Marx, Ed Wynn, Ethel Waters and Alfred Lunt, and directed by Frank Borzage. Songs:
WE MUSTN'T SAY GOODBYE; THE MACHINE GUN SONG; AMERICAN BOY; DON'T WORRY ISLAND; QUICK SANDS; A ROOKIE AND HIS RHYTHM; SLEEP BABY SLEEP; WE MEET IN THE FUNNIEST PLACES; YOU'RE PRETTY TERRIFIC YOURSELF by Al Dubin and Jimmy Monaco; SHE'S A BOMBSHELL FROM BROOKLYN by Sol Lesser, Al Dubin and Jimmy Monaco; THE GIRL I LOVE TO LEAVE BEHIND by Lorenz Hart and Richard Rodgers.

STORMY WEATHER

A 20th Century-Fox picture starring Ethel Waters in a cast that included Lena Horne, Eddie "Rochester" Anderson, Bill Robinson and Fats Waller, and directed by Andrew Stone. Songs:
MY, MY AIN'T THAT SOMETHIN' by Pinky Tomlin and Harry Tobias; THERE'S NO TWO WAYS ABOUT LOVE by Ted Koehler and James P. Johnson; RANG TANG TANG and DAH, DAT, DAH by Cyril J. Mockridge; LINDA BROWN by Al Cowans; THAT AIN'T RIGHT by Nat "King" Cole and Irving Mills; AIN'T MISBEHAVIN' by Harry Brooks, Andy Razaf and Fats Waller; I LOST MY SUGAR IN KANSAS CITY by Johnny Lange and Leon Rene; I CAN'T GIVE YOU ANYTHING BUT LOVE by Dorothy Fields and Jimmy McHugh; GEECHY JOE by Jack Palmer, Andy Gibson and Cab Calloway.

SULTAN'S DAUGHTER, THE

A Monogram picture filmed with a cast headed by Ann Corio, Tim and Irene Ryan, Charles Butterfield, Jack LaRue and Freddie Fisher's orchestra, and directed by A. Dreifuss. Songs, M. Greene and K. Hajos:
CLICKITY CLACK JACK; I'M ALWAYS THE GIRL; I'D LOVE TO MAKE LOVE TO YOU and THE SULTAN'S DAUGHTER.

SWEET ROSIE O'GRADY

A 20th Century-Fox picture starring Betty Grable and Robert Young in a cast that included Adolphe Menjou, Phil Regan, Alan Dinehart, Virginia Grey and Reginald Gardiner, and directed by Irving Cummings. Songs by Mack Gordon and Harry Warren:

MY HEART TELLS ME; THE WISHING WALTZ; GET YOUR POLICE GAZETTE; MY SAM; GOING TO THE COUNTY FAIR and WHERE OH WHERE OH WHERE IS THE GROOM?

SWING FEVER

An M-G-M picture filmed with a cast headed by Kay Kyser, Marilyn Maxwell, William Gargan, Lena Horne, Nat Pendleton and Maxie Rosenbloom, and directed by Tim Whelan. Songs:

MISSISSIPPI DREAM BOAT by Lew Brown, Ralph Freed and Sammy Fain; I PLANTED A ROSE and ONE GIRL AND TWO BOYS by Ralph Freed, Lew Brown and Nacio Herb Brown; YOU'RE SO DIFFERENT by Sammy Fain; SH! DON'T MAKE A SOUND by Sunny Skylar.

SWING YOUR PARTNER

A Republic picture filmed with a cast headed by Lulubelle and Scotty, Vera Vague, Dale Evans and the Tennessee Ramblers, and directed by Frank McDonald. Songs:

CHEESE CAKE and SWING YOUR PARTNER by Charles Henderson; CRACKER BARREL COUNTY by Frank Loesser and Jule Styne; EVERYBODY KISS YOUR PARDNER by Dick Sanford, John Redmond and Frank Weldon; SHUG SHUG YODEL by George Fisher; IN THE COOL OF THE EVENING by Walter Bullock and Jule Styne.

TAHITI HONEY

A Republic picture starring Simone Simon and Dennis O'Keefe in a cast that included Michael Whalen and Dan Seymour, and directed by John T. Auer. Songs by Charles Newman and Lew Pollack:

ANY OLD PORT IN A STORM; IN A TEN-GALLON HAT; KONI PLENTY HU-HU; THIS GETS BETTER EV'RY MINUTE and YOU COULD HEAR A PIN DROP.

THANK YOUR LUCKY STARS

A Warner Brothers' picture filmed with an all-star cast headed by Eddie Cantor, Bette Davis, Olivia DeHaviland, Errol Flynn, John Garfield, Joan Leslie and Ann Sheridan, and directed by David Butler. Songs by Frank Loesser and Arthur Schwartz:

THE'RE EITHER TOO YOUNG OR TOO OLD; HOW SWEET YOU ARE; THE DREAMER; I'M RIDING FOR A FALL; GOOD NIGHT GOOD NEIGHBOR; LOVE ISN'T BORN IT'S MADE; ICE COLD KATY; THANK YOUR LUCKY STARS; WE'RE STAYING HOME TONIGHT; I'M GOING NORTH and THAT'S WHAT YOU JOLLY WELL GET.

THIS IS THE ARMY

A Warner Brothers' picture filmed with a cast of Hollywood stars and GI's that included Irving Berlin, George Murphy, Joan Leslie, George Tobias, Alan Hale, Charles Butterworth, Dolores Costello, Una Merkel, Stanley Ridges, Rosemary DeCamp, Ruth Donnelly, Dorothy Peterson, Frances Langford, Gertrude Niesen, Kate Smith, Lt. Ronald Regan and Ezra Stone, and directed by Michael Curtiz. Songs by Irving Berlin:

THIS IS THE ARMY MR. JONES; THE ARMY'S MADE A MAN OUT OF ME; MANDY; I'M GETTING TIRED SO I CAN SLEEP; WHAT THE WELL-DRESSED MAN IN HARLEM WILL WEAR; GIVE A CHEER FOR THE NAVY; I LEFT MY HEART AT THE STAGE DOOR CANTEEN; AMERICAN EAGLES; OH, HOW I HATE TO GET UP IN THE MORNING; POOR LITTLE ME I'M ON K.P. and GOD BLESS AMERICA.

THOUSANDS CHEER

An M-G-M picture filmed with an all-star cast that included Mickey Rooney, Judy Garland, Red Skelton, Eleanor Powell, Ann Sothern, Lucille Ball, Virginia O'-Brien, Frank Morgan, Kathryn Grayson, Gene Kelly, Mary Astor, John Boles, Ben Blue, Lena Horne and the orchestras of Kay Kyser, Ben Carter and Bob Crosby, and directed by George Sidney. Musical numbers:

THE JOINT IS REALLY JUMPING by Ralph Blane and Hugh Martin; I DUG A DITCH IN WICHITA by Ralph Freed and Burton Lane; THREE LETTERS IN THE MAILBOX by Paul Francis Webster and Walter Jurmann; LET THERE BE MUSIC by E. Y. Harburg and Earl Brent; DAYBREAK by Harold Adamson and Ferde Grofe; HONEYSUCKLE ROSE by Andy Razaf and Fats Waller; UNITED NATIONS ON THE MARCH by E. Y.

Harburg, Harold Rome and Herbert Stot-
hart; CARNEGIE HALL by Ralph Blane,
Hugh Martin and Roger Edens; JUST AS
LONG AS I KNOW KATIE'S WAITIN'
by George R. Brown and Lew Brown; I'M
LOST YOU'RE LOST and WHY DON'T
WE TRY? by Walter Ruick.

THUMBS UP

A Republic picture filmed with a cast
headed by Branda Joyce, Richard Frazer,
Elsa Lancaster, Arthur Margetson, Pat O'-
Malley, Gertrude Niesen, Charles Irwin and
the Hot Spots, and directed by Joseph
Santley. Songs:
FROM HERE ON; LOVE IS A
CORNY THING and WHO ARE THE
BRITISH? by Sammy Cahn and Jule
Styne; ZING WENT THE STRINGS OF
MY HEART by James Hanley.

TRUE TO LIFE

A Paramount picture starring Mary Martin and Franchot Tone in a cast that included Dick Powell, Victor Moore, William
Demarest and Ernest Truex, and directed
by George Marshall. Songs by Johnny Mercer and Hoagy Carmichael:

THERE SHE WAS; OLD MUSIC
MASTER; MISTER POLLYANNA and
SUDSY SUDS THEME SONG.

WHAT'S BUZZIN' COUSIN?

A Columbia picture filmed with a cast
headed by Ann Miller, Eddie "Rochester"
Anderson, John Hubbard, Freddy Martin
and Leslie Brooks, and directed by Charles
Barton. Songs:
EIGHTEEN SEVENTY-FIVE by Wally
Anderson; AIN'T THAT JUST LIKE A
MAN and SHORT, FAT AND 4F by Don
Raye and Gene DePaul; NEVADA by Mort
Greene and Walter Donaldson; KNOCKED
OUT NOCTURNE by Jacques Press.

WINTERTIME

A 20th Century-Fox picture starring Son-
ja Henie in a cast that included Jack Oakie,
Cesar Romero, Carole Landis, S. Z. Sakall,
Cornel Wilde and Woody Herman and his
orchestra, and directed by John Braham.
Songs by Leo Robin and Nacio Herb
Brown:
I'M ALL A-TWITTER OVER YOU;
I LIKE IT HERE; DANCING IN THE
DAWN; WE ALWAYS GET OUR GIRL;
LATER TONIGHT and WINTERTIME.

Feature Films With Songs

ALL BY MYSELF

A Universal picture filmed with a cast
headed by Patric Knowles, Evelyn Ankers
and Rosemary Lane, and directed by Felix
Feist. Songs:
YOU'RE PRICELESS by Morey Amsterdam and T. Ramona; ALL BY MYSELF
by Inez James and Buddy Pepper.

BOMBADIER

An RKO picture starring Pat O'Brien
and Randolph Scott in a cast that included
Anne Shirley, and directed by Richard
Williace. Song by Jack Scholl and M. K.
Jerome:
SONG OF THE BOMBADIERS

CINDERELLA SWINGS IT

An RKO picture filmed with a cast
headed by Guy Kibbe, Gloria Warren,
Helen Parrish, Dick Hogan and Lee 'Lasses
White, and directed by Christy Cabanne.
Songs:
I HEARD YOU CRIED LAST NIGHT
by Jerry Krueger and Ted Grouya; THE
FLAG'S STILL THERE, MR. KEY by
George Jessel and Ben Oakland.

CLAUDIA

A 20th Century-Fox picture starring

Dorothy McGuire and Robert Young, and
directed by Edmund Goulding. Song by Alfred Newman and Charles Henderson:
FROM YESTERDAY TO TOMOR-
ROW

CONSTANT NYMPH, THE

A Warner Brothers' picture starring
Charles Boyer and Joan Fontaine, and di-
rected by Edmund Goulding. Song by Mar-
garet Kennedy and Erich W. Korngold:
TOMORROW (WHEN YOU ARE
GONE).

EIGHT GIRLS IN A BOAT

A Paramount picture filmed with a cast
headed by Dorothy Wilson, Douglas Mont-
gomery and Kay Johnson, and directed by
William Wallace. Songs:
THIS LITTLE PIGGIE WENT TO
MARKET by Harold Lewis and Sam Cos-
low; A DAY WITHOUT YOU by Arthur
Rebner and Sam Coslow.

FOR WHOM THE BELL TOLLS

A Paramount picture starring Gary Cooper and Ingrid Bergman, and directed by
Sam Wood. Songs:
A LOVE LIKE THIS by Ned Washington and Victor Young; FOR WHOM THE

BELL TOLLS by Milton Drake and Walter Kent.

GET GOING
A Universal picture filmed with a cast headed by Grace McDonald, Robert Paige, Vera Vague, Walter Catlett and Maureen Cannon, and directed by Jean Yarbrough. Song by Everett Carter and Milton Rosen:
HOLD THAT LINE

GOOD MORNIN' JUDGE
A Universal picture starring Dennis O'Keefe and Louise Allbritton, and directed by Jean Yarbrough. Songs by Everett Carter and Milton Rosen:
SPELLBOUND and SORT OF A KINDA.

GUY NAMED JOE, A
An M-G-M picture starring Spencer Tracy, Irene Dunne and Van Johnson, and directed by Victor Fleming. Song by Roy Turk and Fred Ahlert:
I'LL GET BY (AS LONG AS I HAVE YOU).

HANGMEN ALSO DIE
A United Artists' picture starring Brian Donlevy, Walter Brennan and Anna Lee, and directed by Fritz Lang. Song by Sam Coslow and Hans Eisler:
NO SURRENDER

HENRY ALDRICH SWINGS IT
A Paramount picture filmed with a cast headed by Jimmy Lydon, Charles Smith, Mimi Chandler, Vaughn Glaser and John Litel, and directed by Hugh Bennett. Song by Kim Gannon and Jule Styne:
DING-DONG—SING A SONG

HERS TO HOLD
A Universal picture starring Deanna Durbin in a cast that included Joseph Cotten and Charles Winninger, and directed by Frank Ryan. Song by Herb Magidson and Jimmy McHugh:
SAY A PRAYER FOR THE BOYS OVER THERE

HIS BUTLER'S SISTER
A Universal picture starring Deanna Durbin, Franchot Tone and Pat O'Brien, and directed by Frank Borzage. Song by Bernie Grossman and Walter Jurmann:
IN THE SPIRIT OF THE MOMENT

HOOSIER HOLIDAY
A Republic picture starring Dale Evans and George Byron, and directed by Frank McDonald. Song by Johnny Marvin:
WHO'S YOUR LITTLE HOOSIER

ISLE OF FORGOTTEN SINS
A Producers Releasing Corporation picture starring John Carradine and Gale Sondergaard, and directed by Edgar G. Ulmer. Songs by June Sillman and Leo Erdody:
SLEEPY ISLAND MOON and IN PANGO (With Ann Levitt).

IT AIN'T HAY
A Universal picture starring Abbott and Costello in a cast that included Patsy O'Connor, Grace McDonald, Eugene Pallette and Eddie Quillan, and directed by Erle C. Kenton. Song by Paul Francis Webster and Harry Revel:
GLORY BE!

LADY TAKES A CHANCE, A
An RKO picture starring Jean Arthur and John Wayne in a cast that included Phil Silvers and Charles Winninger, and directed by William Seiter. Songs:
SWINGING AT THE COTTON CLUB by Bob Bell; JUMPEROO by Bob Bell, Roy Bracker and Walter Williams.

LADY OF BURLESQUE
A United Artists' picture starring Barbara Stanwyck in a cast that included Michael O'Shea, J. Edward Bromberg and Pinky Lee, and directed by William A. Wellman. Songs by Sammy Cahn and Harry Akst:
SO THIS IS YOU and TAKE IT OFF THE E STRING (PUT IT ON THE G STRING).

MAN OF COURAGE
A Producers Releasing Corporation picture starring Barton MacLane and Charlotte Winters, and directed by Alexis Thurn-Taxis. Song by Lew Pollack:
NOW AND THEN

MORE THE MERRIER, THE
A Columbia picture starring Jean Arthur, Joel McCrea and Charles Coburn, and directed by George Stevens. Song by Henry Meyers, Ed Eliscu and Jay Gorney:
DAMN THE TORPEDOS (FULL SPEED AHEAD)

NEVER A DULL MOMENT
A Universal picture starring the Ritz Brothers in a cast that included Frances Langford and Mary Beth Hughes, and directed by Edward Lilley. Songs:
HELLO and YAKIMBOOMBA by Eddie Cherkose and David Rose; MY BLUE HEAVEN by George Whiting and Walter Donaldson.

NORTH STAR, THE

An RKO picture filmed with a cast headed by Anne Baxter, Dana Andrews, Walter Huston, Ann Harding, Jane Withers, Farley Granger and Erich Van Stroheim, and directed by Lewis Milestone. Songs by Ira Gershwin and Aaron Copeland:

NO VILLAGE LIKE MINE and SONG OF THE GUERRILLAS.

OLD ACQUAINTANCE

A Warner Brothers' picture starring Bette Davis and Miriam Hopkins, and directed by Vincent Sherman. Song by Kim Gannon and Franz Waxman:

OLD ACQUAINTANCE

PHANTOM OF THE OPERA, THE

A Universal picture filmed with a cast headed by Nelson Eddy, Susanna Foster and Claude Rains, and directed by Arthur Lubin. Song by George Waggner and Edward Ward:

LULLABY OF THE BELLS

PRINCESS O'ROURKE

A Warner Brothers-First National picture filmed with a cast headed by Olivia De Haviland and Robert Cummings, and directed by Norman Krasna. Song by Ira Gershwin, E. Y. Harburg and Arthur Schwartz:

HONORABLE MOON

SARONG GIRL

A Monogram picture starring Ann Corio in a cast that included Tim Ryan and Irene Murphy, and directed by Arthur Dreifuss. Songs:

SARONGA (AMI MAI) by Louis Herscher and Andy Iona Long; WOOGIE HULA by Marvin Hatley and Louis Herscher.

SHANTYTOWN

A Republic picture starring Mary Lee and John Archer, and directed by Joseph Santley. Song by Kim Gannon and Jule Styne:

ON THE CORNER OF SUNSHINE AND MAIN

SHE HAS WHAT IT TAKES

A Columbia picture starring Jinx Falkenburg and Tom Neal, and directed by Charles Barton. Songs:

MOON ON MY PILLOW by Henry, Harry and Elliot Tobias; TIMBER, TIMBER, TIMBER by Don Reid and Henry Tobias; HONK! HONK! by Gene DePaul and Roy Gordon.

SO PROUDLY WE HAIL

A Paramount picture starring Claudette Colbert, Paulette Goddard and Veronica Lake, and directed by Mark Sandrich. Song by Edward Heyman and Miklos Rozsa:

LOVED ONE

SOMEONE TO REMEMBER

A Republic picture filmed with a cast headed by John Craven, Mabel Paige and Dorothy Morris, and directed by Robert Siodmak. Song by Dorcas Cochran and Walter Scharf:

SUSIE

SONG OF RUSSIA

An M-G-M picture starring Robert Taylor and Susan Peters, and directed by Gregory Ratoff. Song by E. Y. Harburg and Jerome Kern:

AND RUSSIA IS HER NAME

SWING OUT THE BLUES

A Columbia picture filmed with a cast headed by Bob Haymes and Lynn Merrick, and directed by Mal St. Clair. Songs:

THE GREAT AMERICAN HOME by Al Lewis, Al Sherman and Allie Wrubel; OUR CAREER by Walter G. Samuels.

TOP MAN

A Universal picture starring Donald O'Connor and Susanna Foster in a cast that included Lillian Gish, Richard Dix, Count Basie's orchestra and the Harmonica Rascals, and directed by Charles Lamont. Song by Ted Koehler, Harry Barris and Billy Moll:

WRAP YOUR TROUBLES IN DREAMS (AND DREAM YOUR TROUBLES AWAY).

TORNADO

A Paramount picture starring Chester Morris and Nancy Kelly, and directed by William Berke. Songs:

THERE GOES MY DREAM by Frank Loesser and Frederick Hollander; I'M AFRAID OF YOU by Ralph Freed and Frederick Hollander.

YOU'RE A LUCKY FELLOW MR. SMITH

A Universal picture starring Allan Jones and Evelyn Ankers, and directed by Felix Feist. Song by Harry Tobias and Al Sherman:

ON THE CREST OF A RAINBOW

WESTERN FILMS WITH SONGS

ACROSS THE PLAINS

A Republic picture filmed with a cast headed by Bob Steele, Tim Tyler, Jimmy Dodd and Lorraine Miller, and directed by

Howard Bretherton. Song by Jimmy Dodd:
JAILHOUSE BLUES

AVENGING RIDER, THE
An RKO picture starring Tim Holt in a cast that included Cliff Edwards and Ann Summers, and directed by Sam Nelson. Song by Cliff Edwards:
MINNIE MY MOUNTAIN MOOCHER

BLACK MARKET RUSTLERS
A Monogram picture filmed with a cast headed by Ray Corrigan, Dennis Moore, Max Terhune and Evelyn Finley, and directed by S. Roy Luby. Songs:
YOU WINK AT ME AND I'LL WINK AT YOU by Jim Austin; WAITING FOR THE WAGON (Traditional).

COLT COMRADES
A United Artists' picture starring Bill Boyd in a cast that included Andy Clyde, Gayle Lord and Victor Jory, and directed by Leslie Selander. Song by Leo Robin and Ralph Rainger:
TONIGHT WE RIDE

COWBOY COMMANDOS
A Monogram picture filmed with a cast headed by Ray Corrigan, Dennis Moore, Max Terhune and Evelyn Finley, and directed by S. Roy Luby. Song by Johnny Lange:
I'LL GET THE FEUHRER SURE AS SHOOTIN'

COWBOY IN THE CLOUDS
A Columbia picture starring Charles Starrett and Julie Duncan, and directed by Benjamin Kline. Song by James Cavanaugh, John Redmond and Frank Weldon:
COWBOY IN THE CLOUDS

HANDS ACROSS THE BORDER
A Republic picture starring Roy Rogers in a cast that included Ruth Terry, Guinn Williams, Bob Nolan and the Sons of the Pioneers, and directed by Joseph Kane. Songs:
DREAMING TO MUSIC; THE GIRL WITH THE HIGH-BUTTON SHOES; WHEN YOUR HEART'S ON EASY STREET; HEY, HEY and HANDS ACROSS THE BORDER by Ned Washington and Phil Ohman; COOL WATER by Bob Nolan.

IDAHO
A Republic picture starring Roy Rogers in a cast that included Smiley Burnette, Virginia Grey, Ona Munson, Bob Nolan, the Sons of the Pioneers and the Robert Mitchell Boys Choir, and directed by Joseph Kane. Songs:

DON JUAN by Tim Spencer; IDAHO by Jesse Stone; I HOPE I'M NOT DREAMING AGAIN by Roy Rogers and Fred Rose; LONE BUCKAROO and STOP! by Bob Nolan.

IN OLD OKLAHOMA
A Republic picture filmed with a cast that included John Wayne, Martha Scott, Gabby Hayes and Dale Evans, and directed by Albert S. Rogell. Song by Sol Meyer and Walter Scharf:
THEN I'D BE SATISFIED, ALL RIGHT

KING OF THE COWBOYS
A Republic picture starring Roy Rogers in a cast that included Smiley Burnette, Peggy Moran, Bob Nolan and the Sons of the Pioneers, and directed by Joseph Kane. Songs:
RIDE 'EM COWBOY by Tim Spencer; I'M AN OLD COWHAND by Johnny Mercer; A GAY RANCHERO by Abe Tuvin, Francia Lubin and J. J. Espinoza; ROLL ALONG PRAIRIE MOON by Cecil Mack, Ted Fiorito and Albert Von Tilzer; RIDE RANGER RIDE by Vern Spencer; THEY CUT DOWN THE OLD PINE TREE by William Raskin, Edward Eliscu and George Brown; RED RIVER VALLEY (Traditional).

LONE STAR TRAIL
A Universal picture starring Johnny Mack Brown in a cast that included Tex Ritter, Fuzzy Knight and Jennifer Holt, and directed by Ray Taylor. Songs:
ADIOS VAQUEROS and TRAIL DREAMIN' by Oliver Drake and Jimmy Wakely; WELCOME HOME by Everett Carter and Milton Rosen; I GOTTA SEE TEXAS JUST ONCE MORE by Jimmy Wakely.

MAN FROM MUSIC MOUNTAIN, THE
A Republic picture starring Roy Rogers in a cast that included Ruth Terry, Ann Gillis, Bob Nolan and the Sons of the Pioneers, and directed by Joseph Kane. Songs:
KING OF THE COWBOYS; AFTER THE RAIN and WINE, WOMEN AND SONG by Tim Spencer; I'M THINKING TONIGHT OF MY BLUE EYES by A. P. Carter; I'M BEGINNING TO CARE by Gene Autry, Johnny Marvin and Fred Rose; SMILES ARE MADE OF SUNSHINE by Ray Gilbert.

RAIDERS OF SUNSET PASS
A Republic picture filmed with a cast headed by Eddie Drew, Smiley Burnette

and Jennifer Holt, and directed by John English. Song by Smiley Burnette:
WHO'D A THUNK IT?

SILVER SPURS

A Republic picture starring Roy Rogers in a cast that included Smiley Burnette, John Carradine and Phyllis Brooks, and directed by Joseph Kane. Songs: HIGHWAYS ARE HAPPY WAYS by Larry Shay, Tommie Malie and Harry Harris; BACK IN YOUR OWN BACK YARD by Al Jolson, Billy Rose and Dave Dreyer; HORSES AND WOMEN by Smiley Burnette; JUBILATION JAMBOREE by Tim Spencer; WHEN IT'S SPRINGTIME IN THE ROCKIES by Mary Hale Woolsey, Robert Sauer and Milt Taggart; TUMBLIN' TUMBLEWEEDS by Bob Nolan.

SONG OF TEXAS

A Republic picture starring Roy Rogers in a cast that included Sheila Ryan, Barton MacLane, Bob Nolan and the Sons of the Pioneers, and directed by Joseph Kane. Songs: MEXICALI ROSE by Jack Tenney and Helen Stone; ON THE RHYTHM RANGE by Bob Nolan; MOONLIGHT AND ROSES by Edwin H. Lemare, Ben Black and Neil Moret; RAINBOW OVER THE RANGE by Tim Spencer.

TENTING ON THE OLD CAMP GROUND

A Universal picture starring Johnny Mack Brown in a cast that included Tex Ritter, Fuzzy Knight and Jennifer Holt, and directed by Lewis D. Collins. Song by Harold Adamson and Jimmy McHugh:
RIDIN' HOME

THUNDERING TRAILS

A Republic picture filmed with a cast headed by Bob Steele, Tom Tyler, Jimmy Dodd and Nell O'Day, and directed by John English. Song by Jimmy Dodd:
MINSTREL MEDICINE MAN

Jeanne Crain and Dick Haymes in a scene from *State Fair*.

1 9 4 4
"Going My Way" Is Bombarded With Oscars

In the year when Berlin was bombed into rubble, Hollywood staged a blitz of its own. The target was *Going My Way,* and when the all-clear sounded, seven Oscars had been pin-pointed on this film alone, the highly coveted statuettes being awarded to Paramount as the producer of the year's best picture, to Bing Crosby as the best actor, to Barry Fitzgerald as the best supporting actor, to Leo McCarey for the most original story and the best direction, to Frank Butler and Frank Cavett for the best screenplay, and to Johnny Burke and Jimmy Van Heusen for the best film song of 1944—*Swinging On A Star.* In addition, *Going My Way* topped the Ten Best Pictures of the year in a nation-wide poll and grossed $6,500,000 at the box-office.

Going My Way, however, was but one of three 1944 musicals that earned a place in the Golden Circle reserved for productions that show a return of $4,000,000 or better, and shared this honor with *Hollywood Canteen,* the all-star Warner Brothers' revue in which Cole Porter's *Don't Fence Me In* was introduced, and *Meet Me In St. Louis,* starring Judy Garland and yielding two song hits, *The Boy Next Door* and *The Trolley Song,* written by Hugh Martin and Ralph Blane, two comparatively new songwriters in the Hollywood colony.

Neither were Bing Crosby's triumphs confined to *Going My Way,* since the Groaner from Seattle had another sensational box-office draw in *Here Come The Waves,* distinguished by two songs by Johnny Mercer and Harold Arlen: *Let's Take The Long Way Home* and *Ac-cent-chu-ate The Positive,* while Bing's favorite songwriters, Johnny Burke and Jimmy Van Heusen, who took the 1944 Oscar with *Swinging On A Star,* came through with two other hits: *It Could Happen To You* from *And The Angels Sing* and *A Sleigh Ride In July* from *Belle Of The Yukon,* a film that introduced Gypsy Rose Lee to stardom in a field far removed from the strip-tease circuit.

Jerome Kern was represented on the year's honor roll with *Can't Help Singing,* starring Deanna Durbin, and *Cover Girl* in which *Long Ago And Far Away* was the outstanding song, while the younger generation of songwriters could point with pride to Sammy Cahn and Jule Styne who had five Hit Parade favorites in *There Goes That Song Again* and *Poor Little Rhode Island* from *Carolina Blues; I'll Walk Alone* from the Universal all-star revue *Follow The Boys;* and *Come Out, Come Out Wherever You Are* and *And Then You Kissed Me,* sung by Frank Sinatra in *Step Lively.* And while Hollywood was partial to original material, the Broadway stage was represented on the screen by *Knickerbocker Holiday* and *Lady In The Dark,* both with music by Kurt Weill, the Viennese composer who having incurred the wrath of Hitler by writing *Ballad On The Death Of A Caesar*—a most prophetic title—had to flee from Germany before the outbreak of World War II to escape the Gestapo.

From the non-musical pictures of 1944 came three songs that had top priority rating with soldiers and sailors at the juke box—*I'll Be Seeing You* by Irving Kahal and Sammy Fain; *Time Waits For No One* by Cliff Friend and Charles Tobias; and *In My Arms* by Frank Loesser and Ted Grouya and introduced in *See Here Private Hargrove*. And GI Joe's collection of pin-up girls was augmented by pictures of Esther Williams, a swimmer from the Los Angeles Aquacade who first achieved a star's billing on the screen in *Bathing Beauty*. In fact a new day had dawned in Hollywood—for new stars and new songwriters.

Musicals

ALLERGIC TO LOVE
A Universal picture filmed with a cast headed by Noah Beery Jr., Martha O'Driscoll, David Bruce, Franklin Pangborn and Maxie Rosenbloom, and directed by Edward Lilley. Musical numbers:
CARMENCITA by Jack Brooks and Everett Carter; TEPERDI by Jesus Costillon and Mario Santos; FARRUCA by M. G. Matos; MUSIC MAESTRO by Roberto and Marques Roberti and RHUMBA MA-TUMBA by Bobby Collaza.

AND THE ANGELS SING
A Paramount picture starring Dorothy Lamour, Betty Hutton, Diana Lynn and Fred MacMurray, and directed by Claude Binyon. Songs by Johnny Burke and Jimmy VanHeusen.
IT COULD HAPPEN TO YOU; AND HIS ROCKING HORSE RAN AWAY; FOR THE FIRST ONE HUNDRED YEARS; HOW DOES YOUR GARDEN GROW?; KNOCKING ON YOUR OWN FRONT DOOR; BLUEBIRDS IN MY BELFRY; MY HEART'S WRAPPED UP IN GINGHAM and WHEN STANISLAUS GOT MARRIED.

BABES ON SWING STREET
A Universal picture filmed with a cast headed by Ann Blyth, Peggy Ryan, Andy Devine, Leon Errol and Freddy Slack's orchestra, and directed by Edward Lilley. Songs:
JUST BEING WITH YOU; HOTCHA SONYA; I'VE GOT A WAY WITH THE BOYS; WRONG THING AT THE RIGHT TIME; MUSICAL CHAIRS and THE MUSIC AND YOU by Inez James and Sidney Miller; TAKE IT EASY by Mann Curtis and Vic Mizzy; YOUTH IS ON THE MARCH by Everett Carter and Milton Rosen.

BATHING BEAUTY
An M-G-M picture starring Red Skelton and Esther Williams in a cast that included Basil Rathbone, Bill Goodwin, Ethel Smith, Helen Forrest and Xavier Cugat and his orchestra, and directed by George Sidney. Songs by Johnny Green:
FACULTY ROW; SEXY WINDOWS; THAT BOY FLEMING; I'VE GOT A PROBLEM and I'LL TAKE THE HIGH NOTE (lyrics by Harold Adamson).

BEAUTIFUL BUT BROKE
A Columbia picture filmed with a cast headed by Joan Davis, John Hubbard, Jane Frazee and Bob Haymes, and directed by Charles Barton. Songs:
MR. JIVE HAS GONE TO WAR by L. Wolfe Gilbert and Ben Oakland; TAKE THE DOOR TO THE LEFT by James Cavanaugh and Walter G. Samuels; JUST ANOTHER BLUES by Jimmy Paul, Dick Charles and Larry Markes; KEEPING IT PRIVATE by Mort Greene and Walter Donaldson.

BELLE OF THE YUKON
An RKO picture starring Randolph Scott and Gypsy Rose Lee in a cast that included Dinah Shore, Bob Burns and Charles Winninger, and directed by William A. Seiter. Songs by Johnny Burke and Jimmy Van Heusen:
EVERY GIRL IS DIFFERENT; LIKE SOMEONE IN LOVE; SLEIGH RIDE IN JULY and BELLE OF THE YUKON.

BOWERY TO BROADWAY

A Universal picture filmed with a cast headed by Jack Oakie, Donald Cook, Susanna Foster, Terhan Bey and Maria Montez, and directed by Charles Lamont. Songs: THE LOVE WALTZ and THERE'LL ALWAYS BE A MOON by Everett Carter and Edward Ward; MY SONG OF ROMANCE by Don George and Dave Franklin; MONTEVIDEO and CONEY ISLAND WALTZ by Kim Gannon and Walter Kent.

BROADWAY RHYTHM

An M-G-M picture filmed with a cast headed by George Murphy, Ginny Simms, Charles Winninger, Gloria DeHaven, Nancy Walker, Ben Blue, Lena Horne and Eddie "Rochester" Anderson, and directed by Roy Del Ruth. Songs: MILKMAN KEEP THOSE BOTTLES QUIET; WHO'S WHO?; SOLID POTATO SALAD; IRRESISTABLE YOU and I LOVE CORNY MUSIC by Don Raye and Gene DePaul; PRETTY BABY by Gus Kahn, Tony Jackson and Egbert VanAlstyne; BRAZILIAN BOOGIE by Hugh Martin and Ralph Blane; AMOR by Sunny Skylar and Gabriel Ruiz.

CAN'T HELP SINGING

A Universal picture starring Deanna Durbin in a cast that included Robert Paige, Akim Tamiroff and David Bruce, and directed by Frank Ryan. Songs by E. Y. Harburg and Jerome Kern: ELBOW ROOM; MORE AND MORE; ANY MOMENT NOW; CALIFORN-I-AY; SWING YOUR SWEETHEART 'ROUND THE FIRE and FINALE ULTIMO.

CAROLINA BLUES

A Columbia picture filmed with a cast headed by Kay Kyser and his orchestra, Ann Miller and Victor Moore, and directed by Leigh Jason. Songs by Sammy Cahn and Jule Styne: THERE GOES THAT SONG AGAIN; YOU MAKE ME DREAM TOO MUCH; POOR LITTLE RHODE ISLAND and THANKS A LOT, MR. BEEBE (with Dudley Brooks).

CASANOVA IN BURLESQUE

A Republic picture starring Joe E. Brown and June Havoc, and directed by Leslie Goodwins. Songs by Kim Gannon and Walter Kent: CASANOVA JOE; FIVE A DAY FATIMA; MESS ME UP; TAMING OF THE SHREW and WILLIE THE SHAKE.

CHIP OFF THE OLD BLOCK

A Universal picture starring Donald O'-Connor and Peggy Ann Blyth in a cast that included Helen Vinson, Helen Broderick, Arthur Treacher and Patric Knowles, and directed by Charles Lamont. Songs: I GOTTA GIVE MY FEET A BREAK by Inez James and Sidney Miller; IS IT GOOD OR IS IT BAD? by Charles Tobias; MY SONG by Lew Brown and Ray Henderson; SAILOR SONG by Eugene Conrad; LOVE IS LIKE MUSIC by Milton Schwartzwald; SPERLING PREP and IT'S MIGHTY NICE TO HAVE MET YOU by Bill Grage and Grace Shannon.

COVER GIRL

A Columbia picture starring Rita Hayworth and Gene Kelly in a cast that included Phil Silvers, Lee Bowman, Jinx Falkenburg, Otto Kruger and Eve Arden, and directed by Charles Vidor. Songs by Ira Gershwin and Jerome Kern: THE SHOW MUST GO ON; WHO'S COMPLAINING?; PUT ME TO THE TEST; MAKE WAY FOR TOMORROW (with E. Y. Harburg); COVER GIRL; SURE THING and LONG AGO AND FAR AWAY.

DIXIE JAMBOREE

A Producers Releasing Corporation picture starring Frances Langford in a cast that included Guy Kibbe, Eddie Quillan, Charles Butterworth and Fifi D'Orsay, and directed by Christy Cabanne. Songs by Sam Neuman and Michael Breen: NO, NO, NO; YOU AIN'T RIGHT WITH THE LORD; IF IT'S A DREAM; BIG STUFF and DIXIE SHOWBOAT.

EVER SINCE EVE

A Columbia picture filmed with a cast headed by Ina Ray Hutton, Hugh Herbert, Ann Savage, Billy Gilbert and Glenda Farrell, and directed by Arthur Dreifuss. Songs: GLAMOUR FOR SALE and ROSEBUD I LOVE YOU by Lester Lee and Harry Harris; DO I NEED YOU? by Sammy Cahn and Saul Chaplin; WEDDING OF THE BOOGIE AND THE SAMBA by Ben Raleigh and Bernie Wayne.

FOLLOW THE BOYS

A Universal all-star revue filmed with a cast headed by George Raft, Vera Zorina, Maxie Rosenbloom, Jeanette MacDonald, Orson Wells, Marlene Dietrich, Dinah Shore, W. C. Fields, Sophie Tucker, Lon Chaney and the Delta Rhythm Boys, and directed by Edward Sutherland. Songs:

I'LL WALK ALONE and A BETTER DAY IS COMING by Sammy Cahn and Jule Styne; TONIGHT by Kermit Goell and Walter Donaldson; IS YOU IS OR IS YOU AIN'T MY BABY? by Billy Austin and Louis Jordan; I FEEL A SONG COMING ON by Dorothy Fields and Jimmy McHugh; SOME OF THESE DAYS by Shelton Brooks; KITTEN WITH MY MITTENS LACED by Inez James and Buddy Pepper; SHOO SHOO BABY by Phil Moore; BEYOND THE BLUE HORIZON by Leo Robin, W. Franke Harling and Richard Whiting; I'LL GET BY by Roy Turk and Fred Ahlert; MAD ABOUT HIM SAD WITHOUT HIM HOW CAN I BE GLAD WITHOUT HIM BLUES by Dick Charles and Larry Markes.

FOUR JILLS AND A JEEP

A 20th Century-Fox picture filmed with a cast headed by Kay Francis, Carole Landis, Martha Raye, Mitzi Mayfair, Alice Faye, Betty Grable, Dick Haymes and Jimmy Dorsey and his orchestra, and directed by William A. Seiter. Songs by Harold Adamson and Jimmy McHugh:

CRAZY ME; YOU SEND ME; HOW BLUE THE NIGHT; HOW MANY TIMES DO I HAVE TO TELL YOU?; OHIO; IT'S THE OLD ARMY GAME; YOU NEVER MISS A TRICK and HEIL HEEL HITLER.

GHOST CATCHERS

A Universal picture starring Olsen and Johnson in a cast that included Gloria Jean, Leo Carrillo and Morton Downey, and directed by Edward L. Cline. Songs:

BLUE CANDLELIGHT AND RED, RED ROSES and THREE CHEERS FOR THE CUSTOMER by Paul Francis Webster and Harry Revel; QUOTH THE RAVEN by Paul Francis Webster, Harry Revel and Edward Ward; I'M OLD ENOUGH TO DREAM by Everett Carter and Edward Ward; THESE FOOLISH THINGS (REMIND ME OF YOU) by Harry Link, Holt Marvell and Jack Strachey.

GIRL RUSH

An RKO picture filmed with a cast headed by Wally Brown, Alan Carney, Frances Langford, Vera Vague and Robert Mitchum, and directed by Gordon Douglas. Songs by Harry Harris and Lew Pollack:

ANNABELLA'S BUSTLE; RAINBOW VALLEY; IF MOTHER COULD ONLY SEE US NOW and WHEN I'M WALKING ARM-IN-ARM WITH JIM.

GOING MY WAY

A Paramount picture starring Bing Crosby, Risé Stevens and Barry Fitzgerald, and directed by Leo McCarey. Songs:

SWINGING ON A STAR; DAY AFTER FOREVER and GOING MY WAY by Johnny Burke and Jimmy VanHeusen; TOO-RA-LO-TOO-ROO-LA by J. R. Shannon.

GREENWICH VILLAGE

A 20th Century-Fox picture starring Carmen Miranda and Don Ameche in a cast that included William Bendix and Vivian Blaine, and directed by Walter Lang. Songs by Leo Robin and Nacio Herb Brown:

GIVE ME A BAND AND A BANDANA; IT'S ALL FOR ART'S SAKE; IT GOES TO YOUR TOES; THIS IS OUR LUCKY DAY; I'M DOWN TO MY LAST DREAM; OH, BROTHER!; YOU MAKE ME SO MAD; I HAVE TO SEE YOU PRIVATELY; I'VE BEEN SMILING IN MY SLEEP; NEVER BEFORE; TELL ME IT'S YOU; THAT THING THEY TALK ABOUT and COULD IT BE YOU?

HAT CHECK HONEY

A Universal picture filmed with a cast headed by Grace McDonald, Leon Errol, Walter Catlett and the orchestras of Freddy Slack, Harry Owens and Ted Weems, and directed by Edward F. Cline. Songs:

SLIGHTLY SENTIMENTAL; NICE TO KNOW YOU and ROCKIN' WITH YOU by Everett Carter and Milton Rosen.

HERE COME THE WAVES

A Paramount picture starring Bing Crosby and Betty Hutton in a cast that included Sonny Tufts, and directed by Mark Sandrich. Songs by Johnny Mercer and Harold Arlen:

I PROMISE YOU; THERE'S A FELLOW WAITING IN POUGHKEEPSIE; MY MAMA THINKS I'M A STAR; LET'S TAKE THE LONG WAY HOME; HERE COME THE WAVES and ACCENT-CHU-ATE THE POSITIVE

HEY, ROOKIE

A Columbia picture filmed with a cast headed by Joe Besser, Ann Miller, Larry Parks and Hal McIntyre's orchestra, and directed by Charles Barton. Songs:

SO WHAT SERENADE by James Cavanaugh, John Redmond and Nat Simon;

THERE GOES TAPS; TAKE A CHANCE; IT'S GREAT TO BE IN A UNIFORM; IT'S A HELLUVA SWELLUVA HELL-UVA LIFE IN THE ARMY and WHEN THE YARDBIRDS COME TO TOWN by J. C. Lewis Jr.; HEY, ROOKIE; STREAM-LINED SHEIK and YOU'RE GOOD FOR MY MORALE by Ed Eliscu, Henry Meyers and Jay Gorney.

HI, GOOD LOOKIN'
A Universal picture filmed with a cast headed by Harriet Hilliard, Kirby Grant, Roscoe Karns, the Delta Rhythm Boys and the orchestras of Jack Teagarden and Ozzie Nelson, and directed by Edward Lilley. Songs:
YOU'RE JUST THE SWEETEST THING by Buzz Adlam and Walter Bishop; A SLIGHT CASE OF LOVE by Buzz Adlam; I WON'T FORGET THE DAWN by Don Raye and Gene DePaul; BY MIS-TAKE by Inez James and Sidney Miller; PAPER DOLL by Johnny Black; DEACON JONES by Johnny Lange, Hy Heath and Richard Loring; AUNT HAGAR'S BLUES by W. C. Handy; JUST A STOWAWAY (ON A SHIP OF DREAMS) by Vic Knight.

HOLLYWOOD CANTEEN
A Warner Brothers' picture filmed with an all-star cast headed by Jack Benny, Eddie Cantor, Joan Crawford, Bette Davis, Roy Rogers, Barbara Stanwyck, Jane Wyman, the Andrews Sisters and the orchestras of Jimmy Dorsey and Carmen Cavallaro, and directed by Delmer Daves. Musical numbers:
DON'T FENCE ME IN by Cole Porter; YOU CAN ALWAYS TELL A YANK by E. Y. Harburg and Burton Lane; WHAT ARE YOU DOING THE REST OF YOUR LIFE? by Ted Koehler and Burton Lane; I'M GETTING CORNS FOR MY COUNTRY by Jean Barry and Dick Charles; WE'RE HAVING A BABY (MY BABY AND ME) by Harold Adamson and Vernon Duke; SWEET DREAMS SWEET-HEART by Ted Koehler and M. K. Jer-ome; VOODOO MOON by Marian Sun-shine, Julio Blanco and Obdulio Morales; THE GENERAL JUMPED AT DAWN by Larry Neal and Jimmy Mundy; TUMBLIN' TUMBLEWEEDS by Bob Nolan; BALLET IN JIVE by Ray Heindorf; HOLLYWOOD CANTEEN by Ted Koehler, Ray Heindorf and M. K. Jerome.

IN SOCIETY
A Universal picture starring Abbott and Costello in a cast that included Marion Hutton, and directed by Jean Yarbrough. Songs:
NO 'BOUT ABOUT IT and MY DREAMS ARE GETTING BETTER ALL THE TIME by Mann Curtis and Vic Mizzy; WHAT A CHANGE IN THE WEATHER by Kim Gannon and Walter Kent; REHEARSIN' by Bobby Worth and Stanley Cowan; MEMORY LANE by B. G. DeSylva, Larry Spier and Con Conrad.

JAM SESSION
A Columbia picture filmed with a cast headed by Ann Miller, the Pied Pipers and the bands of Charlie Barnet, Louis Arm-strong, Alvino Rey, Jan Garver, Glen Gray and Teddy Powell, and directed by Charles Barton. Musical numbers:
CHEROKEE by Ray Noble; VICTORY POLKA by Sammy Kahn and Jule Styne; MURDER HE SAYS by Frank Loesser and Jimmy McHugh; BRAZIL by S. K. Russell and Ary Barroso; NO NAME JIVE by Glen Gray; ST. LOUIS BLUES by W. C. Handy; JIVE BOMBER by Spud Murphy; I CAN'T GIVE YOU ANYTHING BUT LOVE by Dorothy Fields and Jimmy Mc-Hugh.

KANSAS CITY KITTY
A Columbia picture filmed with a cast headed by Joan Davis, Jane Frazee and Bob Crosby, and directed by Del Lord. Musical numbers:
KANSAS CITY KITTY by Walter Don-aldson; TICO TICO by Ervin Drake and Zequinta Abrau; PRETTY KITTY BLUE EYES by Mann Curtis and Vic Mizzy; NOTHING BOOGIE FROM NOWHERE by Saul Chaplin.

KNICKERBOCKER HOLIDAY
A United Artists' picture starring Nelson Eddy in a cast that included Charles Co-burn and Constance Dowling, and directed by Harry Joe Brown. Songs:
THERE'S NOWHERE TO GO BUT UP; SEPTEMBER SONG and INDIS-PENSIBLE MAN by Maxwell Anderson and Kurt Weill; HOLIDAY by Theodore Paxton and Nelson Eddy; LET'S MAKE TOMORROW TODAY by Furman Brown and Werner Heymann; JAIL SONG by Furman Brown, Nelson Eddy and Kurt Weill; BE NOT HASTY MAIDEN FAIR by Furman Brown and Theodore Paxson; SING OUT by Furman Brown and Franz Steininger; LOVE HAS MADE THIS SUCH A LOVELY DAY; ONE MORE SMILE and ZUYDER ZEE by Sammy Cahn and Jule Styne.

LADY IN THE DARK

A Paramount picture starring Ginger Rogers and Ray Milland in a cast that included Warner Baxter, and directed by Michell Leisen. Songs:
ONE LIFE TO LIVE; GIRL OF THE MOMENT; IT LOOKS LIKE LIZA; THIS IS NEW; MY SHIP and JENNY by Ira Gershwin and Kurt Weill; SUDDENLY IT'S SPRING by Johnny Burke and Jimmy Van Heusen; ARTIST'S WALTZ by Robert E. Dolan; DREAM LOVER by Clifford Grey and Victor Schertzinger.

LADY LET'S DANCE

A Monogram picture filmed with a cast headed by Belita, James Ellison, Walter Catlett, Lucien Littlefield and the orchestras of Henry Busse, Eddie LaBarron, Mitchell Ayres and Lou Bing, and directed by Frank Woodruff. Songs:
DREAM OF DREAMS; RIO; LADY LET'S DANCE; IN THE DAYS OF BEAU BRUMMEL; HAPPY HEARTS and TEN MILLION MEN AND A GIRL by Dave Oppenheim and Ted Grouya; SILVER SHADOWS AND GOLDEN DREAMS by Charles Newman and Lew Pollack.

LOST IN A HAREM

An M-G-M picture starring Abbott and Costello in a cast that included Marilyn Maxwell and John Conte, and directed by Charles Riesner. Songs:
WHAT DOES IT TAKE? and IT IS WRITTEN by Don Raye and Gene De-Paul; SONS OF THE DESERT by Ralph Freed and Sammy Fain.

LOUISIANA HAYRIDE

A Columbia picture starring Judy Canova in a cast that included Ross Hunter and Richard Lane, and directed by Charles Barton. Songs:
YOU GOTTA GO WHERE THE TRAIN GOES and RAINBOW ROAD by Kim Gannon and Walter Kent; I'M A WOMAN OF THE WORLD by Jerry Seelen and Saul Chaplin; PUT YOUR ARMS AROUND ME HONEY by Junie McCree and Albert Von Tilzer; SHORT'NING BREAD.

MEET ME IN ST. LOUIS

An M-G-M picture starring Judy Garland in a cast that included Margaret O'-Brien, Mary Astor, Lucille Bremer, Tom Drake, Marjorie Main and June Lockhart, and directed by Vincent Minnelli. Songs:
THE TROLLEY SONG; THE BOY NEXT DOOR; SKIP TO MY LOU and HAVE YOURSELF A MERRY CHRISTMAS by Ralph Blane and Hugh Martin; MEET ME IN ST. LOUIS by Andrew B. Sterling and Kerry Mills.

MEET MISS BOBBY SOX

A Columbia picture filmed with a cast headed by Bob Crosby, Lynn Merrick and Louise Erickson, and directed by Glenn Tryon. Songs:
I'M NOT AFRAID by Kim Gannon and Walter Kent; COME WITH ME MY HONEY by Mack David, Joan Whitney and Alex Kramer; FELLOW ON A FURLOUGH by Bobby Worth; TWO HEAVENS by Don George and Ted Grouya; DEACON JONES by Johnny Lange, Hy Heath and Richard Loring.

MEET THE PEOPLE

An M-G-M picture filmed with a cast headed by Lucille Ball, Dick Powell, Virginia O'Brien, Bert Lahr and June Allyson, and directed by Charles Riesner. Songs:
IN TIMES LIKE THESE; SCHICKELGRUBER and MEET THE PEOPLE by Ralph Freed and Sammy Fain; I LIKE TO RECOGNIZE THE TUNE by Lorenz Hart and Richard Rodgers; IT'S SMART TO BE PEOPLE by E. Y. Harburg and Burton Lane; SAY THAT WE'RE SWEETHEARTS AGAIN by Earl Brent.

MERRY MONIHANS, THE

A Universal picture starring Donald O'-Connor and Peggy Ryan in a cast that included Jack Oakie and Ann Blyth, and directed by Charles Lamont. Songs:
LOVELY; BEAUTIFUL TO LOOK AT; WE'RE HAVING A WONDERFUL TIME; IMPERSONATIONS and STOP FOOLIN' by Don George and Irving Bibo; I HATE TO LOSE YOU by Grant Clarke and Archie Gottler; IN MY MERRY OLDSMOBILE by Vincent Bryan and Gus Edwards; I'M ALWAYS CHASING RAINBOWS by Joseph McCarthy and Harry Carroll; ISLE D'AMOUR by Earl Carroll and Leo Edwards; WHEN YOU WORE A TULIP by Jack Mahoney and Percy Wenrich; ROSE ROOM by Harry Williams and Art Hickman; WHAT DO YOU WANT TO MAKE THOSE EYES AT ME FOR? by Howard Johnson, Joseph McCarthy and Jimmy Monaco; ROCK-A-BYE YOUR BABY TO A DIXIE MELODY by Sam Lewis, Joe Young and Jean Schwartz.

MINSTREL MAN

A Producers Releasing Corporation picture starring Benny Fields in a cast that included Gladys George, Alan Dinehart and Roscoe Karns, and directed by Joseph H. Lewis. Songs by Paul Francis Webster and Harry Revel:

CINDY; REMEMBER ME TO CAROLINE; I DON'T CARE IF THE WORLD KNOWS ABOUT IT; SHAKIN' HANDS WITH THE SUN and THE BAMBOO CANE.

MOON OVER LAS VEGAS

A Universal picture filmed with a cast headed by Anne Gwynne, David Bruce and Vera Vague, and directed by Jean Yarbrough. Songs:

A DREAM AGO; FAITHFUL FLO; MOON OVER LAS VEGAS and SO GOODNIGHT by Everett Carter and Milton Rosen; A TOUCH OF TEXAS by Frank Loesser and Jimmy McHugh; YOU MARVELOUS YOU by Gene Austin; OKLAHOMA'S ONE WITH ME by Jimmy Dodd; MY BLUE HEAVEN by George Whiting and Walter Donaldson

MOONLIGHT AND CACTUS

A Universal picture filmed with a cast headed by the Andrews Sisters, Leo Carrillo, Elyse Knox, Tom Seidel, Eddie Quillan and Mitchell Ayres' orchestra, and directed by Edward F. Cline. Songs:

HOME by Harry and Jeff Clarkson and Peter Van Steeden; WA HOO by Cliff Friend; SEND ME A MAN, AMEN by Ray Gilbert and Sidney Miller; C'MERE BABY by Lanny Grey and Roy Jordan; HEAVE HO, MY LADS, HEAVE HO by Jack Lawrence; DOWN IN THE VALLEY by Frank Luther; SING by Harold Mooney and Hughie Prince.

MUSIC FOR MILLIONS

An M-G-M picture filmed with a cast headed by Margaret O'Brien, Jose Iturbi, Jimmy Durante, June Allyson, Marsha Hunt, Hugh Herbert, Marie Wilson and Larry Adler, and directed by Henry Koster. Songs:

TOSCANNINI, STOKOWSKI AND ME by Walter Bullock and Harold Spina; UMBRIAGO by Irving Caesar and Jimmy Durante; AT SUNDOWN by Walter Donaldson; SUMMER HOLIDAYS by Helen Deutch and Herbert Stothart.

MUSIC IN MANHATTAN

An RKO picture filmed with a cast headed by Anne Shirley, Dennis Day, Philip Terry, Raymond Walburn, Jane Darwell, Charles Barnet and his orchestra and Nilo Mendendez Rhumba Band, and directed by John H. Auer. Songs by Herb Magidson and Lew Pollack:

DID YOU HAPPEN TO FIND A HEART? WHEN ROMANCE COMES ALONG; ONE NIGHT IN ACAPULCO, MEXICO and I CAN SEE YOU NOW.

MY GAL LOVES MUSIC

A Universal picture filmed with a cast headed by Bob Crosby, Alan Mowbray and Grace McDonald, and directed by Edward Lilley. Songs by Everett Carter and Milton Rosen:

OVER AND OVER; GIVE OUT; PEPITA and SOMEBODY'S ROCKIN' MY RAINBOW.

NIGHT CLUB GIRL

A Universal picture filmed with a cast headed by Vivian Austin, Edward Norris, Maxie Rosenbloom and the Delta Rhythm Boys, and directed by Edward Cline. Songs:

ONE O'CLOCK JUMP by Count Basie; TIGER RAG by the Original Dixieland Jazz Band; THE PEANUT SONG by Nate Wexler, Red Maddock and Al Trace; VINGO JINGO by Don Raye and Gene DePaul; I NEED LOVE by Milton Pascal and Edgar Fairchild; WO-HO by Jimmy Nolan and Jimmy Kennedy; IT'S A WONDERFUL DAY by Harry Tobias and Al Sherman.

PIN-UP GIRL

A 20th Century-Fox picture starring Betty Grable and Martha Raye in a cast that included Joe E. Brown, Gene Pallette and Charley Spivak and his orchestra, and directed by Bruce Humberstone. Songs by Mack Gordon and Jimmy Monaco:

ONCE TOO OFTEN; YOU'RE MY LITTLE PIN-UP GIRL; YANKEE DOODLE HAYRIDE; THE STORY OF THE VERY MERRY WIDOW; DON'T CARRY TALES OUT OF SCHOOL and RED ROBINS, BOB WHITES AND BLUE BIRDS.

RAINBOW ISLAND

A Paramount picture starring Dorothy Lamour and Eddie Bracken in a cast that included Gil Lamb, Barry Sullivan and Olga San Juan, and directed by Ralph Murphy. Songs by Ted Koehler and Burton Lane:

BELOVED; WHAT A DAY TOMORROW; WE HAVE SO LITTLE TIME and THE BOOGIE-WOOGIE BOOGIE

MAN WILL GET YOU IF YOU DON'T
WATCH OUT.

RECKLESS AGE, THE

A Universal picture starring Gloria Jean
in a cast that included Henry Stephenson,
Kathleen Howard, Franklin Pangborn, Jane
Darwell and the Delta Rhythm Boys, and
directed by Felix E. Feist. Songs:
GET ON BOARD LITTLE CHILDREN
by Don Raye and Gene DePaul; VERY
OFTEN ON MY FACE by Bill Grage and
Grace Shannon; CRADLE SONG, based
on a Johannes Brahams' melody, by Irving
Bibo.

ROSIE THE RIVETER

A Republic picture filmed with a cast
headed by Jane Frazee, Frank Albertson,
Vera Vague and Frank Jenkins, and direct-
ed by Joseph Santley. Songs:
I DON'T WANT ANYBODY AT ALL
by Herb Magidson and Jule Styne; ROSIE
THE RIVETER by Redd Evans and John
Jacob Loeb; WHY CAN'T I SING A
LOVE SONG by Sol Meyer and Harry
Akst; FRIENDLY TAVERN POLKA by
Frank DeVol and Jerry Bowne.

SENSATIONS OF 1945

A United Artists' picture starring W. C.
Fields, Eleanor Powell and Dennis O'Keefe
in a cast that included Sophie Tucker and
the orchestras of Cab Calloway and Woody
Herman, and directed by Andrew Stone.
Songs by Harry Tobias and Al Sherman:
MISTER HEPSTER'S DICTIONARY;
WAKE UP MAN YOU'RE SLIPPIN';
ONE LOVE; KISS SERENADE; NO,
NEVER; and SPIN LITTLE PIN BALL.

SEVEN DAYS ASHORE

An RKO picture filmed with a cast head-
ed by Wally Brown, Gordon Oliver and
Marcy McGuire, and directed by John H.
Auer. Songs by Mort Greene and Lew Pol-
lack:
APPLE BLOSSOMS IN THE RAIN;
HAIL AND FAREWELL; JIVE SAMBA;
READY, AIM, KISS and SIOUX CITY
SUE.

SHE'S A SWEETHEART

A Columbia picture starring Jane Frazee
and Larry Parks in a cast that included
Jane Darwell and Nina Foch, and directed
by Del Lord. Songs:
WHO SAID DREAMS DON'T COME
TRUE? by Benny Davis, Al Jolson and
Harry Akst; I'VE WAITED A LIFETIME
by Edward Brandt; I CAN'T REMEMBER
WHEN by Robert Schermann and Jack

Krakeur; MY OTHER LOVE by Bob
Wright and Chet Forrest; WHAT THE
SERGEANT SAID by Jackie Camp; MOM
by Saul Chaplin; AMERICAN PRAYER
by Lawrence Stock, Vincent Rose and Albert Stillman.

SHOW BUSINESS

An RKO picture starring Eddie Cantor
and George Murphy in a cast that included
Joan Davis and Nancy Kelly, and directed
by Edwin L. Marin. Songs:
ALL FOR THE LOVE OF YOU by
Jack Brooks; YOU MAY NOT REMEM-
BER by George Jessel and Ben Oakland;
I'VE HAD THAT FEELING BEFORE by
Sammy Stept; IT HAD TO BE YOU by
Gus Kahn and Isham Jones.

SING A JINGLE

A Universal picture filmed with a cast
headed by Allan Jones, June Vincent and
Edward Norris, and directed by Edward
C. Lilley. Songs:
SING A JINGLE; WE'RE THE JANES
THAT MAKE THE PLANES and MAD-
AME MOZELLE by Inez James and Sidney
Mitchell; THE NIGHT WE CALLED IT
A DAY by Tom Adair and Matt Dennis;
BEAUTIFUL LOVE by Haven Gillespie,
Wayne King and Victor Young; LOVE
YOU ARE MY MUSIC by Dan Twohig
and Gustave Klemm.

SINGING SHERIFF, THE

A Universal picture filmed with a cast
headed by Bob Crosby, Fay McKenzie, Fuz-
zy Knight, Iris Adrian and Spade Cooley
and his orchestra, and directed by Leslie
Goodwins. Songs:
ANOTHER NIGHT by Don George and
Irving Bibo; BESIDE THE RIO TONTO
by Don Raye and Gene DePaul; REACH
FOR THE SKY and YOU LOOK GOOD
TO ME by Inez James and Sidney Miller;
WHO'S NEXT? by Virginia Wicks and Bill
Lava; WHEN A COWBOY SINGS by
Dave Franklin.

SLIGHTLY TERRIFIC

A Universal picture filmed with a cast
headed by Leon Errol, Anne Rooney, Eddie
Quillan and Betty Kean, and directed by
Edward F. Cline. Songs:
HOLD THAT LINE; ME AND MY
WHISTLE; A DREAM SAID HELLO;
RHYTHM'S WHAT YOU NEED; THE
HAPPY POLKA and STARS AND VIO-
LINS by Everett Carter and Milton Rosen;
THE BLUE DANUBE, based on a Johann
Strauss melody, by Katherine Bellamann.

SOMETHING FOR THE BOYS

A 20th Century-Fox picture filmed with a cast headed by Carmen Miranda, Michael O'Shea, Vivian Blaine, Phil Silvers and Perry Como, and directed by Lewis Seiler. Songs by Harold Adamson, Frank Loesser and Jimmy McHugh:

IN THE MIDDLE OF NOWHERE; WOULDN'T IT BE NICE?; EIGHTY MILES OUTSIDE ATLANTA; BOOM BRACHEE; I WISH WE DIDN'T HAVE TO SAY GOODNIGHT and SAMBA BOOGIE.

SONG OF THE OPEN ROAD

A United Artists' picture filmed with a cast headed by Edgar Bergen, Jane Powell, W. C. Fields, Bonita Granville, Reginald Denny and Sammy Kaye and his orchestra, and directed by S. Sylvan Simon. Songs by Kim Gannon and Walter Kent:

ROLLIN' DOWN THE ROAD; DELIGHTFULLY DANGEROUS; TOO MUCH IN LOVE; HERE IT IS MONDAY and FUN IN THE SUN.

SOUTH OF DIXIE

A Universal picture filmed with a cast headed by Ann Gwynne, David Bruce and Jerome Cowan, and directed by Jean Yarbrough. Songs:

NEVER AGAIN; I'M HEADIN' SOUTH; LOU, LOU, LOUISIANA and CROSS MY HEART by Everett Carter and Milton Rosen; WHEN IT'S DARKNESS ON THE DELTA by Marty Symes, A. J. Neiberg and Jerry Livingston; WEEP NO MORE MY LADY by Joan Whitney and Alex Kramer.

STARS ON PARADE

A Columbia picture filmed with a cast headed by Larry Parks, Lynn Merrick, Ray Walker and the King Cole Trio, and directed by Lew Landers. Songs:

WHEN THEY ASK ABOUT YOU by Sammy Stept; TAKING CARE OF YOU by Lew Brown and Harry Akst; JUMPIN' AT THE JUBILEE by Ben Carter and Mayes Marshall; WHERE AM I WITHOUT YOU? by Don Raye and Gene DePaul; MY HEART ISN'T IN IT by Jack Lawrence; TWO HEARTS IN THE DARK by Dave Franklin.

STEP LIVELY

An RKO picture starring Frank Sinatra, George Murphy and Gloria DeHaven in a cast that included Adolphe Menjou, and directed by Tom Whelan. Songs by Sammy Cahn and Jule Styne.

COME OUT, COME OUT, WHEREVER YOU ARE; WHERE DOES LOVE BEGIN (AND WHERE DOES FRIENDSHIP END)?; AND THEN YOU KISSED ME; ASK THE MADAME; AS LONG AS THERE IS MUSIC and WHY MUST THERE BE AN OPENING SONG?

SWEET AND LOW DOWN

A 20th Century-Fox picture filmed with a cast headed by Linda Darnell, Lynn Bari, Jack Oakie, Dickie Moore and Benny Goodman and his orchestra, and directed by Archie Mayo. Songs by Mack Gordon and Jimmy Monaco:

I'M MAKING BELIEVE; HEY, BUB, LET'S HAVE A BALL; TEN DAYS WITH BABY; ONE CHORD IN TWO FLATS; TSK, TSK THAT'S LOVE and CHUG-CHUG, CHOO-CHOO, CHUG.

SWEETHEARTS OF THE U.S.A.

A Monogram picture filmed with a cast headed by Una Merkel and Donald Novis, and directed by Lew Collins. Songs by Charles Newman and Lew Pollack:

THAT REMINDS ME; ALL THE LATINS KNOW IS "SI-SI"; WE'RE THE ONES; HOLD ON TO YOUR HAT and YOU CAN'T BRUSH OFF A RUSSIAN.

SWING IN THE SADDLE

A Columbia picture filmed with a cast headed by Jane Frazee, Guinn Williams, Slim Summerville, the King Cole Trio and the Hoosier Hot Shots, and directed by Lew Landers. Songs:

BY THE RIVER SAINTE MARIE by Edgar Leslie and Harry Warren; SHE BROKE MY HEART IN THREE PLACES by Oliver Drake; WHEN IT'S HARVEST TIME IN PEACEFUL VALLEY by Robert Martin; THERE'LL BE A JUBILEE by Phil Moore; AMOR by Sunny Skylar and Gabriel Ruiz; HEY MABEL by Fred Stryker.

SWINGTIME JOHNNY

A Universal picture filmed with a cast headed by the Andrews Sisters, Harriet Hilliard, Peter Cookson, Tim Ryan and Mitchell Ayres' orchestra, and directed by Edward F. Cline. Songs:

BOOGIE WOOGIE BUGLE BOY by Don Raye and Hughie Prince; SWEET AND LOW and POOR NELL by Everett Carter and Milton Rosen; YOU BETTER GIVE ME LOTS OF LOVIN' by Kermit Goell and Fred Spielman; I MAY BE WRONG BUT I THINK YOU'RE WONDERFUL by Henry Sullivan and Harry

Ruskin; BOOGIE WOOGIE CHOO-CHOO by Johnny Murphy and Roy Jordan; WHEN YOU AND I WERE YOUNG MAGGIE by J. A. Butterfield.

TAKE IT BIG

A Paramount picture starring Jack Haley and Harriet Hilliard in a cast that included Mary Beth Hughes, Richard Lane, Arline Judge, Lucille Gleason, Fuzzy Knight and Ozzie Nelson and his orchestra, and directed by Frank McDonald. Songs by Jerry Seelen and Lester Lee:

LOVE AND LEARN; LIFE CAN BE BEAUTIFUL; TAKE IT BIG and I'M A BIG SUCCESS WITH YOU.

THIS IS THE LIFE

A Universal picture starring Donald O'Connor and Susanna Foster in a cast that included Louise Allbritton, and directed by Felix Feist. Songs:

IT'S THE GIRL; YIPPEE-I-VOTT and GREMLIN WALK by Inez James and Sidney Miller; WITH A SONG IN MY HEART by Lorenz Hart and Richard Rodgers; ALL OR NOTHING AT ALL by Jack Lawrence and Arthur Altman; YOU'RE A LALA PALOOZA by Bill Grage and Grace Shannon.

THREE LITTLE SISTERS

A Republic picture filmed with a cast headed by Mary Lee, Cheryl Walker and Ruth Terry, and directed by Joseph Santley. Songs by Kim Gannon and Walter Kent:

DON'T FORGET THE GIRL BACK HOME; KHAKI WACKY SUE; LITTLE OLD-FASHIONED LOOKING GLASS and SWEET DREAMS SWEETHEART.

TROCADERO

A Republic picture starring Rosemary Lane in a cast that included Johnny Downs, Ralph Morgan, Dick Purcell, Cliff Nazarro, Marjorie Manners and the orchestras of Gus Arnheim and Eddie LaBarron, and directed by William Nigh. Songs:

ROUNDABOUT WAY by Sidney Clare and Lew Porter; BULLFROG JUMP and HOW COULD YOU DO THAT TO ME? by Lew Porter; LOUISIANA LULU by Teepee Mitchell and Lew Porter; THE KING WAS DOING THE RHUMBA by Jay Cheris and Lew Porter; TRYING TO FORGET by Tony Romano; SHOO SHOO BABY by Phil Moore; CAN'T TAKE THE PLACE OF YOU by Walter Colmes and Lew Porter.

TWILIGHT ON THE PRAIRIE

A Universal picture filmed with a cast headed by Johnny Downs, Vivian Austin, Leon Errol, Connie Haines, Eddie Quillan and Jack Teagarden's orchestra, and directed by Jean Yarbrough. Songs:

TEXAS POLKA by Oakley Haldeman, Vic Knight and Lew Porter; NO LETTER TODAY by Frankie Brown; DON'T YOU EVER BE A COWBOY; LET'S LOVE AGAIN and WHERE THE PRAIRIE MEETS THE SKY by Everett Carter and Milton Rosen; I GOT MELLOW IN THE YELLOW OF THE MOON by Jimmy Dodd; SIP NIP SONG by Don George and Branda Weisburg; SALT WATER COWBOY by Redd Evans; THE BLUES by Jack Teagarden.

TWO GIRLS AND A SAILOR

An M-G-M picture filmed with a cast headed by Van Johnson, June Allyson, Gloria DeHaven, Jose Iturbi, Jimmy Durante, Gracie Allen, Lena Horne, Ben Blue, Virginia O'Brien, Henry Stephenson and Harry James and Xavier Cugat's orchestras, and directed by Richard Thorpe. Songs:

YOUNG MAN WITH A HORN by Ralph Freed and George Stoll; YOU DEAR by Ralph Freed and Sammy Fain; IN A MOMENT OF MADNESS and MY MOTHER TOLD ME by Ralph Freed and Jimmy McHugh; A LOVE LIKE OURS by Mann Holiner and Alberta Nichols; SWEET AND LOVELY by Gus Arnheim, Jules Lemair and Harry Tobias; THRILL OF A NEW ROMANCE by Harold Adamson and Xavier Cugat; A TISKET A TASKET by Al Feldman and Ella Fitzgerald.

UP IN ARMS

An RKO picture starring Danny Kaye, Dinah Shore and Dana Andrews, and directed by Elliott Nugent. Songs by Ted Koehler and Harold Arlen:

NOW I KNOW; ALL OUT FOR FREEDOM and TESS'S TORCH SONG.

WAVE, A WAC AND A MARINE, A

A Monogram picture filmed with a cast headed by Elyse Knox, Anne Gillis, Sallie Eilers, Richard Lane, Henry Youngman and Freddie Rich and his orchestra, and directed by Phil Karlson. Songs by Eddie Cherkose, Jacques Press and Freddie Rich:

CARRY ON; TIME WILL TELL and GEE I LOVE MY G.I. GUY.

WEEKEND PASS

A Universal picture filmed with a cast headed by Martha O'Driscoll, Noah Beery

Jr., George Barbier, the Delta Rhythm Boys and the Leo Diamond Quintet, and directed by Jean Yarbrough. Songs:
I AM, ARE YOU?; I LIKE TO BE LOVED; WE BUILD 'EM YOU SAIL 'EM and SHE'S A GIRL A MAN CAN DREAM OF by Everett Carter and Milton Rosen; WE'RE IN THE NAVY by Don Raye and Gene DePaul; ALL OR NOTHING AT ALL by Jack Lawrence and Arthur Altman.

YOU CAN'T RATION LOVE

A Paramount picture starring Betty Jane Rhodes and Johnny Johnston, and directed by Lester Fuller. Songs:
LOOK WHAT YOU DID TO ME; NOTHING CAN REPLACE A MAN; LOVE IS THIS; HOW DID IT HAPPEN? and OOH-AH-OH by Jerry Seelen and Lester Lee; LOUISE by Leo Robin and Richard Whiting.

Feature Films With Songs

ALI BABA AND THE FORTY THIEVES

A Universal picture filmed with a cast headed by Maria Montez, Yvette Duguay, Jon Hall, Turhan Bey and Andy Devine, and directed by Arthur Lubin. Song by J. Keirn Brennan and Edward Ward:
FORTY AND ONE FOR ALL

AMERICAN ROMANCE, AN

An M-G-M picture filmed with a cast headed by Brian Donlevy, Ann Richards and Walter Abel, and directed by King Vidor. Songs by Louis Gruenberg and King Vidor:
LORD PLEASE SEND ME DOWN YOUR LOVE and LULLABY.

ATLANTIC CITY

A Columbia picture starring Constance Moore and Brad Taylor in a cast that included Charley Grapevine and Jerry Colonna, and directed by Ray McCarey. Song by Andrew B. Sterling and Harry Von Tilzer:
ON A SUNDAY AFTERNOON

BARBARY COAST GENT

An M-G-M picture starring Wallace Beery, Binnie Barnes and John Carradine, and directed by Roy Del Ruth. Song by O. B. Ruthven:
STAR OF EVENING

BETWEEN TWO WOMEN

An M-G-M picture starring Van Johnson, Lionel Barrymore and Gloria DeHaven, and directed by Willis Goldbeck. Song by Dorothy Fields and Jimmy McHugh:
I'M IN THE MOOD FOR LOVE

BRAZIL

A Republic picture filmed with a cast headed by Tito Guizar, Virginia Bruce, Edward Everett Horton and Roy Rogers, and directed by Joseph Santley. Songs by Bob Russell and Ary Barrosa:
BRAZIL and RIO DE JANEIRO

CALL OF THE SOUTH SEAS

A Republic picture starring Janet Martin

and Allan Lane, and directed by John English. Song by Ned Washington and Evan Newman:
BLUE ISLAND

CHRISTMAS HOLIDAY

A Universal picture starring Deanna Durbin and Gene Kelly in a cast that included Richard Whorf, Gladys George, Gale Sondergaard and David Bruce, and directed by Charles Lamont. Song by Frank Loesser:
SPRING WILL BE A LITTLE LATE THIS YEAR

CLIMAX, THE

A Universal picture starring Boris Karloff, Susanna Foster and Turhan Bey, and directed by George Waggner. Songs by George Waggner and Edward Ward:
NOW AT LAST and SOME DAY I KNOW

FIGHTING SEABEES

A Republic picture starring John Wayne and Susan Hayward, and directed by Edward Ludwig. Song by Sam Lewis and Peter DeRose:
SONG OF THE SEABEES

GYPSY WILDCAT

A Universal picture starring Maria Montez and Jon Hall in a cast that included Nigel Bruce and Leo Carrillo, and directed by Roy William Neill. Song by George Waggner and Edward Ward:
THE GYPSY SONG OF FREEDOM

HAIL THE CONQUERING HERO

A Paramount picture starring Eddie Bracken and Ella Raines, and directed by Preston Sturges, who contributed the following song:
HOME TO THE ARMS OF MOTHER

HI, BEAUTIFUL

A Universal picture filmed with a cast headed by Martha O'Driscoll, Noah Beery Jr., Hattie McDaniel and Walter Catlett, and directed by Leslie Goodwins. Songs:

BEST OF ALL by Allie Wrubel; DON'T SWEETHEART ME by Charles Tobias and Cliff Friend; SINGIN' IN THE RAIN by Arthur Freed and Nacio Herb Brown.

HOT RHYTHM
A Monogram picture starring Dona Drake and Robert Lowery, and directed by William Beaudine. Songs by Edward J. Kay:
SAY IT WITH YOUR HEART and RIGHT UNDER MY NOSE

I ACCUSE MY PARENTS
A Producers Releasing Corporation picture starring Robert Lowell and Mary Beth Hughes, and directed by Sam Newfield. Songs by Ray Evans and Jay Livingston:
ARE YOU HAPPY IN YOUR WORK?; LOVE CAME BETWEEN US and WHERE CAN YOU BE?

I LOVE A SOLDIER
A Paramount picture starring Paulette Goddard and Sonny Tufts, and directed by Mark Sandrich. Song by Bernie Grossman and Sam Pasternacki:
I LOVE A SOLDIER

I'LL BE SEEING YOU
A United Artists' picture starring Ginger Rogers and Joseph Cotten in a cast that included Shirley Temple and Spring Byington, and directed by William Dieterle. Song by Irving Kahal and Sammy Fain:
I'LL BE SEEING YOU

I'M FROM ARKANSAS
A Producers Releasing Corporation picture filmed with a cast headed by Slim Summerville, Iris Adrain and El Brendel, and directed by Lew Landers. Song by Harry Tobias, Eddie Dean and Judy and Zeke Canova:
DON'T EVER LET ME DOWN LITTLE DARLIN'

IMPATIENT YEARS, THE
A Columbia picture filmed with a cast headed by Jean Arthur, Lee Bowman and Charles Coburn, and directed by Irving Cummings. Song by Benny Davis, Al Jolson and Harry Akst:
WHO SAID DREAMS DON'T COME TRUE?

IMPOSTER, THE
A Universal picture filmed with a cast headed by Jean Gabin, Richard Whorf, Allyn Joslyn, Ellen Drew and Ralph Morgan, and directed by Julien Duvivier. Song by Sam Lerner and A. Renard:
IN SWEET CHERRY TIME

IRISH EYES ARE SMILING
A 20th Century-Fox picture starring June Haver, Dick Haymes and Monte Woolley, and directed by Gregory Ratoff. Songs by Mack Gordon and Jimmy Monaco:
BESSIE IN A BUSTLE and I DON'T WANT A MILLION DOLLARS

JANIE
A Warner Brothers' picture filmed with a cast headed by Joyce Reynolds, Robert Hutton, Edward Arnold and Ann Harding, and directed by Michael Curtiz. Songs:
KEEP YOUR POWDER DRY by Sammy Cahn and Jule Styne; JANIE by Lee David.

LAURA
A 20th Century-Fox picture starring Gene Tierney and Dana Andrews in a cast that included Clifton Webb, Vincent Price and Judith Anderson, and directed by Otto Preminger. Song by Johnny Mercer and David Raskin:
LAURA

MAISIE GOES TO RENO
An M-G-M picture starring Ann Sothern and John Hodiak in a cast that included Tom Drake and Ava Gardner, and directed by Harry Beaumont. Songs by Ralph Freed and Sammy Fain:
PANHANDLE PETE and THIS LITTLE BOND WENT TO BATTLE

MURDER IN THE BLUE ROOM
A Universal picture filmed with a cast headed by Ann Gwynn, Donald Cook, John Litel, Grace McDonald, Betty Kean and June Preisser, and directed by Leslie Goodwins. Songs:
ONE STORMY NIGHT by Don George and Dave Franklin; A-DOO-DEE-DOO-DOO by Teepee Mitchell, Leo Erdody and Lew Porter.

MY BEST GIRL
A Republic picture starring Jane Withers in a cast that included Jimmy Lydon and Frank Craven, and directed by Anthony Mann. Songs by Kim Gannon and Walter Kent:
I'VE GOT THE FLYIN'EST FEELIN'; UPSY DOWNSY and WHERE THERE'S LOVE.

OUR HEARTS WERE YOUNG AND GAY
A Paramount picture starring Gail Russell and Diana Lynn in a cast that included Charles Ruggles, Dorothy Gish and

Beulah Bondi, and directed by Lewis Allen. Song by Kermit Goell and Ted Grouya:
    WHEN OUR HEARTS WERE YOUNG AND GAY

PASSAGE TO MARSEILLES

A Warner Brothers' picture starring Humphrey Bogart and Michele Morgan in a cast that included Claude Rains, Sydney Greenstreet, Peter Lorre and John Loder, and directed by Michael Curtiz. Song by Ned Washington and Max Steiner:
    SOME DAY I'LL MEET YOU AGAIN

PHANTOM LADY

A Universal picture starring Ella Raines and Franchot Tone, and directed by Robert Siodmak. Song by Eddie Cherkose and Jacques Press:
    CHICK-EE-CHICK

PRACTICALLY YOURS

A Paramount picture starring Claudette Colbert and Fred MacMurray, and directed by Mitchell Leisen. Song by Sam Coslow:
    I KNEW IT WOULD BE THIS WAY

PRINCESS AND THE PIRATE, THE

An RKO picture starring Bob Hope and Virginia Mayo in a cast that included Walter Brennan, Walter Slezak and Victor McLaglen, and directed by David Butler. Song by Harold Adamson and Jimmy McHugh:
    HOW WOULD YOU LIKE TO KISS ME IN THE MOONLIGHT?

SEE HERE PRIVATE HARGROVE

An M-G-M picture starring Robert Walker in a cast that included Donna Reed, Keenan Wynn and Robert Benchley, and directed by George Blair. Song by Frank Loesser and Ted Grouya:
    IN MY ARMS

SHINE ON HARVEST MOON

A Warner Brothers' picture starring Ann Sheridan and Dennis Morgan, and directed by David Butler. Songs:
    TIME WAITS FOR NO ONE by Cliff Friend and Charles Tobias; I GO FOR YOU and SO DUMB BUT SO BEAUTIFUL by Kim Gannon and M. K. Jerome.

SINCE YOU WENT AWAY

An M-G-M picture filmed with a cast headed by Claudette Colbert, Jennifer Jones, Joseph Cotten, Shirley Temple, Monte Woolley, Lionel Barrymore, Robert Walker, Hattie McDaniel, Nazimova and Keenan Wynn, and directed by John Cromwell. Songs:
    SINCE YOU WENT AWAY by Kermit

Goell and Ted Grouya; TOGETHER by B. G. DeSylva, Lew Brown and Ray Henderson; THE DIPSY DOODLE by Larry Clinton.

SING NEIGHBOR SING

A Republic picture filmed with a cast headed by Ruth Terry, Lulubelle and Scotty and Brad Taylor, and directed by Frank McDonald. Songs:
    BLAKE SONG and PHRENOLOGY by Jack Elliott and R. Dale Bates; SING NEIGHBOR SING by Fred Rose.

SWING HOSTESS

A Producers Releasing Corporation picture filmed with a cast headed by Martha Tilton, Iris Adrian and Charles Collins, and directed by Sam Newfield. Songs by Ray Evans, Jay Livingston and Lewis Bellin:
    HIGHWAY POLKA and SAY IT WITH LOVE

THEY SHALL HAVE FAITH

A Monogram picture filmed with a cast headed by Gale Storm, Aubrey Smith, Johnny Mack Brown, Conrad Nagel, Mary Boland, Frank Craven and Johnny Downs, and directed by William Nigh. Songs:
    CLOSE YOUR EYES AND JUST PRETEND by Al Jaxton and Neil Rau; YOU'RE THE ANSWER by Robert Watson.

THIRTY SECONDS OVER TOKIO

An M-G-M picture filmed with a cast headed by Van Johnson, Spencer Tracy, Robert Walker and Phyllis Thaxter, and directed by Mervyn LeRoy. Song by Art and Kay Fitch and Bert Lowe:
    SWEETHEART OF ALL MY DREAMS

TO HAVE AND HAVE NOT

A Warner Brothers' picture starring Humphrey Bogart in a cast that included Walter Brennan, Lauren Bacall and Hoagy Carmichael, and directed by Howard Hawks. Song by Johnny Mercer and Hoagy Carmichael:
    HOW LITTLE WE KNOW

UNCERTAIN GLORY

A Warner Brothers' picture filmed with a cast headed by Errol Flynn, Paul Lukas and Jean Sullivan, and directed by Raoul Walsh. Song by Eddie DeLange, Joseph Myrow and Ernesto Lecuona:
    MARIANNE

UNINVITED, THE

A Paramount picture starring Ray Milland and Ruth Hussey, and directed by

Lewis Allen. Song by Ned Washington and Victor Young:
  STELLA BY STARLIGHT

WHEN THE LIGHTS GO ON AGAIN
A Producers Releasing Corporation picture filmed with a cast headed by James Lydon, Regis Toomey, George Cleveland, Grant Mitchell and Dorothy Peterson, and directed by William K. Howard. Song by Eddie Seiler, Sol Marcus and Bennie Benjamin:

WHEN THE LIGHTS GO ON AGAIN ALL OVER THE WORLD

WINGED VICTORY
A 20th Century-Fox picture filmed with a cast headed by Lon McCallister, Jeanne Crain, Edmond O'Brien, Jane Ball, Mark Daniels, Judy Holliday, Lee J. Cobb, Peter Lind Hayes and Red Buttons, and directed by George Cukor. Song by Tod B. Galloway, Meade Minnigerode and George S. Pomeroy:
  THE WHIFFENPOOF SONG

Western Films With Songs

ALASKA
A Monogram picture filmed with a cast headed by Kent Taylor, Margaret Lindsay, John Carradine and Dean Jagger, and directed by George Archainbaud. Songs by Eddie Cherkose and Edward Kay:
  DEAR OLD JOE; A FOOL AND HIS GOLD; FORGET IF YOU CAN and MAYBE HE CAN CAN-CAN TOO.

BOSS OF BOOMTOWN
A Universal picture filmed with a cast headed by Rod Cameron, Tom Tyler, Fuzzy Knight and Vivian Austin, and directed by Ray Taylor. Songs by Johnny Marvin:
  TEXAS; NINETY-NINE DAYS and MY PROUD BEAUTY.

COWBOY AND THE SENORITA, THE
A Republic picture starring Roy Rogers in a cast that included Mary Lee, Dale Evans, John Hubbard, Bob Nolan and the Sons of the Pioneers, and directed by Joseph Kane. Songs by Ned Washington and Phil Ohman:
  ENCHILADA MAN; THE COWBOY AND THE SENORITA and WHAT'LL I USE FOR MONEY?

COWBOY CANTEEN
A Columbia picture starring Charles Starrett and Jane Frazee in a cast that included Vera Vague and Tex Ritter, and directed by Lew Landers. Songs:
  COME ON AND WHISTLE by Irving Bibo and Al Piantadosi; LAZY RIVER by Sidney Arodin and Hoagy Carmichael; BOOGIE WOOGIE SPECIAL; SPOT IN ARIZONA and YOU MAN YOU by Walter G. Samuels and Saul Chaplin; WAIT FOR THE LIGHT TO SHINE by Fred Rose; WALKING DOWN THE LANE WITH YOU by Jimmy Wakely.

LIGHTS OF OLD SANTA FE
A Republic picture starring Roy Rogers in a cast that included Dale Evans, Gabby Hayes, Bob Nolan and the Sons of the Pioneers, and directed by Frank McDonald. Songs:
  THE COWPOKE POLKA; I'M HAPPY IN MY LEVI BRITCHES and TRIGGER HASN'T GOT A PURTY FIGGURE by Tim Spencer; AMOR by Sunny Skylar and Gabriel Ruiz; THE COWBOY JUBILEE by Ken Carson; THE NERVE OF SOME PEOPLE and LIGHTS OF OLD SANTA FE by Jack Elliott; RIDE 'EM COWBOY by Bob Nolan.

MARSHALL OF GUNSMOKE
A Universal picture filmed with a cast headed by Tex Ritter, Russell Hayden, Fuzzy Knight and Jennifer Holt, and directed by Vernon Keays. Songs:
  MY SADDLE SERENADE by Johnny Bond; SUNDOWN TRAIL by Johnny Marvin.

OKLAHOMA RAIDERS
A Universal picture filmed with a cast headed by Tex Ritter, Fuzzy Knight, Dennis Moore, and Jennifer Holt, and directed by Lewis D. Collins. Songs by Johnny Bond:
  OUT ON THE OPEN RANGE and STARLIGHT ON THE PRAIRIE.

RETURN OF THE DURANGO KID
A Columbia picture starring Charles Starrett and Jean Stevens. Song by Eddie Seiler, Al Neiberg and Sol Marcus:
  WHEN THEY FIDDLE OUT THE POLKA.

SAN FERNANDO VALLEY
A Republic picture starring Roy Rogers in a cast that included Dale Evans, Jean Porter, Bob Nolan and the Sons of the Pioneers, and directed by John English. Songs:
  COULD ANYONE BE SWEETER THAN YOU and MY HOBBY IS LOVE

by Charles Henderson; DAYS OF '49 and THEY WENT THAT A-WAY by Tim Spencer; SAN FERNANDO VALLEY by Gordon Jenkins; OVER THE RAINBOW WE'LL RIDE by Ken Carson.

SONG OF NEVADA

A Republic picture starring Roy Rogers in a cast that included Dale Evans, Mary Lee, Bob Nolan and the Sons of the Pioneers, and directed by Joseph Kane. Song by Charles Henderson:
SONG OF NEVADA

TRAIL TO GUNSIGHT

A Universal picture filmed with a cast headed by Eddie Drew, Lyle Talbot, Fuzzy Knight, Ray Whitley, Marie Austin and Sarah Padden, and directed by Vernon Keays. Songs:
OLD NEVADA TRAIL by Joe Carol; SLUMBERTIME OUT ON THE PRAIRIE and AIN'T GOT A GIRL TO COME HOME TO by Oliver Drake; CHUCK WAGON BLUES by Betty Jackson, Jesse Lilley and Harry Walters.

TRIGGER TRAIL

A Universal picture filmed with a cast headed by Rod Cameron, Fuzzy Knight, Eddie Drew and Vivian Austin, and di-

rected by Lewis D. Collins. Songs:
TRAIL DREAMIN' by Oliver Drake, Jimmy Wakely and Milton Rosen; I'M HEADIN' FOR MY OKLAHOMA HOME by Albert Hamilton and Muriel Mays; TWILIGHT ON THE TRAIL by Ray Whitley.

WESTWARD BOUND

A Monogram picture filmed with a cast headed by Ken Maynard, Hoot Gibson and Betty Miles, and directed by Robert Tansey. Songs by Mack David and David Mendoza:
BLAZING THE TRAIL and FRISCO

WHISPERING SKULL, THE

A Producers Releasing Corporation picture filmed with a cast headed by Tex Ritter, Dave O'Brien and Guy Wilkerson, and directed by Elmer Clifton. Songs:
IT'S NEVER TOO LATE by Tex Ritter and Frank Harford; IN CASE YOU CHANGE YOUR MIND by Tex Ritter.

YELLOW ROSE OF TEXAS, THE

A Republic picture starring Roy Rogers in a cast that included Dale Evans, Bob Nolan and the Sons of the Pioneers, and directed by Joseph Kane. Song by Charles Henderson:
DOWN IN THE OLD TOWN HALL

Feature Cartoon With Songs

THREE CABALLEROS

An RKO-Walt Disney production with the following songs:
THREE CABALLEROS by Charles Wolcott; YOU BELONG TO MY HEART by

Ray Gilbert and Augustin Lara; HAVE YOU EVER BEEN TO BAHIA by Norman Ferguson and Dorival Caymmi; SAMBA-JONGO.

Esther Williams in a scene from her first starring film *Neptune's Daughter*

1 9 4 5

"Oklahoma's" Creators Hit The Hollywood Jackpot, Too

In 1943, Oscar Hammerstein II and Richard Rodgers had confounded the Broadway soothsayers, who predicted their forthcoming Theater Guild production wouldn't last four weeks, by collaborating on a musical that hung up an all-time, long-run record of 2248 performances—the fabulous *Oklahoma*. And two and a half years later, they did it again—and in Hollywood, where their past individual success in creating special material for the screen was nothing to cheer about. According to the majority of the top brass of the cinema capital, Rodgers and Hammerstein were strictly Broadway guys and lacking in Hollywood know-how, but this appraisement backfired when *State Fair* grossed better than $4,000,000 at the box-office and the film's most appealing ballad, *It Might As Well Be Spring*, won the Oscar as the best picture song of 1945.

But without detracting from the achievements of Rodgers and Hammerstein, it must be recalled that the year that brought an end to the fighting in both Europe and the Pacific was a great and prosperous year for screen musicals. The war-weary public loved them, and showed its affection at the box-office where in addition to *State Fair, Anchors Aweigh, The Road To Utopia, Thrill Of Romance* and *The Dolly Sisters* won a place in The Golden Circle along with *The Bells Of St. Mary's,* a feature film with songs in which Bing Crosby and Ingrid Bergman co-starred.

Also high on the honor roll of 1945 was *Rhapsody In Blue,* the film biography of George Gershwin in which Robert Alda played the role of the composer who took jazz, born in the brothels and barrelhouses of New Orleans, and transformed her by his genius into a grand lady of bewitching charm.

The famous Dolly Sisters, the toast of Broadway soon after the century's turn, lived again when portrayed by Betty Grable and June Haver in a film for which "Ragtime Jimmy" Monaco wrote his last song, *I Can't Begin To Tell You,* before turning in his battered Tonk piano for a golden harp—or a reasonable facsimile, while Betty Hutton revived in *Incendiary Blonde* the prohibition years when Texas Guinan greeted the patrons of her night club with "Hello, suckers" and introduced George Raft and his brother, Dick, as "the world's greatest dance team."

Bing Crosby, Bob Hope and Dorothy Lamour went out of this world in hitting *The Road To Utopia;* Esther Williams in *Thrill Of Romance* had a much coveted vis-a-vis in Van Johnson; *State Fair* proved the recruiting ground for four future-greats of the screen: Jeanne Crain, Dana Andrews, Dick Haymes and Vivian Blaine; while *Anchors Aweigh* in which Frank Sinatra, Kathryn Grayson and Gene Kelly shared headline billing, was voted one of the Ten Best Pictures of a year that gave birth to such distinguished films as *A Tree Grows In Brooklyn, The Corn Is Green, A Song To Remember* and *The Story Of G.I. Joe,* the latter paying posthumous tribute to Ernie Pyle, the war correspondent, and musically remembered by the song *Linda.*

After completing the score for *Centennial Summer,* scheduled for 1946 release, Jerome Kern left Hollywood for a songwriting mission on Broadway— and never returned, a fatal heart attack bringing an end to a great and glorious career that enriched the world with rare and deathless music.

Musicals

ABBOTT AND COSTELLO IN HOLLYWOOD
An M-G-M picture starring Abbott and Costello, and directed by S. Sylvan Simon. Songs by Ralph Blane and Hugh Martin:
FUN ON THE WONDERFUL MIDWAY; I HOPE THE BAND KEEPS ON PLAYING and AS I REMEMBER YOU.

ANCHORS AWEIGH
An M-G-M picture starring Frank Sinatra, Kathryn Grayson and Gene Kelly in a cast that included Rags Ragland and Jose Iturbi, and directed by George Sidney. Songs:
WE HATE TO LEAVE; WHAT MAKES THE SUN SET?; THE CHARM OF YOU; I BEGGED HER and I FALL IN LOVE TOO EASILY by Sammy Cahn and Jule Styne; THE WORRY SONG by Ralph Freed and Sammy Fain.

BLONDE RANSOM
A Universal picture starring Donald Cook and Virginia Grey in a cast that included Pinky Lee and Collette Lyons, and directed by William Beaudine. Songs by Jack Brooks:
LIFE OF THE PARTY; MUSICAL WEDDING and A MILLION DOLLARS WORTH OF DREAMS.

BRING ON THE GIRLS
A Paramount picture starring Veronica Lake, Sonny Tufts and Eddie Bracken in a cast that included Marjorie Reynolds, Grant Mitchell and Alan Mowbray, and directed by Sidney Lanfield. Songs by Harold Adamson and Jimmy McHugh:
UNCLE SAMMY HIT MIAMI; BRING ON THE GIRLS; HOW WOULD YOU LIKE TO TAKE MY PICTURE?; YOU MOVED RIGHT IN; IT COULD HAPPEN TO ME; TRUE TO THE NAVY and I'M GONNA HATE MYSELF IN THE MORNING.

DELIGHTFULLY DANGEROUS
A United Artists' picture filmed with a cast headed by Jane Powell, Ralph Bellamy, Constance Moore, Arthur Treacher and Morton Gould and his orchestra, and directed by Arthur Lubin. Songs by Edward Heyman and Morton Gould:
I'M ONLY TEASIN'; IN A SHOWER OF STARS; MYNAH BIRD; ONCE UPON A SONG and THROUGH YOUR EYES TO YOUR HEART.

DIAMOND HORSESHOE
A 20th Century-Fox picture starring Betty Grable in a cast that included Dick Haymes, Phil Silvers, William Gaxton, Beatrice Kay and Carmen Cavallaro and his orchestra, and directed by George Seaton. Songs by Mack Gordon and Harry Warren:
I WISH I KNEW; THE MORE I SEE YOU; IN ACAPULCO; PLAY ME AN OLD-FASHIONED MELODY; A NICKEL'S WORTH OF JIVE; MOODY; WELCOME TO THE DIAMOND HORSESHOE and COOKING UP A SHOW.

DOLL FACE
A 20th Century-Fox picture starring Vivian Blaine and Dennis O'Keefe in a cast that included Perry Como and Carmen Miranda, and directed by Lewis Seiler. Songs by Harold Adamson and Jimmy McHugh:
HUBBA, HUBBA, HUBBA (DIG YOU LATER); HERE COMES HEAVEN AGAIN; CHICO CHICO; SOMEONE IS WALKING IN MY DREAM and RED HOT AND BEAUTIFUL.

DOLLY SISTERS, THE
A 20th Century-Fox picture starring Betty Grable and June Haver in a cast that included John Payne and Reginald Gardiner, and directed by Irving Cummings. Songs:

I CAN'T BEGIN TO TELL YOU and DON'T BE TOO OLD-FASHIONED (OLD-FASHIONED GIRL) by Mack Gordon and Jimmy Monaco; GIVE ME THE MOONLIGHT, GIVE ME THE GIRL by Lew Brown and Albert Von Tilzer; WE HAVE BEEN AROUND by Mack Gordon and Charles Henderson; CAROLINA IN THE MORNING by Walter Donaldson; POWDER LIPSTICK AND ROUGE by Mack Gordon and Harry Revel; DARK-TOWN STRUTTERS' BALL by Shelton Brooks; SMILES by Lee Roberts; ARRAH GO ON I'M GONNA GO BACK TO OREGON by Joe Young, Sam Lewis and Bert Grant; OH FRENCHIE by Sam Ehrlich and Con Conrad; I'M ALWAYS CHASING RAINBOWS by Joseph McCarthy and Harry Carroll; ON THE MISSISSIPPI by Ballard MacDonald, Buddy Fields and Harry Carroll.

EARL CARROLL'S VANITIES

A Republic picture starring Dennis O'Keefe and Constance Moore in a cast that included Eve Arden, Otto Kruger and. Alan Mowbray, and directed by Joseph Santley. Musical numbers:
WHO DAT UP THERE? and ENDLESSLY by Kim Gannon and Walter Kent; APPLE HONEY by Woody Herman; RIVERSIDE JIVE by Alfred Newman.

EASY TO LOOK AT

A Universal picture filmed with a cast headed by Gloria Jean, Kirby Grant, J. Edward Bromberg, Eric Blore and the Delta Rhythm Boys, and directed by Ford Beebe. Songs by Charles Newman and Arthur Altman:
COME ALONG MY HEART (WE'RE GOING PLACES); THAT DOES IT; UMBRELLA WITH A SILVER LINING; SWING LOW SWEET LARIAT and JUST FOR THE DEVIL OF IT.

FRISCO SAL

A Universal picture filmed with a cast headed by Susanna Foster, Turhan Bey, Alan Curtis and Andy Devine, and directed by George Waggner. Songs:
BELOVED by George Waggner and Edward Ward; GOOD LITTLE BAD LITTLE LADY by Jack Brooks; I JUST GOT IN by Jack Brooks and Norman Berens.

FRONTIER GIRL

A Universal picture starring Yvonne De Carlo and Rod Cameron, and directed by Charles Lamont. Songs by Jack Brooks and Edgar Fairchild:

SET 'EM UP JOE; JOHNNY'S COMING HOME and WHAT IS LOVE?

GEORGE WHITE'S SCANDALS OF 1945

An RKO picture starring Joan Davis and Jack Haley in a cast that included Phillip Terry, Martha Holliday, Ethel Smith, Rose Murphy and Gene Krupa and his band, and directed by Felix E. Feist. Musical numbers:
HOW'D YOU GET OUT OF MY DREAMS?; I WAKE UP IN THE MORNING; I WANT TO BE A DRUMMER and WHO KILLED VAUDEVILLE? by Jack Yellen and Sammy Fain; WISHING by B. G. DeSylva; LIFE IS JUST A BOWL OF CHERRIES by Lew Brown and Ray Henderson; BOLERO IN THE JUNGLE by Tommy Peterson and Gene Krupa.

HANGOVER SQUARE

A 20th Century-Fox picture starring Laird Cregar, Linda Darnell and George Sanders, and directed by John Brahm. Songs:
ALL FOR YOU; HAVE YOU SEEN JOE?; SO CLOSE TO PARADISE and WHY DO I WAKE UP SO EARLY IN THE MORNING? by Lionel Newman and Charles Henderson; GAY LOVE by Charles Henderson and Bernard Hermann.

HERE COME THE CO-EDS

A Universal picture starring Abbott and Costello in a cast that included Peggy Ryan, and directed by Edgar Fairchild. Songs by Jack Brooks and Edgar Fairchild:
I DON'T CARE IF I NEVER DREAM AGAIN; SOME DAY WE WILL REMEMBER; A NEW DAY; THE HEAD OF THE CLASS; LET'S PLAY HOUSE; JUMPING ON A SATURDAY NIGHT and HURRAY FOR OUR SIDE.

HONEYMOON AHEAD

A Universal picture starring Allan Jones and Grace McDonald, and directed by Reginald LeBorg. Songs by Everett Carter and Milton Rosen:
ROUND THE BEND; TIME WILL TELL; HOW LOVELY and NOW AND ALWAYS.

I'LL TELL THE WORLD

A Universal picture filmed with a cast headed by Lee Tracy, Brenda Joyce and June Preisser, and directed by Leslie Goodwins. Songs:
MOONLIGHT FIESTA by Harry Tobias and Al Sherman; SLAP POLKA by Paul Francis Webster and Harry Revel; WALK

A LITTLE FASTER by Dave Franklin; WHERE THE PRAIRIE MEETS THE SKY by Everett Carter and Milton Rosen.

INCENDIARY BLONDE

A Paramount picture starring Betty Hutton in a cast that included Arturo de Cordova, Charles Ruggles and Barry Fitzgerald, and directed by George Marshall. Songs: RAGTIME COWBOY JOE by Maurice Abrahams and Lewis F. Muir; IDA by Eddie Leonard; OH BY JINGO OH BY GEE by Lew Brown and Albert Von Tilzer; WHAT DO YOU WANT TO MAKE THOSE EYES AT ME FOR? by Howard Johnson, Joseph McCarthy and Jimmy Monaco; ROW, ROW, ROW by William Jerome and Jimmy Monaco; DARKTOWN STRUTTERS' BALL by Shelton Brooks; IT HAD TO BE YOU by Gus Kahn and Isham Jones; SWEET GENEVIEVE by Henry Tucker and George Cooper.

MEXICANA

A Republic picture starring Tito Guizar and Constance Moore, and directed by Alfred Santell. Songs: TIME OUT FOR DREAMING; DE CORAZON A CORAZON; CHILDREN'S SONG; MEXICANA; LUPITA; SEE MEXICO and HEARTLESS by Ned Washington and Gabriel Ruiz; SOMEWHERE THERE'S A RAINBOW by Ned Washington and Walter Scharf.

NAUGHTY NINETIES, THE

A Universal picture starring Abbott and Costello in a cast that included Alan Curtis and Rita Johnson, and directed by Jean Yarbrough. Songs: ROLLIN' DOWN THE RIVER and UNCLE TOM'S CABIN by Jack Brooks and Edgar Fairchild; ON A SUNDAY AFTERNOON by Andrew B. Sterling and Harry Von Tilzer; I'D LEAVE MY HAPPY HOME FOR YOU by Will Heelan and Harry Von Tilzer; NORA MALONE by Junie McCree and Albert Von Tilzer.

ON STAGE EVERYBODY

A Universal picture filmed with a cast headed by Peggy Ryan, Johnny Coy and Jack Oakie, and directed by Jean Yarbrough. Songs: FOR HIM NO LOVE; I'M SO AT HOME WITH YOU; IT'LL ALL COME OUT IN THE WASH and IT WAS THE SULLIVANS by Inez James and Sidney Miller; STUFF LIKE THAT by Ray Evans and Jay Livingston; PUT, PUT, PUT YOUR ARMS AROUND ME by Mann

Curtis, Al Hoffman and Jerry Livingston; TAKE ME IN YOUR ARMS by Mitchell Parish, Fred Markush and Fritz Rotter; WHAT DO I HAVE TO DO TO BE A STAR? by Bobby Kroll; DANCE WITH A DOLLY (WITH A HOLE IN HER STOCKING) by Terry Shand, Jimmy Eaton and Mickey Leader.

OUT OF THIS WORLD

A Paramount picture starring Veronica Lake and Dianna Lynn in a cast that included Cass Daley and Parkyakarkas, and directed by Hal Walker. Songs: JUNE COMES AROUND EVERY YEAR and OUT OF THIS WORLD by Johnny Mercer and Harold Arlen; I'D RATHER BE ME by Eddie Cherkose, Felix Bernard and Sam Coslow; IT TAKES A LITTLE BIT MORE; ALL I DO IS BEAT THAT GOL DARN DRUM and GHOST OF MR. CHOPIN by Sam Coslow; SAILOR WITH AN 8-DAY PASS by Ben Raleigh and Bernie Wayne.

PAN-AMERICANA

An RKO picture filmed with a cast headed by Phillip Terry, Audrey Long, Robert Benchley, Eve Arden and Ernest Truex, and directed by John H. Auer. Musical numbers: RUMBA MATUMBA; MAR (STARS IN YOUR EYES); GUADALAJARA; LA MORINE DE MI COPLA; NEORI LEONG and BARAMBA by Mort Greene and Gabriel Ruiz; BA-BA-LU by Bob Russell and Marguerita Lecuona.

RHAPSODY IN BLUE

A Warner Brothers' picture based on the life of George Gershwin with Robert Alda playing the title role in a cast that included Joan Leslie, Alexis Smith, Charles Coburn, Oscar Levant, Paul Whiteman and his orchestra, Al Jolson, George White and Hazel Scott, and directed by Irving Rapper. Musical numbers by George Gershwin with lyrics by Ira Gershwin except in those cases where names of authors are given in parentheses: SWANEE (Irving Caesar); YANKEE DOODLE BLUES (Irving Caesar); 'S WONDERFUL; SOMEBODY LOVES ME; THE MAN I LOVE; EMBRACEABLE YOU; SUMMERTIME; IT AIN'T NECESSARILY SO; OH LADY BE GOOD; I GOT RHYTHM; LOVE WALKED IN; CLAP YO' HANDS; DO IT AGAIN; I'LL BUILD A STAIRWAY TO PARADISE (Arthur Frances and B. G. DeSylva); LIZA; SOMEONE TO WATCH OVER ME; BIDIN' MY TIME; DELI-

CHIOUS; I GOT PLENTY O' NUTTIN' and RHAPSODY IN BLUE and AN AMERICAN IN PARIS (both instrumental).

ROAD TO UTOPIA, THE

A Paramount picture starring Bing Crosby, Bob Hope and Dorothy Lamour, and directed by Hal Walker. Songs by Johnny Burke and Jimmy Van Heusen:
PUT IT THERE PAL; GOOD TIME CHARLEY; WELCOME TO MY DREAM; IT'S ANYBODY'S SPRING; ROAD TO MOROCCO; WOULD YOU? and PERSONALITY.

SEE MY LAWYER

A Universal picture starring Olsen and Johnson, and directed by Edward F. Cline. Songs:
WE'RE MAKING A MILLION; TAKE IT AWAY and IT'S CIRCUS TIME by Everett Carter and Milton Rosen; MAN ON THE LITTLE WHITE KEYS by Joe Greene and Nat "King" Cole; FUZZY WUZZY by Bob Bell and Roy Branker; PENNY ARCADE by Dave Franklin.

SENORITA FROM THE WEST

A Universal picture starring Allan Jones and Bonita Granville, and directed by Frank Strayer. Songs:
LOU, LOU LOUISIANA by Everett Carter and Milton Rosen; LONELY LOVE by Everett Carter and Ray Sinatra; WHAT A CHANGE IN THE WEATHER by Kim Gannon and Walter Kent.

SHADY LADY

A Universal picture filmed with a cast headed by Charles Coburn, Robert Paige, Ginny Simms, Alan Curtis and Martha O'Driscoll, and directed by George Waggner. Musical numbers:
IN LOVE WITH LOVE and MAM'-SELLE IS ON HER WAY by George Waggner and Milton Rosen; TANGO by Edgar Fairchild.

SING YOUR WAY HOME

An RKO picture starring Jack Haley, Marcy McGuire and Anne Jeffreys, and directed by Anthony Mann. Songs by Herb Magidson and Allie Wrubel:
I'LL BUY THAT DREAM; HEAVEN IS A PLACE CALLED HOME; SEVEN O'CLOCK IN THE MORNING and WHO DID IT?

SONG FOR MISS JULIE, A

A Republic picture filmed with a cast headed by Shirley Ross, Barton Hepburn,

Jane Farrar, Roger Clark and Cheryl Walker, and directed by William Rowland. Songs by Marla Shelton and Louis Herscher:
THAT'S WHAT I LIKE ABOUT YOU; IT ALL COULD HAVE HAPPENED BEFORE; THE COUNTRY AIN'T THE COUNTRY ANYMORE; SWEET SUNDAY and I LOVE TO REMEMBER.

SONG OF THE SARONG

A Universal picture starring Nancy Kelly and William Gargan in a cast that included Eddie Quillan and Fuzzy Knight, and directed by Harold Young. Songs:
RIDIN' ON THE CREST OF A CLOUD and PIPED PIERES OF THE U. S. A. by Jack Brooks; ISLAND OF THE MOON and LOVELY LUANA by Don Raye and Gene DePaul.

STATE FAIR

A 20th Century-Fox picture filmed with a cast headed by Jeanne Crain, Dana Andrews, Dick Haymes, Vivian Blaine, Charles Winninger, Fay Bainter, Donald Meek, Frank McHugh and Henry Morgan, and directed by Walter Lang. Songs by Oscar Hammerstein II and Richard Rodgers:
OUR STATE FAIR; THAT'S FOR ME; IT MIGHT AS WELL BE SPRING; ALL I OWE TO I-O-WAY; ISN'T IT KINDA FUN? and IT'S A GRAND NIGHT FOR SINGING.

STORK CLUB

A Paramount picture starring Betty Hutton in a cast that included Barry Fitgerald, Don DeFore, Andy Russell and Robert Benchley, and directed by Hal Walker. Songs:
DOCTOR, LAWYER, INDIAN CHIEF and BALTIMORE ORIOLE by Paul Francis Webster and Hoagy Carmichael; A SQUARE IN THE SOCIAL CIRCLE by Ray Evans and Jay Livingston; IF I HAD A DOZEN HEARTS by Paul Francis Webster and Harry Revel; LOVE ME by Sammy Cahn and Jule Styne.

SUNBONNET SUE

A Monogram picture starring Gale Storm and Phil Regan, and directed by Ralph Murphy. Songs:
WAIT FOR THE RAINBOW by Ralph Murphy and J. Harold Lewis; SCHOOL DAYS and SUNBONNET SUE by Will Cobb and Gus Edwards; THE BOWERY by Charles H. Hoyt and Percy Gaunt; YIP I ADDY I AY by Will Cobb and James H. Flynn; YOO HOO, AIN'T YOU COMIN' OUT TONIGHT? by Ren Shields and

Henrietta Melson; BY THE LIGHT OF THE SILVERY MOON by Ed Madden and Gus Edwards; IF I HAD MY WAY by Lou Klein and James Kendis; WHILE STROLLING THROUGH THE PARK ONE DAY by Ed Haley.

THAT'S THE SPIRIT

A Universal picture filmed with a cast headed by Peggy Ryan, Jack Oakie, June Vincent and Johnny Coy, and directed by Charles Lamont. Songs:
FELLA WITH A FLUTE and OH, OH, OH by Inez James and Sidney Miller; EVENIN' STAR and NO MATTER WHERE YOU ARE by Jack Brooks and H. J. Salter; NOLA by Felix Arndt; HOW COME YOU DO ME LIKE YOU DO? by Roy Bergere and Gene Austin; BABY WON'T YOU PLEASE COME HOME? by Clarence Williams and Charles Warfield.

THRILL OF A ROMANCE

An M-G-M picture starring Van Johnson and Esther Williams in a cast that included Henry Travers, Spring Byington and Lauritz Melchior, and directed by Richard Thorpe. Songs:
PLEASE DON'T SAY "NO" (SAY MAYBE) by Ralph Freed and Sammy Fain; I SHOULD CARE by Sammy Cahn, Alex Stordahl and Paul Weston; LONELY NIGHT by George Stoll and Richard Connell; VIVE L'AMOUR by George Stoll, Ralph Blane and Kay Thompson; SERENADE by Jack Meskill and Earl Brent.

TONIGHT AND EVERY NIGHT

A Columbia picture starring Rita Hayworth in a cast that included Janet Blair, Lee Bowman, Marc Platt and Professor Lamberti, and directed by Victor Saville. Songs by Sammy Cahn and Jule Styne:
ANYWHERE; THE HEART OF A CITY; TONIGHT AND EVERY NIGHT; WHAT DOES AN ENGLISH GIRL THINK OF A YANK? THE BOY I LEFT BEHIND and YOU EXCITE ME.

UNDER WESTERN SKIES

A Universal picture filmed with a cast headed by Martha O'Driscoll, Noah Beery Jr., Leo Carrillo and Leon Errol, and directed by Jean Yarbrough. Songs by Everett Carter and Milton Rosen:
UNDER WESTERN SKIES; DON'T GO MAKING SPEECHES; OH, YOU KID!; AN OLD-FASHIONED GIRL and A COWBOY'S PRAYER.

WHERE DO WE GO FROM HERE?

A 20th Century-Fox picture starring Fred MacMurray, Joan Leslie and June Haver, and directed by Gregory Ratoff. Songs by Ira Gershwin and Kurt Weill:
IF LOVE REMAINS; ALL AT ONCE; SONG OF THE RHINELAND; CHRISTOPHER COLUMBUS and THE NINA, THE PINTA AND THE SANTA MARIA.

WHY GIRLS LEAVE HOME

A Producers Releasing Corporation picture starring Lola Lane and Sheldon Leonard, and directed by William Berke. Songs by Ray Evans and Jay Livingston:
THE CAT AND THE CANARY; CALL ME and WHAT AM I SAYING?

YOLANDA AND THE THIEF

An M-G-M picture starring Fred Astaire and Lucille Bremer in a cast that included Frank Morgan, Mildred Natwick and Mary Nash, and directed by Victor Minnelli. Songs by Arthur Freed and Harry Warren:
THIS IS A DAY FOR LOVE; ANGEL; WILL YOU MARRY ME?; YOLANDA; COFFEE TIME and CANDLELIGHT.

Feature Films With Songs

AFFAIRS OF SUSAN, THE

A Paramount picture filmed with a cast headed by Joan Fontaine, George Brent, Dennis O'Keefe, Don DeFore, Rita Johnson and Walter Abel, and directed by William Nigh. Song by E. Y. Harburg and Franz Waxman:
SOMETHING IN MY HEART

ALONG CAME JONES

An RKO picture starring Gary Cooper and Loretta Young in a cast that included Dan Duryea and William Demarest, and directed by Stuart Heisler. Song by Arthur Lange and Al Stewart:
ROUND AND ROUND

BELLS OF ST. MARY'S, THE

An RKO picture starring Ingrid Bergman and Bing Crosby in a cast that included Henry Travers and William Gargan, and directed by Leo McCarey. Songs:
AREN'T YOU GLAD YOU'RE YOU? by Johnny Burke and Jimmy Van Heusen; IN THE LAND OF BEGINNING AGAIN by Grant Clarke and George W. Meyer;

THE BELLS OF ST. MARY'S by Douglas Furber and A. Emmett Adams; AVE MARIA.

BIG SHOW-OFF

A Republic picture starring Arthur Lake and Dale Evans, and directed by Howard Bretherton. Song by Dave Oppenheim and Roy Ingraham:
CLEO FROM RIO

BLONDE FROM BROOKLYN

A Columbia picture starring Robert Stanton and Lynn Merrick, and directed by Del Lord. Song by Sid Robin and Teddy Walters:
MY BABY SAID YES

CHRISTMAS IN CONNECTICUT

A Warner Brothers' picture starring Barbara Stanwyck and Dennis Morgan in a cast that included Sydney Greenstreet and Reginald Gardiner, and directed by Peter Godfrey. Song by Jack Scholl and M. K. Jerome:
THE WISH THAT I WISH TONIGHT

CONFIDENTIAL AGENT

A Warner Brothers' picture starring Charles Boyer and Lauren Bacall, and directed by Herman Schumlin. Songs:
TIP-TOE THROUGH THE TULIPS by Al Dubin and Joe Burke; LOVE IS THE SWEETEST THING by Ray Noble.

CRIME, INC.

A Producers Releasing Corporation picture filmed with a cast headed by Leo Carrillo, Tom Neal, Martha Tilton and Lionel Atwill, and directed by Lew Landers. Songs by Ray Evans and Jay Livingston:
I'M GUILTY and LONESOME LITTLE CAMERA GIRL.

DANGEROUS PARTNERS

An M-G-M picture filmed with a cast headed by James Craig, Signo Hasse, Edmund Gwenn and Audrey Totter, and directed by Edward L. Kahn. Song by Earl Brent:
HIS

DUFFY'S TAVERN

A Paramount picture starring Ed Gardner in a cast that included Betty Hutton, Bing Crosby, Paulette Goddard, Dorothy Lamour, Eddie Bracken, Sonny Tufts, Barry Fitzgerald and Veronica Lake, and directed by Hal Walker. Songs:
THE HARD WAY by Johnny Burke and Jimmy Van Heusen; YOU CAN'T BLAME A GIRL FOR TRYIN' by Ben Raleigh and Bernie Wayne.

EADIE WAS A LADY

A Columbia picture filmed with a cast headed by Ann Miller, Joe Besser, William Wright, Jeff Donnell and Hal MacIntyre and his orchestra, and directed by Arthur Dreifuss. Songs:
TABBY THE CAT by Harold Dickinson and Howard Gibeling; SHE'S A GYPSY FROM BROOKLYN by L. Wolfe Gilbert and Ben Oakland.

FALLEN ANGEL

A 20th Century-Fox picture starring Alice Faye, Dana Andrews and Linda Darnell in a cast that included Charles Bickford, Anne Revere, Bruce Cabot and John Carradine, and directed by Otto Preminger. Song by Kermit Goell and David Raskin:
SLOWLY

FLAME OF THE BARBARY COAST

A Republic picture starring John Wayne and Ann Dvorak in a cast that included Joseph Schildkraut and William Frawley, and directed by Joseph Kane. Songs:
HAVE A HEART and BABY BLUE EYES by Jack Elliott; CUBANOLA GLIDE and CARRIE MARRY HARRY (IS A BEAUTIFUL RHYME) by Vincent Bryan and Harry Von Tilzer.

GAY SENORITA

A Columbia picture starring Jinx Falkenburg in a cast that included Jim Bannon, Steve Cochran and Corinna Mura, and directed by Arthur Dreifuss. Song by Don George and Serge Walter:
BUENOS NOCHES

GIRLS OF THE BIG HOUSE

A Republic picture filmed with a cast that included Lynne Roberts, Virginia Christine, Marian Martin, Adela Mura and Richard Powers, and directed by George Archinbaud. Song by Inez James and Jack Elliott:
THERE'S A MAN IN MY LIFE

GREAT JOHN L, THE

A United Artists' picture starring Greg McClure, Linda Darnell and Barbara Britton, and directed by Frank Tuttle. Song by Johnny Burke and Jimmy Van Heusen:
A FRIEND OF YOURS

HER HIGHNESS AND THE BELLBOY

An M-G-M picture starring Hedy Lamarr, Robert Walker and June Allyson in a cast that included Rags Ragland, and directed by Richard Thorpe. Song by Johnny Mercer:
DREAM

HOW DO YOU DO?

A Producers Releasing Corporation picture filmed with a cast headed by Bert Gordon, Harry Von Zell and Cheryl Walker, and directed by Ralph Murphy. Song:
BOOGIE WOOGIE CINDY by Paul Francis Webster and Hal Borne.

IT'S A PLEASURE

An RKO picture starring Sonja Henie and Michael O'Shea, and directed by William A. Seiter. Song by Edgar Leslie and Walter 'Donaldson:
ROMANCE

JOHNNY ANGEL

An RKO picture starring George Raft and Claire Trevor in a cast that included Signe Hasso and Hoagy Carmichael, and directed by Edwin L. Marin. Song by Paul Francis Webster and Hoagy Carmichael:
MEMPHIS IN JUNE

LADY ON A TRAIN

A Universal picture starring Deanna Durbin in a cast that included Ralph Bellamy, Edward Everett Horton, George Coulouris, Patricia Morison and Dan Duryea, and directed by Charles Davis. Songs:
GIVE ME A LITTLE KISS, WILL YA, HUH? by Roy Turk, Jack Smith and Maceo Pinkard; NIGHT AND DAY by Cole Porter.

LOVE LETTERS

A Paramount picture starring Jennifer Jones and Joseph Cotten in a cast that included Ann Richards and Anita Louise, and directed by William Dieterle. Song by Victor Young:
LOVE LETTERS

MASQUERADE IN MEXICO

A Paramount picture starring Dorothy Lamour and Arturo De Cordova in a cast that included Patric Knowles and Ann Dvorak, and directed by Marshall Leisen. Songs:
FOREVER MINE by Bob Russell, Eddie Lisbona and Maria T. Lara; MASQUERADE IN MEXICO by Ben Raleigh and Bernie Wayne.

MISS SUSIE SLAGLE'S

A Paramount picture starring Veronica Lake and Sonny Tufts in a cast that included Joan Caulfield, Lillian Gish, Ray Collins and Billy DeWolfe, and directed by John Berry. Song by Ben Raleigh and Bernie Wayne:
LITTLE ELIZA

MR. EMMANUEL

A United Artists' picture filmed with a cast headed by Felix Aylmer, Greta Gynt, Walter Rilla, Peter Mullins and Ursula Jeans, and directed by Harold French. Song by Mischa Spoliansky:
I DON'T KNOW YOU (YOU DON'T KNOW ME)

MURDER, HE SAYS

A Paramount picture starring Fred MacMurray in a cast that included Helen Walker and Marjorie Main, and directed by George Marshall. Song by Teepee Mitchell and Lew Porter:
MY LIFE IS NO BED OF ROSES

NOB HILL

A 20th Century-Fox picture starring George Raft and Joan Bennett in a cast that included Vivian Blaine, Peggy Ann Garner and Smith and Dale, and directed by Henry Hathaway. Songs by Harold Adamson and Jimmy McHugh:
I DON'T CARE WHO KNOWS IT and I WALKED RIGHT IN WITH MY EYES WIDE OPEN.

PICTURE OF DORIAN GRAY, THE

An M-G-M picture starring George Sanders and Angela Lansbury, and directed by Albert Lewin. Song by C. W. Murphy, William Hargreaves and Dan O'Brien:
GOODBYE LITTLE YELLOW BIRD

PILLOW TO POST

A Warner Brothers' picture starring Ida Lupino and Sydney Greenstreet, and directed by Vincent Sherman. Song by Ted Koehler and Burton Lane:
WHATCHA SAY?

SAN ANTONIO

A Warner Brothers' picture starring Errol Flynn and Alexis Smith, and directed by David Butler. Songs:
SOME SUNDAY MORNING by Ted Koehler, M. K. Jerome and Ray Heindorf; SOMEWHERE IN MONTEREY by Jack Scholl and Charles Kisco; PUT YOUR LITTLE RIGHT FOOT OUT by Larry Spier.

SARATOGA TRUNK

A Warner Brothers' picture starring Gary Cooper and Ingrid Bergman, and directed by Sam Wood. Songs by Charles Tobias and Max Steiner:
AS LONG AS I LIVE and GOIN' HOME

STORY OF G.I. JOE, THE

A United Artists' picture starring Burgess

Meredith and Robert Mitchum, and directed by William A. Wellman. Musical numbers:
LINDA by Jack Lawrence and Ann Ronell; I'M COMING BACK and INFANTRY MARCH by Ann Ronell.

THAT NIGHT WITH YOU
A Universal picture starring Franchot Tone and Susanna Foster in a cast that included David Bruce and Louise Allbritton, and directed by William A. Seiter. Song by Jack Brooks and Hans Salter:
ONCE UPON A DREAM

THEY WERE EXPENDABLE
An M-G-M picture starring Robert Montgomery, John Wayne and Donna Reed in a cast that included Jack Holt and Ward Bond, and directed by John Ford. Song by Earl Brent and Herbert Stothart:
TO THE END OF THE END OF THE WORLD

THIS LOVE OF OURS
A Universal picture starring Merle Oberon, Charles Coburn and Claude Rains, and directed by William Dieterle. Songs by Jack Brooks and Hans Salter:

THEY WENT TO GET MARRIED and DANCE WITH ME

TOO YOUNG TO KNOW
A Warner Brothers' picture filmed with a cast headed by June Leslie, Robert Hutton and Dolores Moran, and directed by Frederick de Cordova. Song by Billy Rose, E. Y. Harburg and Harold Arlen:
IT'S ONLY A PAPER MOON

WEEKEND AT THE WALDORF
An M-G-M picture starring Ginger Rogers, Lana Turner, Walter Pidgeon and Van Johnson in a cast that included Adolphe Menjou. Keenan Wynn, Robert Benchley and Xavier Cugat and his orchestra, and directed by Robert Z. Leonard. Musical numbers by Sammy Fain:
AND THERE YOU ARE (lyrics by Ted Koehler) and GUADALAJARA

WONDER MAN
An RKO picture starring Danny Kaye in a cast headed by Virginia Mayo and Vera-Ellen, and directed by Bruce Humberstone. Musical numbers:
SO IN LOVE by Leo Robin and David Rose; BALI BOOGIE by Sylvia Fine.

Western Films With Songs

ALONG THE NAVAJO TRAIL
A Republic picture starring Roy Rogers in a cast that included Gabby Hayes, Dale Evans, Bob Nolan and the Sons of the Pioneers, and directed by Frank McDonald. Song by Bob Nolan:
COOL WATER

DON'T FENCE ME IN
A Republic picture starring Roy Rogers in a cast that included Gabby Hayes, Dale Evans, Lucille Gleason, Bob Nolan and the Sons of the Pioneers, and directed by John English. Songs:
DON'T FENCE ME IN by Cole Porter; TUMBLIN' TUMBLEWEEDS by Bob Nolan; MY LITTLE BUCKAROO by Jack Scholl and M. K. Jerome; LAST ROUNDUP by Billy Hill; A KISS GOOD NIGHT by Floyd Victor, R. N. Herman and Freddie Slack; CHOO-CHOO POLKA by Mike Shore and Zeke Manners; ALONG THE NAVAJO TRAIL by Eddie DeLange, Larry Markes and Dick Charles; LIGHTS OF OLD SANTA FE by Jack Elliott.

MAN FROM OKLAHOMA, THE
A Republic picture starring Roy Rogers in a cast that included Gabby Hayes, Dale Evans, Roger Pryor, Bob Nolan and the

Sons of the Pioneers, and directed by Frank McDonald. Songs:
CHEERO, CHEERO, CHEROKEE by Gordon Forster; FOR YOU AND ME by Kim Gannon and Walter Kent.

MARKED FOR MURDER
A Producers Releasing Corporation picture filmed with a cast headed by Tex Ritter, Dave O'Brien, Guy Wilkerson and Marilyn McConnell, and directed by Elmer Clifton. Songs:
LONG TIME AGO by Tex Ritter and Frank Harford; TEARS OF REGRET by Don Weston.

PHANTOM OF THE PLAINS
A Republic picture filmed with a cast headed by Bill Elliott, Bobby Blake and Alice Fleming, and directed by Leslie Selander. Songs:
THE FIDDLER AND HIS BOW and IT'S THE PRAIRIE CALLIN' ME by Johnny Lange and Lew Porter; RIDIN' THE TRAIL TO HOME by Johnny Marvin.

SONG OF OLD WYOMING
A Producers Releasing Corporation picture starring Eddie Dean and Jennifer Holt,

and directed by Robert Emmett. Songs:
MY HERDIN' SONG by Eddie Dean
and Milt Mabie; WILD PRAIRIE ROSE
by Eddie Dean and Carl Hoefle; HILLS
OF OLD WYOMING by Earl Robinson
and Ralph Rainger.

SPRINGTIME IN TEXAS
A Monogram picture filmed with a cast
headed by Jimmy Wakely, Lee 'Lasses
White and Dennis Moore. Song by Jimmy
Wakely:
YOU'RE THE SWEETEST ROSE IN
TEXAS

SUNSET IN EL DORADO
A Republic picture starring Roy Rogers
in a cast that included Gabby Hayes, Dale
Evans, Bob Nolan and the Sons of the Pioneers, and directed by Frank McDonald.

THE CALL OF THE PRAIRIE and
IT'S NO USE by Ken Carson; BELLE
OF EL DORADO and THE LADY WHO
WOULDN'T SAY YES by Jack Elliott;
GO WEST, GO WEST YOUNG MAN by
Gordon Forster.

UTAH
A Republic picture starring Roy Rogers
in a cast that included Gabby Hayes and
Dale Evans, and directed by John English.
Songs:
WELCOME HOME, MISS BRYANT by
Ken Carson; THANK DIXIE FOR ME
by Dave Franklin; FIVE LITTLE MILES
by Bob Nolan; UTAH TRAIL by Bob Pal-
mer; LONESOME COWBOY BLUES by
Tim Spencer; BENEATH A UTAH SKY
by Glenn Spencer.

Howard Keel and Kathryn Grayson in a scene from *Show Boat*

1 9 4 6

An Ex-Champ Who's "All Washed Up" Regains His Title

He was the forgotten man of the talkies with a yen to make a comeback, and his reception by Hollywood's top brass came out of the deep-freeze units. The three Warner brothers, whom he had helped to reach heights of eminence in the film capital twenty years before, couldn't see him with a radar range-finder, and they weren't alone in "being in conference" when he asked for an interview. Everybody was convinced he was through, all washed up as a box-office attraction—that is everybody but himself.

Finally, he was given a pacifier, a polite brushoff—the closing spot on the bill of a Sunday night benefit show staged at the Hillcrest Country Club in Beverly Hills, and it was one oclock in the morning before he went on. The acts that had preceded him were out of the top talent drawer, the cream of the screen and radio crop, and tough to follow. But when this ex-champ started punching, he had the audience wide awake, sitting on the edge of their chairs and yelling for more! more! more! And the success of this one-man show convinced Harry Cohn, head of Paramount Pictures, Al Jolson was worth a gamble.

This hunch paid off handsomely. *The Jolson Story* in which the Mammy Singer got a photogenic assist from Larry Parks, grossed $8,000,000 at the box-office, just a half-million dollars shy of the all-time record of *This Is The Army* and equalling the take of *Going My Way,* and was voted the second best picture of a year in which the poignant post-war drama *The Best Years Of Our Lives* took first place by the narrow margin of 59 votes.

What makes the comeback of Al Jolson all the more notable is that it was scored in a year packed with outstanding musicals, seven of which joined *The Jolson Story* in the Golden Circle of films grossing $4,000,000 or more. Two of these box-office bonanzas were biographical pictures that paid tribute to songwriters: *Night And Day* in which Cary Grant played the role of Cole Porter and *Till The Clouds Roll By* with Robert Walker portraying Jerome Kern, whose last screen musical, *Centennial Summer,* was both an artistic and financial triumph and marked by such enduring songs as *All Through The Day* and *In Love In Vain.*

Irving Berlin's songs, some new and some old, plus the box-office magnetism of Bing Crosby and Fred Astaire, put *Blue Skies* in the Golden Circle in company with *The Kid From Brooklyn,* Sammy Kaye's starring picture; *The Harvey Girls* in which Judy Garland introduced Harry Warren's third Oscar-winning song, *On The Atchison, Topeka And The Santa Fe; Ziegfeld Follies,* filmed with a cast of Warner Brothers' stars and notable for two hit songs, *This Love Of Mine* and *Love;* and *Holiday In Mexico,* which was aimed at the pocketbooks of those partial to Xavier Cugat and his Latin-American sambas and rhumbas.

Close up to these seven box-office champions of 1946 were *Three Little Girls In Blue* in which June Haver, Vivian Blaine and Celeste Holm shared headline billing, and *The Time, The Place And The Girl* with three Hit Parade favorites by Leo Robin and Arthur Schwartz: *On A Rainy Night In Rio, A Gal In Calico* and *Oh But I Do,* while Walt Disney was credited with two four-bell productions: *Song Of The South,* the first Disney picture to be filmed with live actors, and *Make Mine Music* in which Nelson Eddy, Dinah Shore and Benny Goodman's orchestra provided the musical background for the capers of the cartoon characters.

Sammy Cahn and Jule Styne upheld the honors of the Johnny-Come-Latelies to the Hollywood branch of Tin Pan Alley by writing a smash song hit, *Give Me Five Minutes More,* for *The Sweetheart of Sigma Chi,* and providing music and lyrics for *Cinderella Jones, Tars And Spars* and *The Kid From Brooklyn,* but in Hollywood's achievement book, the top headline billing for 1946 went to an old-timer—Al Jolson, Mr. Show Business himself—the guy who came back with a resounding bang.

Musicals

BAMBOO BLONDE
An RKO picture starring Frances Langford and Ralph Edwards, and directed by Anthony Mann. Songs by Mort Greene and Lew Pollack:
MOONLIGHT OVER THE ISLANDS; ALONG ABOUT EVENING; I'M GOOD FOR NOTHING BUT LOVE and I'M DREAMING OUT LOUD.

BETTY CO-ED
A Columbia picture filmed with a cast headed by Jean Porter, Shirley Mills and William Mason, and directed by Arthur Dreifuss. Songs:
PUT THE BLAME ON MAME and YOU GOTTA DO WHAT YOU GOTTA DO by Doris Fisher and Allan Roberts; BETTY CO-ED by J. P. Fogarty and Rudy Vallee.

BLUE SKIES
An M-G-M picture starring Bob Hope and Bing Crosby in a cast that featured Joan Caulfield, and directed by Stuart Heisler. Songs by Irving Berlin:
YOU KEEP COMING BACK LIKE A SONG; (RUNNING AROUND IN CIR-CLES) GETTING NOWHERE; SERE-NADE TO AN OLD-FASHIONED GIRL; A COUPLE OF SONG-AND-DANCE MEN; BLUE SKIES; I'LL SEE YOU IN C-U-B-A; EVERYBODY STEP; ALL BY MYSELF; I'VE GOT MY CAPTAIN WORKING FOR ME NOW and PUT-TIN' ON THE RITZ.

CENTENNIAL SUMMER
A 20th Century-Fox picture starring Jeanne Crain, Linda Darnell and Cornel Wilde in a cast that included Walter Brennan and Constance Bennett, and directed by Otto Preminger. Songs by Leo Robin, Oscar Hammerstein II and Jerome Kern:
IN LOVE IN VAIN; ALL THROUGH THE DAY; CINDERELLA SUE; TWO HEARTS ARE BETTER THAN ONE and UP WITH THE LARK.

CINDERELLA JONES
A Warner Brothers' picture starring Joan Leslie and Robert Alda in a cast that included Julie Bishop and Edward Everett Horton, and directed by Busby Berkeley. Songs by Sammy Cahn and Jule Styne:
IF YOU'RE WAITIN' I'M WAITIN' TOO; CINDERELLA JONES; YOU NEVER KNOW WHERE YOU'RE GOIN' TILL YOU GET THERE; and WHEN THE ONE YOU LOVE SIMPLY WON'T LOVE BACK.

CROSS MY HEART

A Paramount picture starring Betty Hutton and Sonny Tufts in a cast that included Rhys Williams, and directed by John Berry. Songs:
THAT LITTLE DREAM GOT NOWHERE; LOVE IS THE DARNDEST THING; HOW DO YOU DO IT?; DOES BABY FEEL ALL RIGHT? and IT HASN'T BEEN CHILLY IN CHILE by Johnny Burke and Jimmy Van Heusen; CROSS MY HEART by Larry Neill and Robert E. Dolan.

CUBAN PETE

A Universal picture starring Desi Arnaz in a cast that included Ethel Smith and Joan Fulton, and directed by Jean Yarbrough. Musical numbers:
EL CUBANCHERO by Rafael Hernandez; LULLABY by Bill Driggs; THE BREEZE AND I by Al Stillman and Ernesto Lecuona; AFTER TONIGHT by Jack Brooks and Desi Arnaz; CUBAN PETE by Jose Norman.

DO YOU LOVE ME?

A 20th Century-Fox picture starring Maureen O'Hara and Dick Haymes in a cast that included Reginald Gardiner and Harry James and his orchestra, and directed by Gregory Ratoff. Songs:
I DIDN'T MEAN A WORD I SAID by Harold Adamson and Jimmy McHugh; AS IF I DIDN'T HAVE ENOUGH ON MY MIND by Charles Henderson, Lionel Newman and Harry James; MOONLIGHT PROPAGANDA by Herb Magidson and Matt Malneck; DO YOU LOVE ME? by Harry Ruby.

DOWN MISSOURI WAY

A Producers Releasing Corporation picture filmed with a cast headed by Martha O'Driscoll, John Carradine and Eddie Dean, and directed by Josef Berne. Songs by Kim Gannon and Walter Kent:
JUST CAN'T GET THAT GUY; BIG TOWN GAL; IF SOMETHING DOESN'T HAPPEN SOON; ROSE OF THE OZARKS; NEVER KNEW I COULD SING; I'M SO IN LOVE WITH YOU; MONKEY BUSINESS and MISSOURI HAYRIDE.

EARL CARROLL SKETCH BOOK

A Republic picture starring Constance Moore and William Marshall, and directed by Albert S. Rogell. Songs by Sammy Cahn and Jule Styne:
LADY WITH A MOP; I'VE NEVER FORGOTTEN; OH, HENRY!; WHAT MAKES YOU BEAUTIFUL, BEAUTIFUL? and I WAS SILLY, I WAS HEADSTRONG, I WAS IMPETUOUS.

EASY TO WED

An M-G-M picture starring Esther Williams and Van Johnson in a cast that included Lucille Ball and Keenan Wynn, and directed by Eddie Buzzell. Songs:
EASY TO WED by Ted Duncan and Johnny Green; GOOSEY-LUCY and IT SHOULDN'T HAPPEN TO A DUCK by Robert Franklin and Johnny Green; CONTINENTAL POLKA and (TELL YOU WHAT I'M GONNA DO) GONNA FALL IN LOVE WITH YOU by Ralph Blane and Johnny Green; COME CLOSER TO ME by Osvaldo Farres.

FREDDIE STEPS OUT

A Monogram picture starring Freddie Stewart and June Preisser, and directed by Arthur Dreifuss. Songs:
LET'S DROP THE SUBJECT by Hal Collins and Joe Sanns; DON'T BLAME ME by Dorothy Fields and Jimmy McHugh; PATIENCE AND FORTITUDE by Billy Moore Jr. and Blackie Warren.

HARVEY GIRLS, THE

An M-G-M picture starring Judy Garland in a cast that included John Hodiak, Ray Bolger, Angela Lansbury, Preston Foster, Virginia O'Brien, Kenny Baker and Marjorie Main, and directed by George Sidney. Songs by Johnny Mercer and Harry Warren:
ON THE ATCHINSON, TOPEKA AND THE SANTA FE; IN THE VALLEY WHEN THE EVENING SUN GOES DOWN; WAIT AND SEE; SWING YOUR PARTNER ROUND AND ROUND; THE WILD, WILD WEST and IT'S A GREAT BIG WORLD.

HIGH SCHOOL HERO

A Monogram picture starring Freddie Stewart and June Preisser, and directed by Arthur Dreifuss. Musical numbers:
FAIRVIEW HIGH by Phil Grayson; SOUTHPAW SERENADE by Freddie Slack; YOU'RE FOR ME; COME TO MY ARMS; WHITNEY HIGH and NIGHT TIME AND YOU by Edward J. Kay; YOU'RE JUST WHAT I CRAVE by Arthur Alexander.

HOLIDAY IN MEXICO

A M-G-M picture filmed with a cast headed by Walter Pidgeon, Jose Iturbi,

Roddy McDowall, Ilona Massey and Xavier Cugat and his orchestra, and directed by George Sidney. Musical numbers:

I THINK OF YOU by Jack Elliott and Don Marcotte; SOMEONE TO LOVE by Ralph Freed and Paul Abraham; THESE PATIENT YEARS and HOLIDAY IN MEXICO by Ralph Freed and Sammy Fain; YOU SO IT'S YOU by Earl Brent and Nacio Herb Brown; AND DREAMS REMAIN by Ralph Freed and Raoul Soler; WALTER WINCHELL RHUMBA by Noro Morales; AND THAT'S THAT by Sammy Stept, Ervin Drake, Xavier Cugat and Noro Morales.

IF I'M LUCKY

A 20th Century-Fox picture filmed with a cast headed by Perry Como. Vivian Blaine, Carmen Miranda, Phil Silvers and Harry James and his orchestra, and directed by Lewis Seiler. Songs by Edgar De-Lange and Joseph Myrow:

IF I'M LUCKY; ONE MORE KISS; BET YOUR BOTTOM DOLLAR; FOLLOW THE BAND; THAT AMERICAN LOOK and PUBLICITY.

JOLSON STORY, THE

A Columbia picture starring Larry Parks as Al Jolson, who sang all the musical numbers; Evelyn Keyes, William Demarest and Bill Goodwin, and directed by Alfred E. Green. Songs:

BY THE LIGHT OF THE SILVERY MOON by Edward Madden and Gus Edwards; YOU MADE ME LOVE YOU by Joseph McCarthy and Jimmy Monaco; I'M SITTING ON TOP OF THE WORLD by Sam Lewis, Joe Young and Ray Henderson; THERE'S A RAINBOW 'ROUND MY SHOULDER by Al Jolson, Billy Rose and Dave Dreyer; MY MAMMY by Sam Lewis, Joe Young and Walter Donaldson; ROCK-A-BYE YOUR BABY TO A DIXIE MELODY by Sam Lewis, Joe Young and Jean Schwartz; LIZA by Ira and George Gershwin; CALIFORNIA HERE I COME by B. G. DeSylva, Al Jolson and Joseph Meyer; SWANEE by Irving Caesar and George Gershwin; WAITING FOR THE ROBERT E. LEE by L. Wolfe Gilbert and Lewis E. Muir; APRIL SHOWERS by B. G. DeSylva and Louis Silvers; ABOUT A QUARTER TO NINE by Al Dubin and Harry Warren; I WANT A GIRL JUST LIKE THE GIRL THAT MARRIED DEAR OLD DAD by Will Dillon and Harry Von Tilzer; ANNIVERSARY SONG by

Al Jolson; THE SPANIARD WHO BLIGHTED MY LIFE by Billy Merson.

JUNIOR PROM

A Monogram picture starring Freddie Stewart and June Preisser, and directed by Arthur Dreifuss. Songs:

TEEN CANTEEN and KEEP THE BEAT by Sid Robin; TRIMBALL FOR PRESIDENT by Stanley Cowan; MY HEART SINGS by Harold Rome and Jamblan Herpin; IT'S ME OH LAWD (Negro spiritual).

KID FROM BOOKLYN, THE

An RKO picture starring Sammy Kaye and Virginia Mayo in a cast that included Walter Abel and Fay Bainter, and directed by Norman Z. McLeod. Songs:

I LOVE AN OLD-FASHIONED SONG; YOU'RE THE CAUSE OF IT ALL; HEY, WHAT'S YOUR NAME?; JOSIE and SUNFLOWER SONG by Sammy Cahn and Jule Styne. PAVLOVA by Sylvia Fine.

LOVER COME BACK

A Universal picture starring Lucille Ball and George Brent in a cast that included Vera Zorina and Charles Winninger, and directed by William Seiter. Songs:

WHERE IS THE SONG OF SONGS FOR ME and THE LITTLE THINGS IN LIFE by Irving Berlin; LITTLE WHITE LIES and SWEET JENNIE LEE by Walter Donaldson; WALKING IN THE SUNSHINE by Cliff Friend; DON'T TELL HER WHAT HAPPENED TO ME by Lew Brown, B. G. DeSylva and Ray Henderson; JUST A GIGOLO by Irving Caesar and Leanello Cassuci.

MAN I LOVE, THE

A Warner Brothers' picture starring Ida Lupino and Robert Alda in a cast that included Andrea King and Bruce Bennett, and directed by Raoul Walsh. Songs:

THE MAN I LOVE and LIZA by Ira and George Gershwin; WHY WAS I BORN? by Oscar Hammerstein II and Jerome Kern; BILL by P. G. Wodehouse, Oscar Hammerstein II and Jerome Kern; IF I COULD BE WITH YOU ONE HOUR TONIGHT by Henry Creamer and Jimmy Johnson; BODY AND SOUL by Edward Heyman and Johnny Green.

MEET ME ON BROADWAY

A Columbia picture filmed with a cast headed by Marjorie Reynolds, Fred Brady and Jinx Falkenburg, and directed by Leigh Jason. Songs by Edgar De Lange and Saul Chaplin:

FIFTH AVENUE; ONLY FOR ME; I NEVER HAD A CHANCE and IS IT WORTH IT?

MY HEART GOES CRAZY
A Universal picture, filmed in England, starring Syd Field and Greta Gynt, and directed by Wesley Ruggles. Songs by Johnny Burke and Jimmy Van Heusen:
SO WOULD I; MY HEART GOES CRAZY; THE 'AMPSTEAD WAY; ANYWAY THE WIND BLOWS; HYDE PARK ON A SUNDAY and YOU CAN'T KEEP A GOOD DREAMER DOWN.

NIGHT AND DAY
A Warner Brothers' picture based on the life of Cole Porter with Cary Grant playing the role of the composer in a cast that included Alexis Smith, Monte Woolley, Ginny Simms and Mary Martin, and directed by Michael Curtiz. Songs by Cole Porter:
IN THE STILL OF THE NIGHT; OLD-FASHIONED GARDEN; LET'S DO IT; YOU DO SOMETHING TO ME; MISS OTIS REGRETS; WHAT IS THIS THING CALLED LOVE?; I'VE GOT YOU UNDER MY SKIN; JUST ONE OF THOSE THINGS; YOU'RE THE TOP; I GET A KICK OUT OF YOU; EASY TO LOVE; MY HEART BELONGS TO DADDY; BEGIN THE BEGUINE and NIGHT AND DAY.

NO LEAVE NO LOVE
An M-G-M picture starring Van Johnson in a cast that included Keenan Wynn, Pat Kirkwood, Marie Wilson and the orchestras of Xavier Cugat and Guy Lombardo, and directed by Charles Martin. Songs:
LOVE ON A GREYHOUND BUS by Kay Thompson, Ralph Blane and George Stoll; ALL THE TIME by Ralph Freed and Sammy Fain; ISN'T IT WONDERFUL by Kay Thompson; IT'LL BE GREAT TO BE BACK HOME by Charles Martin; OLD SAD EYES by Irving Kahal and Sammy Fain; WHEN IT'S LOVE by Edgar DeLange and Nicholas Kharito.

PEOPLE ARE FUNNY
A Paramount release filmed with a cast headed by Jack Haley, Helen Walker, Rudy Vallee, Frances Langford, the Vagabonds and Ozzie Nelson and his orchestra, and directed by Sam White. Songs:
EVERY HOUR ON THE HOUR by Don George and Duke Ellington; HEY JOSE by Ray Evans, Jay Livingston and Jose Guizar; CHUCK-A-LUCKING by Jay

Milton, Walter G. Samuels and Archie Gottler; I'M IN THE MOOD FOR LOVE by Dorothy Fields and Jimmy McHugh; THE OLD SQUARE DANCE IS BACK AGAIN by Don Reid and Henry Tobias; ALOUETTA (French folk song).

SINGIN' IN THE CORN
A Columbia picture starring Judy Canova in a cast that included Allen Jenkins and Guinn Williams, and directed by Del Lord. Songs:
PEPITA CHIQUITA; I'M A GAL OF PROPERTY and AN OLD LOVE IS A TRUE LOVE by Doris Fisher and Allan Roberts; MA HE'S MAKING EYES AT ME by Sidney Clare and Con Conrad.

SONG OF THE SOUTH
Walt Disney's first film with live actors, produced in Technicolor by RKO with a cast headed by Ruth Warwick, Lucille Watson, Hattie McDaniel, James Baskette, Luana Patten and Bobby Driscoll. Songs:
HOW DO YOU DO by Robert MacGimsey; SONG OF THE SOUTH by Sam Coslow and Arthur Johnston; THAT'S WHAT UNCLE REMUS SAID by Johnny Lange, Hy Heath and Eliot Daniel; SOONER OR LATER by Ray Gilbert and Charles Wolcott; EVERYBODY'S GOT A LAUGHING PLACE and ZIP-A-DEE-DOO-DAH by Ray Gilbert and Allie Wrubel; YOU'LL ALWAYS BE THE ONE I LOVE by Sunny Skylar and Ticker Freeman; LET THE RAIN POUR DOWN and WHO WANTS TO LIVE LIKE THAT? by Foster Carling.

SUSIE STEPS OUT
A Comet picture starring David Bruce and Cleatus Caldwell, and directed by Reginald Le Borg. Songs by Hal Borne:
BOP-POP; THAT DID IT; FOR THE RIGHT GUY; WHEN DOES LOVE BEGIN?; WHEN YOU'RE NEAR and I'M SO LONELY.

SWING PARADE OF 1946
A Monogram picture starring Gale Storm and Phil Regan, and directed by Phil Carlson. Songs:
DON'T WORRY ABOUT THAT MULE by William Davis, Duke Groner and Charles Stewart; AFTER ALL THIS TIME by Paul DeFur and Ken Thompson; OH, BROTHER by Matt Malneck and Allie Wrubel; STORMY WEATHER by Ted Koehler and Harold Arlen.

TARS AND SPARS
A Columbia picture filmed with a cast

headed by Janet Blair, Alfred Drake, Marc Platt and Sid Caesar, and directed by Alfred E. Green. Songs by Sammy Cahn and Jule Styne.

KISS ME HELLO, BABY; LOVE IS A MERRY-GO-ROUND; I'M GLAD I WAITED FOR YOU; HE'S A HERO; I LOVE EGGS; AFTER THE WAR, BABY; I HAVE A LOVE IN EVERY PORT; WHEN I GET TO TOWN; DON'T CALL ON ME and I ALWAYS MEANT TO TELL YOU.

THAT'S MY GIRL

A Republic picture filmed with a cast headed by Lynne Roberts, Donald Barry and Pinky Lee, and directed by George Blair. Songs:

THAT'S MY GIRL; THE MUSIC IN MY HEART IS YOU and TAKE IT AWAY by Jack Elliott; FOR YOU AND ME; SENTIMENTAL and HITCH HIKE TO HAPPINESS by Kim Gannon and Walter Kent; 720 IN THE BOOKS by Jan Savitt and Johnny Watson.

THREE LITTLE GIRLS IN BLUE

A 20th Century-Fox picture filmed with a cast headed by June Haver, George Montgomery, Vivian Blaine, Celeste Holm and Vera-Ellen, and directed by Bruce Humberstone. Songs by Mack Gordon and Joseph Myrow:

SOMEWHERE IN THE NIGHT; ALWAYS THE LADY; ON THE BOARD WALK AT ATLANTIC CITY; THREE LITTLE GIRLS IN BLUE; I LIKE MIKE; A FARMER'S LIFE IS A VERY MERRY ONE; YOU MAKE ME FEEL SO YOUNG and THIS IS ALWAYS.

THRILL OF BRAZIL

A Columbia picture starring Evelyn Keyes, Keenan Wynn and Ann Miller, and directed by S. Sylvan Simon. Songs by Doris Fisher and Allan Roberts:

COPA-CABANA; CUSTOM HOUSE; A MAN IS BROTHER TO A MULE; THAT'S GOOD ENOUGH FOR ME; MY SLEEPY GUITAR and THRILL OF BRAZIL.

TILL THE CLOUDS ROLL BY

An M-G-M picture based on the life of Jerome Kern and filmed with an all-star cast that included Robert Walker as Kern, Judy Garland, Lucille Bremer, Van Heflin, Dinah Shore, Van Johnson, June Allyson, Tony Martin, Kathryn Grayson, Virginia O'Brien, Lena Horne and Frank Sinatra, and directed by Richard Whorf. Songs by Jerome Kern with lyricists' name in parentheses:

MAKE BELIEVE (Oscar Hammerstein II); CAN'T HELP LOVIN' THAT MAN (Oscar Hammerstein II); OL' MAN RIVER (Oscar Hammerstein II); TILL THE CLOUDS ROLL BY (P. G. Wodehouse); HOW'D YOU LIKE TO SPOON WITH ME? (Edward Laska); THEY DIDN'T BELIEVE ME (Herbert Reynolds); THE LAST TIME I SAW PARIS (Oscar Hammerstein II); I WON'T DANCE (Otto Harbach and Oscar Hammerstein II); WHY WAS I BORN? (Oscar Hammerstein II); SMOKE GETS IN YOUR EYES (Otto Harbach); WHO? (Otto Harbach and Oscar Hammerstein II); LOOK FOR THE SILVER LINING (B. G. DeSylva); SUNNY (Otto Harbach and Oscar Hammerstein II); CLEOPATTERER (P. G. Wodehouse); LEAVE IT TO JANE (P. G. Wodehouse); GO LITTLE BOAT (P. G. Wodehouse); ONE MORE DANCE (Oscar Hammerstein II); LAND WHERE THE GOOD SONGS GO (P. G. Wodehouse); YESTERDAYS (Otto Harbach); LONG AGO AND FAR AWAY (Ira Gershwin); A FINE ROMANCE (Dorothy Fields); ALL THE THINGS YOU ARE (Oscar Hammerstein II); SHE DIDN'T SAY YES (SHE DIDN'T SAY NO) (Otto Harbach); and the polka from the Mark Twain Suite.

TIME, THE PLACE AND THE GIRL, THE

A Warner Brothers' picture starring Dennis Morgan, Jack Carson and Janis Paige, and directed by David Butler. Songs by Leo Robin and Arthur Schwartz:

A GAL IN CALICO; OH BUT I DO; ON A RAINY NIGHT IN RIO; THROUGH A THOUSAND DREAMS; A SOLID CITIZEN OF THE SOLID SOUTH and I HAPPENED TO WALK DOWN FIRST STREET.

TWO SISTERS FROM BOSTON

An M-G-M picture starring Kathryn Grayson and June Allyson in a cast that included Jimmy Durante, Peter Lawford and Lauritz Melchior, and directed by Henry Koster. Songs:

G'WAN YOUR MUDDER'S CALLIN'; THERE ARE TWO SIDES TO EVERY GIRL; THE FIRE CHIEF'S DAUGHTER; NELLIE MARTIN; DOWN BY THE OCEAN and AFTER THE SHOW by Ralph Freed and Sammy Fain; HELLO, HELLO, HELLO by Jimmy Durante.

WAKE UP AND DREAM

A 20th Century-Fox picture filmed with a cast headed by Clem Bevans, John Payne, June Haver and Connie Marshall, and directed by Lloyd Bacon. Songs: GIVE ME THE SIMPLE LIFE; I WISH I COULD TELL YOU and INTO THE SUN by Harry Ruby and Rube Bloom; WHO KNOWS? by Don Raye and Gene DePaul.

ZIEGFELD FOLLIES

An M-G-M picture filmed with an all-star cast that included Fred Astaire, Lucille Ball, Lucille Bremer, Fanny Brice, Judy Garland, Kathryn Grayson, Lena Horne, Gene Kelly, Victor Moore, Red Skelton, William Powell, Edward Arnold and Esther Williams, and directed by Vincente Minnelli. Musical numbers: THIS HEART OF MINE by Arthur Freed and Harry Warren; THERE'S BEAUTY EVERYWHERE by Arthur Freed and Earl Brent; LOVE by Ralph Blane and Hugh Martin; LIMEHOUSE BLUES by Philip Braham and Douglas Furber; BRING ON THE WONDERFUL MEN by Earl Brent and Roger Edens; HERE'S TO THE GIRLS by Ralph Freed and Roger Edens; THE BABBITT AND THE BROMIDE by Ira and George Gershwin.

Feature Films With Songs

ABILENE TOWN

A United Artists' picture starring Randolph Scott and Ann Dvorak, and directed by Edwin L. Marin. Songs by Kermit Goell and Fred Spielman: SNAP YOUR FINGERS; I LOVE IT OUT IN THE WEST and EVERY TIME I GIVE MY HEART.

BACHELOR'S DAUGHTERS, THE

A United Artists' picture filmed with a cast headed by Gail Russell, Claire Trevor, Ann Dvorak and Adolphe Menjou, and directed by Andrew Stone. Songs: TWILIGHT SONG by Jack Lawrence and Irving Drutman; WHERE'S MY HEART? by Kermit Goell and Fred Spielman.

BEST YEARS OF OUR LIVES

An RKO picture filmed with a cast headed by Fredric March, Myrna Loy, Teresa Wright, Dana Andrews, Virginia Mayo, Cathy O'Donnell, Hoagy Carmichael and Harold Russell, and directed by William Wyler. Song by Sidney Arodin and Hoagy Carmichael: LAZY RIVER

BLACK ANGEL

A Universal picture filmed with a cast headed by Dan Duryea, June Vincent, Peter Lorre and Broderick Crawford, and directed by Roy William Neill. Songs by Jack Brooks: HEARTBREAK; I WANT TO BE TALKED ABOUT; TIME WILL TELL and CONTINENTAL GENTLEMAN.

BOWERY BOMBSHELL

A Monogram picture filmed with a cast headed by Leo Gorcey and Huntz Hall, and directed by Phil Karlson. Song by Ruth and Louis Herscher: WHAT CAN I DO? I LOVE HIM

BREAKFAST IN HOLLYWOOD

A United Artists' picture filmed with a cast headed by Tom Breneman, Bonita Granville, Billie Burke, Zasu Pitts, Hedda Hopper and the King Cole Trio, and directed by Harold Schuster. Songs: IF I HAD A WISHING RING by Marla Shelton and Louis Alter; IT IS BETTER TO BE YOURSELF by Nat "King" Cole.

CALIFORNIA

A Paramount picture starring Ray Milland and Barbara Stanwyck in a cast that included Barry Fitzgerald and George Coulouris, and directed by John Farrow. Songs by E. Y. Harburg and Earl Robinson: SAID I TO MY HEART SAID I; CALIFORNIA OR BUST; CALIFORNIA; I SHOULDA STOOD IN PENNSYLVANIA and LILY-I-LAY-DE-O.

CANYON PASSAGE

A Universal picture filmed with a cast headed by Dana Andrews, Brian Donlevy and Susan Hayward, and directed by Jacques Tourneur. Songs by Hoagy Carmichael: ROGUE RIVER VALLEY; I'M GONNA GET MARRIED IN THE MORNING and OL' BUTTERMILK SKY (with Jack Brooks).

DARK CORNER

A 20th Century-Fox picture filmed with a cast headed by Lucille Ball, William Bendix and Clifton Webb, and directed by Henry Hathaway. Musical number by Eddie Heywood: HEYWOOD BLUES

DRESSED TO KILL

A Universal picture filmed with a cast headed by Basil Rathbone, Nigel Bruce and Patricia Morison, and directed by Roy William Neill. Song by Jack Brooks:
YA NEVER KNOW JUST WHO YER GONNA MEET

FAITHFUL IN MY FASHION

An M-G-M picture filmed with a cast headed by Donna Reed, Tom Drake, Edward Everett Horton and Spring Byington, and directed by Sidney Salkow. Song by Roy Turk and Fred Ahlert:
I DON'T KNOW WHY I JUST DO

GILDA

A Columbia picture starring Rita Hayworth in a cast that included Glenn Ford, George Macready and Joseph Calleia, and directed by Charles Vidor. Songs by Doris Fisher and Allan Roberts:
AMADA MIO and PUT THE BLAME ON MAME.

HER KIND OF MAN

A Warner Brothers' picture starring Dane Clark and Janis Paige in a cast that included Zachary Scott and Faye Emerson, and directed by Frederick De Cordova. Songs:
SOMETHING TO REMEMBER YOU BY by Howard Dietz and Arthur Schwartz; BODY AND SOUL by Edward Heyman and Johnny Green; SPEAK TO ME OF LOVE by Bruce Siever and Jean Lenoir.

INSIDE JOB

A Universal picture filmed with a cast headed by Preston Foster, Alan Curtis and Ann Rutherford, and directed by Jean Yarbrough. Song by Del Courtney:
DO YOU BELIEVE IN LOVING HONEY?

INVISIBLE INFORMER, THE

A Republic picture starring Linda Stirling and William Henry, and directed by Philip Ford. Song by Mort Glickman:
GLOOMY BAYOU

I'VE ALWAYS LOVED YOU

A Republic picture filmed with a cast headed by Marie Ouspenskaya and Philip Dorn, and directed by Frank Borzage. Song by Aaron Goldmark and Ludwig Flato:
I'VE ALWAYS LOVED YOU

JANIE GETS MARRIED

A Warner Brothers' picture filmed with a cast headed by Joan Leslie, Robert Hutton, Edward Arnold, Ann Harding, Robert Benchley, Dorothy Malone and Hattie Mc-

Daniel, and directed by Vincent Sherman. Song by Ted Koehler and M. K. Jerome:
G. I. SONG

KILLERS, THE

A Universal picture starring Burt Lancaster and Ava Gardner, and directed by Robert Siodmak. Song by Jack Brooks and Miklos Rozsa:
THE MORE I KNOW OF LOVE

LITTLE MR. JIM

An M-G-M picture starring Butch Jenkins in a cast that included Frances Gifford and James Craig, and directed by Fred Zinnemann. Song by Ralph Freed and Sammy Fain:
LITTLE JIM

LOVE LAUGHS AT ANDY HARDY

An M-G-M picture starring Mickey Rooney in a cast that included Lewis Stone, Sarah Haden and Bonita Granville, and directed by Willis Goldbeck. Song by Earl Brent:
HAIL TO WAINWRIGHT

MARGIE

A 20th Century-Fox picture starring Jeanne Crain in a cast that included Glenn Langan, Lynn Bari, Hattie McDaniel and Alan Young, and directed by Harry King. Songs:
THREE O'CLOCK IN THE MORNING by Dorothy Terriss and J. Robeldo; WONDERFUL ONE by Dorothy Terriss, Paul Whiteman and Ferde Grofe.

MR. HEX

A Monogram picture filmed with a cast headed by Leo Gorcey and Huntz Hall, and directed by William Beaudine. Songs by Louis Herscher:
ONE STAR-KISSED NIGHT and A LOVE SONG TO REMEMBER

MONSIEUR BEAUCAIRE

A Paramount picture starring Bob Hope and Joan Caulfield, and directed by George Marshall. Songs by Ray Evans and Jay Livingston:
A COACH AND FOUR and WARM AS WINE

MY REPUTATION

A Warner Brothers' picture starring Barbara Stanwyck and George Brent, and directed by Curtis Bernhardt. Song by Stanley Adams and Max Steiner:
WHILE YOU'RE AWAY

NEVER SAY GOODBYE

A Warner Brothers' picture starring Er-

rol Flynn in a cast that included Eleanor Parker and Lucille Watson, and directed by James V. Kern. Song by Al Dubin and Harry Warren:
REMEMBER ME?

NIGHT IN PARADISE, A
A Universal picture starring Merle Oberon and Turhan Bey, and directed by Arthur Lubin. Song by Jack Brooks and Frank Skinner:
A NIGHT IN PARADISE

NOBODY LIVES FOREVER
A Warner Brothers' picture starring John Garfield and Geraldine Fitzgerald, and directed by Jean Negulesco. Song by Jack Scholl and M. K. Jerome:
YOU AGAIN

NOCTURNE
An RKO picture starring George Raft and Lynn Bari, and directed by Edwin L. Marin. Song by Mort Greene and Leigh Harline:
NOCTURNE

ONE MORE TOMORROW
A Warner Brothers' picture starring Ann Sheridan, Alexis Smith and Dennis Morgan, and directed by Peter Godfrey. Song by Edgar DeLange, Josef Myrow and Ernesto Lecuona:
ONE MORE TOMORROW

POSTMAN ALWAYS RINGS TWICE, THE
An M-G-M picture starring Lana Turner and John Garfield in a cast that included Cecil Kellaway and Hume Cronyn, and directed by Tay Garnett. Song by Neil Moret and Richard Whiting:
(I GOT A WOMAN CRAZY 'BOUT ME) SHE'S FUNNY THAT WAY

QUEEN OF BURLESQUE
A Producers Releasing Corporation picture filmed with a cast headed by Evelyn Ankers, Carleton Young, Marian Martin and Craig Douglas, and directed by Sam Newfield. Songs by Gene Lucas:
FLOWER SONG; OH NO NOT MUCH and HOW CAN I TELL YOU?

RAZOR'S EDGE, THE
A 20th Century-Fox picture starring Tyrone Power and Gene Tierney in a cast that included John Payne, Anne Baxter, Clifton Webb and Herbert Marshall, and directed by Edmund Goulding. Song by Mack Gordon and Edmund Goulding:
MAM'SELLE

SEARCHING WIND, THE
A Paramount picture starring Robert Young, Ann Richards and Sylvia Sidney, and directed by William Dieterle. Song by Edward Heyman and Victor Young:
THE SEARCHING WIND

SENTIMENTAL JOURNEY
A 20th Century-Fox picture starring John Payne, Maureen O'Hara, William Bendix and Sir Cedric Hardwicke, and directed by Walter Lang. Song by Les Brown, Ben Homer and Bud Green:
SENTIMENTAL JOURNEY

SING WHILE YOU DANCE
A Columbia picture starring Ellen Drew and Robert Stanton, and directed by D. Ross Lederman. Song by Doris Fisher and Allan Roberts:
I DON'T KNOW HOW YOU DID IT

SO GOES MY LOVE
A Universal picture starring Myrna Loy and Don Ameche, and directed by Frank Ryan. Song by Jack Brooks and Hans J. Salter:
SO GOES MY LOVE

STRANGE LOVE OF MARTHA IVERS
A Paramount picture starring Barbara Stanwyck, Van Heflin and Lizabeth Scott, and directed by Lewis Milestone. Song by Edward Heyman and Miklos Rozsa:
STRANGE LOVE

SUSPENSE
A Monogram picture starring Belita and Barry Sullivan, and directed by Frank Tuttle. Song by B. A. Durham and Dan Alexander:
WHEN YOU ARE IN MY ARMS

SWEETHEART OF SIGMA CHI
A Monogram picture starring Elyse Knox and Phil Regan, and directed by Jack Bernhard. Songs:
(GIVE ME) FIVE MINUTES MORE by Sammy Cahn and Jule Styne; SWEETHEART OF SIGMA CHI by F. D. Vernon and Byron D. Stokes.

TANGIER
A Universal picture starring Maria Montez and Preston Foster in a cast that included Robert Paige, Louise Allbritton, Kent Taylor and Sabu, and directed by George Waggner. Songs:
LOVE ME TONIGHT by George Waggner, Jose Antonio Zorrill and Gabriel Ruiz; POLLY WOLLY DOODLE and SHE'LL BE COMING ROUND THE MOUNTAIN (Both traditional).

TO EACH HIS OWN

A Paramount picture starring Olivia De Haviland and John Lund, and directed by Michael Leison. Song by Ray Evans and Jay Livingston.
TO EACH HIS OWN

TOMORROW IS FOREVER

An RKO picture starring Claudette Colbert and Orson Wells, and directed by Irving Pichel. Song by Charles Tobias and Max Steiner:
TOMORROW IS FOREVER

TWO GUYS FROM MILWAUKEE

A Warner Brothers' picture starring Dennis Morgan, Jack Carson, Joan Leslie and Janis Paige, and directed by David Butler. Song by Charles Lawrence, Joe Greene and Stanley Kenton:
AND HER TEARS FLOWED LIKE WINE

TWO SMART PEOPLE

An M-G-M picture starring John Hodiak, Lucille Ball and Lloyd Nolan, and directed by Jules Dassin. Song by George Bassman and Ralph Blane:
DANGEROUS

VACATION IN RENO

An RKO picture starring Jack Haley and Anne Jeffreys, and directed by Leslie Goodwins. Song by Harry Harris and Lew Pollack:
WHEN I'M WALKING ARM-IN-ARM WITH JIM

VERDICT, THE

A Warner Brothers' picture starring Sydney Greenstreet and Peter Lorre, and directed by Don Siegel. Song by Jack Scholl and M. K. Jerome:
GIVE ME A LITTLE BIT

Western Films With Songs

BAD MEN OF THE BORDER

A Universal picture starring Kirby Grant and Armida, and directed by Wallace W. Fox. Songs by Everett Carter and Milton Rosen:
AND THEN I GOT MARRIED and CARMENCITA (With Jack Brooks).

DESERT HORSEMAN

A Columbia picture starring Charles Starrett in a cast that included Smiley Burnette and Adele Roberts, and directed by Ray Nazarro. Songs:
HE WAS AN AMATEUR ONCE and RING THE BELL by Smiley Burnette; THERE'S A TEAR IN YOUR EYE by Walter Shrum, Robert Hoag and Charles Washburn; I WISH I COULD BE A SINGING COWBOY by Sammy Cahn and Saul Chaplin.

GENTLEMAN FROM TEXAS

A Monogram picture starring Johnny Mack Brown in a cast that included Claudia Drake, and directed by Lambert Hillyer. Song by Phil Grayson and Harvey O. Brooks:
WITH SOMEONE LIKE YOU TO LOVE

GUN TOWN

A Universal picture starring Kirby Grant in a cast that included Fuzzy Knight, Lyle Talbot and Claire Carleton, and directed by Wallace W. Fox. Song by Jack Brooks:
I JUST GOT IN

HOME IN OKLAHOMA

A Republic picture starring Roy Rogers in a cast that included Gabby Hayes and Dale Evans, and directed by William Witney. Songs:
MIGUELITO; HOME IN OKLAHOMA and I WISH I WAS A KID AGAIN by Jack Elliott; THE EVERLASTING HILLS OF OKLAHOMA and COWBOY HAM AND EGGS by Tim Spencer; HEREFORD HEAVEN by Roy J. Turner.

IN OLD SACRAMENTO

A Republic picture starring Bill Elliott and Constance Moore, and directed by Joseph Kane. Songs:
BANKS OF THE SACRAMENTO (Traditional); STRIKE UP THE BAND by Andrew B. Sterling and Charles B. Ward; SPEAK TO ME OF LOVE by Bruce Siever and Jean Lenoir; THE MAN WHO BROKE THE BANK AT MONTE CARLO by Fred Gilbert; SACRAMENTO CAL-I-FOR-NI-AY by Charles Maxwell; MY GAL IS A HIGH-BORN LADY by Barney Fagin; I CAN'T TELL WHY I LOVE YOU BUT I DO by Will Cobb and Gus Edwards.

MAN FROM RAINBOW VALLEY

A Republic picture starring Monte Hale and Adrian Booth, and directed by Robert Springsteen. Song by Mort Glickman:
LITTLE FLOWER IN BLOOM

MY PAL TRIGGER

A Republic picture starring Roy Rogers in a cast that included Gabby Hayes, Dale Evans and Jack Holt, and directed by Frank McDonald. Songs:

HARRIET by Paul Cunningham and Abel Baer; OL' FAITHFUL by Michael Carr and Hamilton Kennedy; ALLA EN EL RANCHO GRANDE by Bartley Costello and Emilio Uranga.

RAINBOW OVER TEXAS

A Republic picture starring Roy Rogers in a cast that included Gabby Hayes and Dale Evans, and directed by Frank McDonald. Songs:

LITTLE SENORITA and RAINBOW OVER TEXAS by Jack Elliott; TEXAS, U.S.A. and COWBOY CAMP MEETING by Gordon Forster; BUST MY BUTTONS by Mort Glickman.

ROLL ON TEXAS MOON

A Republic picture starring Roy Rogers in a cast that included Gabby Hayes and Dale Evans, and directed by William Witney. Songs:

WHAT'S DOIN' TONIGHT IN DREAMLAND?; ROLL ON TEXAS MOON and WON'TCHA BE A FRIEND OF MINE? by Jack Elliott; THE JUMPING BEAN by Tim Spencer.

SIOUX CITY SUE

A Republic picture starring Gene Autry in a cast that included Lynne Roberts, and directed by Frank McDonald. Songs:

YOURS by Jack Sheer and Gonzalo Riog; SIOUX CITY SUE by Dick Thomas and Ray Freedman; RIDIN' DOUBLE by John Rox; SOME DAY YOU'LL WANT ME TO WANT YOU by Jimmy Hodges.

SONG OF ARIZONA

A Republic picture starring Roy Rogers in a cast that included Gabby Hayes, Dale Evans and Lyle Talbot, and directed by Frank McDonald. Songs:

ROUND AND ROUND; HALF-A-CHANCE RANCH; SONG OF ARIZONA and MR. SPOOK STEPS OUT by Jack Elliott; MICHAEL O'LEARY O'BRYAN O'TOOLE by Gordon Forster; WAY OUT THERE by Bob Nolan; WILL YOU BE MY DARLIN'? by Mary Ann Owens.

SOUTH OF THE RIO GRANDE

A Monogram picture filmed with a cast headed by Duncan Renaldo and Armida, and directed by Lambert Hillyer. Songs:

THE CISCO KID RIDES AGAIN by Louis Herscher and Edward J. Kay; ADIOS AMOR by Louis Herscher and J. Castelleone.

WILD WEST

A Producers Releasing Corporation picture filmed with a cast headed by Eddie Dean, Al La Rue and Sarah Padden, and directed by Robert Emmett Tansey. Songs by Dorcas Cochrane and Charles Rosoff:

JOURNEY'S END; RIDE ON THE TIDE OF A SONG; ROLL WAGON WHEELS ROLL ON and I CAN TELL BY THE STARS.

Feature Cartoon With Songs

MAKE MINE MUSIC

An RKO-Walt Disney production that featured Nelson Eddy, Dinah Shore, Benny Goodman and his orchestra, the Andrews Sisters, Jerry Colonna, Andy Russell, Sterling Holloway, the Pied Pipers and the King's Men as unseen talent. Songs:

JOHNNY FEDORA AND ALICE BLUE BONNET by Ray Gilbert and Allie Wrubel; MAKE MINE MUSIC by Ken Darby and Eliot Daniel; BLUE BAYOU by Ray Gilbert and Bobby Worth; CASEY THE PRIDE OF THEM ALL by Ray Gilbert, Ken Darby and Eliot Daniel; TWO SILHOUSETTES by Charles Wolcott and Ray Gilbert; WITHOUT YOU by Charles Wolcott and Osvaldo Farres.

Larry Parks, center, in an early scene from *The Jolson Story*

1 9 4 7

Bing Crosby Makes Some Records—But Not On Wax

If there was any question about Bing Crosby being the top all-time attraction at the country's movie houses, all such doubts were dispelled in 1947 when the Groaner starred in two of the year's three pictures that grossed $4,000,000 or better: *Welcome Stranger* and *The Road To Rio,* both with songs by Johnny Burke and Jimmy Van Heusen, making his overall box-office score read:

Golden Circle Hits, 6; Total Receipts, $35,300,000.

It was a good year, too, for the effervescent Betty Grable and her co-star, Dan Dailey, whose picture with a show business background, *Mother Wore Tights,* also finished in the Golden Circle of top-profit-making productions, and since the 1947 releases provided a change of bill highly spiced with variety, it was a good and rewarding year for movie-goers as well.

They had their choice of long-hair music in *Carnegie Hall,* lowdown jazz in *New Orleans,* sweet syncopation played by Benny on his saxophone and Jimmy on his trombone in *The Fabulous Dorseys,* the lilting melodies written by Viennese-schooled Rudolf Friml for *Northwest Mounted* and the rhumbas and sambas that prevailed in *Carnival In Costa Rica, Copacabana* and *Fiesta.*

The cliff-hanging adventures of Pearl White back in the silent movie days were the inspiration for *The Perils Of Pauline,* starring Betty Hutton. The ballads Chauncey Olcott made famous were revived in *My Wild Irish Rose.* June Allyson and Peter Lawford danced the *Varsity Drag* in the screen adaptation of *Good News,* the Broadway stage hit of 1927. *I Wonder Who's Kissing Her Now?* turned back the clock to the first decade of the Twentieth Century when the ageless Joe Howard, veteran trouper and composer of the picture's songs, started on a matrimonial marathon in which he acquired a total of eight wives. And the inimitable Jimmy Durante, graduate magna cum schnozzola of the much-raided night clubs of the Prohibition era, shared headline billing with Frank Sinatra and Kathryn Grayson in *It Happened In Brooklyn,* and pitted his much-publicized proboscis against Esther Williams' breast stroke and Lauritz Melchior's highly educated pipes in *This Time For Keeps.*

A precious cache of unpublished manuscripts by the late George Gershwin provided Betty Grable and Dick Haymes with the songs they introduced in *The Shocking Miss Pilgrim.* Frank Loesser, who entered the Army as a lyricist, returned to civilian life as an author-composer, thus getting undivided credit for *I Wish I Didn't Love You So, Tallahassee* and the other numbers he wrote for *The Perils Of Pauline* and *Variety Girl.* And Walt Disney came up with something new in *Fun And Fancy Free,* a film that celebrated the wedding of his famous cartoon characters with live talent.

But the Academy of Motion Picture Arts and Sciences had to back track to the sound track of *Song Of The South,* released late in 1946, to find a song worthy of an Oscar—*Zip-A-Dee-Doo-Dah,* and this might be interpreted as an omen of the lean days that lay just ahead—the days that marked the end of the Golden Age of the Hollywood musical.

Musicals

BEAT THE BAND

An RKO picture filmed with a cast headed by Frances Langford, Ralph Edwards, Phillip Terry and Gene Krupa and his band, and directed by John Auer. Songs by Mort Greene and Leigh Harline:
KISSIN' WELL; I'M IN LOVE; I'VE GOT MY FINGERS CROSSED and BEAT THE BAND.

CALENDAR GIRL

A Republic picture filmed with a cast headed by Jane Frazee, William Marshall, Gail Patrick, Kenny Baker, Victor MacLaglen and Irene Rich, and directed by Allan Dwan. Songs by Harold Adamson and Jimmy McHugh:
HAVE I TOLD YOU LATELY? (I'M TELLING YOU NOW); LOVELY NIGHT TO GO DREAMING; CALENDAR GIRL; AT THE FIREMAN'S BALL; A BLUEBIRD IS SINGING TO ME; NEW YORK'S A NICE PLACE TO VISIT and LET'S HAVE SOME PRETZELS AND BEER.

CARNEGIE HALL

A United Artists' picture filmed with a cast headed by William Prince, Marsha Hunt, Frank McHugh and Martha O'Driscoll, featuring Walter Damrosch, Lily Pons, Gregor Piaogorsky, Risé Stevens, Artur Rozinski, Artur Rubenstein, Jan Peerce, Ezio Pinza, Vaughn Monroe and Harry James as guest artists, and directed by Edgar G. Ulmer. In addition to classical numbers, the following songs were introduced:
BEWARE MY HEART by Sam Coslow; SOMETIME WE WILL MEET AGAIN by William LeBarron, Boris Morros and Gregory Stone; THE BROWN DANUBE by Hal Borne.

CARNIVAL IN COSTA RICA

A 20th Century-Fox picture filmed with a cast headed by Dick Haymes, Vera-Ellen, Cesar Romero and Celeste Holm, and di-rected by Gregory Ratoff. Musical numbers:
ANOTHER NIGHT LIKE THIS; I'LL KNOW IT'S LOVE; MI VIDA; COSTA RICA; RHUMBA BAMBA and MARACAS by Harry Ruby and Ernesto Lecuona; QUI PI PIA by Albert Stillman.

CIGARETTE GIRL

A Columbia picture starring Leslie Brooks and Jimmy Lloyd, and directed by Gunther V. Fritsch. Songs by Doris Fisher and Allan Roberts:
IT'S ALL IN THE MIND; HOW CAN YOU TELL?; THEY WON'T LET ME SING; HONEYMOON ON A DIME and THE MORE WE GET TOGETHER.

COPACABANA

A United Artists' picture starring Groucho Marx and Carmen Miranda in a cast that included Andy Russell and Gloria Jean, and directed by Alfred W. Green. Songs by Sam Coslow:
JE VOUS AIME; STRANGER THINGS HAVE HAPPENED; MY HEART WAS DOING A BOLERO; LET'S GO TO COPACABANA; I HAVEN'T GOT A THING TO SELL and WE'VE COME TO COPA.

DOWN TO EARTH

A Columbia picture starring Rita Hayworth in a cast that included Larry Parks, Marc Platt, James Gleason and Edward Everett Horton, and directed by Alexander Hall. Songs by Doris Fisher and Allan Roberts:
THIS CAN'T BE LEGAL; THEY CAN'T CONVINCE ME and LET'S STAY YOUNG FOREVER.

FABULOUS DORSEYS, THE

A United Artists' picture starring Tommy and Jimmy Dorsey and their orchestras in a cast that included Janet Blair, Paul Whiteman, William Lundigan, Mike Pingatore, Charlie Barnet, Ziggy Elman, Henry Busse, Ray Bauduc, Stuart Foster and Helen O'Connell, and directed by Alfred W. Green. Musical numbers:

TO ME by Don George and Allie Wrubel; DORSEY CONCERTO by Leo Shuken; MARIE by Irving Berlin; GREEN EYES by Nilo Menendez and Adolph Utrera; THE OBJECT OF MY AFFECTIONS by Pinky Tomlin, Coy Poe and Jimmy Grier.

FIESTA
An M-G-M picture starring Esther Williams in a cast that included Akim Tamiroff and Ricardo Montalban, and directed by Richard Thorpe. Musical numbers:

LA BAMBA by Luis Martinez Serrano; LA LUNA ENAMORADA by Angel Ortiz De Villajos, Miriano Bolanos Recio and Leocadio Martinez Durango; ROMERIA VASCA by Los Bocheros and LA BARCA DE ORO.

FUN AND FANCY FREE
An RKO picture filmed with a cast headed by Dinah Shore, Edgar Bergen, Billy Gilbert, Cliff Edwards, the Starlighters, the King's Men and the Dinning Sisters in conjunction with Walt Disney's cartoon characters, and directed by William Morgan: Songs:

LAZY COUNTRYSIDE by Bobby Worth; FUN AND FANCY FREE by Bennie Benjamin and George Weiss; SAY IT WITH A SLAP and TOO GOOD TO BE TRUE by Eliot Daniel and Buddy Kaye; BEANERO by Oliver Wallace; MY FAVORITE DREAM by William Walsh and Ray Noble; FEE FI FO FUM by Paul G. Smith and Arthur Quenzer.

GOOD NEWS
An M-G-M picture starring June Allyson and Peter Lawford in a cast that included Mel Torme, Joan McCracken and Patricia Marshall, and directed by Charles Walters. Songs:

TAIT SONG; HE'S A LADY'S MAN; LUCKY IN LOVE; THE BEST THINGS IN LIFE ARE FREE; JUST IMAGINE and VARSITY DRAG by B. G. DeSylva, Lew Brown and Ray Henderson; THE FRENCH LESSON by Betty Comden, Adolph Green and Roger Edens; PASS THAT PEACE PIPE by Ralph Blane and Hugh Martin.

HIT PARADE OF 1947
A Republic picture in which Joan Edwards made her film debut in a cast that

included Eddie Albert, Constance Moore, Gil Lamb, Bill Goodwin, William Frawley and the Sons of the Pioneers, and directed by Frank McDonald: Songs:

I GUESS I'LL HAVE THAT DREAM RIGHT AWAY; CHIQUITA FROM SANTA ANITA; IS THERE ANYONE HERE FROM TEXAS?; COULDN'T BE MORE IN LOVE; THE CUSTOMER IS ALWAYS WRONG and THE CATS ARE GOING TO THE DOGS by Harold Adamson and Jimmy McHugh; BROOKLYN BUCKAROOS by Foster Carling; OUT CALIFORNIA WAY by Tim Spencer.

I WONDER WHO'S KISSING HER NOW
A 20th Century-Fox picture starring June Haver, Mark Stevens and Martha Stewart, and directed by Lloyd Bacon. Songs by Frank Adams, Will Hough and Joe Howard:

HONEYMOON; WHAT'S THE USE OF DREAMING?; HELLO MY BABY; OH GEE BE SWEET TO ME KID; HOW'D YOU LIKE TO BE THE UMPIRE? and I WONDER WHO'S KISSING HER NOW.

I'LL BE YOURS
A Universal picture starring Deanna Durbin in a cast that included Tom Drake, William Bendix and Adolphe Menjou, and directed by William A. Seiter. Songs:

IT'S DREAMTIME and COBBLESKILL SCHOOL SONG by Jack Brooks and Walter Schumann; GRANADA by Augustin Lara; SARI WALTZ by C. C. S. Cushman, E. P. Heath and Emmerich Kalman.

IT HAPPENED IN BROOKLYN
An M-G-M picture starring Frank Sinatra in a cast that included Peter Lawford, Kathryn Grayson and Jimmy Durante, and directed by Richard Whorf. Songs by Sammy Cahn and Jule Styne:

IT'S THE SAME OLD DREAM; TIME AFTER TIME; I BELIEVE; THE BROOKLYN BRIDGE; WHOSE BABY ARE YOU? and THE SONG'S GOTTA COME FROM THE HEART.

IT HAPPENED ON FIFTH AVENUE
A United Artists' picture filmed with a cast headed by Don DeFore, Ann Harding, Charles Ruggles, Gale Storm and Victor Moore, and directed by Roy Del Ruth. Songs by Paul Francis Webster and Harry Revel:

IT'S A WONDERFUL, WONDERFUL

FEELING; SPEAK MY HEART; YOU'RE EVERYWHERE and THAT'S WHAT CHRISTMAS MEANS TO ME.

LADIES' MAN

A Paramount picture filmed with a cast headed by Eddie Bracken, Cass Daley, Virginia Weekes and Spike Jones and his City Slickers, and directed by William D. Russell. Songs: I GOTTA GIRL (IN NORTH AND SOUTH DAKOTA); WHAT AM I GONNA DO ABOUT YOU?; AWAY OUT WEST and I'M AS READY AS I'LL EVER BE by Sammy Cahn and Jule Styne; COCKTAILS FOR TWO by Sam Coslow and Arthur Johnston; HOLIDAY FOR STRINGS by David Rose; MAMA YE QUIERA (I WANT MY MAMA) by Al Stillman and Vincente and Jaraca Paiva.

LINDA BE GOOD

An Eagle-Lion picture filmed with a cast headed by Elyse Knox, Marie Wilson and John Hubbard, and directed by Frank McDonald. Songs: MY MOTHER SAYS I MUSTN'T by Jack Mason and Sy Miller; LINDA BE GOOD by Jack Mason and Charles Herbert; YOUNG GIRLS OF TODAY and OLD LADY WITH A ROLLIN PIN by Sir Launcelot.

LITTLE MISS BROADWAY

A Columbia picture filmed with a cast headed by Jean Porter, John Shelton and Ruth Donnelly, and directed by Arthur Dreifuss. Songs: CHEER FOR THE TEAM by McElbert Moore, Charles Newman and Walter G. Samuels; JUDY AND DICK by Betty Wright, Victor McLeod and Fred Karger; THAT'S GOOD ENOUGH FOR ME and A MAN IS A BROTHER TO A MULE by Doris Fisher and Allan Roberts.

LOVE AND LEARN

A Warner Brothers' picture filmed with a cast headed by Jack Carson, Robert Hutton, Janis Paige and Martha Vickers, and directed by Frederick De Cordova. Songs: HAPPY ME and IF YOU ARE COMING BACK TO ME by Jack Scholl and M. K. Jerome; WOULD YOU BELIEVE ME? by Charles Tobias, M. K. Jerome and Ray Heindorf.

MOTHER WORE TIGHTS

A 20th Century-Fox picture starring Betty Grable and Dan Dailey in a cast that included Mona Freeman, and directed by

Walter Lang. Songs: YOU DO; KOKOMO, INDIANA; THERE'S NOTHING LIKE A SONG; ON A LITTLE TWO-SEAT TANDEM; THIS IS MY FAVORITE CITY; ROLLING DOWN TO BOWLING GREEN and FARE-THEE-WELL DEAR ALMA MATER by Mack Gordon and Josef Myrow; TRA-LA-LA-LA by Mack Gordon and Harry Warren.

MY WILD IRISH ROSE

A Warner Brothers' picture filmed with a cast headed by Dennis Morgan, Arlene Dahl, Andrea King and Alan Hale, and directed by David Butler. Songs: WEE ROSE OF KILLARNEY; MISS LINDY LOU; THERE'S ROOM IN MY HEART FOR THEM ALL and THE NATCHEZ AND THE ROBERT E. LEE by Ted Koehler and M. K. Jerome; COME DOWN MA EVENIN' STAR by Robert B. Smith and John Stromberg; MY NELLIE'S BLUE EYES by William J. Scanlon; ONE LITTLE SWEET LITTLE GIRL by Dan Sullivan; MY WILD IRISH ROSE by Chauncey Olcott; A LITTLE BIT OF HEAVEN by J. Keirn Brennan and Ernest Ball; MOTHER MACHREE by Rida Johnson Young, Chauncey Olcott and Ernest Ball.

NEW ORLEANS

A United Artists' picture filmed with a cast headed by Dorothy Patrick, Arturo De Cordova, Irene Rich and Louis Armstrong and his orchestra, and directed by Arthur Lubin. Songs: BLUES ARE BREWIN'; ENDIE and DO YOU KNOW WHAT IT MEANS TO MISS NEW ORLEANS? by Edgar DeLange and Louis Alter; WHERE THE BLUES ARE BORN IN NEW ORLEANS by Bob Carleton and Cliff Dixon.

NORTHWEST OUTPOST

A Republic picture starring Nelson Eddy in a cast that included Ilona Massey, Lenore Ulrich and Joseph Schildkraut, and directed by Allan Dwan. Songs by Edward Heyman and Rudolf Friml: ONE MORE MILE TO GO; RAINDROPS ON A DRUM; LOVE IS THE TIME; NEARER AND DEARER; TELL ME WITH YOUR EYES; RUSSIAN EASTER HYMN and WEARY (CONVICT SONG).

PERILS OF PAULINE

A Paramount picture starring Betty Hutton in a cast that included John Lund,

Constance Collier, Billy DeWolfe and William Demarest, and directed by George Marshall. Songs:
POPPA DON'T PREACH TO ME; RUMBLE, RUMBLE, RUMBLE; THE SEWING MACHINE and I WISH I DIDN'T LOVE YOU SO by Frank Loesser; POOR PAULINE by Raymond Walker and Charles McCarron.

ROAD TO RIO, THE
A Paramount picture starring Bing Crosby, Bob Hope and Dorothy Lamour, and directed by Norman Z. McLeod. Songs by Johnny Burke and Jimmy Van Heusen:
BUT BEAUTIFUL; EXPERIENCE; YOU DON'T HAVE TO KNOW THE LANGUAGE and APALACHICOLA, FLORIDA.

SHOCKING MISS PILGRIM, THE
A 20th Century-Fox picture starring Betty Grable in a cast that included Dick Haymes, Gene Lockhart, Ann Revere and Allyn Joslyn, and directed by George Seaton. Songs by Ira and George Gershwin:
AREN'T YOU KINDA GLAD WE DID?; FOR YOU, FOR ME, FOR EVERMORE; BUT NOT IN BOSTON; STAND UP AND FIGHT; CHANGING MY TUNE; ONE, TWO, THREE; SWEET PACKARD; WALTZ ME NO WALTZES and WALTZING IS BETTER THAN SITTING DOWN.

SOMETHING IN THE WIND
A Universal picture starring Deanna Durbin and Donald O'Connor, and directed by Irving Pichell. Songs by Leo Robin and Johnny Green:
THE TURNTABLE SONG; I'M HAPPY-GO-LUCKY AND FREE; I LOVE A MYSTERY; IT'S ONLY LOVE; SOMETHING IN THE WIND and YOU WANNA KEEP YOUR BABY LOOKIN' RIGHT.

SONG OF SCHEHERAZADE
A Universal picture with Pierre Aumont in the role of Rimsky-Korsakoff and heading a cast that included Yvonne De Carlo, Brian Donlevy and Eve Arden; directed by Walter Reisch. Songs by Jack Brooks based on the melodies of N. Rimsky-Korsakoff:
GYPSY SONG; FANDANGO; SCHEHERAZADE; SONG OF INDIA and HYMN TO THE SUN.

THIS TIME FOR KEEPS
An M-G-M picture starring Esther Williams, Jimmy Durante and Lauritz Melchior, and directed by Richard Thorpe. Songs:
TEN PER CENT OFF and 'S 'NO WONDER THEY FALL IN LOVE by Ralph Freed and Sammy Fain; LITTLE BIT OF THIS AND LITTLE BIT OF THAT; INKA DINKA DOO and I'M THE MAN WHO FOUND THE LOST CHORD by Jimmy Durante; WHY DON'T THEY LET ME SING A LOVE SONG? and LITTLE BIG SHOT by Benny Davis and Harry Akst; I LOVE TO DANCE by Ralph Freed and Burton Lane; WHEN IT'S LILAC TIME ON MACKINAC ISLAND by Leslie Kirk.

TWO BLONDES AND A RED HEAD
A Columbia picture filmed with a cast headed by Jean Porter, Jimmy Lloyd, June Preisser and Judy Clark, and directed by Arthur Dreifuss. Songs:
IT'S SO EASY and ALL I KNOW IS SI SI by Doris Fisher and Allan Roberts; BOOGIE WOOGIE FROM NOWHERE by Saul Chaplin; ON THE SUNNY SIDE OF THE STREET by Dorothy Fields and Jimmy McHugh.

VARIETY GIRL
A Paramount picture filmed with a cast headed by Mary Hatcher, Olga San Juan, DeForest Kelley and William Demarest, and directed by George Marshall. Songs by Frank Loesser:
TALLAHASSEE; HE CAN WALTZ; YOUR HEART CALLING MINE; I MUST HAVE BEEN MADLY IN LOVE; I WANT MY MONEY BACK; IMPOSSIBLE THINGS and THE FRENCH.

WELCOME STRANGER
A Paramount picture starring Bing Crosby in a cast that included Barry Fitzgerald and Joan Caulfield, and directed by Elliott Nugent. Songs by Johnny Burke and Jimmy Van Heusen:
AS LONG AS I'M DREAMING; MY HEART IS A HOBO; COUNTRY STYLE; SMILE RIGHT BACK AT THE SUN and SMACK IN THE MIDDLE OF MAINE.

WHEN A GIRL'S BEAUTIFUL
A Columbia picture filmed with a cast headed by Adele Jurgens, Marc Platt and Patricia White, and directed by Frank McDonald. Songs by Allan Roberts and Lester Lee:
I'M SORRY I DIDN'T SAY I'M SORRY (WHEN I MADE YOU CRY LAST NIGHT); WHEN A GIRL'S BEAUTIFUL and AS LONG AS I'M IN LOVE.

Feature Films With Songs

ANGEL AND THE BAD MAN, THE
A Republic picture filmed with a cast headed by John Wayne, Gail Russell, Irene Rich, Harry Carey and Bruce Cabot, and directed by James Edward Grant. Song by Kim Gannon and Walter Kent:
A LITTLE BIT DIFFERENT

BIG TOWN
A Paramount picture filmed with a cast headed by Philip Reed, Hillary Brooke and Richard Travis, and directed by William C. Pine. Song by Harold Adamson and Walter Donaldson:
IT'S A SMALL WORLD

BISHOP'S WIFE, THE
An RKO picture starring Cary Grant and Loretta Young in a cast that included David Niven, and directed by Henry Koster. Song by Edgar DeLange, Emil Newman and Herbert Spencer:
LOST APRIL

BLAZE OF NOON
A Paramount picture filmed with a cast headed by Anne Baxter, William Holden, Sonny Tufts, William Bendix and Sterling Hayden, and directed by John Farrow. Song by Charles Henderson and Adolph Deutsch:
BLAZE OF NOON

CALCUTTA
A Paramount picture filmed with a cast headed by Alan Ladd, Gail Russell, William Bendix and June Duprez, and directed by John Farrow. Song by Ben Raleigh and Bernie Wayne:
THIS IS MADNESS

CHEYENNE
A Warner Brothers' picture starring Dennis Morgan and Jane Wyman in a cast that included Janis Paige and Bruce Bennett, and directed by Raoul Walsh. Songs:
I'M SO IN LOVE I DON'T KNOW WHAT I'M DOING by Ted Koehler and M. K. Jerome; GOIN' BACK TO OLD CHEYENNE by Ted Koehler and Max Steiner.

CORPSE CAME C.O.D., THE
A Columbia picture starring George Brent and Joan Blondell, and directed by Andrew Levin. Song by Doris Fisher and Allan Roberts:
WARM KISS (AND A COLD HEART)

CYNTHIA
An M-G-M picture starring Elizabeth Taylor and George Murphy in a cast that included S. Z. Sakall, Mary Astor and Gene Lockhart, and directed by Robert Z. Leonard. Song by Ralph Freed and Johnny Green:
MELODY OF SPRING (Based on a Johann Strauss melody).

DAISY KENYON
A 20th Century-Fox picture starring Joan Crawford, Dana Andrews and Henry Fonda in a cast that included Ruth Warwick, Martha Stewart and Peggy Ann Garner, and directed by Otto Preminger. Song by Mack Gordon and David Raskin:
YOU CAN'T RUN AWAY FROM LOVE

DARK PASSAGE
A Warner Brothers' picture starring Humphrey Bogart and Lauren Bacall in a cast that included Bruce Bennett and Agnes Morehead, and directed by Delmer Daves. Song by Johnny Mercer and Hoagy Carmichael:
HOW LITTLE WE KNOW

DEAD RECKONING
A Columbia picture starring Humphrey Bogart and Lizabeth Scott in a cast that included Morris Carnovsky, and directed by John Cromwell. Song by Doris Fisher and Allan Roberts:
EITHER IT'S LOVE OR IT ISN'T

DEAR RUTH
A Paramount picture starring Joan Caulfield and William Holden in a cast that included Mona Freeman, Edward Arnold and Billy DeWolfe, and directed by William D. Russell. Song by Johnny Mercer and Robert Emmett Dolan:
FINE THINGS

DEEP VALLEY
A Warner Brothers' picture starring Ida Lupino and Dane Clark in a cast that included Wayne Morris, Fay Bainter and Henry Hull, and directed by Jean Negulesco. Song by Charles Tobias and Max Steiner:
DEEP VALLEY

EASY COME EASY GO
A Paramount picture filmed with a cast headed by Barry Fitzgerald, Diana Lynn, Sonny Tufts, Dick Foran and Frank McHugh, and directed by John Farrow. Song by Ray Evans and Jay Livingston:
EASY COME EASY GO

ESCAPE ME NEVER
A Warner Brother's picture starring Ida Lupino and Errol Flynn in a cast that included Gig Young, Eleanor Parker and Reginald Denny, and directed by Peter Godfrey. Songs by Ted Koehler and Erich W. Korngold:
LOVE FOR LOVE and O NENE

GOLDEN EARRINGS
A Paramount picture starring Marlene Dietrich and Ray Milland in a cast that included Murvyn Vye and Quentin Reynolds, and directed by Mitchell Leisen. Song by Ray Evans, Jay Livingston and Victor Young:
GOLDEN EARRINGS

GREEN DOLPHIN STREET
An M-G-M picture starring Lana Turner and Van Heflin in a cast that included Donna Reed, Richard Haydn, Frank Morgan, Edmund Lowe and Dame May Whitty, and directed by Victor Saville. Song by Ned Washington and Bronislaw Kaper:
ON GREEN DOLPHIN STREET

GUILT OF JANET AMES, THE
A Columbia picture starring Rosalind Russell and Melvyn Douglas in a cast that included Sid Caesar, Betsy Blain and Nina Foch, and directed by Henry Levin. Song by Doris Fisher and Allan Roberts:
CAN YOU IMAGINE

HONEYMOON
An RKO picture starring Shirley Temple and Franchot Tone in a cast that included Guy Madison and Corinna Maura, and directed by William Keighley. Songs by Mort Greene and Leigh Harline:
I LOVE GERANIUMS and VEN AQUI

HUCKSTERS, THE
An M-G-M picture starring Clark Gable and Deborah Kerr in a cast that included Sydney Greenstreet, Adolphe Menjou, Ava Gardner and Edward Arnold, and directed by Jack Conway. Song by Buddy Pepper:
DON'T TELL ME

I WALK ALONE
A Paramount picture starring Burt Lancaster, Lizabeth Scott and Kirk Douglas, and directed by Byron Haskins. Song by Ned Washington and Allie Wrubel:
DON'T CALL IT LOVE

IF WINTER COMES
An M-G-M picture starring Walter Pidgeon and Deborah Kerr in a cast that included Angela Lansbury, Binnie Barnes, Janet Leigh and Dame May Whitty, and directed by Victor Saville. Song by Kim Gannon and Imogene Carpenter:
IF WINTER COMES

IMPERFECT LADY
A Paramount picture starring Teresa Wright and Ray Milland in a cast that included Sir Cedric Hardwicke, Virginia Field, Reginald Owen, Melville Cooper and Rhys Williams, and directed by Lewis Allen. Song by Ray Evans and Jay Livingston:
PICCADILLY TILLY

IVY
A Universal picture starring Joan Fontaine, Patric Knowles and Herbert Marshall, and directed by Sam Wood. Song by Hoagy Carmichael:
IVY

KISS OF DEATH
A 20th Century-Fox picture starring Victor Mature, Brian Donlevy and Coleen Gray, and directed by Henry Hathaway. Song by Alfred Newman:
SENTIMENTAL RHAPSODY

LIVING IN A BIG WAY
An M-G-M picture starring Gene Kelly in a cast that included Marie McDonald and Charles Winninger, and directed by Gregory La Cava. Song by Edward Heyman and Louis Alter:
FIDO AND ME

LONG NIGHT, THE
An RKO picture starring Henry Fonda and Barbara Bel Geddes in a cast that included Vincent Price and Ann Dvorak, and directed by Anatole Litvac. Song by Ned Washington and Dimitri Tiomkin:
THE LONG NIGHT

MAGIC TOWN
An RKO picture starring James Stewart and Jane Wyman in a cast that included Kent Smith, Ned Sparks, Regis Toomey, Wallace Ford and Donald Meek, and directed by William A. Wellman. Songs:
MY BOOK OF MEMORY by Edward Heyman, Johnny Burke and Jimmy Van Heusen; MAGIC TOWN by Robert Wells and Mel Torme.

MICHIGAN KID, THE
A Universal picture filmed with a cast headed by Jon Hall, Victor McLaglen, Rita Johnson and Andy Devine, and directed by Ray Taylor. Song by Jack Brooks and Hans J. Salter:
WHOOPS MY DEAR

MONSIEUR VERDOUX

A United Artists' picture starring Charlie Chaplin in a cast that included Mady Carrell, Allison Roddan, Robert Lewis, Audrey Betz and Martha Raye, and directed by Charlie Chaplin, Robert Florey and Wheeler Dryden. Musical numbers by Charlie Chaplin:

A PARIS BOULEVARD; TANGO BITTERNESS and RHUMBA.

MY FAVORITE BRUNETTE

A Paramount picture starring Bob Hope and Dorothy Lamour in a cast that included Peter Lorre and Lon Chaney, and directed by Elliott Nugent. Songs by Ray Evans and Jay Livingston:

BESIDE YOU and MY FAVORITE BRUNETTE

NIGHT SONG

An RKO picture starring Dana Andrews, Merle Oberon and Ethel Barrymore in a cast that included Hoagy Carmichael, and directed by John Cromwell. Songs:

WHO KILLED 'ER (WHO KILLED THE BLACK WIDDER)? by Fred Spielman, Janice Torres and Hoagy Carmichael; NIGHT SONG by Jack Brooks and Leith Stevens.

NORA PRENTISS

A Warner Brothers' picture starring Ann Sheridan and Kent Smith in a cast that included Robert Alda and Bruce Bennett, and directed by Vincent Sherman. Songs by Jack Scholl, Eddie Cherkose and M. K. Jerome:

WHO CARES WHAT PEOPLE SAY? and WOULD YOU LIKE A SOUVENIR?

PRIVATE AFFAIRS OF BEL AMI, THE

A United Artists' picture starring George Sanders and Angela Lansbury in a cast that included Ann Dvorak, Francis Dee and Marie Wilson, and directed by Albert Lewis. Song by Jack Lawrence and Irving Drutman:

MY BEL AMI

RAMROD

A United Artists' picture starring Veronica Lake and Joel McCrea in a cast that included Arleen Whalen, Don DeFore, Preston Foster and Charles Ruggles, and directed by Andre De Toth. Songs by Adolph Deutsch:

THE MOON AND I and SONG OF THE RAMROD

ROMANCE OF ROSY RIDGE

An M-G-M picture starring Van Johnson, Thomas Mitchell and Janet Leigh, and directed by Roy Rowland. Songs by Lewis Allan and Earl Robinson:

I COME FROM MISSOURI; FIDDLIN' FOR A FROLIC; LONELY LOVERS and PIG IN THE PARLOR.

ROSE OF SANTA ROSA

A Columbia picture starring Patricia White and Eduardo Noriega, and directed by Ray Nazarro. Song by Allan Roberts and Jerry Livingston:

ROSE OF SANTA ROSA.

SECRET LIFE OF WALTER MITTY, THE

An RKO picture starring Danny Kaye in a cast that included Virginia Mayo, Boris Karloff, Fay Bainter and Ann Rutherford, and directed by Norman Z. McLeod. Songs by Sylvia Fine:

ANATOLE OF PARIS and SYMPHONY FOR UNSTRUNG TONGUES

SMASH UP

A Universal picture starring Susan Hayward, Marsha Hunt and Lee Bowman, and directed by Stuart Heisler. Songs by Harold Adamson and Jimmy McHugh:

LIFE CAN BE BEAUTIFUL; HUSH-A-BYE ISLAND and I MISS THAT FEELING.

SMOKY RIVER SERENADE

A Columbia picture filmed with a cast headed by Paul Campbell, Ruth Terry, Billy Williams, Virginia Hunter, the Hoosier Hot Shots and the Sunshine Boys, and directed by Derwin Abrahams. Song by Doris Fisher and Allan Roberts:

ALL I KNOW IS SI SI

SONG OF LOVE

An M-G-M picture starring Katherine Hepburn, Paul Henreid and Robert Walker, and directed by Clarence Brown. Song by Charles Tobias and Peter De Rose:

AS YEARS GO BY

SONG OF MY HEART

An Allied Artists' picture filmed with a cast headed by Frank Sundstrom, Audrey Long and Sir Cedric Hardwicke, and directed by Benjamin Glazer. Songs by Janice Torre and Fred Spielman:

SOMEONE and I LOOK FOR LOVE

SONG OF THE THIN MAN

An M-G-M picture starring William Powell and Myrna Loy in a cast that included Keenan Wynn, Dean Stockwell and Patricia Morison, and directed by Eddie Buzzell. Songs:

YOU'RE NOT SO EASY TO FORGET by Herb Magidson and Ben Oakland; YOU'VE GOT TO HAVE A BEAT by Henry Nemo.

STAGE STRUCK

A Monogram picture filmed with a cast headed by Kane Richmond, Audrey Long and Conrad Nagel, and directed by William Nigh. Song by E. Y. Harburg and Harold Arlen:

IN YOUR OWN QUIET WAY

SWEET GENEVIEVE

A Columbia picture filmed with a cast headed by Jean Porter, Jimmy Lydon and Gloria Marlen, and directed by Arthur Dreifuss. Songs by Doris Fisher and Allan Roberts:

FIVE OF THE BEST and MAMA KEEP AWAY FROM THAT JUKE BOX

TRAIL STREET

An RKO picture starring Randolph Scott in a cast that included Robert Ryan, Anne Jeffreys and Gabby Hayes, and directed by Ray Enright. Songs:

YOU MAY NOT REMEMBER by George Jessel and Ben Oakland; YOU'RE NOT THE ONLY PEBBLE ON THE BEACH by Stanley Carter and Harry Braisted.

TROUBLE WITH WOMEN, THE

A Paramount picture starring Ray Milland and Teresa Wright in a cast that included Brian Donlevy, Rose Hobart and Charles Smith, and directed by Sidney Lanfield. Song by Ben Raleigh and Bernie Wayne:

TRAP THAT WOLF

UNFINISHED DANCE, THE

An M-G-M picture starring Margaret O'Brien in a cast that included Cyd Charisse and Danny Thomas, and directed by Henry Koster. Musical numbers:

I WENT MERRILY, MERRILY ON MY WAY by Irving Kahal and Sammy Fain; HOLIDAY FOR STRINGS by David Rose.

WALLFLOWER

A Warner Brothers' picture filmed with a cast headed by Joyce Reynolds, Robert Hutton, Janis Paige and Edward Arnold, and directed by Frederick De Cordova. Songs:

ASK ANYONE WHO KNOWS by Eddie Seiler, Sol Marcus and Al Kaufman; I MAY BE WRONG BUT I THINK YOU'RE WONDERFUL by Harry Ruskin and Henry Sullivan.

Western Films With Songs

APACHE ROSE

A Republic picture starring Roy Rogers in a cast that included Dale Evans and Olin Howlin, and directed by William Witney. Songs by Jack Elliott and Tim and Glenn Spencer:

THERE'S NOTHING LIKE COFFEE IN THE MORNING; WISHING WELL; RIDE VAQUERO; JOSE and APACHE ROSE.

BELLS OF SAN ANGELO

A Republic picture starring Roy Rogers in a cast that included Dale Evans and Andy Devine, and directed by William Witney. Song by Jack Lawrence:

I LIKE TO GET UP EARLY IN THE MORNING

HELLDORADO

A Republic picture starring Roy Rogers in a cast that included Gabby Hayes and Dale Evans, and directed by William Witney. Songs:

GOOD NEIGHBOR by Jack Elliott; SILVER STARS, PURPLE SAGE, EYES

OF BLUE by Denver Darling; MY SADDLE PALS AND I and HELLDORADO by Roy Rogers and Bob Nolan.

LAND OF THE LAWLESS

A Monogram picture starring Johnny Mack Brown in a cast that included Raymond Hatton and Christine McIntyre, and directed by Lambert Hillyer. Song by Louis Herscher:

A GAL A MAN LOVES TO KISS.

LAST ROUNDUP, THE

A Columbia picture starring Gene Autry in a cast that included Jean Heather, Ralph Morgan, Carol Thurston, Mark Daniels and the Texas Rangers, and directed by John English. Song by David Kapp:

ONE HUNDRED AND SIXTY ACRES

RANGE BEYOND THE BLUE

A Producers Releasing Corporation picture filmed with a cast headed by Eddie Dean, Roscoe Ates, Helen Mowery and Bob Duncan, and directed by Ray Taylor.

Song by Hal Blair and Eddie Dean:
THE PONY WITH UNCOMBED HAIR

SADDLE PALS

A Republic picture starring Gene Autry in a cast that included Lynn Roberts and Sterling Holloway, and directed by Leslie Selander. Songs:
YOU STOLE MY HEART by Stanley Adams and Harry Sosnik; WHICH WAY'D THEY GO? by Ray Allen and Perry Botkin; THE COVERED WAGON ROLLED RIGHT ALONG by Britt Wood, Hy Heath and Ernest Gold; AMAPOLA by Albert Gamse and Joseph M. LaCalle; I WISH I'D NEVER MET SUNSHINE by Gene Autry, Dale Evans and Oakley Haldeman.

STARS OVER TEXAS

A Producers Releasing Corporation picture filmed with a cast headed by Eddie Dean, Roscoe Ates, Shirley Patterson and Lee Bennett. Songs by Eddie Dean, Hal Blair and Glen Strange:
SANDS OF THE OLD RIO GRANDE; STARS OVER TEXAS and 1501 MILES OF HEAVEN.

TRAIL TO SAN ANTONE

A Republic picture starring Gene Autry in a cast that included Peggy Stewart, Sterling Holloway and William Henry, and directed by John English. Songs:
DOWN THE TRAIL TO SAN ANTONE by Deuce Spiggins; COWBOY BLUES by Cindy Walker and Gene Autry; SHAME ON YOU by Spade Cooley; THAT'S MY HOME by Sid Robin; BY THE RIVER OF ROSES by Marty Symes and Joe Burke.

WILD COUNTRY

A Producers Releasing Corporation picture filmed with a cast headed by Eddie Dean, Roscoe Ates, Peggy Wynn and Douglas Fowley, and directed by Ray Taylor. Songs:
SADDLE WITH THE GOLDEN HORN and AIN'T NO GAL GOT A BRAND ON ME by Pete Gates; WILD COUNTRY by Eddie Dean and Hal Blair.

Scene from the Oscar-winning musical *An American In Paris,* starring Gene Kelly

1 9 4 8

That Big Bad Wolf Television Gives Hollywood A Scare

Perhaps the men and women who had made Hollywood the capital of the amusement world were tired and disillusioned. Who wasn't in 1948? Perhaps the top brass of Cinemaland were out to make a fast buck instead of outstanding pictures. And then there was that upstart Television, making its first serious bid for favor, offering entertainment for free in the home, and probably giving rise to the question: Why invest big money in the production of films that may not break even let alone show a profit in the face of such competition? But whatever the reason, the Hollywood musical, which had soared to glorious heights during the war and in the years immediately following, suddenly plunged to a lacklustre low in 1948.

Of the song-and-dance films released that year, only two rated an "E" for excellence: *Easter Parade* with songs by Irving Berlin, the Old Reliable Music Man, and starring Judy Garland and Fred Astaire, and *The Emperor Waltz,* which raised Bing Crosby's total of Golden Circle pictures to seven. Add *The Paleface,* a comedy with songs in which Bob Hope and Jane Russell shared headline billing, and you have only three musical shows in 1948 that grossed $4,000,000 or better compared to seven that hit the big jackpot the year before.

Three Broadway musicals that were adapted to the screen: *Are You With It?,* Kurt Weill's *One Touch Of Venus* and *Up In Central Park,* Sigmund Romberg's last contribution to pictures, all fell short of their stage popularity as films. Cole Porter was far from his best in the songs he wrote for *The Pirate,* starring Judy Garland and Gene Kelly. There were no Oscar-winning numbers in the music Harry Warren, a three-time Oscar winner, composed for *Summer Holiday,* based on Eugene O'Neill's stage success, *Ah, Wilderness.* And Nacio Herb Brown, who returned to Hollywood after a five-year sabbatical in Mexico, had no songs in either *The Kissing Bandit,* starring Frank Sinatra and Kathryn Grayson, or *On An Island With You,* a showcase for Esther William's charms and Jimmy Durante's clowning, to match *Singin' In The Rain, You Were Meant For Me, Pagan Love Song* and other hits he wrote when the talkies were in swaddling clothes.

In fact, most of the veteran songwriters of Hollywood had to give way to the younger generation, and the credit for the smash hits went to Sammy Cahn and Jule Styne, who had three top-riding tunes on the 1948 Hit Parade in *Every Day I Love You A Little Bit More, It's Magic* and *Put 'Em In A Box (Tie 'Em With A Ribbon And Drop 'Em In The Deep Blue Sea)* from *Two Guys From Texas* and *Romance On The High Seas,* while Ray Evans and Jay Livingston, two former cruise ship musicians who had anchored in the cinema capital two years before, were awarded the 1948 Oscar for *Buttons and Bows,* introduced in *The Paleface.*

Although everybody had money and was not averse to spending it, *The Countess Of Monte Cristo* didn't cut as sharp a figure at the box-office as Sonja Henie did on the ice, which like the film story was artificial, and Eddie Cantor's rendition of *What Do I Want With Money?* in *If You Knew Susie* struck a sour note with thousands of movie house operators. They not only wanted money . . . they had to have it to survive as the daily receipts kept dropping, dropping until eventually they plunged lower than Faye Emerson revealing TV neckline. For that "big bad wolf" Television was on the prowl with a greedy eye on the fabulous house for which Al Jolson had laid the foundation twenty years before.

Musicals

APRIL SHOWERS
A Warner Brothers' picture starring Ann Sheridan and Jack Carson in a cast that included Robert Alda and S. Z. Sakall, and directed by James V. Kern. Songs:
WORLD'S MOST BEAUTIFUL GIRL by Kim Gannon and Ted Fetter; LITTLE TROUPER by Kim Gannon and Walter Kent; MR. LOVEJOY AND MR. JAY by Jack Scholl and Ray Heindorf; IT'S TU-LIP TIME IN HOLLAND by Dave Radford and Richard Whiting; APRIL SHOW-ERS by B. G. DeSylva and Louis Silvers; CAROLINA IN THE MORNING by Gus Kahn and Walter Donaldson.

ARE YOU WITH IT?
A Universal picture starring Donald O'Connor, Olga San Juan and Martha Stewart, and directed by Jack Hively. Songs by Inez James and Sidney Miller:
DADDY SURPRISE ME; WHAT DO I HAVE TO DO TO MAKE YOU LOVE ME?; IT ONLY TAKES A LITTLE IM-AGINATION; I'M LOOKING FOR A PRINCE OF A FELLOW; ARE YOU WITH IT? and DOWN AT BABA'S AL-LEY.

CAMPUS HONEYMOON
A Republic picture filmed with a cast headed by Lyn Wilde, Lee Wilde, Adele Mara and Richard Crane, and directed by Will Jason. Songs by Richard Sale:
ARE YOU HAPPENING TO ME?; HOW DOES IT FEEL TO FALL IN LOVE?; IT'S NICE TO HAVE A MAN AROUND THE HOUSE; WHO'S GOT A TENT FOR RENT? and THE OPA-LOCKA SONG (With Nathan Scott).

CASBAH
A Universal picture starring Yvonne De Carlo in a cast that included Tony Martin, Peter Lorre and Marta Toren, and directed by John Berry. Songs by Leo Robin and Harold Arlen:
IT WAS WRITTEN IN THE STARS; HOORAY FOR LOVE; THE MONKEY SAT IN THE COCOANUT TREE; FOR EVERY MAN THERE'S A WOMAN and WHAT'S GOOD ABOUT GOODBYE?

COUNTESS OF MONTE CRISTO, THE
A Universal picture starring Sonja Henie in a cast that included Olga San Juan and Michael Kirby, and directed by Frederick De Cordova. Songs by Jack Brooks and Saul Chaplin:
COUNT YOUR BLESSINGS; THE FRIENDLY POLKA and WHO BE-LIEVES IN SANTA CLAUS?

DATE WITH JUDY, A
A M-G-M picture starring Wallace Beery, Jane Powell and Elizabeth Taylor in a cast that included Carmen Miranda, Rob-ert Stack and Xavier Cugat and his orches-tra, and directed by Richard Thorpe. Songs:
JUDALINE by Don Raye and Gene De-Paul; IT'S A MOST UNUSUAL DAY by Harold Adamson and Jimmy McHugh; I'M STRICTLY ON THE CORNY SIDE by Stella Unger and Alec Templeton; I'VE GOT A DATE WITH JUDY and I'M GONNA MEET MY MARY by Bill Katz and Calvin Jackson.

EASTER PARADE
An M-G-M picture starring Judy Gar-

land and Fred Astaire in a cast that included Peter Lawford and Ann Miller, and directed by Charles Walters. Songs by Irving Berlin:
A FELLA WITH AN UMBRELLA; IT ONLY HAPPENS WHEN I DANCE WITH YOU; BETTER LUCK NEXT TIME; STEPPING OUT WITH MY BABY; A COUPLE OF SWELLS; DRUM CRAZY; HAPPY EASTER and EASTER PARADE.

EMPEROR WALTZ, THE
A Paramount picture starring Bing Crosby and Joan Fontaine in a cast that included Roland Culver, Richard Haydn and Lucille Watson, and directed by Billy Wilder. Musical numbers:
GET YOURSELF A PHONOGRAPH by Johnny Burke and Jimmy Van Heusen; FRIENDLY MOUNTAINS (melody based on Swiss airs with lyrics by Johnny Burke); A KISS IN YOUR EYES by Richard Heuberger and Johnny Burke; I KISS YOUR HAND MADAME by Ralph Erwin and Fritz Rotter; WHISTLER AND HIS DOG by Arthur Pryor; THE EMPEROR WALTZ (melody based on music by Johann Strauss with lyrics by Johnny Burke).

FEUDIN', FUSSIN' AND A-FIGHTIN'
A Universal picture starring Donald O'Connor in a cast that included Marjorie Main, Percy Kilbride, Penny Edwards and Joe Besser, and directed by George Sherman. Songs:
FEUDIN,' FUSSIN' AND A-FIGHTIN' by Al Dubin and Burton Lane; S'POSIN' by Andy Razaf and Paul Denniker; ME AND MY SHADOW by Al Jolson, Billy Rose and Dave Dreyer.

FOREIGN AFFAIR, A
A Paramount picture starring Jean Arthur, Marlene Dietrich and John Lund, and directed by Billy Wilder. Songs by Frederick Hollander:
BLACK MARKET; ILLUSIONS; RUINS OF BERLIN; IOWA CORN SONG and MEADOWLAND.

GLAMOUR GIRL
A Columbia picture filmed with a cast headed by Susan Reed, Virginia Grey and Gene Krupa and his band, and directed by Arthur Dreifuss. Musical numbers:
ANYWHERE by Sammy Cahn and Jule Styne; WITHOUT IMAGINATION by Doris Fisher and Allan Roberts; GENE'S BOOGIE by Segar Ellis and George Williams.

I SURRENDER DEAR
A Columbia picture starring Gloria Jean and David Street in a cast that included Don McQuire and Alice Tyrrell, and directed by Arthur Dreifuss. Songs:
I SURRENDER DEAR by Harry Barris and Gordon Clifford; HOW CAN YOU TELL AMADA MIO? by Doris Fisher and Allan Roberts; WHEN YOU ARE IN THE ROOM by Oscar Hammerstein II and Ben Oakland; NOBODY ELSE BUT ELSIE by Allie Wrubel.

IF YOU KNEW SUSIE
An RKO picture starring Eddie Cantor and Joan Davis, and directed by Gordon M. Douglas. Songs by Harold Adamson and Jimmy McHugh:
LIVIN' THE LIFE OF LOVE; MY HOW THE TIME GOES BY and WHAT DO I WANT WITH MONEY?

ISN'T IT ROMANTIC?
A Paramount picture starring Veronica Lake and Mary Hatcher in a cast that included Mona Freeman, Billy DeWolfe and Pearl Bailey, and directed by Norman Z. McLeod. Songs by Ray Evans and Jay Livingston:
WON'DRIN WHEN; I SHOULDA QUIT WHEN I WAS AHEAD; MISS JULIE JULY; INDIANA DINNER and AT THE NICKELODEON

KISSING BANDIT, THE
An M-G-M picture starring Frank Sinatra and Kathryn Grayson in a cast that included J. Carroll Naish and Mildred Natwick, and directed by Laslo Benedek. Songs by Edward Heyman, Earl Brent and Nacio Herb Brown:
IF I STEAL A KISS; SENORITA; LOVE IS WHERE YOU FIND IT; TO-MORROW MEANS ROMANCE; WHAT'S WRONG WITH ME?; I LIKE YOU; DANCE OF FURY and SIESTA.

LULU BELLE
A Columbia release starring Dorothy Lamour and George Montgomery in a cast that included Albert Dekker, Otto Kruger and Glenda Farrell, and directed by Leslie Fenton. Songs:
LULU BELLE by Edgar DeLange and Henry Russell; I'D BE LOST WITHOUT YOU by Henry Russell; SWEETIE PIE by John Lehman and Henry Russell; ACE IN THE HOLE by George Mitchell and James Dempsey; SWEETHEART OF THE BLUES by Lester Lee and Allan Roberts.

MARY LOU

A Columbia picture filmed with a cast headed by Robert Lowery, Joan Barton and Glenda Farrell, and directed by Arthur Dreifuss. Musical numbers:
LEARNING TO SPEAK ENGLISH by Ben Blossner; FRANKIE CARLE'S BOOGIE by Frankie Carle; WASN'T IT SWELL LAST NIGHT? by Doris Fisher and Allan Roberts; MARY LOU by Abe Lyman and J. Russell Robinson; DON'T MIND MY TROUBLES by Lester Lee and Allan Roberts.

MELODY TIME

An RKO-Walt Disney production filmed with a cast headed by Roy Rogers and Trigger, Dennis Day, the Andrews Sisters, Fred Waring and his Pennsylvanians, Freddy Martin, Frances Langford, Ethel Smith and Buddy Clark. Songs:
BLAME IT ON THE SAMBA by Ray Gilbert and Ernesto Nazareth; PECOS BILL and BLUE SHADOWS ON THE TRAIL by Johnny Lange and Eliot Daniel; MELODY TIME by Bennie Benjamin and George Weiss; LITTLE TOOT by Allie Wrubel; ONCE UPON A WINTERTIME by Ray Gilbert and Bobby Worth; THE PIONEER SONG; THE LORD IS GOOD TO ME and APPLE SONG by Kim Gannon and Walter Kent.

MYSTERY IN MEXICO

An RKO picture filmed with a cast headed by William Lundigan, Jacqueline White and Ricardo Cortez, and directed by Robert Wise. Songs by Johnny Burke and Jimmy Van Heusen:
SOMETHING IN COMMON; AT THE PSYCHOLOGICAL MOMENT; I COULD GET ALONG WITH YOU and ROLLING IN RAINBOWS.

ON AN ISLAND WITH YOU

An M-G-M picture starring Esther Williams, Peter Lawford and Jimmy Durante, and directed by Richard Thorpe. Songs by Edward Heyman and Nacio Herb Brown:
TAKING MISS MARY TO THE BALL; IF I WERE YOU; ON AN ISLAND WITH YOU; THE DOG SONG and BUENOS NOCHES BUENOS AIRES.

ONE SUNDAY AFTERNOON

A Warner Brothers' picture starring Dennis Morgan and Janis Paige in a cast that included Don DeFore, Dorothy Malone and Ben Blue, and directed by Raoul Walsh. Songs:
GIRLS WERE MADE TO TAKE CARE OF BOYS; ONE SUNDAY AFTERNOON; THE RIGHT TO VOTE; SOMEDAY and JOHNNY AND LUCILLE by Ralph Blane; MARY YOU'RE A LITTLE BIT OLD FASHIONED by Marion Sunshine and Henry Marshall.

ONE TOUCH OF VENUS

A Universal picture starring Ava Gardner and Robert Walker in a cast that included Dick Haymes, Eve Arden and Olga San Juan, and directed by William A. Seiter. Songs:
MY WEEK and DON'T LOOK NOW BUT MY HEART IS SHOWING by Ann Ronell and Kurt Weill; SPEAK LOW; THAT'S HIM and THE TROUBLE WITH WOMEN by Ogden Nash and Kurt Weill.

PIRATE, THE

An M-G-M picture starring Judy Garland and Gene Kelly in a cast that included Walter Slezac and Reginald Owen, and directed by Vincent Minnelli. Songs by Noel Coward and Cole Porter:
LOVE OF MY LIFE; MACK THE BLACK; YOU CAN DO NO WRONG; BE A CLOWN; NINA and VOODOO.

ROMANCE ON THE HIGH SEAS

A Warner Brothers' picture starring Jack Carson and Janis Paige in a cast that included Doris Day, Don DeFore and Oscar Levant, and directed by Michael Curtiz. Songs by Sammy Cahn and Jule Styne:
IT'S YOU OR NO ONE; I'M IN LOVE; THE TOURIST TRADE; IT'S MAGIC; RUN, RUN, RUN; TWO LOVERS MET IN THE NIGHT and PUT 'EM IN A BOX, TIE 'EM WITH A RIBBON AND THROW 'EM IN THE DEEP BLUE SEA.

SO DEAR TO MY HEART

An RKO-Walt Disney production filmed with a cast headed by Bobby Driscoll, Beulah Blondi, Burl Ives, Luana Patten and Harry Carey. Songs:
SO DEAR TO MY HEART by Irving Taylor and Ticker Freeman; IT'S WHAT YOU DO WITH WHAT YOU'VE GOT by Don Raye and Gene DePaul; OL' DAN PATCH; LAVENDER BLUE and STICK-TO-IT-IVITY by Larry Morey and Eliot Daniel; COUNTY FAIR by Bob Wells and Mel Torme.

SONG IS BORN, A

An RKO-Samuel Goldwyn production starring Danny Kaye in a cast that included Hugh Herbert and Virginia Mayo, and di-

rected by Howard Hawks. Songs by Don Raye and Gene DePaul:
STEALIN' APPLES; DADDY-O; FLYING HOME and A SONG IS BORN.

SUMMER HOLIDAY
An M-G-M picture, based on the Eugene O'Neill play *Ah, Wilderness,* starring Mickey Rooney, Gloria DeHaven, Walter Huston and Frank Morgan, and directed by Rouben Mamoulain. Songs by Ralph Blane and Harry Warren:
IT'S OUR HOME TOWN; AFRAID TO FALL IN LOVE; ALL HAIL DANVILLE HIGH; STANLEY STEAMER; IT'S INDEPENDENCE DAY and I THINK YOU'RE THE SWEETEST KID I'VE EVER KNOWN.

THAT LADY IN ERMINE
A 20th Century-Fox picture starring Betty Grable and Douglas Fairbanks Jr., and directed by Ernst Lubitsch. Songs:
THIS IS THE MOMENT; THE MELODY HAS TO BE RIGHT; THERE'S SOMETHING ABOUT MIDNIGHT; THE JESTER'S SONG and OH, WHAT I'LL DO (TO THAT WILD HUNGARIAN) by Leo Robin and Frederick Hollander; IT'S ALWAYS A BEAUTIFUL DAY by Leo Robin and Ernst Lubitsch.

TWO GUYS FROM TEXAS
A Warner Brothers' picture starring Dennis Morgan, Jack Carson, Dorothy Malone and Penny Edwards, and directed by David Butler. Songs by Sammy Cahn and Jule Styne:
EVERY DAY I LOVE YOU A LITTLE BIT MORE; HANKERIN'; I DON'T CARE IF IT RAINS ALL NIGHT; THERE'S MUSIC IN THE LAND; I

NEVER MET A TEXAN and I WANNA BE A COWBOY IN THE MOVIES.

UP IN CENTRAL PARK
A Universal picture starring Deanna Durbin in a cast that included Dick Haymes and Vincent Price, and directed by William Seiter. Songs by Dorothy Fields and Sigmund Romberg.
CAROUSEL IN THE PARK; WHEN SHE WALKS IN THE ROOM and OH SAY DO YOU SEE WHAT I SEE?

WHEN MY BABY SMILES AT ME
A 20th Century-Fox picture starring Betty Grable, Dan Dailey, and June Havoc in a cast that included Jack Oakie, James Gleason and Richard Arlen, and directed by Walter Lang. Songs:
BY THE WAY and WHAT DID I DO? by Mack Gordon and Josef Myrow; WHEN MY BABY SMILES AT ME by Andrew B. Sterling and Harry Von Tilzer.

YOU WERE MEANT FOR ME
A 20th Century-Fox picture starring Jeanne Crain and Dan Dailey in a cast that included Oscar Levant, and directed by Lloyd Bacon. Songs:
GOOD NIGHT SWEETHEART by James Campbell, Reginald Connelly and Ray Noble; CRAZY RHYTHM by Irving Caesar, Roger Wolfe Kahn and Joseph Meyer; AIN'T MISBEHAVIN' by Andy Razaf and Fats Waller; IF I HAD YOU by James Campbell, Reginald Connelly and Ted Shapiro; I'LL GET BY (AS LONG AS I HAVE YOU) by Roy Turk and Fred Ahlert; AIN'T SHE SWEET? by Jack Yellen and Milton Ager; YOU WERE MEANT FOR ME by Arthur Freed and Nacio Herb Brown.

Feature Films With Songs

ALBUQUERQUE
A Paramount picture starring Randolph Scott and Barbara Britton in a cast that included Gabby Hayes and Lon Chaney, and directed by Ray Enright. Song by Darrell Calker:
ALBUQUERQUE

ANGEL ON THE AMAZON
A Republic picture filmed with a cast headed by George Brent, Vera Rawlston, Constance Bennett and Brian Aherne, and directed by John H. Auer. Song by Stanley Wilson and Nester Amaral:
UNCLE SAMBA

ARCH OF TRIUMPH
A United Artists' picture starring Ingrid Bergman, Charles Boyer and Charles Laughton, and directed by Lewis Milestone. Song by Ervin Drake, Jimmy Shirl and Ruby Polk:
LONG AFTER TONIGHT

ARKANSAS SWING
A Columbia picture filmed with a cast headed by Gloria Henry and the Hoosier Hot Shots. Song by Frances Clark and Robert Bilder:
THAT LUCKY FEELING

BEYOND GLORY

A Paramount picture starring Alan Ladd and Donna Reed in a cast that included George Macready and George Coulouris, and directed by John Farrow. Song by Jay Evans and Ray Livingston:
BEYOND GLORY

BIG CITY

An M-G-M picture starring Margaret O'-Brien in a cast that included Robert Preston, Danny Thomas, George Murphy and Butch Jenkins, and directed by Norman Taurog. Songs:
OK'L BABY DOK'L by Inez James and Sidney Miller; I'M GONNA SEE A LOT OF YOU by Janice Torre and Fred Spielman; DON'T BLAME ME by Dorothy Fields and Jimmy McHugh, YIPPEE-O YIPPEE-AY by Jerry Seelen and Walter Pepp.

BIG CLOCK, THE

A Paramount picture filmed with a cast headed by Ray Milland, Charles Laughton, Maureen O'Sullivan and Rita Johnson, and directed by John Farrow. Song by Ray Evans and Jay Livingston:
THE BIG CLOCK

CAMPUS SLEUTH

A Monogram picture starring Freddie Stewart and June Preisser, and directed by Will Jason. Songs by Sid Robin and Will Jason:
BABY YOU CAN COUNT ON ME; WHAT HAPPENED? and NEITHER COULD I.

DON'T TRUST YOUR HUSBAND

A United Artists' picture filmed with a cast headed by Fred MacMurray, Madeleine Carrol, Charles "Buddy" Rogers, Rita Johnson and Louise Allbritton, and directed by Lloyd Bacon. Songs:
THESE THINGS ARE YOU and AN INNOCENT AFFAIR by Kim Gannon and Walter Kent; JEALOUS by Jack Little, Tommie Malie and Dick Finch.

DREAM GIRL

A Paramount picture starring Betty Hutton and MacDonald Carey in a cast that included Virginia Fields, Patric Knowles and Walter Abel, and directed by Mitchell Leisen. Songs by Ray Evans and Jay Livingston:
CINCINNATI; DRUNK WITH LOVE and DREAM GIRL.

DUEL IN THE SUN

An RKO picture starring Jennifer Jones and Joseph Cotten in a cast that included Gregory Peck, Lionel Barrymore, Herbert Marshall and Walter Huston, and directed by King Vidor. Song by Allie Wrubel:
GOTTA GET ME SOMEBODY TO LOVE

ENCHANTMENT

An RKO picture filmed with a cast headed by David Niven, Teresa Wright, Evelyn Keyes and Farley Granger, and directed by Irving Reis. Song by Don Raye and Gene DePaul:
ENCHANTMENT

GIVE MY REGARDS TO BROADWAY

A 20th Century-Fox picture filmed with a cast headed by Dan Dailey, Charles Winninger, Nancy Guild, Charles Ruggles and Fay Bainter, and directed by Lloyd Bacon. Songs:
GIVE MY REGARDS TO BROADWAY by George M. Cohan; WHEN FRANCES DANCES WITH ME by Benny Ryan and Sol Violinsky.

JULIA MISBEHAVES

An M-G-M picture starring Greer Garson and Walter Pidgeon in a cast that included Peter Lawford, Elizabeth Taylor and Cesar Romero, and directed by Jack Conway. Song by Jerry Seelen and Hal Borne:
WHEN YOU'RE PLAYING WITH FIRE

KEY LARGO

A Warner Brothers' picture starring Humphrey Bogart, Edward G. Robinson and Lauren Bacall in a cast that included Lionel Barrymore and Claire Trevor, and directed by John Huston. Song by Howard Dietz and Ralph Rainger:
MOANIN' LOW

LADY FROM SHANGHAI, THE

A Columbia picture starring Rita Hayworth and Orson Wells, who also directed the film. Song by Doris Fisher and Allan Roberts:
PLEASE DON'T KISS ME

LOVES OF CARMEN, THE

A Columbia picture starring Rita Hayworth in a cast that included Glenn Ford, Ron Randell and Victor Jory, and directed by Charles Vidor. Song by Fred Karger and Morris Stoloff:
THE LOVE OF A GYPSY

LUXURY LINER

An M-G-M picture filmed with a cast headed by George Brent, Jane Powell,

Lauritz Melchior and Frances Gifford, and directed by Richard Whorf. Song by Janice Torre, Fred Spielman and Fritz Rotter:
SPRING CAME BACK TO VIENNA

MEXICAN HAYRIDE
A Universal picture starring Abbott and Costello in a cast that included Virginia Grey, Luba Malina, John Hubbard and Pedro de Cordoba, and directed by Charles T. Barton. Song by Jack Brooks and Walter Scharf:
IS IT YES OR IS IT NO?

MR. PEABODY AND THE MERMAID
A Universal picture starring William Powell and Ann Blyth, and directed by Irving Pichel. Song by Johnny Mercer and Robert Emmett Dolan:
THE CARIBEES

MOONRISE
A Republic picture starring Ethel Barrymore, Gail Russell and Dane Clark, and directed by Frank Borzage. Songs:
IT JUST DAWNED ON ME by Harry Tobias and Bill Lava; MOONRISE by Edgar De Lange and Louis Alter.

MY GIRL TISA
A United Artists' picture filmed with a cast headed by Lilli Palmer, Sam Wanamaker and Akim Tamiroff, and directed by Elliott Nugent. Song by Mack David:
AT THE CANDLELIGHT CAFE

MY OWN TRUE LOVE
A Paramount picture starring Melvyn Douglas, Phyllis Calvert and Wanda Hendrix, and directed by Compton Bennett. Song by Ray Evans and Jay Livingston:
MY OWN TRUE LOVE

NIGHT HAS A THOUSAND EYES, THE
A Paramount picture starring Edward G. Robinson and Gail Russell in a cast that included John Lund, Virginia Bruce and William Demarest, and directed by John Farrow. Song by Buddy Bernier and Jerry Brainen:
THE NIGHT HAS A THOUSAND EYES

PALE FACE, THE
A Paramount picture starring Bob Hope and Jane Russell, and directed by Norman Z. McLeod. Songs:
BUTTONS AND BOWS and MEET-CHA ROUND THE CORNER by Ray Evans and Jay Livingston; GET A MAN by Joseph J. Lilley.

RACE STREET
An RKO picture filmed with a cast headed by George Raft, Marilyn Maxwell and William Bendix, and directed by Edward L. Marin. Songs:
LOVE THAT BOY by Don Raye and Gene DePaul; I'M IN A JAM WITH BABY by Ted Koehler and M. K. Jerome.

RACHEL AND THE STRANGER
An RKO picture starring Loretta Young and William Holden in a cast that included Robert Mitchum, and directed by Norman Foster. Songs by Ray Webb and Waldo Salt:
OH HE, OH HI, OH HO; TALL DARK STRANGER; JUST LIKE ME; SUMMER SONG and FOOLISH PRIDE.

ROAD HOUSE
A 20th Century-Fox picture filmed with a cast headed by Ida Lupino, Cornel Wilde and Celeste Holm, and directed by Jean Negulesco. Songs:
AGAIN by Dorcas Cochrane and Lionel Newman; THE RIGHT KIND by Don George, Charles Henderson and Lionel Newman.

ROGUE'S REGIMENT
A Universal picture filmed with a cast headed by Dick Powell, Marta Toren and Vincent Price, and directed by Robert Florey. Songs by Jack Brooks and Serge Walter:
JUST FOR A WHILE and WHO CAN TELL? (NOT I)

SAINTED SISTERS, THE
A Paramount picture starring Veronica Lake and Joan Caulfield in a cast that included Barry Fitzgerald and William Demarest, and directed by William D. Russell. Song by Ray Evans and Jay Livingston:
PLEASE PUT OUT THE LIGHT

SIGN OF THE RAM, THE
A Columbia picture filmed with a cast headed by Susan Peters, Alexander Knox, Phyllis Thaxter and Peggy Ann Garner, and directed by John Sturges. Song by Allan Roberts and Lester Lee:
I'LL NEVER SAY I LOVE YOU (TO ANYONE BUT YOU)

SINGIN' SPURS
A Columbia picture filmed with a cast headed by Pat White and the Hoosier Hot Shots, and directed by Ray Nazarro. Song by Allan Roberts and Lester Lee:
SINGIN' SPURS

SLEEP MY LOVE

A United Artists' picture starring Claudette Colbert and Don Ameche, and directed by Douglas Sirk. Song by Sam Coslow:
SLEEP MY LOVE

SMART GIRLS DON'T TALK

A Warner Brothers' picture filmed with a cast headed by Virginia Mayo, Bruce Bennett and Robert Hutton, and directed by Richard Bare. Song by Lee Towers and Don Pelosi:
THE STARS WILL REMEMBER

STATION WEST

An RKO picture starring William Powell and Jane Greer in a cast that included Agnes Moorhead, Burl Ives, Tom Powers and Steve Brodie, and directed by Sidney Lanfield. Songs by Mort Greene and Leigh Harline:
THE SUN IS SHINING WARM; SOMETIME REMIND ME TO TELL YOU and A MAN CAN'T GROW OLD.

TEXAS, BROOKLYN AND HEAVEN

A United Artists' picture filmed with a cast headed by Guy Madison, Dianna Lynn, James Dunn and Lionel Standing, and directed by William Castle. Song by Ervin Drake and Jimmy Shirl:
TEXAS, BROOKLYN AND HEAVEN

THREE DARING DAUGHTERS

An M-G-M picture filmed with a cast headed by Jeanette MacDonald, Jose Iturbi, Jane Powell and Edward Arnold, and directed by Fred M. Wilcox. Song by Howard Dietz and Sammy Fain:

THE DICKEY BIRD SONG
TO THE VICTOR

A Warner Brothers' picture starring Dennis Morgan and Viveca Lindfors, and directed by Delmer Daves. Songs:
LA VIE EN ROSE by Edith Paif and Louiguy; YOU'RE TOO DANGEROUS CHERIE by Mack David and Louiguy.

VARIETY TIME

An RKO picture filmed with a cast headed by Edgar Kennedy, Leon Errol, Pat Rooney and Frankie Carle, and directed by Hal Yates. Songs:
C'EST MON COEUR by Stephen Morgan; BA-BA-LU by Bob Russell and Marguerita Lecuona.

WHIPLASH

A Warner Brothers' picture starring Dane Clark and Alexis Smith in a cast that included Zachary Scott, Eve Arden, Jeffry Lynn and S. Z. Sakall, and directed by Lewis Seiter. Songs:
JUST FOR NOW by Dick Redmond; THE GIRL WITH THE SPANISH DRAWL (WOW! WOW! WOW!) by Mack David, Fauste Curbelo and Johnny Camacho.

WHISPERIN' SMITH

A Paramount picture filmed with a cast headed by Alan Ladd, Brenda Marshall, Robert Preston and Donald Crisp, and directed by Leslie Fenton. Song by Ray Evans and Jay Livingston:
LARAMIE

Western Films With Songs

BLACK HILLS

An Eagle-Lion picture filmed with a cast headed by Eddie Dean, Roscoe Ates and Shirley Patterson, and directed by Ray Taylor. Songs by Eddie Dean and Hal Blair:
LET'S GO SPARKIN' and BLACK HILLS

CALIFORNIA FIREBRAND

A Republic picture filmed with a cast headed by Monte Hale, Adrian Booth, Paul Hurst and Alice Tyrell, and directed by Philip Ford. Songs by Sid Robin and Foy Willing:
TRAIL TO CALIFORNIA and GONNA HAVE A BIG TIME TONIGHT

COURTIN' TROUBLE

A Monogram picture filmed with a cast headed by Jimmy Wakely, Cannonball Taylor and Virginia Belmont, and directed by Ford Beebe. Songs:
MOON OVER MONTANA by Oliver Drake, Jimmy Wakely and Edward Kay; A NEW THRILL FROM AN OLD FLAME by Tommy Dilbeck.

COWBOY CAVALIER

A Monogram picture filmed with a cast headed by Jimmy Wakely, Cannonball Taylor, Jane Bryant and Claire Whitney, and directed by Derwin M. Abrahams. Songs:
SHE'S MINE ALL MINE by Lee 'Lasses White; THIS OLD WHITE MULE OF MINE by Bob Nolan; NIGHT AFTER NIGHT by Doris Mayer and Jimmy Wakely.

EYES OF TEXAS

A Republic picture starring Roy Rogers in a cast that included Lynne Roberts, Andy Devine and Nana Bryant, and directed by William Witney. Songs:

TEXAS TRAILS and GRAVE DIGGER OF THE WEST by Tim Spencer; PADRE OF OLD SAN ANTONE by Tim Spencer and Aaron Gonzales.

FAR FRONTIER, THE

A Republic picture starring Roy Rogers in a cast that included Gail Davis, Andy Devine and Nana Bryant, and directed by William Witney. Songs by Jack Elliott:

THE FAR FRONTIER and THE CASUAL COWBOY'S SONG

GALLANT LEGION, THE

A Republic picture filmed with a cast headed by Bill Elliott, Adrian Booth and Joseph Schildkraut, and directed by Joseph Kane. Songs by Jack Elliott:

A KISS OR TWO; A GAMBLER'S LIFE and LADY FROM MONTEREY.

GAY RANCHERO, THE

A Republic picture starring Roy Rogers in a cast that included June Frazee, Andy Devine and Tito Guizar, and directed by William Witney. Songs:

A GAY RANCHERO by Abe Tuvin, Francia Lubin and J. J. Espinosa; GRANADA by Augustin Lara; COWBOY COUNTRY by Tim Spencer; WAIT TILL I GET MY SUNSHINE IN THE MOONLIGHT by Jack Lambert and D. Olson; YOU BELONG TO MY HEART by Ray Gilbert and Augustin Lara.

GRAND CANYON TRAIL

A Republic picture starring Roy Rogers in a cast that included Jane Frazee and Andy Devine, and directed by William Witney. Songs:

COLORADO JOE and GRAND CANYON TRAIL by Jack Elliott; THE RUNAWAY MARE by Nathan Scott; EVERYTHING'S GOING MY WAY by Foy Willing.

NIGHTTIME IN NEVADA

A Republic picture starring Roy Rogers in a cast that included Adele Mara and Andy Devine, and directed by William Witney. Songs:

OVER NEVADA by Tim Spencer; SWEET LAREDO SUE by Bob Nolan and Ed Morrissey; BIG ROCK CANDY MOUNTAIN (Traditional).

OLD LOS ANGELES

A Republic picture filmed with a cast headed by Bill Elliott, John Carroll and Catherine McLeod, and directed by Joseph Kane. Song by Jack Elliott and Aaron Gonzales:

EVER FAITHFUL

RANGE RENEGADES

A Monogram picture starring Jimmy Wakely and Jennifer Holt, and directed by Lambert Hillyer. Song by Buddy Feyne and Irving Miller:

ARIZONA SUNSET

SMOKY MOUNTAIN MELODY

A Columbia picture starring Roy Acuff and the Smoky Mountain Boys, and directed by Ray Nazarro. Song by Robert Bilder:

PARTY TIME ON THE PRAIRIE

SONS OF ADVENTURE

A Republic picture starring Russell Hayden and Lynne Roberts, and directed by Yakima Canutt. Song by Sammy Cahn and Jule Styne:

IF IT'S LOVE

STRAWBERRY ROAN, THE

A Republic picture starring Gene Autry in a cast that included Gloria Henry and Jack Holt, and directed by John English. Songs:

WHEN THE WHITE ROSES BLOOM IN RED VALLEY by Paul Herrick and Allie Wrubel; STRAWBERRY ROAN by Fred Holland and Nat Vincent; ANGEL SONG by Gene Autry, Curt Massey and Mary Milland.

UNDER CALIFORNIA SKIES

A Republic picture starring Roy Rogers in a cast that included Jane Frazee and Andy Devine, and directed by William Witney. Songs:

LITTLE SADDLE PAL; ROGERS KING OF THE COWBOYS and UNDER CALIFORNIA SKIES by Jack Elliott; DUST by Johnny Marvin; SERENADE TO A COYOTE by Andy Parker.

1 9 4 9

"Jolson Sings Again" For A Triumphant Bow-off at 63

On March 26, 1949, Al Jolson celebrated his sixty-third birthday. Fifty of these sixty-three years had been spent in show business. And five months later, the skies over Hollywood were flooded with the beams of searchlights heralding the premiere of the Mammy Singer's latest and last picture: *Jolson Sings Again,* a film that gladdened the hearts of movie house owners by grossing $5,000,000 at the ticket windows. And $5,000,000 wasn't hay in a year when the box-office harvest was pitifully poor.

In November of that same year, the searchlights beamed again for another premiere: *Always Leave Them Laughing,* in which Milton Berle made his debut as a film star. But Uncle Miltie, the hottest thing in TV, was no ball of fire on the screen, and his box-office appeal, or lack of it, again had the wise men of show business pondering over a question that had plagued them for years:

"Where were the future stars of stage and screen to get their schooling now that minstrelsy, burlesque, vaudeville and the road show, all alma maters of Al Jolson and other truly greats of show business, were dead?"

Again, as in 1947, Al Jolson was the screen headliner of the year, and in the Golden Circle reserved for musical films grossing $4,000,000 or more, had to share honors only with the whimsical creatures created by Walt Disney's cartoonists for the story-book fantasy *Cinderella.*

Bing Crosby, as always, was a contender for box-office laurels with two pictures: *The Connecticut Yankee* and *Top O' The Morning* with songs by Johnny Burke and Jimmy Van Heusen ,and among the tunesmiths on Hollywood's sharps-and-flats team, Frank Loesser batted better than .300 with *Baby It's Cold Outside,* the Oscar-winning song of 1949, and other hits he authored and composed for *Neptune's Daughter,* starring Esther Williams and Red Skelton, and *Red Hot And Blue* in which Betty Hutton, Victor Mature and June Havoc had top billing on the marquee boards.

But in 1949 the old songs were the best songs—the "pop" numbers Al Jolson revived in *The Jolson Story*—the songs from the Broadway musical of 1931, *The Bandwagon,* that had a rebirth in *Dancing In The Dark*—the immortal Jerome Kern songs June Haver sang in *Look For The Silver Lining,* a screen tribute to Marilyn Miller—the songs that bore on their title pages the name of Fred Fisher, whose colorful Tin Pan Alley career was made the basis of the film *Oh, You Beautiful Doll.*

These oldtime songs, like Al Jolson, had a nostalgic appeal. But probably there was another reason for their popularity in 1949. They recalled the years many would have traded for those of the "bright new world" already tarnished by economic unrest and impending strife—the years when it wasn't "so cold outside" the executive offices and real estate concerns for millions of disillusioned young men and women seeking gainful employment and a decent place to live.

Musicals

ALWAYS LEAVE THEM LAUGHING
A Warner Brothers' picture starring Milton Berle in a cast that included Virginia Mayo, Bert Lahr, Alan Hale and Grace Hayes, and directed by Roy Del Ruth. Songs:
YOU'RE TOO INTENSE and ALWAYS LEAVE THEM LAUGHING by Milton Berle and Sammy Cahn; SAY FAREWELL by Sammy Cahn and Ray Heindorf; CLINK YOUR GLASSES by Johnny Mercer and Sammy Cahn; EMBRACEABLE YOU by Ira and George Gershwin; BY THE LIGHT OF THE SILVERY MOON by Edward Madden and Gus Edwards.

BARCLAYS OF BROADWAY, THE
An M-G-M picture starring Ginger Rogers and Fred Astaire in a cast that included Billie Burke and Oscar Levant, and directed by Charles Walters. Songs:
YOU'D BE HARD TO REPLACE; WEEK-END IN THE COUNTRY; MANHATTAN DOWNBEAT; SHOES WITH WINGS ON and MY ONE AND ONLY HIGHLAND FLING by Ira Gershwin and Harry Warren; THEY CAN'T TAKE THAT AWAY FROM ME by Ira and George Gershwin.

BEAUTIFUL BLONDE FROM BASHFUL BEND
A 20th Century-Fox picture starring Betty Grable in a cast that included Cesar Romero, Rudy Vallee and Olga San Juan, and directed by Preston Sturges. Songs:
EVERYTIME I MEET YOU by Mack Gordon and Josef Myrow; BEAUTIFUL BLONDE FROM BASHFUL BEND by Don George and Lionel Newman; IN THE GLOAMING by Meta Orred and Annie F. Harrison.

CONNECTICUT YANKEE, A
A Paramount picture starring Bing Crosby and Rhonda Fleming in a cast that included Sir Cedric Hardwicke and William Bendix, and directed by Tay Garnett. Songs by Johnny Burke and Jimmy Van Heusen:
ONCE AND FOR ALWAYS; IF YOU STUB YOUR TOE ON THE MOON; WHEN IS SOMETIME?; BUSY DOING NOTHING and TWIXT MYSELF AND ME.

DANCING IN THE DARK
A 20th Century-Fox picture, based on the Broadway musical The Band Wagon, filmed with a cast headed by William Powell, Mark Stevens, Betsy Drake, Adolphe Menjou, Randy Stuart, Hope Emerson and Walter Catlett, and directed by Irving Reis. Songs by Howard Dietz and Arthur Schwartz:
DANCING IN THE DARK; NEW SUN IN THE SKY; SOMETHING TO REMEMBER YOU BY and I LOVE LOUISA.

HOLIDAY IN HAVANA
A Columbia picture starring Desi Arnaz and Mary Hatcher, and directed by Jean Yarbrough. Musical numbers:
RUMBA RUMBERO by Albert Gamse and Miguelito Valdez; COPA CABANA by Doris Fisher and Allan Roberts; I'LL TAKE ROMANCE by Oscar Hammerstein II and Ben Oakland; STRAW HAT SONG by Fred Karger and Allan Roberts; MADE FOR EACH OTHER by Ervin Drake, Jimmy Shirl and Rene Touzet; HOLIDAY IN HAVANA by Desi Arnaz.

IN THE GOOD OLD SUMMERTIME
An M-G-M picture starring Judy Garland and Van Johnson in a cast that included S. Z. Sakall, Spring Byington and Buster Keaton, and directed by Robert Z. Leonard. Songs:
MERRY CHRISTMAS by Janice Torre and Fred Spielman; MEET ME TONIGHT IN DREAMLAND by Beth Slater Whitson and Lee Friedman; PUT YOUR ARMS AROUND ME HONEY by Junie McCree and Harry Von Tilzer; PLAY THAT BARBER SHOP CHORD by Ballard MacDonald, William Tracey and Lewis Muir; I DON'T CARE by Jean Lenox and Harry Sutton.

INSPECTOR GENERAL, THE
A Warner Brothers' picture starring Danny Kaye in a cast that included Walter

Slezac, Barbara Bates, Elsa Lanchester and Rhys Williams, and directed by Henry Koster. Songs by Sylvia Fine:
ONWARD, ONWARD; THE MEDICINE SHOW; THE INSPECTOR GENERAL; LONELY HEARTS; GYPSY DRINKING SONG; SOLILOQUY FOR THREE HEADS; HAPPY TIMES and BRODNY.

IT'S A GREAT FEELING
A Warner Brothers' picture starring Dennis Morgan, Doris Day and Frank Carson in which Gary Cooper, Joan Crawford, Errol Flynn, Edward G. Robinson and Jane Wyman made guest appearances, and directed by David Butler. Songs by Sammy Cahn and Jule Styne:
BLAME MY ABSENT-MINDED HEART; AT THE CAFE RENDEZVOUS; THERE'S NOTHING ROUGHER THAN LOVE; GIVE ME A SONG WITH A BEAUTIFUL MELODY; IT'S A GREAT FEELING and FIDDLE-DEE-DEE.

JOLSON SINGS AGAIN
A Columbia picture starring Larry Parks as Jolson in a cast that included Barbara Hale, William Demarest and Bill Goodwin, and directed by Henry Levin. Songs:
I ONLY HAVE EYES FOR YOU by Al Dubin and Harry Warren; I'M JUST WILD ABOUT HARRY by Noble Sissle and Eubie Blake; MA BLUSHIN' ROSIE by Edgar Smith and John Stromberg; APRIL SHOWERS by B. G. DeSylva and Louis Silvers; SWANEE by Irving Caesar and George Gershwin; I'M LOOKING OVER A FOUR-LEAF CLOVER by Mort Dixon and Harry M. Woods; CALIFORNIA HERE I COME by B. G. DeSylva, Al Jolson and Joseph Meyer; CHINATOWN MY CHINATOWN by Joe Young, Sam Lewis and Jean Schwartz; CAROLINA IN THE MORNING by Gus Kahn and Walter Donaldson; PRETTY BABY by Gus Kahn, Tony Jackson and Egbert Van Alstyne; BABY FACE by Benny Davis and Harry Akst.

LADIES OF THE CHORUS
A Columbia picture filmed with a cast headed by Adele Jurgens, Marilyn Moore, Rand Brooks, Nana Bryant and Eddie Garr, and directed by Phil Karlson. Songs by Allan Roberts and Lester Lee:
ANYONE CAN SEE; CRAZY FOR YOU; EV'RY BABY NEEDS A DA-DA-DADDY; YOU'RE NEVER TOO OLD and LADIES OF THE CHORUS.

LOOK FOR THE SILVER LINING
A Warner Brothers' picture based on the life of Marilyn Miller, who was played by June Haver in a cast that included Ray Bolger, Gordon MacRae and Charles Ruggles, and directed by David Butler. Musical numbers:
WHO and SUNNY by Otto Harbach, Oscar Hammerstein II and Jerome Kern; LOOK FOR THE SILVER LINING and WHIP-POOR-WILL by B. G. DeSylva and Jerome Kern; PIROUETTE by Herman Frinck; JUST A MEMORY by B. G. DeSylva, Lew Brown and Ray Henderson; TIME ON MY HANDS by Mack Gordon, Harold Adamson and Vincent Youmans; A KISS IN THE DARK by B. G. DeSylva and Victor Herbert; WILD ROSE by Clifford Grey and Jerome Kern.

MAKE BELIEVE BALLROOM
A Columbia picture filmed with a cast headed by Jerome Courtland, Ruth Warrick, the King Cole Trio and Frankie Carle and his orchestra, and directed by Joseph Santley. Songs:
LITTLE MISS IN BETWEEN by Allan Roberts and Lester Lee; THE WAY THE TWIG IS BENT by Allan Roberts and Doris Fisher; MAKE BELIEVE BALLROOM by Leon Rene, Johnny Mercer and Al Jarvis.

MAKE MINE LAUGHS
An RKO picture filmed with a cast headed by Ray Bolger, Anne Shirley, Dennis Day, Joan Davis, Jack Haley, Leon Errol, Frances Langford and Frankie Carle and his orchestra, and directed by Richard Fleischer. Musical numbers:
DID YOU HAPPEN TO FIND A HEART? by Herb Magidson and Lou Pollack; YOU GO YOUR WAY by Mack Gordon and Harry Revel; CARLE MEETS MOZART by Frankie Carle and Frank DeVol; MOONLIGHT OVER THE ISLANDS by Mort Greene and Lou Pollack; POOR LITTLE FLY ON THE WALL by Freddy Fisher.

MANHATTAN ANGEL
A Columbia picture filmed with a cast headed by Gloria Jean, Ross Ford, Patricia White, Thurston Hall and Toni Harper, and directed by Arthur Dreifuss. Songs:
CANDY STORE BLUES by Nick Castle, Herb Jeffries and Eddie Beal; NAUGHTY ALOYSIUS by Robert Bilder; IT'S A WONDERFUL, WONDERFUL FEELING by Jack Segal and Dewey Bergman; I'LL

TAKE ROMANCE by Oscar Hammerstein II and Ben Oakland.

MY DREAM IS YOURS
A Warner Brothers' picture starring Jack Carson and Doris Day, and directed by Michael Curtiz. Songs:
SOMEONE LIKE YOU; LOVE FINDS A WAY; FREDDIE GET READY; MY DREAM IS YOURS and TIC, TIC, TIC by Ralph Freed and Harry Warren; (YOU MAY NOT BE AN ANGEL BUT) I'LL STRING ALONG WITH YOU by Al Dubin and Harry Warren; CANADIAN CAPERS by Guy Chandler, Bert White, Henry Cohen and Earle Burtnett.

MY FRIEND IRMA
A Paramount picture starring Marie Wilson and John Lund in a cast that included Diana Lynn and Don DeFore, and directed by George Marshall. Songs by Ray Evans and Jay Livingston:
HERE'S TO LOVE; JUST FOR FUN; MY FRIEND IRMA; MY ONE, MY ONLY, MY ALL.

NEPTUNE'S DAUGHTER
An M-G-M picture starring Esther Williams and Red Skelton in a cast that included Betty Garrett, Keenan Wynn and Xavier Cugat and his orchestra, and directed by Eddie Buzzell. Songs by Frank Loesser:
MY HEART BEATS FASTER; BABY IT'S COLD OUTSIDE and I LOVE THOSE MEN.

OH YOU BEAUTIFUL DOLL
A 20th Century-Fox picture based on the life of Fred Fisher, filmed with a cast headed by S. Z. Sakall, June Haver, Mark Stevens, Charlotte Greenwood and Jay C. Flippen, and directed by John M. Stahl. Songs by Fred Fisher with lyricists' name in parentheses:
OH YOU BEAUTIFUL DOLL (Nat Ayer and A. Seymour Brown); PEG O' MY HEART (Alfred Bryan); CHICAGO; I WANT YOU TO WANT ME TO WANT YOU (Bob Schafer and Alfred Bryan); COME JOSEPHINE IN MY FLYING MACHINE (Alfred Bryan); THERE'S A BROKEN HEART FOR EVERY LIGHT ON BROADWAY (Howard Johnson); WHO PAID THE RENT FOR MRS. RIP VAN WINKLE? (Alfred Bryan); DADDY YOU'VE BEEN MORE THAN A MOTHER TO ME; WHEN I GET YOU ALONE TONIGHT (Joseph McCarthy and Joe Goodwin).

ON THE TOWN
An M-G-M picture starring Gene Kelly, Frank Sinatra, Betty Garrett and Ann Miller in a cast that included Jules Munshin and Vera-Ellen, and directed by Gene Kelly and Stanley Doren. Songs by Adolph Green, Betty Comden and Leonard Bernstein:
ON THE TOWN; COUNT ON ME; PREHISTORIC MAN; COME UP TO MY PLACE; YOU'RE AWFUL; MISS TURNSTILES; MAIN STREET; A DAY IN NEW YORK and NEW YORK, NEW YORK.

RED, HOT AND BLUE
A Paramount picture starring Betty Hutton, Victor Mature and June Havoc in a cast that included William Demarest, and directed by John Farrow. Songs by Frank Loesser:
THAT'S LOYALTY; HAMLET; I WAKE UP IN THE MORNING FEELING FINE and (WHERE ARE YOU) NOW THAT I NEED YOU?

SLIGHTLY FRENCH
A Columbia picture starring Dorothy Lamour and Don Ameche in a cast that included Janis Carter, Willard Parker, Adele Jergens and Jeanne Manet, and directed by Douglas Sirk. Songs:
I WANT TO LEARN ABOUT LOVE; I KEEP TELLING MYSELF; NIGHT and FIFI FROM THE FOLIES BERGERE by Allan Roberts and Lester Lee; LET'S FALL IN LOVE by Ted Koehler and Harold Arlen.

TAKE ME OUT TO THE BALL GAME
An M-G-M picture starring Esther Williams, Frank Sinatra and Gene Kelly in a cast that included Edward Arnold, Betty Garrett and Jules Munshin, and directed by Busby Berkeley. Songs by Betty Comden, Adolph Green and Roger Edens:
THE RIGHT GIRL FOR ME; IT'S FATE BABY IT'S FATE; O'BRIEN TO RYAN TO GOLDBERG; STRICTLY U.S.A. and YES INDEEDY.

THERE'S A GIRL IN MY HEART
An Allied Artists' picture filmed with a cast headed by Lee Bowman, Elyse Knox, Gloria Jean, Peggy Ryan and Lon Chaney, and directed by Arthur Dreifuss. Songs by Robert Bilder:
BE CAREFUL OF THE TIDAL WAVE; WE ARE THE MAIN ATTRACTION; ROLLER SKATING SONG and

THERE'S A GIRL IN MY HEART (Lyrics by Arthur Dreifuss).

TOP O' THE MORNING
A Paramount picture starring Bing Crosby, Ann Blyth and Barry Fitzgerald in a cast that included Hume Cronyn, and directed by David Miller. Songs by Johnny Burke and Jimmy Van Heusen:
YOU'RE IN LOVE WITH SOMEONE; TOP O' THE MORNING; OH 'TIS SWEET TO THINK and THE DONOVANS.

YES SIR THAT'S MY BABY
A Universal picture starring Donald O'-Connor and Gloria De Haven, and directed by George Sherman. Songs by Jack Brooks and Walter Scharf:
MEN ARE LITTLE CHILDREN; THEY'VE NEVER FIGURED OUT A WOMAN and LOOK AT ME.

Feature Films With Songs

ADAM'S RIB
An M-G-M picture starring Katharine Hepburn and Spencer Tracy in a cast that included Judy Holliday, Tom Elwell and David Wayne, and directed by George Cukor. Song by Cole Porter:
FAREWELL AMANDA

ALIMONY
An Eagle-Lion picture starring Martha Vickers and John Beal, and directed by Kurt Neumann. Songs by L. Wolfe Gilbert and A. Laszlo:
THAT'S HOW DREAMS ARE MADE and YOU'RE ALL THE WORLD TO ME

BAD BOY
An Allied Artists' picture filmed with a cast headed by Lloyd Nolan, Jane Wyatt, Audie Murphy and James Gleason, and directed by Kurt Neumann. Song by Gene Austin:
DREAM ON LITTLE PLOWBOY

BAGDAD
A Universal picture filmed with a cast headed by Maureen O'Hara, Paul Christian and Vincent Price, and directed by Charles Lamont. Songs by Jack Brooks and Frank Skinner:
SONG OF THE DESERT; BAGDAD and LOVE IS STRANGE.

BRIBE, THE
An M-G-M picture starring Robert Taylor, Ava Gardner and Charles Laughton, and directed by Robert Z. Leonard. Song by William Kantz and Nacio Herb Brown:
SITUATION WANTED

BRIDE OF VENGEANCE
A Paramount picture starring John Lund, Paulette Goddard and MacDonald Carey, and directed by Mitchell Leisen. Song by Ray Evans, Jay Livingston and Troy Sanders:
GIVE THY LOVE

CHICAGO DEADLINE
A Paramount picture starring Alan Ladd, Donna Reed and June Havoc, and directed by Lewis Allen. Song by Victor Young:
OVERNIGHT

COME TO THE STABLE
A 20th Century-Fox picture starring Loretta Young and Celeste Holm, and directed by Henry Koster. Songs:
MY BOLERO by James Kennedy and Nat Simon; THROUGH A LONG AND SLEEPLESS NIGHT by Mack Gordon and Alfred Newman.

DEPUTY MARSHAL
A Lippert picture starring Jon Hall and Frances Langford, and directed by William Berke. Songs by Irving Bibo:
THERE'S A HIDEOUT IN HIDDEN VALLEY and LEVIS, PLAID SHIRT AND SPURS.

GIRL FROM JONES BEACH, THE
A Warner Brothers' picture filmed with a cast headed by Ronald Reagan, Virginia Mayo, Eddie Bracken and Dona Drake, and directed by Peter Godfrey. Songs:
THE GIRL FROM JONES BEACH by Sol Marcus and Eddie Seiler; I ONLY HAVE EYES FOR YOU by Al Dubin and Harry Warren.

GREAT LOVER, THE
A Paramount picture starring Bob Hope and Rhonda Fleming in a cast that included Roland Young and Roland Culver, and directed by Alexander Hall. Songs by Ray Evans and Jay Livingston:
A THOUSAND VIOLINS and LUCKY US

HEIRESS, THE
A Paramount picture starring Olivia De-Haviland and Montgomery Clift in a cast that included Sir Ralph Richardson and

Miriam Hopkins, and directed by William Wyler. Song by Ray Evans and Jay Livingston:
MY LOVE LOVES ME.

IT HAPPENS EVERY SPRING
A 20th Century-Fox picture starring Ray Milland, Jean Peters and Paul Douglas, and directed by Lloyd Bacon. Song by Mack Gordon and Joseph Myrow:
IT HAPPENS EVERY SPRING

LUCKY STIFF
A United Artists' picture starring Dorothy Lamour, Brian Donlevy and Claire Trevor, and directed by Lewis R. Foster. Song by Ned Washington and Victor Young:
LOVELINESS

MALAYA
An M-G-M picture filmed with a cast headed by Spencer Tracy, James Stewart, Valentina Cortesa, Sydney Greenstreet, John Hodiak and Lionel Barrymore, and directed by Richard Thorpe. Songs:
TEMPTATION by Arthur Freed and Nacio Herb Brown; BLUE MOON by Lorenz Hart and Richard Rodgers; A FULL MOON AND AN EMPTY HEART by Mort Greene and Harry Revel; PAGAN LULLABY by Frank Loesser and Jule Styne.

MRS. MIKE
A United Artists picture starring Dick Powell and Evelyn Keyes, and directed by Lewis King. Songs by Ned Washington and Max Steiner:
KATHY; BEN HUR DRIP and TALL IN THE SADDLE.

MY FOOLISH HEART
An RKO picture starring Dana Andrews and Susan Hayward, and directed by Mark Robson. Song by Ned Washington and Victor Young:
MY FOOLISH HEART

PINKY
A 20th Century-Fox picture filmed with a cast headed by Jeanne Crain, Ethel Barrymore, Ethel Waters and William Lundigan, and directed by Elia Kazan. Song by Harry Ruby and Alfred Newman:
BLUE (WITH YOU OR WITHOUT YOU)

ROSEANNA McCOY
An RKO picture based on the Hatfield-McCoy feud, filmed with a cast headed by Farley Granger, Joan Evans, Charles Bick-

ford and Raymond Massey, and directed by Irving Reis. Song by Frank Loesser:
ROSEANNA

SAMSON AND DELILAH
A Paramount picture starring Hedy Lamarr, Victor Mature and George Sanders, and directed by Cecil B. De Mille. Song by Ray Evans, Jay Livingston and Victor Young:
SONG OF DELILAH

SONG OF SURRENDER
A Paramount picture filmed with a cast headed by Wanda Hendrix, Claude Rains, MacDonald Carey, Andrea King and Henry Hull, and directed by Mitchell Leisen. Songs:
NOW AND FOREVER by Ray Evans, Jay Livingston and Victor Young; SONG OF SURRENDER by Ray Evans and Jay Livingston.

SOUTH OF ST. LOUIS
A Warner Brothers' picture filmed with a cast headed by Joel McCrea, Alexis Smith, Zachary Scott and Dorothy Malone, and directed by Ray Enright. Songs:
TOO MUCH LOVE by Ralph Blane and Ray Heindorf; AS THE BRASS BAND PLAYED by Jack Scholl and Ray Heindorf.

SORROWFUL JONES
A Paramount picture starring Bob Hope and Lucille Ball, and directed by Sidney Lanfield. Songs by Ray Evans and Jay Livingston:
HAVING A WONDERFUL WISH and ROCK-A-BYE BANGTAIL

STREETS OF LAREDO
A Paramount picture filmed with a cast headed by MacDonald Carey, William Holden, William Bendix and Mona Freeman, and directed by Leslie Fenton. Song by Ray Evans and Jay Livingston:
STREETS OF LAREDO

SUN COMES UP, THE
An M-G-M picture filmed with a cast headed by Jeanette MacDonald, Lloyd Nolan, Claude Jurman, Jr. and Lewis Stone, and directed by Richard Thorpe. Songs by William Katz and Andre Previn:
IF YOU WERE MINE and COUSIN EBENEEZER

THAT MIDNIGHT KISS
An M-G-M picture filmed with a cast headed by Kathryn Grayson, Jose Iturbi, Ethel Barrymore and Mario Lanza, and di-

rected by Norman Taurog. Songs by Bob
Russell and Bronislaw Kaper:
I KNOW, I KNOW, I KNOW and
THAT MIDNIGHT KISS

TULSA

An Eagle-Lion picture starring Susan
Hayward and Robert Preston, and directed
by Stuart Heisler. Song by Mort Greene

and Allie Wrubel:
TULSA

UNDER CAPRICORN

A Warner Brothers' picture starring Ingrid Bergman and Joseph Cotten, and directed by Albert Hitchcock. Song by Kay
Twomey and Richard Addinsell:
ONE MAGIC WISH

Western Films With Songs

BIG SOMBRERO, THE

A Republic-Autry picture starring Gene
Autry in a cast that included Elena Verdugo,
and directed by Frank McDonald. Songs:
I'M THANKFUL FOR SMALL FA-
VORS by Don Raye and Gene De Paul;
RANCHO PILLOW by Charles Newman
and Allie Wrubel; MY ADOBE HACI-
ENDA by Louise Massey and Lee Penny;
GOODBYE TO OLD MEXICO by Dwight
Butcher.

DOWN DAKOTA WAY

A Republic picture starring Roy Rogers
in a cast that included Dale Evans, and
directed by William Witney. Songs:
UNCLE SAMBA by Stanley Wilson and
Nestor Amoril; DOWN DAKOTA WAY
by Dale Butts and Sloan Bibly; ABC SONG
by Sid Robin and Foy Willing; CANDY
KISSES by George Morgan.

GOLDEN STALLION, THE

A Republic picture starring Roy Rogers
in a cast that included Dale Evans, and
directed by William Witney. Songs:
NIGHT ON THE PRAIRIE by Al Par-
enteau and N. Gluck; DOWN MEXICO
WAY by Eddie Cherkose, Sol Meyer and
Jule Styne; GOLDEN STALLION and
THERE'S ALWAYS TIME FOR A SONG
by Sid Robin and Foy Willing.

HELLFIRE

A Republic picture starring Bill Elliott
and Marie Windsor, and directed by R. G.
Springsteen. Song by Sol Meyer, B. Reeves
and Frank Campbell:
SHOO FLY

LAST BANDIT, THE

A Republic picture starring Bill Elliott
and Adrian Booth, and directed by Joseph
Kane. Song by Jack Elliott:
LOVE IS SUCH A FUNNY THING

RIDERS IN THE SKY

A Columbia-Autry picture starring Gene
Autry in a cast that included Gloria Henry,
Pat Buttram and Mary Beth Hughes, and
directed by John English. Songs:
GHOST RIDERS IN THE SKY by Stan
Jones; IT MAKES NO DIFFERENCE
NOW by Jimmy Davis and Floyd Tillman.

RIDERS OF THE WHISTLING PINES

A Columbia-Autry picture starring Gene
Autry in a cast that included Patricia White,
and directed by John English. Songs:
IT'S A LAZY DAY and LET'S GO
ROAMIN' ROUND THE RANGE by
Smiley Burnette; LITTLE BIG DRY by
Billy Weber; TOOLIE OOLIE DOOLIE
(YODEL POLKA) by Art Beul and Vaughn
Horton; HAIR OF GOLD EYES OF
BLUE by Sunny Skylar.

RIM OF THE CANYON

A Columbia-Autry picture starring Gene
Autry in a cast that included Nan Leslie,
and directed by John English. Songs:
YOU'RE THE ONLY STAR IN MY
BLUE HEAVEN by Gene Autry; RIM
OF THE CANYON by Johnny Lange and
Hy Heath.

STALLION CANYON

An Astor picture starring Ken Curtis and
Carolina Cotton, and directed by Harry
Fraser. Song by Hy Heath:
HILLS OF UTAH

SUSANNA PASS

A Republic picture starring Roy Rogers
in a cast that included Dale Evans and Es-
telita Rodriguez, and directed by William
Witney. Songs:
A GOOD, GOOD MORNIN' by Sid
Robin and Foy Willing; SUSANNA PASS
by Jack Elliott and Aaron Gonzales; TWO-
GUN RITA by Jack Elliott; THAT'S MY
GAL by Frank Perkins.

Feature Cartoons With Songs

CINDERELLA

An RKO-Walt Disney cartoon fantasy with songs by Mack David, Al Hoffman and Jerry Livingston:

A DREAM IS A WISH YOUR HEART MAKES; SO THIS IS LOVE; BIBBIDI-BOBBIDI-BOO; OH SING SWEET NIGHTINGALE; CINDERELLA and THE WORK SONG.

ICHABOD AND MR. TOAD

An RKO-Walt Disney production with narration by Bing Crosby, Basil Rathbone, Eric Blore and Pat O'Malley. Songs:

ICHABOD CRANE; KATRINA and THE HEADLESS HORSEMAN by Don Raye and Gene DePaul; THE MERRILY SONG by Larry Morey, Ray Gilbert, Charles Wolcott and Frank Churchill.

Scene from *Jolson Sings Again* with Larry Parks in the title role

Betty Hutton in the "I'm An Indian Too" number of *Annie Get Your Gun*

1 9 5 0

"Annie" Hits The B.O. Bull's-eye With a Song-Loaded Gun

"You can't get a man with a gun!"

Ethel Merman made this declaration nightly (and at the Wednesday and Saturday matinees, too) during the 1159-performance run of *Annie Get Your Gun* on Broadway. Betty Hutton reiterated it on the sound track in the adaptation of this highly successful stage musical to the screen. And when the picture grossed $4,650,000 at the movie box-office, Hollywood discovered that while the male is invulnerable to buckshot, movie-goers were sitting ducks waiting to be bagged if "Annie's" gun was loaded with the right kind of ammunition—drama, color, glamour, wholesome comedy and most important of all, songs by Irving Berlin.

"Annie", in fact, had a field day all her own in the box-office shooting match since the picture glorifying "Little Sure Shot" of the Buffalo Bill show was the only 1950 musical to hit the bull's-eye—the Golden Circle. All the other song-and-dance films missed the mark entirely. For the most part, they were loaded with BB shot at a time when 16-inch shells were needed to shatter the apathy of John Q. Public and his wife Mary, who were absorbed with their TV sets and preferred Uncle Miltie, Howdy Doody and the grunt-and-groaners to the low-budget pictures showing at the neighborhood movie house.

A pair of zany comics that had panicked John and Mary in guest appearances on television shows, wooed them away from their 12-inch screen when Dean Martin and the unpredictable Jerry Lewis made their film debut, first as featured players in Marie Wilson's starring picture, *My Friend Irma Goes West,* and later as headliners in *At War With The Army,* and Mr. and Mrs. Public heard *Be My Love* so often on the radio, they eventually developed a yen to have a look-see at the newly discovered tenor, Mario Lanza, who introduced this treacle-drenched ballad in *The Toast of New Orleans.*

John and Mary also found their perennial favorite, Bing Crosby, worth the admission price in both *Mr. Music* and *Riding High,* and held hands just like the high school kids in the darkened balcony did while listening to Vincent Youman's romantic ballads in *Tea For Two* and the songs from the Turbulent Twenties revived in *Three Little Words,* the film biography of two Tin Pan Alleyites, Bert Kalmar and Harry Ruby.

But the veteran songwriters under contract to the picture studios seemed to have lost their Sunday punch just as Joe Louis had, and the committee delegated to select an Oscar-winning song for 1950 had to go outside the musical productions to find one—*Mona Lisa,* written by Ray Evans and Jay Livingston for *Captain Carey of the U. S. A.*

And had you asked the film critics what they thought of the year's output

256   [1950]

of musical pictures as a whole, this probably would have been their answer: "They should have processed them with that magic drug chlorophyll. They were stinkers!"

Musicals

ANNIE GET YOUR GUN
An M-G-M picture starring Betty Hutton and Howard Keel in a cast that included Louis Calhern, Edward Arnold, Keenan Wynn and J. Carroll Naish, and directed by George Sidney. Songs by Irving Berlin:
COLONEL BUFFALO BILL; DOIN' WHAT COMES NATURALLY; THE GIRL THAT I MARRY; YOU CAN'T GET A MAN WITH A GUN; THERE'S NO BUSINESS LIKE SHOW BUSINESS; MY DEFENSES ARE DOWN; I'M AN INDIAN TOO; I GOT THE SUN IN THE MORNING; ANYTHING YOU CAN DO and THEY SAY IT'S WONDERFUL.

AT WAR WITH THE ARMY
A Paramount picture starring Dean Martin and Jerry Lewis in a cast that included Polly Bergen, and directed by Hal Walker. Songs by Mack David and Jerry Livingston:
YOU AND YOUR BEAUTIFUL EYES; THE NAVY GETS THE GRAVY AND THE ARMY GETS THE BEANS and TANDA WANDA HOY.

BUCCANEER'S GIRL
A Universal picture starring Yvonne De Carlo in a cast that included Philip Friend, Robert Douglas and Elsa Lanchester, and directed by Frederick De Cordova. Songs by Jack Brooks and Walter Scharf:
HERE'S TO THE LADIES; MONSIEUR; BECAUSE YOU'RE IN LOVE and A SAILOR SAILS THE SEVEN SEAS.

DUCHESS OF IDAHO
An M-G-M picture starring Esther Williams and Van Johnson in a cast that included Mel Torme and Eleanor Powell, and directed by Robert Z. Leonard. Songs:
OF ALL THINGS; OR WAS IT SPRING?; WARM HANDS, COLD HEART; YOU CAN'T DO WRONG DOIN' RIGHT and LET'S CHOO CHOO CHOO TO IDAHO by Al Rinker and Floyd Huddlestone; SINGLEFOOT SERENADE by G. M. Beilenson and M. Beelby; BABY COME OUT OF THE CLOUDS by Lee Pearl and Henry Nemo; YOU

WON'T FORGET ME by Kermit Goell and Fred Spielman.

HIT PARADE OF 1951
A Republic picture filmed with a cast headed by John Carroll, Marie McDonald, Estelita Rodriguez, Frank Fontaine, Grant Withers and Bobby Rames' Rhumba Band, and directed by John H. Auer. Musical numbers:
YOU'RE SO NICE; HOW WOULD I KNOW?; WISHES COME TRUE; YOU DON'T KNOW THE OTHER SIDE OF ME and A VERY HAPPY CHARACTER AM I by Al Rinker and Floyd Huddleston; SQUARE DANCE SAMBA AND BOCA CHICA by Sy Miller and Buddy Garrett.

I'LL GET BY
A 20th Century-Fox picture filmed with a cast headed by June Haver, William Lundigan, Gloria De Haven, Dennis Day and Harry James and his orchestra, and directed by Richard Sale. Songs:
TAKING A CHANCE ON LOVE by John LaTouche, Ted Fetter and Vernon Duke; ONCE IN A WHILE by Bud Green and Michael Edwards; FIFTH AVENUE and THERE WILL NEVER BE ANOTHER YOU by Mack Gordon and Harry Warren; I'VE GOT THE WORLD ON A STRING by Ted Koehler and Harold Arlen; YOU MAKE ME FEEL SO YOUNG by Mack Gordon and Josef Myrow; YANKEE DOODLE BLUES by B. G. DeSylva, Irving Caesar and George Gershwin; IT'S BEEN A LONG, LONG TIME by Sammy Cahn and Jule Styne; I'LL GET BY (AS LONG AS I HAVE YOU) by Roy Turk and Fred Ahlert; McNAMARA'S BAND by Shamus O'Connor and J. J. Stamford.

LET'S DANCE
A Paramount picture starring Betty Hutton and Fred Astaire in a cast that included Roland Young, Ruth Warwick and Lucille Watson, and directed by Norman Z. McLeod. Songs by Frank Loesser:
I CAN'T STOP THINKING ABOUT HIM; WHY FIGHT THAT FEELING?; OH THEM DUDES; TUNNEL OF LOVE; JACK AND THE BEANSTALK and THE HYACINTH.

MILKMAN, THE
A Universal picture starring Donald O'
Connor and Jimmy Durante in a cast that
included Joyce Holden, and directed by
Charles T. Barton. Songs:
IT'S BIGGER THAN BOTH OF US
and THE EARLY MORNING SONG by
Jack Barnett and Sammy Fain; THAT'S
MY BOY and NOBODY WANTS MY
MONEY by Jack Barnett and Jimmy Dur-
ante.

MR. MUSIC
A Paramount picture starring Bing Cros-
by in a cast that included Nancy Olson,
Charles Coburn, Ruth Hussey, Dorothy
Kirsten, Peggy Lee and the Merry Macs,
and directed by Richard Haydn. Songs by
Johnny Burke and Jimmy Van Heusen:
LIFE IS SO PECULIAR; HIGH ON
THE LIST; ACCIDENTS WILL HAP-
PEN; THEN YOU'LL BE HOME;
WOULDN'T IT BE FUNNY?; ONCE
MORE THE BLUE AND WHITE; MI-
LADY; WASN'T I THERE? and MR.
MUSIC.

MY BLUE HEAVEN
A 20th Century-Fox picture starring
Betty Grable and Dan Dailey in a cast
that included David Wayne, Jane Wyatt
and Mitzi Gaynor, and directed by Henry
Koster. Songs:
LIVE HARD, WORK HARD, LOVE
HARD; THE FRIENDLY ISLANDS; IT'S
DEDUCTIBLE; HALLOWE'N; DON'T
ROCK THE BOAT DEAR; WHAT A
MAN; I LOVE A NEW YORKER and
COSMO COSMETICS by Ralph Blane
and Harold Arlen; MY BLUE HEAVEN
by George Whiting and Walter Donaldson.

MY FRIEND IRMA GOES WEST
A Paramount picture starring John Lund
and Marie Wilson in a cast that included
Dianna Lynn, Dean Martin, Jerry Lewis
and Corinne Calvert, and directed by Hal
Wallis. Songs by Ray Evans and Jay Liv-
ingston:
BABY OBEY ME; I'LL ALWAYS
LOVE YOU and FIDDLE AND GITTAR
BAND.

NANCY GOES TO RIO
An M-G-M picture filmed with a cast
headed by Jane Powell, Ann Sothern, Carmen Miranda and Danny Scholl, and directed by Robert Z. Leonard. Songs:
LOVE IS LIKE THIS by Ray Gilbert
and J. DeBarro; CA-BOOM PA PA and
YIPSEE-I-O by Ray Gilbert; TIME AND

TIME AGAIN by Earl Brent and Fred
Spielman; NANCY'S GOIN' TO RIO by
George Stoll and Earl Brent.

OF MEN AND MUSIC
An M-G-M picture filmed with a cast
headed by Arthur Rubenstein, Jan Peerce,
Nadine Connor, Jascha Heifetz, Dimitri
Mitropoulos and Deems Taylor, and directed by Irving Reis. The score consisted
solely of classical numbers.

PAGAN LOVE SONG
An M-G-M picture starring Esther Wil-
liams and Howard Keel, and directed by
Robert Alton. Songs:
TAHITI; SEA OF THE MOON;
HOUSE OF SINGING BAMBOO; SING-
ING IN THE SUN; WHY IS LOVE SO
CRAZY?; MUSIC ON THE WATER;
HERE IN TAHITI WE MAKE LOVE
and ETIQUETTE by Arthur Freed and
Harry Warren; MATA by Roger Edens;
PAGAN LOVE SONG by Arthur Freed
and Nacio Herb Brown.

PETTY GIRL, THE
A Columbia picture filmed with a cast
headed by Robert Cummings, Joan Caul-
field, Elsa Lanchester and Melville Cooper,
and directed by Henry Levin. Songs by
Johnny Mercer and Harold Arlen:
FANCY FREE; AH LOVES YA; CA-
LYPSO SONG and THE PETTY GIRL.

RIDING HIGH
A Paramount picture starring Bing Cros-
by in a cast that included Coleen Gray,
Charles Bickford, Frances Gifford, William
Demarest, Raymond Walburn and Jimmy
Gleason, and directed by Frank Capra.
Songs by Johnny Burke and Jimmy Van
Heusen:
SUNSHINE CAKE; THE HORSE
TOLD ME; SURE THING and SOME
PLACE ON ANYWHERE ROAD.

SUMMER STOCK
An M-G-M picture starring Judy Garland
and Gene Kelly in a cast that included
Eddie Bracken, Gloria DeHaven, Marjorie
Main and Phil Silvers, and directed by
Charles Walters. Songs by Mack Gordon
and Harry Warren:
FRIENDLY STAR; MEM'RY ISLAND;
DIG-DIG-DIG FOR YOUR DINNER; IF
YOU FEEL LIKE SINGING, SING;
HAPPY HARVEST; BLUE JEAN POLKA
and YOU WONDERFUL YOU (Lyrics by
Jack Brooks and Saul Chaplin.)

TEA FOR TWO
A Warner Brothers' picture starring Doris Day and Gordon MacRae, and directed by David Butler. Songs:
I KNOW THAT YOU KNOW by Anne Caldwell and Vincent Youmans; CRAZY RHYTHM by Irving Caesar, Roger Wolfe Kahn and Joseph Meyer; I ONLY HAVE EYES FOR YOU by Al Dubin and Harry Warren; TEA FOR TWO and I WANT TO BE HAPPY by Irving Caesar and Vincent Youmans; DO DO DO by Ira and George Gershwin; OH ME OH MY by Arthur Francis and Vincent Youmans.

THREE LITTLE WORDS
An M-G-M picture based on the life of Bert Kalmar and Harry Ruby, filmed with a cast headed by Fred Astaire, Red Skelton, Vera-Ellen and Arlene Dahl, and directed by Richard Thorpe. All songs were by Kalmar and Ruby with the exception of those whose collaborators' names are in parentheses:
WHERE DID YOU GET THAT GIRL? (with Harry Puck); COME ON PAPA (lyrics by Edgar Leslie); THINKING OF YOU; NEVERTHELESS; SHE'S MINE ALL MINE; MY SUNNY TENNESSEE (with Herman Ruby); THREE LITTLE WORDS; SO LONG OO-LONG; WHO'S SORRY NOW? (with Ted Snyder); ALL ALONE MONDAY; I WANNA BE LOVED BY YOU; HOORAY FOR CAPTAIN SPAULDING and I LOVE YOU SO MUCH.

TOAST OF NEW ORLEANS, THE
An M-G-M picture starring Mario Lanza and Kathryn Grayson in a cast that included David Niven, and directed by Norman Taurog. Songs by Sammy Cahn and Nicholas Brodszky:
THE BAYOU LULLABY; BOOM BIDDY BOOM BOOM; I'LL NEVER LOVE YOU; THE TINA-LINA and BE MY LOVE.

WABASH AVENUE
A 20th Century-Fox picture starring Betty Grable and Victor Mature in a cast that included Jimmy Barton and Phil Harris and his orchestra, and directed by Henry Koster. Songs by Mack Gordon and Josef Myrow:
CLEAN UP CHICAGO; WILHELMINA; DOWN ON WABASH AVENUE; MAY I TEMPT YOU WITH A BIG RED APPLE? and BABY SAY YOU LOVE ME.

WEST POINT STORY, THE
A Warner Brothers' picture starring James Cagney, Virginia Mayo and Doris Day in a cast that included Jean Nelson and Gordon MacRae, and directed by Roy Del Ruth. Songs by Sammy Cahn and Jule Styne:
TEN THOUSAND FOUR HUNDRED AND THIRTY-TWO SHEEP; BY THE KISSING ROCK; YOU LOVE ME; MILITARY POLKA; LONG BEFORE I KNEW YOU; BROOKLYN; IT COULD ONLY HAPPEN IN BROOKLYN and THE CORPS.

Feature Films With Songs

CAPTAIN CAREY OF THE U.S.A.
A Paramount picture starring Alan Ladd and Wanda Hendrix in a cast that included Francis Lederer and Joseph Calleia, and directed by Mitchell Leisen. Song by Jay Evans and Ray Livingston:
MONA LISA

CHAIN LIGHTNING
A Warner Brothers' picture starring Humphrey Bogart, Eleanor Parker and Raymond Massey, and directed by Stuart Heisler. Song by J. Hughes, Frank Lake and Al Stillman:
BLESS 'EM ALL

COPPER CANYON
A Paramount picture starring Ray Milland, Hedy Lamarr, MacDonald Carey and Mona Freeman, and directed by John Far-

row. Song by Ray Evans and Jay Livingston:
COPPER CANYON

DARK CITY
A Paramount picture filmed with a cast headed by Charles Heston, Lizabeth Scott, Viveca Lindfors, Dean Jagger and Don DeFore, and directed by William Dieterle. Song by Jack Elliott and Harold Spina:
(WHAT WOULD I DO) IF I DIDN'T HAVE YOU?

DAUGHTER OF ROSIE O'GRADY, THE
A Warner Brothers' picture starring June Haver, Gordon MacRae and James Barton, and directed by David Butler. Songs:
AS WE ARE TODAY by Charles Tobias and Ernesto Lecuona; THE DAUGHTER OF ROSIE O'GRADY by M. C. Brice and Walter Donaldson.

DOUBLE CROSSBONES

A Universal picture starring Donald O'
Connor and Helena Carter in a cast that
included Will Geer, John Emery and Hope
Emerson, and directed by Charles T. Bar-
ton. Songs by Lester Lee and Dan Shapiro:
PERCY HAD A HEART and SONG OF
ADVENTURE

FURIES, THE

A Paramount picture starring Barbara
Stanwyck, Wendell Corey, Walter Huston
and Judith Anderson, and directed by An-
thony Mann. Song by Ray Evans and Jay
Livingston:
T. C. ROUNDUP TIME

GREAT RUPERT, THE

An Eagle-Lion picture starring Jimmy
Durante, Terry Moore and Tom Drake,
and directed by Irving Pichel. Songs:
TAKE AN L by Jimmy Durante;
CHRISTMAS SONG by Jimmy Durante
and Harry Crane; RUPERT by Buddy
Kaye and Fred Spielman.

HARVEY

A Universal picture starring Jimmy Stew-
art and Josephine Hull, and directed by
Henry Koster. Song by Albert Goetz, Al
Stillman and Peter De Rose.
HARVEY

LIFE OF HER OWN, A

An M-G-M picture starring Lana Turner
and Ray Milland in a cast that included
Tom Elwell, Louis Calhern, Ann Dvorak
and Barry Sullivan, and directed by George
Cukor. Song by Paul Francis Webster and
Bronislaw Kaper:
A LIFE OF HER OWN

MONTANA

A Warner Brothers' picture starring Errol
Flynn and Alexis Smith, and directed by
Ray Enright. Song by Mack David, Al
Hoffman and Jerry Livingston:
RECKON I'M IN LOVE

NEVER A DULL MOMENT

An RKO picture starring Irene Dunne
and Fred MacMurray, and directed by
George Marshall. Songs by Kay Swift:
ONCE YOU FIND YOUR GUY; A
MAN WITH A BIG FELT HAT and
SAGEBRUSH LULLABY.

NO MAN OF HER OWN

A Paramount picture starring Barbara
Stanwyck and John Lund in a cast that included Jane Cowl and Phyllis Thaxter, and
directed by Mitchell Leisen. Song by Ray

Evans and Jay Livingston:
THE LIE

NO SAD SONGS FOR ME

A Columbia picture starring Margaret
Sullavan and Wendell Corey in a cast that
included Viveca Lindfors, Natalie Wood,
John McIntyre and Ann Doran, and di-
rected by Rudolph Mate. Song by Doris
Fisher and Allan Roberts:
NO SAD SONGS FOR ME

PAID IN FULL

A Paramount picture starring Lizabeth
Scott, Diana Lynn and Robert Cummings,
and directed by William Dieterle. Song by
Ray Evans and Jay Livingston:
YOU'RE WONDERFUL

RED HEAD AND THE COWBOY, THE

A Paramount picture filmed with a cast
headed by Glenn Ford, Edmund O'Brien,
Rhonda Fleming and Alan Reed, and directed by Leslie Fenton. Song by Ray Evans
and Jay Livingston:
TRAV'LIN' FREE

SOUTH SEA SINNER

A Universal release filmed with a cast
headed by MacDonald Carey, Shelley Win-
ters and Helena Carter, and directed by
Bruce Humberstone. Songs:
IT HAD TO BE YOU by Gus Kahn and
Isham Jones; I'M THE LONESOMEST
GAL IN TOWN by Lew Brown and Albert
Von Tilzer; BLUE LAGOON by Frederic
Herbert and Arnold Hughes; ONE MAN
WOMAN by Jack Brooks and Milton
Schwartzwald.

STAGE FRIGHT

A Warner Brothers' picture starring Marlene Dietrich, Jane Wyman, Mitchell Wild-
ing and Richard Todd, and directed by Alfred Hitchcock. Song by Cole Porter:
THE LAZIEST GAL IN TOWN

STELLA

A 20th Century-Fox picture starring Ann
Sheridan, Victor Mature and David Wayne
in a cast that included Randy Stuart, Marion Marshall and Frank Fontaine, and directed by Claude Binyon. Song by Allan
Roberts and Alfred Newman:
STELLA

SUNSET BOULEVARD

A Paramount picture starring John Holden, Gloria Swanson and Erich Von Stroheim in a cast that included Nancy Olson,
Cecil B. De Mille, Hedda Hopper, Buster
Keaton, Anna Nelsson, H. B. Warner, Ray

Evans and Jay Livingston, and directed by Billy Wilder. Song by Ray Evans and Jay Livingston:
PARAMOUNT - DON'T - WANT - ME BLUES

THIRD MAN, THE
An Alexander Korda production starring Orson Wells, Joseph Cotten, Valli and Trevor Howard, and directed by Carol Reed. Instrumental music composed by Anton Karas, who played it on his zither:
HARRY LIME THEME; CAFE MOZART WALTZ; CASANOVA MELODY; CEMETERY BLUES and LE PREMIER HOMME.

TRAVELING SALESWOMAN
A Columbia picture starring Joan Davis in a cast that included Andy Devine and Adele Jergens, and directed by Charles F. Reisner. Songs by Allan Roberts and Lester Lee:
HE DIED WITH HIS BOOTS ON and EVERY BABY NEEDS A DADDY

TWO WEEKS WITH LOVE
An M-G-M picture starring Jane Powell and Ricardo Montalban in a cast that included Louis Calhern and Ann Harding, and directed by Ray Rowland. Song by Arthur Fields and Walter Donovan:
ABA DABA HONEYMOON

UNDER MY SKIN
A 20th Century-Fox picture starring John Garfield, Michelene Prelle and Luther Adler, and directed by Jean Negulesco. Song by Mack Gordon and Alfred Newman:
STRANGER IN THE NIGHT

WAGONMASTER, THE
An RKO picture filmed with a cast headed by Ben Johnson, Harry Carey Jr., Joanne Dru, Ward Bond, Charles Kempner, Alan Mowbray and Jane Darwell, and directed by John Ford. Songs by Stan Jones:
CHUCKAWALLA SWING; WAGONS WEST; ROLLIN' DUST and SONG OF THE WAGONMASTER.

WYOMING MAIL
A Universal picture filmed with a cast headed by Stephen McNally, Alexis Smith and Howard Da Silva, and directed by Reginald Le Borg. Songs by Lester Lee and Dan Shapiro:
TAKE ME TO TOWN and ENDLESSLY

YOUNG MAN WITH A HORN
A Warner Brothers' picture starring Kirk Douglas, Lauren Bacall, Doris Day and Hoagy Carmichael, and directed by Michael Curtiz. Song by Sammy Cahn and Ray Heindorf:
MELANCHOLY RHAPSODY

Western Films With Songs

ACROSS THE BAD LANDS
A Columbia picture filmed with a cast headed by Charles Starrett, Smiley Burnette and Helen Mowery, and directed by Fred F. Sears. Songs by Smiley Burnette:
HARMONICA BILL and I'M TELLING MYSELF I'M NOT AFRAID

BELLS OF CORONADO
A Republic picture starring Roy Rogers in a cast that included Dale Evans, Pat Brady and Grant Withers, and directed by William Witney. Songs by Sid Robin and Foy Willing:
GOT NO TIME FOR THE BLUES; SAVE A SMILE FOR A RAINY DAY and BELLS OF CORONADO.

BLAZING SUN, THE
A Columbia picture starring Gene Autry in a cast that included Lynne Roberts, Pat Buttram and Anne Gwynne, and directed by John English. Songs:
ALONG THE NAVAJO TRAIL by Edgar DeLange, Larry Markes and Dick Charles; BRUSH THOSE TEARS FROM

YOUR EYES by Oakley Haldeman, Al Trave and Jimmy Lee.

COW TOWN
A Columbia picture starring Gene Autry in a cast that included Gail Davis and Harry Shannon, and directed by John English. Song by Stanley Richinski and Carmen Lombardo:
POWDER YOUR FACE WITH SUNSHINE

INDIAN TERRITORY
A Columbia picture starring Gene Autry in a cast that included Pat Buttram and Gail Davis, and directed by John English.
CHATTANOOGA SHOESHINE BOY by Harry Stone and Jack Stapp; WHEN THE CAMPFIRE IS LOW ON THE PRAIRIE by Sammy Stept.

LIGHTNING GUNS
A Columbia picture starring Charles Starrett in a cast that included Smiley Burnette and Gloria Henry, and directed by Fred F. Sears. Songs by Smiley Burnette:

THE BATH TUB KING; RAMBLIN' BLOOD IN MY VEINS and OUR WHOLE FAMILY'S SMART.

MULE TRAIN
A Columbia picture starring Gene Autry in a cast that included Pat Buttram and Sheila Ryan, and directed by John English. ROOMFUL OF ROSES by Tim Spencer; MULE TRAIN by Johnny Lange, Hy Heath and Fred Glickman; OLD CHISHOLM TRAIL (Traditional).

NORTH OF THE GREAT DIVIDE
A Republic picture starring Roy Rogers in a cast that included Penny Edwards, and directed by William Witney. Songs by Jack Elliott:
JUST KEEP A'MOVIN'; NORTH OF THE GREAT DIVIDE and BY THE LAUGHING SPRING.

OUTCAST OF BLACK MESA
A Columbia picture filmed with a cast headed by Charles Starrett, Smiley Burnette and Martha Hyer, and directed by Nat Nazarro. Songs by Smiley Burnette:
DONKEY ENGINE; NOBODY FIRES THE BOSS and JUST SITTIN' AROUND IN JAIL.

RAIDERS OF TOMAHAWK CREEK
A Columbia picture starring Charles Starrett in a cast that included Smiley Burnette, Edgar Dearing and Kay Buckley, and directed by Fred F. Sears. Songs by Smiley Burnette:
I'M TOO SMART FOR THAT and GRASSHOPPER POLKA

ROCK ISLAND TRAIL
A Republic picture filmed with a cast headed by Forrest Tucker, Adele Mara, Adrian Booth and Bruce Cabot, and directed by Joseph Kane. Song by William Roy:
ROCK ISLAND TRAIL

SINGING GUNS
A Republic picture starring Vaughn Monroe, Ella Raines and Walter Brennan, and directed by R. J. Springsteen. Songs:
MULE TRAIN by Johnny Lange, Hy Heath and Fred Glickman; SINGING MY WAY BACK HOME by Wilton Moore and Al Vann; MEXICALI TRAIL by Sunny Skylar and Wilton Moore; ONE MORE HAND ON THE RANGE by Milton Drake.

SONS OF NEW MEXICO
A Columbia picture starring Gene Autry in a cast that included Gail Davis and Robert Armstrong, and directed by John English. Musical numbers:
CAN'T SHAKE THE SANDS OF TEXAS FROM MY SHOES by Gene Autry, Diane Johnstone and Kenneth Pitts; THERE'S A RAINBOW ON THE RIO COLORADO by Gene Autry and Fred Rose; HONEY I'M IN LOVE WITH YOU by Curt Massey and Abbie Gibbon; NEW MEXICO MILITARY INSTITUTE MARCH by F. E. Hunt.

SUNSET IN THE WEST
A Republic picture starring Roy Rogers in a cast that included Estelita Rodriguez and Penny Edwards, and directed by William Witney. Songs by Jack Elliott:
ROLLIN' WHEELS and WHEN A PRETTY GIRL PASSES BY.

TRAIL OF ROBIN HOOD
A Republic picture starring Roy Rogers in a cast that included Penny Edwards, Gordon Jones and Jack Holt, and directed by William Witney. Songs by Jack Elliott:
EV'RY DAY IS CHRISTMAS IN THE WEST and GET A CHRISTMAS TREE FOR JOHNNY.

TRIGGER, JR.
A Republic picture starring Roy Rogers in a cast that included Dale Evans and Pat Brady, and directed by William Witney. Song by Foy Willing:
THE BIG RODEO

TWILIGHT IN THE SIERRAS
A Republic picture starring Roy Rogers in a cast that included Dale Evans, Estelita Rodriguez and Pat Brady, and directed by William Witney. Songs by Sid Robin and Foy Willing:
PANCHO'S SANCHO; ROOTIN' TOOTIN' COWBOY; TWILIGHT IN THE SIERRAS and IT'S ONE WONDERFUL DAY.

VANISHING WESTERNER, THE
A Republic picture filmed with a cast headed by Monte Hale, Paul Hurst, Aline Towne and Roy Bancroft, and directed by Philip Ford. Song by Irwin Coster:
THERE'S NO USE WORRYIN'

WEST OF THE GREAT DIVIDE
A Republic picture starring Roy Rogers in a cast that included Penny Edwards, and directed by William Witney. Songs by Hy Heath:
MOVE ALONG LITTLE DOGIE and YOU'RE WEST OF THE GREAT DIVIDE.

1 9 5 1

A Sleeper Carrying Gershwin's Colors Wins The Oscar Derby

When the nominations for the annual Academy Awards were announced, two highly dramatic pictures, *A Street Car Named Desire* and *A Place In The Sun,* were made the odds-on favorites with *The African Queen* being rated as a possible contender, but on the night the statuettes were awarded, the Oscar for the best picture of 1951 went to a lightly favored outsider, *An American In Paris,* with music by George Gershwin and starring Gene Kelly and Leslie Caron.

In making this song-and-dance production the third musical to be accorded such top honors since the birth of the talkies in 1927, Hollywood gave belated recognition to the genius of a highly sensitive man who had been continually humiliated and brushed off during the two years he spent in the film capital. A perfectionist in his craft and a trail-blazer in the realms of popular music, George Gershwin repeatedly offered suggestions for the improvement of the films on which he was working that were repeatedly turned down in favor of hackneyed ideas with tried-and-true box-office appeal. And while the medical report said that Gershwin died of a brain tumor, a broken heart probably speeded his untimely end in 1937.

If the popularity of the three Golden Circle musicals of 1951 are a just criterion, the public still was partial to the songs of the past. *An American In Paris* revived the music that had captivated Broadway in the 1920's. *Show Boat* represented Jerome Kern at his glorious best. And *The Loveliest Night Of The Year,* the most popular number in *The Great Caruso,* which also offered the arias with which the celebrated Italian tenor had first thrilled "Met" audiences at the century's turn, was based on the melody of a Viennese waltz, *Over The Waves,* written when hoopskirts and brocaded waistcoats were fashionable.

Thus a group of dead composers was largely instrumental in breathing new life in the Hollywood musical, badly in need of a blood transfusion in 1951 when more than a thousand movie houses capitulated unconditionally to TV and closed.

Among the less profitable musicals of 1951, the old songs also proved a box-office lure. For *Mr. Imperium,* Ezio Pinza, who had demonstrated in *South Pacific* that a suitor with greying hair had better than an equal chance of getting the gal in competition with a youthful juvenile with a crew cut, had to go to the music catalogue of 1941 for a show-stopping tune: *You Belong To My Heart. I'll See You In My Dreams,* the film biography of Gus Kahn, the lyricist, was brimming over with nostalgic numbers, most of them written before the radio landed the K.O. punch on the five-and-dime-store music counter. And in a year when songs from the buried past proved to be the salvation of an enfeebled musical present, only two alive-and-kicking songwriters rated a 21-gun salute: Johnny Mercer and Hoagy Carmichael, who collaborated on the Oscar-winning song of 1951: *In The Cool, Cool, Cool Of The Evening,* introduced by Bing Crosby in *Here Comes The Groom.*

Musicals

AMERICAN IN PARIS, AN
An M-G-M picture starring Gene Kelly and Leslie Caron in a cast that included Oscar Levant, Georges Guetary and Nina Foch, and directed by Vincenti Minnelli. Songs by Ira and George Gershwin:
I GOT RHYTHM; EMBRACEABLE YOU; 'SWONDERFUL; BY STRAUSS; TRA-LA-LA; OUR LOVE IS HERE TO STAY; I'LL BUILD A STAIRWAY TO PARADISE (lyrics by E. Ray Goetz and B. G. DeSylva); CONCERTO in F and AN AMERICAN IN PARIS (both instrumental numbers).

CALL ME MISTER
A 20th Century-Fox picture starring Betty Grable, Dan Dailey and Danny Thomas, and directed by Lloyd Bacon. Songs:
JAPANESE GIRL LIKE AMERICAN BOY; I JUST CAN'T DO ENOUGH FOR YOU BABY; LOVE IS BACK IN BUSINESS and WHISTLE AND WALK AWAY by Mack Gordon and Sammy Fain; IT'S A MAN'S WORLD by Mack Gordon and Josef Myrow; LAMENT TO POTS AND PANS by Jerry Seelen and Earl K. Brent; CALL ME MISTER; THE GOING-HOME TRAIN and MILITARY LIFE by Harold Rome.

CASA MANANA
A Monogram picture starring Robert Clarke and Virginia Welles, and directed by Jean Yarbrough. Songs:
FIFTY GAMES OF SOLITAIRE ON SATURDAY NIGHT by Ruth and Louis Herscher; I HEAR A RHAPSODY by Jack Baker and George Fragos; CIELITO LINDO; BOUNCE by Olsen and Johnson, Ray Evans and Jay Livingston; PEOPLE LIKE YOU by Otis Bigelow and Harold Cooke; MADAME WILL DROP HER SHAWL by Sam Brown and Herb Pine.

COMIN' ROUND THE MOUNTAIN
A Universal picture starring Abbott and Costello and Dorothy Shay, and directed by Charles T. Lamont. Songs:
AGNES CLUNG by Hessie Smith and Dorothy Shay; YOU BROKE YOUR PROMISE by George Wyle, Irving Taylor and Eddie Pola; WHY DON'T SOMEONE MARRY MARY ANN by Wilbur Beatty and Britt Wood; SAGEBRUSH SADIE by Britt Wood; THERE'LL NEVER BE ANOTHER NOTCH ON FATHER'S SHOTGUN.

DISC JOCKEY
A United Artists' release filmed with a cast headed by Ginny Simms, Tom Drake, Jane Nigh, Lenny Kent, Russ Morgan, Tommy Dorsey and his orchestra, George Shearing, Nick Lucas, Herb Jeffries, Sarah Vaughn and the Weavers, and directed by Will Jason. Musical numbers:
SHOW ME YOU LOVE ME and LET'S MEANDER THROUGH THE MEADOW by S. Steuben and Roz Gordon; AFTER HOURS and NOBODY WANTS ME by Roz Gordon; DISC JOCKEY and IN MY HEART by Herb Jeffries and Dick Hazard; PEACEFUL COUNTRY by Foy Willing; BRAIN WAVE by George Shearing; OH LOOK AT ME NOW by John DeVries and Joe Bushkin; THE ROVING KIND by Jessie Cavanaugh and Arnold Stanton; GO TELL AUNT RHODY (Traditional).

EXCUSE MY DUST
An M-G-M picture starring Red Skelton and Monica Lewis in a cast that included Sally Forrest, MacDonald Carey and William Demarest, and directed by Roy Rowland. Songs by Dorothy Fields and Arthur Schwartz:
GET A HORSE; SPRING HAS SPRUNG; THAT'S FOR CHILDREN; GOIN' STEADY; LORELEI BROWN; I'D LIKE TO TAKE YOU OUT DREAMING; IT COULDN'T HAPPEN TO TWO NICER PEOPLE and WHERE CAN I RUN FROM?

FOOTLIGHT VARIETIES
An RKO picture filmed with a cast headed by Leon Errol, The Sportsmen, Jack Parr, Liberace and Frankie Carle and his orchestra, and directed by Hal Yates.

Musical numbers:

HI TIME by Marty Sperzel and John Rarig; THE SHOW MUST GO ON by Tom Adair and Gordon Jenkins; YOU ONLY WANT IT 'CAUSE YOU HAVEN'T GOT IT by Harry Parr Davies, Barbara Gordon and Basil Thomas; SWINGING IN THE CORN by Herb Magidson and Allie Wrubel and LIBERACE BOOGIE by Liberace.

G.I. JANE

A Lippert Pictures release filmed with a cast headed by Jean Porter, Tom Neal and Iris Adrian, and directed by Reginald La Borg. Songs:

GEE I LOVE MY G.I. JANE and I LOVE GIRLS by Jimmy Dodd; BABY I CAN'T WAIT by Diane Manners and Johnny Clark; WHAT'S TO BE IS GONNA BE by Johnny Anz and Teepee Mitchell.

GOLDEN GIRL

A 20th Century-Fox release filmed with a cast headed by Mitzi Gaynor, Dale Robertson, Dennis Day, James Barton and Una Merkel, and directed by Lloyd Bacon. Songs:

CALIFORNIA MOON by George Jessel, Sam Lerner and Joe Cooper; NEVER by Eliot Daniel and Lionel Newman; SUNDAY MORNIN' by Eliot Daniel and Ken Darby; KISS ME QUICK AND GO by Eliot Daniel.

GREAT CARUSO, THE

An M-G-M picture starring Mario Lanza and Ann Blyth in a cast that included Dorothy Kirsten, Jarnilo Novotna and Blanche Thebom, and directed by Richard Thorpe. In addition to the arias that Enrico Caruso made famous, there was one popular song in the score, based on the melody of the Viennese waltz *Over The Waves* with lyrics by Paul Francis Webster:

THE LOVELIEST NIGHT OF THE YEAR

HERE COMES THE GROOM

A Paramount picture starring Bing Crosby, Jane Wyman, Franchot Tone and Alexis Smith in a cast that included James Barton, and directed by Frank Capra. Songs:

MISTO CHRISTOFO COLUMBO; BONNE NUIT and YOUR OWN LITTLE HOUSE by Ray Evans and Jay Livingston; IN THE COOL, COOL, COOL OF THE EVENING by Johnny Mercer and Hoagy Carmichael.

HONEYCHILE

A Republic release starring Judy Canova in a cast that included Eddie Foy Jr., Alan Hale Jr. and Walter Catlett, and directed by R. J. Springsteen. Songs:

HONEYCHILE by Jack Elliott and Harold Spina; MORE THAN I CARE TO REMEMBER by Ted Johnson and Matt Terry; RAG MOP by Johnny Lee Wills and Deacon Anderson; TUTTI FRUITI by Jack Elliott and Ann Canova.

I'LL SEE YOU IN MY DREAMS

A Warner Brothers' picture based on the life of Gus Kahn, the songwriter; starring Doris Day and Danny Thomas in a cast that included Frank Lovejoy, Patrice Wymore and James Gleason, and directed by Michael Curtiz. All the following songs had lyrics by Gus Kahn, and their composers' names are shown in parentheses:

I WISH I HAD A GIRL (Grace LeBoy Kahn); MEMORIES (Egbert Van Alstyne) PRETTY BABY (Egbert Van Alstyne and Tony Jackson); NOBODY'S SWEETHEART (Billy Meyers, Elmer Schoebel and Ernie Erdman); MY BUDDY (Walter Donaldson); IT HAD TO BE YOU (Isham Jones); SWINGING DOWN THE LANE (Isham Jones); CAROLINA IN THE MORNING (Walter Donaldson); MAKIN' WHOOPIE (Walter Donaldson); YOUR EYES HAVE TOLD ME SO (Walter Blaufuss and Egbert Van Alstyne); I'LL SEE YOU IN MY DREAMS (Isham Jones); I NEVER KNEW (Ted Fiorito); AIN'T WE GOT FUN? (Richard Whiting); THE ONE I LOVE BELONGS TO SOMEBODY ELSE (Isham Jones); YES SIR THAT'S MY BABY (Walter Donaldson); TOOT TOOT TOOTSIE GOODBYE (Al Jolson and Ernie Erdman); LOVE ME OR LEAVE ME (Walter Donaldson); NO NO NORA (Ted Fiorito and Ernie Erdman); UKELELE LADY (Richard Whiting).

LEMON DROP KID, THE

A Paramount picture starring Bob Hope and Marilyn Maxwell in a cast that included Lloyd Nolan and Jane Darwell, and directed by Sidney Lanfield. Songs by Ray Evans and Jay Livingston:

SILVER BELLS; IT DOESN'T COST A DIME TO DREAM and THEY OBVIOUSLY WANT ME TO SING.

LULLABY OF BROADWAY

A Warner Brothers' picture starring Doris Day, Gene Nelson and S. Z. Sakall in a cast that included Billy DeWolf and Florence Bates, and directed by David Butler. Songs:

YOU'RE DEPENDABLE by Jerry Seelen and Sy Miller; I LOVE THE WAY YOU SAY GOOD NIGHT by George Wyle and Eddie Pola; JUST ONE OF THOSE THINGS by Cole Porter; YOU'RE GETTING TO BE A HABIT WITH ME and LULLABY OF BROADWAY by Al Dubin and Harry Warren; ZING WENT THE STRINGS OF MY HEART by James Hanley; PLEASE DON'T TALK ABOUT ME WHEN I'M GONE by Sidney Clare and Sammy Stept; IN A SHANTY IN OLD SHANTY TOWN by Joe Young, Little Jack Little and Joe Siras.

MEET ME AFTER THE SHOW

A 20th Century-Fox picture starring Betty Grable, MacDonald Carey and Rory Calhoun in a cast that included Eddie Albert and Fred Clark, and directed by Richard Sale. Songs by Leo Robin and Jule Styne:

LET GO OF MY HEART; MEET ME AFTER THE SHOW; BETTIN' ON A MAN; IT'S A HOT NIGHT IN ALASKA; NO TALENT JOE and I FEEL LIKE DANCING.

MR. IMPERIUM

An M-G-M picture starring Ezio Pinza and Lana Turner in a cast that included Marjorie Main and Sir Cedric Hardwicke, and directed by Don Hartman. Songs:

LET ME LOOK AT YOU; MY LOVE AND MY MULE and ANDIAMO by Dorothy Fields and Harold Arlen; YOU BELONG TO MY HEART by Ray Gilbert and Augustin Lara.

ON MOONLIGHT BAY

A Warner Brothers' picture starring Doris Day and Gordon MacRae, and directed by Roy Del Ruth. Songs:

LOVE YA by Charles Tobias and Peter De Rose; CHRISTMAS STORY by Pauline Walsh; ON MOONLIGHT BAY by Edward Madden and Percy Wenrich; CUDDLE UP A LITTLE CLOSER by Otto Harbach and Karl Hoschna; TELL ME WHY NIGHTS ARE LONELY by W. J. Callahan and Max Kortlander; I'M FOREVER BLOWING BUBBLES by Jean Kenbrovin and John W. Kellette; EVERY LITTLE MOVEMENT HAS A MEANING ALL ITS OWN by Otto Harbach and Karl Hoschna; TILL WE MEET AGAIN by Ray Egan and Richard Whiting; PACK UP YOUR TROUBLES IN YOUR OLD KIT BAG by Felix Powell and George Asaf.

ON THE RIVIERA

A 20th Century-Fox picture starring Danny Kaye, Gene Tierney and Corrinne Calvet, and directed by Walter Lang. Songs:

HAPPY ENDING; ON THE RIVIERA; POPO THE PUPPET and RHYTHM OF A NEW ROMANCE by Silvia Fine; BALLIN' THE JACK by Chris Smith.

ON THE SUNNY SIDE OF THE STREET

A Columbia picture filmed with a cast headed by Frankie Laine, Billy Daniels, Terry Moore and Toni Arden, and directed by Richard Quine. Songs:

I GET A KICK OUT OF YOU by Cole Porter; THE LOVE OF A GYPSY by Morris Stoloff and Fred Karger; ON THE SUNNY SIDE OF THE STREET by Dorothy Fields and Jimmy McHugh; COME BACK TO SORRENTO by Ernesto de Curtis; LET'S FALL IN LOVE by Ted Koehler and Harold Arlen; TOO MARVELOUS FOR WORDS by Johnny Mercer and Richard Whiting; I HADN'T ANYONE TILL YOU by Ray Noble; I'M GONNA LIVE TILL I DIE by Al Hoffman, Mann Curtis and Walter Kent; I MAY BE WRONG BUT I THINK YOU'RE WONDERFUL by Harry Ruskin and Henry Sullivan.

PAINTING THE CLOUDS WITH SUNSHINE

A Warner Brothers' release filmed with a cast headed by Dennis Morgan, Virginia Mayo, Gene Nelson, Lucille Norman, S. Z. Sakall and Virginia Gibson, and directed by Ralph Butler. Songs:

PAINTING THE CLOUDS WITH SUNSHINE and TIP-TOE THROUGH THE TULIPS by Al Dubin and Joe Burke; VIENNA DREAMS by Irving Caesar and Rudolf Sieczy; WITH A SONG IN MY HEART by Lorenz Hart and Richard Rodgers; BIRTH OF THE BLUES by Lew Brown, B. G. DeSylva and Ray Henderson; YOU'RE MY EVERYTHING by Mort Dixon and Harry Warren; JEALOUSIE by Vera Bloom and Jacob Gabe; MAN IS A NECESSARY EVIL and MAMBO MAN by Jack Elliott and Sonny Burke.

PURPLE HEART DIARY

A Columbia release filmed with a cast headed by Frances Langford, Judd Holdren, Ben Lessy and Tony Romano, and directed by Richard Quine. Songs:

HOLD ME IN YOUR ARMS; HI, FELLOW TOURISTS and WHERE ARE YOU FROM? by Johnny Bradford, Barbara Hayden and Tony Romano; BREAD AND BUTTER WOMAN by Allan Roberts and Lester Lee; TATTLE-TALE EYES by John Bradford and Tony Romano.

RHYTHM INN
A Monogram picture filmed with a cast headed by Jane Frazee, Kirby Grant, Charles Smith and Lois Collier, and directed by Paul Landres. Musical numbers:
LOVE by Bill Raynor and Edward J. Kay; CHI CHI by Armida; B FLAT BLUES; RETURN TRIP and WHAT DOES IT MATTER? by Edward J. Kay; WITH A TWIST OF THE WRIST by Irvin Graham; I LOVE YOU THAT IS by Dewey Bergman, Jack Segal and Patrick Lewis; WINDOW WIPER'S SONG by Olsen and Johnson, Ray Evans and Jay Livingston; IT'S A BIG WIDE WONDERFUL WORLD by John Rox.

RICH, YOUNG AND PRETTY
An M-G-M picture starring Jane Powell, Vic Damone, Fernando Lamas, Danielle Darrieux and Wendell Corey, and directed by Norman Taurog. Songs by Sammy Cahn and Nicholas Brodszky:
DARK AS THE NIGHT; WONDER WHY?; I CAN SEE YOU; WE NEVER TALK MUCH; HOW D'YA LIKE YOUR EGGS IN THE MORNING?; TONIGHT FOR SURE; PARIS and C'EST FINI.

ROYAL WEDDING
An M-G-M picture starring Fred Astaire, Jane Powell, Peter Lawford and Susan Churchill in a cast that included Keenan Wynn and Albert Sharpe, and directed by Stanley Donen. Songs by Alan Jay Lerner and Burton Lane;
YOU'RE ALL THE WORLD TO ME; HOW COULD YOU BELIEVE ME WHEN YOU KNOW I'M THE BIGGEST LIAR IN THE WORLD?; SUNDAY JUMPS; EVERY NIGHT AT SEVEN; OPEN YOUR EYES; THE HAPPIEST DAY OF MY LIFE; I LEFT MY HAT IN HAYTI; TOO LATE NOW; WHAT A LOVELY DAY FOR A WEDDING and I GOT ME A BABY.

SAILOR BEWARE
A Paramount release starring Dean Martin and Jerry Lewis in a cast that included Corrinne Calvet and Marion Marshall, and directed by Hal Walker. Songs by Mack David and Jerry Livingston:

THE OLD CALLIOPE; SAILORS' POLKA; NEVER BEFORE; MERCI BEAUCOUP and TODAY, TOMORROW, FOREVER.

SHOW BOAT
An M-G-M picture filmed with a cast headed by Kathryn Grayson, Howard Keel, Joe E. Brown, Ava Gardner, Agnes Moorehead, Robert Sterling, William Warfield and Marge and Gower Champion, and directed by George Sidney. Songs by Oscar Hammerstein II and Jerome Kern:
WHY DO I LOVE YOU?; MAKE BELIEVE; OL' MAN RIVER; CAN'T HELP LOVIN' THAT MAN and BILL (With P. G. Wodehouse).

STARLIFT
A Warner Brothers' release filmed with a cast headed by Doris Day, Gordon MacRae, Virginia Mayo, Gene Nelson and Ruth Roman, and directed by Roy Del Ruth. Songs:
YOU'RE GONNA LOSE YOUR GAL by Joe Young and Jimmy Monaco; 'SWONDERFUL and LIZA by Ira and George Gershwin; YOU OUGHT TO BE IN PICTURES by Edward Heyman and Dana Suesse; YOU DO SOMETHING TO ME and WHAT IS THIS THING CALLED LOVE? by Cole Porter; IT'S MAGIC by Sammy Cahn and Jule Styne; GOOD GREEN ACRES OF HOME by Irving Kahal and Sammy Fain; I MAY BE WRONG BUT I THINK YOU'RE WONDERFUL by Harry Ruskin and Henry Sullivan; LOOK OUT STRANGER I'M A TEXAS RANGER by Ruby Ralesin and Phil Harris; NOCHE CARIB by Percy Faith.

STRIP, THE
An M-G-M picture starring Mickey Rooney, Sallie Forrest and Vic Damone in a cast that included James Craig and the orchestras of Louis Armstrong and Jack Teagarden, and directed by Leslie Kardos. Musical numbers:
A KISS TO BUILD A DREAM ON by Bert Kalmar, Oscar Hammerstein II and Harry Ruby; BASIN STREET BLUES by Spencer Williams; LA BOTA by Haven Gillespie II and Charles Wolcott; DON'T BLAME ME by Dorothy Fields and Jimmy McHugh; SHADRACK (Negro spiritual).

TEXAS CARNIVAL
An M-G-M release starring Esther Williams, Red Skelton, Howard Keel and Keenan Wynn, and directed by Charles

Walters. Songs:
  WHOA, EMMA!; YOUNG FOLKS SHOULD GET MARRIED; IT'S DYNA-MITE and CORNIE'S PITCH by Dorothy Fields and Harry Warren; CLAP YOUR HANDS by David Rose and Earl K. Brent.

TWO GALS AND A GUY

A United Artists' picture starring Robert Alda, Janet Paige and the Three Suns, and directed by Alfred E. Green. Songs by Hal David and Marty Nevins:
  LAUGH AND BE HAPPY; SO LONG FOR NOW; SUN SHOWERS and WE HAVE WITH US TONIGHT.

TWO TICKETS TO BROADWAY

An RKO picture filmed with a cast headed by Tony Martin, Janet Leigh, Gloria DeHaven, Eddie Bracken, Ann Miller and Bob Crosby, and directed by Charles V. Kern. Songs:
  THE CLOSER YOU ARE; ARE YOU JUST A BEAUTIFUL DREAM?; BABY YOU WON'T BE SORRY; THE WORRY BIRD; BIG CHIEF HOLE-IN-THE-GROUND; PELICAN FALLS; IT BE-GAN IN YUCATAN; LET'S DO SOME-THING NEW; THAT'S THE TUNE and NEW YORK (LET ME SING) by Leo Robin and Jule Styne; THERE'S NO TO-MORROW by Al Hoffman, Leo Corday and Leon Carr; LET'S MAKE COM-PARISONS by Sammy Cahn and Bob Crosby.

Feature Films With Songs

ACROSS THE WIDE MISSOURI

An M-G-M picture filmed with a cast headed by Clark Gable, Ricardo Montalban, John Hodiak, Adolphe Menjou and Maria Elena Marques, and directed by Frank Wellman. Song by Alberto Colombo.
INDIAN LULLABY

ALONG THE GREAT DIVIDE

A Warner Brothers' picture starring Kirk Douglas, Virginia Mayo and Walter Brennan, and directed by Raoul Walsh. Kentucky mountain folk song:
DOWN IN THE VALLEY

ANNE OF THE INDIES

A 20th Century-Fox picture starring Jean Peters and Louis Jourdan, and directed by Jacques Tourneur. Song by George Jessel, Sam Lerner and Joe Cooper:
ANNE OF THE INDIES

BIG CARNIVAL, THE

A Paramount picture starring Kirk Douglas, Jan Sterling and Bob Arthur, and directed by Billy Wilder. Song by Ray Evans and Jay Livingston:
WE'RE COMING, LEO

BIRD OF PARADISE

A 20th Century-Fox picture filmed with a cast headed by Louis Jourdan, Debra Paget, Jeff Chandler and Everett Sloane, and directed by Delmer Daves. Songs:
LEGEND OF THE RAIN and SONG OF KALUA by Ken Darby; APAPANE by Queen Liliuokalani.

BLUE VEIL, THE

An RKO release starring Jane Wyman, Charles Laughton, Joan Blondell and Richard Carlson, and directed by Curtis Bernhardt. Songs:
I COULDN'T SLEEP A WINK LAST NIGHT by Harold Adamson and Jimmy McHugh; THERE'LL BE SOME CHANGES MADE by Billy Higgins and W. Benton Overstreet.

BULLFIGHTER AND THE LADY, THE

A Republic picture starring Robert Stack and Joy Page, and directed by Budd Boetticher. Musical numbers by Jack Elliott and Victor Young:
ESTA NOCHE and CIELO ANDALUX

CALLAWAY WENT THATAWAY

An M-G-M release starring Fred Mac-Murray, Dorothy McGuire and Howard Keel, and directed by Norman Panama and Melvin Frank. Songs:
WHERE THE TUMBLEWEED IS BLUE by Charles Wolcott; CALLAWAY WENT THATAWAY by Al Stillman and Peter DeRose.

CROSSWINDS

A Paramount picture starring John Payne and Rhonda Fleming, and directed by Lewis Foster. Song by Ray Evans and Jay Livingston:
CROSSWINDS

CUBAN FIREBALL

A Republic picture starring Estelita Rodriguez and Warren Douglas, and directed by William Beaudine. Songs by Jack Elliott:
LOST AND FOUND and TOBACCO

DOUBLE DYNAMITE

An RKO release starring Jane Russell, Groucho Marx and Frank Sinatra, and di-

rected by Irving Cummings: Songs by Sammy Cahn and Jule Styne:
IT'S ONLY MONEY and KISSES AND TEARS

FIGHTING COAST GUARD, THE
A Republic picture starring Brian Donlevy, Forrest Tucker and Ella Raines, and directed by Joseph Kane. Songs:
SEMPER PARATUS by Francis S. Von Boskerck; HOME ON THE RANGE (Traditional); I LOVE THE PRAIRIE COUNTRY.

FLAMING FEATHER, THE
A Paramount release filmed with a cast headed by Sterling Hayden, Forrest Tucker, Barbara Rush, Arleen Whelan, Victor Jory and Richard Arlen, and directed by Ray Enright. Song by Frank Loesser and Manning Sherwin:
NO RING ON HER FINGER

GO FOR BROKE
An M-G-M picture starring Van Johnson, and directed by Robert Pirosh. Song by Robert Pirosh, Alberto Colombo and Ken Okamoto:
THE MEANING OF LOVE

GUY WHO CAME BACK, THE
A 20th Century-Fox picture starring Paul Douglas, Joan Bennett and Linda Darnell, and directed by Joseph Newman. Song by Ken Darby:
KEEP YOUR EYE ON THE BALL

HALF ANGEL
A 20th Century-Fox picture starring Loretta Young and Joseph Cotten, and directed by Richard Sale. Song by Ralph Blane and Alfred Newman:
MY CASTLE IN THE SAND

HAPPY GO LOVELY
An RKO picture starring Vera-Ellen, David Niven and Cesar Romero, and directed by Bruce Humberstone. Song by Jack Fishman and Mischa Spoliansky:
WOULD YOU, COULD YOU?

HAVANA ROSE
A Republic release filmed with a cast headed by Estelita Rodriguez, Bill Williams, Hugh Herbert and Florence Bates, and directed by William Beaudine. Musical numbers:
BA-BA-LU by Bob Russell and Marguerita Lecuona; NOCHE DE RONDA by Augustin Lara; REPIQUETEA TIMBARLERO.

HIS KIND OF WOMAN
An RKO picture starring Jane Russell,

Robert Mitchum and Vincent Price, and directed by John Farrow. Songs:
FIVE LITTLE MILES FROM SAN BERDOO and KISS AND RUN by Sam Coslow; YOU'LL KNOW by Harold Adamson and Jimmy McHugh.

I WAS AN AMERICAN SPY
A United Artists' picture starring Ann Dvorak, Gene Evans and Douglas Kennedy, and directed by Leslie Selander. Song by Arthur Hammerstein and Dudley Wilkinson:
BECAUSE OF YOU

INSIDE STRAIGHT
An M-G-M picture filmed with a cast headed by David Brian, Arlene Dahl and Barry Sullivan, and directed by Gerald Mayer. Songs by Charles E. Horn and H. B. Farnie:
UP IN A BALLOON and WHAT CAN A POOR MAIDEN DO?

KATIE DID IT
A Universal picture starring Ann Blyth and Mark Stevens, and directed by Frederick De Cordova. Song by Lester Lee and Dan Shapiro:
A LITTLE OLD CAPE COD COTTAGE

LITTLE BIG HORN
A Lippert picture filmed with a cast headed by Lloyd Bridges, John Ireland and Marie Windsor, and directed by Charles M. Warren. Song by Stanley Adams, Maurice Sigler and Larry Stock:
ON THE LITTLE BIG HORN

LONE STAR
An M-G-M picture starring Clark Gable and Ava Gardner in a cast that included Broderick Crawford and Lionel Barrymore, and directed by Vincent Sherman. Song by Earl K. Brent:
LOVERS WERE MEANT TO CRY

MAN IN THE SADDLE, THE
A Columbia release starring Randolph Scott, Joan Leslie and Ellen Drew, and directed by Andre De Toth. Song by Ralph Murphy and Harold Lewis:
MAN IN THE SADDLE

MAN WITH A CLOAK, THE
An M-G-M picture starring Barbara Stanwyck and Joseph Cotten, and directed by Fletcher Markle. Song by Earl K. Brent:
ANOTHER YESTERDAY

MATING SEASON, THE
A Paramount picture starring Gene Tierney, John Lund and Miriam Hopkins, and

directed by Michell Leisen. Songs:
MY LOST MELODY by Marguerite
Monnot and Raymond Asso; THE MAT-
ING SEASON by Ray Evans and Jay Liv-
ingston; WHEN I TAKE MY SUGAR TO
TEA by Irving Kahal and Sammy Fain.

MY FAVORITE SPY
A Paramount picture starring Bob Hope,
Hedy Lamarr and Francis L. Sullivan, and
directed by Norman Z. McLeod. Songs:
I WIND UP TAKING A FALL by
Johnny Mercer and Robert Emmett Dolan;
JUST A MOMENT MORE by Ray Evans
and Jay Livingston.

NEW MEXICO
A United Artists' picture starring Lew
Ayres and Marilyn Maxwell, and directed
by Irving Reis. Songs:
SOLDIER, SOLDIER WON'T YOU
MARRY ME (Traditional); NEW MEX-
ICO by Lynn Cowan and Irving Bibo.

PANDORA AND THE FLYING
DUTCHMAN
An M-G-M picture starring James Mason
and Ava Gardner, and directed by Albert
Lewin. Song by Albert Lewin and Johnny
Green:
PANDORA

RACKET, THE
An RKO release starring Robert Mitch-
um and Lizabeth Scott, and directed by
John Cromwell. Song by Harold Adamson
and Jimmy McHugh:
A LOVELY WAY TO SPEND AN EVE-
NING

RHUBARB
A Paramount picture filmed with a cast
headed by Ray Milland, Jan Sterling, Gene
Lockhart, William Frawley, Elsie Holmes
and Taylor Holmes, and directed by Ar-
thur Lubin. Song by Ray Evans and Jay
Livingston:
IT'S A PRIVILEGE TO LIVE IN
BROOKLYN

ROADBLOCK
An RKO release starring Charles Mc-
Graw and Joan Dixon, and directed by Har-
old Daniels. Song by Leona Davidson:
SO SWELL OF YOU

ST. BENNY THE DIP
A United Artists' picture starring Dick
Haymes, Nina Foch and Roland Young,
and directed by Harry Lee Danziger. Song
by Bob Stringer:
I BELIEVE

SEA HORNET, THE
A Republic picture filmed with a cast
headed by Rod Cameron, Adele Mara, Adri-
an Booth and Chill Wills, and directed by
Joseph Kane. Songs:
I'M AFRAID OF YOU and A DREAM
OR TWO AGO by Jack Elliott; SOME-
ONE TO REMEMBER by Jack Elliott and
Nathan Scott.

SELLOUT, THE
An M-G-M release filmed with a cast
headed by Walter Pidgeon, John Hodiak,
Audrey Totter and Paul Raymond, and di-
rected by Gerald Mayer. Song by Al Rinker
and Floyd Huddleston.
YOU CAN'T DO WRONG DOIN'
RIGHT

SIERRA PASSAGE
A Monogram picture starring Wayne
Morris, Lola Albright and Alan Hale, and
directed by Frank McDonald. Song by
Charles Dixon and Max Goodwin:
LOVE IS MUSIC

SKIPALONG ROSENBLOOM
A United Artists' release filmed with a
cast headed by Maxie Rosenbloom, Max
Baer, Jackie Coogan and Fuzzy Knight, and
directed by Sam Newfield. Songs:
YOU'VE GOT PLENTY TO LEARN
ABOUT LOVE by Eddie Forman and Jack
Kenney; SKIPALONG ROSENBLOOM by
Dean Reisner and Jack Kenney.

SLAUGHTER TRAIL
An RKO release filmed with a cast
headed by Brian Donlevy, Gig Young, Virginia Grey, Andy Devine and Robert Hutton, and directed by Irving Allen. Songs:
HOOFBEAT SERENADE; BALLAD OF
THE BANDELIER and I WISH I WUZ
by Sid Kuller and Lyn Murray; 'CEPTIN'
ME by Sid Kuller and Terry Gilkerson.

STRICTLY DISHONORABLE
An M-G-M picture starring Ezio Pinza,
Janet Leigh and Gale Robbins, and di-
rected by Melvin Frank and Norman Pan-
ama. Song by Harold Adamson and Burton
Lane:
EVERYTHING I HAVE IS YOURS

TAKE CARE OF MY LITTLE GIRL
A 20th Century-Fox picture starring
Jeanne Crain, Dale Robertson, Mitzi Gay-
nor and Jean Peters, and directed by Jean
Negulesco. Song by Harry Ruby and Alfred
Newman:
TAKE CARE OF MY LITTLE GIRL

TERESA

An M-G-M picture starring Pier Angeli and John Ericson, and directed by Fred Zinnemann. Song by Mack David and Jerry Livingston:
TERESA

THAT'S MY BOY

A Paramount picture starring Dean Martin and Jerry Lewis in a cast that included Ruth Hussey, Eddie Mayehoff and Polly Bergen, and directed by Hal Walker. Songs: BALLIN' THE JACK by Chris Smith; I'M IN THE MOOD FOR LOVE by Dorothy Fields and Jimmy McHugh; RIDGE-VILLE FIGHT SONG by Ray Evans and Jay Livingston.

TWO DOLLAR BETTOR

A Realart Picture release filmed with a cast headed by John Litel, Marie Windsor, Steve Brodie and Barbara Logan, and directed by Edward Leven. Song by Jean Logan:
QUERIDA

VARIETIES ON PARADE

A Lippert picture filmed with a cast headed by Jackie Coogan, Eddie Garr, Tom Neal and Iris Adrian, and directed by Ron Ormond. Songs:
OLD LAZY MOON; OH WHERE IS MY DARLIN' TONIGHT? and PEGGY LEE by Rene Lamarr; THAT'S SHOW BUSINESS by Diane Manners and Johnny Clark.

WESTWARD THE WOMEN

An M-G-M release starring Robert Taylor, Denise Darcel, Hope Emerson and John McIntyre, and directed by William A. Wellman. Song by Henry Russell:
TO THE WEST! TO THE WEST!

WHISTLE AT EATON FALLS, THE

A Columbia release starring Lloyd Bridges and Dorothy Gish, and directed by Robert Siodmak. Song by Carleton Carpenter:
EV'RY OTHER DAY

WILD BLUE YONDER, THE

A Republic picture starring Wendell Corey, Vera Ralston, Forrest Tucker and Phil Harris, and directed by Allan Dwan. Musical numbers:
THE THING by Charles Randolph Green; THE HEAVY BOMBER SONG by Ned Washington and Victor Young; ARMY AIR FORCE SONG by Robert Crawford; MAN BEHIND THE ARMOR-PLATED DESK.

WILD NORTH, THE

An M-G-M picture filmed with a cast headed by Stewart Granger, Cyd Charisse, Wendell Corey, Morgan Farley and John War Eagle, and directed by Andrew Marton. Songs by Charles Wolcott:
NORTHERN LIGHTS and WINTER WHEN WINTER COMES

Western Films With Songs

BANDITS OF EL DORADO

A Columbia picture starring Charles Starrett, and directed by Ray Nazarro. Songs:
THE RICH GET RICHER and TRICKY SENOR by Smiley Burnette; THAT LAST GREAT DAY by Frank Rice and Ernest L. Stokes.

HEART OF THE ROCKIES

A Republic picture starring Roy Rogers in a cast that included Penny Edwards, and directed by William Witney. Songs by Jack Elliott:
WANDERIN'; RODEO SQUARE DANCE and HEART OF THE ROCKIES.

IN OLD AMARILLO

A Republic picture starring Roy Rogers in a cast that included Penny Edwards and Estelita Rodriguez, and directed by William Witney. Songs by Jack Elliott and Foy Willing:
IF I EVER FALL IN LOVE; UNDER THE LONE STAR MOON and IN OLD AMARILLO.

KID FROM AMARILLO, THE

A Columbia picture starring Charles Starrett, and directed by Ray Nazarro. Song by Smiley Burnette:
THE GREAT BURNETTE FROM CHIHUAHUA

OH SUZANNA

A Republic picture starring Rod Cameron and Adrian Booth, and directed by Joseph Kane. Song by Jack Elliott:
IS SOMEONE LONELY?

OVERLAND TELEGRAPH

An RKO picture filmed with a cast headed by Tim Holt, Richard Martin and Gail Davis, and directed by Leslie Selander. Songs:
OH SUZANNA; NELLY BLY and DOLLY DAY by Stephen Foster; I'SE GWINE BACK TO DIXIE by C. W. White.

RODEO KING AND THE SENORITA, THE

A Republic picture filmed with a cast headed by Rex Allen, Mary Ellen Kay and Buddy Ebsen, and directed by Philip Ford. Two folk songs:
STRAWBERRY ROAN and JUANITA

SILVER CANYON

A Columbia picture starring Gene Autry in a cast that included Gail Davis, and directed by John English. Songs:
RIDIN' DOWN THE CANYON WHEN THE DESERT SUN GOES DOWN by Gene Autry and Smiley Burnette; FORT WORTH JAIL by Dick Reinhart.

SNAKE RIVER DESPERADOES

A Columbia picture starring Charles Starrett, and directed by Fred F. Sears. Song by Larry Conley and Samuel Short, Jr.:
BRASS BAND POLKA

SOUTH OF CALIENTE

A Republic picture starring Roy Rogers in a cast that included Dale Evans, and directed by William Witney. Songs:
MY HOME IS OVER YONDER and WON'TCHA BE A FRIEND OF MINE? by Jack Elliott; GYPSY TRAIL by Jack Elliott and Geri Gallian.

SPOILERS OF THE PLAINS

A Republic picture starring Roy Rogers in a cast that included Penny Edwards, and directed by William Witney. Songs by Jack Elliott:
IT'S AN OLD CUSTOM and IT'S A LEAD PIPE CINCH.

UTAH WAGON TRAIN

A Republic picture filmed with a cast headed by Rex Allen, Penny Edwards and Buddy Ebsen, and directed by Philip Ford. Songs by Rex Allen:
THE BIG CORRAL and THE STREETS OF LAREDO

VALLEY OF FIRE

A Columbia picture starring Gene Autry in a cast that included Pat Buttram and Gail Davis, and directed by John English. Songs:
HERE'S TO THE LADIES by Gene Autry and Cindy Walker; ON TOP OF OLD SMOKY (Traditional).

WHIRLWIND

A Columbia picture starring Gene Autry in a cast that included Smiley Burnette and Gail Davis, and directed by John English. Songs:
AS LONG AS I HAVE MY HORSE and TWEEDLE-O-TWILL by Gene Autry and Fred Rose; WHIRLWIND by Stan Jones.

Feature Cartoon With Songs

ALICE IN WONDERLAND

An RKO-Walt Disney production with Ed Wynn, Richard Haydn, Sterling Holloway, Jerry Colonna and Kathryn Beaumont supplying the speaking and singing voices. Songs:
VERY GOOD ADVICE; IN A WORLD OF MY OWN; ALL IN A GOLDEN AFTERNOON; ALICE IN WONDERLAND; THE WALRUS AND THE CARPENTER; THE CAUCUS RACE; I'M LATE; PAINTING THE ROSES RED and MARCH OF THE CARDS by Bob Hilliard and Sammy Fain; 'TWAS BRILLIG by Don Raye and Gene DePaul; A VERY MERRY UN-BIRTHDAY by Mack David, Al Hoffman and Jerry Livingston; WE'LL SMOKE THE BLIGHTER OUT; OLD FATHER WILLIAM and A-E-I-O-U by Oliver Wallace and T. Sears.

David Wayne and Susan Hayward in *With A Song In My Heart*

1952

Hollywood Pays Tribute To A Courageous Lady Of Song

This is being written on a July afternoon. The weather is hot and muggy, the kind that's apt to becloud a crystal ball, but many film critics already are predicting that eight months from now the Oscar for the best picture of 1952 will go to a musical: *With A Song In My Heart*. And they may be right—right as rice in the empty rice bowl of a starving Korean orphan.

For *With A Song In My Heart* is more than a four-bell picture enriched with twenty or more songs the public knows and remembers with affection. It is more than a glowing tribute to a gallant lady of song, Jane Froman. It is as American as the Fourth of July—an inspiring saga of determination, patriotism, sacrifice and indomitable courage, qualities that will be the sole salvation of a country now beset by crime and corruption from within and menaced by Communism from without.

This picture also points up a lesson Hollywood would do well to heed if the talkies are to meet the great and growing competition that television offers —free entertainment in the home. For that competition can't be met with B pictures on the screen and popcorn machines in the lobby. It is competition that demands of the top brass of the cinema capital a rebirth of the courage that brought the talkies into being, and a return to that pride of craftsman-ship on the part of producers, directors, authors and songwriters that was re-flected in both the early musicals and the song-and-dance films of the wartime years.

That such a lesson has struck home is evidenced in several of the musical productions that were released during the first six months of 1952, the most notable of which in addition to *With A Song In My Heart,* being *The Merry Widow, Lovely To Look At* and *Singing In The Rain*. The first of these re-vives the music written a half-century ago by Franz Lehar, the second is a revised edition of Jerome Kern's *Roberta,* and the sound track of the third is packed with the songs that unrolled the red carpet in Tin Pan Alley for Ar-thur Freed and Nacio Herb Brown in the late 1920's.

The selection of old music rather than new for these four films, a policy carried over from the preceding years, can lead to but one conclusion: That one of Hollywood's greatest needs today is for songwriters who can write en-during songs rather than tunes the movie-goers "forget to remember" as they file out of the theater. The reason for this lack, which can't be hidden with Technicolor, challenges explanation, but recalling that most of the great songs in our catalogue of popular music, like most of the great novels and great poetry, were written strictly from hunger, it could be due to an era in our national life when the all-too-common ambition is to make a fast and easy buck and to hell with the future and how that future may regard you.

Apparently, there's nothing new under the sun even in fabulous Hollywood for during 1952, the year that marks the silver anniversary of the talkies, the producers went into the deep freeze for screen material that would woo the *I Love Lucy* fans away from their T-V sets. *What Price Glory,* a silent film classic, was embellished with World War I songs for a 1952 revival. *Singing In The Rain* brought back for a reprise the many song hits Arthur Freed and Nacio Herb Brown wrote when sound pictures were still a novelty. The turn-of-the-century music of Franz Lehar was taken out of moth balls for a retake of *The Merry Widow* in technicolor. Finally, the pendulum completed a full swing back to 1927 in September when the cameras started rolling on a modernized version of *The Jazz Singer* with Danny Thomas playing the Al Jolson role that first brought music and dialogue to the silver screen. And that's where we came in!

Musicals

AARON SLICK FROM PUNKIN CRICK
A Paramount picture filmed with a cast headed by Alan Young, Dinah Shore, Robert Merrill and Adele Jergens, and directed by Claude Binyon. Songs by Ray Evans and Jay Livingston:
LIFE IS A BEAUTIFUL THING; WHY SHOULD I BELIEVE IN LOVE; MARSHMALLOW MOON; I'D LIKE TO BABY YOU; PURT 'NIGH BUT NOT PLUMB; STILL WATER; CHORES; SATURDAY NIGHT IN PUNKIN CRICK; THE GENERAL STORE; WILL YOU BE AT HOME IN HEAVEN?; STEP RIGHT UP; SODA SHOP and THE SPIDER AND THE FLY.

ABOUT FACE
A Warner Brothers' picture filmed with a cast headed by Aileen Stanley Jr., Gordon MacRae, Eddie Bracken, Larry Keating, Dick Wesson and Virginia Gibson, and directed by Roy Del Ruth. Songs by Charles Tobias and Peter De Rose:
PIANO, BASS AND DRUMS; NO OTHER GIRL FOR ME; I'M NOBODY; SPRING HAS SPRUNG; WOODEN INDIAN; REVEILLE; S. M. I. MARCH; TAR HEELS and THEY HAVEN'T LOST A FATHER YET.

BECAUSE YOU'RE MINE
An M-G-M picture starring Mario Lanza and Doretta Morrow in a cast that included James Whitmore and Dean Miller, and directed by Alexander Hall. In addition to excerpts from *Cavalleria Rusticana,*

Rigoletto, Il Trovatore and *Norma,* the following songs were introduced:
BECAUSE YOU'RE MINE by Sammy Cahn and Nicholas Brodszky; LEE-AH-LOO by John Leeman and Ray Sinatra; THE SONG ANGELS SING by Paul Francis Webster and Irving Aaronson; YOU DO SOMETHING TO ME and ALL THE THINGS YOU ARE by Cole Porter, THE LORD'S PRAYER by Albert Hay Malotte; GRANADA by Augustin Lara.

BELLE OF NEW YORK, THE
An M-G-M picture starring Fred Astaire and Vera-Ellen in a cast that included Marjorie Main, Keenan Wynn, Alice Pearce and Clinton Sundberg, and directed by Charles Walters: Songs:
BRIDE'S WEDDING DAY; WHEN I'M OUT WITH THE BELLE OF NEW YORK; OOPS; BABY DOLL; NAUGHTY BUT NICE; SEEING'S BELIEVING; BACHELOR'S DINNER SONG; THANK YOU MR. CURRIER, THANK YOU MR. IVES; and I LOVE TO BEAT A BIG BASS DRUM by Johnny Mercer and Harry Warren! I WANNA BE A DANCING MAN by A. J. Lerner and Burton Lane; LET A LITTLE LOVE COME IN by Roger Edens.

EVERYTHING I HAVE IS YOURS
An M-G-M release starring Marge and Gower Champion in a cast that included Dennis O'Keefe, Monica Lewis and Dean Miller, and directed by Robert Z. Leonard. Songs:

DERRY DOWN DILLY by Johnny Mercer and Johnny Green; SERENADE TO A NEW BABY by Johnny Green; CASABLANCA by Richard Priborsky; SEVENTEEN HUNDRED TELEPHONE POLES by Saul Chaplin; LIKE MONDAY FOLLOWS SUNDAY by Johnny Green, Clifford Grey, Rex Newman and Douglas Furber; MY HEART SKIPS A BEAT by Bob Wright, Chet Forrest and Walter Donaldson; GENERAL HIRAM JOHNSON JEFFERSON BROWN by Gus Kahn and Walter Donaldson; EVERYTHING I HAVE IS YOURS by Harold Adamson and Burton Lane.

I DREAM OF JEANIE

A Republic release filmed with a cast headed by Ray Middleton, Bill Shirley, Muriel Lawrence and Eileen Christy, and directed by Allan Dwan. Songs:
MY OLD KENTUCKY HOME; OLD FOLKS AT HOME; OH SUZANNA; OLD DOG TRAY; RING DE BANJO; CAMPTOWN RACES; JEANIE and COME WHERE MY LOVE LIES DREAMING by Stephen Foster; A RIBBON IN YOUR HAIR; I SEE HER STILL IN MY DREAMS and HEAD OVER HEELS, all based on Stephen Foster melodies with lyrics by Allan Dwan; ON WINGS OF SONG by Mendelssohn; LO HEAR THE GENTLE LARK.

JACK AND THE BEANSTALK

A Warner Brothers' release starring Abbott and Costello in a cast that included Buddy Baer, Dorothy Ford, Shaye Cogan, James Alexander, Barbara Brown and William Farnum, and directed by Jean Yarbrough. Songs by Lester Lee and Bob Russell:
DREAMER'S CLOTH; JACK AND THE BEANSTALK; HE NEVER LOOKED BETTER IN HIS LIFE; I FEAR NOTHING and DARLENE.

JUMPING JACKS

A Paramount picture starring Dean Martin and Jerry Lewis in a cast that included Mona Freeman and Don DeFore, and directed by Norman Taurog. Songs by Mack David and Jerry Livingston:
DO THE PARACHUTE JUMP; WHAT HAVE YOU DONE FOR ME LATELY?; THE BIG BLUE SKY IS THE PLACE FOR ME; I KNOW A DREAM WHEN I SEE ONE; I CAN'T RESIST A BOY IN UNIFORM and KEEP A LITTLE DREAM HANDY.

JUST FOR YOU

A Paramount picture starring Bing Crosby, Jane Wyman and Ethel Barrymore, and directed by Elliott Nugent. Songs by Leo Robin and Harry Warren:
THE LIVE OAK TREE; CHECKIN' MY HEART; I'LL SI-SI YA IN BAHIA; ON THE 10:10 (FROM TEN, TEN TENNESSEE); MAIDEN OF QUADALUPE; ZING A LITTLE ZONG; HE'S JUST CRAZY FOR ME; A FLIGHT OF FANCY; CALL ME TONIGHT; JUST FOR YOU and THE OL' SPRING FEVER.

LOVELY TO LOOK AT

An M-G-M picture filmed with a cast headed by Kathryn Grayson, Red Skelton, Howard Keel, Ann Miller, Sza Sza Gabor, Kurt Kasznar and Marge and Gower Champion, and directed by Mervyn LeRoy. Songs by Otto Harbach and Jerome Kern:
OPENING NIGHT; I'LL BE HARD TO HANDLE; LAFAYETTE; YESTERDAYS; I WON'T DANCE; YOU'RE DEVASTATING; LOVELY TO LOOK AT; SMOKE GETS IN YOUR EYES; THE MOST EXCITING NIGHT and THE TOUCH OF YOUR HAND.

MEET DANNY WILSON

A Universal picture filmed with a cast headed by Frank Sinatra, Alex Nicol, Shelley Winters and Raymond Burr, and directed by Joseph Pervey. Songs:
WHEN YOU'RE SMILING by Mark Fisher, Joe Goodwin and Larry Shay; ALL OF ME by Seymour Simons and Gerald Marks; THAT OLD BLACK MAGIC by Johnny Mercer and Harold Arlen; HOW DEEP IS THE OCEAN? by Irving Berlin; A GOOD MAN IS HARD TO FIND by Eddie Green; SHE'S FUNNY THAT WAY by Neil Moret and Richard Whiting; YOU'RE A SWEETHEART by Harold Adamson and Jimmy McHugh; LONESOME MAN BLUES by Sy Oliver; I'VE GOT A CRUSH ON YOU by Ira and George Gershwin.

MERRY WIDOW, THE

An M-G-M picture starring Lana Turner and Fernando Lamas in a cast that included Thomas Gomez, Una Merkel and Richard Haydn, and directed by Curtis Bernhardt. Songs by Paul Francis Webster and Franz Lehar:
VILIA; MAXIM'S; NIGHT; MERRY WIDOW WALTZ; GIRLS, GIRLS, GIRLS and CAN-CAN.

RAINBOW 'ROUND MY SHOULDER

A Columbia release starring Frankie Laine, Billy Daniels, Charlotte Austin and Arthur Franz, and directed by Richard Quine. Songs:

WONDERFUL, WASN'T IT? by Hal David and Don Rodney; GIRL IN THE WOOD by Neal Stuart and Terry Gilkyson; THERE'S A RAINBOW 'ROUND MY SHOULDER by Al Jolson, Billy Rose and Dave Dreyer; WRAP YOUR TROUBLES IN DREAMS (AND DREAM YOUR TROUBLES AWAY) by Harry Barris, Ted Koehler and Billy Moll; SHE'S FUNNY THAT WAY by Neil Moret and Richard Whiting; BYE, BYE BLACKBIRD by Mort Dixon and Ray Henderson; THE LAST ROSE OF SUMMER by Thomas Moore; BUBBLE, BUBBLE, BUBBLE (PINK CHAMPAGNE) by Bob Wright and George Forrest.

SHE'S WORKING HER WAY THROUGH COLLEGE

A Warner Brothers' picture starring Virginia Mayo and Donald Reagan in a cast that included Gene Nelson, Don DeFore, Phyllis Thaxter and Patrice Wymore, and directed by Bruce Humberstone. Songs:

I'LL BE LOVING YOU; THE STUFF THAT DREAMS ARE MADE OF; GIVE 'EM WHAT THEY WANT; AM I IN LOVE?; LOVE IS STILL FOR FREE and SHE'S WORKING HER WAY THROUGH COLLEGE by Sammy Cahn and Vernon Duke; WITH PLENTY OF MONEY AND YOU by Al Dubin and Harry Warren.

SINGING IN THE RAIN

An M-G-M picture starring Gene Kelly, Donald O'Connor and Debbie Reynolds in a cast that included Jean Hagen, Millard Mitchell and Cyd Charisse, and directed by Gene Kelly and Stanley Dowen. Songs:

WOULD YOU?; SINGING IN THE RAIN; ALL I DO IS DREAM OF YOU; I'VE GOT A FEELING YOU'RE FOOLING; WEDDING OF THE PAINTED DOLL; SHOULD I?; MAKE 'EM LAUGH; YOU WERE MEANT FOR ME; YOU ARE MY LUCKY STAR; FIT AS A FIDDLE AND READY FOR LOVE and GOOD MORNING by Arthur Freed and Nacio Herb Brown; MOSES by Betty Comden, Adolph Green and Roger Edens.

SKIRTS AHOY

An M-G-M picture filmed with a cast headed by Esther Williams, Vivian Blaine, Billy Eckstine, Joan Evans, Barry Sullivan, Debbie Reynolds, Margalo Gillmore and the DeMarco Sisters, and directed by Sidney Lanfield. Songs:

THE NAVY WALTZ; HILDA MATILDA; WHAT GOOD IS A GUY WITHOUT A GIRL?; WHAT MAKES A WAVE?; I GOT A FUNNY FEELING; GLAD TO HAVE YOU ABOARD; WE WILL FIGHT and HOLD ME CLOSE TO YOU by Ralph Blane and Harry Warren; OH BY JINGO by Lew Brown and Albert Von Tilzer.

SOMEBODY LOVES ME

A Paramount release starring Betty Hutton and Ralph Meeker in a cast that included Robert Keith and Adele Jergens, and directed by Irving Brecher. Songs:

LOVE HIM; THANKS TO YOU and HONEY OH MY HONEY by Ray Evans and Jay Livingston; JEALOUS by Jack Little, Tommy Malie and Dick Finch; JUNE NIGHT by Cliff Friend and Abel Baer; I CRIED FOR YOU by Gus Arnheim, Arthur Freed and Abe Lyman; I'M SORRY I MADE YOU CRY by N. J. Clesi; ON SAN FRANCISCO BAY by Vincent Bryan and Gertrude Hoffman; SOMEBODY LOVES ME by B. G. DeSylva and George Gershwin; ROSE ROOM by Harry Williams and Art Hickman; WAY DOWN YONDER IN NEW ORLEANS by Henry Creamer and J. Turner Layton; SMILES by J. Will Callahan and Lee S. Roberts; I CAN'T TELL WHY I LOVE YOU by Will J. Cobb and Gus Edwards; WANG WANG BLUES by Gus Mueller, Buster Johnson and Henry Busse; DIXIE DREAMS by Arthur Johnston, George W. Meyer, Grant Clarke and Roy Turk; THAT TEASING RAG by Joe Jordan; TODDLING THE TODALO by E. Ray Goetz and A. Baldwin Sloane; A DOLLAR AND THIRTY CENTS.

SON OF PALEFACE

A Paramount picture starring Bob Hope, Jane Russell and Roy Rogers, and directed by Frank Tashlin. Songs:

WING DING TONIGHT; CALIFORNIA ROSE and WHAT A DIRTY SHAME by Ray Evans and Jay Livingston; AM I IN LOVE?; FOUR-LEGGED FRIEND and THERE'S A CLOUD IN MY VALLEY OF SUNSHINE by Jack Brooks, Jack Hope and Lyle Moraine.

STOOGE, THE

A Paramount release filmed with a cast headed by Dean Martin, Jerry Lewis, Polly

Bergen, Eddie Mayehoff and Marion Marshall, and directed by Norman Taurog. Songs:

A GIRL NAMED MARY AND A BOY NAMED BILL by Mack David and Jerry Livingston; WHO'S YOUR LITTLE WHOZIS? by Al Goering, Ben Bernie and Walter Hirsch; JUST ONE MORE CHANCE by Arthur Johnston and Sam Coslow; WITH MY EYES WIDE OPEN I'M DREAMING by Mack Gordon and Harry Revel; LOUISE by Leo Robin and Richard Whiting; I'M YOURS by E. Y. Harburg and Johnny Green.

STORY OF ROBIN HOOD, THE
A Walt Disney-RKO picture filmed with a cast headed by Richard Todd, Joan Rice, James Hayton, James R. Justice, Bill Owen and Elton Hayes, and directed by Kenneth Annakin. Songs:
WHISTLE MY LOVE and RIDDLE DE DIDDLE DE DAY by Eddie Pola and George Wyle; THE SWEET RHYMING MINSTREL; COME SWING LOW COME SWING HIGH and ROBIN HOOD BALLADS by Lawrence E. Watkins and Elton Hayes.

WHERE'S CHARLEY?
A Warner Brothers' picture starring Ray Bolger and Allyn McLerie in a cast that included Robert Shackleton and Mary Germaine, and directed by David Butler. Songs by Frank Loesser:
ONCE IN LOVE WITH AMY; MAKE A MIRACLE; MY DARLING, MY DARLING; THE YEARS BEFORE US; BETTER GET OUT OF HERE; SERENADE WITH ASIDES; WHERE'S CHARLEY?; AT THE RED ROSE COTILLON; LOVELIER THAN EVER and THE NEW ASHMOLEAN MARCHING SOCIETY.

WITH A SONG IN MY HEART
A 20th Century-Fox release filmed with a cast headed by Susan Hayward, Thelma

Ritter, Rory Calhoun, David Wayne and Robert Wagner, and directed by Walter Lang. The following songs were sung by Jane Froman, the heroine of this biographical picture:
BLUE MOON and WITH A SONG IN MY HEART by Lorenz Hart and Richard Rodgers; THAT OLD FEELING by Lew Brown and Sammy Fain; I'VE GOT A FEELING YOU'RE FOOLING by Arthur Freed and Nacio Herb Brown; TEA FOR TWO by Irving Caesar and Vincent Youmans; DEEP IN THE HEART OF TEXAS by June Hershey and Don Swander; CARRY ME BACK TO OLD VIRGINNY by James Bland; DIXIE by Dan Emmett; THEY'RE EITHER TOO YOUNG OR TOO OLD by Frank Loesser and Arthur Schwartz; IT'S A GOOD DAY by Peggy Lee and Dave Barbour; I'LL WALK ALONE by Sammy Cahn and Jule Styne; GIVE MY REGARDS TO BROADWAY by George M. Cohan; ALABAMY BOUND by Bud Green, B. G. DeSylva and Ray Henderson; CALIFORNIA HERE I COME by B. G. DeSylva, Al Jolson and Joseph Meyer; CHICAGO by Fred Fisher; AMERICA THE BEAUTIFUL by Katherine Lee Bates and Samuel A. Ward; I'M THROUGH WITH LOVE by Gus Kahn, Fud Livingston and Matty Malneck; EMBRACEABLE YOU by Ira and George Gershwin; ON THE GAY WHITE WAY by Leo Robin and Ralph Rainger; THE RIGHT KIND OF LOVE by Don George and Charles Henderson; MONTPARNASSE by Alfred Newman and Eliot Daniel; MAINE STEIN SONG by E. A. Fenstad and Lincoln Colcord; (BACK HOME AGAIN IN) INDIANA by Ballard MacDonald and James F. Hanley; GET HAPPY by Ted Koehler and Harold Arlen; HOE THAT CORN by Max Showalter and Jack Woodford; JIM'S TOASTED PEANUTS and WONDERFUL HOME SWEET HOME by Ken Darby.

Feature Films With Songs

AFFAIR IN TRINIDAD
A Columbia release starring Rita Hayworth and Glenn Ford, and directed by Vincent Sherman. Songs by Lester Lee and Bob Russell:
I'VE BEEN KISSED BEFORE and TRINIDAD LADY

BAL TABARIN
A Republic release filmed with a cast headed by Muriel Lawrence, William Ching,

Claire Carleton and Steve Brody, and directed by Philip Ford. Songs by Jack Elliott and Tom Mack:
NOW AND FOREVERMORE; YOU'VE NEVER BEEN IN LOVE and MY HEART SAYS YES

BELA LUGOSI MEETS A BROOKLYN GORILLA
A Realart release starring Bela Lugosi in a cast that included Duke Mitchell, Sammy

Petrillo, Charlita and Muriel Sanders, and directed by William Beaudine. Songs:
'DEED I DO by Walter Hirsch and Fred Rose; TOO SOON by Tim Gayle, Jack Fascinato and Frances M. Gnass.

BELLES ON THEIR TOES
A 20th Century-Fox picture filmed with a cast headed by Jeanne Crain, Myrna Loy, Debra Paget, Jeffry Hunter, Edward Arnold and Hoagy Carmichael, and directed by Henry Levin. Songs:
LINGER AWHILE by Harry Owens and Vincent Rose; WHISPERING by John and Malvin Schonberger; WHEN YOU WORE A TULIP by Jack Mahoney and Percy Wenrich; THREE O'CLOCK IN THE MORNING by Dorothy Terris and Julian Robeldo.

CLASH BY NIGHT
An RKO release filmed with a cast headed by Barbara Stanwyck, Paul Douglas and Bob Ryan, and directed by Fritz Lang. Song by Dick Gasparre, Jack Baker and George Fragos:
I HEAR A RHAPSODY

DEVIL MAKES THREE, THE
An M-G-M release starring Gene Kelly and Pier Angeli, and directed by Andrew Marton. Songs by Jack Brooks and Bronislaw Kaper:
CAN LOVE COME BACK AGAIN? and OH CHRISTMAS TREE!

FABULOUS SENORITA
A Republic picture filmed with a cast headed by Estelita Rodriguez, Robert Clarke and Nestor Paiva, and directed by R. G. Springsteen. Song by Edward Heyman, Tony Martin and Victor Young:
YOU'VE CHANGED

GLORY ALLEY
An M-G-M release filmed with a cast headed by Ralph Meeker, Leslie Caron, Kurt Kasznar, Gilbert Roland and Louis Armstrong, and directed by Raoul Walsh. Songs:
ST. LOUIS BLUES by William C. Handy; GLORY ALLEY by Mack David and Jerry Livingston; THAT'S WHAT THE MAN SAID by Willard Robison; JOLLY JACQUELINE.

GREATEST SHOW ON EARTH, THE
A Paramount picture filmed with a cast headed by Betty Hutton, James Stewart, Cornel Wilde, Dorothy Lamour, Gloria Grahame, Charlton Heston and the cast of the Ringling Brothers Barnum & Bailey Circus, and directed by Cecil B. DeMille. Songs:
BE A JUMPING JACK and THE GREATEST SHOW ON EARTH by Ned Washington and Victor Young; POPCORN AND LEMONADE; SING A HAPPY SONG and A PICNIC IN THE PARK by John Murray Anderson and Henry Sullivan; LOVELY LUAWANA LADY by E. Ray Goetz and John Ringling North.

HALF-BREED, THE
An RKO release filmed with a cast headed by Robert Young, Janis Carter, Jack Buetel and Barton MacLane, and directed by Stuart Gilmore. Songs:
WHEN I'M WALKIN' ARM IN ARM WITH JIM by Harry Harris and Lew Pollack; REMEMBER THE GIRL YOU LEFT BEHIND by Mort Greene and Harry Revel.

HAPPY TIME, THE
A Columbia release filmed with a cast headed by Charles Boyer, Louis Jourdan, Marsha Hunt, Kurt Kasznar, Linda Christian and Bobby Driscoll, and directed by Richard Fleisher. Song by Ned Washington and Dimitri Tiomkin:
THE HAPPY TIME

HAS ANYBODY SEEN MY GAL?
A Universal release filmed with a cast headed by Piper Laurie, Rock Hudson, Charles Coburn, Gigi Perreau and Lynn Bari, and directed by Douglas Sirk. Songs:
FIVE FOOT TWO EYES OF BLUE by Sam Lewis, Joe Young and Ray Henderson; GIMME A LITTLE KISS WILL YA HUH? by Roy Turk, Jack Smith and Maceo Pinkard; IT AIN'T GONNA RAIN NO MORE by Wendell Hall; WHEN THE RED RED ROBIN COMES BOB, BOB BOBBIN' ALONG by Harry M. Woods; TIGER RAG by the Original Dixieland Jazz Band.

HIGH NOON
A United Artists' release filmed with a cast headed by Gary Cooper, Thomas Mitchell, Lloyd Bridges, Katy Jurado and Grace Kelly, and directed by Fred Zinnemann. Song by Ned Washington and Dimitri Tiomkin:
HIGH NOON

INVITATION
An M-G-M picture starring Van Johnson and Dorothy McGuire in a cast that included Ruth Roman and Louis Calhern,

and directed by Gottfried Reinhardt. Instrumental number by Bronislaw Kaper:
INVITATION

LADY POSSESSED
A Republic release filmed with a cast headed by James Mason, June Havoc, Stephen Dunne, Fay Compton and Pamela Kellino, and directed by William Spier and Roy Kellino. Songs:
IT'S YOU I LOVE by Allie Wrubel; MORE WONDERFUL THAN THESE by Kay Thompson and William Spier; MY HEART ASKS WHY by Hermoine Hannen and Hans May.

LAS VEGAS STORY, THE
An RKO release starring Jane Russell and Victor Mature in a cast that included Vincent Price and Hoagy Carmichael, and directed by Robert Stevenson. Songs:
I GET ALONG WITHOUT YOU VERY WELL and THE MONKEY SONG by Hoagy Carmichael; MY RESISTANCE IS LOW by Orrin Tucker.

LOST IN ALASKA
A Universal release starring Abbott and Costello in a cast that included Mitzi Green, Tom Elwell and Bruce Cabot, and directed by Jean Yarbrough. Songs by Frederick Herbert and Arnold Hughes:
A COUNTRY GAL and THERE'LL BE A HOT TIME IN THE IGLOO TO-NIGHT

MACAO
An RKO picture starring Robert Mitchum, Jane Russell and William Bendix in a cast that included Gloria Grahame and Brad Dexter, and directed by Joseph Von Sternberg. Songs:
YOU KILL ME; TALK TO ME TO-MORROW and OCEAN BREEZE by Leo Robin and Jule Styne; ONE FOR MY BABY (AND ONE MORE FOR THE ROAD) by Johnny Mercer and Harold Arlen.

NIGHT WITHOUT SLEEP
A 20th Century-Fox release starring Linda Darnell, Gary Merrill and Hildegarde Neff, and directed by Roy Baker. Songs:
TOO LATE FOR SPRING by Haven Gillespie and Alfred Newman; LOOK AT ME by Ken Darby and Alfred Newman.

OKLAHOMA ANNIE
A Republic release starring Judy Canova and John Russell in a cast that included Grant Withers, Roy Bancroft and Emmett

"Pappy" Lynn, and directed by R. G. Springsteen. Songs:
BLOW THE WHISTLE by S. Sherwin and Harry McClintock; NEVER, NEVER, NEVER by Jack Elliott and Sonny Burke; HAVE YOU EVER BEEN LONELY (HAVE YOU EVER BEEN BLUE)? by George Brown and Peter De Rose.

ONE MINUTE TO ZERO
An RKO release starring Robert Mitchum and Ann Blyth, and directed by Tay Garnett. Song based on a Japanese-Korean melody with lyrics by Norman Bennett:
TELL ME GOLDEN MOON

OUTLAW WOMEN
A Lippert Picture release filmed with a cast headed by Marie Windsor, Richard Rober, Alan Nixon and Carla Balenda, and directed by Ben Ormond and Samuel Newfield. Songs:
CRAZY OVER YOU by June Carr; FRISCO KATE by Ben Young.

QUIET MAN, THE
A Republic release filmed with a cast headed by John Wayne, Maureen O'Hara, Barry Fitzgerald, Ward Bond and Victor McLaglen, and directed by John Ford. Songs:
GALWAY BAY by Dr. Edward Colahan; and three traditional Irish songs: THE WILD COLONIAL BOY; THE HUMOUR IS ON ME NOW and MUSH MUSH (TREAD ON THE TAIL OF ME COAT).

RANCHO NOTORIOUS
An RKO release filmed with a cast headed by Marlene Dietrich, Mel Ferrer, Arthur Kennedy, William Frawley and Jack Elam, and directed by Fritz Lang. Songs by Ken Darby:
LEGEND OF CHUCK-A-LUCK and GET AWAY YOUNG MAN

SOUND OFF
A Columbia release filmed with a cast headed by Mickey Rooney, Anne James and Sammy White, and directed by Richard Quine. Songs:
MY LADY LOVE by Bob Russell and Lester Lee; BLOW YOUR OWN HORN by Mickey Rooney.

SUDDEN FEAR
An RKO picture starring Joan Crawford and Jack Palance. Song by Jack Brooks and Elmer Bernstein:
AFRAID

TROPICAL HEAT WAVE

A Republic release starring Estelita in a cast that included Robert Hutton and Grant Withers, and directed by R. J. Springsteen. Songs:
MY LONELY HEART AND I by Arthur T. Horman and Sammy Wilson; I WANT TO BE KISSED by Nester Amaral and Sammy Wilson; WHAT SHOULD HAPPEN TO YOU by Sammy Wilson.

WAIT TILL THE SUN SHINES NELLIE

A 20th Century-Fox picture filmed with a cast headed by Jean Peters, David Wayne, Hugh Marlowe and Albert Dekker, and directed by Henry King. Songs:
WAIT TILL THE SUN SHINES NELLIE by Andrew B. Sterling and Harry Von Tilzer; ON THE BANKS OF THE WABASH by Paul Dresser; BREAK THE NEWS TO MOTHER by Charles K. Harris; GOODBYE DOLLY GRAY by Paul Barnes and Will Cobb; SMILES by J. Will Callahan and Lee J. Roberts; IT'S A LONG WAY TO TIPPERARY by Harry Williams and Joe Judge; PACK UP YOUR TROUBLES IN YOUR OLD KIT BAG by Felix Powell and George Asaf; LOVE'S OLD SWEET SONG by G. Clifton Bingham and James Lyman Molloy.

WHAT PRICE GLORY?

A 20th Century-Fox release starring James Cagney, Corinne Calvet and Dan Dailey, and directed by John Ford. Songs:
MY LOVE MY LIFE by Ray Evans and Jay Livingston; OUI, OUI MARIE by Fred Fisher, Alfred Bryan and Joseph McCarthy; IT'S A LONG WAY TO TIPPERARY by Harry Williams and Joe Judge; SMILES by J. Will Callahan and Lee J. Roberts; PACK UP YOUR TROUBLES IN YOUR OLD KIT BAG by Felix Powell and George Asaf.

Western Films With Songs

APACHE COUNTRY

A Columbia release starring Gene Autry in a cast that included Pat Buttram and Carolina Cotton, and directed by George Archainbaud. Songs:
THE COVERED WAGON ROLLED RIGHT ALONG by Britt Wood and Hy Heath; I LOVE TO YODEL by Carolina Cotton; (MELT YOUR) COLD COLD HEART by Hank Williams; CRIME WILL NEVER PAY by Jack Pepper.

BARBED WIRE

A Columbia release starring Gene Autry in a cast that included Pat Buttram and A. James, directed by G. Archainbaud. Songs:
MEXACALI ROSE by Jack B. Tenney; OLD BUCKAROO by Gene Autry and Fleming Allen; EZEKIEL SAW THE WHEEL (Traditional).

BORDER SADDLEMATES

A Republic release filmed with a cast headed by Rex Allen, Mary Ellen Kay and Slim Pickens, and directed by William Witney. Song by Jack Elliott:
ROLL ON BORDER MOON

COLORADO SUNDOWN

A Republic release filmed with a cast headed by Rex Allen, Mary Ellen Kay, Slim Pickens and June Vincent, and directed by William Witney. Songs:
UNDER COLORADO STARS by Jack Elliott; DOWN BY THE RIVERSIDE (Traditional); NEW RIVER TRAIN

HAWK OF WILD RIVER, THE

A Columbia release filmed with a cast headed by Charles Starrett, Smiley Burnette, Jack Mahoney, Clayton Moore and Donna Hall, and directed by Fred F. Sears. Songs:
PEDRO ENCHILADA and CHIEF POCATELLO by Smiley Burnette.

JUNCTION CITY

A Columbia release starring Charles Starrett in a cast that included Smiley Burnette, Jack Mahoney and Kathleen Case, and directed by Ray Nazarro. Song:
LITTLE INJUN by Smiley Burnette.

KID FROM BROKEN GUN

A Columbia release starring Charles Starrett in a cast that included Smiley Burnette, Jack Mahoney and Angela Stevens, and directed by Fred F. Sears. Song:
IT'S THE LAW by Smiley Burnette.

LAST MUSKETEER, THE

A Republic release starring Rex Allen, and directed by William Witney. Songs:
I STILL LOVE THE WEST by Foy Willing; AURA LEE by W. Fosdick and G. Poulton; DOWN IN THE VALLEY.

MONTANA TERRITORY

A Columbia release starring Lon McCallister and Wanda Hendrix. Dir. Ray Nazarro.
DOWN IN THE VALLEY (Traditional)

NIGHT STAGE TO GALVESTON

A Columbia release starring Gene Autry in a cast that included Pat Buttram and

Virginia Huston, and directed by George Archainbaud. Songs:

YELLOW ROSE OF TEXAS by David W. Guion; A HEART AS BIG AS TEXAS by Oakley Haldeman and Buddy Feyne; DOWN IN SLUMBERLAND by Burnette; THE EYES OF TEXAS by J. L. Sinclair.

OLD OKLAHOMA PLAINS

A Republic release starring Rex Allen in a cast that included Slim Pickens, Elaine Edwards and Roy Bancroft, and directed by William Witney. Three traditional songs: OLD CHISHOLM TRAIL; THE LONESOME ROAD and DESE BONES (GONNA RISE AGAIN)

OLD WEST, THE

A Columbia release starring Gene Autry in a cast that included Pat Buttram and Gail Davis. Dir. George Archainbaud. Songs: SOMEBODY BIGGER THAN YOU AND I by Johnny Lange, Hy Heath and Sonny Burke; MUSIC BY THE ANGELS by Marty Symes and Arthur Altman.

PALS OF THE GOLDEN WEST

A Republic picture starring Roy Rogers in a cast that included Dale Evans, Estelita Rodriguez and Pinky Lee, and directed by William Witney. Songs by Jack Elliott: YOU NEVER KNOW WHEN LOVE MAY COME ALONG; SLUMBER TRAIL; PALS OF THE GOLDEN WEST and BEYOND THE GREAT DIVIDE.

ROUGH, TOUGH WEST, THE

A Columbia picture starring Charles Starrett in a cast that included Smiley Burnette, Carolina Cotton and Pee Wee King and orchestra; Dir. R. Nazarro. Songs: CAUSE I'M IN LOVE by Stan Jones; THE FIRE OF "41" by Smiley Burnette; YOU GOTTA GET A GUY WITH A GUN by Carolina Cotton.

TOUGHEST MAN IN ARIZONA

A Republic release starring Vaughn Monroe and Joan Leslie in a cast that included Edgar Buchanan, Victor Jory, Jean Parker and H. Morgan. Dir. B.G. Silversteen. Songs: MAN DON'T LIVE WHO CAN DIE ALONE by Bobby Sherwood and Johnny Schram; A MAN'S BEST FRIEND IS HIS DOG; HOUND DOG (BAY AT THE MOON).

WAGON TRAIN

A Columbia release starring Gene Autry in a cast that included Pat Buttram, Gail Davis and Dick Jones, and directed by George Archainbaud. Songs: IN AND OUT OF THE JAIL HOUSE by Paul Mertz; I'VE BEEN INVITED TO A JUBILEE by V. O. Stamps; HOWDY FRIENDS AND NEIGHBORS by Jack Pepper; BACK IN THE SADDLE AGAIN by Gene Autry and Ray Whiteley.

ERRATA

The following films will not be found in their proper chronological period due to an oversight in makeup:

HALFWAY TO HEAVEN (1929)

A Paramount picture starring Buddy Rogers and Jean Arthur, and directed by George Abbott. Song by Leo Robin and Richard Whiting:
LOUISE

ONE MORE TOMORROW (1937)

A Warner Brothers' picture with Ann Sheridan and Alexis Smith heading the cast. Songs by Jack Scholl and M. K. Jerome: HAVE YOU MET MY LULU? and THE LITTLE WHITE HOUSE ON THE HILL

GIRL FROM BROOKLYN (1938)

A 20th Century-Fox picture starring Alice Faye and Warner Baxter. Songs by Les Brown and Lew Pollack:
THERE'LL BE OTHER NIGHTS

MOONLIGHT MASQUERADE (1942)

A Republic picture starring Jane Frazee and Dennis O'Keefe, and directed by John H. Auer. Song by Mort Greene and Harry Revel:
WHAT AM I DOING HERE IN YOUR ARMS?

FROM THIS DAY FORWARD (1946)

An RKO picture starring Joan Fontaine and Mark Stevens, and directed by John Barry. Song by Mort Greene and Leigh Harline:
FROM THIS DAY FORWARD

FANCY PANTS (1950)

A Paramount picture starring Bob Hope and Lucille Ball, and directed by George Marshall. Songs by Ray Evans and Jay Livingston:
HOME COOKIN'; FANCY PANTS and YES M'LORD.

Albums and Long-Playing Records of Hollywood Musicals

AARON SLICK FROM PUNKIN CRICK
RCA Victor WP-342 (45 rpm), Dinah
Shore, Robert Merrill, Alan Young and
orchestra.

ALICE IN WONDERLAND
RCA Victor Y-437 (78 rpm), Kathryn
Beaumont, Ed Wynn, Sterling Holloway,
Jerry Colonna and orchestra.

AMERICAN IN PARIS, AN
MGM-93 (78 rpm), E-93 (33 rpm) and
K-93 (45 rpm), Gene Kelly, Georges
Guetary, Leslie Caron and orchestra.

ANNIE GET YOUR GUN
MGM-50 (78 rpm), E-50 (33 rpm) and
K-50 (45 rpm), Betty Hutton, Howard
Keel and orchestra.

BECAUSE YOU'RE MINE
RCA Victor DM-7015 (78 rpm) and
LPM-7015 (33 rpm), Mario Lanza and
orchestra.

BELLE OF NEW YORK, THE
MGM E-108 (33 rpm), Fred Astaire,
Anita Ellis and orchestra.

BELLS OF ST. MARY'S and GOING MY
WAY
Decca DL-5052 (33 rpm), Bing Crosby
and orchestra.

BLUE SKIES
Decca DL-5042 (33 rpm), Bing Crosby,
Fred Astaire and orchestra.

FOR ME AND MY GAL
Victor P-3059 (78 rpm) and LPM-3059
(33 rpm), Frankie Laine and orchestra.

HOLIDAY INN
Decca DL-5092 (33 rpm), Bing Crosby,
Fred Astaire and orchestra.

HOLLYWOOD'S BEST (Eight songs that
have won the Academy Award).
Columbia CL-6224 (33 rpm), Rosemary
Clooney and Harry James' orchestra.

I'LL SEE YOU IN MY DREAMS
Columbia CL-6198 (33 rpm), C-289
(78 rpm) and B-289 (45 rpm), Doris Day,
Danny Thomas and Paul Weston's orchestra.

JOLSON SINGS AGAIN
Decca 9-4 (45 rpm), DL-5006 (33 rpm)
and A-716 (78 rpm), Al Jolson and orchestra.

JOLSON STORY, THE
Decca 9-9 (45 rpm) and DL-5026 (33
rpm), Al Jolson and orchestra.

JUST FOR YOU
Decca 9-350 (45 rpm) and DL-5417 (33
rpm), Bing Crosby, Jane Wyman, the Andrews Sisters and orchestra.

LOVELY TO LOOK AT
MGM E-150 (33 rpm), MGM-150 (78

rpm) and K-150 (45 rpm), Kathryn Grayson, Red Skelton, Howard Keel and orchestra.

MERRY WIDOW, THE
MGM 157 (78 rpm), K-157 (45 rpm)
and E-157 (33 rpm), Lana Turner, Fernando Lamas and orchestra.

MR. MUSIC
Decca 9-101 (45 rpm) and DL-5284
(33 rpm), Bing Crosby, Dorothy Kirsten,
the Andrews Sisters and orchestra.

PINOCCHIO
Decca DL-5151 (33 rpm), Cliff Edwards,
Ken Darby Singers and Victor Young's orchestra.

RAINBOW 'ROUND MY SHOULDER
Columbia B-302 (45 rpm) and C-302
(78 rpm), Frankie Laine and orchestra.

SINGING IN THE RAIN
MGM E-113 (33 rpm), MGM-113 (78
rpm) and K-113 (45 rpm), Gene Kelly,
Donald O'Connor, Debbie Reynolds and orchestra.

SHOW BOAT
MGM-84 (78 rpm), E-559 (33 rpm)
and K-84 (45 rpm), Kathryn Grayson, Ava
Gardner, Howard Keel and orchestra.

*SNOW WHITE AND THE SEVEN
DWARFS*
Decca DL-5015 (33 rpm), Evelyn Knight
and Lyn Murray orchestra.

SOMEBODY LOVES ME
Victor LPM-3097 (33 rpm), Betty Hutton and orchestra; Decca DL-5424 (33
rpm) and 9-357 (45 rpm), Blossom Seeley,
Benny Fields and orchestra.

THIS IS THE ARMY
Decca DL-3108 (33 rpm), All-soldier cast
with orchestra.

THREE LITTLE WORDS
Decca DL-5160 (33 rpm), Bob Hannon,
Sunny Skylar, Dianne Courtney, Honey
Dean and Leo Reisman orchestra.

TOP O' THE MORNING and *THE
EMPEROR WALTZ*
Decca DL-5272 (33 rpm), Bing Crosby
and orchestra.

WITH A SONG IN MY HEART
Capitol DDN-309 (78 rpm), L-309 (33
rpm) and KDF-309 (45 rpm), Jane Froman
and orchestra.

WIZARD OF OZ, THE
Decca DL-5152 (33 rpm), Judy Garland,
Ken Darby Singers and Victor Young's orchestra.

Hollywood's Foremost Singing and Dancing Stars

With places and dates of birth, films in which they made their
debut, and in some instances, their real names in parentheses

— o —

ASTAIRE, FRED..............Omaha, Neb., May 10, 1900. *Dancing Lady* (1933).

AUTRY, GENE.................Tioga, Texas, September 29, 1907. Ascot shorts (1934).

BAKER, KENNY...............Monrovia, Calif., September 30, 1912. *King Of Burlesque* (1936).

BALL, LUCILLE...............Butte, Mont., August 6, 1911. *Roman Scandals* (1933).

BLONDELL, JOAN.............New York City, August 30, 1909. *Sinner's Holiday* (1929).

BOLES, JOHN..................Greenville, Texas, October 27, 1900. *Love Of Sunya* (1927).

BOLGER, RAY.................Dorchester, Mass., January 10, 1908. *Great Ziegfeld* (1936).

BOW, CLARA..................Brooklyn, N. Y., 1905. *Down To The Sea In Ships* (1923).

BRICE, FANNY................(Fanny Borach). New York City, October 20, 1891. *My Man* (1929).

CAGNEY, JAMES..............New York City, July 1, 1904. Screen debut 1931.

CANTOR, EDDIE..............(Edward Iskowitz). New York City, January 31, 1892. Kid Boots (1926).

CHEVALIER, MAURICE........Paris, France, 1889. *Innocents Of Paris* (1929).

CROSBY, BING................Tacoma, Washington, May 2, 1904. *The King Of Jazz* (1930) as a member of the Three Rhythm Boys.

DAVIS, JOAN..................St. Paul, Minn., 1912. *Way Up Thar* (1934).

DAY, DORIS...................(Doris Kappelhoff). Cincinnati, Ohio, April 3, 1924. *Romance On the High Seas* (1949)

DeCARLO, YVONNE...........Vancouver, B. C., September 1, 1922. *This Gun For Hire* (1942).

De HAVEN, GLORIA...........Los Angeles, Calif., ...*Susan And God* (1940).

Del RIO, DOLORES............(Dolores Ansunsolo), Durango, Mexico, August 3, 1905. *Joanna* (1925).

DUNNE, IRENE................Louisville, Ky., December 20, 1904. *Cimarron* (1931).

DURANTE, JIMMY.............New York City, February 10, 1893. *Roadhouse Nights* (1929).

DURBIN, DEANNA.............(Edna Mae Durbin). Winnipeg, Canada, December 4, 1922. *Three Smart Girls* (1936).

DVORAK, ANN . . . . New York City, August 2, 1912. *Hollywood Revue* (1929) as a chorus girl.

DIETRICH, MARLENE . . . . (Mary Magdalene Von Losch). Berlin, Germany, December 27, 1904. American screen debut *The Blue Angel* (1930).

EDDY, NELSON . . . . Providence, R. I., June 29, 1901. *Broadway To Hollywood* (1933).

EDWARDS, CLIFF . . . . Hannibal, Mo., ... *Hollywood Revue* (1929).

FAYE, ALICE . . . . New York City, 1915. *George White's Scandals* (1934)

GARLAND, JUDY . . . . (Judy Gumm). Grand Rapids, Mich., 1923. *Pigskin Parade* (1936).

GARRETT, BETTY . . . . St. Joseph, Mo., May 23, ... *The Big City* (1947).

GODDARD, PAULETTE . . . . Great Neck, N. Y., June 3, 1911. *Modern Times* (1936).

GRABLE, BETTY . . . . St. Louis, Mo., December 18, 1916. *What Price Innocence* (1933).

HARLOW, JEAN . . . . (Harlean Carpentier). Kansas City, Mo., March 3, 1911. *Hell's Angels* (1930).

HAVER, JUNE . . . . Rock Island, Ill., June 19, 1926. *Home In Indiana* (1944).

HAVOC, JUNE . . . . (June Hovick). Seattle, Wash., 1916.

HAYWORTH, RITA . . . . (Margarita Cansino). New York City, October 17, 1919. *Dante's Inferno* (1935).

HENIE, SONJA . . . . Oslo, Norway, April 8, 1913. *One In A Million* (1937).

HOPE, BOB . . . . Eltham, England, 1903. Universal shorts (1934-35).

HORNE, LENA . . . . Brooklyn, N. Y., 1918. *Panama Hattie* (1942).

HUTTON, BETTY . . . . Battle Creek, Mich., February 26, 1921. *The Fleet's In* (1942).

JEAN, GLORIA . . . . (Gloria Jean Schoonover). Buffalo, N. Y., April 14, 1928. *The Under Pup* (1939).

JOLSON, AL . . . . (Asa Yoelson). St. Petersburg, Russia, May 28, 1886. *The Jazz Singer* (1926)

KAYE, DANNY . . . . Brooklyn, N. Y., June 18, 1913. *Up In Arms* (1944).

KEELER, RUBY . . . . Halifax, Nova Scotia, 1909. *Forty-second Street* (1933).

KEEL, HOWARD . . . . (Harold Keel). Gillespie, Ill., April 13 . . . . . *The Small Voice* (London).

KELLY, GENE . . . . Pittsburgh, Pa., 1912. *For Me And My Gal* (1942).

KEYES, EVELYN . . . . Port Arthur, Texas, ... *The Buccaneer* (1938).

LAMOUR, DOROTHY......... New Orleans, La., December 10, 1914. *Jungle Princess* (1938).

LANGFORD, FRANCES......... Lakeland, Fla., 1913. *Every Night At Eight* (1935).

LANZA, MARIO............... New York City, January 31, 1921. *That Midnight Kiss* (1949).

LESLIE, JOAN................. (Joan Brodell). Detroit, Mich., January 26, 1905. *Two Thoroughbreds* (1939).

LEWIS, JERRY................ Newark, N. J., March 16, 1926. *My Friend Irma Goes West* (1949)

LOUISE, ANITA............... (Anita Louise Fremault). New York City, 1915. *The Music Master* (1929)

LOVE, BESSIE................. Midland, Texas, September 10, 1898.

LYNN, DIANA................. (Dolly Loehr). Los Angeles, Calif., October 7, 1926. *There's Magic In Music* (1941).

MacDONALD, JEANETTE....... Pittsburgh, Pa., June 18, 1907. *The Love Parade* (1929).

MARTIN, DEAN............... Steubenville, Ohio, June 17, 1917. *My Friend Irma Goes West* (1949).

MARTIN, MARY............... Wetherford, Texas, December 1, 1914. *The Great Victor Herbert* (1939).

MAYO, VIRGINIA............. (Virginia Jones). St. Louis, Mo., 1920.

MIRANDA, CARMEN.......... (Maria Do Cormo Miranda da Cunha). Marco Canavozes, Portugal, 1914. *Down Argentine Way* (1940).

MOORE, CONSTANCE......... Sioux City, Ia., January 18, 1922. *Prison Break* (1938).

MORGAN, DENNIS............ (Stanley Morner) Prentice, Wis., December 10, 1920. *Suzy* (1936).

MURPHY, GEORGE........... New Haven, Conn., July 4, 1904. *Kid Millions* (1934).

NOVARRO, RAMON........... (Ramon Samaniegoes). Durango, Mexico, February 6, 1905. Screen debut in 1920.

OAKIE, JACK................. Sedalia, Mo., 1903.

O'BRIEN, VIRGINIA........... Los Angeles, Calif., ... *Hullabaloo* (1940).

O'CONNOR, DONALD......... Chicago, Ill., August 28, 1925. *Sing You Sinners* (1938).

O'DRISCOLL, MARTHA....... Tulsa, Okla., March 4, 1922. *Collegiate* (1935).

PAIGE, JANIS................. (Donna Mae Jaden) Tacoma, Wash., September 16, 1923. *Hollywood Canteen* (1944).

PARKS, LARRY............... Olathe, Kansas.

PINZA, EZIO................. Rome, Italy, May 18, 1892. *Carnegie Hall* (1947).

PORTER, JEAN................ Cisco, Texas, ... *Babes On Broadway* (1941).

POWELL, DICK . . . . Mount View, Ark., November 14, 1904. *Blessed Event* (1932).

POWELL, ELEANOR . . . . Springfield, Ohio, 1912. *George White's Scandals* (1935).

POWELL, JANE . . . . (Suzanne Bruce). Portland, Ore., April 1, 1929. *Song Of The Open Road* (1944).

RAYE, MARTHA . . . . Butte, Mont., ... *Rhythm On The Range* (1936).

RAYMOND, GENE . . . . (Raymond Guion) New York City, August 13, 1908. *Personal Maid* (1931).

REGAN, PHIL . . . . Brooklyn, N. Y., May 28, 1908. *The Key* (1934).

REYNOLDS, DEBBIE . . . . (Mary Francis Reynolds). El Paso, Texas, April 1, ... *Daughter Of Rosie O'Grady* (1950).

ROBBINS, GALE . . . . Mitchell, Ind., May 7, 1924. *In The Meantime Darling* (1944).

ROGERS, CHARLES "BUDDY" . . Olathe, Kansas, August 13, 1904.

ROGERS, GINGER . . . . (Virginia Katherine McMath). Independence, Mo., July 16, 1911. *Young Man Of Manhattan* (1929).

ROGERS, ROY . . . . (Leonard Slye). Cincinnati, Ohio, November 5, 1912. *Old Barn Dance* (1938).

ROONEY, MICKEY . . . . (Joe Yule, Jr.) Brooklyn, N. Y., September 23, 1922. *Orchids And Ermine* (1927).

ROSS, SHIRLEY . . . . (Bernice Gaunt). Omaha, Neb., ... *Manhattan Melodrama* (1934).

RYAN, PEGGY . . . . (Margaret Orene Ryan). Long Beach, Calif., August 28, 1924. *Top Of The Town* (1936).

SHORE, DINAH . . . . Winchester, Texas, March 1, 1917. *Thank Your Lucky Stars* (1943).

SINATRA, FRANK . . . . Hoboken, N. J., 1918. *Higher And Higher* (1943).

TEMPLE, SHIRLEY . . . . Santa Monica, Calif., April 23, 1929. *Red Haired Alibi* (1932).

VALLEE, RUDY . . . . (Hubert Prior Vallee). Island Pond, Va., July 28, 1901. *The Vagabond Lover* (1929).

VERA-ELLEN . . . . (Vera-Ellen Rohe). Cincinnati, Ohio, February 16, 1926. *Wonder Man* (1945).

WATERS, ETHEL . . . . Chester, Pa., October 13, 1900. *On With The Show* (1929).

WEST, MAE . . . . Brooklyn, N. Y., 1892. *Night After Night* (1932).

WILLIAMS, ESTHER . . . . Los Angeles, Calif., 1923. *Andy Hardy Steps Out* (1942).

WITHERS, JANE . . . . Atlanta, Ga., 1927. *Bright Eyes* (1934).

INDEX

E R R A T A

Last lines in Table of Contents should read:

Songs Linked With Silent Pictures

Back in the days of silent movies, producers often depended on specially written music, played by pit orchestras in the first-run houses, to set the mood for the action on the screen and aid in the exploitation of the film. Several of these songs have lived to this day, and include:

THE PERFECT SONG (1915) by Clarence Lucas and James Carl Breil. This was used as the background music for the love scenes between Lillian Gish and Henry B. Walthall in *The Birth Of A Nation*, and in 1928, when "Amos 'n' Andy" first went on the air, they revived the melody for their opening signature music and have used it ever since.

MICKEY (1918) by Harry Williams and Neil Moret, written for the motion picture of the same title in which Mabel Normand starred.

COVERED WAGON by Will Morrissey and Joe Burrows and WESTWARD HO! by R. A. Barnet and Hugo Rosenfeld, both used in the exploitation of *The Covered Wagon*, released in 1923 and one of the first western film epics.

CHARMAINE (1926) by Lew Pollack and Erno Rapee, written for the exploitation of *What Price Glory?* in which Edmund Lowe and Victor McLaglen were starred.

RAMONA (1927) by L. Wolfe Gilbert and Mabel Wayne, and before the release of the picture of the same title, based on Helen Hunt Jackson's famous novel, Dolores Del Rio, the star of the film, introduced the song on a personal appearance tour that took her from coast to coast.

JEANNINE I DREAM OF LILAC TIME (1928) by L. Wolfe Gilbert and Nat Shilkret, used in the exploitation of the picture *Lilac Time*, starring Colleen Moore.

POOR PAULINE by Charles McCarron and Raymond Walker also might be included in this category. It was a gag song, written in 1914, and inspired by the miraculous escapes from death experienced weekly on the screen by Pearl White, star of the serial *The Adventures Of Pauline*.